Miracle on the Mesa

MIRACLE
ON THE
MESA

A History of the University of New Mexico

1889–2003

WILLIAM E. DAVIS

The University of New Mexico Press

for the Office of the President

Albuquerque

Library of Congress Cataloging-in-Publication Data

Davis, William E. (William Eugene), 1929–
    Miracle on the mesa : a history of the University of New Mexico,
       1889–2003 / William E. Davis.
    p. cm.
Includes bibliographical references and index.
    ISBN-13: 978-0-8263-4016-0 (cloth : alk. paper)
    ISBN-10: 0-8263-4016-4 (cloth : alk. paper)
    ISBN-13: 978-0-8263-4017-7 (pbk. : alk. paper)
    ISBN-10: 0-8263-4017-2 (pbk. : alk. paper)
1. University of New Mexico—History.
2. College presidents—New Mexico.
    I. Title.
    LD3781.N52D38 2006
    378.789´61—dc22
                         2005027467

DESIGN AND COMPOSITION: *Mina Yamashita*

Contents

MIRACLE ON THE MESA

Dedication

The great philosopher and historian Will Durant once said that before we die we should gather up our heritage and pass it on to our posterity. It is in that spirit that I have endeavored to acknowledge in this book some of the people responsible for the development of the University of New Mexico in its first 114 years. I would hope that if the University, like Oxford and Cambridge, endures for eight or more centuries, students and faculty in that far-off time might pick up this book and learn something about the birth and early life of this campus and the people who made it happen.

Writing a history is a humbling but exhilarating experience, as is being a university president. As the presiding officer at UNM commencements between 1975 and 1982, I was acutely aware that those crossing the platform and receiving diplomas symbolized a long, adventuresome journey to reach that moment in time—not just the University's moment, but their own. The words were spoken, the degrees conferred, and the graduates went their separate ways, never to be assembled in that company again. They had come from many backgrounds. They went on to represent the University in all parts of the world, embodying its mission of scholarship and service.

Given my experience I could not resist organizing this history chronologically around the tenure of its presidents. In truth, though, the real vision and achievement of a university come from teachers, scholars, and students, those in the hallowed groves of academe, or more realistically in the library stacks and at the lab benches and in the classroom seats.

UNM has been blessed with some great presidents and many other great teachers, researchers, administrators, and coaches. The right people were in the right place at the right time in the early days: Charles E. Hodgin, John D. Clark, M. Custers, Josephine S. Parsons, Lynn B. Mitchell, Simon P. Nanninga, George I. Sanchez, Marshall E. Farris, and Roy W. Johnson, to mention only a few.

Later, during the days of President Popejoy and President Heady, there was another generation of leaders and scholars: Sherman E. Smith, Harold L. Enarson, Hoyt Trowbridge, Henry Weihofen, Dudley Wynn, Pete McDavid, Reginald Fitz, Marshall R. Nason, and Frank C. Hibben. If you were a youngster at UNM in the first two-thirds of the twentieth century you could add many more names to this brief list, and you should. These people bequeathed us a legacy.

We, and the students of today, are the heirs of that legacy. In 2003 the University's mission is still the education of students and the advancement of knowledge

"Swede" Johnson

Tony Hillerman

through research. When these are done well, the University is in a strategic position to enrich the lives of the people of New Mexico by providing leadership in all fields of endeavor, leadership that has an impact not only on the economy but also on the cultural and intellectual vitality of the state.

All this occurs when great teachers interact with great students and transmit both knowledge and the passion for seeking knowledge. UNM has had many teachers who are still very much alive in the hearts and minds of their students. Less visible but just as important are the nonteaching employees who create the conditions for learning. Each person ever associated with UNM should make such a list, for who among us has not experienced the influence of a truly great teacher or colleague?

V. B. Price, one of New Mexico's preeminent authors, wrote the chapter in this book on the Davis presidency. I was both flattered and embarrassed by his account of the years between 1975 and 1982, and most grateful for his kind remarks. But I must credit an array of people for all the good things that happened. What better place to do this than at the beginning of this history? With gratitude and humility, I dedicate my remembrances of those years to the following friends and colleagues:

Marvin D. "Swede" Johnson—Vice president for student affairs, alumni relations, and development, he had a real soft spot for students. He liked them so much that he lived in one of the residence halls for a semester until his family arrived from Tucson. Johnson came to New Mexico from the University of Arizona, where he had earned degrees and served as vice president. Perhaps because he was so in tune with students, he also was highly effective in collaborating with them after graduation, especially when they were able to become benefactors. He also inspired greatness in his staff. While at UNM he served as the national president of the powerful Council for the Advancement and Support of Education (CASE).

Tony Hillerman—The month I assumed the presidency of UNM I read my first Hillerman novel, *Dance Hall of the Dead.* That same month I attended a gathering at Zuni Pueblo. After a dinner with the pueblo council, one of the elders cornered me and asked in a conspiratorial tone, "Do you know this Tony Hillerman?" I acknowledged I did indeed know him. The next question was, "Who's he been talking to?" The elders were leery about his insight into Zuni religion and culture.

Returning to the campus, I told the story to Tony, who roared with laughter and replied, "Tell them I just go to the stacks in Zimmerman Library."

I had been told that Tony had been the administrative assistant to Tom Popejoy. Since Popejoy seemed to have done pretty well, I decided to follow his lead and asked Tony to be my assistant. He agreed. As the years passed my admiration for him grew. I learned that he was a mediocre poker player, a good friend, and a superb mentor for an itinerant Gringo seeking to learn more about New Mexico and its people.

Chester C. Travelstead—Few people have the guts to put their job and home on the line to stand up for a principle, but he did. He lost his job, too, but then found a better one at the University of New Mexico. There his virtue, wisdom, and just plain old love of people, especially faculty and students, garnered him a reputation as a master teacher and a master administrator. His son, Coleman, also has a niche in the UNM historical hall of fame. As a teenager, he was a soda jerk in the old Student Union, which became the Anthropology Building, and was later president of the Alumni Association.

John Perovich—He ranks right up there with Popejoy and Zimmerman for his contributions to the greatness of UNM. For fifty years as a student, finance wizard, chief advisor to presidents, then as president himself, and finally as active retiree, he has exerted a powerful influence. Like Popejoy, he had great credibility with legislators, but he also has a special sparkle. When he walks into a room, the whole place lights up. He has the same expression as a boy spying a shiny bicycle beneath the Christmas tree, always expectant, always smiling. And I suspect he bleeds cherry and silver.

Robert G. Lalicker—First director of the University of New Mexico Foundation, Lalicker headed up the campaign for the Presidential Scholars program, designed to keep New Mexico's best and brightest at home through scholarships that recognized and rewarded their academic prowess. He also served his alma mater as alumni director. The ex-four-striper Navy captain got all aboard to support fund-raising efforts on behalf of UNM and put together a team of alumni and business leaders to rally 'round the Lobo flag with gifts, grants, and boundless enthusiasm.

Clinton Adams—Certainly one of the best academic administrators I have ever known or worked with, Clinton Adams was dean of the College of Fine Arts, then associate provost, and served as interim provost after the retirement of Chester Travelstead. A cofounder of the Tamarind Lithography Workshop, he also was a gifted painter, historian, and author of the definitive history of lithography and more than a hundred articles. He was known and respected as one who did not suffer fools gladly. He also was a superb poker player who could draw to an inside straight and hit it. Rarely was he caught bluffing. In 1985, he received the Governor's Award for Outstanding Contributions to the Art of New Mexico.

Dick Pfaff—An inspiration to generations of students working on newspapers and yearbooks, he had the wisdom and patience to guide them through troubled times. When protests plagued the campus, when the sports reporters missed their deadlines, when the advertising budget disallowed a special section on the latest fad, Dick was the calm at the heart of the storm. Armed with the cool confidence of a Christian holding four aces, his real contribution was on the business and management side: advertising, distribution, payroll, equipment, and all the details of going to press.

Clinton Adams

Dick Pfaff

Henry Ellis

Jess Price

McAllister H. Hull—An expert on all matters known to God and man, and a few that are not, Mac served as provost and helped organize and solidify the University's research mission, particularly in the sciences. A physicist by training, he was literally a man for all seasons, one who enjoyed the thrill of jumping out of airplanes and white-water rafting on Niagara Falls.

Henry Ellis—A professor of psychology by academic title, he thinks of himself as a poor man's Pete Sampras with a wounded knee. He smiles too much for a real shrink, which makes his students suspicious. Deep down, though, they love and trust him and have deep respect for his developing one of the finest psychology programs in the whole country right here at UNM.

Jess Price and Melissa Howard—They were a potent team, Jess as director of public information and Melissa as editor of the *Alumnus* and *Campus News.* Each had the knack of turning a phrase. Best of all, they dug deep into the lives of faculty and students and the research and academic programs, enlightening generations of readers about the good things going on at UNM.

Jack Campbell—Always effervescent, he came across as a typical undergraduate Yalie, wandering around digging up bones in the tundra of the Arctic or in the Southwestern deserts, camera dangling from his neck. As professor and chairman of anthropology and director of the Maxwell Museum of Anthropology, he wrote books, took pictures, and talked and talked and talked. One of his exploits ended badly for the woodpeckers nesting in a totem pole outside Scholes Hall. His colleague Frank Hibben had had this totem pole towed through the ocean and delivered to UNM as a trophy. Over time, woodpeckers made their homes in the pole, and their relentless pecking annoyed faculty and students. So Campbell was ordered to shoot the woodpeckers and did. The totem pole survived and today is in the courtyard of the Anthropology Building.

Bob and Florence Lister—They were a team, whether collecting sherds in Spain or excavating ruins in Chaco Canyon. They also wrote books, guided eastern dudes through western mysteries, and charmed generations of students with their hospitality and boundless knowledge.

Jim Belshaw—A UNM alum and guest lecturer as well as a cynical, hard-bitten journalist, he writes with a scalpel instead of a pen. Deep down, however, he is a real softy with a dogged loyalty for all underdogs—he has been cheering for the Chicago White Sox for fifty years. He is also famous. He and Tony Hillerman were once having lunch at a local beanery. When they had paid their bill and departed, another diner walked up to the cashier and asked, "Wasn't that one of New Mexico's greatest writers?" The cashier agreed it was, and the diner commented, "I thought so! That was Jim Belshaw! I read his column every day!"

Timothy R. MacCurdy—Not only a scholar, but also a novelist, MacCurdy displayed a distinguished demeanor on the UNM campus that made him stick out like Tight's windmill. A renowned student and teacher of Spanish literature, he spoke the language with a Louisiana accent. MacCurdy was more than a good role model; he was a walking, talking example of the "Good Gringo."

Rupert Trujillo—Through his extension programs, he had more students off campus than the University had on campus. An early pioneer of extension and distance learning, he brought education to thousands of part-time, place-bound, working students. He also toted his load in developing the branch campuses in Los Alamos, Gallup, Zuni, and Valencia County.

Ferenc Morton Szasz, Richard W. Etulain, John L. Kessell, Richard Ellis, and Gerald D. Nash—These distinguished historians wrote about the greatness of the Southwest, ranging from Kessell's endeavors to make don Diego de Vargas the real "father of our country" to Szasz's documenting the story of the Trinity Site that day the sun rose twice. Great scholars, great lecturers, great teachers, they lit a lot of fires in aspiring students of western history.

Bill Weeks

Bill Weeks—When I was an undergraduate football player at the University of Colorado, my special job was to quarterback the "scouting" team. So for three years, I got to be "Bill Weeks" the week Colorado played Iowa State, where he was the passingest quarterback in the old Big Eight. He later coached the UNM Lobos to Western Athletic Conference football championships in 1962, 1963, and 1964. Still later, he was a highly effective ambassador to the New Mexico Legislature, whether lobbying for a new law library or raises for the faculty. He also spread a lot of goodwill, which in many cases made it possible for good things to happen at UNM.

David Hamilton—The jolly leprechaun of the Economics Department, Hamilton, with his beaming countenance and good humor, became a powerful force in campus politics. He had the knack of getting to the center of gravity of problems and producing acceptable solutions.

David Darling

David W. Darling—Not really mean enough to be a dean, David Darling nonetheless was relentless in his mission to increase the number of bilingual teachers in the public schools and Native American teachers on the reservations. UNM's federally sponsored program, which brought students from the two-year Gallup branch to summer courses on the UNM campus and then returned them to reservation schools as student teachers, served as a model for increasing the numbers of Native American teachers. His summer program for administrators from Central and South America, with courses taught in Spanish, helped establish UNM as a focal point for Latin American studies.

John Clark

Paul Vassallo

Warren Heffron

The Karens—UNM could boast two fourteen-carat Karens, Glaser and Abraham. Karen Glaser plied her trade in Student Affairs, while Karen Abraham headed Alumni Affairs. Although both alleged that neither students nor alumni of UNM had affairs, their leadership had a tremendous impact on the lives of students while they were on the campus and after they had departed. Once a Lobo, always a Lobo, was the motto of these two cherry and silver gems.

John Miller Clark—He was director of the Collegiate Singers, those traveling troubadours who displayed UNM at its best as they sang their way into the hearts of admiring audiences around the state. They were front and center at the governor's mansion in Santa Fe when UNM alum Bruce King entertained Great Britain's Princess Anne. The Collegiate Singers wowed New Mexico's most prestigious citizens and the visiting royalty with western ballads.

Don McRae—He looked too human to be a dean, especially a dean of the College of Fine Arts, but in his casual, down-home, workaday manner that is what he was. He not only managed those prima donnas of the arts, but also massaged their creative instincts and tempered their fiery individualism with the touch of a master soothing souls. Not only that, he convinced the tight-fisted financial vice president to junk the decrepit practice pianos and replace them with shiny black concert pianos that for the most part were in tune. Choirs of admirers sang his praises.

Paul Vassallo—The bearded, mustachioed chief librarian looked a lot like a medieval Maltese nobleman, complete with furrowed brow, bushy eyebrows, and piercing black eyes. His vision and industry overshadowed his impressive demeanor, however. He sought to increase the UNM library holdings from four hundred thousand to a million books. To do this, he needed an additional million dollars a year for five years for acquisitions. He got it, and the University celebrated its millionth volume in 1981. Its holdings in Hispanic, Native American, and Southwestern topics are among the best in the country.

Anne Brown—She began as John Durrie's assistant as secretary to the University and the Regents and then succeeded him. She did the hands-on work of organizing the University's records, preparing agendas, taking minutes, and overseeing the pomp and protocol of academic processions and gatherings. An elegant lady, she added dignity and charm to any occasion—and carefully selected, soft-spoken words in an unreconstructed Alabama accent dropped from her lips like pearls in a puddle.

Warren Heffron—Meanwhile, far from the clash and conflict of medical administration are the practitioners. These are the dedicated and semihidden doctors who teach the students and treat the patients, doctors like Warren Heffron in Family Practice. His influence extends worldwide as he travels and brings to the UNM Hospital men and women who assist, observe, and learn.

Leonard Napolitano—In the old days, Napolitano without a cigarette would be as conspicuous as an emperor without clothes. Seeing him puffing away, it is difficult to picture him as the back-up quarterback for the Santa Clara football team when it played Oklahoma in the Orange Bowl in 1950. Born to lead, as a quarterback or as a dean, Napolitano was kind of a maverick in medical education, what with having a PhD in anatomy rather then the more prevalent MD of medical circles. Roughly a decade after the med school was founded, however, it was Napolitano who helped put together the respective empires consisting of the School of Medicine, the hospitals, the Schools of Pharmacy and Nursing, and the Dental Hygiene Program. This became the basic administrative structure for today's Health Sciences Center. Not only that, he presided over the transformation of the old Bernalillo County Medical Center to the UNM Hospital with control vested in the Board of Regents. All the while, he charmed, beguiled, and browbeat those recalcitrant philanthropists in the legislature to support what has emerged as one of the finest medical, educational, research, and treatment centers in the Southwest. So, as he might say, put that in your pipe and smoke it.

Leonard Napolitano

Alex Mercure—Alex was one of the survivors of the raid on the courthouse at Tierra Amarilla by land-grant activist Reies López Tijerina in 1967. Traveling in a UNM-marked state car, Alex thought the atmosphere very strange when he pulled into town. When he got out of the car, he was greeted by shotgun fire and dived into a nearby ditch. There, he spent the rest of the day keeping his head and his fanny out of the line of fire. He survived to be a vice president at UNM in 1974. A Hispanic from northern New Mexico, Mercure later left his post at UNM to go to Washington, D.C., as assistant secretary of agriculture.

Alex Mercure

Linda Estes—Like Joan of Arc she waded into many a fray, slaying dragons and heretics with gleeful abandon. A champion of women's sports and Title IX, she was one of the first women picked to serve on the powerful NCAA executive committee when championships for women were first authorized in 1980. Her competitive and political instincts matched her common sense and good judgment, which made her an effective spokesperson for women's rights both on and off the campus.

Jerry Apodaca and Bruce King—Both alumni of UNM, Apodaca and King were New Mexico governors, and both were outspoken champions of higher education. Their strong backing, along with that of the legislatures under their governorships, provided special funding for library acquisitions, development of engineering and the sciences, and construction of facilities for research. This support enabled the University to forge alliances with scientific laboratories in the area. Apodaca and King were also particularly instrumental in the expansion of the Health Sciences Center. During their time in office, the State of New Mexico was among the national leaders in support of higher education as measured by percentage of increase in appropriations and expenditures per capita income.

Linda Estes

Joe Scaletti

Tow Diehm

Joe Scaletti—The Italian stallion, Joe Scaletti, became the University's research czar. A former microbiologist in the School of Medicine, he helped write the grant proposals and led the charge to procure funds from federal and private sources to finance advanced research. Under his watch, the University doubled and then doubled again the funds for sponsored research and laid the groundwork for UNM to become a national leader in federal support. Among his many contributions was convincing the legislature that grant overhead should be returned to the University. On campus he never corrected anyone who assumed he was somehow related to the great Domenico Scarlatti, a noted Italian Baroque composer.

Albert E. Utton—In the land of little rain, it is said that more men have been killed fighting over water than over women. So an expert on water law is welcomed like a summer rain after a long drought. Utton, a UNM graduate and a Rhodes Scholar, made the University's School of Law a Mecca for aspiring attorneys who sought to know more about water rights and other aspects of environmental law in the West. He inspired both respect and confidence, and his early death was a great loss to the University and his profession.

Jerry Slavin—Slim, shy, and soft-spoken, Jerry Slavin was a true friend and mentor to hundreds of foreign students. His fluency in the Spanish language strengthened his role as their counselor and advisor. He was my guide when we visited the Universidad Autónoma in Guadalajara. He impressed even the mariachis when he sang the "Mañanita" outside the window of a black-eyed señorita at four o'clock in the morning. After that we were treated like native sons returned for the family reunion.

Tow Diehm—Not many athletic trainers end up as associate directors of athletics, but Tow Diehm proved to be the exception. In all, he served UNM for a total of thirty-six years until his retirement in 1993. In addition to being a mentor and confidante of UNM athletes as well as the one who taped their ankles or attended to multiple injuries, he designed a five-year physical therapy athletic trainer curriculum that colleges and universities nationwide copied. He also served as the primary lobbyist for a tuition-waiver bill for athletes and spearheaded the drive to raise funds for UNM's athletic training facility, which was named for him. He is a member of the UNM, Albuquerque, and trainers' halls of fame.

Fred Hart, Robert J. Desiderio, and Joe Goldberg—The three caballeros of the School of Law served as dean, professor, and University attorney during those rip-roaring days when the school was adding a library, offices, and classrooms so it would have something to name in honor of Fred Hart. The pride of the school, however, was its ability to tailor learning of the law to the needs of the students through practical experience in clinical law and special programs for Hispanics and Native Americans.

Bill Huber—Renowned for his acerbic tongue, he never had a critical thought he did not utter. Beneath that stern countenance, however, his quiet chuckle and crooked smile revealed his inner self. Whatever he did, he wanted the best—from himself and from all involved. Dean of the University College, he was the author of the program of targeted recruiting, which meant the University should identify the leaders in academic prowess, leadership, and special talent in the high schools in the state, then go and get them for UNM. He wanted UNM to have the pick of the best and the brightest, and he made it happen. He also chaired the Student Publications Board and refereed many tough battles about excess editorial zeal as well as participating in the tough job of picking editors for the *Lobo*.

John Durrie—"Chief of Protocol" was not his official title, but it might have been, because Durrie's arrival on campus brought order out of chaos. Before he became the University secretary, commencements had become hilarious occasions rather than celebrations of academic pomp and circumstance. Students, faculty, families, and sometimes even administrators on the platform could not refrain from outright laughter when deans from the wrong school presented degrees to graduates of the right school or vice versa or when an obviously male name was announced and a diploma was handed to a woman. Durrie brought his professional experience from Princeton with him, and over time put UNM in line with academic rules and traditions. He also organized the University's records, including indexing the minutes of Regents' meetings, and served as secretary to the Board of Regents. He gained a reputation of always being proper, leading to a rumor that he slept in shirt, tie, and suit.

Bill Byrne—A refugee from Idaho State University, Bill Byrne came to UNM as associate athletic director in charge of raising money for the athletic program through the Lobo Club, an organization of athletic boosters. After Albuquerque, he went to San Diego State University in a similar capacity, then to the University of Oregon, where he became athletic director. His next appointment was to the same position at the University of Nebraska, followed by his current position as athletic director at Texas A&M. His humble beginnings at UNM launched him into a career in which he became one of the most powerful leaders in the nation's collegiate athletic programs.

Ted Martinez—He had more titles than a Russian nobleman in the days of the czar. A Marine colonel, he looks like a poster boy for the Corps—size 17 collar, size 4 hat. A reputation for getting things done augmented his genial manner and jovial disposition. He was elected to the Albuquerque Board of Education several times while serving as director of the New Mexico Student Union and assistant to President Ferrel Heady. Later he became director of the state Board of Educational Finance, a Peace Corps volunteer, and president of Albuquerque Technical Vocational Institute. He was convinced he could do anything, and we all believed him.

Bill Huber

John Durrie

Ted Martinez

Bub Henry

Gerald Boyle

Gwinn "Bub" Henry—He led the cheers for UNM as a student, track star, alumni director, and volunteer track coach. Perhaps most important, he organized and led the fund raising for renovating Hodgin Hall, the University's first building, which today houses the Alumni Office. Bub is a part of UNM's Henry dynasty, which dates back to the 1930s when his father Gwinn Henry was head football coach. Bub's twin sons, Matt and Mark, are track coaches at UNM at the turn of the twenty-first century. His other son, Patrick, who attended UNM, coached men's and women's track and field teams to twenty-seven NCAA championships at Louisiana State University before moving on to become head coach at Texas A&M in 2003.

Peter Johnstone—This graduate of the UNM Law School was the attorney who prepared the University's response to more than fifty NCAA allegations of improprieties in the Athletic Department during the affair known as Lobogate. Called "the poor man's Columbo," Peter conducted the investigation and sweet-talked the NCAA into something less than a public hanging. He tried his best to be humble afterward, but he failed.

Floyd Williams—He maintained the campus with pride and passion. Presiding over a staff of hundreds of employees, Floyd Williams set high standards of loving care, ranging from the upkeep of buildings to the landscaping of the grounds. Thanks to him and all like him, the campus of the University of New Mexico became a bouquet of beauty.

John Bridgers—A bulldog by temperament, John Bridgers hailed from Alabama where he played his college football at Auburn University. After coaching in the pros with the Baltimore Colts, he was head coach at Baylor University and Florida State University before becoming athletic director at the latter institution. He came to UNM in 1980 to reorganize the Athletic Department following wholesale turnovers in staff. Among his chief appointees were head coaches Joe Morrison for football and Gary Colson for basketball. Under his stern, firm direction, a program in chaos quickly recovered, and both UNM football and basketball teams flourished. Bridgers, however, had his sights set high and aspired to improve the program by expanding the stadium, thus increasing the revenue. His plans went awry with changes in the governing board and presidents, and, saddened and discouraged, he resigned in 1986.

Gerald Boyle—There are few persons more valuable to a university than a professor of economics and public administration who has the respect and confidence of the chairman of the Legislative Finance Committee, and such was the case with Gerald Boyle. Boyle's stature as an academician, his detailed knowledge of public finance, and his credibility with the legislature strongly influenced the University's development of its professional programs, enhancement of its library holdings, and expansion of its research capabilities.

R. Philip Eaton—Inventor of an insulin pump for diabetics, the brilliant, energetic Eaton progressed through the ranks to become vice president for health sciences. Perhaps his greatest achievement was garnering for UNM a reputation for educating and placing Hispanic and Native American health-care practitioners in rural areas of the Southwest. Further, he initiated programs for the early identification of prospective doctors and ways to fund their education. He became a quiet giant in his field.

David Stuart—If one were to name an all-around great professor, cherubic Dave Stuart would be at the top of the list. It is said that standing ovations followed his anthropology lectures. His research led to numerous scholarly publications. His passion for learning helped create outreach and service programs for dropouts, many of whom returned to finish their degrees. Stuart is the author of *Anasazi America*, an important book on Chaco Canyon archaeology and the links between the ancient people and ourselves. He has also published memoirs based on his adventures in Mexico and Latin America.

Those Nameless Student Advisees—Toward the end of my administration, I asked for volunteers from the faculty who wanted to advise five freshmen each year. Roughly four hundred faculty responded. Members of the professional staff were all thanked for volunteering before they knew they had volunteered. Going through the adventures and agonies of getting freshmen registered for the first time and working with them through their first year taught all of us volunteers a lot. It was a refreshing, educational experience for all who participated, one none of us will ever forget.

The Regents—As president of UNM, I had the good fortune to work closely with a governing board of outstanding and supportive Regents. Board presidents during my time were Calvin Horn, an oil tycoon, historian, author, and former legislator; and Henry Jaramillo, a Belen banker. Other members of the board in 1975 were Dr. Albert Simms, a physician and philanthropist, nephew of a former governor; Austin Roberts, an attorney from Farmington; and Ann Jourdan of Hobbs, a wife and mother, public servant, and dynamic leader. Later appointees to the board were Phillip Martinez, a neurosurgeon from Albuquerque, and Colleen Maloof, a Raton native who was part of the Maloof family of business leaders. All were wise, caring people who shared one thing in common: their love for the University of New Mexico.

The Committee for *Miracle on the Mesa*—In the fall of 2000, Van Dorn Hooker, University architect emeritus, and Joe Scaletti, recently retired associate vice president for research, set up a lunch meeting to discuss the idea of producing a history. Soon after, they met with President F. Chris Garcia, who made the idea a reality by offering financial support. The committee was expanded to include

R. Philip Eaton

David Stuart

Bud and Polly Davis

Anne Brown, University secretary emerita; the UNM Press director, Luther Wilson; Professor Emeritus Rudolfo A. Anaya; the University archivist, Terry Gugliotta, who provided much valuable research material; Coleman Travelstead, president of the Alumni Association; and Melissa Howard, a former UNM publications staffer. Chris Garcia served as an occasional consultant after leaving the presidency. The committee members read drafts of the history and offered helpful comments. Van Dorn Hooker, author of *Only in New Mexico,* the acclaimed architectural history of the University, made valuable suggestions and selected many of the photos. Melissa Howard edited the manuscript and prepared the appendices. She and Terry Gugliotta organized the photos (which came from the University's archives) and wrote the captions.

Presidential and Other Spouses—Thus far in the history of the University of New Mexico, the presidential spouses have all been women. It has been my good fortune and honor to have known most of them since the era of Bess Popejoy: Charlotte Heady, Polly Davis, June Perovich, Mary Joyce May, Donna Peck, Kathy Gordon, Sandy Garcia, and now Eva Caldera. Each has been an integral part of the life of the University, a full partner in striving to fulfill its many missions. Also great contributors are the spouses of faculty and staff who have been strong allies in the commitment to generations of students. To all, a salute and special thanks.

Pollyanne Peterson Davis—For more than fifty years she has raised the children, managed the household, and served as untitled and unpaid assistant coach, assistant alumni director, assistant professor, assistant president, and assistant chancellor. She has soothed the savage beast of her itinerant educator of a husband in whatever "big house" they currently inhabited.

Polly loves parties and tennis, which gives rise to the saying that she is a kitten in the kitchen but a panther at the net. One of her twin daughters, when asked by a first-grade teacher what her mother did, replied, "Oh, Mother doesn't work. She just gives parties." One of her most memorable parties was the dinner at 1901 Roma on the UNM campus for our houseguests: the British ambassador and his wife, the daughter of the prime minister. The plumbing backed up in the guest bathroom, triggering frantic calls to campus maintenance. Promptly at 7:00 P.M. everyone—the governor, legislators, Regents, faculty, administrators, and students—arrived, along with the caballeros with their rotors to rip out the plumbing, the Daughters of the British Empire, a bagpipe band and a mariachi band, and the incredulous British Secret Service. Now that was some party.

Over the years, Polly has fallen in love with many campuses and literally generations of faculty, students, and friends of universities. She has been the first reader for rough drafts of manuscripts, including this one, has listened to my dull speeches with rapt attention, and has laughed at my jokes because she always forgot the punch lines. We have shared a lifetime of adventures, beginning back in August 1944 when we met as sophomores at Loveland High School in Colorado. And, as Randy Newman sings, "I loved her the first time I saw her, and I love her still." ■

Prologue

The Miracle on the Mesa

Delving into the lives and events that shape the character and history of an institution, the question arises: what makes this institution special, this University of New Mexico? Well, let me count the ways.

For starters, this University annually touches the lives of more than two million New Mexicans, beginning with the students and their families, the faculty and staff and their families, and all those people who avail themselves of the academic programs on the various campuses or through the extension and continuing education programs. The University also touches those who are patients in its clinics and hospitals and those who attend its athletic events, visit its museums and galleries, enjoy its concerts and performing arts, participate in its workshops and public forums, read its publications, use its libraries and research services, and view or hear its television and radio programs. Then there are the New Mexicans who sell goods and services to the University, who develop their businesses with help from University researchers, who are part of its relationships with government agencies, and who are its partners in the public schools. In all, the University is in many ways a public treasure.

Such a list includes many repeated contacts with the same people. Nonetheless over the lifetime of an institution like the University of New Mexico the cumulative impact is awesome.

But that is only the beginning. There are other characteristics that make the University of New Mexico very special. Since early in the twentieth century, the Pueblo Style of architecture has defined the campus, pulling it together, making it more than a cluster of eclectic buildings. The blended traditions of American Indian and Hispanic architecture are preserved and applied in a modern idiom for an environment that can be found only in New Mexico.

Similarly, some of the University's academic offerings have been built upon the Southwestern culture and locale, producing outstanding programs in anthropology, archaeology, history, geology, literature, political science, architecture, and education, among others. In its role as the state's flagship institution, UNM has built strong programs for graduate and professional study, research, and public service as capstones to the core offerings for undergraduates. These include:

The Health Sciences Center has developed a national reputation for cutting-edge research, for excellence in family practice, and for success in

Facing page: Photo by Tom Brahl

educating and placing American Indians and Hispanics in health-related services in rural areas.

The Law School is noted for its expertise in water and environmental law and its special programs in practical law. Further, its summer courses to prepare American Indians and Hispanics for the law profession have served as models for other institutions.

The Anderson Schools of Management have prepared graduates for all levels of leadership in the economic development of the state.

School administrators and classroom teachers educated in the halls of the University occupy positions of leadership in the schools of virtually every community in the state, including many from pueblos and tribes who received specialized training for their people's needs. Many more educators in Latin America received advanced training at UNM.

Excellence in the sciences and engineering programs, the Research Park, and strong alliances with national laboratories have provided ever-expanding opportunities for scholars and teachers and have won the University an international reputation as a center for research and scientific training.

The University of New Mexico Press, together with a superb program in creative writing, have made the UNM campus a gathering place and incubator for aspiring authors, including some of the premier American Indian and Hispanic writers. New Mexico and its cultures are known throughout the world thanks to people like Rudolfo Anaya and Tony Hillerman.

The University Library system has become one of the top hundred research libraries in the country while maintaining its emphasis on fields related to the Southwest and Latin America.

The impact of the University of New Mexico is not confined within the city limits of Albuquerque. Its spirit and mission can be found at the D. H. Lawrence Ranch or the Harwood Foundation and Art Museum in Taos, or the branch and "twig" campuses at Taos, Los Alamos, Gallup, Zuni, and Valencia County. As the twenty-first century advances, the University is sending its curriculum to all corners of the state by means of computers and satellites.

Of even more importance, the University of New Mexico has a presence wherever its alumni go. Where they are at work, so is the University. It can be found in the members of the New Mexico Legislature who were educated at UNM. It is reflected in the lithographs of R. C. Gorman, a Native American artist, whose work was printed at the Tamarind Institute brought to UNM by Dean Clinton Adams and Professor Garo Z. Antreasian. Every summer Santa Fe's Spanish Market features the work of santero Charlie Carrillo, a UNM graduate and one of thousands of talented New Mexicans who have stayed home to get an education and pursue a career.

Photo by Tom Brahl

The University of New Mexico has carved out niches of excellence in academic areas and research programs associated with its cultural roots and geographic locale while at the same time striving to meet standards by which all great universities are evaluated. If universities are judged by their impact on the people of a state, then the University of New Mexico ranks among the very best.

This, of course, is a very personal opinion, but the vision of the University of New Mexico as a "miracle on the mesa" is not far-fetched. It is actually a take-off on *Pueblo on the Mesa,* Dorothy Hughes's book of 1939. "Miracle" seems to be a fitting word, one derived from Old English and medieval Latin, meaning something to be wondered at, "an extremely outstanding or unusual . . . accomplishment."

In 2003, as you travel north on Interstate 25 and reach the outskirts of Albuquerque, signs for the UNM South Golf Course greet you. Minutes later, you can exit the freeway on Gibson, then take a left on University Boulevard, and you are soon passing the University athletic complex that includes the football stadium and the famed Pit. Then, across the street from the Pit to the north is the Research Park.

Photo by Tom Brahl

Continuing on University Boulevard, in minutes you are looking east to the Central Campus, where the Administration Building, now Hodgin Hall, was erected in 1892. Further along, across Lomas Boulevard, is the North Campus that houses one of the premier medical centers in the Southwest.

Whether zooming along I-25 or cruising along University Boulevard, all this flashes by in a matter of minutes, but it took more than a century to build. It took time and the toil and talents of some truly great people who could look into the future and see the potential of a wilderness of sagebrush and rocks transformed into an oasis of learning and culture.

The University of New Mexico truly is a place where miracles occur, where lives are changed and made better as, one by one, students prepare themselves for positions of leadership and personal fulfillment. While faculty must receive a lot of the credit for the success of UNM's graduates, let us not forget those other talented and dedicated people who work for the University: the Regents, clerks, gardeners, coaches, all successors to the farsighted founders of the flagship institution. They may not realize it, but they are part of a century-long success story that shows every sign of continuing.

Today's University of New Mexico is indeed a "miracle on the mesa." To paraphrase N. Scott Momaday, it is the "house made of dawn" and "the way to Rainy Mountain," the place where those who hunger for education can seek, find, and disperse knowledge. It has been and will be a source of wonder for all who are touched by its influence and carry on its spirit.

Now, though, let us roll back the years and embark upon a journey that begins in the days of the old Wild West. Let us explore the evolving history of this University and its people who made possible this "miracle on the mesa." ■

The railroad had ignited a growth spurt for the riverside village of Albuquerque, shown here with the volcanoes on the western horizon and a horse and rider in the foreground. Courtesy of the Albuquerque Museum Photo Archive

CHAPTER ONE

Early New Mexico to 1889

It was not very much to begin with, this University of New Mexico, mostly just a vision, a dream. In the year 2003, one can get the feeling of what those beginnings must have been like in 1880s. Travel a few miles south of today's Albuquerque on Interstate 25. Look east toward the mesas rising in swells against the backdrop of mountains and imagine no roads or houses, nothing but sand, saltbush, and desert critters, no water, trees, or vestiges of civilization.

In the latter part of the nineteenth century, Tijeras Canyon provided a gateway to the east, while rutted wagon tracks on a dirt road led west toward Gallup and California. South was El Paso, then Mexico. North was Santa Fe, the capital. The city of holy faith was hard to reach by rail, so the first railway line in 1880 bypassed it, cutting across the mountains from Las Vegas and dropping down to Albuquerque, which was developing as a trade and transportation center for the territory.

Old Town Albuquerque on the east bank of the Rio Grande traced its history back to the coming of Coronado in 1540. The Duke City, named in 1706 for the Spanish Duke of Alburquerque, was a small village 70 years before the American Revolution and 166 years after Coronado first arrived in the valley below the Sandia Mountains. The new Albuquerque did not arrive until the Santa Fe Railroad laid its tracks one and a half miles east of Old Town in 1880.

In the spring of 1889, four families donated twenty acres on a mesa some two miles east of New Albuquerque with the intent that the land serve as a site for a territorial institution of higher learning, the University of New Mexico. Valued at about $5 per acre, the land was literally dirt cheap. Anyone who has ever tried to nurture a tree or bush on New Mexico's high desert will appreciate the foresight or imagination, perhaps the courage, of visualizing anything ever blossoming on that barren mesa, let alone a full-blown university.

In 1889 the Territory of New Mexico was still a wild frontier. The Lincoln County War had barely ended, and the Apaches and Navajos raided the isolated ranches with frequency and fury. The Santa Fe Ring, a shadowy coalition of politicians, federal officials, and land and cattle barons, controlled the legislature, law enforcement, and courts and exerted power in Washington.[1] With spreads of land so big they almost defied imagination, these barons ruled virtually unchallenged.

The Albuquerque of the 1880s was a trade and railroad center, a far cry from the metropolis it would become a century later. Even the combined population of Old Town (the original Spanish colonial settlement) and New Town (the business and residential area around the railroad head after 1880) was only about six thousand, about the present size of Belen or Bernalillo. In addition to warehouses and general stores fit for selling and trading, Albuquerque also had hotels for its highly transient population, as well as bars, brothels, and gambling dens. One might get educated in such an environment, but not with much promise of such education leading to degrees in higher learning.

If the social climate had some downsides, the high, dry, clean air did attract "lungers" from back East and other more civilized parts of the world. For health reasons, those afflicted with tuberculosis came to New Mexico. Some died, but many lived and recovered enough of their health to make lasting contributions to this sparsely populated territory.

La Tierra Encantada—Land of Enchantment

Tony Hillerman is not a native New Mexican, much as most natives would like to claim him. He grew up in Oklahoma and graduated from college there before coming to New Mexico as a newspaperman. He then became an administrator and professor at UNM. Meanwhile, he kept writing, until ultimately his mystery novels outsold even the Sherlock Holmes books. Hillerman paints beautiful word pictures. He often is most eloquent when writing about New Mexico, lovingly describing it as a place "where edges meet." Hillerman wrote the narrative that accompanied the photographs of David Muench for a book entitled *New Mexico*. In eleven pages, he captures the beauty, majesty, and history of the region, tracing the geological and cultural developments back to the very beginnings.

> It is here that the Rocky Mountains finally end in a chaos of parallel ridges. Here the Great Plains lap at last against the edge of these mountains. And here the Sonoran Desert—spread over an immensity of Mexico—is finally overcome by too much altitude and too many late summer thunderstorms. No other state offers such an abrupt contrast in landscape. Six of the continent's seven biological life zones are found within her borders—ranging from the cold and windy arctic-alpine country above timberline to the sometimes torrid Lower Sonoran Desert . . .
>
> The net effect of location and altitude is a sort of cancellation—a climate basically dry, mild and dominated by the sun. The thin, dry air moderates the summer's heat and almost constant sunlight warms the winters.
>
> Something like this might also be said about its culture. Its population, too, has been formed by edges and over-lappings—the meetings of migrations which had lost their force with cultures which had lost their intolerance.

Hillerman goes on to trace the successive New Mexican cultures from the Athabascans and Ancestral Puebloans (the ancient ones, until recently called the

Anasazi) to the Navajos and Apaches and on to the Spanish conquistadores and Franciscan missionaries and then the Mexicans. These were finally engulfed by the westward sweep of the Anglo-Americans.

> But without the magnet of material wealth to attract it, even Manifest Destiny lost force and ferocity . . . and allowed other cultures to survive. For once, the American melting pot failed to operate. New Mexico produced a mosaic of cultures instead of a mixture.[2]

To understand and appreciate the impact of the University of New Mexico, one must be *simpático* (attuned) to the geography, history, and culture of the people of this "place where edges meet," this New Mexico.

The Educational Climate in New Mexico

Michael Welsh, a professor of history at the University of New Mexico in the 1980s, wrote an excellent history of the University from its beginnings to 1938. Though never finished nor published, this work provides a superb account of the development of public education in New Mexico in the latter half of the nineteenth century. On numerous occasions, he cites the 1982 PhD dissertation of Jane Atkins, entitled "Who Shall Educate: The Schooling Question in Territorial New Mexico, 1846–1911."

Atkins observed that "when the American Army descended upon Santa Fe in 1846, it opened a path for settlement and domination by a nation expanding more rapidly than it could comprehend. What the United States found in New Mexico were established Hispanic and Indian populations of long standing, and a scarcity of land and water resources for latecomers."[3]

When newcomers from the eastern states arrived in New Mexico, they did not see environment and economics as determining influences in the glaring deficiencies in public education. Instead, they convinced themselves that the Hispanic culture, "especially its focus on the Roman Catholic faith," had hindered progress. As reported by Welsh, "Government officials, Protestant missionaries, educators, and civic boosters raised a chorus of voices denouncing the Catholic influence on New Mexicans, and pressed for reforms to free the territory from this vestige of medieval sorcery."[4]

For these early settlers, religious tension seemed to overwhelm all other elements in the debate over public schooling for the territory. This attitude did not escape the attention of New Mexican Hispanic Roman Catholics. In the 1850s, French-born Archbishop Jean Baptiste Lamy attempted to resolve this issue by importing foreign priests and resisting the spread of sectarian schooling. Protestants viewed the issue as proof of the Roman Catholic evil, while at the same time accepting Lamy's "simplistic explanation of New Mexican illiteracy as nothing more than 'the Mexican national vice.'"[5]

Much as they coveted education for their children, residents of New Mexico soon realized that the territory had few trained teachers and very little money for salaries. There were no teachers' colleges and therefore no instructors who understood the dynamics of the territory. Further, it is interesting that, given the predominance of native Hispanics and Indians, there were virtually no native speakers in New Mexican classrooms. Thus, local communities often hired their teachers from Catholic religious orders, the only source of instructors who fit the unique criteria for education in the territory.

Unwilling to leave the education of their children to nuns and priests, various religious groups ventured into New Mexico to fight what were then perceived to be the dual enemies of the frontier West: illiteracy and the Roman Catholic Church. In 1879, the New West Education Commission (NWEC) was founded and opened schools in Santa Fe (the New West Academy) and Albuquerque (the Albuquerque Academy). The NWEC, which the Congregationalists funded and directed from the church's western outpost (Colorado College in Colorado Springs), offered the only school in either Albuquerque or Santa Fe with grades one through twelve. Most of the student body came from the Anglo merchant class. The curriculum reflected the influence of eastern academies and included classical languages, literature, philosophy, and the natural sciences. It was basically a program of studies designed for a small number of rich kids in New England and the upper Midwest, young men and women from affluent backgrounds who could look forward to positions in the family businesses. Their families believed that their sons and daughters needed polish and sophistication more than intellectual challenge and breadth of learning.[6]

The presence of the NWEC schools, with their network of eastern contributors, provided Albuquerque leaders with what they believed to be the best possibilities for public education. In 1881, the Presbyterians began the U.S. Indian Training School (known commonly as the Albuquerque Indian School) in rented quarters a mile north of the Old Town Plaza. Later, this site was the home of Menaul School, sponsored by the Presbyterians. In addition, the Methodists sent Thomas and Emily Harwood to open a school for Hispanic youth. The Harwoods eventually established the Albuquerque Methodist Episcopal College, which offered a bachelor of arts degree. The school closed in 1891, however, with the passage of the public school bill in the territorial legislature.

These activities energized the Roman Catholic Church to meet the challenge of Protestant influences. Thus by 1889, the Duke City had several convent schools, which nuns operated in their living quarters, as well as the Highland School.[7]

Meanwhile, in Santa Fe the Roman Catholic Church established Saint Michael's High School and College for boys and Loretto Academy for girls. A Jesuit college opened in Las Vegas but was soon moved to Denver, where it became Regis College.

For the record, Congregational minister Horatio O. Ladd founded the first institution named the University of New Mexico in Santa Fe in 1881. The school was not well accepted by the public and closed its doors in 1888. Located at the corner of Santa Fe's Garfield and Guadalupe streets, the building's next occupant was Saint Mary's Convent. Years later it was remodeled into a housing facility called University Apartments.[8]

The Coming of the Railroad

Philosophers and historians have waxed eloquent on the lofty motives of advocates for the development of higher learning on the western frontier. Typical of this romantic idealism, Henry Ward Beecher, in 1859, picturesquely described the western emigrants.

> They drive schools along with them as shepherds drive flocks. They have herds of churches, academies, lyceums; and the religious and educational institutions go lowing along the western plains as Jacob's herds lowed along the Syrian Hills.[9]

The Territory of New Mexico was not the western plains, but mountains and semidesert, a battlefield for conflicting cultures, a haven for outlaws, and a magnet to land and cattle barons. The entrepreneurs in the central Rio Grande valley, with its cattle and sheep, agricultural products, and the boom in mining, coveted the coming of the railroads, and Albuquerque was considered to be the hub of the territory. It had suffered a major setback in 1875, however, when the territorial legislature combined Bernalillo County and its northern neighbor, Santa Ana County, into one. After a series of delays, in March 1878 the county commissioners called a general election to determine where the county seat would be located. Albuquerque lost, Bernalillo won, and the county records and offices were transferred to the village of Bernalillo.[10]

As Marc Simmons reported in his book *Albuquerque: a Narrative History*, rails in the direction of Albuquerque had actually been laid in 1866. Congress had authorized the Atlantic and Pacific Railroad (A&P) to build a transcontinental line from Springfield, Missouri, to San Francisco via the thirty-fifth parallel through central New Mexico. The A&P, however, went into receivership in 1872. It was succeeded by the Atchison, Topeka, and Santa Fe (AT&SF), which by 1878 had laid rails to Trinidad, Colorado. Many New Mexicans viewed the railroad as a giant corporation with unlimited funds and treated its representatives accordingly. This attitude was to cost several New Mexico towns dearly.[11]

In February 1878 Bernalillo had its chance for the railhead. A delegation of five "advance men" representing AT&SF met with leaders in the community. The company apparently had selected Bernalillo as the chief division point on its transcontinental line and proposed to build a bridge across the Rio Grande, offices, a roundhouse, and extensive railroad yards, which would transform Bernalillo into the foremost town in the territory. Bernalillo's premier citizen, Leandro Perea, let these representatives know that if the railroad wanted his land, it should be prepared to pay $425 an acre. This prompted the AT&SF officials to roll up their maps and depart for Albuquerque, where the atmosphere proved more hospitable.

The story of the coming of the railroads to New Mexico in the 1880s would make a book in itself. The tales of avarice, greed, and blown chances would haunt communities like Bernalillo, Las Vegas, and Santa Fe for years. Old Las Vegas envisioned huge profits from land sales and ended up with the rails laid a mile or two east of the original settlement, and a new Las Vegas grew up.

The Santa Fe tale took another twist. So confident and haughty in their demands were town officials in negotiating for a rail line through their city, the railroad representatives broke off talks and chose the more expedient and economical route through Galisteo to Albuquerque. Eventually a trunk line was established to and from Lamy (which was really Galisteo renamed) to the capital city.

The net effect of the railroad executives' decisions was the eventual blooming of Albuquerque as the commercial and transportation hub of the middle Rio Grande valley and, over time, as the largest metropolitan center of New Mexico. As a result Albuquerque soon became the logical site for the University of New Mexico.

Simmons commented: "After seeing Las Vegas bypassed by a mile and Santa Fe missed by a good deal more than that, with the main line at least, nervous Albuquerqueans knew one thing for a certainty: haggling with the AT&SF was risky business."[12]

Much to the disappointment of the residents of old Albuquerque, the key decision was where the AT&SF would decide to place its offices and yards. Old Town was nestled in a bend of the Rio Grande, about a mile and a half west of a straight line surveyors had drawn down the east side of the valley. AT&SF officials announced in January 1880 that they had chosen the straighter, more direct route, which meant the depot and yards would be built about two miles east of Old Town on the barren semidesert. The last rails were laid in early April 1880, and April 22 was selected for a gala celebration welcoming the railroad. Only stacks of rails, ties, and other construction materials marked the site of what would become the new Albuquerque, which a decade later on a sandy mesa two miles further east would serve as the home of the University of New Mexico.

If such dreams existed in 1880, they were not readily apparent in that raw setting. What emerged was a typical frontier railroad town, a haven that attracted a restless, even shiftless class of transient railroad employees who had money to spend. Assorted vagrants, criminals, and confidence men were drawn to the brawling, sprawling Albuquerque. In addition, fires and floods occurred with disturbing frequency, all reminding the town fathers of the precarious existence of their frontier community.

Old Town versus New Town

As related earlier, the beginnings of Albuquerque reach back to the founding of the villa in 1706. That was Old Town, mostly Hispanic, with adobe buildings, the plaza, and the old church, San Felipe de Neri. The booming metropolis that Albuquerque became, however, had its origins in the arrival of the railroad in 1880. This was New Town, mostly Anglo, with government buildings, hotels, mercantile shops, business establishments, and later tall stone buildings reflecting the architecture that accompanied the new arrivals from the eastern part of the nation.[13]

Simmons captured the flavor of this growth of New Town, which in 1880 was nothing but barren prairie or desert.

City developers in 1880 had expected the Old and the New Towns to undergo parallel expansion until the space between them was filled, and they merged to form a single metropolis. But in fact, New Albuquerque spurted ahead, leaving its aging sister lolling in the doldrums over by the river. Old Town became like a barnacle clinging to the hull of the fast-moving central city, going nowhere on its own and glad for a free ride on the swelling tide of progress.[14]

Old Town and New Town remained separated by a depressingly bare floodplain. Rivalries included squabbles over the locations of the post office and county courthouse. (The latter was returned to Old Town from Bernalillo in 1873.) Equally divisive were the social distinctions, with Old Town dominated by Hispanics and New Town by Anglos arriving on the railroad. The merger of the two communities did not take place until the mid-twentieth century, thanks to urban sprawl.[15]

While these intramural skirmishes between Old Town and New Town were going on, Albuquerqueans were trying vigorously to win the capital away from Santa Fe. Throughout the 1880s and well into the 1890s, money and energy were poured into an intense lobbying effort. In the final years of the century, however, the campaign was abandoned as hopeless.[16]

Mariano S. Otero and Elias S. Stover

The coming of the railroad brought prosperity and change to the Albuquerque area. The cattle business of Lincoln and Colfax counties and the trade in wool and sheep from Hispanic and Navajo herds stimulated the flow of capital and the hunger for durable and luxury goods. The combination of transport and trade provided expanded opportunities for entrepreneurs. Two in particular, one Hispanic whose family had strong roots in the middle valley and one Anglo from the Midwest, were to play strong roles in the development of Albuquerque and the founding of the University of New Mexico.

Mariano Otero, son of Miguel Otero, Sr., former territorial delegate to Congress, merchant-investor, and the founder of the San Miguel County Bank of Las Vegas, became an important entrepreneur in Bernalillo County, where his interests included the railroad. With his Hispanic lineage and his entrepreneurial leadership, he was to become a prominent figure in the University of New Mexico, serving as the first president of its Board of Regents.[17]

Elias Stover also was to become a prime mover in the establishment of the University of New Mexico. Marc Simmons related this colorful account of Stover's arrival in Albuquerque and his rise to prominence.

On a bright day in 1876, Stover had climbed off the stagecoach in front of Tom Post's Exchange Hotel, beat the dust from his clothes, and looking about told himself that this sun-blistered, dirt-coated Albuquerque had the pulse of a town with a future. A Union veteran, former lieutenant-governor of Kansas (1872–74), and a merchant by trade, Elias Stover, at age forty, believed in keeping ahead of the crowd. Kansas, before he left, had been in a frenzy of railroad building, and at least one of the lines, the Atchison, Topeka, and Santa Fe, was pointing toward the Southwest. Stover's nose for business must have told him that once the rails reached New Mexico, the land's vast reservoir of resources would be ripe for tapping, and that could only be done by the men who were out front. Whether by chance or by unerring instinct, he had singled out the one town ordained by circumstance to become the chief metropolis of the Territory. Quickly he set himself up in a store on the [Old Town] plaza and by the spring of 1878, Stover and Co. was being referred to in print as "the most liberal, enterprising, and public spirited of any house in town." . . . In an unbelievably short time, Elias S. Stover had won a slot among the ranks of the community's business elite. And from that position, he was on his way to becoming a central figure in the lively events that were soon to follow.[18]

Among Stover's many business enterprises, he established the Stover, Crary and Company grocery concern, operated a livery stable, and purchased the Albuquerque Publishing Company, which produced the *Albuquerque Morning Journal*. He joined forces with Judge William Hazeldine and a local trader, Franz Huning, to form the New Mexico Town Company, which bought large sections of land east of the Old Town plaza, some of which they donated for a depot and yards for the railroad.

For the latter part of the nineteenth century, Stover and his business associates created an economic cartel that would rival Santa Fe's merchant class. Stover, Hazeldine, and Huning were among the foremost boosters and devoted great energy to creating an attractive, prosperous business climate. As stated by Judge Hazeldine, "The bell of the locomotive tolls the death knell of . . . superstition and ignorance." He predicted that the power of technology in New Mexico would lead to "knowledge, education, advancement and progress" for the people.[19]

Albuquerque, 1880–90

The years from 1880 to the new century sometimes were referred to as Albuquerque's gilded age, an ebullient time of rapid growth and progress. Marc Simmons pointed out, however: "Though the times were magnificent in the prosperity and opportunity they held out to men of industry and imagination, they were also hectic and sometimes dangerous." There were man-made disasters, like fires, and natural disasters, like floods. Simmons added that lawlessness remained unchecked. In colorful terms, he described the people of Albuquerque in that era. "The railroad workers with silver coin to throw away were the magnet that drew professional gamblers, ladies of ill repute, bunko men, saloon keepers, and outlaws of several stripes."[20]

Had a group of no-nonsense experts been commissioned in the early 1880s to study New Albuquerque and to submit a forecast as to its possibilities of one day attaining the respectability that goes with the development of religious, educational, and cultural institutions, the experts might well have concluded, on that score at least, that the town had little future. Like frontier communities throughout the West, Albuquerque at the start seemed to feed and grow on its saloons, gambling parlors, and brothels, and to derive a certain perverse vitality from gunfights, public hangings, and night rides of vigilantes. But here, as elsewhere, both the loose living and the violence were to prove a transitory stage in the ongoing process of forming a new municipality in the standard American mold.[21]

Thus, as Albuquerque grew, it began to attract other professionals who recognized the need for more advanced education. With fervor and passion, ministers of the various Protestant denominations brought civilization and virtue to the community with imposing churches, missionary societies, and sectarian schools. These augmented the Roman Catholic convent schools. Civic leaders began to realize that in order to attract a better class of migrant they had to establish and support not only institutions of worship, but also of learning, namely, a system of public schools. Further, they were also aware that surrounding states, like Colorado, and territories, like Arizona, had formed systems of higher education in the 1870s and 1880s. The importance of institutions of higher learning in the economic development of a region also did not go unnoticed nor was it limited to the visionaries of Albuquerque. South, in the Mesilla valley (Las Cruces), agitation had begun for a land-grant college as early as 1886. The people around Socorro were lobbying for a school of mines, while representatives from Las Vegas were bidding for a territorial normal school to produce teachers in anticipation of a new system of public education.[22]

Meanwhile, on the national scene the election of a Republican president, Benjamin Harrison, was not good news for Albuquerque. Supporters of Territorial Governor Edmund G. Ross and the Democratic Party knew that they had less than three months (in late 1888 and early 1889) to enact territorial legislation for higher education. They were apprehensive that when the Republicans entered the White House on March 4, 1889, they would appoint new federal officials who were sympathetic to the Santa Fe Ring and the capital city. Consequently, when the territorial legislature opened for business in December 1888, several bills appeared calling for institutions of higher learning in Albuquerque, Las Cruces, and Las Vegas.[23]

So the stage was set for the dramatic events leading to the establishment of the University of New Mexico. ■

Fred Simms is at his stenograph machine, and Bernard Rodey is behind his desk.

Bernard S. Rodey

CHAPTER TWO

Founding of the University of New Mexico
1889–92

To anyone reviewing the time, place, and people involved with the establishment of a western university in the last half of the nineteenth century, there is always a nagging question. What motivated people of little or no formal education to strive for public institutions of higher learning in an intellectual desert that did not even have a system of public elementary or high schools? The editors of the *Literary History of the United States* perhaps answer the question in part.

> A tincture of social vanity, mingled with a sincere wish for the good life, set the tone for aspiration on this Western frontier. If the prospector, mountain man, or cattle king be scorned because he reckoned culture by weight and bulk, or recognized beauty only when certified by convention, it must be added that he was faithfully striving for better things. By the building of schools and colleges and free libraries, the West was trying, according to its lights and with admitted future success, to enhance the cultural perception of its children.[1]

In *Pueblo on the Mesa,* a volume commemorating the fiftieth anniversary of the founding of the University, Dorothy Hughes cites an unnamed *escudero* (nobleman) who in 1849 exclaimed, "May Heaven grant to New Mexico some institution of learning where its sons may receive educational training according to the requirements of the century!" Hughes then added, "And it was only to Heaven and to themselves that the early New Mexican inhabitants could look."[2]

While Hughes pointed out that the territory had in meager fashion made a beginning of schools, it had always been in the face of opposition. Many New Mexicans were not content to leave schooling in the hands of the Roman Catholic Church where it had been during the Spanish and Mexican occupation. Hughes noted that some parents opposed schools because their children were needed to herd sheep and some were exempted from mandatory school attendance or bound out "under the law of masters and servants." So the proponents of higher education struggled with the public's rather indefinite longing for public education and its contrasting reluctance to pay for it. Many also viewed colleges and universities as economic development tools.[3]

Higher education needed a champion, and it found one in Bernard Shandon Rodey.

"Father of the University"

Early historians of the University of New Mexico bequeathed upon Rodey the title of "Father of the University." Only thirty-two years old in 1889, he was reported to be "inspired by tremendous enthusiasm plus courage, independence, persistence and intelligence," and he was identified as the person who was elected to the territorial legislature "to fight almost single-handed for the University of New Mexico."[4]

Michael Welsh, citing the work of Lee Ann Pricer, who wrote a student paper on Rodey, stated that Rodey's background made him a logical person to promote higher education for New Mexico and seek the territorial university for his adopted hometown. Rodey, born March 1, 1856, had come to North America from his native Ireland at age seven. His was a farm family, and they lived in Canada and Vermont. Self-educated, he had only about three months of formal schooling. Like many young Irishmen, Rodey found work with the westward-expanding railroad lines. He took a position in Boston with the Atlantic and Pacific Company as the private secretary and stenographer for the general manager of the railroad. In the evening he read law books in preparation for a career as an attorney. When the A&P sent its general manager to live in Albuquerque in 1881, Rodey also came.

Soon after his arrival, Rodey sought entry into the legal profession. He worked for the Second Judicial District in Socorro as a stenographer and then moved to Albuquerque, where he earned admission to the territorial bar association in 1884. The connections he made among Duke City political and civic leaders brought him attention and linked him to the reform movement in Albuquerque opposed to the Santa Fe Ring. In 1888 he ran successfully for the Territorial Assembly as a representative from Bernalillo County, where he joined with others to advance the cause of his community through territorial appropriations.

For reasons unknown, Rodey served only one two-year term, 1888–90. Later he represented the New Mexico Territory in Congress, served as a federal judge in Puerto Rico, and became the United States attorney for the territory of Alaska.[5]

In the 1889 legislative session, Rodey felt compelled to gain some distinction as a reformer and one of a new breed of politicians. To this end he introduced a number of measures, including bills relating to justices of the peace, irrigation projects, and banking.[6]

Many years later, in a 1942 speech to the Newcomen Society, UNM President Tom Popejoy identified some of the other men also responsible for the legislation authorizing the founding of the University of New Mexico: Neill B. Field, Elias S. Stover, O. E. Cromwell, Colonel Ralph E. Twitchell, Judge John R. McFie (later appointed to the Supreme Court of the New Mexico Territory), and others. Popejoy added, however, that Rodey actually wrote the legislation.[7]

Gary Karsh, writing for the *UNM Alumnus* in 1979, described the adverse conditions that faced Rodey and the legislators seeking to found and locate the state university in Albuquerque.

> It was a complicated situation. A new federal law promised territories revenues from leases of federal lands. It was proposed to use the income to support three territorial institutions: a penitentiary, an insane asylum and a university. Legislators from the Santa Fe and Las Vegas areas, who had traditionally dominated the Territorial Legislature, were now apprehensive about the growing power of the Albuquerque delegation. They joined forces to ensure location of the supposedly more lucrative institutions in their areas, perhaps because they believed there would always be criminals and lunatics, but not necessarily college students. That political line-up was an advantage for Bernard Shandon Rodey . . . for it removed powerful obstacles to his plan to open the school in his hometown. As the 1889 session drew to a close, agreement had not yet been reached on locations of the three institutions.[8]

Tony Hillerman's version reports that two days before the passage of the bill creating the University of New Mexico, Rodey was still hammering away in a "smoke-filled caucus room in the rococo splendor of Santa Fe's famous old Palace Hotel."

> Bernard Rodey had been there for days, arguing with a visionary's eloquence that the Territory must have a university, and gradually persuading those who felt that a hundred other more pressing problems had prior call on what little cash the impoverished territory could muster.
>
> How Rodey prevailed in the political struggle is lost to posterity. Then as now, no minutes were kept of the hard-nosed bargaining sessions held behind the locked doors of the caucuses. Suffice to say that fortune gave Rodey and his handful of allies an opportunity. In this session the struggle centered around locating important territorial institutions—the penitentiary, insane asylum, agricultural experiment station, and others. Rodey's plan for a university would add another small plum to the spoils available. Perhaps it would be enough to swing the votes of a small county which otherwise received nothing. Whatever happened inside the room, when the meeting adjourned decisions had been made. . . . Among the smaller parcels delivered was the University of New Mexico, to be located in Bernalillo County.[9]

Dorothy Hughes also described those last hours in Santa Fe's Palace Hotel, located at the corner of Washington and Marcy streets, though later destroyed by fire and replaced by a filling station. She reported that Albuquerque attorney Neill B.

Field delivered to Rodey a rough draft of the bill. On the night of February 26, John McFie and Rodey began framing the final version.

> For thirty-six hours Rodey and McFie did not leave that room. Meals were brought to them; there was no time to go out for such trivialities as food, not if there was to be a University. The sixty sections of the bill were dictated almost in their entirety by the indefatigable Mr. Rodey to Fred Simms, a negro stenographer. The bill was introduced into the Legislature in its last waning hours and was passed just before adjournment. The University had been born.[10]

Marc Simmons reports that when the bill was introduced three days before the end of the legislative session, other towns, sensing a commercial advantage that must certainly go with such an undertaking, suddenly became contenders for the home of the new school. By adroit maneuvering, Albuquerque's partisans managed to allot other public institutions to their rivals and thus preserve the university for themselves. Socorro got a school of mines, Las Cruces a college of agriculture, and Las Vegas the insane asylum. The bill also provided additional funds for the penitentiary in Santa Fe.

Rodey's bill, which a coalition of progressive forces supported, succeeded in overcoming the opposition and won passage on February 28, 1889, literally the last hours of the session. The bill provided that the new school was "intended to be the state university when New Mexico should be admitted as a state to the Union."[11]

Drawing upon the research published by Frank D. Reeve in his master's thesis on the history of the University of New Mexico, Michael Welsh commented:

> The clauses in the seventy-three-section Omnibus Bill contain interesting suggestions about the school's purpose and function. The succeeding century would be occupied with the search for meaning about these statements.
>
> The religious tensions of New Mexico prompted the writing of Section 17: "No sectarian tenets or opinions shall be required to entitle any person to be admitted as a student or employed as a tutor."
>
> The faculty would have "immediate governance of the social departments," but the five-member Board of Regents "shall have the power to regulate the course of instruction, and prescribe the books and authorities to be used in the several departments."
>
> The question of religion would mix with ethnicity, leading many Hispanic Catholics to see UNM as a bastion of Anglo Protestantism. Likewise, the Regents-faculty debate would recur on several occasions . . .
>
> Of all the clauses in the enabling legislation, UNM's future evolved most directly from Sections 7 and 8. The former declared that "the University of New Mexico . . . is intended to be the State University."

The latter stated "The object of the University . . . shall be to provide the inhabitants of the Territory of New Mexico and the future state with the means of acquiring a thorough knowledge of the various branches of literature, science and arts."[12]

Michael Welsh noted that Albuquerque itself still found the idea of a university somewhat puzzling.

> Albuquerque . . . did not quite know what Bernard Rodey had bequeathed to it . . . The instruction at UNM would be for an urban-industrial society, which neither the Duke City nor New Mexico at large possessed until the boom growth of the post-World War II era. The institution sat upon the east mesa distant from both Hispanic Old Town and Anglo New Town, with a forty-five minute wagon ride to campus in good weather. Albuquerque had no public schools until 1891 . . . and few students came from families imbued with the spirit of higher education.[13]

Simmons also commented on the problems that had arisen during the drafting and politicking for the omnibus bill. He pointed out that during the weeks preceding its final passage, when it began to appear likely that Albuquerque would be chosen as the site for the state university, some people wanted it placed near the river in the vicinity of Old Town. Others supported a location in Barelas. The farsighted Rodey resolved the question by adding a clause that the University should be located on a third site. With deliberate intent, the location was described as being "near the town of Albuquerque, in the County of Bernalillo, within two miles of Railroad Avenue, upon a tract of good, high and dry land, of not less than twenty acres." As Simmons noted, such a site would place the University well outside the limits of Albuquerque and far up on the east mesa "where there was room to grow and the forthcoming institution would be well removed from the floods that plagued the valley."[14]

Simmons went on to say that Rodey knew precisely what he was doing and carefully spelled out the method of land acquisition. The act read: "The said land shall be donated and conveyed, free of any cost or expense, to the Territory of New Mexico, by G. W. Meylert."[15]

Meylert at that time was mayor of Albuquerque. He also was well known as one of the builders of the San Felipe Hotel and the man who convinced his fellow investors that it should be supplied with a library in place of a saloon. A ten-chimneyed structure, it proclaimed itself one of the greatest hostelries in the Southwest.[16]

While the principal donor of the site was C. W. Kennedy, upon whose gift of land the first University buildings were located, little has been said or written about the other three donors. In researching his book on the architectural history of the University, *Only in New Mexico,* Van Dorn Hooker discovered a map showing the original twenty acres. On the map's legend, Mr. and Mrs. C. W. Kennedy and Mr.

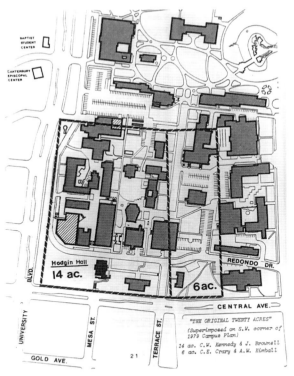

The University's first twenty acres are superimposed on a 1979 campus map. Map by Edward B. T. Glass

and Mrs. J. Brownell were given credit for the donation of fourteen acres, and Mr. and Mrs. C. E. Crary and Mr. and Mrs. A. W. Kimball were listed as donors of the remaining six acres.[17]

A newspaper of the day printed a glowing account of the land, describing it as "magnificent mesa land" that "overlooks the city of the valley with its progressive people." Others observed, however, that it was two rocky, steep miles from New Town (Old Town was another mile and a half west) and connected to civilization by only the rutted wagon tracks that would become Central Avenue.

Governor Edmund Ross signed the omnibus bill on February 28, 1889, a date identified forever thereafter as the official founding of the University of New Mexico, though there were no students, faculty, or buildings until the summer of 1892. Ross left office as governor the next day, and the territorial legislature adjourned. As Michael Welsh and other historians have pointed out, however, no one was quite sure what the departing governor and legislature had bequeathed to New Mexico. Ross, an outspoken proponent of advanced education as a means of modernizing the territory, relegated the "college bill" to the middle of his report to the secretary of the federal Department of the Interior for 1889. More prominent in the report were references to formation of a new finance system, a clarification of the codes of conduct for lawyers, and regulation of public health and welfare.[18]

The First Board of Regents

In his last day in office, Governor Ross was anxious to select a board of regents for the new university before his departure. His list included his old friend from Kansas, Elias Stover, Albuquerque businessman Mariano S. Otero, and Gurdon Meylert. His other two choices were John A. Lee, vice president of the Aztec Coal Company (which Stover ran) and W. B. Childers, also of Albuquerque.

A Republican appointee, L. Bradford Prince, replaced Ross as territorial governor. One of his first actions was to demand the resignations of all five appointees. Stover, reportedly seeking to ingratiate himself with the new governor, urged him to reappoint the Republicans. Meanwhile, Bernard Rodey, who described himself as the "Daddy of the Omnibus Bill" and one who took a "great interest in all the affairs of the University," submitted a list of nineteen candidates, all of whom lived in or near Albuquerque.[19]

Territorial Governor Prince announced his selections to the University of New Mexico Board of Regents on September 2, 1889. While Stover, Meylert, and Otero all had seats, Lee and Childers were dropped in favor of territorial Judge Henry Waldo and Frank W. Clancy of Santa Fe, a leading member of the New Mexico Bar Association and a future territorial attorney general. This group held its first meeting on November 3, 1889, at Meylert's San Felipe Hotel at Fifth and Gold avenues. The hotel was also the site of subsequent meetings before the completion of the University's first building in 1892.

The board's first order of business was to elect officers and begin the task of authorizing construction of a physical plant. Mariano Otero was elected by acclamation as the board's first president. Meylert was named secretary-treasurer and instructed to advertise in Denver, Kansas City, Santa Fe, and Albuquerque for an architect to plan a university building.[20]

Planning for the First Building

At its next meeting, December 9, 1889, the Regents drafted a letter to prospective architectural firms informing them that UNM had $25,000 to spend on a three-story brick building. The Regents envisioned "a chemical laboratory, janitor's room, furnaces, coal bins . . . patent dry closets (for both sexes) and two good rooms for a gymnasium." The building also needed "three recitation rooms on each of these floors, and three small rooms for professors."[21]

Welsh reported that because several months were allowed for the responses to the proposals, the Board of Regents chose to meet only once before May 28, 1890. At that time, the Regents received the last of the architectural bids and moved to accept the preliminary sketches of Albuquerque's Jesse M. Wheelock, who suggested that the cost of the structure the Regents proposed would be roughly $30,000. Based on Wheelock's concepts, construction bids were solicited. By September 13, the board had in hand statements from five firms and awarded the contract to Santa Fe contractors Palladino and Digneo. Specifically, the board prohibited purchasing bricks from the prison shops of the Santa Fe penitentiary, preferring Albuquerque red brick instead. Apparently, bricks made at the penitentiary were too soft and not suitable for exterior work.[22] Records reveal that most of the activities of the year 1890 revolved around the management of the architectural and construction contracts.

By 1891, however, the Regents were turning their attention to the academic structure and leadership of the University. That year the board named Elias Stover as the institution's first president for a six-month term. (In all, he was to serve as president until 1897.) Welsh pointed out that the selection of a member of the governing board as president was not an uncommon move for western universities, as the organizers wanted to keep close watch on the management of their schools. The selection of a "nonacademic" as president, however, would lead to friction with the faculty, some of whom were of the opinion that the appointment ignored the intellectual life of the campus. The Regents, however, believing that building a university from the ground up demanded a businessman's guidance, stuck with Stover.

Preceding the completion of the first building and the formal opening of the University, in the spring of 1892 the Regents authorized the planting of 150 shade trees and the construction of a barbed-wire fence around the twenty-acre site. One of the jokes of the time was that the fence was to keep the livestock out and the students in.

With its first building in the final stages of construction and the improvement of the site under way in the late spring of 1892, the governing board began to focus on the hiring of a faculty and the enrollment of the first students. As for the curriculum, there was heavy pressure from many sources to emphasize teacher training. The *Albuquerque Daily Citizen* stressed that teacher training might well be one of the most successful ventures for the fledgling university since only a third of all New Mexican children attended school. The newspaper also pointed out the lack of educators who were "acquainted with the habits and customs" of New Mexico.[23]

When it came to hiring faculty, the University, still on the drawing board, had little money and no prestige. The Regents approved the hiring of George S. Ramsey and Marshall Gaines, two former principals of the "Old UNM" that the New West Education Commission operated as a private school in Santa Fe from 1881 to 1888. Ramsey received an annual salary of $1,500. He served as principal and also took charge of the college-preparatory section. At Ramsey's suggestion, Marshall Gaines was appointed to teach in the Normal Department (the teacher-training program, sometimes referred to as the Normal School) for $150 per month.[24]

Thus, the summer term of the UNM Normal Department began on June 15, 1892, when the two teachers, Ramsey and Gaines, opened the doors for twenty-five pupils. "Because the UNM campus was so far from town, and roads were non-existent, the Regents authorized Ramsey to rent space in the New West Education Commission's Albuquerque Academy for $125 per month."[25] The building that housed the University's first students in that summer session was known as Perkins Hall, located on the northwest corner of Edith and Railroad Avenue. It had previously housed the Albuquerque Academy. When the University moved to its permanent campus in 1892, it continued to use the building until 1905 as the quarters for the Department of Music. The building later became the Albuquerque Public Library.[26]

During the course of the summer, as many as eighty-two students were enrolled in the Normal School. Among the attendees there were only five with Hispanic surnames: David Chaves, Albino Cordova, Adolfo Gallegos, Alberto Luna, and Atanasio S. Montoya. Charles Hodgin, later a distinguished faculty member and administrator at UNM, was one of the students, as was Robert Menaul, son of the founder of the Albuquerque Indian School and later the Menaul School of the Presbyterian Church.[27]

UNM's First Building

Meanwhile, the first building on the campus was nearing completion. Over the years, including at the time of fiftieth, seventy-fifth, and centennial celebrations, UNM historians have offered their own versions of that first official structure on the UNM campus.

Professor and administrator John D. Clark, who annually addressed the incoming freshmen at UNM, said in the 1930s that he remembered very distinctly "when the University seemed as far from the center of Albuquerque as Santa Fe now seems from this city, for the road to the University was just a trail over the sand hills, so poor in condition that those few who owned early automobiles often abandoned the cars in favor of the horse when coming to the University."[28]

Clark went on to relate some reminiscences of the fabled Charles Hodgin. He had written in 1928:

The heavy roof, the crowning glory of UNM's first building, had been framed when this photo was taken.

The University consisting of one building, its students had to live in town. A long rambling hack, driven by an old Indian fighter, Sandy Wardwell, made a trip to the University in the morning and a trip back to Albuquerque in the afternoon. The late Miss Josephine Parsons collected five cents from each passenger on the hack. A large percentage of the students rode saddle horses to and from the University, and it was found necessary to erect wooden sheds to shelter these animals.[29]

Clark offered his own description of that first building, a large three-story brick building, with a top-heavy, barn-like roof.

It was conspicuous standing alone in the great space of the open mesa. Visualize it if you can: without a tree, with no houses between it and the town, and none between it and the mountains, and no street leading to the mesa except the extension of Railroad Avenue, by the mere scratching of the gravel over the undulating and ungraded foothills. The only approaches for vehicles before this newly outlined way were two sandy arroyos, one coming up at the north line of the Campus, and one several blocks to the south.[30]

In what she described as the beginning of the "Pueblo on the Mesa," Dorothy Hughes stated:

There had not been a finer school building in the territory in 1892 than that first red brick structure, standing on a mesa, about two miles east of the village of Albuquerque. You know that building. It was not unlike any other

Animals—from this donkey to Tight's horse and Custers's cow—were popular for student pranks.

of that era of architectural destitution, the unimaginative and practical age of Victoria. Doubtless you yourself spent your early school days in just such an [*sic*] one, red brick and white stone, a chimney flanking each wing, an arched entrance, and windows, long windows, everywhere. This particular schoolhouse differed from its contemporaries in but one respect which set it apart then and for years to come as something far more precious than any like building, at least within the borders of New Mexico. That something was carved in stone above the arch. It read: "University N. M."[31]

Tony Hillerman, in celebration of the seventy-fifth birthday of the University of New Mexico, said of that first building of 1892:

> A tall, two-story brick building with Gay 90s gables rose in lonely majesty, jutting like a red pinnacle amid unbroken oceans of grassland. A wagon trail wound two miles down the mesa to link (except in wet weather) the center of learning with the center of civilization below.[32]

Gary Karsh in 1979 described the first building as "a stylish Richardson Romanesque structure of red brick with sandstone trim, a barn-like roof and rows of narrow, arched windows. Within its walls were housed the complete facilities of the University."[33]

By 1988, UNM was beginning to celebrate the centennial anniversary of its founding. Melissa Howard wrote on the hundred years of partnership with the Albuquerque business community and gave this description of that first building. "The red brick building, with its eyebrowed windows, arched doorways and identical east and west facades, was proclaimed the 'finest school building in the territory.' For decades it was UNM: classrooms, labs, library, administrative offices, even the dormitory . . ."[34]

Campus architect and author Van Dorn Hooker gives a detailed account of the contracts for and construction of the building. Hooker relates that Jesse M. Wheelock, who designed the building, patterned it after the Richardsonian style, which was popular in 1890.

> The University's Main Building . . . was red brick with light-colored stone trim, typical of midwestern school architecture. . . . It was symmetrically designed so that both east and west facades had inscription blocks above the arched entrance panels reading "University N.M. 1890." The main entrance was on the west side, and there was no back door as such for many years. The roof, a complex combination of hipped and gabled framing, added twenty-six feet to the already imposing structure. . . . The building was situated on the southwest corner of the campus, easily visible from the valley below.[35]

That it was a warm and lively place is attested to many times. Charles Hodgin, for whom the building was later named, recalled those early days, writing in 1928:

> When the first building was erected, there was a large hay-loft-like room immediately under the heavy roof—third floor above ground. For some time the assembly was held, a daily proposition, in this immense room, notwithstanding the hard stair climb for the young ladies, already over-burdened with superfluously extended dress skirts.[36]

The third floor also became the target of one of the first student pranks, as told by Hodgin:

> It happened on a certain hollowe'en that the lads—some of the lads—those who had more human nature than others—centered their attention upon a carriage, cautiously kept on the campus. They took it to pieces and wheel by wheel, and part by part carried it up to the assembly room and put all parts together on the platform by the speakers' stand, ready for the lads to enjoy the next morning at the 9 o'clock assembly. But alas the janitor discovered the prank in time to prevent the commotion.[37]

It is well that the University has pictures and descriptions of this first building, because in 1909 it was modified in the Pueblo Style of architecture, which has been the campus's chief characteristic for almost a century. It still occupies its original site on the southwest corner of the Central Campus.

On June 6, 1942, President Tom Popejoy addressed the Newcomen Society. Referring to those turbulent days leading up to the founding of the state university and the flurry of activities that accompanied its initial academic year in 1892, he reminded his audience: "To me it is important to suggest that the creation by the legislature of a territorial university to be located in Albuquerque was a stupendous decision."[38] A more accurate remark could scarcely be made. ▪

Roy Stamm (back row, fourth from left) played on the University's first football team in 1894. The coach, W. A. Zimmer, stands at right.

CHAPTER THREE
Administration of Elias S. Stover and Hiram Hadley
1892–97

President Stover served as the chief administrative officer until 1897.

W hen the first classes at the University of New Mexico were inaugurated in the summer of 1892, the institution was a university in name only. Records show that seventy-three or perhaps seventy-five students enrolled, most of them from New Mexico. At the outset, inasmuch as the territory lacked public high schools, the newly created university addressed itself to establishing a Preparatory Department (sometimes called the Preparatory School) to prepare students for regular university work. This department offered courses at the secondary level and continued functioning until 1905. Also added in that first year was the Normal Department (or School), designed to train teachers to staff the anticipated public schools in the territory.[1]

The Regents had appointed one of their own, Albuquerque businessman Elias Stover, as the first president. He served as president until 1897 and as Regent until 1911. Because he had no experience in education, however, Hiram Hadley was appointed vice president of the faculty in 1894, a position that was said to place him "in charge of the University."[2]

Anticipating the problem of having no students in the territory prepared for college, the Regents in the spring of 1892 authorized letters to be sent out to county school superintendents to "ascertain who may desire to attend a Normal Department in the University, provided one should be opened during the summer months." Apparently the letter was effective.

Hiram Hadley oversaw the academic operations during the University's first years.

During the summer of 1892, the University issued and distributed its first catalog, "a small, pinkish, thin-paper pamphlet numbering fifteen pages." Dorothy Hughes says the catalog, in an "informal, almost heart-to-heart fashion," proudly announced that the University had a "'well-fitted laboratory'; a library with books, periodicals, and 'the leading Encyclopaedias,' which the Regents were buying 'on time.'" The catalog also praised the climate and the new University building. Hughes noted in *Pueblo on the Mesa* that "nothing had been overlooked to attract the students; there were reduced railroad rates on return fares (only if you stayed out the term); good boarding facilities; free tuition."

George Ramsey (back row, center) and his Normal Class students posed in the doorway of the Main Building in 1892.

Further, the catalog pointed out that the University "is not a reform school. The largest liberty consistent with good work and good order will be given," and "its bounty is intended for the earnest and industrious student." It warned, however, that "the indolent or unworthy will not be retained in the institution."[3]

The catalog was distributed widely to the four corners of the territory with good results. Several teachers enrolled, desiring to obtain a degree and update their credentials and knowledge, as did numerous students who aspired to enter the teaching profession. Thus, when the University opened the doors of its own building on September 21, 1892, 108 students had signed up for the academic year.[4]

The catalog specified the curriculum, which reflected the classical tradition and listed Latin, Greek, English, and mathematics as the core courses. These included four years of Latin and Greek grammar and prose (Caesar, Cicero, Anabasis, Virgil, and Homer); algebra, geometry, physics; and a choice of French, German, or Spanish, with "rhetorical work through the course" on the side. Hughes observed: "What might seem a strange over-emphasis on Latin and Greek in this new wilderness is explainable in that 'for admission to the Freshman Class, the same degree of accuracy and thoroughness will be insisted on as in our best colleges.'"[5]

> It didn't matter that these young folk of a desert land, sons of pioneers and actually pioneers themselves, probably would have little use for Latin and Greek in their battle for existence in an undeveloped territory. The founders were not attempting to fit a university to the needs of a frontier population; their purpose was to prepare students to meet the exacting requirements of other universities in the United States. Latin and Greek were an integral part of the curriculum of the day.[6]

When the fall semester of 1892 opened, George Ramsey was principal of both the Preparatory and Normal departments and administered the academic affairs of the University. In addition, he taught mathematics and physics. In all there were six faculty members, five of whom held the master's degree: Ramsey, Alcinda Morrow (education, English, and Spanish), Marshall R. Gaines (Latin, Greek, and natural sciences), Albert Christy (elocution), and G. R. Stouffer, master of accounting (penmanship and the sixth grade). The sixth member of the faculty, Andrew Groh, taught German and French. He also was listed as a student. The courses in Latin, Greek, sciences, and literature were for students in the Preparatory Department since college-level courses were not offered until 1897.[7]

In late October 1892 the Regents approved the appointment of Josephine Parsons as an instructor of stenography and bookkeeping. Parsons remained on the faculty for thirty-five years and became the highest-ranking woman in the UNM administration as financial secretary.[8]

As the first academic year (1892–93) drew to a close, the UNM Regents and faculty believed they had given to the territory what the legislature had intended in 1889. Sixty-three students had enrolled in the various programs, although none were taking courses on the college level. Expenditures for the year were $12,998.02, of which $9,481.92 was for salaries.[9]

In the second year of operations (1893–94), Stouffer left, and two newcomers were added to the faculty: Martha L. Taylor, MA, who taught English grammar, history, and geography, and Harriet E. Jenness, for drawing, penmanship, music, and calisthenics. Of the eight faculty members, four were women.

The catalog for 1893 announced programs leading to three baccalaureate degrees in arts (which required preparation in Latin, Greek, and mathematics, as well as electives), philosophy (calling for Latin, mathematics, literature, and philosophy), and science (for which mathematics, physics, chemistry, and biology were necessary). Historian William C. Dabney, however, noted that this was all on paper and added: "During the first five years there was no college-level program in operation. The catalog announced that the college was not yet open being 'not fully equipped with professors and appliances.'"[10]

Although enrollment that year reached 142 (or perhaps 140, depending on the source), no students were taking college courses. In fact, the Regents and faculty lamented that most students were not even ready for the preparatory program. This motivated the Regents to create a "subpreparatory" department, which offered basics of arithmetic, language, history and geography of the United States, reading, spelling, and nature studies.[11]

In the spring of 1894 several Albuquerque physicians and druggists approached the UNM Regents with a request for a program to prepare people to pass the licensing examination in pharmacy. W. A. Zimmer of Cedar Rapids, Iowa, a business associate of Regent Meylert, spoke on behalf of the proposed pharmacy program. He pointed out that the territory had no medical school or professional programs, but had already begun to attract persons who suffered from respiratory ailments, mainly tuberculosis. He further suggested that UNM could link its chemistry program to outside lectures by prominent Albuquerque physicians. President Stover recommended approval of the program with Zimmer as its chair, and the Regents concurred.[12]

At the spring commencement of 1894, held in the B. F. Davis Opera House in Albuquerque, five women and one man were awarded the first bachelor of pedagogy degrees. All recipients were from the Normal Department and had taken some of the course work elsewhere to meet the requirements. The recipients of those first degrees were Kate Adams and Mary James, who had attended Bethany College in Topeka, Kansas; Fannie Nowlen from the Missouri State Normal School at Kirksville, Missouri; Elizabeth Menaul, who had studied at Granville Female College in Ohio; Jessie Keith of El Paso; and Charles Hodgin, who had attended Indiana State Normal in Terre Haute.

During the summer of 1894, the Regents and faculty engaged in a series of meetings concerning the status and future of UNM. Lack of dormitory space forced students to live in town, where they often paid exorbitant rates for rooms at local hotels. Further, the faculty wanted Albuquerque public schools to assume

The student body consisted mostly of "preps" in the early years, although the lads in knee pants look too young even for pre-high school studies.

One of the University's first graduates, Josephine Parsons became one of its longest-serving and most valuable employees.

more responsibility for the preparation of students entering college. The faculty also asked for a longer school year, from September to June, and termination of the summer program. In addition, they petitioned the board to ask the president of the United States to detail an Army officer to teach drill and military subjects at the University. Finally, the faculty requested that the Regents adopt their suggestions for registration and expulsion of students, courses of study, curricula, and textbooks.[13]

The Regents were busy that summer of 1894. They decided that the University needed more sophisticated management and on July 17 named Alcinda Morrow principal of the Normal Department. Two days later, they accepted the resignation of George Ramsey, who had been the first academic administrator at UNM. Other changes included naming Marshall Gaines as head of the Preparatory Department.

A third department, the Commercial Department, was opened that year. It offered nondegree courses in stenography, bookkeeping, and arithmetic. Josephine Parsons was named department head. Students respected her policy of "no pets," and regarded her as strict but sympathetic. In addition to collecting fares for the hack that transported students to and from "the Hill" and presiding at the dining table at noon, she was reputed to be able to converse on almost every conceivable topic; in her later years as a faculty member, she taught Spanish. It was said that her hair grew white in her service to the University, and she was remembered by students as "a perfect lady." She was memorialized on the campus by Parsons Grove at the corner of Central and Yale.[14]

Another favorite professor in those first years of UNM was James Hay Paxton, a brilliant young southerner who had graduated first in his class at the University of Virginia. Described as tall and handsome, he won student admiration for his ability to quote Shakespeare on almost any occasion.[15]

The most significant change in the summer of 1894 was the Regents' decision to create the position of vice president of the faculty and put that person in charge of the administration of the University. Their intent was for the vice president to set future policy for the institution and lead in upgrading the intellectual standards for both faculty and students.[16] Facing a limited time frame, since the opening of fall classes was only a few weeks away, and a salary limitation for a vice president of only $200 per month, the Regents had little hope of drawing candidates from other, more prosperous regions of the country. Thus, the Regents stayed within the territory and hired the recently cashiered president of the land-grant university at Las Cruces, Hiram Hadley.[17]

Vice President Hiram Hadley

Hiram Hadley had impressive credentials as an educator, lay minister of the Quaker faith, and speculator in southern New Mexico land schemes. He had founded and led Hadley Normal Academy in Richmond, Indiana, where one of his students had been Charles Hodgin, who played a role in bringing his former mentor to UNM in 1894. Hadley had reportedly migrated to Las Cruces in 1887 because his son, Walter, needed a dry climate for his respiratory ailments.

Active in the development of public education in the territory, Hadley acquired a reputation for advocacy of public schools. In the spring of 1888, a group of Las Cruces business and civic leaders had solicited Hadley's help in establishing Las Cruces College to educate the Presbyterian youth of the Mesilla valley. The school, with elementary, college-preparatory, and business offerings, opened that fall with sixty-four students.

A year passed while Hadley worked closely with southern New Mexico promoters to locate the land-grant agricultural school for the territory in Las Cruces. His efforts impressed the "boosters," and he was named the first president of the faculty of the agricultural college. The head of that institution's board of regents was John McFie, who, as previously noted, worked closely with Bernard Rodey in locating the territorial university in Albuquerque. The opening of the land-grant school in January 1890 gave New Mexico College of Agriculture and Mechanic Arts (NM A&M) the distinction of being the first public institution of higher learning in the territory. It also marked the demise of Las Cruces College.[18]

Simon Kropp ably documented the story of the early years of the Las Cruces school in *That All May Learn: New Mexico State University, 1888–1964*. He reported that Hadley had played a major role in the early successes of the agricultural college and, as president, earned an annual salary of $3,000, thanks to federal laws authorizing funds for land-grant colleges. No UNM president would receive a salary that high until 1912.[19]

Welsh praises Kropp's account, writing,

> Unfortunately, the financial security guaranteed by federal monies also spawned political interference, and Hadley's ties to the local Republican party did not please Democrats like Albert Fall, owner of the *Las Cruces Independent Democrat* and himself an ambitious politician. The NM A & M leader had labored to expand support for the school through his public appearances around the territory. Fall and his cohorts saw Hadley as an elitist and sycophant of Judge McFie's political machine. The new governor, William Thornton, named regents who preferred Samuel McCrea, a former instructor at Las Cruces College and a local businessman, to lead NM A & M. They ordered Hadley's contract terminated on July 1, 1894, thus removing from office an individual as knowledgeable of higher education as anyone else in New Mexico.[20]

The University of New Mexico Regents, mostly Republicans, had no problem with Hadley's political affiliations, and New Mexico A&M's loss became UNM's gain.

Over the years, Hadley had maintained his friendship with his former pupil, Charles Hodgin, and on several occasions visited Hodgin in Albuquerque. Hadley also had spoken at the UNM Normal Department and had the dubious honor of arranging the first football game between UNM and NM A&M. UNM won that contest, 18–6, and Hadley had to go back to Las Cruces and face criticism of the game as well as the outcries of those who abhorred the violence of college football, both on the field and in the stands.[21]

Hadley's pay cut from $250 a month to $200 reflected the salary disparities between the two territorial universities. His appointment was a three–two vote by the Regents, with F. W. Clancy and Gurdon Meylert opposing. This division on the board was serious, and Hadley was to struggle with finances, standards, and interference by Regents throughout his three-year tenure at UNM. Having the former president of NM A&M as vice president of UNM was a difficult pill to swallow for those who remembered his role as a competitor in his previous post.

Hadley's early successes included procuring funds to add books to the small UNM library, the purchase of a gong to signal class time, the acquisition of notepaper for instructors' use, and distribution of promotional leaflets at the 1894 Territorial Fair.[22]

By the spring of 1895, the financial woes of the state and national fiscal panic of '93 had taken their toll and threatened the economic status of the University. In Albuquerque, the city's largest employer, the Santa Fe Railroad, had gone into receivership and hundreds of employees had lost their jobs. Many families relied on charity for their survival, which left them unable to afford higher education for their children. The uncertainty of these events upset UNM faculty members, provoking them to petition the Regents in March 1895 with a request to be informed as to whether the school could offer them contracts for the 1895–96 academic year.[23]

That same spring the territorial legislature reduced a source of funds that UNM had used for its operations by channeling all delinquent taxes for 1894–95 into the treasuries of New Mexico's counties, rather than to the territorial government in Santa Fe.

Internally, Hadley was apprehensive over what he regarded as a loss of direction affecting UNM and its Regents. He wrote a detailed summary of his thoughts on the school's policies and lamented the fact that substantive discussions could not be held at Regents' meetings. He was particularly concerned over UNM's lack of a "college atmosphere," and believed it was a mistake to admit students with a history of low scholarship. In the fall of 1894, he had turned down twenty-five applicants, and he planned removal of the lower levels of classes as soon as possible. Enrollment dropped to sixty (or perhaps seventy-four) students in 1895–96, a figure that Hadley hoped would double once students and parents learned of UNM's increased standards.[24]

Hadley urged the Regents to run the school like a business, hire the best professors, offer the public every "phase and whim" of elective education, and enroll six hundred students per year. He also made an impassioned plea to maintain the best of the classical tradition. The vice president wanted UNM to spend its money on its "best risk," the advanced student. Hadley also found fault with UNM's policy of free tuition, saying that UNM had been "annoyed by adventurers who had no purpose in view but to transfer their place of loafing to the University." He also complained about the shortcomings of UNM's physical plant, including the lack of dormitory space, laboratory equipment, and a gymnasium. Finally, he stated that UNM needed good public relations to "neutralize the false statements and scurrilous squibs that smart editors entirely ignorant of facts . . . delight to set afloat." He proposed mailing brochures to every post office in New Mexico and some in Arizona to attract attention and prospective students.[25]

As the academic year 1894–95 drew to a close, the territorial legislature appointed what was called the Select Committee to Investigate the University of New Mexico. That its forthcoming report was highly favorable was no great surprise, inasmuch as Walter Hadley, the son of the UNM vice president, was a member of the committee. The committee found that the University's finances were in good order and it had adhered to its admissions standards despite the temptation to lower them. Highly important to the struggling University, however, was the recommendation of the committee that UNM should remain "as it is now, the chief educational institution of New Mexico." The committee could find nothing to criticize and commended the Regents for having made good use of the funds provided them.[26]

Also in the spring of 1895, the Regents reviewed the pharmacy program and agreed they had acted prematurely in creating it. They moved to shut it down, but allowed the three students enrolled to complete their coursework. Alcinda Morrow, who had taken over as principal of the Normal Department, announced that four seniors had completed the program and would make excellent schoolteachers.[27]

The 1895 catalog reported that a "committee of ten" had developed standards for classifying the preparatory students and recommended "Latin-scientific" and English curricula. The committee's recommendation that students study German or French was rejected, however, because "it was thought that local reasons justified the substitution of Spanish."[28]

Entering the 1895–96 academic year, the Regents and Hadley moved to implement many of the select committee's suggestions. Capital construction got a boost when UNM notified contractors of its intent to build a gymnasium. In February 1896, the custodian, M. Custers, was directed to install three hundred feet of irrigation pipe to create a sprinkler system for improving the vegetation on the east mesa property. Meanwhile, the New Mexico Printing Company of Santa Fe, publishers of that community's daily newspaper, agreed to print 1,500 copies of the UNM catalog. Matriculation fees entering students paid in the fall of 1895 went toward purchases of library books.

Perhaps the most significant of the changes that year, however, was when the Regents on August 24, 1896, officially terminated the "subpreparatory" (elementary-level) program. The board directed Hadley to work with the Albuquerque Public Schools to make proper provision for students who were not prepared to enter the University. This action met with hearty approval from the UNM faculty, whose members had long felt that it was a waste of time and energy to occupy themselves with "this class of students."[29]

All these actions were on the plus side, but there were some downers, too, namely woes brought on by politics and finances. As for politics, rumors circulated in Albuquerque that the water on campus was unfit to drink and that UNM wanted to purchase alcohol in spite of territorial prohibition. As for finances, Vice President Hadley had to reduce salaries nearly 25 percent from the levels of the previous year. Dormitories remained a high priority, as the University was still struggling to overcome the lurid reputation of the Duke City as a haven for gambling, drugs, and prostitution. Rural New Mexico families, understandably, wanted closer supervision of their sons and daughters than was available in downtown hotels and boarding houses.[30]

A prank triggered a series of events that embroiled the campus in chaos, confrontation, and confusion, ultimately leading to the resignations of the University's first president and its vice president. It all began one evening following a lecture by Clarence L. Herrick, at the time a faculty member at the School of Mines in Socorro, but destined to be the next president of UNM. After the lecture, Hadley, a close friend of Herrick, drove the University's guest from the campus to his hotel. Meanwhile, someone had taken a hand bell and attached explosives to it, then left it in the Main Building. As planned, it blew up, shattering the bell and driving one large piece of metal into the wooden stairway. All evidence pointed to Roderick Stover, a student who also happened to be the son of UNM's Regent/president, Elias Stover. Roderick, good lad that he was, did not deny the accusation.[31]

Hadley conducted a hearing, and Roderick Stover was expelled. The faculty upheld Hadley's actions, agreeing with his refusal to tolerate "the evil and corruption of the times."

The boy's father, Elias, a pillar of the Albuquerque community and one of the founders of the University, thought otherwise. He could not and would not countenance "the social trauma of a miscreant child." Thus, on February 8, 1897, Stover brought before the Regents his appeal for the reinstatement of his son and also pressed for Hadley's resignation from the University.

The Hadley-Stover confrontation convulsed the University for months, affecting Regents, faculty, and students. At the request of the board, the faculty prepared a detailed account of their reasons for the suspension of young Stover. For his part, Hadley prepared a lengthy letter to Regent Frank W. Clancy. He rebutted Stover's charges, waxing eloquent on the difficulties of disciplining unruly teenagers who were members of prominent Albuquerque families, including sons of Regents Stover and Mariano Otero. Offenses he listed ranged from ringing class bells at the wrong times to thefts of oranges and schoolbooks from the desks of students.

Hadley singled out Hispanics for special mention. "Under a pressure to take in nearly everything that applied," he noted, "especially if they were Mexicans, I spent very nearly one-half of my energies last year in teaching two Mexicans who scarcely belonged in the third grade of a Common School."[32]

Michael Welsh summed up these events.

> Upon calling the President's son before them, the Regents heard him
> declare his guilt and accept his punishment. The Board then upheld

Hadley's actions and found President Stover's charges groundless. Hadley, a veteran of the political wars of Doña Ana County, knew that Stover's influence in the community would make any future endeavors problematic. Thus he [Hadley] resigned on April 19, 1897, prompting Stover to relinquish the President's chair. The Board agreed to Stover's continued presence as a member (a position he held until 1911), and then asked the faculty to remain loyal to UNM despite the damaging effects of the year-long battle.[33]

Roderick Stover won the day, for he is listed in the 1912 UNM alumni roster as an electrical engineer in Albuquerque and a member of the Class of 1909.

In his short but turbulent three-year tenure as UNM's vice president, Hiram Hadley had struggled with finances, standards, and Regents. Welsh says:

The departure of Hiram Hadley left him free to return to Las Cruces, where the ascendance of Republicans to the presidency in Washington and the governor's chair in Santa Fe created new opportunities for him. In 1898, the NM A&M hired its former faculty president to teach history. In 1901 he became head of the school, and in 1905 Governor Miguel A. Otero, Jr., named Hadley as superintendent of public instruction for the territory. When Herbert J. Hagerman replaced Otero as governor, he asked Hadley to sit on the NM A&M Board of Regents, a post he held from 1907–1912. Las Cruces kept his memory alive by naming a street for him in the northern part of town, and the college he helped establish remembers him with Hadley Hall for the offices of the school's central administration.[34]

Early Days of the University

One can picture Hadley's frustration during his stint as vice president of what was called the University of New Mexico. It was with real pathos, that Hadley wrote in 1895 that the University was an "institution with a large name and a small capital."

If that lone building on the east mesa did not seem like much of a college, there were good reasons, the most important being it was not much of a college. It was more like a high school, or pre-high school. The students were young, some boys still in knickers. The classes were small, and during Hadley's turbulent tenure, no students were taking college-level courses.

The isolation of the campus was also a significant issue. It was two miles from town with no residence halls, food services, or amenities suggesting a campus life. Students, most of whom lived in the town, had to walk to the campus. The legendary refrain passed down to future generations about having to walk uphill in heat and cold, dust and wind, and snow and rain was a reality. As Robert Knight Barney wrote in *Turmoil and Triumph:* "A person's oldest shoes continued to be pressed into service for the two mile trek to and from town."[35] Women often carried another pair of shoes in a bag and changed after arriving on the campus.

Four horses labored to pull the "hack," or wagon, and the students up the hill to the campus.

Travel by horse and buggy was a rare luxury, as not many students were lucky enough to have them. Hughes says having his own horse and buggy enhanced Roderick Stover's popularity, although "the condition of Railroad Avenue, to say nothing of less traveled lanes, wasn't conducive to buggy riding."[36]

The University did, however, provide some transportation to get students up and down "the Hill." At 8:30 in the morning, groups of students gathered in the village awaiting the arrival of "Jumbo," the old-fashioned hack drawn by four coach horses that carried them up to the schoolhouse atop the mesa in time for the daily assembly at nine o'clock. In back of the hack was the head of the Commercial Department, "Miss Josie," Josephine Parsons. She greeted each student with a brisk "Good morning," then collected the five-cent fare and signaled the driver. He cracked his whip, and the long pull up to the University was under way.[37]

Hughes paints a vivid word picture of the female students in the nineties.

We turn back the pages to see the students of earlier days, the girls in voluminous skirts hiding their "wine-colored tans" or the more usual high-laced black shoes, and all wearing the high-necked, full-bosomed shirtwaists with the popular leg-o-mutton sleeve. Their hair, under the great wide hats, was in a neat center part, drawn back into a knot, later worn in pompadour.[38]

Then Hughes describes the young gents of that era.

The boys dressed with formality for school. The necktieless shirt and old pair of trousers were beneath the dignity of gentlemen; for best they wore the heavy broadcloth frock coat with wing or high collar, ascot or string tie, or the "pussy-cat" tie called more correctly "Windsor," like those we see in photographs of our fathers or grandfathers. And for everyday at school, they wore stiff collars, stiff cuffs, and heavily starched stiff-bosom shirts. Some students discovered that by pressing the forefinger on the bosom of the shirt and then releasing it, a rhythmic click could be produced. This was entertainment for classes until the boys were ousted from the room to learn better behaviour. Some boys were bearded, some mustachioed, but the majority clean-shaven; their hair, too, was slicked from a center part. "Boughten" cigarettes were effeminate; pipes and roll-your-own, of course, were the thing, for this was the cow country. Smoking was not prevalent among students, and no man smoked at parties nor when with women. The "sports," campus playboys, sometimes would slip off and drink a whole glass of beer. However, this was only for the wild ones.[39]

Picnics in the Sandia Mountains were popular outings. Hughes reports that at Bear Canyon there was a long climb, with a welcome break at a hole in the rocks termed "Fat Man's Misery." This break provided opportunities that often would

The spartan gymnasium was supplemented by swings, climbing bars, and other apparatus.

Neckties and long skirts were standard attire even for picnics in the Sandia foothills.

lead to "the budding of romance, as here the girls would have to be helped through by the boys. Some girls would swoon at this dangerous pass while others found a turn of the ankle enough to make sure of gentlemanly attention for the rest of the afternoon."

Hughes reports that the Castelar Literary Society was mentioned in the catalog of 1893, but otherwise was not recalled. The four-member class of 1895 decorated the opera house in Albuquerque for the first graduating class. Following the completion of the decorations, there was a "grand sleigh-ride and skating."[40] In this era, obviously, most of the activities outside the classroom were informal, influenced by the isolation of the campus, the limitations on travel, and by a careful observance of the formalities of relations with the opposite sex.

Athletics

Athletics, which in the last half of the nineteenth century became a lasting part of the campus scene nationally, had a slow start at the University of New Mexico. The 1895 wood-frame gymnasium, designed by Albuquerque architect Edward Buxton Cristy, was barely large enough for basketball games and had no room for spectators. Gymnasium equipment was added outside.[41] It was described at the time as "most modern and equipped with the best new apparatus." In reality, however, it was of little use in carrying out any exercise programs. In his 1969 history of UNM athletics, *Turmoil and Triumph*, Robert Knight Barney wryly reported that "most of the exertion experienced in this building was related to the changing of one's clothing."

As for playing fields, "the practice field for football was a weed-strewn, goathead-infested patch of mesa ground located on the eastern edge of the diminutive campus." Between seasons of play "the University's outdoor athletic facilities suffered badly

Old Town's San Felipe de Neri Church is in the background of this 1896 photo, with the varsity boys posed in their "flying wedge" formation.

from the ravages of New Mexico dust storms and a fanatical weed growth which denied the common belief that nothing could grow in arid New Mexico except when inundated by water."[42]

In this era the "varsity" teams of UNM played their contests in a variety of places, hardly any of which were located on the campus itself.

> Basketball games were played first at Colombo Hall, across Second Street from where today's Greyhound Bus Station is located, and later at the town Armory building, remodeled now, but still standing just south of the modern and towering Federal Courthouse building. Football games were played in a trio of places—originally in a vacant lot behind the town's ice factory and later at either the Albuquerque Indian School grounds or at the Territorial Fair Grounds in Old Albuquerque (Old Town). Track and field activity was held at Traction Park, which, if still in existence today, would straddle Route 66 where Central Avenue intersects with Rio Grande Boulevard. Traction Park formed the end of the line for the first horse-drawn trolleys which much later gave way to an electrically operated coach line. Traction Park was really an extension of the Fair grounds . . . Baseball games, if possible, were played at the Fair grounds diamond which was carefully maintained by the professional nines of the town and readily acknowledged as the finest diamond in the entire Territory.[43]

The first football contest of record for the University of New Mexico was against Albuquerque High School on October 27, 1892, played in a vacant lot north of the town's ice factory. UNM lost, 0–5. Three weeks later the two teams met again on the same site and once more Albuquerque High prevailed, 8–0 (a touchdown scored four points in those days).

The following year forty-eight boys were enrolled. Football practices were organized early in the fall term, and a game was scheduled with Albuquerque High. It was reported that the football players were "rather concerned" that the local newspapers were giving far more publicity to a "spelling bee" than to the game. On November 18, 1893, UNM defeated Albuquerque High 4–0 by scoring a lone touchdown late in the game. This was UNM's first victory ever in a varsity sport.

New Mexico College of Agriculture & Mechanic Arts had issued a challenge for a friendly game. The game was played at the Fair Grounds in Albuquerque on New Year's Day, 1894, with UNM winning, 25–5. This was UNM's first game against a collegiate opponent.

Boosters of NM A&M and newspapers from Las Cruces vehemently protested that UNM had used a large number of "outsiders" in the game. Later discoveries revealed that of the thirteen UNM participants, only ten were registered students. This was shrugged off with the rationale that use of "outsiders" was common practice until shortly after the turn of the century.

In 1894, for the first time, UNM had the services of a coach for its football team: Pharmacy Professor W. A. Zimmer. While he acted more in the role of manager than coach, he nevertheless contributed to the first faculty control and supervision of the University's athletic program. That year, all three games were against the Indian School. UNM lost the first game, tied the second, and won the third. In that final game, a crowd of nearly fifteen hundred people was on hand, and a twenty-five-cent admission charge was solicited.

The University's colors in the early years were black and gold until Harriet Jenness, who taught drawing, drama, music, and penmanship, proposed new colors: crimson for the effect of sunset on the Sandia Mountains and silver for the ribbon of the Rio Grande. Her idea was adopted in 1897, although the crimson was later changed to cherry.

The year 1894 marked the formulation of the University's first official cheer.

> Chickee-currunk-currunk-curooo!
> Varsity, Varsity, N.M.U.
> Razzle, Dazzle, Boom!
> Varsity, Varsity, Rah, Rah, Ree!

No football was organized at UNM from 1895 through the fall of 1898, as student and faculty interest ebbed at an all-time low.[44]

The first UNM player to be a football hero was Roy Allen Stamm. He graduated from Albuquerque High School in 1892 and entered the University in the fall of 1893. Barney describes Stamm as "a stocky, compact lad; handsome and endowed with qualities of leadership which made him one of the most popular University students of the period." Stamm went on to become a championship tennis player, president of his class, an accomplished debater, and an outstanding student of the classical languages.[45]

Mathias Lambert Custers

The legendary Stamm had a colorful description of the equipment football players wore in the nineties.

> Our canvas suits—those who were fortunate enough to have them— carried little padding except where towels were stuffed over shoulders and knees. Head-gears, nose-guards, and helmets were not yet introduced and all players cultivated heavy heads of hair for protection.[46]

M. Custers—A Man for All Seasons

Every era has its unsung heroes or heroines. Mathias Lambert Custers, known to everyone as M. Custers, was such a man. He was custodian, librarian, faculty member, and more. He truly blossomed as a man for all seasons at the University of New Mexico. A Civil War veteran, Custers had come to the territory for health reasons and worked for the *Albuquerque Journal* until 1892, when he took a job as the University's first custodian. He soon became its first librarian, when the library occupied a single room on the north side of the Main Building. Custers had a great knowledge of mathematics, surveying, and trigonometry, and was later appointed a member of the faculty.[47]

Dorothy Hughes paid tribute to the legendary Custers.

> M. Custers—his name appears in no other form, in either catalog or regents' reports—a versatile man with long chin whiskers and bald head, was employed as janitor at the opening of the University. But he was no ordinary janitor . . . In the records he appears time and again before the Board of Regents asking [sic] a length of hose, planning a way to protect the basement windows from their frequent breakage by wind-storm, or discussing what kind of coal should be bought; at other places in the records we see him inaugurating irrigation, building with his own money the first frame dining and residence hall across from Rodey Hall, before there was a Rodey Hall, becoming a member of the faculty to teach surveying and later trigonometry, but continuing his janitorship under the more dignified title of custodian, and probably sandwiching in the library position between stoking the old coal furnace in winter and watering the few trees in spring. He did all of his tasks unaided, for the most part; his appeals to the first board asking for an occasional helper were seldom successful. When his sight began to fail, he continued to keep order in the library, recognizing each student by his or her voice.[48]

Van Dorn Hooker goes into more detail on M. Custers's role in the development of UNM's first dormitory and eating facility.

> When the Board of Regents met on July 14, 1898, Custers, who had been provided living quarters for his family in the Main Building, proposed to

This photo of the Custers family home first appeared in a 1922 report of a commission appointed by Governor Merritt Mechem to study "the status and needs" of the University. The commission reported that the building, now used as a women's dorm and, in the addition on the left, a dining hall, was "one of the most efficiently managed units of the plant of the University."

advance money to construct a residence of his own design on the campus. The board accepted the offer, with the provision to pay him back if the University needed the house or land. The Custers family lived in what was called the Custodian's House only a short time before the regents relieved Custers of his custodial duties because they thought they could get the services he performed for less money and he was losing his eyesight. They paid off the balance of the note he held on his house on June 4, 1902. The first floor became the Dining Hall, and the second floor housed a few women. It was called the Ladies' Cottage.[49]

In retrospect, it appears that back there in the 1890s that was one tight-fisted, hard-hearted Board of Regents. As related by Dabney: "Custers petitioned the Board of Regents for a ten-dollar increase. Winter was approaching, he said, and his job was more demanding in cold weather. The Regents responded by increasing his pay to $80 a month, beginning in October, with the understanding that once winter was over he would be cut to $70 for the warmer half of the year."[50]

Custers stayed on at UNM until 1902, when a combination of advancing age, blindness, and poor pay led to his retirement. The legend of his multiple contributions in a variety of responsibilities at UNM was reported in a 1968 story in *Ripley's Believe It or Not.*[51]

From its very beginnings, the University of New Mexico was a colorful place with a full complement of heroes and heroines, plus a few rascals and villains. The nineties were years of hard work and adventuresome beginnings, a time for planting trees and traditions. Students, faculty, presidents, and regents all had an uphill climb to that once-barren mesa that became a Mecca, a destination and repository for strong loyalties and deep memories. The change was forever. The University became a place where miracles happened. Through education, lives were made better and visions expanded. From those lofty heights, the view and the future were magnificent. ◼

The words Hadley Laboratory were carved in sandstone over the door.

CHAPTER FOUR
Administration of Clarence L. Herrick
1897–1901

Clarence Luther Herrick

In the numerous historical updates of the University, Clarence Luther Herrick, the institution's second president, receives brief reviews and few accolades. One prolific author who wrote numerous pieces on UNM history, for example, covered Herrick's tenure in two sentences, reporting: "The second president, Clarence Luther Herrick, was famed for his diverse scholarship, his ability to draw two pictures simultaneously with his two hands, and for a prodigious memory. But his tenure brought no great spurt of growth."[1]

A closer look at Herrick's tenure, however, reveals that he was undoubtedly the University's first academic president. Elias Stover, who held the title from 1892 to 1897, probably had little to do with providing academic leadership for the institution. After all, like most members of the University's first Board of Regents, he was a hard-nosed, self-educated Albuquerque businessman who delegated administrative and academic responsibilities to the principal, George Ramsey, and, later, to the vice president, Hiram Hadley.

Herrick, however, was hailed as a bona fide academician, a man with a national and international reputation as a scholar and scientist. Under his leadership the first students began taking college-level courses leading to bachelor's degrees. UNM had awarded six bachelor's degrees in pedagogy, a three-year program, in 1894, three years before Herrick's arrival. As was the custom of the times, courses and degrees in pedagogy were not considered to be college level nor were the programs in the commercial curriculum. Apparently, only the traditional classical curriculum, which included Latin, Greek, advanced mathematics, and the sciences and led to the bachelor of arts or sciences degree, counted as collegiate credits. Therefore, when Herrick is praised for moving UNM to the collegiate level, it has to be recognized as a significant step in the evolution of what ultimately became a major research university.

It should also be noted that in the 1890s, when progress and prestige often were measured by "body count," what was labeled the University of New Mexico was in reality a small prep school with roughly one hundred pupils, smaller than high schools that by the year 2000 were classified for athletic purposes in New Mexico as 1A high schools, the lowest category.

In 1900, though, the number of college students began to increase. The prepreparatory program had been eliminated just before Herrick took office. He made a conscious decision, which the faculty enthusiastically supported, to begin phasing out the preparatory program and make UNM a true university with classics-oriented collegiate courses and even graduate work. These decisions marked a monumental change in the development of a true university.

As a part of this emphasis on college-level work, in 1899 Herrick created the College of Literature and Arts (the forerunner of today's College of Arts and Sciences). He initiated the first graduate courses and put a high priority on research. He also was the primary mover in raising the funds and overseeing the construction of the second major building on the campus.

Throughout his brief but brilliant four-year tenure, Herrick continued his own scholarship and research, wrote leading articles for prestigious scientific journals, and brought in scholars, especially in the sciences, who attracted national attention for their teaching and research. Under his leadership, this small, relatively unknown territorial institution began the transition from prep school to university. In retrospect, he may have been one of UNM's great presidents.

One who did appreciate and extol the virtues of Herrick was Charles Hodgin, who left his post as superintendent of the Albuquerque Public Schools in 1897 to join the faculty at UNM. In a memorial tribute to Herrick in 1932, Hodgin described the young president as "quiet, reserved, refined, unassuming, disliking show, despising sham, manifesting genuine zeal for life and knowledge, showing real originality in thought, working with tireless energy, revealing breadth and depth of scholarship, and maintaining always the highest moral ideals."

Hodgin continued by relating that Herrick was born June 21, 1858, near Minneapolis. Herrick graduated from Minneapolis High School before going on to the University of Minnesota, where he finished a four-year course in three years. He traveled abroad, studying at universities in Leipzig and Berlin, where he became acquainted with many internationally renowned scientists. Herrick was often referred to as "Dr. Herrick," as were many who studied at a European institution, but there is no record that he had an earned doctorate in the modern sense. Before coming to New Mexico in 1897, he taught at his alma mater, the University of Minnesota, at Denison College in Ohio, and at the University of Cincinnati, where he held a chair in the Department of Biology. He came to UNM in 1897.[2]

Herrick's strenuous work schedule was the direct cause of his being diagnosed with tuberculosis when he was but thirty-five years old. His illness came at the time he had been called to the University of Chicago's chair of geology.[3] Herrick had contracted respiratory ailments while in the East and in Europe, conditions exacerbated by the demands of his teaching and scholarship. He declined the Chicago position and "sought the more salubrious climate of the Southwest." He first appeared in New Mexico in 1894, where he utilized his geological expertise in the mines of the Magdalena Mountains. He also taught classes on mining engineering and conducted field research at the newly opened New Mexico School of Mines.[4]

Michael Welsh, citing Hodgin's 1932 memorial tribute to Herrick, wrote that the new president gave UNM "a touch of the college atmosphere." Hodgin also noted that Herrick was not a dramatic speaker, but "his quiet, earnest, confident manner . . . commanded attention." He further commented on Herrick's encyclopedic mind, his interesting assembly lectures, his piano playing at student gatherings, and his ability to draw diagrams on the blackboard simultaneously with both hands.[5]

Herrick was a prolific scientific and philosophical writer, founding and for several years editing the *Journal of Comparative Neurology*. At the time of his death in 1904 at the age of forty-six, his publications totaled more than 150 scientific articles. His own health problems instilled a deep interest in the effect of the New Mexico climate on lung trouble, and he persuaded Mrs. Walter Hadley to donate most of the funds to build a science building, Hadley Hall, with a climatology laboratory.[6]

The Health Seekers

The history of the University of New Mexico includes repeated references to the health seekers, those afflicted by respiratory ailments who were seeking a cure. In his unpublished account of the University's first decades Welsh wrote that the University benefited enormously from such persons, because they could not return to their more prestigious positions elsewhere and therefore had to work for the low salaries the impoverished university in the New Mexico Territory could provide.[7] Two such persons were Walter Hadley, the son of Vice President Hiram Hadley, and later Clarence Herrick.

Perhaps the best account of the health seekers is the one Marc Simmons offers in his *Albuquerque: A Narrative History*. He observes that the New Mexico Territory was gaining renown as a health center and promoting itself as one with statements like this: "Albuquerque is one of the cities of the West that is so openly, so rampantly healthy, so gloriously deluged with vivifying sunshine and purified with healing breezes that it invites with open arms the sick and the ailing to enter its portals."[8]

The health benefits derived from two favorable geographical conditions: the high altitude and thin atmosphere. Both relieved the pressure on lungs weakened by consumption and other respiratory ailments, aided by the relatively low humidity.[9]

Health-seeking newcomers proved to be an economic boon to merchants and real-estate operators, particularly in Albuquerque. Simmons reports that by 1910 there were more than three thousand tuberculars among a population of ten thousand. Cynically, he noted that the flood of money apparently "clouded the judgment of the municipal fathers," who either did not understand the highly contagious nature of tuberculosis or deliberately overlooked the health problem caused by large numbers of diseased people.[10]

The menace to public health was quite real. There was no attempt to confine or quarantine tuberculosis victims, and those who were ambulatory freely circulated

Charles E. Hodgin

among the general populace. A number of domestic servants, Indian or Hispanic, contributed to the spread of the illness, both in Albuquerque and in their pueblos and reservations.

A large number of those who came to Albuquerque with health problems were beyond help, but for others it was different. As reported by Simmons: "In the bracing atmosphere at Albuquerque they regained health and happiness, and with a merry twinkle in their eyes, or a contented chuckle, enjoyed telling in a good-humored manner how wrong their doctor's diagnosis had proved."[11]

Charles E. Hodgin

Among the faculty members added in 1897 was Charles Elkanah Hodgin, who was to occupy a hallowed place in the history of UNM and the lives of generations of students. Hodgin's career deserves a close look. In March 1979, the *UNM Alumnus* published Van Dorn Hooker's moving, poignant profile entitled "The Right-Hand Man." The slender, "very thin man with blue eyes and slightly reddish hair" was a major part of the University scene.

Hodgin hailed from Indiana, where he was born in the small village of Lynn in 1857. He grew up in Richmond, Indiana, where he graduated from the Friends' Academy conducted by Professor Hiram Hadley. After attending Indiana State Normal School, Hodgin moved on to his first teaching position in Wayne County, Indiana, for $50 a month. He continued teaching in various schools in Indiana until he came to New Mexico. Hodgin arrived in Albuquerque with his wife, Sallie, on September 25, 1883. Sallie was ill, and the doctors in Indiana thought the dry New Mexico climate would aid in her recovery, but she lived only a few years longer.

There were only two schools in Albuquerque, a convent and the Albuquerque Academy. Hodgin was offered a new one-room school, which was in a remodeled fire station on South Edith. His salary was whatever tuition he could collect, which amounted to about $40 a month. "From there, he went on to teach at the Academy and later became its principal. In September 1891, Albuquerque started a public school system, and Charles Hodgin was made the first superintendent."

Hodgin was among the first students to attend UNM when it opened its doors for the first time in the summer session of 1892. He also was among the first graduates of the institution, receiving a bachelor of pedagogy degree in 1894.

In 1897, when Herrick became president of UNM, Hodgin was appointed principal of the Normal Department. This launched a twenty-eight-year career at UNM, where he served as head of the Education Department, dean of the University, and, finally, as vice president from 1917 to 1925, when he retired. Hodgin died in 1934 at the age of seventy-seven.

[Hodgin] was obviously a modest man. In 1927, the University awarded him a Doctor of Laws Degree in honor of his service to education. He never framed the diploma, but folded it, placed it in an envelope, and filed it away. At one time he was offered the presidency of the University, but declined because he felt that his having earned only a Bachelor's Degree would diminish the academic standing of the school.[12]

During the early 1930s, Hodgin frequently spoke at the UNM memorial services honoring persons who had made distinctive contributions to the University. These proceedings were edited by Dean Lynn B. Mitchell and published as *Remembrance Wakes* in 1941.[13]

Moving from Prep School to University

One of the problems confronting President Herrick and the Regents in 1897 was redirecting the curriculum to accommodate the more pragmatic needs of an impoverished territory. Hadley and the Regents continued to support those branches of study that appeared to offer some immediate pecuniary return to students. Cited as an example was the Spanish program at UNM, staffed by an 1896 graduate and the University's first Hispanic faculty member, Atanasio Montoya, Jr., a native of Bernalillo County. Throughout the territory, there was a dire need for Spanish-speaking teachers for New Mexico's public schools. The UNM course in Spanish was thus deemed to have great career value to students who aspired to be teachers.[14]

The first college courses were offered in the fall of 1897, to four freshmen and one sophomore: Douglas W. Johnson of West Virginia, who had followed Herrick to New Mexico and who was one of the University's first two graduates.[15] He became a professor at the Institute of Technology in Boston. The other member of the Class of 1901 was Eva W. Johnson, a "trained nurse" who soon moved to Los Angeles. Both received bachelor of science degrees. The next college degrees had been awarded to Gustav Alfred Magnusson in 1903 and Josephine Parsons in 1904.[16]

Within days of his arrival on the campus in 1897, Herrick approached the Board of Regents with a request that was to characterize his efforts to professionalize UNM. He proposed establishing a joint laboratory with the New Mexico Territorial Board of Health for research relating to tuberculosis. Specifically, he wanted the Bacteriology Laboratory to collect throat cultures of tubercular patients, study them for potential cures, and disseminate statistical data to the medical profession.[17] By the spring of 1898, the work of this project had grown to such an extent that Herrick requested permission to publish a bulletin to report the ongoing research.

Looking back, it seems these pioneering efforts in recording and treating tuberculosis paved the way for UNM's emergence as one of the nation's great health science centers in the latter half of the twentieth century. Certainly these early efforts laid the foundation for the University's emphasis on teaching, research, and treatment.

As Herrick began to better understand UNM's place in the territory, he established a cooperative teacher-training program between the University and the Albuquerque Public Schools. Further, he began to attack what was to endure as one of the most vexing problems for higher education in the territory: namely, the duplication of academic services for political and economic advantage, particularly in Las Vegas, Silver City, and Socorro. As a first step, he advocated an affiliation between UNM and the School of Mines at Socorro, an idea that failed. Likewise, efforts to shut down the normal schools were also thwarted. These institutions were still operating at the beginning of the twenty-first century, but by that time their names had been changed to universities.

As the academic year closed in June 1898, the newly appointed territorial governor, Miguel A. Otero, Jr., the first and only Hispanic to lead New Mexico during the territorial era, wanted to prove to Anglo New Mexicans and officials in Washington that the territory could manage its own affairs and develop public institutions and policies recognizable to easterners. This hit a responsive note in Herrick, who realized that on a raw frontier there was a temptation to lower the standards of admission and requirements for graduation. He strongly believed that such reduced expectations made a mockery of the rigorous training and scholarship expected of flagship universities. He further believed that such a policy deceived students who sought advancement by attending schools like UNM.[18]

This debate over access versus excellence was to trouble UNM and its sister institutions in the territory and, later, the state, throughout the next century, and perhaps still does. Several questions were raised. Could practical knowledge coexist on a campus devoted to classical thought? Could students trained in the average public high school meet the standards of elitist private institutions? Could public funds be taken from all taxpayers to sponsor academic programs that by their nature excluded all but the students who took the traditional classical courses necessary to enter the best of the nation's colleges and universities?

Herrick's answer, which was to adhere to universally accepted standards of the best eastern colleges, set the tone for UNM's collegiate program. He received strong faculty support for this stance.

Herrick also knew that few New Mexico students were ready for a college curriculum, and he assured Governor Otero that UNM would continue to assist students with deficiencies in their preparation for college. Thus, the preparatory program would continue, at least for a while. Within the institution, though, changes were being made. The Classics Department grew and required a chair to administer the program. The Normal Department availed itself of the talents of the entire faculty, and a model school was established at Albuquerque High School to give advanced students practice in teaching. Herrick likened the relationship of the model school to the clinic of a medical college.

He specifically focused on building the sciences at UNM, both to prepare students for future study and generate original thought that would assist in the development of the resources of the territory. This led him to bring to the campus E. P. Childs of the University of Michigan to be chair of chemistry and physics. A year later, Childs was the first person at UNM to be called a dean when he became the head academic administrator of the College of Literature and Science. Herrick also hired a tuberculosis patient, John Weinzirl of the University of Wisconsin, to work in the Bacteriology Laboratory and conduct research on illnesses in the territory.

Several graduate students also came to UNM in 1897–98, including Weinzirl, who completed his master of science degree, Frank S. Maltby of the Johns Hopkins University, and George S. Coghill of Brown University. Their presence at UNM brought attention and prestige to the University it had never received before.[19]

As noted previously, the first catalog of the University in 1892 had boasted about the library. It was housed on the first floor of the Main Building in a small, poorly lighted room, and later moved across the hall. By 1897, the library was also a depository for congressional and territorial publications and contained 935 bound volumes and 390 pamphlets. Additional funding for the enlargement of the library was a part of the annual appeal to the legislature.[20]

With the advent of the Spanish-American War in 1898, all UNM students underwent physical examinations and took some sort of physical training in the new gymnasium. The physical training served to demonstrate the territory's potential for developing strong physiques and enlarging lung capacity, although the catalog noted that "athletics are encouraged within the bounds of moderation."[21] UNM had acquired a full set of "anthropometrical" instruments, which were used in the physical examinations. The results indicated that those boys who had been in the territory for five years or more had a lung strength and capacity of 295 cubic inches, some 100 above normal. The University used these amazing figures for advertising the benefits of living in New Mexico. President Herrick was hopeful that the healthful effects of attending UNM would lessen its chances "of collecting in the Territory a race of feeble-lunged descendents of immigrant invalids."[22]

Inspired by Governor Otero, reforms in management of higher education led to four studies of UNM and higher education by state officials between November 1898 and March 1899. Prominent in the reports was the lack of sufficient financial support for UNM with particular emphasis on abysmally low faculty salaries. Regent Frank Clancy contended that "the public is receiving a greater return for the small amount of money expended than is given by any institution of like character anywhere in the United States."[23]

In 1898 the territorial superintendent for public instruction wanted to know how UNM met its obligations to the diverse population of New Mexico. Herrick responded that the youth of New Mexico were no less capable or ambitious than their counterparts in other and older colleges. He also pointed out that the model school gave students practical experience and there would be no excuse for any public school in the territory to remain without competent teachers. Further, he cited UNM's Commercial Department and the steady advance in those programs New Mexico's native people enjoyed.

Herrick also seized on this opportunity to stress the need for more adequate appropriations, a dormitory, a department of electrical engineering, funds for more geological survey work, and scholarship funds for impecunious students from the territory. He further suggested that as the head of the educational system of the territory, UNM belonged "above local and partisan interest and should be jealously cared for and cherished by the citizens of the entire Territory."[24]

In January 1899, Governor Otero requested Herrick's opinion on centralization of services among the territory's public institutions. Herrick had long been frustrated by the duplication of higher education in the territory, and he charged that the legislature had "frittered away" money in "fruitless attempts to create more or less competitive or antagonistic centers for college culture." He believed that there should be one institution of the first rank employing the most eminent talent.[25]

He expressed his fear that New Mexico parents would never patronize the home institutions for their sons and daughters unless they had standards that were the same as those of eastern colleges. Students who went away to college might never come back to serve New Mexico, he said.

This led to a report drafted by Holm O. Bursum, head of a special legislative committee. While agreeing with Herrick's call for better salaries, a larger physical plant, and support for applied scientific research, Bursum's committee also expanded on a theme that was to become popular in twentieth-century New Mexico: the health- and life-giving qualities of the territory's climate, which, if generally known, would attract "many persons suffering from physical ailments who would naturally bring with them their money—something that New Mexico is desirous of obtaining."[26]

A second legislative committee, this time the Committee on Finance, under the leadership of Frank H. Winston, also issued a report on UNM in 1899. The committee found no fault with UNM's bookkeeping or management and praised its efforts to maintain academic standards. It did assert, however, that all the territory's institutions of higher learning attempted to cover too much ground, resulting in expensive duplication. Tax increases, the committee reported, were distasteful, so it recommended closing certain schools, but this recommendation fell on deaf ears.[27]

Student Life

Herrick had a more relaxed, informal style in his relations with students than his predecessor, although "he was rather reserved and had plenty of dignity," a student told Hughes. The younger boys reportedly vied for the privilege of pedaling Herrick's "bicycle lathe" while he prepared rock sections. Two students, John Bascom Terry and Herrick's son, Harry, "had the honor of supplying axolotes (water dogs) [salamanders] for neurological experiments," getting their specimens from the old reservoir. "When they glutted the market with too many in one lot, young Herrick started his own breeding farm in the pool" behind the Administration Building.[28]

It was said Presideent Herrick knew how to deal with students and their pranks, including rattlesnakes on the study-room floor, the biology skeleton dressed in a professor's clothing, or the discovery of M. Custers's cow in the assembly room. As students reported, "We were made to realize the undesirability of these pranks without any unpleasant aftermath."

There were not many outside activities for students in those days, but with the small enrollment, they knew each other, and friendliness was a matter of course. Special events included candy-pulls, bicycling, picnics, and dances. Going to public

dances in Albuquerque was regarded as "slumming," though, and students seldom attended unless in a crowd of other UNM students for moral support. One student of the nineties era remarked: "We were rather 'small town prigs' with social lines strictly drawn."[29]

With the passage of years, other organized activities sprouted. The *Mirage* yearbook was first published in 1898. The preceding classes of UNM were each given a page for their history. That same spring, Professor John Weinzirl sponsored the formation of two literary societies, Estrella and Ben Hur. Both soon passed into history, but they signaled the beginning of fraternity, sorority, dramatic, debating, poetic, and other club life on the campus, presenting programs and plays and sponsoring social gatherings. Also organized in 1898 was the Camera Club, whose members took "pictures of pueblos and Indians and burros and queer rock formations" as well as shots of the rapid changes in the life of the Anglos and their environment. Some of these were printed in the 1898 *Mirage*.[30]

Track at UNM had its beginnings in the annual Field Day, but the competition was strictly intramural. Following the dashes, running races, jumping, and putting

Among the girls eating lunch on the campus in the spring of 1901 are Minnie Craig (left), editor of the student newspaper Mirage *in 1901–2, and Mata Tway, editor in 1900–1901 and president of the Alumni Association in 1902. The basketball court in the background featured goals made from the football field's goal posts. After the basketball season, the same posts were cut up and used for the net on the tennis court.*

Hadley Hall doubled the number of substantive buildings, but the campus still looked somewhat less than imposing.

the shot, there were bicycle races and potato and sack races. Tennis, basketball, and baseball games were another part of Field Day, and Albuquerque merchants donated prizes for events. Students laid out the first adobe-base tennis courts in the nineties. Roy Stamm, a state tennis champion, was one of the students who climbed to the third floor of the Main Building to get a bird's-eye view of the campus before selecting a site for the tennis courts, and he later helped in their construction.[31] In the spring of 1898, Stamm won the first New Mexico intercollegiate tennis championship, but tennis as a varsity sport did not start until 1908.

Construction of Hadley Hall

In May 1899, Mrs. Walter C. Hadley, the widow of Walter Hadley, son of the former UNM vice president, offered the University Regents $10,000 for construction of a clinical laboratory. Together Mrs. Hadley and President Herrick worked out the plans for a memorial to her late husband, who had been a health seeker and who, as a mining engineer, had amassed a considerable fortune. In addition to Mrs. Hadley's major contribution, the Board of Regents raised another $5,000 in donations, including $300 from the student body.[32]

Mrs. Hadley was anxious to support the work of UNM to ease the burden carried by people like her husband who came to New Mexico for relief. She received a commitment from the Regents to name the building after Walter Hadley and

The University's first basketball players were the young women. In 1898 they called themselves the "Gladiators," and apparently they played in high-button shoes and bloomers. Their coach was Myra Lukens (standing at left), a graduate of an Ohio normal school, whose title was director of women's gymnasium work.

maintain it "so long as the University shall continue in existence." Under the plan, the newly formed Department of Climatology would study the biological and physiological problems relating to the climate of the plateau region of the Southwest.[33] In addition, Mrs. Hadley wanted the new building to supply facilities for investigation and instruction in other branches of science. This generous gift gave great emphasis to scientific research at UNM.

What was to become Hadley Hall was the second major building on the UNM campus. The Board of Regents accepted architect Edward Buxton Cristy's plans in June 1899. Several changes were made in the plans to reduce the cost, including using Cerrillos sandstone in place of granite and installing roof tile instead of galvanized steel. Contractor John McQuade finished the building on February 1, 1900. By May it was ready for dedication.[34] Rooms in Hadley Hall were set aside for research in histology, zoology, botany, and geology. The building also contained a herbarium and laboratories for physics, chemistry, and bacteriology. In the basement was a "constant temperature vault," while on the roof a large deck was provided for the United States Weather Bureau and special meteorological investigations.[35]

Athletics

In 1900, an outdoor basketball court was laid out atop the tennis court's playing surface, and two rickety shooting goals were put up at each end of the court. The unsteady shooting targets, wind, and a somewhat less than smooth dribbling surface forced the sport indoors.

The first organized basketball team in the history of UNM was the 1898 girls' team. The members played with great enthusiasm and success against New Mexico A&M and local high schools.[36]

Terry Gugliotta, then the University's archivist, reported in 2003 that in those days in some quarters it was considered "unladylike" for young women to participate in sports, and physicians sometimes proclaimed it was harmful to their reproductive organs. Nonetheless, in their bloomers and bows with the letters UNM sewn across their "chests," the women represented the University in its first varsity basketball competition.[37]

The young men of UNM may have been chagrined by having their masculinity infringed upon by the distaff members of the student body. Perhaps for this reason, a men's basketball team was organized in 1900.[38] In February, the UNM male "hoopsters" played their first basketball game in the town armory against the Albuquerque Guards, an amateur team. UNM rallied to earn an 8–6 victory.

Meanwhile, in 1899 UNM organized its first baseball team and played two practice games against the Albuquerque Indian School, losing both. The regular season consisted of one game, on May 12, against a team composed of the combined talents of the Albuquerque High School and the Goss Military Institute (later New Mexico Military Institute). The University won, 18–9. From 1900 through the spring of 1903, no baseball teams were organized at UNM.[39]

It was truly a time of many firsts for UNM athletics. One occurred in 1898 when Frank S. Maltby, a member of the class of 1899, was named the University's first "physical director" in charge of the gym and exercise. In that year the gym was remodeled by adding lockers and a bath. Although athletics were only beginning at the University, an athletic association was organized, "absolutely debarring professionalism, and insisting upon 'strict observance of business principles in all financial dealings.'"[40]

Herrick's Resignation

An issue that may have exacerbated Herrick's failing health and led to a tragic relapse was the continued financial problem that plagued the fledgling University. By March 1900, Herrick and the Board of Regents realized that positions would be lost if the faculty did not accept pay cuts of 7.5 percent. This was a blow to the faculty, which had received no salary increases since the first two years of UNM's operations. Most members of the faculty, including Herrick, agreed to the reductions.

What Herrick feared most at this time was the possibility of losing faculty he had worked so hard to obtain. "As a health-seeker himself, he [Herrick] knew that UNM's list of accomplished teachers owed much to the climate of New Mexico, and not as an approximation of eastern centers of learning."[41]

In September 1900, as his health continued to deteriorate, Herrick asked to resign. The Regents, eager to keep him, offered him leave with pay, which he declined. The Regents then agreed upon a leave without pay, and Herrick left his post as president in the spring of 1901.[42] He lived only three more years, dying in 1904 at the age of forty-six.

For too brief a time Herrick was a brilliant flame in the history of UNM. By the time he left the campus in 1901, the University of New Mexico was on its way to being a center of higher learning prepared to serve the territory and in a few years, New Mexico, the state. ■

Arabella and the baby posed with a lavishly bearded Tight in Granville, Ohio.

CHAPTER FIVE

Administration of William George Tight

1901–9

William George Tight

When the University of New Mexico's third president, William George Tight, took office in 1901, he was not fantasizing about some Harvard on the Rio Grande. Quite the contrary, he reasoned that red brick was for the green East. For this arid land of New Mexico, he believed the Native American builders had recognized what would be fitting and so began to study Pueblo Indian construction as he went around the territory. He photographed Pueblo buildings. He ferreted out detailed information and carefully studied the lines, walls, windows, and roofs of the homes of New Mexico natives, both Indian and Hispanic. He also traveled to Arizona to study the Hopi villages. Professionally, Tight was a scientist, a nationally acclaimed field geologist, but he was also a dreamer, a man of vision. As reported by Gary Karsh, Tight became "fascinated by the pueblos of the Rio Grande and Hopi Indians and dreamed of borrowing from their unique building style." Further, "he was impressed by the pueblos' practicality as well as their aesthetic quality of blending with the environment and began to study these structures during his travels around the Territory."[1]

Tight believed that this twenty-acre site on the hill where sand and cactus thrived in lieu of trees and shrubs, this desolate patch of raw frontier where coyotes vied with students in moonlight strolls, could one day be an academic oasis in the wilderness. He had the vision to see it as a "pueblo on the mesa"—a place that would stand as the world's finest example of what would come to be called the Pueblo Style of architecture.[2]

While his years at UNM marked great changes in the growth and development of the institution, perhaps his best-remembered and most-appreciated contribution was the initiation of the unique indigenous architecture. Every single one of the many authors who have written about the development of the University acknowledges Tight and his dream of the "pueblo on the mesa." That was the title of Dorothy Hughes's history written for the fifty-year anniversary of the University. Tony Hillerman referred to it when he wrote "Birthday for a College," published in *New Mexico Magazine* in 1964 as the University celebrated its seventy-fifth birthday. It was cited in Karsh's "Birth of a Frontier University" in the *UNM Alumnus* in 1975. When UNM, New Mexico State University, and New Mexico Institute of

Mining and Technology celebrated their centennial in 1988–89, *New Mexico Magazine* published a special supplement, "Century of Scholarship," with Melissa Howard's article "UNM: For 100 Years a 'Pueblo on the Mesa.'" The article praised Tight, saying that the architectural style "symbolized his vision of a university that both drew from and nourished its physical and cultural environment."[3]

The Appointment of Tight

The relationship between Tight and Clarence Herrick, his predecessor as UNM president, began at Denison University in Ohio in 1881, when Herrick was a professor and Tight his bright and shining pupil and then his colleague. When Herrick resigned as president of UNM because of failing health in the spring of 1901, he recommended "the tall, muscular, virile William G. Tight" as his replacement. The Regents found the suggestion quite appealing, and the only vote against Tight came from the board's secretary-treasurer, James H. Wroth. As the keeper of the University's books, Wroth disliked hiring someone who could not fill UNM's void in teaching mathematics and physics.[4]

None of the Regents, including Wroth, could find fault with Tight's impressive academic vita. Tight had been professor of geology and botany at Denison University, Granville, Ohio, during the last decade of the nineteenth century. He was born on March 12, 1865, on a farm near Granville, where he attended the public schools. In 1881, he entered Denison University, where he devoted special attention to science. Tight received a BS degree from Denison in 1886 and in 1887 was one of the first two students at that institution to complete a postgraduate degree, the MS. He was appointed instructor of science, succeeding Professor Herrick, who had taken a post at the New Mexico School of Mines. Tight was advanced to assistant professor of geology and botany (1889–92) and to professor (1892–1901). During the summer term of 1888 and the winter of 1893, he pursued special studies at Harvard University. Tight then went on to earn the PhD (1901) from the University of Chicago, stopping in Chicago en route to Albuquerque to pick up his diploma.[5]

Interestingly, in the various accounts of the appointment of Tight, there is no reference to his marital status. He had a wife, Arabella, and a child, whom he left in Granville, Ohio. There was gossip that he had abandoned them, which was the basis of a divorce on December 14, 1905. The court held that he had been willfully absent for three years and was guilty of gross neglect of duty. Arabella received custody of the child and Tight was to pay $65 per month alimony.[6]

In June 1901, at the age of thirty-six, Tight was hired to become president of the University of New Mexico for the annual salary of $2,000. Tony Hillerman described Tight as a scientist of international repute, a Midwesterner "who resembled Prince Albert except for his blacksmith's hands."[7] John Clark, who came to UNM in 1907 as a member of the faculty, remembered Tight as a "human dynamo," words often used to describe the young and vigorous president.[8]

In February 1931, UNM held a memorial service honoring Tight. Clark tells of his initial acquaintance with Tight in 1907.

I first arrived in Albuquerque late on an August evening, and the next morning walked over the sand hills up to the University. The first person with whom I became acquainted was President Tight. I found him dressed in overalls, doing carpenter work in the auditorium of the present Administration Building [Hodgin Hall]. Many times afterward the new instructor was carpenter's, painter's, or plumber's assistant to Dr. Tight. U.N.M. had little money. There was much to be done, and we did our duty. I loved the man from the very first day I knew him.[9]

In the same memorial service another close friend and colleague, Charles Hodgin, said of Tight:

John Clark later lamented the loss of his youthful head of hair.

Physically, nature had well endowed him. He was tall, broad shouldered, robust, and wholesome looking. For many years he wore a full beard, well trimmed, which gave him rather a distinguished appearance. He was genial, approachable, and enthusiastic. He was accommodating and loyal to friends, and held as little lasting resentment to enemies as is usually found in a well balanced man. He was brimful of the spirit and joy of youth, tending generally to inspire confidence and action from faculty and students, such as is characteristic of a leader. He was a genius in doing things—a practical plumber, a carpenter, a painter, and he did not hesitate to don his overalls, and use his mechanical ingenuity to help over any emergency that might arise.[10]

Like so many who worked closely with Tight, Hodgin had his own special remembrances. He told of a time when Tight was working on the underground irrigation of vegetation.

On this occasion he had his rough clothes on and was spading the soil, when a nicely dressed lady drove up and asked if Dr. Tight lived there. He answered that he did and that he would go and call him. So he went in the house, hastily changed his apparel and returned to receive the waiting lady, and introduced himself to her.[11]

Hodgin had plenty of opportunities to know Tight well. After all, they lived together for seven years. Hodgin explains that when Tight first arrived at the University, he wanted to move into the Hodgin house and live with the family.

We told him more than once we were not taking in anybody. But one day an expressman drove up to the house, and delivered a trunk which he said Dr. Tight had sent, and a little later the owner of the trunk himself appeared on the scene, and again announced his desire to live with us. He stayed until he had permission to put his trunk in a room where he

Tight and Julia Asplund appear in front of Hadley Hall; the horse may well be the beloved Billy.

followed, and then remained with us in our home for seven years . . . When he entered the house, he would fill it like a breeze, always happiest when he had something favorable to report regarding the University.[12]

Dorothy Hughes commented: "He [Tight] didn't merely say, 'Do this;' he put on his work clothes and dug in the earth himself." She, too, had her own favorite anecdotes.

Although a product of the East, Dr. Tight had fast become a Westerner upon his arrival in New Mexico, in part because he early found it necessary to add the herding of cattle to his many and often self-appointed duties. Cattle and horses from the many little ranches, then in the foothills beyond the University, were let roam down to the campus at night where they made havoc of the new trees and shrubs which were being planted by Dr. Tight. The requests to the sheriff for aid were received with a spirit of levity, almost understandable in that the hilltop mesa had always been a roaming spot for cattle, and it was not to be expected that its accustomed desolation could be harmed by even a hundred head. There was the further fact that the University in its country setting was considered with no more than an "amused tolerance" by the most of the town in those days. "William George," however found a way to force action. Many a night he spent on the back of Billy, the horse he had bought after considerable dickering, out of a rodeo because it was the "best roper of steers." The University President and Billy rounded up the strays and drove them, not home-wards, but down across the Barelas bridge, knowing full well that when they appeared next morning in the residential sections of the town, something indeed would be done about the wanderers. After a few such roundups the marauding cattle disappeared from the campus, partly because the townspeople were indignant at the encroachment upon their lawns and gardens and partly because of the difficulty the owners had in getting their stock back home from downtown. It was not discovered how the marauders happened to wander so far from their accustomed nocturnal pasture.[13]

As Hillerman reported, "Tight was popular with the students, who slaved in unpaid enthusiasm on his endless building projects."[14] Cottonwood trees were planted in 1905, but they soon littered the campus with cotton and were plagued with worms. This led Tight and the students to plant hardier trees in 1907, elms and hemlocks, pines and cedars, black locusts and white ashes, and they flourished.

Then, as the story goes, there were the squirrels. Tight arranged for six gray squirrels to be sent from the Cincinnati Zoological Gardens. Placed near the fountain that the Class of 1906 donated, they all ran away. Tight persevered, however, and arranged for another shipment of gray squirrels, this time from the Washington, D.C., zoo.[15]

Definitely not a part of the plan for campus beautification was a large cesspool, located about where the Civil Engineering Building is in 2003. All campus sewage drained into it. As Professor John Clark reminisced on the occasion of his seventy-fourth birthday in 1956, "It was covered with a heavy coating of oil and the water in it did not smell very badly, not much, and I remember very well that one time my younger daughter was up there and fell in and my older daughter pulled her out . . . Mama didn't seem a bit pleased."[16]

The Groves of Academe

President Tight, however, had more on his agenda than the beautification of the campus and the beginnings of Pueblo Style architecture. As a scholar and educator with impressive credentials, including a significant portfolio of learned publications, Tight raised the level of expectations of future faculty at UNM. His own stature in the world of academe indicated to New Mexicans that UNM resided in good hands. Those New Mexicans promoting economic development and statehood could point to both Herrick and Tight as proof that the New Mexico Territory deserved attention from outside investors and recalcitrant congressmen who consistently had voted against the territory's admission to the Union.[17]

Tight's assessment was that the University had carried out the legislative mandate to serve as New Mexico's premier academic institution, that the gift of Hadley Hall represented an important bond between UNM and private donors, and that the faculty had responded by creating lines of demarcation between disciplines, "giving to each department individuality and character." In his Report to the Governor, 1901, Tight also stressed that as the flagship university of the territory, UNM needed a close affiliation with the new public school system.[18]

Finances, Academic Affairs, and Enrollment

Tight's influence on UNM in the areas of finances, academic affairs, and enrollment came early, as did his aggressive posture toward its maintenance and expansion. In his first two years he increased the school's revenues by 60 percent, paid all outstanding debts, and held a cash balance of $2,250. To finance more growth, Tight and the Regents also solicited increased support from the legislature. Financial stringencies ended the relationship with the Albuquerque Public Schools' model school for training student teachers. In 1902, UNM faculty again faced new contracts with no pay raises. Josephine Parsons, for example, earned the same $100 monthly salary she had accepted in 1893. Charles Hodgin convinced Tight to add to his pay by adding responsibility to head the Normal Department and serve as dean of faculty and registrar. Atanasio Montoya, Jr., UNM's first Hispanic graduate and the only Hispanic instructor, refused to sign another contract with no salary increase and left the school.[19]

President Tight reported to Governor Otero in December 1902, pointing out that UNM's enrollment had risen by 48 percent over the previous year. We must take his word on this, as no reliable figure is now available.

John Weinzirl took this photo of the Bacteriology Laboratory he directed in Hadley Hall in 1903.

Tight also continued his personal scholarly interests with an emphasis on the geological phenomena of New Mexico. The U.S. Reclamation Service hired the president as a consulting geologist for its preliminary surveys for the proposed Elephant Butte reservoir and dam in southern New Mexico. Further, in the summer of 1903, Tight joined a mountain-climbing expedition in Chile.[20]

On June 6, 1903, at Tight's urging, UNM established a sabbatical program for faculty, wherein every seven years they could receive one year's leave with pay for research and writing. The policy also required faculty members to provide for the satisfactory performance of their classes during their absence without expense to the University. That year the Regents also approved the appointment of two new faculty members, Rupert Asplund in history and Aurelio Espinosa for languages.[21]

The matter of royalties received for leases for cattle grazing on territorial land held in trust for UNM consumed much of the time of the Regents and the president in 1904–5. Welsh reported that erratic funding levels from the legislature and the policy of free tuition for New Mexico residents kept UNM constantly in search of additional revenues.[22]

In order to learn more about western land questions and establish ties with other state and territorial universities, Tight in 1905 attended the annual meeting of an organization of state university presidents in Washington, D.C. A year later, he persuaded the Geological Society of America to hold its annual conference at UNM. He prevailed upon the Santa Fe Railroad to offer reduced excursion rates so that those scholars attending the meeting could see other parts of the Southwest. Tight served as organizer and social director for the group, including a trip to the Sandia Mountains and a more extended journey to the Grand Canyon in Arizona. The success of this endeavor attracted the attention of the National Irrigation Congress, an organization of prominent western water users and political leaders, which met on the UNM campus in 1908.[23]

By the 1908–9 school year, enrollment at UNM had risen to 173, including 5 graduate students, 67 college students, 91 preps, and 10 extension students.[24] These numbers indicated what Tight and others had believed all along regarding UNM's appeal to the territory. Tight noted that before the opening of dormitories for men and women, UNM never had more than three or four New Mexican counties represented. By 1908, students were attending UNM from two-thirds of the territory's counties.

In addition, the University had matured enough to require work in "advanced lines of study." Tight, however, warned that if the demands for professional schools (such as law and medicine) and graduate work were not met, it would be impossible to hold New Mexican students in the territory. Further, he believed that academic excellence served all citizens of the territory. In 1905 only three New Mexico high schools could send graduates prepared for the college course at UNM. Three years later, the number of high schools coordinating their programs with the University had grown to ten.[25]

Advanced scholarship by members of the faculty also brought UNM added prestige. One of the prime examples was the publication *Language Series*, devoted to research in the humanities. Professor Aurelio Espinosa, a native New Mexican, published in the series a play about colonial Hispanic life entitled *Los Comanches*, which attracted wide attention. At the same time requests for the UNM catalog increased from five hundred to two thousand.[26]

An academic milestone for the University occurred in 1905 when Thomas S. Bell was selected as the institution's first Rhodes Scholar. (Bell received his BA degree from the University in May 1905. Upon completion of his courses at Oxford in 1908, he studied under a fellowship at Columbia University for a year. He passed the New York state bar examinations in 1909 and then taught international law at the University of Washington for a short time. For the next thirty years, he lived in Pasadena, California, where he practiced law before retiring. At UNM, Bell was captain and center of the varsity basketball team in 1904–5. Upon his death, Bell left a substantial gift to UNM.)[27] Another Rhodes Scholar from that era, Frank C. Light, a student from Silver City, was selected in 1908.

The College of Letters and Science

What had begun as the College of Literature and Arts in 1899 became the College of Letters and Science in 1903. A School of Engineering had been established within the college in 1906, offering courses in civil, electrical, mechanical, and mining engineering. It became the College of Engineering, the University's second college, three years later. Expansion of philosophy, language, and science also occurred during this decade. Over time, the names and affiliations of other academic areas, such as education, fine arts, home economics, business, and architecture, changed. They were sometimes separate colleges or schools or departments, and at other times they were under the umbrella of the liberal arts college, by whatever name. For several years after the departure of Dean Edward Childs in 1901, no person was designated as dean of the college, and the title was used imprecisely. As related previously, Charles Hodgin was called dean of the faculty, but the post was neither defined nor did it seem to have carried with it any particular duties or powers.[28] William M. Dabney wrote in "A History of the College of Arts and Sciences" in 1989–90:

> In the early part of the twentieth century a student who wanted to be admitted to the college had to be at least sixteen years old and a graduate of either the University's preparatory school or one of a list of secondary schools the catalog listed as accredited. A secondary school graduate from outside of New Mexico was acceptable if his school was accredited by its state university. Provision was made, also, for entrance examinations for those youngsters who did not otherwise qualify. . . .
>
> Once in the college the student chose from three curricula: the classical, the philosophical, and the scientific. The classical scholar studied Greek, Latin, Spanish, mathematics, rhetoric, and literature. The philosophical would take Latin, German or Spanish, mathematics, rhetoric, literature, physics, and philology. The scientific course included modern language, mathematics, science, and rhetoric. In each of the three the student would also choose some electives. There were changes in these curricula with almost every new catalog, but the degree requirements remained quite rigorous. For several years a thesis was required for graduation, but later this statement was amended to read that a thesis might be required.
>
> In the earliest years of the college thirty-six credits were needed to graduate, none of them in the major. (A credit was defined as five hours per week, or two hours per day laboratory, for one quarter.) Freshmen and sophomores had to do "rhetoricals," and juniors and seniors could elect to do so but were not required to. Every semester each student had to deliver one declamation and one memorized essay.[29]

Among Tight's many accomplishments was the establishment in 1902 of a School of Music, which ultimately led to the College of Fine Arts. Although William George, as the students affectionately called him, could not carry a tune or even distinguish one from another, music was important to him. He compiled and published the first UNM songbook, and the campus sings were great events during his presidency. Space was rented for the music program in the old Perkins Hall at

Edith and Central, which had been vacant since the closing of Albuquerque Academy. Quarters consisted of a large assembly hall in addition to several classrooms, and some of the program was conducted in the roughly finished basement. A faculty was responsible for vocal training, piano, violin, public reading, and musical kindergarten. The University solicited the community for $1,500 to support the Music School operations. This action received warm town approval, while the faculty regarded it as a strong bond with the city.[30] Tight also included music in the institution's first extension work, cooperating with music programs in the territory.[31]

A New Century

Changes in the early twentieth century greatly affected the University of New Mexico. In particular, new modes of transportation and communication linked semi-isolated communities like Albuquerque to the rest of the world. Improved accommodations for railroad passengers brought an influx of easterners to the territory while new highways and automobiles captured the fancy of the adventurous. They turned to the horseless carriage to get them not only up the hill to the University but also up and back from Santa Fe in a single day.

Breakthroughs in communications were also dramatic. The telegraph and telephone brought the news within hours. Then, during and after World War I, the radio connected the frontier of New Mexico to other places worldwide.

For the University, improved transportation and communication were supplemented by other expanded contacts, such as ties to prestigious universities in other parts of the country. Contacts were also established with the national accrediting agencies as the young institution sought to set goals and implement plans to join the elite of the nation's institutions of higher learning.

Student Life

Changes in student life accompanied the new century. By 1904, caps and gowns were worn at commencement. In 1907, as reported by Clark, the ceremony for those earning bachelor's degrees was held at the Elks Theatre downtown, while "the preparatory graduation exercises were held on campus under trees which had grown large enough to be noticeable."[32]

From the time of his arrival on campus in 1901, President Tight's relationship with students was warm and cordial. He enjoyed their company and looked upon their campus pranks with good humor. Neither the city fathers nor the UNM faculty always appreciated this attitude. As reported in an article in the alumni magazine *Mirage* in the spring of 1988, "Tight sometimes ruffled the feathers of the townspeople. He irritated others (notably some members of the faculty) by being one of the best friends the students had."[33]

As Kirk Bryan wrote of Tight in the 1910 student yearbook *Mirage*, "That rare quality, common sense, was uppermost in his dealings with students, while its close ally, a sense of humor, saved many a one who was at outs with authority after some college prank."[34]

Among the college pranks that gained enduring recognition was the painting of zebra stripes on Billy, the president's big bay horse. Hodgin related the tale:

It was on a hollowe-en when it fell to the lot of "Billy" to be sneaked out of his stable about 2 A.M. and stealthily guided across the street, into the campus, up the steps of the administration building, and into the library room . . . There the horse was securely tied to the librarian's desk, and thoroughly treated to a coat, in stripes of different colored paints to represent the zebra of the circus. And "Bill" was left till morning to browse among the books, surrounded by Plato, Socrates, Shakespeare and Josh Billings. It was the ardent hope of the boys that the librarian and students would enter the library the next morning to behold the unusual. But again disappointment was theirs for the janitor discovered the out-of-placeness of the horse, notified the president at once, and the camp was all astir. Several of us laboriously removed the paint, and at half past eight President Tight hitched "Billy" to his buggy and slowly drove to town as students were plodding up the hill to school. As he expected, certain boys stared at the horse while passing and looked back with more than usual interest, and by that revelation, suspicion was aroused and convictions followed.[35]

Charlie Lembke, a student under Tight, explained how he dealt with misbehavior.

President Tight was a great big man, and strong, my God! He was strong. He would come up to a couple of us students, grab us by the backs of our necks, pick us up off the ground, and then hold us out (his arms spread as upon a cross) until we agreed to stop doing whatever wrong we were busily engaged in. The students loved him . . . [36]

Early in his administration, Tight began transforming the dusty mesa into a garden. In 1904, he sent boys into the Sandias to fetch ponderosa pines for the first trees on the campus. He also planted or oversaw the planting of hedges of tamarisk, rose bushes, and honey locusts. In February 1905, he traveled to Silver City and arranged for a shipment of yuccas. In April of that year, he planted thirty pines west of the Administration Building and promised that the students would plant two hundred more before spring break. They did.[37]

Tight was successful in rallying the students for the hard labor of planting trees and shrubs. He convinced the students that beauty and shade were necessary to make the campus an attractive place. This was a real challenge for the rocky hillside, poor soil, and expensive irrigation, especially when most people predicted that the transplanted trees would never grow. For several years Tight made Arbor Day a special holiday devoted to campus improvement, as well as a high spot in fun and student morale. Charles Hodgin, writing in 1928, described the gala occasion.

A grove of poplar trees was planted next to the Main Building. What would be called Tight Grove was soon added in front.

The day before Arbor Day groups of boys with teams and wagons were dispatched to the mountains and down the river after trees. On that same day other groups with shovels and spades were set to work digging holes. On Arbor Day morning tree planting according to plans became the all absorbing interest. Lovers planted trees in pairs and certain trees were named for individuals. . . . At noontime a group of good girls . . . were ready in Hadley Laboratory to serve a sumptuous, and satisfying dinner, where appetites were amply appeased.[38]

Arbor Day also included the annual faculty-varsity baseball game. According to Hodgin, Tight, "a well-built man, 6 feet and 2 inches, was himself a fine athlete, and several men on the faculty were choice players." He also reported that perhaps a "ringer" or two from the town helped beef up the faculty team, so it turned into an entertaining battle for the students and townspeople.[39]

Another major annual event for the students at UNM was the Territorial Fair. On one occasion, President Tight and his helpers built a dragon that was mounted on sixteen wagons drawn by thirty-two horses. But, as related by Hughes, it was the University exhibit in the 1908 fair that really caused "wonder and amazement." Reflecting what Tight was trying to do in promoting Pueblo Style architecture, the president, members of the faculty, and the student body "erected a three-storied pueblo building, complete with primitive ladders leading from roof to roof." The "typical Indian *horno*" (oven) was clearly visible, with the "circular symbol with the figure of No-ma-ta, mythical hog-human of Indian legends, painted in red and black on the facade." Tight had driven out into the country in his buggy to bring back strands of red chile to decorate the building, and varieties of yucca and cactus were planted around it. The beauty and perfection of detail of this Pueblo building were viewed as outstanding. It was not built of adobe, however, and was really no

The University's exhibit at the 1908 Territorial Fair, built by President Tight and some students, was an early attempt to show New Mexicans their architectural heritage.

more than a "movie set" constructed for its temporary purpose. The cost to the University was only $138, the Fair Association having contributed $275.[40]

Fraternities and sororities made their appearance on the campus in 1903, when President Tight helped establish the men's first fraternity, Alpha Alpha Alpha, which had formerly been the Yum Yum Society. At the same time he sponsored the Sigma Sigma sorority, which had begun as the Minnehaha Social Club. For the latter group, which was allotted space in the Administration Building, Tight arranged for the room to be "newly furnished" and repapered in the sorority colors of green and white.

Three years later Tight helped found the Society of Engineers, and in 1906, the first dramatic society was formed. Professor Weinzirl reorganized the literary society for girls under a new name, Estrella. For the boys, a debating society, Khiva, was initiated. Musical organizations also thrived.

Student government made its first formal appearance in 1908 under the label of The Associated Student Body, although it was another ten years until there was a student council. The weekly student paper of the era was known as the *Mirage.* It later became the *U.N.M. Weekly* and finally the *Lobo.* The yearbook, *Mirage,* had been published since 1898, and by Tight's tenure was an established tradition.[41] After the yearbook ceased publication in the early 1970s, the alumni magazine took the name "Mirage" for itself.

Contributions to the enhancement of life on the campus during the Tight era were improved travel to and from the campus, the purchase of Custers's six-room house for a dormitory and dining hall, the construction of Kwataka Hall and a few cottages to house male students and Hokona Hall for female students, as well as modification of the second floor of the Administration Building for a few men.

Pueblo on the Mesa paints a vivid picture of student life at the turn of the century and described it as a time of "more college fun."

Every possible holiday, in particular Hallowe'en, Washington's Birthday, Valentine's and April Fool's Day, was a cause for celebration. A social treat of 1904 was when the Sigma Sigma sorority entertained a "large crowd of students" with a trolley ride. The "jolly ride" continued until ten in the evening when the guests gathered at O'Rielly's drug store, "one of the college paper advertisers," it was noted, to patronize "that popular soda fountain." After refreshments there, the ride proceeded to Old Town and back, ending at the Alvarado switch. "College songs and jokes and yells made the welkin ring," it was reported, "and brought people to the doors to see what kind of a performance was in progress. The trolley managers were patient. Several members of the faculty were along and entered heartily into the fun."

The Alpha Alpha Alpha gave a "frat party" that same year "with continuous performance" by Bell and Allen, who led the grand march, appeared in a cake walk, and presented themselves with the cake "which they made that afternoon," acted as waiters, and orated. There were games later for those who did not indulge in dancing.

The new dorms were christened at the "Sing" of 1906, but with no "Mumm's Extra Dry," the students commented; it was "strictly a temperance affair." On the night of the christening there was an Indian Harvest Dance about a bonfire, given "by braves from Kwataka." The Dorm and the University picnics always ended with Indian dances about the bonfire, and the popular song riding home was "Ta-ra-ra-ra-boom-de-ay." The picnic spot continued to be Bear Canyon and the sports would climb to the top and roll rocks down the canyon to watch the trees break and crash, until the law stopped the practice. Ice cream and watermelon were the picnic climax. The ice cream freezer was too heavy to carry to the Upper Falls where the students climbed, but was left at the foot of the hill, enabling the boys to make a race downward later to be first for dessert.[42]

Some of the highlights on campus during Tight's era included the time the circus came to town in 1906, and the girls were furious because the boys would not escort them to the event. Two anonymous male students invited town preachers to toil up the hill to judge a debate, a debate that had never been scheduled and never took place. After President Tight gave a stern lecture against "spooning" in an assembly, the cuddling and kissing continued despite his good advice. That same year, the basketball team, returning from Las Vegas, celebrated its victory by playing another game on the train. The conductor gave the impossible order to the train porter to eject them if they kept it up.

The 1908 school year was remembered for the raid on the Sigma Sigma party for the women's basketball team in the University Dining Hall. A dramatic part of the "raid" was a fake shooting. As the story goes, John Marshall shot Frank Light with a blank pistol, and the latter lay covered with red-ink blood. With all distracted by this phony ploy, the student body president, Ralph Tascher, stole the ice cream and cake from the kitchen, leaving the girls without dessert. Light, who was a Rhodes Scholarship recipient that year, played his part as the hapless victim until a volunteer nurse began to unbutton his shirt. At that point he recovered and jumped through a window.

In 1908, the "sports" were wearing wide ties "like gigantic butterflies," blue spotted socks, fobs without watches, jerseys of every shade of red, shoes that "arch and bow" extremely, coats of every hue, and "verdant vests."

Arbor Day continued to be a resounding success. Highlights of the 1909 celebration included a "gondola race" on the UNM reservoir. Washtubs were used for gondolas and brooms for paddles. A light was placed on President Tight's large windmill as well as on the sundial bench, but it was said that neither dimmed those places of nocturnal popularity. The stone bench memorial of the Class of 1905 and the sundial love seat of 1907 were still havens for spooners. Preps were ducked under the rustic pump, a gift of the class of 1904. Rodey Hall, adjacent to the remodeled Administration Building, was the scene of dancing, with refreshments served across the way in the Dining Hall. The engineering students held their first banquet that year and introduced their famous yell:

> Three Cheers,
> Three Beers,
> Varsity, Varsity,
> Engineers!

The great social event of Albuquerque in that era was the annual Montezuma Ball at the Alvarado Hotel. One student who wangled an invitation wrote that he attended in a borrowed dress suit and white kid gloves, but had difficulty in keeping his coat tails out of the fountain at the hotel.[43]

The lack of a financial aid program for students handicapped the efforts of UNM to increase its enrollment. Important as a college education was to New Mexicans, many families could not meet even the modest costs of fees, room and board, books, and incidental expenses. In 1905, when UNM learned that it would receive $500 per year from a Connecticut family fund to help poor and deserving girls receive an education, it marked a major step forward. This in turn led to the 1907 territorial legislature approving the Indigent Students Act, allowing each lawmaker to nominate one student for $200 a year in financial aid at a New Mexico college of the student's choice. The county commissioners of the territory also received the right to nominate a student for financial aid. This program prompted many Hispanic youths from northern New Mexico to avail themselves of higher education for the first time, and it contributed to the establishment of the Spanish American Normal School in El Rito in 1909.[44]

Campus Development and Construction

Throughout these middle years of his tenure as UNM's president, Tight continued his efforts to develop the physical plant. As related previously, in 1903 he decided

Kwataka and Hokona dormitories each had a solar-heated water tank on the roof, concealed in a replica of a Pueblo horno, *or oven (left corner in this photo). President Tight and English Professor Ethel Hickey painted this depiction of a "man eagle," or* kwataka, *on the front of the building.*

that the architectural plan of the University had no central theme. He became enamored of the "simplicity and other-worldliness" of Pueblo Indian adobe and the relatively low cost of frame or stone, what with all the materials and labor being readily available. He believed the use of adobe to be both economical and aesthetically pleasing. Tight and architect Edward Buxton Cristy, a former UNM instructor, fashioned a "hybrid of Pueblo forms" into a master plan for the new facilities at UNM. It was said that the proposed architectural style at first appealed to the Regents, who recognized both its uniqueness and economy.[45]

What with Tight's enthusiasm and boundless energy and a lot of unpaid student labor, the once wild and barren mesa did indeed become a blooming oasis. All those trees, shrubs, and vines needed water in this arid land, however. By the end of his tenure as president, what today is called Tight Grove consisted of some forty or fifty pine trees, each about eighteen inches high, located west and slightly south of the Administration Building.

Early on it was discovered that the pressure from the city reservoir was insufficient to throw water above the first floors of the University buildings, so a deep well was dug with a high windmill for power. The well and windmill were located north and east of the Administration Building, and for years this windmill was one of the landmarks of the campus. It was painted cherry and silver. The tower was seventy feet high and the wind-driven pump added another twenty feet.

The opening to the well was about ten feet below ground level, inside a small building made of galvanized corrugated steel. There was an electrical pump at the bottom of the well, and water tanks were placed on the third story of Hadley Hall.

The campus reservoir was constructed in 1905. It was walled with brick and covered with tar. The eight-foot-deep reservoir, which held 250,000 gallons of water, also was used as a swimming pool. It lacked any type of filtration system or sanitation measures, however, and soon became the chief supplier of aquatic animals

The campus landscaping was becoming more substantial when the windmill was photographed, but sidewalks were still only a dream. The dirt road in the foreground would become Railroad Avenue and then Central Avenue.

for study and dissection in the biology laboratory. The water was also subsequently used for experimental irrigation projects.

Another phase of improvement of the campus resulted from President Tight's encouraging each senior class to leave some memorial. These included a fish pool, a fountain, some concrete seats, a pyramid (a mound of stones), and a rustic sundial. Several were placed in the middle of Terrace Street, which for many years served as the entrance to the campus. Some of the benches are still outside Hodgin Hall.[46]

In July 1904, the Regents leased the Solon Rose House just east of the campus for $100 per year and authorized another $100 for putting it in good shape. The campus newspaper reported: "The boys' dorm has been removed from the Main Building to the neat little cottage just over the campus line, so that hereafter there need be no conflict between the recitation and sleeping rooms." The University later purchased the house.[47]

In June 1905, the Regents approved a contract for the construction of a boiler plant. Designed by E. B. Cristy, it was the first campus building done in the Pueblo Style. A year later, in March, the Regents approved plans for a dormitory, which would be divided into two wings, one for women and one for men. The contract was let to Wallace Hesselden, but was canceled two months later because of financing problems. Hesselden then submitted a proposal to build two separate dormitories with his own funds and rent them to the University for a dollar a year until they were paid for. The University agreed to purchase them within four years and borrowed money to make the payments.

The dormitories were given Indian names: Kwataka, meaning "man-eagle," for the men's and Hokona, signifying "butterfly-maiden," for the women. President Tight and Miss Ethel Hickey, an English teacher, painted these symbols on the walls. Kwataka accommodated twenty-four men and Hokona, thirty women. Rooms were arranged in suites with two bedrooms and a study room. Interior walls were painted plaster with no decorations. Curtains were emblazoned with Indian symbols, and light fixtures were in the shape of Indian swastikas.

The unique designs of the dormitories and the heating plant attracted national attention in newspaper and magazine articles that had titles such as "Prehistoric Home for University," "A University Pueblo," and "University Buildings of Adobe."[48]

College banners supplemented the Indian décor of the first men's and women's dormitories, which were wired for electricity.

Sometime between 1906 and 1908, the president showed some of the Yum Yum boys how to make and lay adobe bricks to build what was to be called the Estufa, a term meaning "sweathouse." Early Spanish settlers in New Mexico used the word for the Pueblo Indians' kivas, since they got so hot and smoke-filled during ceremonials. This structure is still in use in 2003 on Redondo Drive at the Martin Luther King Boulevard entrance to the campus. The Estufa had no ventilation, which no one seemed to mind, and the only entrance was through a hole in the roof with a ladder to the room below. By midcentury, more than one thousand members had been initiated into the fraternity in the hallowed structure. As noted previously, the Yum Yum Society was soon transformed into the Alpha Alpha Alpha fraternity, which later became a chapter of the national fraternity Pi Kappa Alpha.[49]

By 1908, it was clear to the president and the Regents that winds battering the roof of the Administration Building were causing severe damage to the supporting walls. The danger was so obvious that there was even talk of razing the whole structure. President Tight seized this opportunity to remodel the building in keeping with his dream of a Pueblo Style campus. Cristy presented plans to the Regents on May 18 to remove the pitched roof and replace it with a viga-supported

*Decades later, a student would say of the Estufa:
"Many things go in; only smoke comes out."*

flat roof, cover the brick walls with stucco, block off the top of the arched window openings, and modify the interior. All bids were rejected as being over the budget, and Cristy revised his plans. Bids were received again on June 12, with A. Y. Hayden being awarded the contract. The *U.N.M. Weekly* proclaimed

> The Administration Building, as we used to know it, is gone. In its place stands an immense three storied pueblo. It is easily larger than anything of similar style erected in modern times and seems more pleasing to the eyes than any specimen of pueblo architecture on the campus. It is almost incredible that a building of such pronounced character, could be, in so short a time so completely changed. . . . Arches have been removed or straightened, doors cut through, walls torn out, porches made, a room built on the south side, the old top heavy third floor torn down and two new rooms built in the center, a flat roof built to replace the old one, a thousand and one changes made. North of the Main Building, and seemingly a part of it is Rodey Hall, the new assembly building. . . . It is cross shaped, the platform occupying the shorter arm of the cross. The ceiling is quite high and a balcony is being constructed in the upper part of the longer arm of the cross. Large rough pine logs are used for rafter, joists, and pillars in both this and the Administration Building. The walls and corners are heavily buttressed and the general effect of this building is that of an old Pueblo church.[50]

Gary Karsh, writing in 1979 about the "Birth of a Frontier University," also gave us a vivid picture of the remodeled building and its additions:

> The Hodgin Hall that we see today is the product of that 1909 remodeling. Stucco was applied over the brick exterior; the gables, cornices and chimneys were removed from the roof; wood vigas, pillars and balconies were added;

The remodeling of Hodgin Hall by President Tight and architect Cristy began as a structural imperative and was later hailed as the first step toward the Pueblo Revival style that gives the campus its identity.

the stone arches over doors and windows were covered and some windows were filled in; buttresses were added at the corners and porches were built on the east and west entrances. In addition, two new wings were added: Rodey Hall, a 500-seat auditorium inspired by the church at Ranchos de Taos, on the north and new quarters for Dean Hodgin's department of education on the south. By this time the main entrance had become the east door, facing the rapidly expanding campus instead of downtown Albuquerque.[51]

Bainbridge Bunting, a distinguished architectural historian on the UNM faculty, wrote in 1978 that Hodgin Hall, by then on the state and national registers of historic cultural properties, is a "very significant" building:

> Interestingly enough, however, this importance relates not so much to the structure as it was built in the early 1890s but as it was remodeled in the Spanish Pueblo style less than two decades later. As such it stands as the first significant step in the rediscovery and revival of the traditional architecture of the Rio Grande valley. The architectural fashion exemplified by the remodeled building is sometimes termed the "Santa Fe style," which was to achieve widespread recognition in the 1920s and '30s, but it is important to remember that the movement got its start here on the UNM campus several years before Santa Fe followed suit with the restoration of the Palace of the Governors or the construction of the Museum of Art.[52]

Despite all the acclaim and even worldwide excitement the "pueblo on the mesa" generated, Hooker observed that "not everyone agreed with Tight's use of Pueblo Style architecture on the campus."[53] Charles Hodgin recollected some of the opposition:

Basketball was apparently serious business for the members and coaches of the 1905 women's team. Photo courtesy of Adah Vaughn, Normal Class of 1905

One man said to me one day, "How foolish to go back 300 years for a type of building—not much evidence of progress in that." I said, "What about going back two or three thousand years to copy Greek architecture?" "Well," he said, "if you are going to be consistent, the President and faculty should wear Indian blankets around their shoulders, and feathered coverings on their heads!"[54]

Athletics

In the beginning years of organized athletics at UNM, the athletic team commonly was referred to as the varsity. Most of UNM's athletic contests, however, were against local or regional high schools, such as Albuquerque High School, Menaul High School, Albuquerque Indian School, and the Santa Fe Indian School. Other competition included various amateur and professional teams in the area. Robert Knight Barney pointed out that "the long distances and expense involved in traveling to other collegiate institutions, inside and outside of the territory, made it apparent that the young University must develop its athletic programs by competing chiefly against nearby competition or have them perish from complete inactivity. . . . Travel away from Albuquerque for any appreciable distance usually entailed a train trip."[55]

The early organization of athletics at the University was for the most part a haphazard affair with little faculty interest and control. Roy Stamm, a pioneer University student-athlete in the nineties, proclaimed: "To play football, baseball, or tennis, you had to have real zest for the game. You made your own diamonds, fields,

The basketball players apparently proclaimed themselves the champions in 1903 after winning their only game.

and courts. You paid your own expenses and bought all equipment and clothing. No lettermen were named and if injured, certainly you settled your own hospital and doctor's fees."[56] Barney goes on to report,

> In 1902, an Athletic Association was formed and a constitution drawn up to regulate athletic competition. Chief among the concerns was the practice of recruiting boys who had no connection with the University to represent the institutions in athletic contests. Because there were so few male students taking college courses, the early teams relied heavily on the "preppers."[57]

At the beginning of the twentieth century, UNM began phasing out its contests with high school and independent teams, replacing them with competitors from other colleges and universities in the area. Home football games continued to be played in a vacant lot behind the town's ice factory, the Albuquerque Indian School grounds, or the Territorial Fair Grounds in Old Town.[58]

In 1901 the University played its first away game when the varsity football team journeyed to Las Vegas to meet the New Mexico Normal College, losing 0–32. Despite efforts to upgrade its schedule, UNM continued playing mostly high school teams. The 1905 team won five games and lost one. In the final game of the season, UNM was drubbed by its downstate collegiate rival, New Mexico College of Agriculture and Mechanic Arts (A&M) of Las Cruces, 0–40.

Football at UNM took on a more collegiate tone in 1908, as in addition to two contests with the Albuquerque Indian School, it defeated teams from New Mexico Mines, the New Mexico Military Institute, and A&M. Highlight of the season, however, was the beginning of what would be a long rivalry, the scheduling of the University of Arizona. UNM lost, 5–10. The 1908 season also marked the first time the University was given a guarantee to play away from home, $400 to play New Mexico Military Institute in Roswell. Ticket revenues were only $15, so apparently the military institute had to supply the remaining $385. To add insult to injury, UNM won the game 16–12.

Basketball games were more limited in this period, notwithstanding the fact that the sport generated a great deal of enthusiasm among the University's student body as well as the local townspeople. As an added attraction, dances were almost always held following the games played at the Albuquerque Armory (south of the courthouse), Colombo Hall (across Second Street), or the Casino at Traction Park.[59]

In 1903–4, UNM played only one game, beating New Mexico A&M 21–9. In the season of 1905–6, the University split games with Albuquerque High School, lost to the Albuquerque Minors, and finished the season by beating A&M 28–16. In the season of 1906–7, UNM won by one point over A&M, 18–17, and lost to the Las Vegas YMCA.

The pattern of playing mostly high school and independent teams continued in 1907–8, with UNM playing six games, of which the only one against collegiate competition was A&M. UNM won 44–25. All three games in 1908–9 were against independent teams.

The years between 1901 and 1909 marked a bleak period for baseball at UNM. The only games against collegiate teams were those against A&M in 1903, which UNM won, 12–5, and 1908, which A&M won 12–10.

Track began as a varsity sport at UNM in 1903, at which time construction began on a one-fifth-mile oval track for practice and meets. The track was literally and laboriously carved from the mesa. UNM's first track competition consisted of a three-way meet at the Albuquerque Fair Grounds in 1903 with the Albuquerque Indian School and New Mexico A&M. The latter overwhelmed its two opponents, scoring 81 points against UNM's 16 and the Indian School's 2. The meet, however, was hailed as a rousing success and served to initiate an interest in track and field in the territory.

Tennis made a brief appearance at UNM in 1908, when the University won its only match, 2–0, against the School of Mines. Frank Light, the aforementioned Rhodes Scholar, won the singles match and then teamed with Fred Johnson to win the doubles competition. The match was played in gusty winds, which were to become quite standard during tennis seasons of the future.[60]

The Firing of Tight

Meanwhile, Tight, who had been divorced in December 1905, remarried in June 1908. He took the train to Gallup and at a friend's home married Mabel L. Hackman, formerly of Glendale, California. The couple returned to Albuquerque by train after the ceremony.[61]

Professor John Clark, a close friend of Tight, referred to the events surrounding the firing of the president in 1909 as "one of those eruptions so volcano-like in its severity and all too common in state institutions in the distant West."[62]

In retrospect, perhaps it was not one but several items of seemingly unrelated discontent that brought the popular president down. Among them were the unhappiness over his changes in the architecture, the termination of two faculty members and suspension of a student, concern over his alleged impropriety in taking a female faculty member on buggy rides, and, although not documented, speculation about his divorce and remarriage.

Several UNM historians referred to the criticism of campus architecture. Tony Hillerman wrote in 1964: "Tight was popular with the students, who slaved in unpaid enthusiasm on his endless building projects, but his dream of a pueblo on the mesa was much too much for more conservative thinkers."[63] Gary Karsh, in referring to the remodeled Administration Building, commented, "Possibly the resulting appearance was too much for the forces opposing the Pueblo idea to take. Soon after the remodeling of the administration building was completed, Tight received a letter from the Regents asking for his resignation."[64] Marc Simmons stated:

> It was in the design of new buildings . . . that President Tight chalked up his greatest achievement, and at the same time unexpectedly touched off an avalanche of public criticism. . . . Citizens of Albuquerque had watched with undisguised alarm while the university head indulged his fancy for maverick architecture—"a reversion to the primitive," many called it.[65]

In 1983, reporter Bart Ripp noted that the Regents were not supportive. "A college campus, they reasoned, should be brick and ivy, not vigas and adobe."[66] Professor William Dabney commented: "There were those who believed that this style (Pueblo), so widely admired in years to come, simply was not suitable for a university campus."[67] Melissa (Noland) Howard wrote in the *UNM Alumnus* in March 1979, "The controversy over architecture was only one of his [Tight's] problems in 1909. That spring the Regents censured him 'for exceeding his authority in asking for [two faculty members'] resignations before consulting the board.' Without citing any other reasons, the Regents then asked Dr. Tight to resign."[68]

The official reason for Tight's termination was thus not his quest for an architectural style for the campus, but his handling of a problem of two faculty members and, as it turned out, a recalcitrant, bitter student. This became the official party line.

Michael Welsh supported this theory. "The eight-year tenure of William Tight came undone for reasons of discipline, involving both faculty and students." Each incident "exacerbated campus and community opinion" and ultimately involved the territorial governor and attorney general.

President Tight looked forward to a well-deserved sabbatical leave in 1909–10. Before his departure, however, he sought to remove two instructors, Rupert Asplund and John Crum, whose attitudes he considered to be unprofessional, and a student, Roy Baldwin, who was expelled for bringing liquor into the men's dormitory. Tight cited Asplund's poor performance as secretary of the faculty, his revisions of galley proofs for the University catalog, and manipulation of transcripts of a student Asplund had tutored one summer. While Tight liked Asplund personally, he found his scholarship lacking and the latter's demands for a sabbatical leave not in keeping with University policy.

Tight had received complaints from students about Crum's lack of dependability and indifference in the classroom. Crum had supervision of the drama and debating programs. When he was hired, Crum's salary was so low that he was allowed to solicit drama students for additional funds and keep a portion of the profits from student plays. It had been agreed that when Crum's salary was brought up to par, the solicitations and holdbacks would cease. When Tight learned that Crum had continued the practice, he demanded that Crum quit the University. Crum refused.

The dismissals of the two faculty members reportedly polarized the small faculty and student body and spilled over into the town of Albuquerque. Two Regents, the Reverend Fletcher Cook and Father A. M. Mandalari, had for some time disliked Tight's style and had endeavored to have him removed. Cook, particularly, played an active role in the opposition to Tight and took his case to selected students. He did not limit his efforts to the Asplund-Crum case, but also intervened in the Baldwin case. He allegedly sought to bring pressure on the beleaguered president and urged a student, David Lane, to respond to a Portland, Oregon, newspaper that was soliciting "gossip" pertaining to Tight. Lane suspected that Regent Cook had already been in contact with the newspaper.[69]

Cook had just been appointed to the Board of Regents and served only one year, 1908 to 1909. Father Mandalari also had just been appointed and served but three years, 1909 to 1912. W. J. Johnson was also appointed Regent in 1909 and served one year. Of the five-member board, only Frank Clancy and James Wroth had been on when Tight was appointed in 1901.

In the midst of all of this, an unnamed correspondent had sent an article to the *El Paso Herald*, which was printed on March 27, 1909. He had written that the Regents had met the previous day, which they had not, that Tight had demanded not only Crum's and Asplund's resignations, but also Hodgin's, and that all three had refused. The article added that it was rumored that the entire faculty would be terminated, a new president would be appointed, and sixty students in a body had visited the Regents and declared that Tight had to be removed. It also asserted that an investigation of Tight had been conducted but was kept under wraps so as not to endanger the school's appropriation.

The board president, Frank Clancy, refuted these charges, stating there had been no such meeting of the board and that no sixty students had visited the board in a body. "As President of the Board, it is likely I should have known of it."[70]

When Tight came before the Regents on March 30, 1909, he seemed genuinely surprised that Asplund had prepared a lengthy diatribe against his administration. Asplund's charges, however, were deemed groundless, and the board upheld the termination of both instructors.[71] Hodgin reported that a stunned Tight received a letter the following morning from the Regents asking for his resignation.

> No opportunity was to be allowed him in answering any charges or making any explanations. I shall never forget the expression that clouded his face as he read to me that fateful letter. To thus be torn away so suddenly, just in his prime, from his deepest life interest, with no chance for defense, quite broke his heart and spirit, and doubtless a little later on, his health.[72]

For the next thirty days President Tight struggled to save his position and his reputation. Having had no previous criticism about his administration from the Regents, he found it absurd that they would uphold his dismissal of Asplund and Crum and then cashier him summarily. The Regents meanwhile made no public response to the case of their president.

The newspapers, however, turned their attention to young Roy Baldwin, who had undertaken a crusade to discredit the president. Baldwin sent the *Albuquerque Journal* a list of accusations about Tight, including rumors about immoral behavior with a female employee of the University. Baldwin claimed that the faculty and community wanted the president removed. The *Journal*, however, took the stance that the University would be better off without Baldwin. Baldwin tried to appeal to the Board of Regents, but the board declined and told him to go to the Faculty Council. The council refused to reconsider.

Tight, meanwhile, made a direct appeal to the territorial governor, George Curry, asking him to convince the board that he deserved a fair deal. Regent Wroth had supported Tight, ironic, as Wroth had been the lone Regent to vote against Tight's appointment as president. Stover had apparently sided with Cook and Mandalari against him. That left only the president of the board, Frank Clancy, who also was the territory's attorney general. The governor dodged the issue by referring the matter to Clancy, who disagreed that the UNM president had been denied due process. The negative response from the governor left Tight with no options. The board informed President Tight that his usefulness to the University had been greatly impaired and, irrespective of whether he was guilty of any wrong, it was in the best interest of the University that he resign. Welsh relates: "The publicity surrounding these maneuverings delighted the news media throughout the West and Midwest, which carried wire-service stories of the latest developments. Rarely did flagship public universities conduct such sordid business openly."[73]

Almost eighty years later, in 1988, yet a third scenario pertaining to Tight's dismissal came to light in an article in the alumni magazine, *Mirage*. "Tight's introduction of the regional architecture inspired disbelief and derision by some, and outright contempt by others. But architecture was at best a bit player on a stage of scandal and intrigue that led to Tight's firing in 1909. . . . Tight, who came to UNM in 1901, was a divorced man in a time when divorce was not looked on with favor."[74]

The article cited Charlie Lembke, a student under Tight and a prestigious alumnus of UNM. In an interview of unknown date, Lembke explained:

> President Tight made the mistake . . . of taking the art teacher out for a ride on the mesa without a chaperone. . . . Tight would come riding up to the dormitory on the wagon, pick up the teacher and off they would go. Sometimes they would be gone for several hours and not come back until after dark. Well, you can imagine the kind of ammunition that provided the old busybodies all over town. You couldn't go anywhere in Albuquerque, I guess anywhere in the territory, without hearing about the scandalous behavior at the University.[75]

The *Mirage* article also reported that Asplund had openly criticized Tight and gossiped about his buggy romance. In the meeting with the Regents Asplund charged that the president had flaunted the "ordinary conventions of respectable society and was clearly morally corrupt." Flabbergasted, Tight asked that he be allowed to respond to Asplund, but was refused.[76]

For one of these reasons, or for all of them, on May 1, 1909, the Regents formally sought and received Tight's resignation. The board was firm in its belief that Tight's action in terminating the faculty members without consulting the board overstepped his authority and was "exceedingly embarrassing." At the same time the board praised him for "the executive ability displayed by him in the upbuilding of the University" and commended him for his "great eminence in his special line of work as a geologist." The Regents also agreed to recommend him "as an experienced and talented educator."[77]

Following his resignation, Tight literally was without a job in academe and was not optimistic about his chances of finding one. He took a temporary post for the annual Territorial Fair in Albuquerque in the fall of 1909, then moved to Roswell, where he was a local representative of a California insurance company. By November 1909, a stomach disorder forced him to give up his job and move to a sanitarium in Glendale, California, where he hoped to find a cure. Shortly thereafter, because of an acute condition that terminated in blood poisoning, he died on January 15, 1910, at the early age of forty-four. At his request his body was cremated, and the little urn of ashes was sent back through Albuquerque to his former Granville, Ohio, home.

The sad news reached the UNM campus on January 16, 1910, when Charles Hodgin received a brief telegram from Tight's widow. "Billy passed away last night. There was nothing that could save him. Mable Tight." The venerable Charlie Lembke said, "We always thought he died of a broken heart."[78] A long-time friend and colleague, Lawrence F. Lee of Raleigh, North Carolina, in a moving tribute to William George Tight in 1931, wrote that many times Tight had stated:

A state university never fails. Its buildings and plant may be wiped off the face of the earth by conflagration, its faculty may leave or its students may temporarily withdraw, but the alumni and the state will open the state university the next day and it will always go on.[79]

At the University of New Mexico, William George Tight will always be remembered as the man who brought to fruition the beginnings of the dream of "a pueblo on the mesa." A memorial on Hodgin Hall acknowledges the contributions of Tight. "His monument stands before you." ■

Tight served as president of the 1909 Territorial Fair after leaving the University. Photo courtesy EXPO New Mexico State Fair archives

The slow, heavy camera of its day captured the high point of a pole vault on campus. Hokona Hall is in the background.

Chapter Six
Administration of Edward D. M. Gray
1909–12

Edward D. M. Gray

President Tight's dream of "a pueblo on the mesa" quickly faded with the appointment of Edward Dundas McQueen Gray in the spring of 1909. Historian William Dabney states that Gray was an "erudite Scottish clergyman, highly educated, an author of note," but "there was no doubt in Gray's mind what a university campus should look like and be like, and pueblo architecture and such courses as New Mexico history were not it." Gray was also the first president of UNM who was "unmistakably inclined toward the liberal arts and away from the sciences, especially the applied sciences." His dream was to make the University of New Mexico an "Oxford on the Rio Grande."[1]

Michael Welsh noted, "Unlike his predecessors, Gray was steeped in the ancient humanities traditions of European universities, and often appeared amused at the pragmatism and present-mindedness of American higher education." He had developed his standards of learning in English schools.[2]

Gray (MA, PhD) was born in Lanarkshire, Scotland, in 1854 and educated in Victoria College at Oxford. He also attended the University of Bonn and the University of Heidelberg. At London University, he received the bachelor's degree with honors in Latin, Greek, philosophy, mathematics, history, French, and theology. Gray resided at different times in various localities in Europe, Africa, the West Indies, and the United States. He was a fellow of the Royal Historical Society and Royal Society of Arts and had taken holy orders in the Episcopal Church and the Church of England. He also received decorations from the governments of France, Venezuela, Egypt, and Turkey and was renowned as a world traveler, linguist, publicist, author, poet, musician, educator, and parish priest.[3]

In the United States, Gray was a member of the prestigious Cosmos Club of Washington, D.C., as well as the British and University clubs. What was especially significant to some of the UNM Regents, however, was that he was an ordained minister in the Episcopal Church.[4]

Gray was described by E. Dana Johnson, a friend and local writer, as "genial, engaging, and humorous," with a "scintillate" personality, "very, very British with all the British mannerisms and accent," and "a kindly and courteous man of great savoir faire."[5]

Like so many others, Gray came to New Mexico in 1884 because of its healthful climate, hoping the dry desert could cure his wife's sister, who suffered from a respiratory ailment. Gray first lived near the southeastern New Mexico town of Loving and set about building a baronial country manor he named Croftonhill. There, from 1884 to 1893, he operated his estate like an English lord of the manor, including constructing a private racetrack and hosting an annual market for farmers up and down the Pecos valley.

When fire destroyed the family home, the Grays relocated to Carlsbad, a move that connected him with the economic and political life of the territory. He also accepted the pastorate of the Grace Episcopal Church. In 1907 Gray visited Albuquerque at the request of two UNM students, Hugh Bryan and Frank Light, who were applying for Rhodes Scholarships. "Gray's knowledge of Greek and Latin far eclipsed that of [UNM professor] Rupert Asplund . . . and [Gray's] successful tutoring of Bryan and Light may have prompted [UNM President] William Tight to seek Asplund's removal in the fateful spring of 1909."

Edward Gray was hired as president of UNM in June 1909. Among their first decisions pertaining to Gray, the Regents approved travel funds for him to attend the Denver meeting of the National Education Association in July, as well as the Congress of College Presidents in Seattle in August. The Regents also directed him to visit the towns of the territory and call upon parents and guardians of students who might be interested in attending the University.[6]

The year of 1909–10 was a short honeymoon, however. Members of the faculty still loyal to Tight resented Gray's imperious manner. Dabney was later to write, "It was not long before faculty and Regents alike were looking back on the Tight years with nostalgia." In addition, the University faced a fiscal crisis in the athletic program.

By the spring of 1910, President Gray had begun to put his mark on the future direction of the University. His suggestions for reorganization, however, disturbed some of the Regents, and the board directed Regent Mandalari to visit the campus as often as practicable to familiarize himself with the details of management and instruction and strengthen the president in his work. This was a response in part to rumors circulating among the faculty that Gray contemplated wholesale terminations of their contracts.[7]

As it turned out, the most significant firing that spring was the dismissal of Aurelio Espinosa. It had all begun when he sought an increase in salary and an allocation to purchase some books necessary for his research on Spanish dialectology and folklore. The president refused and labeled Espinosa's research superfluous. He also believed the professor was unfit to teach even the elementary Spanish courses, which he had done since 1902. As a New Mexico native and the first Hispanic faculty member at UNM with a PhD (University of Chicago, cum laude, 1909), Espinosa charged that the president's action was malicious and an insult. He took his case to the Regents, telling them that not only should he be retained, but also that his salary should be raised by $1,800. The board rejected his plea, which left

Espinosa unemployed until Stanford University hired him. He ultimately became chair of the Department of Classical Languages at that prestigious institution.[8]

With the close of the academic year of 1909–10, several issues were bothering Gray. He found it absurd that the University had made no provisions for a campus residence for him and his family. Hodgin, on Gray's behalf, reminded the Regents that a "proper" university provided such accommodations, so in May 1910 the board called for architectural designs and construction bids. The house was not built. Meanwhile, still unresolved was the matter of insufficient student housing.[9]

The Fire in Hadley Hall

Tragedy struck on the evening of May 23, 1910, when the science building, Hadley Hall, burned to the ground. Most of the students at UNM missed the big fire, which came three days after the close of school for the summer. As related by Dorothy Hughes:

> The fire department was called when the fire was first discovered, but because of the condition of the road at the time became stuck in the sand and arrived far too late. There was no way of saving the building, no matter how heart-breaking it was to stand on the sidelines and know that the precious materials within, many of which could never be replaced, were doomed.[10]

Among the losses were the geological collection of President Herrick, the botanical collection, and the Ethnological Museum with its ancient specimens. Also, gold and silver ores, regarded as among the finest specimens from the mines of the territory, were melted down. In addition, the entire mineralogy collection, which had been part of the exhibition at the St. Louis World's Fair, was lost.

> The destruction of the chemicals made it dangerous to go near the building during the fire. There were countless explosions, which by their colors at the time of the detonation allowed the scientific watchers to know just what was being destroyed. After the fire was over, Dr. Clark raked through the hot ashes on the Hadley Hall site and recovered all but one tiny piece of the platinum. . . . The gold, silver, and other precious metals had all melted into the earth, making that particular site to this day potentially most valuable of all campus land.[11]

The fire also threatened other buildings in the area, particularly the home of Charles Hodgin. He and others, armed with wet mops or brooms, crawled along the roof and extinguished flying sparks.[12]

While the loss of Hadley Hall, the only privately funded building on the campus, was a major disaster in itself, also destroyed in the fire were the engineering and science equipment and the personal papers and library of William Tight, which

1.

CHAPEL in Rodey Hall; you may see how
Each devout worshiper his head doth bow,
But why so many empty seats and chairs?
Oh, where are all the Varsity students now?

2.

Dancing in Rodey Hall: music and cheer;
Far through the night the lights shine bright and clear;
And now the hall is full—no space nor room—
For now at last is every student here.

THE dining hall where students wise,
Fill themselves with cakes and pies;
Waiters answer at your beck,
And spill the soup right down your neck.

The 1910 Mirage *featured whimsical drawings and doggerel.*

the Regents had purchased from his widow seven weeks earlier. The insurance policies on Hadley Hall covered $13,300 for the structure and $1,300 for the furnishings. The Regents, however, decided to seek private donations to rebuild the science building and directed Gray to tour the territory asking New Mexicans to sign "joint notes for the purpose of providing security on a Hadley Hall note." The plan was for the president and the Regents to then apply to the legislature for an appropriation to retire these notes, thus placing their cosigners at no financial risk for their generosity.[13] The scheme apparently was unsuccessful, as neither significant contributions nor legislative appropriations were forthcoming.

Campus Development and Construction

Within a year Hadley Hall was replaced by an unattractive, one-story masonry building with a pitched roof, and UNM's adherence to the Pueblo Style was abandoned. Originally called the College of Science and Engineering Building, it later housed many other departments, including music, engineering laboratories and offices, and some art studios. President Gray defended the architecture, stating that the building had "a good foundation and good walls" and adding that he was planning as economically as possible so that when "a uniform architecture is decided upon, the building can be remodeled without undue loss." The building was never remodeled and remained an eyesore until it was removed in 1971 to make way for Logan Hall, the Psychology Building.[14]

At the time there was some conjecture as to whether Gray's negative attitude was related to his displeasure with his predecessor, Tight, who had brought the Pueblo Style to campus, or his objection to the architecture itself, which some people reasoned struck Gray's sensibilities as primitive. Whatever the reason, Gray informed the Regents there would be no new facilities designed in the Pueblo Style.

Gray's position irritated UNM alumni, and they undertook a campaign to determine what the public's view on the matter might be. They were joined by Regent R. W. D. Bryan, who appreciated the deep cultural and historical significance of the Pueblo architecture. Even the territorial governor, William J. Mills, came out in favor of the Pueblo design for the campus. Supporters argued that such buildings would give UNM an indigenous style that not even the Ivy League schools, with their imitations of Oxford and Cambridge, could claim. The publicity Bryan and the Alumni Association generated failed to dissuade President Gray, who persisted in his directive that all new construction should have a generic style that could be modified to suit the tastes of later generations. He continued to view the Pueblo architecture as "an inspiration to barbarism," and stated that it was "belittling for the head of the educational system of the Territory."[15]

While architecture continued to be a subject of widespread debate on the campus and in the territory, the student newspaper related one piece of good news in September 1910.

> The Old Varsity Road [Railroad, later Central, Avenue] is dead. Long live the new road. . . . Formerly, one walked on one side of a ditch, or sometimes on both sides, when strolling up the road in the calm moonlight. Now, the students are all wearing smiles of great width and gladness in memory of the deceased worst road in Bernalillo County. The old road was a nightmare. The new one is a dream. Upon the old road, frequent sights were panting horses and stalled automobiles. Upon the new road is now heard the gay honk of the autoist's Klaxon as he shoos from out his path the strolling Varsity students who are walking because the new road is so good.

The writer warned that the new macadam road was not for heavy wagons, for "if used by them, it will soon be as bad as the old one." He added that two gallons of water and a half day with the road roller would keep it in shape.[16]

Student Life

Life on the campus in the Gray era was lively and fun. There were fudge parties, chafing-dish parties, and smokers; mandolin-guitar selections were popular; the noodle glide was the new dance; and the Arens Brothers' orchestra played for parties. There was excitement when a herd of goats visited the campus. The winter of 1909–10 was characterized by heavy snows as well as ice skating on the reservoir. The chemistry professor from New England, John Clark, entertained students with his prowess as a skater.[17]

In May 1911, school was dismissed for a morning to allow students to attend a speech by Governor Woodrow Wilson of New Jersey, who was campaigning for the

"Four-footed Pete Woods" was photographed in front of Kwataka dorm.

presidency of the United States. On the steps of the Alvarado Hotel in downtown Albuquerque, the "University Youngsters" gave Wilson several yells before the speech, and the "Varsity bunch" encored him with a college yell, "which for heartiness even though not for volume reminded him of his own college, Princeton."[18] Between 1903 and 1912, UNM students had the opportunity to see and hear both Theodore Roosevelt and Woodrow Wilson, not bad for what generally was considered to be a backwater territory.

One of the biggest events of 1911 was the installation of Phi Mu as the first national sorority to be installed in either the New Mexico or Arizona territory.

The next year, 1912, the big news centered around Erna Fergusson, who had a reputation for always losing her keys. With great ceremony, she was presented a key ring, which she also promptly lost. Fergusson, later a noted New Mexico author, was editor in chief of the *Mirage,* and Charles Lembke, president of the senior class, served as business manager.

A favorite pastime was eating at Fred Harvey's in the Alvarado Hotel. Students were advised against such ordinary slang as "kiddo" and "believe me." Bull-fighter handkerchiefs were worn on the campus. The lights went out on the windmill and "campustry (spooning) became very interesting." President Gray sponsored tours of the girls' glee club and the U.N.M. Entertainers, the boys' group. With the cooperation of the Santa Fe Railroad the girls toured through Arizona and California, and the boys through Texas and Kansas. The latter also had engagements in southern Colorado and northern New Mexico on the return trip. On Halloween, Professor Clark's horse was painted with zebra stripes (similar to what had been done to President Tight's horse a few years earlier). The president's reception in September was described as a brilliant event, with the horse-drawn Jumbo making three trips from town to carry the guests. Many others came in automobiles, carriages, and cabs.[19]

The relationship between the president and the students was often rigid and formal. The aforementioned Hugh M. Bryan, the 1910 Rhodes Scholar, had these recollections.

> From his own funds, Dr. Gray outfitted the Men's Glee Club in tuxedoes, and thereby introduced formal dress on the University campus. He thought that it was a waste of effort to educate non-gentlemen and that it was impossible to produce gentlemen without some of the usual accoutrements.
>
> Dr. Gray wondered that so few students admitted a zeal for knowledge and that classroom work failed to attain his idea of accuracy. . . .
>
> Dr. Gray's own educational requirement slogan was, "Accuracy, Speed, and Style." He wanted the three requirements attained in that order. First, the correct information, then the statement or use of the information with freedom and quickness. . . . After the first two came style, which was his idea of crowning attainment.[20]

In the spring of 1911, Charles Hodgin helped President Gray form a Bureau of Student Employment. More than half of UNM students had part-time jobs, with New Mexico students receiving preference for employment over out-of-state students. Distances from town, however, severely limited the opportunities for work.[21]

Athletics

In his first fall at UNM, 1909, President Gray was the beneficiary of good news and bad from the fields of friendly strife, intercollegiate athletics. The good news was that the varsity football team won the University's first football championship, the territorial championship, by defeating the University of Arizona, New Mexico A&M, and the military institutes at Roswell and El Paso. The only blemish was a whomping 0–53 loss to the University of Colorado. It also marked the year that the team had its first professional football coach, S. L. "Mac" McBirnie, a former football player at the University of Oklahoma.[22]

The bad news was that with the addition of salaries and travel costs, the football program overspent its budget by $1,800. The president was understandably angry and called upon the Regents for a decision. Albuquerque Judge Neill B. Fields appeared before the Board of Regents and told them that good business sense dictated payment of these bills. He believed that to do otherwise would endanger the morale of the boys on the team. He placed the blame for this crisis on the athletic officials of the University, whom he described as having "a bad effect in forming the players' character."

After lengthy debate, the Regents agreed to allocate existing funds to meet the athletic office's obligations. They added, with misplaced confidence or naïveté, "that no athletic indebtedness will be permitted to be incurred in the future." The Regents directed President Gray to design new fiscal guidelines to prohibit recurrences of this embarrassing problem.[23]

More bad news followed as the football program went downhill. McBirnie could not be induced to return to UNM, and the 1910 team struggled through a winless season. A 0–80 loss to New Mexico Military Institute was particularly galling. The next year UNM won only one game.

Overall the Gray era of UNM athletics was rather bleak. In competition against both high school and college teams the varsity just about broke even. The only track and field meet during Gray's tenure was in 1912, with UNM losing to the Albuquerque Indian School 11–45. No baseball games were played in 1909. The 1910 season was successful as UNM won seven games while losing one, but mostly playing against high school teams. In 1911, however, the team lost five games and posted its only win against St. Michael's College.

Despite continued problems with funding, the most significant development in the athletic program at UNM in this era came in 1911, when the University for the first time hired a professional coach of all sports, essentially an athletic director. Ralph L. "Hutch" Hutchinson held the job until 1917, when World War I drew him away from the campus. The hiring of Hutchinson was perceived as reflecting the

Charles Lembke is listed in the 1912 yearbook as a participant in virtually every athletic, forensic, dramatic, choral, and social activity on campus. He went on to found a construction company that built Johnson Gym and other campus structures.

University's increasingly serious approach to the role of athletics on the campus. A graduate of Princeton University, where he had played football and baseball, "Hutch" was described as "likable," but also was regarded as a stern disciplinarian.[24]

Two stalwart athletes of this period were Charles Lembke and Gillette Cornish. Both had grown up in Albuquerque and matriculated at UNM in 1907 from the local high school. They were natural leaders and excelled in academic as well as athletic activities. The popular, articulate Lembke also was president of his 1912 class. Both played multiple positions on the football team, with Lembke presiding as quarterback. In basketball, Cornish, an excellent scorer, was the team star. Lembke stood out as a defensive player. They also excelled in baseball. Lembke went on to serve as an infantry lieutenant in France during World War I, was wounded in action, and incorrectly reported as being killed, and received several decorations for valor.[25]

By 1912, UNM athletic facilities included an oval running track around the crude football field, the old, small, and seldom-used gymnasium, a baseball diamond, and two tennis courts in bad condition. Athletic boosters believed, however, that the years ahead would mark a time when intercollegiate sports would play a vital role in the University's affairs.[26]

The Beginning of the End

Meanwhile, President Gray faced a sullen, unhappy faculty, and the local boosters fell woefully short, raising only $750. Gray's personal appeal to Albuquerque businessmen raised a mere $80. Reluctantly, the Regents agreed to appropriate an additional $500 toward the $1,800 shortfall after December 1, 1910.[27]

By the spring of 1911, the new College of Science and Engineering Building was near completion. Academic standards had risen, and it was said that the University finished the year on a high note. Community outreach programs had begun, and more students who were prepared for college courses had enrolled. Gray proudly announced at commencement that UNM's scholarship ranked among the best in the West. He also proclaimed that a collegiate atmosphere finally predominated over the high-schoolish life the University had known.

The responses to mailings to prospective students during the summer of 1911 heartened Gray, who reportedly took a personal interest in resolving problems of student moral behavior, employment, and academic potential. When a divorced woman requested to live in the women's dormitory to save money, however, Gray led the parade to turn her down. He believed that a formerly married woman would be a bad influence on the young girls.

In 1911, Gray also discontinued the University's practice of accrediting New Mexico high schools. He replaced the accreditation program with new standards of classes and grades deemed necessary for admission to UNM and admitted only students whose transcripts included a sufficient number of such courses.

The president was disturbed by what he regarded as the general American indifference to the Rhodes Scholar program from England. As the U.S. national chairman of the Rhodes program, Gray had been encouraged to publicize it widely in New Mexico. He gladly obliged.[28] The only UNM Rhodes Scholar during Gray's tenure was the 1910 recipient, Hugh M. Bryan, the son of Regent Bryan, who never liked Gray very much. The young Bryan was one of the persons invited to speak at the memorial service for Gray in 1933, and he related that:

> I asked him [Gray] . . . for a letter to send with my application for admission to an Oxford College which Dr. Gray gave me, and which, after a very proper salutation, began: "Not a bright boy, nor a good student . . ." The letter gave me a peculiar reputation at Oxford which I spent three years in a vain effort to live down.[29]

Gray believed that the nation's intellectual immaturity was especially striking in his adopted home of New Mexico. In his opinion, both the citizenry of the territory and its students rarely rose above their provincial tastes to appreciate the academic experience UNM could provide.

As the 1911–12 school year approached, Gray realized he had inherited two obstacles from his predecessor: UNM's poverty and faculty discontent. He believed these and New Mexico's impending statehood threatened his tenure as president. The poverty issue had haunted the institution since its inception and seemed to grow worse in 1911. The summer session overran its budget by $37. Gray covered the debt out of his own pocket, and the Regents reimbursed him in September. The faculty, however, did not fare so well, as declining revenues motivated Gray to suspend the sabbatical-leave policy adopted less than a decade earlier. The fiscal crisis within the University, along with faculty unrest, served to heighten the tensions between Gray and the Regents. Three Regents expressed discontent with Gray's performance but did not act to remove him from office. The board decided instead to extend his contract for six months, at which time the Regents would evaluate his performance sometime after the new year, 1912.[30]

Statehood

In 1910 New Mexico sent its constitution to the U.S. Congress for its approval. The New Mexico Territory had petitioned for admission to the United States fifty times since the Americans had taken over in 1846, but each time it had been rejected. For New Mexicans, this was a real insult, inasmuch as by 1910 the territory had a population of more than 250,000, far more than the 60,000 minimum required by law. One of the reasons Congress gave for declining to grant statehood was that the territory was thought to be unable to govern itself, despite the presence of federal officials appointed to take charge of local government. Senator Albert Beveridge, who had visited New Mexico in 1905–6, also irritated New Mexicans when he reported that the territory was too populated with non-English-speaking citizens and lacked a credible public school system.[31]

These sentiments still haunted New Mexico in 1911 as the territory struggled with the uncertainty of budget projections and the presence of federal officials. Finally, on August 21, 1911, President William Howard Taft signed a statehood bill, "using a gold-banded quill plucked from a great American eagle that had been captured near Taos."[32] The bill also granted statehood to Arizona, provided that its constitution was amended to eliminate voter recall of judges. The election was held in November, and New Mexico became the forty-seventh state on January 6, 1912.[33]

Among the clauses in the legislation granting New Mexico statehood was a section calling for the regents of UNM and the other institutions in the state to resign so the newly elected governor could make his own selections for the various governing boards. The UNM Regents cleared their calendar of unfinished business but declined to renew Gray's contract, which triggered an immediate search for Gray's successor. The new governor, William C. McDonald, a Democrat, sensing that great change was in the wind, came to Albuquerque to discuss the institution's "future welfare."

His new appointees were R. W. D. Bryan, a holdover member, and Nathan Jaffa, A. W. Cooley, Howard L. Bickely, and John A. Reidy. Before the first gathering of these new Regents, President Gray cast them into "the maelstrom of campus politics." Newspapers reported that four members of the old board had told Gray to leave and that President Gray had resigned. Regent Clancy, who was winding up a tenure of twenty years on the board, denied these assertions and rallied to Gray's defense. He maintained that Gray had done nothing to alienate the faculty, despite the fact that most of them had supported his predecessor. Clancy asserted that Gray's mere presence in the president's office brought him unfavorable comparisons to the "ebullient and aggressive Tight." In defense of Gray's English demeanor, Clancy argued: "A very large portion of people in the United States have a dislike of anything that is English." Because Gray had not officially severed his connection with the University, Clancy hoped the new Board of Regents would reconsider the action of the previous Regents and retain Gray.

Gray's Resignation

The issue of Gray's dismissal did not come before the new Board of Regents until March 25, 1912. After dispensing with other business, President Gray asked the new president of the board, R. W. D. Bryan, for permission to deliver some remarks on the status of the University. Perhaps against his better judgment, Bryan allowed the president to speak.

Gray then proceeded to unleash a barrage of complaints, including an allegation of conspiracy against him by the members of the faculty of the College of Science and Engineering. He identified Martin Angell, dean of the college, as the leader of these conspirators and recommended that he be summarily fired. Gray alleged that this group had persuaded L. B. Stephan, an assistant professor of German, "to spy" on Gray and other faculty members. He further accused Stephan and other faculty of enlisting members of campus fraternities to "make life miserable" for Gray and his faction. In addition, he charged that the Angell faction had freely circulated stories in the town critical of his management of the University. He labeled the Department of Physics and Engineering "ridiculously inefficient," with "utterly inadequate" equipment and "impractical and unskilled" instructors. Gray continued his diatribe, blasting the faculty almost person by person and department by department.[34]

Gray reiterated these charges to the governor. As summarized by William Dabney, they included:

His predecessors had let politics play a part in his appointments, [Gray] said. Thus an instructor in modern languages owed her appointment to the fact that she was the niece of a prominent New Mexico politician. The head of the English Department was inefficient, and a woman, to boot. Incompetence was rife, according to Gray, and he included in this blanket condemnation the librarian and even Hodgin, who had made no bones of his dismay at the ousting of Tight and appointment of Gray. Indeed, Gray asserted, there were only two of the Science and Engineering faculty and four of the College of Letters and Arts who were thoroughly competent. One of those who did pass muster with him was his assistant in the teaching of English, Erna Fergusson, who though still an undergraduate was teaching under his direction, and doing an excellent job. The head of the English Department, a jealous person in Gray's estimation, had tried to turn the students against Miss Fergusson.

Worse still, the students were becoming involved. Fraternities took sides. If we are to believe Gray, the unscrupulous Dr. Angell roped the Tri-Alpha fraternity into the conspiracy and fostered among its members animosity toward non-fraternity men and toward members of Sigma Tau.[35]

Gray concluded his tirade to the board by asking its members to award no contracts to faculty until he conferred with the new board president on personnel matters. The board, no doubt stunned by this outburst, concurred with the request but took no action at that time on Gray's reappointment. Within two weeks, however, Gray learned that the new Regents had selected David Ross Boyd to succeed him in office.

Gray stepped down at the end of the 1912 spring term and accepted an appointment with the Episcopal Church as a missionary in the Pecos valley. With the outbreak of World War I in Europe in 1914, he returned to England to serve as a chaplain with the British Expeditionary Forces. After the conclusion of the war in 1918, he became pastor of the Forest Green Episcopal Church in Dorking, England, where he ministered until his death in 1932 at the age of seventy-eight.[36]

UNM's Renaissance man, John Clark, wrote of Gray that "his whole educational background was that of England, and when I tell you that he went around the campus at times in a cap and gown, you may know how well he was received in Albuquerque."[37] Michael Welsh had these thoughts on Gray's tenure as president:

Edward Gray's presence at UNM, though brief and controversial, did bring attention to the limitations placed upon the university by the larger content of New Mexico, and by the community's understanding of the currents of higher education. . . . Gray knew that UNM needed both high standards and practical application of knowledge to accommodate the young and inexperienced society surrounding the university. He became frustrated at the narrow vision and present-mindedness of his detractors, yet could not see his own limits emanating from his background as an Englishman in the rural southwest, or as an Episcopal minister in a region divided between Catholics and Protestants, Hispanics and Anglos.[38]

All in all, this union between Gray and the University was not a happy marriage. True, the erudite Scot had impressive academic credentials, including almost as many degrees as the entire UNM faculty combined. After a glorious entry into the job as president, his British mannerisms began to wear on Regents, townspeople, faculty, and students. His open resentment of the continued loyalty to Tight was apparent and certainly came to the fore in his last meetings with the outgoing Regents and his first meeting with the new board. In comparing students with those in British or Eastern schools of higher learning, he could never reconcile himself to the lack of preparation of New Mexican youngsters entering UNM or their lack of zeal for what he perceived to be the true values of an education: accuracy, speed, and style. In the end, he wound up as a reminder of that old adage of college presidents, "Don't think you're paranoid just because everyone is after you."

The Spanish Language in New Mexico

Gray was indeed a complex man, sometimes obtuse, often brilliant, certainly eloquent. He was at his best when he wrote his article, "The Spanish Language in New Mexico: A National Resource," for the *UNM Bulletin* in February 1912. Unfortunately, however, it was published about the same time he was being fired as president. For timeliness, vision, and just plain common sense, it was right on target. Gray suggested that New Mexico's leaders think about one resource that had never been fully comprehended: the Spanish language of most of the state's citizens. Far too often, the bilingualism of many of New Mexico's citizens had been a matter of reproach rather than an asset, even among those who spoke both English and Spanish. Gray believed that bilingualism made New Mexico unique. He wrote: "The man equipped with two mother tongues is . . . doubly armed." He also believed that the American sentiment toward the Spanish language in particular would enlarge the minds of New Mexicans, saying "there is no foreign language which possesses so great a practical value for the American citizen as Spanish does."

In classic style, Gray proclaimed that "in the opinion of all thinking men [a state must] stand or fall according to the manner in which the question of race and languages is handled by its citizens. . . . The right of the Spanish American citizen to the unrestricted development of his racial inheritance in language is incontestable."

Gray closed his appeal by calling for racial harmony in New Mexico to further the interest of UNM and the state, saying that "a union of such character [Anglo and Hispanic] would go far to obliterate the lines of division which have too long marred the fair face of our Sunshine State." His remarks were eerily prophetic. Gray believed that New Mexico must "stand or fall according to the manner in which the question of race and languages" was handled by its citizens.[39]

Gray's personal style may not have blended well with the lack of intellectualism on a raw frontier, but he gave New Mexicans a lot to think about. Many years later, as we look back on his turbulent presidency, what must be asked is: "Was the writer of this eloquent tribute to the Spanish language the same person who fired Aurelio Espinosa?" ■

Members of the World War I Student Army Training Corps assembled in front of Hodgin Hall in about 1918.

David Ross Boyd

Chapter Seven
Administration of David Ross Boyd
1912–19

As New Mexico made the transition from territory to state between 1912 and 1919, it experienced significant growth. Albuquerque's population roughly doubled in ten years, reaching 12,500 by 1920. The city outgrew its reputation as a tough little cattle and railroad town and began to be regarded as a rapidly progressing city with considerable metropolitan promise.

In particular, land development provided expanded possibilities for the future. One of the first developments in 1913 stretched the city north and east: the Luna Circle Development, straddling what today is called Lomas Boulevard. Three years later, University Heights was developed on a huge rectangular land parcel bounded by Central Avenue, Carlisle and Garfield streets, and Yale Boulevard. Residences soon were constructed on streets named for eastern colleges.

Improvement of Central Avenue (until 1907, Railroad Avenue) enhanced access to the University and these land developments. As described by Robert Barney, "Time-worn ruts and the ever-present cavities caused by desert erosion were removed and the thoroughfare was smoothed to a state never before experienced." A sidewalk was not built, however, so "throughout the era, foot traffic to and from the University trudged along on a mantle of sand and weed growth."[1]

Automobiles, first seen in Albuquerque in 1899, increased rapidly in number, and by 1913 a total of 1,869 motorcars had been licensed by the state. The appearance of the automobile in New Mexico was in many ways responsible for "extinguishing the romanticized deeds of the western cattle rustler," and "the rustling of livestock was soon replaced by a more profitable undertaking—automobile hi-jacking."[2]

Albuquerque newspapers also underwent considerable change in this era. News coverage was expanded with national and international wire services, and reporting of domestic news was more thorough. New developments included feature articles, sports news, comics, and advertising. The number of pages per edition increased, and Sunday editions often were twice the size of daily publications.

The silent movie made its appearance in Albuquerque early in this period, and stars such as Douglas Fairbanks, Lionel Barrymore, and Mary Pickford became national idols. One young man who had been run out of town by the Albuquerque sheriff for brawling became a legend in early Western films: Tom Mix.

Education in Albuquerque also experienced a great spurt of growth. The federal government's Indian School had the largest enrollment in the state with more than four hundred students. Menaul School continued to thrive, and St. Mary's, a small Catholic elementary and secondary school, opened. The permanent Albuquerque High School campus was built in 1914 and was said to "forever end the need for a high school in the community."[3]

While the Santa Fe Railroad shops were acknowledged as the most significant business enterprise in the city, a new venture of tremendous importance was the health sanatorium. New Mexico's climate attracted health seekers from around the world to new hospital-like establishments, including Presbyterian, Methodist, and St. Joseph sanatoriums.[4]

When New Mexico entered the Union in 1912, people may have hoped that self-government would bring unbounded prosperity and deliverance from the clutches of an oppressive federal bureaucracy, that the old patterns of business and politics would evaporate, and that intellectual life would blossom. Instead, territorial officials continued in most public offices and the cultural divisions among the Hispanics, Anglos, and Indians persisted. Statehood also failed to relieve the ever-present conditions of distance, isolation, and aridity.

The University of New Mexico continued to be haunted by its reputation for firing three of its first four presidents and having highly politicized governing boards that meddled in administrative affairs.[5] The history of parsimonious support from the governor and the legislature also lingered. The University ranked at the bottom of most lists in appropriations.

While the institution was a university in name, it still had large numbers of students enrolled in preparatory courses. Then, too, in 1912 it was aspiring to be an urban school, but it was set in a small town that lacked the critical mass of capital, professionals, and educated citizens. In addition, there were few job opportunities in the new state for college graduates.

These were the conditions when David Ross Boyd was appointed president of the University of New Mexico on April 6, 1912. Judge Clarence M. Botts, speaking at a memorial service for President Boyd in 1938, stated that Boyd "found a school little known and less respected—filled with internal dissension. He saw nearly all of the high school graduates going to other states for their university training."[6]

Boyd was the first president the UNM Regents hired who had extensive managerial experience at a college or university. He had been president of the University of Oklahoma from its founding in 1892 and served until fired by its governing board in 1908. Overall, the Regents were impressed by his broad "range of experience, his Midwestern Protestantism, and his sophisticated and pragmatic demeanor."[7]

Boyd was born on a farm in southern Ohio in 1853, attended Wooster College, where he received a bachelor's degree, and taught and administered in several Ohio school districts during the post–Civil War era. In addition, throughout his life he maintained close ties with the Presbyterian Church.

Unlike his predecessors at UNM and Gray, Boyd did not have an earned PhD. As Judge Botts noted, "I am told that his degree of doctor of philosophy was an honorary degree; but I have never heard anyone question that it was 'earned' in the sense that it was deserved."[8]

Boyd moved west in 1888 to engage in real-estate speculation in Salt Lake City, but turned back to his true love, public education. He landed a job as superintendent of schools in Arkansas City, Kansas, which led to his appointment as the first president of the University of Oklahoma in 1892. There he demonstrated many of the skills that would make him so successful at UNM, including developing a well-designed campus, recruiting faculty and students, raising private funds, lobbying for federal and state funds, encouraging coeducation, and developing outreach programs to bond the university with the taxpayers. By the time Boyd left OU in 1908, the university catalog advertised 361 courses in thirty-eight college-level programs. He also served as the head of the Territorial Board of Education for Oklahoma.

The creation of state government in Oklahoma in 1908, when Democrats ousted the Republicans from virtually all political posts, left Boyd without the support of the new governor or legislators. Boyd's detractors leveled accusations of "rampant immorality" (drinking, dancing, playing cards, and smoking) on the Norman campus, and in June 1908 the Board of Regents bowed to demands for Boyd's removal. Years later, Oklahoma's Governor Charles N. Haskell admitted that Boyd's firing was the greatest mistake of his administration.

His dismissal left the fifty-five-year-old Boyd in need of another career. He prevailed upon the Presbyterian Church to appoint him superintendent of education of the Women's Board for Home Missions. In this capacity, he spent the next few years coordinating and often visiting the far-flung system of mission schools, including many in the Hispanic Southwest. He became acquainted with economic and political leaders in New Mexico, who played a strong role in advocating his candidacy for the presidency at UNM.[9]

Thus, there was great joy as well as high expectations when his appointment became official. Among those heartened by the appointment was "the father of the University," Bernard S. Rodey, at that time the U.S. attorney in Seattle, said Boyd was "the right man, in the right place at the right time."[10]

In assessing the problems that would confront him in his new post at UNM, Boyd listed the loss of Hadley Hall; a population more than 50 percent Hispanic, 90 percent of whom were illiterate and unable to speak or understand the English language; and recently arrived easterners, who demanded services they had known elsewhere but that strained the impoverished state treasury.

The UNM student population was around two hundred for the two semesters of 1912–13, but few of the students were enrolled in upper-division courses. The campus still had only its twenty original acres, and statehood had clouded land titles on property surrounding the campus.[11]

Boyd at once began his travels around the state. High on his agenda was the study of the bilingualism of the populace. Boyd also received the support of

Governor William McDonald in defusing the allegation that UNM was a local rather than a state institution. McDonald broke Albuquerque's grip on the UNM Board of Regents by appointing members from across the state. As the first statehood governor, he appointed a completely new board in 1912: R. W. D. Bryan and A. W. Cooley (who served less than two years), John A. Reidy, Howard L. Bickley, Nathan Jaffa (who had been elected Albuquerque's first mayor in 1885), and George L. Brooks. The next year McDonald brought William G. Hayden to the board.

A letter survives that Boyd wrote to a former faculty member at the University of Oklahoma, Vernon L. Parrington. The latter had also been a part of the 1908 purge, having been dismissed for excessive smoking. He went on to become a professor of history at the University of Washington and winner of a Pulitzer Prize. In his letter Boyd expressed his chief concerns for the upcoming year at UNM: more land, a landscape architecture scheme, appropriations for physical equipment that would command the interest and respect of people, an adjustment to the imbalance between junior and senior faculty, full professors to guide and advise the less experienced instructors, and proper dormitory facilities.[12]

The new president found he also had to deal with more mundane issues, including the firing of Erna Fergusson from her teaching job in the English Department, allegedly for lack of advanced degrees. Her dismissal met with widespread disapproval inasmuch as she was a popular teacher, had been an outstanding student leader, was a gifted writer, and was the daughter of Harvey Fergusson, the former territorial delegate and at that time New Mexico's representative to Congress. Fergusson had pressed her case for reinstatement with Amado Chavez, the first superintendent of public instruction in New Mexico. Boyd did not appreciate her failure to approach him through proper channels and also wanted faculty with more experience than a recent bachelor's degree. He turned her down.

Boyd apparently held a bias against women on the faculty. When he started at UNM there were six women on a faculty of fifteen. He noted that nearly all the precollege instruction of native New Mexicans was under the direction of women, whether in public or parochial schools. He preferred a strong masculine influence, especially on the university level.[13] Among his first actions, Boyd reappointed all three faculty members who had been denounced by Gray: Hodgin, Angell, and Stephan.

The Boyd Administration from 1912 to 1917

The UNM fall semester opened on September 9, 1912, and the new president was ready to go. Despite his efforts at recruitment over the summer, attendance in the college program dropped to seventy-eight students. Boyd attributed part of this attrition to his termination of such programs as typewriting, bookkeeping, and reviews of elementary subjects for teachers. When he assumed office, Boyd returned the academic organizational structure of UNM to the single-college plan. At first he announced that he would be acting dean of the College of Letters and Science, but during his administration there was no faculty member officially designated as dean of the college. There were, however, officials designated as dean of the

University, first Charles Hodgin and later Lynn B. Mitchell. As time passed, Boyd left most of the internal administration of the University to Hodgin and Mitchell while he concentrated on external affairs.[14]

A graduate of Cornell University, Lynn Boal Mitchell arrived on the campus in 1912 as an associate professor of Latin and Greek. At that time there was a faculty of twenty-one, and Mitchell was one of only three who had a PhD. As the years passed, he became the first assistant to President Boyd. Often referred to by his colleagues and students as the "Old Roman," Mitchell became dean of the College of Arts, Philosophy, and Science in 1917 and headed the college until 1929. He continued to teach classes until his retirement in 1950.[15]

Lynn Boal Mitchell

Although a Republican himself, Boyd was pleased with the election of Democrat Woodrow Wilson as president of the United States in the fall of 1912. He calculated that the continuation of the Democrats in office would not throw New Mexico into another round of political change. That first year also brought Boyd a warm friendship with Edgar L. Hewett, director of the Archaeological Institute of America in Santa Fe, the predecessor of the School of American Research. This relationship ultimately led to a close, advantageous working relationship between the two educational and research institutions and to the University's excellent programs in anthropology.

The 1913 spring term also marked Boyd's first interactions with the state legislature, which, for the most part, went very well. Internally, he also took the first steps in restructuring the curricula, including adding languages and humanities to the College of Letters and Science; creating schools of education and applied science, mostly engineering; and initiating new departments of Household Economics, Music and Fine Arts, and Physical Education. A Division of University Extension also was created. Much to Boyd's satisfaction, the state's lawmakers responded positively to his blueprint for the future.

Boyd's major disappointment with the legislative session included rejection of a plan to close all New Mexico colleges and universities except UNM. He argued that seven state institutions of higher learning were six too many. The measure passed the Senate with no dissent, but it was defeated in the House by three votes.

Once the spring term was over, Boyd concentrated on promoting the University both within and without New Mexico. He established strong bonds with artists, writers, and historians in Taos, the Four Corners area, and Santa Fe.

In the spring term, 1914, UNM began preparation for the twenty-fifth anniversary of the 1889 higher education omnibus bill. Those attending the celebration included Judge Bernard S. Rodey; Professor Charles Hodgin, who had been on the faculty for seventeen years and was second only to Josephine Parsons in tenure at the University; and UNM's first president, Elias Stover.[16]

Boyd spent the summer and fall of 1914 planning UNM's ambitious budget request to the state legislature. That fall the University enrolled only 6 students in the Preparatory Department and, according to one source, 118 in college courses, an increase of nearly two-thirds from Boyd's first year. The campus grounds included

This postcard shows UNM students outside the remodeled Administration Building in about 1915. Photo by Paul Lynn Menaul

315 acres, and its physical plant and equipment were valued at $202,000. The library contained more than twelve thousand volumes. Furthermore, UNM boasted five recipients of Rhodes Scholarships: Thomas S. Bell, Frank C. Light, Hugh M. Bryan, Karl G. Karsten, and William Coburn Cook.[17]

In preparing his budget request, Boyd also reported that the advancing enrollment had strained classroom facilities and laboratory equipment, especially in chemistry, where thirty students shared space intended for ten. More than half the students were freshmen, with a similar number anticipated to enroll for the fall semester. Summer enrollment had exceeded all expectations, and the Extension Program needed support to carry UNM's program throughout the state.[18]

Boyd, in January 1915, closed his remarks to the Regents by noting an ominous trend among other New Mexican governing boards to assert their influence on campus affairs. He pointed out that when he took the job, it had been with the understanding that he, not the Regents, would run the University. An editorial in the *Albuquerque Morning Journal,* which warned against Regents' intrusions into administrative matters, strongly supported Boyd. It stated that the governing board had financial responsibility and the duty to set overall policy, but should let the president do his job. As a matter of principle the president should have an absolute voice in the selection, reappointment, or discharge of his assistants and faculty. The editorial concluded that regents who distrusted their presidents in matters of personnel should not intrude, but should hire a leader who inspired their confidence.

Shortly after the editorial appeared, the UNM board took note of it and officially accepted the recommendation as policy.[19]

During Boyd's tenure as president, the Board of Regents met infrequently. An executive committee, which ordinarily consisted of the board members who lived in Albuquerque, plus Boyd, carried on most of the business, while the board as a whole convened only two or three times a year to ratify what the executive committee had done.[20]

The hard work of Boyd and the Regents, resulting in burgeoning enrollments and higher academic standards, bore fruit in 1915 when the legislature increased its appropriation to $180,000 for the biennium, in addition to $4,000 in land royalties (as compared to an annual appropriation of $32,500 in 1912). The legislature also awarded the University $85,000 for a new science building. The campus had grown to 340 acres, and college enrollment had increased to a reported 120 of the total 137 attendees over two semesters. Negotiations had also begun with Walter Burley Griffin, the well-known Chicago architect, to develop a unified architectural plan for the campus.[21] Boyd took a strong personal interest in architecture and planning.

Despite these achievements, Boyd could not rest in his efforts to make UNM a "real" university. Thus, late in the spring of 1915, he hired H. B. Hening, a former editor of the *Albuquerque Morning Journal*, as UNM's first "director of publicity," at a salary of $600 a year. (One wonders if Hening had written the editorial on roles of regents.)

Also that spring, prestigious eastern universities made offers to three prominent UNM faculty members, but all chose to stay with the University. The president did raise Lynn Mitchell's salary by $300 and gave him the title of registrar. Josephine Parsons, who had handled the duties of registrar as well as financial secretary, was now free to devote full time to the University's finances.[22]

In 1915 President Boyd strengthened the graduate program, including setting new requirements for the degree of master of arts. The more stringent requirements included reading knowledge of one foreign language, completion of a thesis, and passing of oral and/or written examinations.[23]

A significant change occurred in the summer of 1916 when Boyd hired Roscoe Hill to teach Latin American history. Boyd wanted to take advantage of New Mexico's recognition as a bilingual state, including organizing a School of Latin American Affairs. He believed that young Hispanics would feel more comfortable if UNM held their heritage in higher regard and offered academic training in business, diplomacy, and language. That year the number of Hispanics at the University included only 3 students out of a total of 206. This seemed quite discouraging in that there had almost always been at least one Hispanic member of the Board of Regents.[24]

Roscoe Hill, thirty-five years old when he joined UNM, had already established himself as a specialist in Latin American affairs. Unfortunately, he was at UNM for only three years, after which he went on to become a diplomat, scholar, and author. During his short time in Albuquerque, he not only started the School of

This official University seal first appeared on the 1916 catalog. The Latin words can be translated as "Life," "Man," and "Light."

Latin American Affairs, but also completely reorganized the history curriculum, adding several courses in Spanish, Latin American, and New Mexico history. Hill also traveled to small New Mexico communities to speak—in Spanish—to parents of prospective students.[25]

That same year Boyd endeavored to expand professional program development by offering a bachelor's degree in commerce, following patterns established earlier at eastern universities. He wanted to make it clear, however, that the commerce courses were not a continuation of courses offered in the old Commercial Department, but stressed subjects related to business management, principles of banking, and similar topics.

When classes opened in September 1916, there was rejoicing that enrollment had doubled since 1913. The catalog listed 207 students: 3 graduate students, 118 in the College of Letters and Sciences, 42 in the School of Applied Science, 11 in the School of Education, 29 "special" students, and 4 extension students.[26] UNM could claim that it had students from every county in the state. Boyd resolved to continue his efforts to link the state to its flagship university and personally canvassed rural school districts in search of students and moral support.[27]

Strong legislative and professional backing for UNM continued, but by the academic year 1916–17, the optimism gave way to anxiety and confusion as the United States edged closer to participation in World War I. While the battlefields in Europe seemed far away, New Mexico experienced its own invasion when in 1916 the Mexican revolutionary, Pancho Villa, crossed the southern border of the state and attacked the village of Columbus. This was followed by the U.S. Army assembling an expeditionary force headed by General John J. Pershing to pursue Villa into Mexico. The perceived romance of that expedition captivated the hearts and led to enlistments of many college-age New Mexican males on the eve of the nation's entry into World War I.[28]

As the fall session of 1917 opened, state universities across the nation were projected into wartime programs, among which was the Student Army Training Corps (SATC). It was designed both to provide some military training to young male students and maintain enrollments and keep the universities open to meet professional needs such as engineering and medicine. UNM shared this national excitement and concern.

Meanwhile, the president of the Board of Regents, George Brooks, became disenchanted with the efforts of the publicity director, Hening. Despite advertisements in more than forty newspapers throughout the Midwest and Southwest that attracted more than a thousand inquiries, only two or three students actually enrolled as a result of these campaigns. Hening had also incurred the disfavor of the outgoing Democratic governor, William C. McDonald, who demanded Hening's resignation. Brooks, as president of the Regents and business manager of the University, on his own initiative summarily fired Hening.

All this occurred shortly after the board adopted a strong policy opposing Regents' interference in internal affairs. No one seemed to notice, except, perhaps,

President Boyd, who hurriedly extended a contract to Hening for $600 to complete an advertising campaign on time. Boyd then proceeded to hire A. S. Hunt as the University's first executive assistant to the president. Hunt's duties included overseeing the president's office, the buildings and grounds, and the Student Employment Bureau.[29]

New Mexico had a new governor in January 1917, Ezequiel C de Baca. Unfortunately, he died two months after taking office and was succeeded by Lieutenant Governor Washington Lindsey. The latter appointed a new Board of Regents for UNM, retaining Nathan Jaffa, George Brooks, and John A. Reidy, and adding Antonio Lucero of San Miguel County and John R. McFie, Jr., of McKinley County.[30]

The legislature of 1917 was unsure of the future of the state with the impending rumors of war. It was also concerned with what it regarded as unnecessary duplication of educational services and the high cost of funding seven institutions of higher learning, but these matters became less pressing in April when the United States went to war.

Campus Development and Construction

Most of the activity pertaining to the campus in the Boyd era focused on acquisition of more land, both for immediate expansion of the campus and for later sale or use. In 1912 the University was deeded 273,000 acres under the federal Ferguson Act. The state Land Office would administer the land, which included some oil and gas fields, and the University would receive the income.

Van Dorn Hooker provides a detailed rendition of the land-acquisition efforts and credits George Brooks, elected president of the Regents in 1913, with providing most of the leadership. Brooks operated a large food store in Albuquerque, invested in mining operations, and was a prosperous property owner. His ambition was to beautify the campus along the lines the late President Tight had envisioned. He also sought to expand the campus and volunteered to serve without remuneration as business manager for the University. Professor John Clark quoted Regent Brooks as saying, "I'll attend to the physical plant. Dr. Boyd will run the academic side."[31]

Capitalizing on his dual positions, Brooks took over many aspects of the operation of UNM, much to the consternation of President Boyd, who did not like the idea of dual management. Brooks personally supervised the campus landscaping, improved the irrigation system, and restored life to the neglected greenery. Later, another Regent, William G. Hayden, paid tribute to Brooks, saying that he had once been depressed by the appearance of the campus. When he visited it a few years later, however, Hayden observed: "It looked to me as if a magic hand had touched the picture. The beautiful flowers, grass, trees, and vegetation, the fine buildings on the grounds which met my eye, form a greater monument to his [Brooks's] memory than any tribute that can be written."[32]

In the fall of 1913, Boyd and Regent Brooks set out to buy an eighty-acre tract east of the small campus called the Ghost Lands. Because the faculty opposed use of University funds to buy land "which would never be needed,"[33] they proposed using $12,000 gained by selling lands granted to the University at statehood. They asked Attorney General Frank W. Clancy, a former Regent, to rule on the legality of the plan. Clancy upheld the deal, and the land, including the site of today's Jefferson Middle School, was purchased.

A year later, Brooks negotiated the purchase of 277 acres just north of the campus. Another forty-acre site was acquired through a surrogate, who immediately deeded it to UNM. The University also bought the Methodist Sanatorium land. Brooks had heard that acreage in the vicinity of today's Louisiana Boulevard might be available, and the property was purchased for $3 an acre at 4 percent interest with nothing down.[34] Van Dorn Hooker reported that some of this land was later sold at a huge profit, while one of the three parcels became part of the Winrock Center lease arrangement.

Brooks also commissioned John Clark of the Chemistry Department and Charles Kirk of Geology to survey some of the land in northern and northeastern New Mexico granted to UNM by the federal government. They were to report on possibilities for agriculture, grazing, or other uses, collect soil and grass samples, and take photographs. By wagon and saddle horse, the two professors began the task during the summer of 1915, fording rivers, climbing mountains, and confronting the elements. The following summer they used Clark's new car. Their report included valuable maps and recommendations that later resulted in profitable land leases for the University.[35]

Boyd's interests in campus development went far beyond landscaping and acquisition of new land. Shortly after his arrival on the campus he became enamored of Tight's dream of an original, distinctive campus. Boyd envisioned Pueblo Style dormitories and social halls based around a quadrangle. He wanted something "purely American." Not long after his arrival at UNM, Boyd was ready to move forward on a unified architectural plan and entered into negotiations with Walter Griffin, one of the nation's premier architects, who had just won an international competition to design a new capital for Australia. Van Dorn Hooker uncovered previously unknown information about Griffin's career in researching his history of UNM architecture. He reports that Boyd went to Chicago and discussed the proposed campus development with Griffin, who was enthusiastic about the Pueblo Style and the possibilities of the desert setting of the University. Griffin was on his way to Australia, however, so he authorized an assistant, Francis Barry Byrne, to take over the UNM project. While in Australia Griffin nonetheless designed both a science building and a "nucleus plan" for the entire campus, whose "general scheme is a compact, contiguous pueblo," although the buildings were not in Pueblo Style. The plan apparently never reached Boyd or the Regents, and the planning process was further muddled when Regent Brooks contacted Byrne directly.[36]

In December 1915, President Boyd finally submitted to the Regents the proposal of the firm of Griffin and Byrne, which the latter had prepared, to develop "plans for the laying out of the University grounds and campus," covering approximately

320 acres. The firm also was to design a science building and a second building. The sketches for the buildings revealed a Mayan influence. The Regents approved the contract, which Byrne signed on Griffin's behalf. Griffin was reported to be furious when he found out what had happened, but in the end Byrne did the work for UNM.[37]

Byrne's campus plan went through several revisions before it was finally completed in February 1918, but few of its elements were ever implemented, nor was his first science building built. What was built was the Chemistry Building (called the Engineering and Science Computer Pod in 2003), which Byrne designed as a simple one-story structure. Says Hooker: "The feeling of pre-Columbian architecture is no longer preserved and except for a vague relationship to a pueblo, the design is free from historical precedent."[38]

In June 1919, after Boyd's resignation but before his departure, bids were opened for construction of a mechanical arts building to be located west of the Chemistry Building and due north of Rodey Hall. It was to provide space for the Civil Engineering and Practical Mechanics departments, plus some elements of the Electrical Engineering program, the Department of Mathematics, a pattern shop, a mechanical drawing room, and a machine shop.[39]

Sometime between 1914 and 1916, thirteen wood-frame cottages were erected around Kwataka Hall. Each had a study room and two open-air sleeping porches, steam heat and electricity, but no toilets. Students had to use the facilities at Kwataka or Hokona Hall.[40]

Student Life

Under the Boyd administration, the growth of clubs and national societies went hand in hand with the growth of departments and schools. Musical organizations such as quartets, brass quintets, band, orchestra, and glee clubs were among the first additions. National honorary societies began to appear on the campus, the first being Phi Kappa Phi. A group of professors, including John Clark and Lynn Mitchell, both of whom belonged to other honorary scholastic fraternities, founded it in 1915. Outstanding senior men were honored by membership in Khatali, the women in Mortar Board.

Local fraternities at UNM now began to affiliate with national organizations. The Tri-Alphas became Pi Kappa Alpha in 1915, and Sigma Tau, a local organized in 1906, became Sigma Chi. In rapid order, other national fraternities and sororities came to the campus. The Kappa Sigma house was the first fraternity house to be built. Before this, the Sigma Chis had purchased the Pueblo Style home of President Tight, on the southwest corner of Central and University; and the Phi Mus purchased the home of Professor Nelson on Gold Avenue.[41]

By 1914, UNM students were dancing the one-step in Rodey Hall, as well as the two-step and tango. The young sports wore striped suits with trousers well above the ankles, and the girls appeared in long tube-like dresses, split in front. The girls were also reported as affecting to walk as if they had not had any breakfast and only a bowl of soup for lunch. Hughes reports that there was a campaign against cigarette smoking, and the *U.N.M. Weekly* published a letter from Thomas Edison to Henry Ford, which began:

> The injurious agent in cigarettes comes principally from the burning paper wrapper. The substance thereby formed is called "acrolein." It has a violent action on the nerve centers, producing degeneration of the cells of the brain which is quite rapid among boys. Unlike most narcotics this degeneration is permanent and uncontrollable. I employ no person who smokes cigarettes.

The student paper printed a college glossary to bring slang up-to-date. "Campustry" meant the same as "dialing," no doubt a reference to the popular sundial, or "mesa-ing," previously known as "spooning." "Pike" still meant to cut a class. "Queening" was the same as "fussing." "Knobby" meant up-to-date and was synonymous with "classy," "spuzzy," and "spiffy." A girl was a "chicken," "doll," or "skirt." A "fusser" or "masher" was "any young thing calling on ladies," and a "nice machine" was "any car offering a student a lift."[42]

In the eyes of Professor Clark and other members of UNM's faculty and student body, the building of a street car line to the campus in 1916 was a significant event in the life of the young university.

> Before that time (1916) going to town meant getting cleaned up when one arrived, if he was to appear at all presentable. One of our professors kept a shoe brush hidden in a tamarisk hedge down near the present Santa Fe hospital. To get the car line to be extended to the University, they [UNM officials] had purchased enormous quantities of street car tickets, and these were sold at very low prices so that student patronage of the street cars was very great and the cars were always crowded.[43]

Hooker also commented on this historic development.

> M. P. Stamm and the University Heights Development Company offered a bonus to the City Electric Company, which owned the street car system, for such an extension [street car service to the campus]. The University agreed to buy 2,500 special transportation tickets for $2,000 and to remove the "hump" in Central Avenue. The "hump," in front of Presbyterian Sanitarium, was several feet high, steeper than the cars could climb. Twelve-minute service was started on July 22, 1916, with Professor Charles Hodgin driving the first car to the campus from First Street and Central Avenue.[44]

Professor Clark also recalled that in the early years of the University, there was no place to buy anything east of Broadway. So in 1915, an enterprising student, Earl Gerhardt, received permission to establish a store in one of the cottages near Kwataka Hall and called it Earl's Grotto. It soon became a place where students could play cards and buy candy and soda pop. Tobacco was forbidden on campus but was bootlegged at the Grotto. (The University eventually took over the establishment and renamed it the Varsity Store.)[45]

One of the last decisions of Boyd's presidency was to impose a $5 per semester tuition in 1919. By then enrollment had reached 348, with only 4 preparatory students.[46]

Athletics

Intercollegiate athletics at UNM took some giant strides during the 1912–19 era, with football, basketball, baseball, and track and field enjoying notable success. Financial support from the University had improved but was limited chiefly to buying football and baseball uniforms and paying the traveling expenses of players. The administration also began to control athletics more tightly.

By 1912, home football games were played at either the University's rough field just east of the women's dormitory or at Hopewell Field, near Albuquerque High School. A season ticket for UNM home games cost $2.

Rivalries with New Mexico A&M, New Mexico Military Institute, and the University of Arizona were continued, and the University of Colorado, Colorado A&M, the Colorado School of Mines, and Colorado College were added to the schedule, along with the Texas School of Mines and Arizona State Normal at Flagstaff. In 1916 UNM was given provisional membership in the Class B division of the Rocky Mountain Faculty Athletic Conference, along with the University of Wyoming and the University of Montana. Governing only competition in football, the conference marked UNM's first attempt to align its athletic programs with those of other institutions in hopes of gaining prestige.

The 1916 season was particularly outstanding even though UNM lost its first two games by large scores (2–47 to Colorado College and 0–23 to Colorado Mines). Traditional rival New Mexico A&M was shut out 51–0. Arizona State Normal was overwhelmed 108–0.

Many of the University's athletes enlisted in the nation's armed forces during the late spring of 1917, shortly after the United States entered World War I. When school opened that fall, of the fourteen men who reported for practice, only one had played for UNM previously, and most of the others had never played football. "There were few substitutes and scrimmage sessions often saw one side of the line bucking against the other side." Coach Hutchinson had also left for the armed forces, and his place was taken by the well-meaning but inexperienced Professor E. L. Wood. This makeshift team split games against high school opponents, then journeyed to Las Cruces for a season-ending game against New Mexico A&M. On a cold, gray November afternoon, the Aggies thrashed the University by the score of

110—3. So humiliating was that defeat that the members of the UNM varsity refused the award of their football letters. This episode attracted coverage in many of the nation's leading newspapers.[47]

UNM baseball between 1912 and 1919 underwent spurts of progression and depression. Some years only one or two games were played, while other seasons had as many as eight or nine. Almost all competition was against high school teams, while collegiate opponents included old rivals such as St. Michael's College of Santa Fe, the School of Mines from Socorro, and New Mexico A&M. The overall record was twenty wins against twelve losses, with one tie.[48]

The biggest development in basketball in this era was the coming together of three governing factions: the colleges, the Young Men's Christian Association, and the Amateur Athletic Union. Representatives met in 1914 and formed a joint rules committee. The rules changes brought about new styles of play. The dribbling and shooting of the best player on the team gave way to the new strategy involving patterned plays and zone defenses. This resulted in higher scores and provided better entertainment for spectators.

Many of the games in this era were preceded by preliminary games featuring the UNM women's basketball team. Unfortunately, however, the results of those games were not recorded.[49]

These were lean years for most of the other varsity sports. There was growing concern pertaining to recruitment and financial support of athletes. University officials strongly disapproved of some institutions that recruited talented athletes and paid them, supposedly for some menial task on campus, but in fact for their sports performances. The evils of athletic recruiting in the larger colleges and universities had not yet gained a foothold in the frontier-like state of New Mexico.[50]

The University during World War I

On April 6, 1917, President Woodrow Wilson announced that the United States would enter the European war against Germany. This greatly affected UNM as well as other colleges and universities across the country, as male students withdrew to enlist in the armed forces. Wilson's crusade "to make the world safe for democracy" also had a profound impact on higher education. Thrust into a new world, towns like Albuquerque, universities like UNM, and states like New Mexico were no longer island communities. They were a part of a bigger but closer world with new expectations and demands.

The federal government called upon the states to train troops at home for eventual transport overseas. A "Committee for Securing a Mobilization Camp for the National Guard for Albuquerque" asked UNM to locate New Mexico's training camp, eventually known as Camp Funston, adjacent to the campus. President Boyd agreed, but with the stipulation that the soldiers could not trespass on University property and that students would be prohibited from visiting the military camp.[51]

To accommodate the irregularity of wartime academic planning, Boyd changed the University calendar to a four-quarter system. Many students worked during the summer of 1917 on a federal program to supply agricultural products to beleaguered European allies. UNM remained closed until October to permit students to complete the fall harvest.[52]

When the fall term of 1917 began, UNM officials discovered that more than 70 percent of the male students had enlisted in the armed forces. Students who did return found a campus transformed, as Dorothy Hughes noted.

> "Camp Funston" had taken over the land east of the football field during the summer, and there were more than 1,500 members of Battery A, New Mexico National Guard, encamped there. The preceding May there had been no evidence of this "soldier's city of barracks and tents," Red Cross hospitals, Y.M.C.A. buildings, supply houses, horse corrals, nor of the several hundred horses and mules, army wagons, caissons and cannons, and pack tents. Kwataka Hall was now the dwelling of the officers. The Gymnasium was used for physical examinations of soldiers, and the Federal Army Board occupied much of the Administration Building. City-like traffic on rechristened Railroad Avenue began in those days. . . . The sight of army wagons pulled by four or six horses was common, hauling endless supplies. The campus was khaki-clad, and the drill of soldiers, the martial music of the Camp Funston military band, made the war seem real in New Mexico. Refreshment stands sprang up to serve the soldiers. Nor was social life entirely neglected despite the overemphasis on war.[53]

One of the sad episodes in this era occurred in April 1918, when the chairman of the State War Defense Board brought charges against Johann Walter Gruner, an instructor of German at the University. Gruner had been born in the Sudeten region of what was then the German Empire and had come to the United States in 1912, where he learned English and got a job as a civil engineer for a railroad. He became interested in geology and enrolled at UNM, graduating in 1917. He was then appointed as an instructor in German and geology. The exact charges against Gruner are unknown, but it is likely they amounted to no more than the fact that he was a German by birth, probably spoke with an accent, and taught classes on the German language. President Boyd pointed out that there were only two students studying German at the time, so he determined that they would be given credit for the remainder of the semester and the class would be discontinued. The executive committee of the Regents also decided that a public announcement should be made that "German would no longer be taught at the University of New Mexico." The next University catalog showed no Johann Gruner, but did list a John W. Gruner, assistant professor of geology.[54]

Gruner left UNM soon thereafter and earned his PhD at the University of Minnesota, where he became a member of the faculty and went on to a distinguished career. In March 1963 he was awarded the Roebling Medal, the highest recognition that the field of mineralogical science bestows. He also received, in a more peaceful time on June 14, 1963, the honorary degree, doctor of science, from the University of New Mexico.[55]

By the end of the summer of 1918, as the war escalated and the draft replaced voluntarism, the War Department tightened its regulations about SATC enlistment and college attendance. It also directed a new curriculum for SATC students that strongly emphasized languages and the hard sciences. President Boyd and his administrative colleagues became acutely aware that the War Department would essentially manage college campuses for the duration of the war. Thus, as SATC students arrived on the UNM campus in September, what had first been a welcome, rational relationship with the War Department had degenerated into an academic and logistical nightmare. To meet the anticipated increases in "soldier students," the University had erected temporary barracks and classrooms, but the Army rejected requests for reimbursement of the costs of their construction. Included in these transactions was UNM's decision to expand the temporary quarters for the SATC unit before receiving official approval. Welsh reports: "The circus atmosphere at UNM transferred from the administration building to the campus at large once classes started on October 1. No one could anticipate the impact of the new curriculum, or the instability engendered by servicemen awaiting impending calls to duty."[56]

The opening of school in the fall of 1918 found all males pledged to the SATC and required to live in the barracks. The University doors closed after only seven days because of the Spanish influenza epidemic. City students were under quarantine until December 2, although members of the SATC and dorms were allowed to return to school in November. Many of the University girls acted as nurses at the camp during the epidemic, with some contracting the disease.[57] While millions died of Spanish influenza worldwide, including many in New Mexico, there were no fatalities at UNM. The fall semester of 1918, however, which was never orderly in its planning or implementation, was essentially lost.

The signing of the armistice ending the war on November 11, 1918, brought jubilation. President Boyd canceled classes so that UNM students, faculty, and staff could participate in the celebration in downtown Albuquerque. Boyd knew, however, that once the cheering stopped, the wartime enrollments would also cease. The Army announced in December that the SATC units would disband immediately, but that the military-academic relationship would continue through a Reserve Officer Training Corps program (ROTC). President Boyd asked for student support for such a unit, and the students responded with unanimous consent. In April 1919, Captain Charles Purviance of the U.S. Army accepted an appointment to direct the UNM ROTC unit.[58]

Following the UNM commencement exercises in June 1919, there was a special ceremony to acknowledge those persons from the University who had been in the armed forces. In all, 395 had seen military service; 1 had been killed in action, 3 others had died overseas, and 1 had died in the United States. Some 136 had been trained in the University's SATC.[59]

Resignation of Boyd

In the months after the war, President Boyd ambitiously outlined a bold plan for the University that entailed a significant increase in legislative appropriations. His request, however, shocked many lawmakers who feared an economic recession triggered by the sudden termination of lucrative wartime contracts and programs. They further asserted they had many other public institutions and programs to support. The new governor, Octaviano Larrazolo, cited a depressed state economy when he slashed the proposed UNM operating budget for the 1919–20 biennium from $250,000 to $150,000. He also denied any funds for campus construction.

President Boyd resigned soon after the final budget figures arrived in his office, stating that the appropriation was so inadequate that it would be impossible to meet reasonable expectations or demands upon the institution.[60] His resignation triggered an emotional response from the Regents, the campus, and even the governor. George Brooks, who had been so active in UNM affairs through the trauma of statehood and war, resigned, as did Regents John R. McFie, Jr., and Antonio Lucero. Governor Larrazolo reportedly had little to say other than to regret the wholesale resignations.[61]

Boyd was sixty-six at the time of his retirement. Professor John Clark wrote in 1958 that the president had decided he had had enough of the unrelenting battle for funds for UNM and interference by Regent Brooks. "One day he [Boyd] came to my office, pulled out two cigars and told me he was going to resign. He said, 'If I were younger I'd not put up with this [meaning Brooks's interference], but I don't need the job and I'll resign.'"[62]

As Boyd cleared out his office to leave UNM, he did not face the same uncertain future that had accompanied his leaving the University of Oklahoma eleven years earlier. He had purchased extensive tracts of land on the west side of the Rio Grande and sold them at a handsome profit. He and his wife stayed in Albuquerque until 1921, when they moved to Glendale, California. Through his investments, they lived comfortably in southern California until his death on November 17, 1936. In 1927, under the Zimmerman administration, Boyd received an honorary doctor of laws degree from the University of New Mexico. Three years later, the University of Oklahoma, which by this time looked back with pride at its first leader, honored Boyd by naming him president emeritus.[63] ■

Picnics at Supper Rock in Tijeras Canyon were still popular in the 1920s, and cars made the going easier. Freshmen engineering students kept the U painted on the rock until the 1950s. Photo courtesy of Butch Worthington, class of 1942

CHAPTER EIGHT
Administration of David Spence Hill
1919–27

David Spence Hill

It was called the Roaring Twenties and the Jazz Age, this era following the war to end wars, a time of great social and cultural change in America. The Victrola provided music for the foxtrot, the Charleston, and the lindy hop. Radio sets became a household staple. One could buy twenty smokes for a dime. Liquor, while hard to get during Prohibition, was still consumed in great quantities.

Perhaps the greatest change was in the women—how they looked, what they did. Gone were the long skirts and high-buttoned blouses, the corsets and stays. Hair was bobbed, cut straight and short. Gone, too, was the scandal that accompanied a revealed ankle. To the watchful male observers, much more of the feminine anatomy was observable than in the late, unlamented Victorian Age.

The development of household appliances was trumpeted as a great emancipator of women. Freed from the drudgery of housework and linked to family, friends, and merchants by the telephone, many women sought employment to supplement the family income or acquire a bankroll of their own.

Advances in technology affected the men, too, especially the mania accompanying cars. By the time the 1920s were in full swing, the open-air roadster was giving way to the covered sedan, and $550 could buy a new Chevrolet coupe with a rumble seat. The roads and streets improved. In Albuquerque, it was a day to celebrate in 1921 when Central Avenue was paved from High Street all the way—all four blocks— east to Mulberry, the city limit. Robert Barney noted:

> To Americans everywhere, the twenties represented an era of a dramatic new social philosophy, catering to the desires, comforts, and general welfare of the average citizen. Americans wanted a better, easier, and more fun-filled life and the developments seen during the period responded to those types of desires.[1]

Sadly, for the students and most of the faculty at UNM, the University was to have an 1890s president.

The Appointment of President David Hill

When David Boyd resigned in the late spring of 1919, the Board of Regents had ample time to conduct a search and appoint a new president before the fall semester began. There was no lack of candidates. Even Governor Octaviano Larrazolo had an interest, advocating the appointment of the state superintendent of public instruction, Jonathan H. Wagner. The latter, however, had no earned degrees. The president of the Board of Regents, Nathan Jaffa, insisted that the next president of UNM should be a college graduate. Other Regents also held firm to the belief that the institution needed an out-of-state candidate to ensure that the new president would have no state or local political affiliation.[2]

In the course of the search, the Regents discovered David Spence Hill, a forty-six-year-old native of Nashville, Tennessee, who had a puzzling record of academic experiences. He held a PhD from Clark University. At the time of his candidacy, Hill, a bachelor, was an acting professor of education at the University of Illinois, a "temporary" post he had held since 1917. His other teaching positions included two years at Tulane University and two at Peabody Teachers College in Nashville. He had also taught summer courses at institutions in Montana, New York (Cornell), California (Berkeley), and Wisconsin. He had received word that he would not be reappointed at Illinois despite his "excellent ability in scholarship and research." An appeal to the university's president had failed. As the months passed, Hill feared that his professional career was over. He was thus elated, and perhaps surprised, when the UNM Regents invited him to New Mexico for an interview. The Regents were impressed by his record of scholarship, which included several lengthy reports he had written when he directed the New Orleans (Louisiana) Department of Education Research.

K. C. Babcock, dean of the University of Illinois College of Education, wrote a recommendation for Hill, but added "a minor qualifying" statement. "Perhaps the severest criticism which could be made of him" was that Hill "sometimes put a higher estimate on his accomplishments than all his friends would agree to."

Although never officially a candidate for the post, Hill came to the UNM campus, was interviewed on July 14, 1919, and later that same day was offered the presidency at a salary of $5,000 per year. The Regents' vote was unanimous.

Hill revealed his inexperience in managing a university soon after his appointment by writing to the executive secretary of the University of Illinois president, requesting a chart, diagram, or other explanation showing the business organization of the university, the articulation between academic departments, and the relationship of the various offices to the affairs of each other.[3] While such a request might have appeared to some as a weakness, others may have thought it only a prudent inquiry that might be of value in organizing the University of New Mexico.

President Hill's Administration

Not much in Hill's background prepared him for his experiences at UNM. He literally walked into bad news when, a week before the opening of the fall semester, the War Department announced that it would not authorize formation of the previously announced ROTC unit on the UNM campus. Hill, however, took the news in stride and launched into what would be a seven-and-a-half-year tenure.

One of Hill's first tasks was to respond to a general demand for a hygiene program at UNM. On the same day he was appointed president, the Regents approved a plan to raise $10,000 to construct a building on the campus for a public-health facility. Soon the State of New Mexico entered into an agreement with UNM to house a joint public-health laboratory on the campus.

The 1919 fall semester began in October with an enrollment of 220 students.[4] The new president lost no time in launching a campaign to upgrade curriculum standards as the first step in moving UNM closer to his goal of national accreditation. He also expressed his intent to improve the academic credentials of faculty by encouraging them to undertake graduate instruction at the earliest possible moment, a bold move considering the small library and lack of graduate courses.[5]

Hill also brought back Atanasio Montoya, who had resigned over a pay dispute in 1902, to be the University's specialist in rural education. During his brief tenure Montoya recruited students, including Tom Popejoy of Raton High School, and gave workshops for schoolteachers.[6]

While attending his first meeting of the National Association of State Universities in 1919, Hill was impressed by the commitment of major schools to engineering instruction and research. He envisioned a similar goal for UNM.

Toward the end of that first year, state Senator George A. Kaseman contributed $2,000 for a building for the Home Economics Department. Kaseman's generosity inspired President Hill to solicit a total of $12,000 from local sponsors in less than six months. The largest donor was Joshua Raynolds, a member of a prominent territorial-era family and president of a bank in El Paso. Raynolds gave $5,000 to purchase equipment for the building. In return, Hill agreed to name the facility Sara Raynolds Hall, in honor of Raynolds's mother. Its first supervisor, Professor Elizabeth Simpson, stated that the structure became "a showplace for the field of domestic science." At the time it was dedicated, it was the only building on the campus built exclusively with private funds.[7]

In 1919 the name of the largest college was again changed, this time to the College of Arts and Sciences, which was still in effect in 2003. The reorganization of the former College of Arts, Philosophy, and the Sciences was regarded as more than a mere change of name. To members of the faculty it meant that the liberal arts had acquired an identity and the college a sense of collegiality. They also thought that the change would allow them to assume control of the various rules and regulations, curricula requirements, and standards; they were unaware at the time that the president had his own thoughts on those issues. The new format, however, did give the faculty many opportunities to meet and talk. They also displayed a deep interest in the students' morale and social welfare and thoughtfully passed a resolution condemning all improper forms of dancing, including that form known as "cheek dancing," and "other unseemly conduct not approved by people of good breeding."[8]

Also identified in Hill's organizational chart were a College of Engineering and a long-awaited, much-debated Graduate School.

The president, as he had promised, in that first year also initiated a new, more stringent system of grading designed to eliminate both grade inflation and the practice of awarding grades of incomplete at the end of a term.[9]

Meanwhile, signs of discontent among the faculty began to emerge. Some of UNM's liberal arts–oriented faculty were allegedly irritated by the prominence of technical coursework during the war years and took secret delight in the impending demise of engineering. Hill, himself a product of a liberal arts education, moved quickly to dispel such rumors and blamed any morale problems in engineering on the collapse of federal funding. He brought several new instructors to the campus, including faculty with degrees in physics, spent more money on the engineering program than ever before, and promised to acquire new equipment and provide better salaries to attract good faculty in that field.[10]

Dabney reported that:

> From the beginning of Dr. Hill's presidency he encountered opposition and criticism. His objectives were respected but his means drew fire. He was efficient, but he did not get along well with people, especially his faculty and his deans.[11]

The faculty applauded Hill's determination to be a strong president, believing that meant he would practice a managerial type of administration and involve faculty in academic and administrative decisions. Much to their horror, they discovered that Hill believed in presidential power as opposed to delegation of power. Faculty were even more alarmed when they learned that Hill frequently was at odds not only with the dean of the College of Arts and Sciences, Lynn Mitchell, but also with the dean of engineering, Thomas Eyre, and the Graduate School dean, John Clark.

In that first year of Hill's presidency, several faculty members began to grumble, and the news of their dissatisfaction reached the Regents. The Regents accordingly planned a series of meetings and invited disgruntled faculty members to air their concerns. At the end of the gripe sessions, the Regents took a vote and expressed their confidence in Hill. It soon became apparent, however, that Hill was taking careful note of what was said.[12]

Faculty unhappiness over low salaries and other concerns led many to apply to other schools. The board responded that the faculty members had had every opportunity to voice their discontent, which Regents attributed to years of faculty management under Hill's predecessor, Boyd. The emphasis on credentialism, meaning advanced degrees from prestigious institutions, also irked many faculty members.

Armed with support from the board, in the summer of 1920 Hill embarked upon a tour of universities to recruit new faculty. He had some success, hiring Wilma Loy Shelton from the University of Illinois as librarian and Roy W. Johnson from the University of Michigan as athletic director and coach.[13]

The 1920 fall term marked increased pressure for stronger academic standards as an antidote to a shift in student life that was causing problems at universities nationwide: the "collegiate syndrome," where social activities often overshadowed the more serious intellectual aspects of higher education. In September 1920, the Regents approved the appointment of Edna Mosher "to perform the duties that generally pertain to a dean of women" and act as an advisor to all women students. The following month the president drafted regulations for women that included standards of behavior for residence halls, chaperones, and sororities. Among other regulations, women were not allowed to loiter in front of fraternity houses or other residences of the men students; they had to leave the campus swimming pool by 6:00 P.M.; they needed to register their place of residence with Edna Mosher; and they had to seek permission if they left town while school was in session. Undergraduate women needed escorts to travel downtown at night to attend social functions, and all social activities on campus required the approval of Miss Mosher.[14]

At this time talk about consolidation of New Mexico's public higher education system caught the attention of outgoing Governor Larrazolo. He selected a committee of outside experts who recommended consolidating all higher education under a single board and merging the schools at Socorro and Las Vegas with UNM in Albuquerque. As had been the case in the past, these suggested changes were not adopted.

When the fall 1920 semester neared its end, Hill prepared for his first appearance with the New Mexico Legislature. He outlined what he thought to be his "remarkable accomplishments" in his first eighteen months in office, including upgrading the faculty by recruiting graduates of prestigious universities, phasing out the preparatory program, and operating fiscal affairs without debt. He concluded by pointing to UNM as "an increasingly good educational investment" for the citizens of the state. However, the deepening financial crisis within New Mexico gave the lawmakers little inclination to support UNM's requested increase in funding. The University was lucky to receive a general appropriation of only $92,500 for the coming year.[15]

A somewhat chastened president devoted most of the spring term of 1921 to reorganization of student government and athletics, academic program development, and expansion of the physical plant.

The federal government's termination of support for the UNM Hygiene Department did not close it down, as the president was able to arrange for the New Mexico Bureau of Public Health to fund the program. Public reaction to the dedication of Sara Raynolds Hall prompted Hill to seek additional private funding for a new women's dormitory. The existing facility lacked parlor space, and Edna Mosher, the women's supervisor, reported: "It's almost impossible for the girls to entertain callers." According to her, this forced women students "to entertain their gentleman friends in the street, in automobiles, or anywhere they find a corner." Mosher also requested a separate rest room "for the town girls to use between classes instead of running to the dormitory and upsetting things there."[16]

Before Hill's departure that summer to recruit faculty in the East, he terminated the employment of Joseph Landers in philosophy and psychology, stating he doubted that Landers could master the social science techniques of any future research projects UNM might undertake. In addition, he fired Ethel Hickey in English, who had been at UNM for two decades, because she had no advanced degrees. In his letter of dismissal Hill added that Hickey's expression of hostility to his administration further justified the decision to terminate her, so "the 'free and frank' session with the Regents in which the disgruntled faculty had a chance to voice their complaints came back to haunt [her]."[17]

Far more inflammatory was Hill's dismissal of Hannibal Ibarra y Rojas, the Romance language instructor. Dean Mitchell had pressed Hill to remove Ibarra on the grounds of "neglect of duty and inefficient teaching." Hill, however, at first elected to retain him as he was one of the few Hispanic faculty members. Late in the spring term, Women's Supervisor Edna Mosher wrote a "serious complaint" against Ibarra. While there is no record of the specifics, there was speculation that the complaint stemmed from Ibarra leaning out a window in his room to address a woman faculty member. Whatever the cause of the complaint, it convinced Hill to agree to his dismissal. The University purchased the remaining months on Ibarra's contract, and he was gone.

George S. Hubbell, a PhD from Princeton University, accepted the position in English, while Benjamin F. Haught of Peabody Teachers College in Nashville was appointed to replace Landers. Helen Evers, a Bryn Mawr PhD at Grinnell College in Iowa, was hired to teach Romance languages, and Katherine McCormick of Columbia University joined UNM as a physical education instructor.[18]

By the third year of Hill's administration, fall enrollment was reported to be 236 (or 273) students, a slight increase over the previous year. While this was less than the number of students in the preWorld War I years, Hill attributed the drop to the rigor of the new admission standards. The legislature, while not increasing UNM's appropriation, did pass a bill providing grants for indigent students to attend various state educational institutions.[19]

The announcement of UNM's accreditation by the North Central Association (NCA) came in April 1922, making the University the first of New Mexico's colleges and universities to meet the NCA's national standards. It was hailed as the most significant advance in the school's thirty-year history. The accreditation meant that UNM graduates would have better standing for employment purposes and for admission to prestigious professional schools. UNM students transferring to other schools would also be spared the embarrassment of taking entrance exams, while UNM's education majors could meet the licensing criteria of surrounding states. A delighted President Hill was also pleased with the recommendations of the accrediting team inasmuch as they closely paralleled his own, including a call for more funds to attract PhD-holding faculty and better-prepared students.[20]

Another historic milestone was celebrated in 1922, when the University proclaimed that the preparatory program had been terminated. For the first time since the University opened its doors in 1892, UNM could boast that its entire student body was enrolled in collegiate degree programs.

Concerned with presenting a higher Hispanic profile, the Regents pushed the hiring of a UNM graduate, Anita Osuna, in the Romance Languages Department. She became the first Hispanic woman to receive a permanent faculty appointment at the University. Osuna had received her bachelor's degree from UNM in 1921 and her master's the following year from Stanford University. There she had been a teaching fellow for another UNM graduate and former faculty member, Aurelio Espinosa.

Outreach efforts at UNM that year included further development of the Extension Division, which attracted 140 students to the campus and included such nondegree programs as home economics, journalism, child psychology, and "Platonic Influence in Literature and Thought."[21]

President Hill announced a major new initiative in 1922: the School of Spanish Literature and Life. Echoing unsuccessful proposals by Presidents Gray and Boyd, he proposed a regional study center to research Spanish literature and culture, train teachers, and study conditions affecting the welfare of Spanish-speaking people. Hill obtained endorsements from former Governor Octaviano Larrazolo; Regent Antonio Sedillo, whose daughter Mela had organized the nation's first Anglo-Hispano sorority at UNM; and Adelina Otero-Warren, an influential Santa Fe club woman. The president asked the Carnegie Foundation for almost $300,000, more than four times the University's operating budget, for the project. The foundation's executives were interested but found flaws in the proposal and turned it down.[22]

Meanwhile, in Santa Fe there was another change of governors, as James Hinkle of Roswell replaced the departing Merrit C. Mechem. This was not good news for Hill, inasmuch as Hinkle was reported to be more conservative than his predecessor. Adding to Hill's consternation was the criticism of higher education mounting around the state. Herbert Hagerman, speaking to a farmers' picnic at Dexter, was highly critical of all levels of education for draining the public treasury while not producing graduates capable of serving in the modern economy. Hagerman lamented the fact that there was little or no surplus wealth in New Mexico. He charged that education placed the greatest demands on the limited financial resources of the state, but the schools were so bad that the expenditures were far too high for the results achieved.[23]

In 1923, midway in his presidential tenure at UNM, Hill witnessed a slow deterioration of the quality he had worked so hard to establish. Governor Hinkle began his term in January by exhorting the legislature to cut expenditures and maintain taxes at their current rate. He recommended that UNM's appropriation for the fiscal year 1923–24 be reduced by 10 percent to $83,500, which would bring the school to its lowest rate of funding since World War I. Mercifully, the legislature retained UNM's appropriation at $92,500, far less than Hill had requested, but better than the governor's recommendation. The lawmakers also passed an act to regulate fiscal matters more carefully, including a requirement that University employees request permission from the governor to travel out of state on business.

This was particularly galling to Hill as the regulation stemmed from criticism of his recruiting trips to the East.[24]

More bad news for the University was yet to come. When Governor Hinkle began formulation of the 1924–25 state budget, his accountants questioned the entire salary structure of all state institutions with particular emphasis on what critics considered to be the "elaborate programs" at UNM. Despite the growing criticism, though, the institution moved forward on improving salaries and developing academic programs as well as financial constraints allowed.

The strain on the faculty took its toll in many ways. Edna Mosher, the women's supervisor, took exception to Hill's failure to raise her salary for 1923–24, complaining that it mattered little for her to have an advanced degree when every other professor on the campus could make as much or more without the qualifications she had. Further, Laurence Lee, an Albuquerque insurance executive, called upon the president to remove Roy Johnson and hire someone who could build a winning football team.[25]

A bright spot on the troubled campus was the selection of Fred Wagner as a Rhodes Scholar in 1923. An excellent student and tennis player, Wagner had graduated in May and accepted a position in the Magdalena public schools to teach Latin and Spanish. His real interest, however, was international law, and the opportunity to attend Oxford was the chance of a lifetime. President Hill considered Wagner's selection a vindication of his efforts to improve academic life at the University.[26] The University's tenth Rhodes Scholar, an English major and oratorical-contest winner named Woodford A. Heflin, would be named in 1926.[27]

As 1924 began, Hill prepared to present his budget proposal to a fourth governor in the span of five years. He was sobered by the fact that the voters would go to the polls again in November to select a new governor, which he believed would guarantee the politicization of the appropriations process.[28]

The economic outlook for the state was depressing. New Mexico had gone from poor to impoverished. Farm products fell over one-quarter in value; four thousand farms statewide had been abandoned and six thousand more were without means or credit to purchase seeds; and the herds and flocks of stockmen had overgrazed the grasslands, resulting in huge losses. Businesses closed, and bankruptcies increased. Forty percent of the state and federal banks ceased operation, and the state lost more than $30 million in personal savings and investments. Property owners and taxpayers pressed for a freeze in state spending. Under these conditions, any plans devised by President Hill for the expansion of UNM were doomed.[29]

There was brighter news at the June 6, 1924, commencement ceremony, when the University's first honorary degree was presented to John James Tigert, the United States commissioner of education. Also presented were twenty bachelor's degrees in the College of Arts and Sciences and three in the College of Engineering.[30]

The strain caused by enrollment growth, cramped facilities, and meager pay for the faculty took its toll in 1924. President Hill, however, persisted in his demands for more services and stronger credentials without any promise of improvement of conditions or salaries. In 1925 the legislature once again appropriated $92,500 but added another $10,000 to repair the campus heating system. To get more output from his staff, Hill asked Deans Clark, Hodgin, Mitchell, and Eyre to work an extra thirty days over the summer, with no salary increase. Hodgin (who had been appointed in 1897), Clark (1907), and Mitchell (1912) informed Hill that they had routinely worked in the summers for no salary and rarely any verbal recognition. Clark particularly was outspoken, pointing out that the principal of the high school in Albuquerque was paid more than any of the deans. Hill's combative style did not permit his backing down.

The president's discussion with Eyre did not turn out well. Eyre had come to UNM because of respiratory problems and had missed several months of work in 1923 because of poor health. Hill had had to petition the legislature for special permission to grant Eyre an exception to a new law that prohibited employment of tubercular patients in state classrooms. Unfortunately Eyre suffered a relapse in the summer of 1924 and had little interest or energy for Hill's demands for more work. Eyre's attitude exacerbated their ongoing quarrel about the decline of enrollments in engineering. Eyre had proposed a revised curriculum with a decreased emphasis on intense specialization, which he believed was a deterrent to graduates obtaining jobs in New Mexico. Eyre left UNM in 1926 to accept a faculty position at the University of Southern California.

President Hill also frowned upon faculty working on projects outside the University to supplement their pay. He targeted a popular, productive professor of history, Charles F. Coan, who had contracted with the American Historical Society in Chicago to write a history of New Mexico. Hill charged that the writing of the history reduced Coan's committee work on the Athletic Council and also resulted in a lowering of scholarship in his classes. Tragically, Coan died suddenly in 1928. The Charles Florus Coan Award was established in 1930 to be awarded to students in history and political science.

Hill's crusade pertaining to faculty standards in teaching and grading had even stranger repercussions during the 1924–25 academic year. Several instructors were charged with maintaining high enrollment by resorting to grade inflation, where everyone passed courses, many with high marks to encourage their continued attendance. A survey by the campus registrar revealed that Dean Eyre, Professor Coan, and even "the venerable" Dean Hodgin had almost no students receiving incomplete or failing grades. Hill chastised his faculty and recommended that they eliminate from 5 to 15 percent of their students. He pointedly asked Hodgin, the twenty-seven-year veteran, "to be a little more rigid in the standards of scholarship that you require."[31]

Unfortunately the president's relations with faculty and students deteriorated further when he insisted on mandatory assemblies as part of the student socialization process. Faculty members were directed to attend, take roll, and see that students also attended the sessions, duties that faculty members detested. Hill persisted, declaring that "faculty regularly absent themselves for personal or selfish reasons." He wanted the faculty to consider the tedious assemblies "a privilege, and not a favor."[32]

Hoping to inspire his faculty, President Hill invited the review committee of the Association of American Universities (AAU) to visit the UNM campus in the fall of 1924. The AAU served as the accrediting agency for graduate programs and in 1900 had organized to set standards for curricula, libraries, facilities, and instruction at the graduate level. The committee came, it saw, it left. In November the AAU reported that UNM's request for graduate accreditation had been rejected.[33]

Hill regarded the election of Governor Arthur T. Hannett in November 1924 as yet another disaster. Hannett, an avowed fiscal conservative, immediately targeted higher education as wasteful and inefficient. While this merely echoed criticism that had arisen over the years about the funding of the state's colleges and universities, it also gave rise to pressures to remove Hill from his post as president.

When Hannett submitted his first budget to the legislature in January 1925, he revealed his frustration at the absurdity of funding higher education. He charged that the state had indulged in pork-barrel politics by establishing seven schools and protecting them by constitutional fiat. The intensity of the criticism in the legislative session shocked Hill and the UNM Regents. Hill immediately retracted proposals for physical plant improvements and recalculated and resubmitted the University's budget request.[34]

Hill's problems in Santa Fe were merely an extension of a growing crisis of leadership within the University itself. Hill had systematically managed to alienate almost all his internal constituencies: the deans, the faculty, and the students. A student disciplinary case, remarkably similar to the Roddy Stover dismissal in 1897, added to the furor and was one of the incidents that inspired public outcry in February 1926.

Owen Marron, Jr., was dismissed from the University by the Committee on Student Discipline because he failed to secure the requisite number of chaperones for a fraternity dance, encouraged the invitation of women high school students to the party, and then dimmed the house lights to leave only the fraternity crest illuminated at the end of what must have been a very dark room. Owen, Jr., just happened to be the son of a prominent Albuquerque attorney, Owen Marron, Sr., president of the Kappa Sigma fraternity alumni group. A representative of the Interfraternity Council named Tom Popejoy told Dean Clark that he and his fellow fraternity members would willingly accept any punishment the Committee on Student Discipline might recommend or impose. The Marron case might have gone no further had the political climate not been so heated by the rhetoric of the governor and other critics of the University.

Owen Marron, Jr., was not an unknown student; he stood out. He had been placed on probation for poor scholastic work, skipped weekly assembly programs, and been threatened with dismissal from classes by angered professors. When dismissed from the institution, he countered with complaints of abusive treatment and autocratic management of UNM by its president. Francis E. Wood, who was Marron, Sr.'s, law partner, marched into Hill's office and demanded a retraction of the suspension. Hill understandably resented Wood's accusatory style and told him so. Wood backed down, seemingly embarrassed by his own behavior.[35] The bitterness lingered, though, and spread. Marron was eventually reinstated and, interestingly, was appointed by Professor James F. Zimmerman to represent UNM when the debating team from Oxford University came to the campus in the fall of 1926.

In retrospect, it appears that Hill just had a natural penchant for trouble. In February 1926, he took on Carl Magee, editor of the *New Mexico State Tribune.* Magee had attracted national notoriety for his crusading editorials that exposed Interior Secretary Albert Fall's involvement in the Teapot Dome oil scandal. Hill, however, was unimpressed with Magee and publicly described him as "an egocentric, aristocratic sycophant of Old Guard Republicans." Magee, who had lost the Republican nomination for the U.S. Senate in 1924, looked upon Hill as one of his personal enemies. It is unwise to be any kind of an enemy to a person who buys ink by the barrel.

Magee clearly sympathized with Governor Hannett's dislike of higher education management and campaigned to undermine Hill's reputation and authority. Hill counterattacked by rallying support from influential friends of the University. Magee rose to the challenge after Hill had described Magee as a victim of "ego mania." Magee gleefully informed the psychology professor-turned-president: "I have no recollection of having employed you to make a diagnosis of my condition, but perhaps my failure of memory is a part of my infirmity, in which event I suggest that you enclose a bill for your services."[36]

Late in December 1925, Carl Magee began blasting Hill in his newspaper and openly asked for the president's ouster. In their meeting of January 2, 1926, the Regents took note of Magee's accusations but accepted Hill's explanation that they were inaccurate. Suddenly, however, ten prominent Albuquerque citizens appeared and demanded to speak to the board about Hill's alleged mismanagement of the University. Two of their number, Clyde Tingley, a member of the City Commission, and Edward Swope, state land commissioner, claimed to be merely bystanders. The other eight expressed bitter opposition to Hill and called for his removal. The members of the self-appointed Committee of Eight were people of stature within the community. Perhaps the most ominous of the critics, however, was a young reporter and insurance salesman, Clinton P. Anderson, who was to serve as New Mexico's senator for twenty years. The Regents heard them out, but took no action. As for Hill, he dismissed these criticisms as unfounded or minor in nature.[37]

A week later, the Board of Regents conducted an intensive hearing that included testimony from supporters of Hill as well as from the Committee of Eight; Deans Mitchell, Eyre, and Clark; and the president. Then the Regents held a closed executive session. That evening the board reconvened at eleven o'clock and voted three to two to retain Hill. The president, feeling quite insecure, wanted to know if this close vote would be repeated in future reviews of his presidential actions. The board members made no reply. He then asked if the board's vote should be interpreted as an "an entire exoneration of himself." The Regents agreed.[38]

Members of Alpha Rho gathered in front of their fraternity house.

Dean Nanningga

By March 1926, however, the combination of Carl Magee's charges, the dismissal of Owen Marron, Jr., and the doomed UNM budget were beginning to wear down the beleaguered president. Hill, apparently without friends on the campus, chafed at the travel restrictions placed upon him and sought comfort in corresponding and visiting with colleagues in other parts of the country. He seemed to revel in describing how bad things really were in New Mexico or lamenting the demise of other college presidents because of meddling, politicized governing boards. At the depths of despair, the weary chief executive finally received some good news. The discoveries of oil and natural gas deposits on UNM trust lands near Artesia increased UNM's royalty payments, and by year's end the properties were worth more than $40 million. This meant that the University could establish a permanent fund whose interest would supplement legislative appropriations.[39]

The Democratic legislature, however, hard-pressed for funds and jealous of UNM's good fortune, proposed to change the language of the constitution so that all public land royalties would revert to the state's general fund. Just before the end of the session the lawmakers voted to refer the matter to the voters in the fall of 1926. The voters in November defeated the referendum, and the land royalties continued to accrue to the University.

Throughout the summer, Hill was uncertain about the availability of any income from the land fund. Confident that UNM ultimately would prevail, he kept plunging ahead and in June publicized a plan to issue bonds for campus construction by using $110,000 of endowment as collateral. First priority for the campus was a library, then dormitories, and a larger assembly hall and dining area.[40]

By the beginning of the fall term money woes continued to restrict efforts to recruit new faculty and upgrade credentials. UNM benefited once again from its reputation as a healthful place for tubercular patients when a young doctoral candidate in history from Harvard, France V. Scholes, was appointed to the faculty. He was offered a part-time position at $45 monthly, launching him on an illustrious career at the University, which included outstanding research in Latin America, service as vice president, and the naming of the Administration Building in his honor.

Also hired on the UNM faculty in 1925 were James F. Zimmerman of Columbia University in political science and Simon P. Nanninga of the University of California, Berkeley, as dean of education. Nanninga's experience included serving six months as an aide to General John J. Pershing during World War I.

Hill considered his appointment of Nanninga a coup and expected him to take over for the Hodgin and reorganize the program in education. Hill's growing displeasure with Hodgin stemmed chiefly from comments by one of the visitors at the time UNM was rejected for graduate accreditation by the Association of American Universities. The educator told Hill that one of the reasons for the rejection was that many of the deans and faculty members lacked advanced degrees. He specifically mentioned Hodgin, saying the dean had only a two-year degree in pedagogy, a subject no longer taught by the better colleges of education. Perhaps the pressure worked, because Hodgin retired that year after twenty-eight years at UNM.

Hill's relationships with his remaining deans continued to deteriorate. He expected Clark to serve as chair of the Chemistry Department as well as an instructor in that discipline, chair of the Committee on Student Affairs, and dean of the Graduate School. Hill believed that a dean should have been able to inspire more than one graduate degree candidate in six years. In addition to what the president referred to as a "light" teaching load, twenty-two hours, Clark also performed chemical analyses on demand from city officials and private organizations. Hill further expected him to conduct original research and publish scholarly articles in his field. Hill notified Clark that he intended to strip him of his deanship, including the stipend, and restructure the Graduate School.[41]

Hill's personal vendetta also included members of the faculty. His dealings with some appeared to be ruthless and tactless. When an economics professor asked that his salary be raised by $200, the president wrote back that in view of the professor's statement that he could not live with the offered salary, the position was vacant. A professor of psychology declined to take steps toward obtaining his doctorate, and the president terminated the position. The president also alluded to the fact that the professor had expressed his dissatisfaction with the administration in the Regents' gripe session in 1920. When a woman professor of biology had surgery, Hill wrote her a letter expressing his high regard for her and hopes for a complete recovery. He added that he thought it better that she not return to her position the next academic year. He ended the letter by saying that he took some consolation in the fact that she had recently come into an inheritance, so the hardship of not returning to her professorial position would be mitigated.

When Hill heard that a history professor was unhappy that a new political science professor had been hired at a higher salary than his, Hill replied that the simple fact was that the new professor was worth more.

The faculty neither loved nor admired Hill, and opposition to his leadership mounted and coalesced. Some of his chief opponents, who later testified against him, were among the most highly respected scholars and teachers at UNM. When President Hill removed Lynn Mitchell as dean of the College of Arts and Sciences, the criticism reached a new intensity. The academic pot was boiling.[42]

Student Life

Tension and confrontation marked student life under the Hill administration as the president sought to impose Victorian regulations on Jazz Age students. Many of the male students had fought in the big war, as World War I was referred to in that era. The females were far more daring than the girls of the long skirts and tight morals of another age. Hill was a fastidious male chauvinist in a coeducational environment. He had no children, but he held to the doctrine of in loco parentis. He had degrees in psychology, but no experience, tact, or diplomacy in working with young people, and particularly with women.

Hill had barely arrived on the campus in 1919 when he began to worry about the quality of student life and morality on the campus after the exposure to war.

Members of Pi Kappa Alpha sorority posed in their spring finery at the steps of their house after an Easter breakfast in 1926.

He detected a cult of masculinity attributed to the male veterans. He was also concerned about consumer culture, which he viewed as relying upon gratification, avoidance of responsibility, and lax standards of social conduct. This led Hill to create the Committee on Conduct of Women Students in January 1920. He then prohibited all dances on Sundays through Thursdays, required that chaperones be appointed for all dances, and promised prompt discipline of any individual who indulged in improper forms of dancing. He also endeavored to protect the virtue of women students who used the swimming pool. He was unconcerned with matters of health, safety, and maintenance, focusing on the issue of "mixed bathing."[43]

What really attracted Hill's attention, however, was the development of the fraternities and sororities. The most disturbing issue for Hill was the physical punishment inflicted upon fraternity initiates known as hazing, or, as a newspaper characterized it in 1920, "undergraduate mob law." Hill considered the practice appalling, illegal, and contrary to the purpose for which state universities were maintained. He had as little success in curbing the practice as did other college presidents around the country.

Not surprisingly, students resented and resisted his authority. Because of the University's isolation on the east mesa, students had few venues for social functions other than in the town. Earl's Grotto, the small store and cafe that had been operating in one of the cottages, was considered unsanitary and a source of disorder, so Hill had it refurbished as the Varsity Shop. Run by students, it diligently carried out the president's directives, which included restrictions on nighttime hours, the sale of cigarettes, gambling, dancing, music, habitual loafing, and improper language.

Lena C. Clauve, a 1925 graduate of UNM and later its dean of women, remembered Hill as "distant and aloof" from his students. She added that "his haughty manner" made him the target of jokes and sarcastic comments. Hill further incurred the displeasure of students by mandating class attendance the Friday after the Thanksgiving holiday.[44]

While troubles with students continued for the harried Hill, he also held the University's staff accountable. He reprimanded the campus superintendent, Harry Frank, charging that he was doing nothing about the gambling on automobile and horse races that went on just east of the reservoir on the UNM athletic field. He expressed his deep concern about pickpockets and thieves in the parking lots during athletic events and about fans surging on the field while the teams played and tearing down goal posts at the end of games. He could not know that the same problems still plague college presidents almost a century later.

In the eyes of the women's supervisor, Edna Mosher, the institution still had problems of moral turpitude on the part of the women, alcohol abuse at social functions, and heavy automobile traffic past the women's residence hall on warm spring mornings. She was particularly irate over the men's track team parading past the women's dorm in their training outfits.

Student conduct at dances persisted as a troublesome issue. Hill and Edna Mosher could not condone the "suggestive movements" spawned by the fashionable jazz music UNM students preferred. Hill therefore instructed all chaperones to prohibit vulgar, cheap jazz, immoral jerky half-steps, and shimmy dancing, which Hill defined as "a shaking of the upper body while taking short steps, or standing still." Students also were admonished not to hold each other too closely, use "neckholds," or dance from the "waist up."[45]

In the latter part of Hill's administration, student life on the campus continued to follow the uneven course of his relationships with faculty. The president called upon twenty-nine student organizations to draft by-laws and constitutions that would enable the administration to more closely supervise their activities. He also had repeated run-ins with student publications, the *Lobo*, the student newspaper, and the *Mirage*, the yearbook. As early as 1922, students began to show little enthusiasm for the yearbook. In 1924 the administration canceled publication of the *Mirage* as funds were not available for "incidentals like yearbooks." The publication was revived in 1926, but had problems when advertisers failed to reimburse the student managers for $500 worth of ads, thus leaving its editor liable to creditors' suits.

In regard to the *Lobo*, Hill complained that there were times when the University had been ashamed to send the paper to high schools around the state. On at least one occasion, however, he applauded the student editor's efforts in publicizing the University. He encouraged the editor to include in his paper book reviews written by students to give it a "more scholarly tone." He also asked the editor to refrain from the unpleasantness of making "jocular or facetious reference to young women." With a change of editors, the *Lobo* reverted to its old practices and received harsh criticism from the president over the "Razz" issue of May 21, 1926, which Hill charged echoed the *Harvard Lampoon* for its "suggestiveness and questionable taste."

The president also had problems with former students, the alumni, over poor management of the Alumni Association. Acting on the advice of former alumni presidents, Hill finally determined that students who had attended UNM could

Wilma Lay Shelton

belong to the organization, but only students who had graduated from UNM could vote and hold office.[46]

Hill just could not give up on his efforts to monitor and dictate the lifestyle of students. Even in the twilight years of his presidency, he proclaimed, "Men should regard girls and young women as objects to be protected as surely as they so regard their own sisters and mothers."[47]

Campus Development and Construction

The "not-so-roaring twenties" was a period of little planning and building for UNM. Most of this was because of a change of governors every two years, each of whom seemed determined to spend less money than his predecessor. Governor Arthur T. Hannett visited the UNM campus on January 13, 1925, and mentioned that he did not favor erecting new buildings at any of the educational institutions.

The University nevertheless continued to submit detailed capital construction requests to the legislature, which were turned down with depressing regularity. In 1920, the Regents and the president presented one to the legislature for $331,500 for construction projects. In July 1921 the legislature approved $6,000 for an addition of sixteen rooms to Hokona Hall, the women's dormitory. As reported by Hooker: "What resulted was a much skinned-down building omitting exterior buttresses, between-floor insulation, plaster and other finishes."

Of the thirteen wood-frame cottages erected around Kwataka Hall between 1914 and 1916, only five were still in use as residences in 1923. Some had been modified for other functions, including the Varsity Shop, student publications, and a laundry. All the cottages were removed by the late 1920s.

The New Library

The Regents were meanwhile focusing on what was considered to be the greatest need on the UNM campus: a new library. At the urging of Librarian Wilma Loy Shelton, on April 5, 1924, the board approved construction of the facility. The Regents and the president had identified $35,000 (through savings, land royalties, and private gifts) to authorize the project and began an effort to raise another $10,000 from private donations.[48]

A new library was certainly needed, wrote Dorothy Hughes.

The library was still in its small quarters in the old Administration Building, now Hodgin Hall, when Miss Wilma Loy Shelton came to the campus in 1920. Combined with it was the University post office. The duties of a librarian were evidently still considered something to be tossed off in one's spare time, as Miss Shelton was also put in charge of Rose Cottage, annex to the girl's dormitory, . . . was sorority chaperon to the Alpha Chi Omega, . . . and finally spent four years as "temporary" dean of women.

Students and staff liked their new library, although they complained the lights were inadequate at night.

In the latter capacity, Shelton kept office hours, supervised the women's dormitories, attended every social function of the student groups, and oversaw the enforcement of strict rules and regulations. After attending to these minor duties, she was the main custodian in a library always overcrowded with students. She did have the assistance of one student helper, a Miss Russell.

Serving as head of the largest university library in New Mexico made Shelton an unusual figure in her profession, noted Mary Ellen Hanson and Carl A. Hanson in a *New Mexico Historical Review* article in 1989. In 1920 women held 88 percent of all librarian jobs but few of the top ones. By 1970, twenty years after Shelton's retirement (when she had been succeeded by a man), women were 82 percent of the library work force and held only 8 percent of the highest administrative posts.[49]

Construction began on the new library in 1924 on the site where the original Hadley Hall had been. When completed at a cost of $80,000, it was believed that the facility would take care of all of the library needs at UNM for years to come. Hughes also reports:

> The building was finished and used for commencement exercises before the money for the necessary stacks to house the books was forthcoming. But on the afternoon of the seventeenth of May in 1926, for the first time in history there was a real University library. With appropriate ceremony, the faculty, students, and campus force carried the books from the outgrown corner of the old Administration Building to the new building, the library being open for business as usual the next morning. With the move, the library was open for night hours as well as for day, which meant that Miss Shelton and Miss Russell . . . were necessarily in attendance day and night. The library was quite the place for students' "social hours" in those days, and because of the limited space there was usually disturbance of those

who attempted serious study. With all books given over the one desk, the "rush hour" between classes will not soon be forgotten.[50]

In all, the students, faculty, and staff moved more than fifty-seven thousand volumes, including thirty thousand bound books, as well as other items such as pine tables and chairs. No one regarded the task as finished until the stacks were in place. Meanwhile, the campus basked in the aura of its very own library.[51]

The UNM Wireless Station

Another historical event was recorded in the 1920s when UNM began radio broadcasting. With the help of gifts from members of Albuquerque's Korber family and others, UNM purchased surplus wireless telegraph and telephone equipment at large discounts. By October 1921 the equipment was on hand, and students had begun construction on two steel towers. The first broadcast was on December 16, 1921. Features of the Korber Radio Station (with the call letters RYU and later KFLR) included weather reports, music, and in 1924 the first live radio broadcast of a sporting event in New Mexico, a play-by-play account of a UNM-versus-A&M football game in Las Cruces. A sophomore from Raton, Tom Popejoy, offered to work as a student assistant to keep weather records at the radio station, one of his first, but not his last, managerial duties at the University.[52]

Athletics

The postwar era marked the rising importance of collegiate sports as governing boards and presidents became aware of the opportunity to get more visibility for their institutions, build stronger links with their communities, and attract spectators in huge numbers. The money-making potential of big-time football had special appeal. As so often had been the case in higher education, the prestigious universities in the East and upper Midwest set the pattern with huge stadiums and crowds that often numbered in the thousands. "The university's Saturday game marked the high point of many a college town's social calendar."[53]

The most significant event in the upgrading and development of the athletic program at UNM was the 1920 appointment of Roy W. Johnson as director of athletics and coach of all sports. Described as a man of extreme dedication and immense integrity, Johnson came to New Mexico from the University of Michigan, where he had played for the legendary Fielding Yost, one of the early icons of intercollegiate football.

Johnson had an impressive vita. Born in Grand Rapids, Michigan, in 1892, he had worked hard in high school to support a widowed mother and his sister. His prowess in sports earned him the reputation of being one of the finest all-around athletes in his community. He went on to work his way through the University of Michigan while competing in football, track, baseball, and gymnastics. The war interrupted his education, and he saw action in most of the major battles in France and was a much-decorated commissioned officer in the U.S. Army. He was gassed on the battlefield and suffered lung damage. During his convalescence he studied theatre arts at the University of Poitiers while living with a French family.

He returned to the University of Michigan in September 1919 and despite shortness of breath earned a second football letter and a degree in play production. Coach Yost had known David Hill at Tennessee, and the two men arranged for Johnson to come to New Mexico, yet another health seeker who made great contributions to his new home state.

From the time of his arrival on campus, Johnson earned respect and deep loyalties. Sometimes he labored almost alone as athletic director, coach of all sports, groundskeeper, athletic business manager, equipment custodian, faculty member, and participant and leader in many community endeavors. His influence extended far beyond the playing fields, as he was also admired for his talents as an actor and a gifted singer with a rich bass voice. As described by his biographer, Robert Knight Barney:

> Johnson, personally, was a quiet, rather aloof individual who kept his respect and fondness for his players and fellow colleagues on the University's faculty well hidden beneath the ominous countenance of his bushy eyebrows and formidable frame. Because of Johnson's stubborn dedication to principle and unyielding stands on the aspects of issues which he felt in his own mind to be right, he was soon accorded the nickname "Old Iron Head" and was often referred to by this moniker—though never to his face.[54]

Coach Roy Johnson

Johnson took the lead in improving the athletic plant. Mostly on his own, armed with a hoe, a rake, and an abundance of enthusiasm and energy, he spent countless hours weeding, raking, and leveling the football field.[55]

In 1926 the football field was resurfaced with drift dirt and silt from arroyo bottoms. The ground was harrowed to dig out the rocks and replace the rough surface that was taking a heavy toll on knees, elbows, and noses.[56]

The first development in renovating the athletic facilities came with the construction of a new grandstand for the football field in 1921. On a game day the old field had usually been surrounded by a solid ring of automobiles from which the spectators could watch the activities on the "gridiron." Johnson raised $800 from alumni to purchase materials and, with the help of the male students, bleachers were erected on the west side of the field. The grandstand was built in twelve sections, each of which was twelve tiers high, and could accommodate fifteen hundred people.[57]

Most members of the campus community were delighted with the new grandstand, but not Edna Mosher, the women's supervisor. She was appalled by the height of the steps and said: "It is impossible for the women to reach their places without listening to vulgar comments on their appearance at that time, and it is also impossible for them to present a proper appearance [in the short flapper-girl skirts of the day] in mounting such high steps."[58]

The chrysanthemum bouquets suggest this may have been a Homecoming football game, with the fans watching from the sidelines because there was no grandstand.

The University's Athletic Department in this period became more or less self-sustaining. The gate receipts for football and basketball were expected to pay for expenses those two sports incurred, as well as for all other varsity sports. If there were deficits, they were underwritten by loans from local banks. For purely fiscal reasons UNM began to schedule games with big-name teams to pay off its debts. This led to playing a game against highly rated Texas A&M in 1926. UNM lost, 0–63, but profited from the hefty gate.

President Hill's biggest worry, however, was eligibility of University athletes. Consequently, in 1920 he organized a new Faculty Athletic Board of Control that placed severe restrictions on academically deficient athletes. The president further demanded that opposing teams submit prior to game day a list of all eligible players and the conditions for eligibility mandated by their school.[59]

At the end of hostilities in Europe in 1918, war-hardened young men from all branches of the armed forces streamed back to college. After what these veterans had been through on the battlefields, football, with its body contact and intensity, appealed to them. The former old college try was replaced by a quality of performance never seen before. Great coaches and great teams from the nation's most prestigious schools made this a period of football's greatest boom.

When Coach Johnson came to UNM from Michigan, he brought along his play books and formations, mostly single wing and double wing in those days. He was also a master of teaching the fundamentals of the game: blocking and tackling.

The size and quality of the players on the squad progressed, as in the fall of 1921 forty-one players tried out. Football uniforms changed, and numbers appeared on the backs of jerseys in 1924. Although helmets were worn in the 1920s, many players still opted to have only a heavy shock of hair to protect their heads.

The University's football teams enjoyed mixed success as the schedules got tougher. In 1922 Johnson discontinued playing high school teams. His first four years as coach were mostly break-even years. The season of 1924, however, became a year to remember as UNM beat five college teams while losing 0–6 to New Mexico A&M. High point of the season was Tom Popejoy's dropkick for a field goal in the waning minutes against the University of Arizona for a 3–0 victory.[60]

The UNM football season usually ended sometime around Thanksgiving Day weekend, and then all eyes turned to basketball. Johnson's tenure as basketball coach was long and successful. Things got off to a slow start in his first two seasons but improved considerably by 1924–25 when the team won the Far Southwestern Conference. Between 1924 and 1927 UNM beat downstate rival A&M ten times and lost none. They also defeated the University of Arizona basketball team four times in six games.

1923

With a decline in interest in baseball and tennis in this era, track and field became the dominant spring sport and was considered one of the big three in UNM athletics. For the most part, competition was arranged to include an annual meeting with the University of Arizona, as well as a yearly intracity meet that included Albuquerque High School and sometimes other Albuquerque schools. Coach Johnson was also successful in scheduling dual meets with the powerful University of Nebraska track squad. The latter stopped by Albuquerque on return trips from the Pacific Coast. These dual meets were always one-sided but did enable the people from the University and the region to see some of the finest track and field athletes in the nation. Although UNM track and field teams in the 1920s were only moderately successful, the sport continued to grow in strength and in its schedule by the end of the decade.[61]

The Lobo Nickname and Mascot

Over the years many legends have arisen over how UNM adopted Lobo as its official nickname. When the University first began playing football in the 1890s, the team was referred to as the University boys, or the Varsity, to distinguish them from the prep school boys. In 1917 the student body began exploring the possibilities for an official nickname and/or mascot for athletics as well as a name for the student newspaper, at that time known as the *U.N.M. Weekly*.

Through his own research, Athletic Director Johnson had learned that one of the chief gods worshiped by the ancient Natives was the wolf, a war god of extreme prominence and admired for his power, courage, and cunning.

On September 22, 1920, sophomore George S. Bryan, editor of the *U.N.M. Weekly* and student manager of the football team, appeared at a student council meeting and proposed that University teams be given a mascot and name. Specifically, he suggested "Lobo," the Spanish word for "wolf." His proposal was received with enthusiasm, and the Lobo, "feared for his prowess and the leader of the pack," became the official University mascot.[62]

Not long after, 1923, a real, live *lobo* became the UNM mascot. Bruno Dieckmann, a member of the UNM class of 1902 who had become a successful Albuquerque insurance and real-estate agent, acquired a live wolf pup, which he gave to the

The 1921 Lobos were warming up on their newly improved gridiron, but the Lobo, tugging on two chains, looks eager to get away.

University. The cub became the responsibility of the cheerleaders, and it appeared in harness at every football game. At one of the games in the late 1920s, however, a child teased the wolf and was bitten. UNM officials were forced to dispose of the wolf, and it was never again a part of the University athletic scene.

In the early 1960s a costumed human mascot was created and given the name Lobo Louie. A female counterpart, Lobo Lucy, was created in 1980, and both became members of the school's cheerleading squad.[63]

Seeds of Discontent and the Resignation of Hill

As Hill's presidential tenure extended into the fall of 1926, the seeds of discontent continued to sprout. The friction among his own administrative chiefs was obvious to members of the UNM community. Hill, ensnared in the conflicts with Owen Marron and Carl Magee, grew angry at what he called the timidity of Dean Lynn Mitchell. Hill accused Mitchell of passing on to the president the responsibility for every petty matter of discipline.[64]

Hill also continued his vendetta against Thomas Eyre, dean of the College of Engineering, having been unable to persuade the dean to upgrade his credentials. In addition, Hill was distressed that the enrollment in engineering had slumped to a mere fifty-two students in the fall of 1926. He further noted with chagrin that the State of Texas had opened Texas Technological University (Texas Tech), a technological college in Lubbock, using oil-royalty funds to build a physical plant at the cost of $2 million and offer instruction almost tuition-free to resident students. To the north, the University of Colorado had eight hundred students enrolled in engineering courses. Eyeing and envying their success, Hill reached a point of almost total despair in improving engineering under Eyre.

During this same time, Washington State University was offering big money to James F. Zimmerman to join that institution as dean of men. Zimmerman had shown in eighteen months signs of true brilliance as a teacher and administrator, and Hill was determined to keep him at UNM. So, in view of his deteriorating personal relationships with the graduate dean, John Clark, Hill offered Clark up as an alternative candidate for the Washington State post. He wrote a glowing recommendation, which is interesting considering the strong animosity between the two. Hill stated that Clark wanted to leave New Mexico and UNM, that Clark had "a pleasing personality and was exceedingly diplomatic," and if offered $3,500 for the position, would "accept it on the spot."[65] Either the offer was not made or Clark did not accept it.

The Regents, at their meeting of February 20, 1926, were confronted by two former judges, M. R. Hickey and Clarence M. Botts, as well as newspaperman Carl Magee. The trio, though not included in the official agenda, demanded time to explain their case for Hill's dismissal. The Regents agreed to hear them. The three antagonists charged that the president had been arrogant, autocratic, and unjust to faculty members and referred to correspondence to Clark that they described as "harsh and even brutal."

Most of the Regents defended Hill. The president also defended himself and reminded the Regents that Judge Botts had been reprimanded by a campus watchman about picnicking with his family on University grounds. As for Hickey, the president reminded the Regents that he had terminated his sister, Ethel, from her long-time position in the UNM English Department for a lack of advanced degrees. The meeting adjourned with no action, but the rumor mills churned. The *Albuquerque Herald* acknowledged that pressure for the president's departure had become intense, but found it outrageous that Hill's greatest sin was nothing more than "unpopularity."[66]

The political situation in the fall of 1926 also took a turn for the worse. The incoming governor, Richard C. Dillon, a rancher from Encino, identified himself as a conservative on economic and social matters. Furthermore, the Republicans, restored to office after several years of Democrats, were described as desperate for the governorship with its power of patronage. The anti-Hill sentiment in Albuquerque influenced Dillon greatly. When he took office he accepted the resignations of the entire Board of Regents of UNM, something that had not happened since the "statehood purge" of 1912. Among Dillon's selections for the new board were John F. Simms, a lawyer for some aggrieved subcontractors on a campus building project; Mrs. Laurence Lee, the wife of the disgruntled football fan; Frank Light, who owned the *Silver City Enterprise* and was a strong advocate of the normal college in that town; Mrs. Reed Holloman, the wife of a Santa Fe judge; and A. C. Torres, publisher of a Spanish-language newspaper in Socorro. With great anguish, the UNM president labeled the appointees the Get-Hill Gang. He was not far wrong.

The outgoing Regents met for the last time in early January 1927 and went on record as supporting Hill, but it was to no avail. The new board convened on January 18 to act on Governor Dillon's pledge to remove the UNM president. Attending the meeting were the members of the Committee of Eight, along with Deans Mitchell and Clark, who testified against their president. Under these circumstances, Hill presented a brief statement asking the board not to renew his contract when it expired in the fall. The new Regents responded by agreeing to pay Hill for seven months' vacation and put him on leave for the remainder of the academic and fiscal year. The Regents then appointed thirty-eight-year-old James F. Zimmerman to be acting president until September 1, 1927.[67]

Hill's departure from UNM was "swift, and regretted by few." After leaving the UNM presidency, David Hill lived a long, full life. He moved to Alabama, where he accepted a position as research professor of psychology at the University of Alabama in Tuscaloosa. Hill died in his native South in 1950, at the age of seventy-seven.[68] His fate, Welsh later noted, "paralleled that of five of his six predecessors, and he left the University both better and worse upon his departure than he had found it on his arrival."[69] ■

Women appear in many of the undated, unidentified photos of UNM anthropology.

James Fulton Zimmerman

CHAPTER NINE
Administration of James F. Zimmerman, Part 1
1927–39

It was the best of times to be president of the University of New Mexico. After almost seven years of anguish, anxiety, and sometimes brutal insensitivity, everyone was looking for a change: students, faculty, deans, townspeople, legislators, even governors. They sought a messiah, someone who could lead the University out of the wilderness. They were ready for someone they could admire, cheer for, work for. Whoever succeeded Hill, they wanted him to succeed. Even the looming specter of the Great Depression could not affect New Mexico; it was already depressed. The Depression was kind of a leveling-down process where more prosperous states began to be as impoverished as New Mexico.

The people wishing for a messiah found one in young James F. Zimmerman. He had credibility and compassion, as well as vision and vigor. He was gracious without being ingratiating, proud, but with a true humility, and aggressive but not arrogant. Best of all, he could lead; but he also could listen. While he didn't walk upon the Rio Grande, at least he didn't sink in the quicksand. Zimmerman was ready for New Mexico, and New Mexico was ready for Zimmerman.

The first person ever chosen to lead the University who had previously been a member of its faculty, Zimmerman was destined to preside over the institution for seventeen years, more than twice as long as any of his predecessors. Unlike five of the six former UNM presidents who had been hounded out of office, Zimmerman would die in office, and a grateful and loving campus and state mourned his loss.

The 1930s

The 1930s were a dark period in the nation's and New Mexico's efforts at economic growth and development. The decline of the stock market in 1929 launched a decade-long economic collapse. Scenes of men standing in soup lines; thousands of unemployed workers milling about in an atmosphere of tense uncertainty; rises in crime, particularly bank robberies and kidnappings; bank failures; closings and bankruptcies of businesses; and extremely depleted public buying power were not pleasant to observe.

The impact of the Great Depression on New Mexico was partly offset by the fact that the state had never enjoyed prosperity. "To New Mexicans in general,

Mrs. James F. Zimmerman

the great depression was something which arrived late, lasted briefly, and exited rapidly."[1] Although there were severe cuts in appropriations for higher education and thus in faculty salaries, few of the state's businesses closed and most banks weathered the storm.

During the Depression era, the Democratic Party in New Mexico built a substantial majority in state and national politics, with roughly 70 percent of the populace voting Democrat. New Mexicans were primarily interested in "seeing that their well-being was secured immediately—not tomorrow, or the day after."[2]

Advances in technology in the 1930s included the development of gas furnaces, water heaters, electric refrigerators, and washing machines. Hydraulic brakes appeared on almost all automobiles, and aviation became a significant part of Albuquerque's physical environment.

Social developments included decreased consumption of alcohol as people began to save their money. The nation's "noble experiment," Prohibition, finally ended in 1933 when Congress repealed the Eighteenth Amendment.

The used-car business thrived while sales of new cars decreased. Beef became the meat of choice. Albuquerque established a city garbage collection service in 1931, and in 1932 milk delivery to homes began. A state sales tax was implemented in 1934, the real-estate industry boomed, and the city began to expand in all directions.[3]

James Fulton Zimmerman

James Zimmerman arrived in Albuquerque before the Depression. After eleven days of travel and camping in the spring of 1925, he and his wife, Willa, and their two daughters drove into Albuquerque and pitched their tent in the Camp in the Woods, now the site of the Rio Grande Zoo on Tenth Street. As the story goes, President David Hill learned of their accommodations and rushed to the camp to order UNM's new history professor to register in a local hotel. Hill, highly conscious of the image he wanted UNM to project, could not condone a faculty member and his family sleeping on the ground with "common tourists."[4]

Zimmerman was born September 11, 1887, and grew up in rural Missouri. He received bachelor's and master's degrees from Vanderbilt University. After graduation in 1913 he taught high school courses in history and government in his home state and in several schools in Tennessee before serving as an instructor in economics and sociology at Vanderbilt University in Nashville, Tennessee (1917–19).

As a doctoral student at Columbia University, Zimmerman studied with several great scholars and was exposed to the latest trends in scholarship and higher learning. When he received his PhD at Columbia in 1925, he was offered a position in history at the Ohio State University. He had also received a letter from David Hill at the faraway University of New Mexico. He thought the latter offered the perfect laboratory in which to test his ideas about government, society, culture, and public service. Thus, he accepted Hill's offer to teach at UNM for one year to experience the exotica of the Southwest. He never left, spending his entire professional career at the University of New Mexico.

From his arrival on campus, Zimmerman's diplomatic manner and his commitment to learning endeared him to the Regents, deans, faculty, and students. Only a year and a half later the shifting political forces sufficed to remove Hill from the presidency. The Regents and faculty and students, the media and townspeople and legislators, indeed, all of the many constituencies of UNM, saw in the thirty-nine-year-old historian someone who could lead the University. Zimmerman was appointed acting president in January 1927.[5]

The Zimmerman Administration

When he moved into the president's office in the spring of 1927, Zimmerman undertook management of an institution in a state that ranked forty-seventh of forty-eight states in per capita income and forty-sixth in density of population and in tangible wealth (such as bank deposits and property ownership), but fifth in per capita expenditures for education. New Mexico had more than $6 million in uncollected taxes outstanding. Zimmerman's work with the legislature was phenomenal and included authorization to sell $200,000 worth of bonds for campus facilities based on the collateral to come from twenty years of projected oil royalties. He also enticed the legislature to raise the general appropriation by $10,000 for 1927–28 and then consider a major increase for the 1929–31 biennium to $250,000 annually.

Mrs. Reed Holloman in 1959

This good fortune and the potential for significant advances for the University prompted the Regents to dispense with the formalities of a national search. On March 14, 1927, the board's first woman president, Mrs. Reed Holloman, acting on its behalf, offered Zimmerman the UNM presidency on a permanent basis. He took some time to consider, sensitive to the cultural shock of his wife, Willa, who missed her native South. On April 1, 1927, Zimmerman finally accepted the board's offer. This launched what at that time was the longest term in office of any UNM president, seventeen years, to be exceeded only by Tom Popejoy's twenty years.[6]

With a few weeks remaining in the 1927 spring term, Zimmerman focused his attention on the internal organization of the University and sought the support of the faculty before developing any long-range programs. He established an Advisory Council of Administration and developed a clear chain of authority from the president through the deans to faculty, staff, and students. He also made counseling freshmen students a high priority for all faculty and worked to increase the number of scholarships and student-job opportunities.

Much of the increase in appropriations was devoted to faculty pay raises and the creation of new faculty positions. Among the new appointments was Loyd S. Tireman of the University of Iowa, who became one of the nation's foremost academicians in the area of bilingual education.[7] In 1930 he opened the San José Experimental School in the South Valley to train teachers in bilingual instruction. The Rockefeller Foundation's General Education Board and the federal government provided funds, through the efforts of New Mexico Senator Bronson Cutting, who later donated $10,000 himself.

Loyd S. Tireman

The University entered the fall semester of 1927 with forty-five returning faculty members. One prickly case demanded Zimmerman's attention. The dean of engineering, Carl E. Hanson, had been appointed by the former president, Hill. With the change in administration, Hanson found he had the support of neither the new president nor the other deans. Zimmerman sought to remove Hanson by offering a lower salary and reducing his academic rank to instructor. After failing to gain the support of state officials or University administrators, Hanson filed a grievance with the American Association of University Professors. The organization sympathized with Hanson, but Zimmerman held fast in refusing to reinstate the engineering dean, appointing Phillip Donnell instead.[8]

More tragic news was the death of Josephine Parsons, the University's long-time financial secretary, in June 1927. For thirty-four years she had symbolized the perseverance and continuity of the institution and had set high standards for the management of UNM's business affairs. President Zimmerman praised her "loyalty, punctuality, regularity, and constant application to duty" and prevailed upon the Regents to name the new biology building in her honor.

The president in 1927 determined that the relationship of UNM to the city and state had to be improved and that the people of New Mexico had to be convinced that the University indeed served their interests. To this end, he scheduled numerous speaking engagements and meetings with public school educators throughout the state. In addition, he proposed several initiatives to meet the needs of New Mexico's diverse cultural milieu.

The Arrival of Anthropology
The founding of the Anthropology Department can be seen in retrospect as a milestone, because the program was both destined for national acclaim and focused on the rich and little-known prehistory of the Southwest. The farsighted Zimmerman invited Edgar Lee Hewett, the widely respected archaeologist, writer, and teacher who had worked to gain public control of the antiquities on public lands in the West, to visit the campus in May of 1927. The two quickly came to terms on the creation of a Department of Anthropology and Archaeology affiliated with the School of American Research (SAR) in Santa Fe. Zimmerman hoped a unique regional studies program would improve the University's chances for graduate accreditation by the Association of American Universities.[9]

Hewett certainly was the right person for the job. He had taught school in Missouri and Colorado and earned a master's degree while spending summers exploring the ruins on the Pajarito Plateau west of Santa Fe. He pushed for establishment of national parks there and at Chaco Canyon.

In 1897 Hewett was named the first president of New Mexico Normal School (now Highlands University) in Las Vegas, where he organized the first university-level anthropology and archaeology courses west of the Mississippi River. He was instrumental in the 1907 founding of the SAR, a pioneer in preserving and studying antiquities. He also led in the creation of the Museum of New Mexico in 1909. And he was responsible for the establishment of an anthropology museum in San Diego and the anthropology department at what is now San Diego State University.

UNM's first archaeology field schools were held at Chaco Canyon and the Jemez Pueblo ruin in the summer of 1928 with sixty students. The skeletons and artifacts from Jemez became the nucleus of the anthropology museum, which opened in 1932. In the early years, the focus was on the ethnology, particularly linguistics, of indigenous people. The first three bachelor's and two master's degrees were conferred in 1932 and the first doctorate in 1948. Under Hewett's leadership, students and their mentors worked for many years at Chaco Canyon and the pueblos of Jemez, Tijeras, and Pecos. They collected thousands of artifacts and skeletal remains, along with field notes and photographs, and began to form theories about what had happened a thousand years previously. During the Depression the federal Works Progress Administration funded UNM studies of cultivated plants in the New World and Navajo material culture and mythology, among other subjects.

Zimmerman's cooperative programs with the School of American Research also brought the *New Mexico Historical Review* to the campus when its first editor, Lansing B. Bloom, joined the history faculty in 1929. Founded in 1926, the quarterly was a project of the SAR, the Museum of New Mexico, and the Historical Society of New Mexico. Bloom brought back microfilmed records from archives in Spain and Mexico. He retired in 1945 but continued editing the *NMHR* until his death the following year. He once wrote that he and the journal had been invited because the University "wanted 'in' on" a successful publication.[10]

Other Academic Initiatives

Zimmerman continued to work with the other state institutions of higher education through an association of their presidents. In November 1928, the association called for standardization of credits among New Mexican colleges, and UNM agreed to accept transfer students who had completed their sophomore year.

In 1928 Zimmerman and the UNM faculty supported granting college status to the Education Department with Simon P. Nanninga named as its first dean. This was a significant move in professionalization of the teaching business statewide. The concept included two years of subject matter in the College of Arts and Sciences, while education methods courses were limited to the upper division and graduate school. In 1930 fifteen courses were offered in the College of Education's new Physical Education Department, capping several years of effort by Roy Johnson, who developed the curricula and facilities and taught most of the courses.

The Regents, still headed by Mrs. Holloman, accepted architects' plans for a new gymnasium, a biology building, a science lecture hall, and a new dormitory for men in March 1927. These buildings were made possible by the $200,000 bond issue approved by the 1927 legislature. All were designed in the Pueblo Style. Van Dorn Hooker noted that "there is no record of the board at that time making a formal statement establishing the style of architecture to be used on the campus, but the regents' actions reestablished, with no elaboration, the style initiated by President

The Pueblo Indians' regalia at President Zimmerman's inauguration outside the Estufa may have been authentic, but it looks as though a car seat was used as a kneeling platform.

Tight."[11] When the buildings were dedicated, during Zimmerman's presidential inauguration, the Pueblo Style architecture was celebrated by the presence of the governors of all the Indian pueblos in the state, all attired in their native dress.[12]

The occasion of Zimmerman's formal installation as president on June 4, 1928, gave the University good reason to celebrate. Republican Governor Richard C. Dillon attended, as did public school officials from all over the state. Ray Lyman Wilbur, president of Stanford University, who six months later became secretary of interior in President Herbert Hoover's cabinet, was the featured speaker. This ceremony also enabled Zimmerman to declare his love for his adopted home and his vision for its state university.[13]

With the glow of his early successes, Zimmerman prepared for the 1929 legislative session. He had no idea at the time of the difficulties that lay ahead, as no one predicted the collapse of the stock market that October or the effect it would have on the 1929–31 biennial budget. The picture Zimmerman painted for the lawmakers was both optimistic and grim. Enrollment at UNM had increased to 1,000, up 103 percent since 1926, while the appropriation had grown a mere 20 percent. The legislature did not disapprove of Zimmerman's request but felt somewhat overwhelmed by the scale of increases requested by all institutions.

Zimmerman had the opportunity to appoint no fewer than thirty faculty and staff members in 1929–30. Stepping down were two venerable deans, Lynn Mitchell and John Clark. Zimmerman was able to bring on board several appointees who were to serve the institution long and well as teachers and administrators, including Lansing Bloom and Marion Dargan in history, Ralph W. Douglass in art, Jay Carroll Knode as dean of men, and George P. Shannon as dean of arts and sciences. On the downside, once again the president was looking for a dean of engineering as Philip Donnell left to become dean at Oklahoma State University.[14]

President Zimmerman had a strong belief that the University should emphasize those areas of scholarly activities that were related to New Mexico's heritage and its region. Spanish would thus be emphasized in the foreign language field. Rather than general history, UNM would specialize in Southwestern, borderlands, and Latin American history. Professor Dargan, for example, turned his talents and energies to the history of territorial New Mexico.[15]

Not all new faculty were pleased with the University. Physics and mathematics Professor Carroll Newsom later wrote in his autobiography that he disliked the presence of so many tubercular patients, the pervasive desert wind storms, and the "desperate" financial situation of the University. Other new faculty members either did not share Newsom's views of the University or kept their opinions to themselves.

Much more serious was the criticism of the women who began to assert themselves in 1929. They expressed their concern about the lack of female administrators at UNM. Meekly, futilely, the president replied that UNM had four women department chairs and three administrators: dean of women, registrar, and head librarian. The criticism, however, was but the tip of an iceberg that would not thaw in the remainder of the twentieth century or the beginning of the twenty-first.[16]

One of the department chairs was Grace Thompson Edmister of music, who held the post from the department's founding in 1925 until 1942. She would also become the first American woman to conduct a city symphony, the predecessor to the New Mexico Symphony Orchestra.[17]

In 1929, Zimmerman was elected president of the New Mexico Education Association, which included both K–12 and higher education members. Among the problems confronting New Mexican educators were the obvious: language, poverty, isolation, and distance, as well as inadequate teacher training. Studies showed that while in most subjects New Mexican high school seniors compared favorably with those from other states, they were seriously behind in mathematics, physics, and chemistry. What further disturbed Zimmerman was the relative decline of New Mexico educationally in the 1920s. School districts in some parts of the state faced actual budget reductions that ranged from 5 to 30 percent, and the near future looked bleak. H. B. Kimball, a state representative from Springer, reminded the UNM president "that political instability kept New Mexican higher education in check. Every governor could appoint new boards of regents to all state colleges and universities, and the combination of two-year terms and the failure of any governor to gain re-election prior to 1928 almost guaranteed perpetual volatility." School officials recommended a more aggressive advertising campaign by the University, especially in the eastern part of New Mexico. They also called for a better explanation of the rationale for UNM's higher standards for admission and retention and requested more emphasis on training for professional and technical careers.[18]

Zimmerman weathered these criticisms and settled into the job. In 1930 he appointed Paul Walter, Sr., of Santa Fe to become director of publications for the University. The president also established the *New Mexico Quarterly* to enhance the

A new University seal was created in 1928. It featured two New Mexico founders—a Spanish conquistador and a frontiersman—and, in the center, seals of the state and nation and a Spanish coat of arms. The Latin phrase had been revised, reportedly by Classics Professor Lynn B. Mitchell, and was now translated as "Light is the Life of Man."

*These UNM Band members of 1932–33
look like extras for* Casablanca *with their
square-topped hats and jaunty capes. This
photo appeared in the* Mirage, *which reported
that the drum major (perhaps the man in
the center with the dark sweater) was
J. C. MacGregor, Jr., who would become
the University's admissions director.*

regional literary culture. He missed what might have been a great coup, however, when he declined the services of Conrad Richter, who came to New Mexico for his wife's health in 1928. Richter, struggling at that time in the early stages of his career, sought to supplement his meager income by teaching a class at UNM on short-story writing. He later won a Pulitzer Prize for his New Mexico–based novel, *Sea of Grass.*

In the fall of 1930, the new governor, Arthur Seligman, won the election after campaigning with "fanatical zeal" on a platform to reduce state expenditures. The New Mexico Taxpayers Association was delighted that its two-decades-old crusade to reduce public spending had finally found a champion. Undaunted, Zimmerman cited the expanding enrollment at UNM, one thousand in fall 1931. The faculty had doubled in size from thirty-three to sixty-seven members, who, Zimmerman said, were overworked and underpaid. While some legislators agreed with Zimmerman, others saw in the president's remarks an "arrogant disregard" for the New Mexican way of life. The legislature recommended a 25 percent increase in UNM's appropriation, but this was nowhere near Zimmerman's requested 80 percent increase. He argued that UNM educated half of all college students in the state, but received less than 30 percent of the higher education appropriation.

These protests did not please Governor Seligman, who was determined to slash spending. He targeted UNM as a special offender in budgetary mismanagement and allowed UNM a small 8 percent increase of $17,500. He then used an administrative tactic to restrain UNM in the future. He replaced the five-member Board of Regents with bankers and businessmen, but included no women, and reinstated the 1920s practice of gubernatorial review of all University travel expenditures.[19] One of the Regents in this era was Dr. William Randolph Lovelace, a tuberculosis patient who had come to Albuquerque in the early twentieth century as a surgeon for the Santa Fe Railway. As a physician he worked among fellow tuberculosis sufferers for many years before opening Lovelace Clinic in 1931.[20]

Both the tightened budget at UNM and the Depression haunted Zimmerman's presidency throughout 1931. Among the high points was the appointment of Marshall E. Farris as dean of the College of Engineering. Zimmerman also aimed for a higher standard for student life on the campus. Retention of first-year students became critical to the intellectual and financial health of UNM, and in 1930 he inaugurated a series of activities called Freshman Week and called upon faculty to discuss more substantive work with new students. UNM then instituted more waivers of prerequisite courses, offers of better-paid student employment, and freer access to faculty. The president also agreed to assist the state chapter of the League of Women Voters in their organization of a conference on international affairs. In the summer of 1931, Zimmerman served in a prestigious capacity when he sailed to Europe with other academics for the Carnegie Endowment for International Peace. The trip not only enlightened Zimmerman on world affairs but also enhanced the University's reputation, since it put him in touch with dignitaries from world powers and American government and foundations.[21]

Marshall E. Farris

In 1931 the College of Arts and Sciences had eighteen departments. That year the Regents approved a recommendation by the college's faculty to divide it into upper and lower divisions. Students in the lower division were expected to satisfy the group requirements in their first two years of study, while students in the upper division would be free to direct their attention to the major and minor courses. Although passed in 1931, this change did not take effect until 1934.[22]

Zimmerman's endeavors to expand programs in research and instruction, particularly in archaeology and anthropology, paid off in 1931 when UNM and the National Park Service reached an agreement on Chaco Canyon in the northwest region of the state. The Park Service received title to the lands, which individuals and energy companies had held, to unify the monument, while UNM retained access for scientific research and field-school training for its faculty and students.[23]

Frank C. Hibben

By then the collection of artifacts and field notes stored in the basement of Scholes Hall demanded organization. A young Frank C. Hibben was hired to establish the Museum of Anthropology in 1932. He held the job until 1970 and was also a faculty member and active researcher, becoming something of a living legend. A graduate of Princeton and holder of a Harvard doctorate, Hibben formulated a dual mission for the new museum: public education through exhibits and oversight of actual field research. Reflecting Hibben's eclectic interests, the museum's scope broadened to include most of the world's diverse cultures while at the same time retaining its Southwest emphasis.

Recurring disappointments for Zimmerman during his long tenure at UNM were the repeated rejections of the University's efforts to be admitted to the Association of American Universities. In April 1931 the AAU turned down UNM yet again. Once more the reasons for the rejection were hazy, but references to the lack of graduate degrees for Dean of Women Lena Clauve and the head of home economics, Elizabeth Simpson, led University officials to view this as a key. In an effort to enable UNM to reapply for certification by another national organization, the American Association of University Women, Clauve and Simpson took academic leaves of absence in the spring term of 1932 to work toward master's degrees.[24]

Interest in minority issues began to emerge in 1931. At the request of Ralph Brown, a newly appointed Regent, the University prepared some information pertaining to the 1,037 students enrolled for the fall term. Ninety percent of the students were from New Mexico, where the Hispanic population, in those days called Spanish-Americans, was more than 50 percent. Only ninety-nine Spanish-Americans were enrolled at UNM, 9 percent of the student body, and only nine Indians (as they were then called), less than 1 percent. Three-fourths of the student body came from Bernalillo County, which invited charges that UNM was still a predominantly local institution.

The prolonged impact of the Depression made Zimmerman's life as president nearly unbearable. The delicate balance of regional programs, physical plant, faculty appointments, and outreach efforts was subject to the winds of persecution and prejudice. The president could do little more than hang on until the political temperament nationally and within the state changed in the election of 1932.[25]

The New Mexico Taxpayers Association charged that pork-barrel influences drove higher education appropriations, resulting in high expenditures and unnecessary duplication of programs and facilities. The association was also highly critical of voters for showing little inclination for a system with a central board of regents. As had been the pattern in the past, however, those favoring any restructuring of higher education were spitting in the wind. The national economic crisis persisted, as did the prejudices against the University. Some of the charges were serious, some petty, and none offered any substantive solutions.

Zimmerman was personally singled out for criticism. The Internal Revenue Service had learned from confidential sources that the president allegedly had not reported all of his compensation in previous years. The charges lacked substance, and Zimmerman refuted them.

Of a more serious nature, the state auditor reported a drastic shortage of tax revenues. Zimmerman and the board restructured the budget to limit salary cuts to 10 percent, but warned faculty and staff that the board could not guarantee full salary payments for 1932–33. The president directed that all purchase orders come to his office for approval. While the economic plight of faculty overshadowed all other concerns, the faculty members committed themselves to maintenance of standards and even advancement of programs where money was not the critical factor.

The coming of Franklin Delano Roosevelt and the New Deal in 1933–34 had a profound effect on higher education all across the nation as a host of federal programs showered millions of dollars on campuses and students. The National Industrial Recovery Act was passed, leading to the creation of the National Recovery Administration (NRA), the Federal Emergency Relief Act (FERA), the National Youth Administration (NYA), the Public Works Administration (PWA), the Works Progress Administration (WPA), and the Civilian Conservation Corps (CCC). These programs helped keep the floundering public institutions afloat, providing the means to keep young people in college, off the streets, and out of the labor market. At UNM, federal stipends supported student employees, and federal contracts and grants were gained for programs in Latin American and Southwest studies, particularly anthropology. In addition, the WPA financed a veritable building boom.[26]

As President Zimmerman prepared for the 1933 legislative session, he had to adjust to a proposed 10 percent reduction in the University's operating budget. Governor Seligman, reelected for a second term, proposed a 25 percent cut in higher education appropriations for the biennium, including 35 percent for UNM.[27]

In January 1933, the Regents informed members of the faculty that it was necessary to cut salaries by 25 percent. As reported by William Dabney, the faculty members accepted this bad news with "relatively good grace." No professors were dismissed, but a few instructors were terminated, although none had been permanent members of the faculty.[28]

Governor Seligman, who had appointed five new Regents in 1931, named three more in 1933, an unhealthy trend of high turnover. Five new members, of course, had been appointed with the founding of the University in 1889. There was a complete turnover in 1912. In 1919, four new Regents were appointed. Zimmerman took office in 1927, along with five new Regents. Five more were appointed in 1931, three in 1933, and four in 1935. With a governing board that had no corporate memory or continuity and was susceptible to strong political influence, it is amazing that Zimmerman not only outlasted all these board members but also accomplished so much.

Neither the University nor its president was immune from strong criticism coming from political figures. R. H. Grissom, educational auditor for the state comptroller's office, in 1933 wanted the president to explain the duties of every UNM employee, especially the faculty teaching courses with limited enrollments. The state comptroller, J. M. Lujan, cited a $10,000 discrepancy attributed to unauthorized out-of-state travel, losses in the management of the dining and residence halls, and overcharges for utility lines to the newly constructed President's House. The latter was the object of scorn for its alleged lavishness in an age of financial hardship. On one occasion Zimmerman was called before the Senate Finance Committee to explain why he had bought with state funds a rug that cost $25,000. Zimmerman had to prove he had spent only $250 of the $750 authorized for purchase of rugs. The governor himself denied UNM's request to send representatives from the board and administration to the annual meeting of the North Central Association of Colleges and Schools, even though the University's ten-year renewal of accreditation hung in the balance.

Internally, a former student, Mary Coan, the spouse of the late history professor Charles Coan, lobbied hard for a seat on the Board of Regents. She charged that many of the policies pursued at the University were "nothing short of educational suicide." She attributed much of UNM's problem to the imperious attitude of its faculty and administrators.[29]

The Zimmerman family was the first to live in the President's House. The day the family moved in, Dean Lena Clauve helped Mrs. Zimmerman unpack while the president went fishing.

Ethnic Tensions Escalate

New Mexico, with a Hispanic population of 52 percent and another 7 percent Native American, actually had a minority Anglo population. With the exception of the national Office of Negro Affairs (a part of the NYA), however, there was no national force to guide or coerce the nation toward equal opportunity for all groups at all levels of education. Schools like UNM had to go it alone in addressing the problems of educating students with Hispanic or Native backgrounds.

In the mid-1930s Hispanic leaders statewide began charging UNM with tolerating racial unpleasantness between Anglo and Hispanic students. These critics complained that no Hispanics were members of UNM fraternities or sororities. Michael Welsh noted that even the administration was aware of the problem.

> President Zimmerman had recognized the cliquishness and discriminatory practices from the time of his arrival on campus in 1925. Yet the appeal of membership among middle-class and upper-class Anglos, a segment of the student population able to finance its own education in the Depression, kept Zimmerman and his peers nationwide from punishing such transgressions too severely.[30]

This criticism was unusual in an age when ethnic tensions rarely generated notoriety. By 1932, Hispanic enrollment was 16 percent of UNM's student population. Hispanic enrollment had grown 1,500 percent in the 1920s, which could be considered remarkable because there was no state or federal pressure to admit Hispanics. There was no getting around the fact that in 1932 more than 70 percent of UNM students belonged to one or another social or fraternal organization, and few were Hispanics.

Opinion was divided. Some Hispanics downplayed the value of fraternity membership. Others saw the division as indicative of UNM's preference for the Anglo culture in a heavily Hispanic state. Five Hispanic legislators agreed that the lawmakers should correct issues the University could not or would not resolve. This led to the introduction of a resolution "urging that the President and the Board of Regents . . . in some positive and immediate manner attempt to lessen and eventually do away [with] the proved class discrimination that surely exists on the part of the membership of fraternities and sororities at UNM." Dubbed the "anti-fraternity" resolution, it failed, but it did exacerbate the prevailing criticism of UNM and its president.[31]

An article in the 1986 *New Mexico Historical Review* provided context for the controversy. Spanish Americans took pride in their descent from natives of Spain and tended to romanticize the New Mexico colonial period and shun protests over discrimination, wrote Phillip B. Gonzales. "As an extension of glorifying the past, Spanish Americans also reacted to racism's taint of anyone labeled Mexican by calling themselves 'white' and denying any Indian mixture in their past." What Gonzales called Hispano "cultural and physical distinctiveness" clashed with the "extreme cliquishness" of the Greek organizations. One victim was Juan A. Sedillo, son of a UNM Regent, who lost a childhood friend when the latter joined a fraternity. It was Sedillo who introduced the anti-fraternity bill.[32]

The worst was yet to come. In the spring of 1933, two young UNM scholars, Richard Page, professor of psychology, and George I. Sanchez of the College of Education, attempted to apply state-of-the-art methodologies to the ethnicity question. Page, who had been hired four years earlier from the University of Texas, did not hold to the theory that Hispanics were "uneducable." Sanchez, a native of Albuquerque and former schoolteacher in Bernalillo County, had deep concerns about bilingual education and a demonstrated gift for statistical research. Upon graduation from UNM, he accepted a fellowship from the General Education Board (GEB) to attend the University of Texas, followed by an additional year of work in social science at the University of Chicago to refine his research techniques. This led to negotiations among UNM, the GEB, and Sanchez for a $27,000 grant from the GEB to employ Sanchez under the joint sponsorship of UNM and the state government. Following receipt of his master's degree in 1931 in educational psychology and Spanish, Sanchez returned to New Mexico. In his native state, he conducted a whirlwind tour of schools and communities.

Sanchez also entered into negotiations with Richard Page to conduct a study of the attitudes Anglo high school students held about Hispanics and drafted a questionnaire to solicit opinions of Anglo and Hispanic students pertaining to alleged tension between the races. He planned to publish the research and reveal the bitterness both cultures harbored. Sanchez and Page formulated a twenty-page questionnaire and sent it to all senior high schools in New Mexico. The questions puzzled many recipients, though, as they could not interpret the pointed language of such queries as: "No matter how much you educate Spanish-speaking people, they are nothing but greasers." A political firestorm followed, once described as "the saddest moment in the history of UNM." As noted by Welsh:

All the forces of politics, economics, and culture that have shaped the state came into play, revealing the gulf between the urban university and its rural state, between Hispanic and Anglo leaders, and between warring political factions eager to seize power in the midst of chaos.[33]

All hell broke loose. Governor Seligman received an avalanche of mail, and newspapers rushed copies of the questionnaire into print. Sanchez was mystified and did not think much would come of the issue. Zimmerman considered the publicity "ridiculous" but found himself "helpless in the matter."

The naïveté of the two, however, soon crumbled amidst the escalating rhetoric. Mass meetings were held in Old Town and Barelas with speakers demanding an end to the discrimination at UNM and immediate dismissal of all parties responsible for the questionnaire. Rumors circulated about the existence of a lynching party in Old Town targeting the president and Page. On the night of April 27, there was a large outdoor meeting in Old Town Plaza where an angry mob carried weapons and shouted curses at UNM. Hispanic students reportedly told about the shame and embarrassment they felt at UNM, and others related they had been referred to as Greasers or Mexicans. Another said that Hispanics served but two functions for Anglos: "to provide votes on election day and to give Anglos all that could be obtained from the native and leave him poor and downtrodden." The most fiery speaker was Mrs. E. A. Perrault, a former New Mexico secretary of state. She scolded her fellow citizens and challenged the men in the audience to protest, saying, "The men are afraid to come to brass tacks and defend their own people."[34]

The governor responded quickly, advocating the dismissal of both Page and Sanchez. Zimmerman demurred, but appointed a committee to investigate the matter. The president, aware of Sanchez's respect and concern for fellow Hispanics, did not believe that such a "little mistake" in the phrasing of some questions should merit such drastic punishment as dismissal.

Sanchez received unexpected support from New Mexico's powerful senator, Bronson Cutting, who calmly reminded the governor, "I have been familiar with Mr. Sanchez's work in the state, and think that, on the whole, it has been of great value." He also stated to Zimmerman, "I did not believe drastic action should be taken on account of what was no doubt a mistake of judgment."

As the fateful day neared for the start of the investigation, Hispanic groups, primarily in northern New Mexico, were demanding Sanchez's dismissal, often adding that his retention would be an affront to Spanish Americans in New Mexico and a discredit to his position and his origin.

The investigative committee Zimmerman appointed, by this time referred to as the Espinosa Committee, met on May 2, 1933, in the offices of its chairman, Gilbert Espinosa. After listening to testimony from several persons, the committee recommended censure of Zimmerman and Sanchez and dismissal of Page.

The committee then turned to the larger problem of anti-Hispanic sentiment at UNM and reported that almost every witness was concerned about the social relationship between Hispanics and Anglos. The panel attributed this to the fraternities and sororities, whose members had testified there was not a single person with a Spanish surname in any of the fraternities at that time. While the committee found no open policy of discrimination, it did direct UNM to redouble its efforts to rid itself of an unjust and discriminatory situation. It asked for a Hispanic member on the Board of Regents.

Professor Page, finding himself with few friends and no options at UNM, resigned on May 10. He left Albuquerque under cover of darkness. His departure brought calm to the campus and for a brief period seemed to ease the tensions.[35]

The faculty, however, was up in arms and blamed the newspapers and anti-UNM factions outside the University. They expressed confidence in Page's professional competence and responsibility and believed UNM could and should put its own house in order on matters relating to the fraternities and sororities. In the city of Albuquerque, a mass meeting with more than seven hundred persons attending passed a vote of confidence in President Zimmerman and the Regents.

Despite the apparent backing for Sanchez, there were many who believed it would be better for all if he were to leave the state. The General Education Board concurred and offered to fund a one-year fellowship for Sanchez in the doctoral program in education at the University of California–Berkeley. On this note, Sanchez left New Mexico. Beyond the borders of New Mexico, however, few people knew of the anguish and anger that had swept the campus.[36]

Returning to New Mexico in 1934, Sanchez still had funding from the GEB for his statistical work. He resumed his ties with President Zimmerman, who had committed the University to enrolling larger numbers of Hispanic students in return for New Deal funding and sought ways to improve public schools so more Hispanics could meet entrance standards. Sanchez was elected president of the New Mexico Educational Association and successfully lobbied the legislature for a school funding equalization bill. Senator Cutting died in 1935, however, thus weakening Sanchez's ties to the Rockefeller Foundation's GEB and his political support in New Mexico. The legislature voted to withhold funds from the San José bilingual training program and the demographic research.[37]

Meanwhile, in 1933, there was cause for celebration on the campus when UNM was notified that its academic programs had been placed on the accreditation list of the Association of American Universities. New Mexico was the last of the forty-eight states to have an AAU-recognized school. Much to its disappointment, UNM was not granted membership in that prestigious organization, even though the College of Engineering was approved by the Engineering Council for Professional Development in 1937.

Governor Seligman died in 1934. His replacement was the equally conservative A. W. Hockenhull.[38]

Bronson Cutting played a brief but significant role in the development of UNM in the mid-1930s. Governor Dillon had appointed him to a vacancy in the U.S. Senate in 1927. Nominally a Republican, Cutting had been a strong supporter of Franklin D. Roosevelt and the New Deal in the national election of 1932. In response, Roosevelt initially granted Cutting control of some New Deal patronage in New Mexico, which allowed the state and UNM to receive large amounts of federal funding. New Mexico and Louisiana, with Senator Huey Long, soon led the nation in federal largesse.

Cutting was known as the Prince of Santa Fe. He had come to New Mexico as a tubercular in 1910 and soon dominated Santa Fe's cultural, political, and economic affairs. He was widely respected as a stockholder in its largest bank, benefactor of its museums and academic institutions, friend to artists and intellectuals, and publisher of the *Santa Fe New Mexican*. He was fluent in Spanish, French, German, and Arabic. He was both patron and *patrón* in Santa Fe.

In the election of 1934, his opponent was two-term Representative Dennis Chavez, a Democrat. In a bitterly contested election Cutting prevailed, winning after a recount by only 1,251 votes. Cutting was the only Republican candidate for the Senate elected that year. Chavez challenged the election, and an official inquiry was launched. Cutting was seated temporarily in the Senate while the investigation was under way.

After returning to New Mexico to gather some documents pertaining to the election, Cutting was flying back to Washington, D.C., on a TWA airplane when it crashed in a Missouri field in the middle of a thunderstorm on May 6, 1935. Cutting was killed, and the newly elected Democratic governor of New Mexico, Clyde Tingley, almost immediately appointed Dennis Chavez to the vacated Senate seat. UNM had lost a friend whose personal efforts made possible dramatic changes in the University.[39] Many feared that Cutting's death meant that UNM would no longer have the same access to New Deal agencies or private donors.

However, Tingley, Albuquerque's former City Commission chairman, had long been a strong advocate of the University and had close ties with many on the campus, including President Zimmerman. With this personal backing, UNM blossomed in the last half of the 1930s, with generous funding and support for programs and facilities from both state and federal sources.

More sad news came to the campus in 1934, with the death of Charles Hodgin. He died just six days after his seventy-seventh birthday while he was visiting in Pasadena, California. In a memorial service in March 1936, President Zimmerman said, "No one who ever walked with him on this campus, no one who ever studied with him in these halls, or who ever talked with him along the way, will ever need a material monument to recall to mind the nobility of his life and work among us."[40]

In Dean Shannon's last biennial report on the College of Arts and Sciences (1933–34), he acknowledged a substantial gift to the library from the Carnegie Foundation. Faculty strength had increased by 10 percent, but this was chiefly because of additions in the lower ranks and the use of part-time instructors. Only six tenured faculty members had resigned, all under circumstances that implied no dissatisfaction with the University. There had been an increase of about 40 percent in the number of professors with doctoral degrees, and research and publications by faculty over the four Depression years included more than 160 books and articles. Dean Shannon left at the end of the 1935 academic year to take a position at the University of Alabama.

By the fall of 1935, the College of Arts and Sciences had forty-seven full-time faculty. The salary range for professors was $3,000 to $3,500; for academic deans, $3,800 to $3,995; for the president, $7,000; and for the football coach, $4,800. The increase to the appropriation for UNM in 1935 was $100,000, which gave some reason to cheer.[41]

The General College was established in 1935. It was designed to direct attention to freshmen and sophomores and make special provisions for their remedial needs, if necessary.

The College of Fine Arts came a year later. George St. Clair was appointed dean. He was a poet and writer, a discerning critic, and a student and lover of art, the theatre, and music.[42] The 1934–35 catalog listed a summer field school in painting in Taos. Acting as "critic teachers" were the nationally prominent Taos painters who were putting New Mexico on the art map: Kenneth Adams, Oscar Berninghaus, Ernest Blumenschein, Victor Higgins, Ward Lockwood, Bert Phillips, Joseph Henry Sharp, and Walter Ufer.[43] The first prearchitecture concentration classes were offered in 1937 by Santa Fe architect William Burk, with five students enrolled. There had previously been architectural engineering courses and, in the Art Department, architectural design and history courses.[44] In 1936, the Home Economics Department was moved to the College of Education.

The College of Arts and Sciences was reorganized in 1936 as well. Upon the departure of Dean George Shannon, George P. Hammond assumed duties as head of the History Department, dean of the Graduate School, and dean of the upper division of the college. Jay Carroll Knode, a philosophy professor, became dean of both the General College and the lower division of arts and sciences. By 1938 it was determined that the system of two deans had not proved to be useful. Hammond thus continued as dean of the Graduate School, while Knode assumed the duties for the whole College of Arts and Sciences.

At approximately the same time, a Faculty Senate was created, consisting of the president, registrar, and bursar, all deans, department heads, and full professors, as well as two associate professors, two assistant professors, and one instructor.[45]

As the University, state, and nation entered into a period of economic recovery at the end of the 1930s, the number of degrees the College of Arts and Sciences granted increased by 40 percent over a two-year period. The beginning of the doctoral programs in the Graduate School was likewise hailed as progress for advanced studies.[46] Thirty-three master's degrees were awarded in 1936, and several academic programs began to achieve reputations throughout the West as among the best, especially anthropology, geology, and engineering.[47] The first PhD was awarded in 1937 in the field of history, and other departments, anthropology, biology, English, government, and modern languages, were also accepting candidates for doctoral degrees.

Dean J. C. Knode

Regent Jack Korber (shown here at commencement in 1952 between Governor Edwin Mechem and Regent Ethel Bond) had received hours of physical therapy from Roy Johnson as a boy after suffering polio. The coach came to the Korber home every morning for grueling exercises; when he was at an away game he sent his graduate athletic manager, Tom Popejoy, in his place. Korber progressed from being bedridden to using a wheelchair, then crutches. As a UNM student he was manager of Johnson's track team.

By fall 1939, the University's enrollment had reached 1,482. A year later it was 1,565. As an added feature, by 1936 Hispanic enrollment had increased to 28 percent of the total student body. By 1939, thirty-seven Latin American content courses were being taught in ten departments, and two new interdisciplinary undergraduate programs were developed, Latin American Diplomatic, Consular and Commercial Relations, and Latin American Studies.[48] By the time John Miles succeeded Clyde Tingley as governor in 1939, the University could also boast of a physical plant of nineteen buildings. Governor Miles appointed three Regents, including Jack Korber, who served from 1939 to 1959, a tenure exceeded only by Elias Stover's twenty-two years and Frank Clancy's twenty-one. Further signs of UNM's growing reputation were the elections of Professor George Hammond as president of the national history honorary, Phi Alpha Theta, and Professor Carroll Newsom from mathematics as president of the national math fraternity, Kappa Mu Epsilon. Enhancing UNM's reputation for serving the state, professors were flown from Albuquerque to Roswell, Clovis, Hobbs, and Carlsbad to offer courses for degree programs.

The University Press

Books and publications are like old gold to a University, as their value increases with age. A strong university press is one of the hallmarks of a great university. UNM can trace the beginnings of its press back to 1913 when Paul A. F. Walter, Sr., a former newspaperman and at that time secretary and business manager of the Museum of New Mexico and School of American Research, along with Edgar L. Hewett, director of these organizations, founded El Palacio Press in the historic Palace of the Governors at Santa Fe. Their publication, *El Palacio*, started as a monthly covering scientific, literary, and art news of the Spanish Southwest. Soon it became a weekly, the first to be devoted to archaeology and museum activities.

In 1929, President Zimmerman entered into a cooperative agreement with Hewett to coordinate the activities of the University with the museum and School of American Research. Walter donated the printing press, which was moved to the campus. His son, Paul Walter, Jr., a sociology professor, served briefly as director of the press, followed by Fred E. Harvey. The change of name to University of New Mexico Press was not made with the move, but happened gradually. The first book, *Givers of Life, the American Indians as Contributors to Civilization*, by Emma Franklin Estabrook, was published in 1931. Another early publication, *Practical Spoken Spanish*, by Francis M. Kercheville, became a perennial best seller and was still in print at the turn of the twenty-first century. By the time Hughes wrote the semicentennial history in 1939 the press was self-supporting, and its publications included the UNM catalog, *New Mexico Quarterly*, and the *New Mexico Business Review*; *El Palacio* had returned to the Museum of New Mexico.[49] The University of New Mexico Press not only published history, it made history by establishing a national reputation for quality.

A new fraternity house was added to the list in 1935: Alpha Delta Pi at the corner of University and Ash. The aerodynamic car is a Nash. Photo by Bill Winnie

Student Life

Images of the model student at UNM during the late 1920s and early 1930s were projected in advertisements in the student newspaper, the *Lobo*. Ads for clothing and cigarettes glamorized the sophistication of college life. Old Gold cigarettes encouraged students to smoke and issued disclaimers about the hazards of tobacco by the slogan, "Not a cough in a class-full."

As the Depression took hold, students took more pride in campus life, seemed more serious in their social behavior, and became more conservative in their political views. A *Lobo* survey revealed that more than half favored retaining the Prohibition laws. The debate team competed with football for feature coverage. Other polls revealed that political science students did not believe that conditions in the Pacific suggested an eventual war between Japan and the United States. A poll of women students showed that less than 30 percent admitted to attending UNM to find a husband and a plurality declared teaching careers were their main reason for enrolling. They also protested the lack of women in student government.[50]

Marie Hays, a 1936 graduate, provided a glimpse of life on the small campus.

> The relationship between the faculty and students probably was the most important thing about [the 1930s]. A very close relationship was fostered by President Zimmerman and his staff. We were all known by our first names—and when we did poorly on a test, it was a personal conference. You did not cut class as you knew the professor would call you on it. A great example was Dr. John Clark, Professor of Chemistry, who held 7:00 A.M. Help Sessions.[51]

One issue of this era was the admission of those who were then called Negro students to New Mexico public institutions of higher learning. In 1930, three Negro

Their clothes show individuality, but almost every one of these sorority members parted her hair severely.

Paul Brock, class of 1940, was proud of his letter sweater, earned for basketball, and he was also proud of his dirty corduroy pants. A 1930s alumna once told University Archivist Terry Gugliotta that the boys bought a new pair at the beginning of the school year and wore them, over and over, without washing them, so the pants could stand up on their own by the end of spring semester.

students who had graduated from New Mexico high schools were denied admission at New Mexico College of Agriculture and Mechanic Arts (A&M). When queried as to whether Negro students were allowed to enroll at UNM, President Zimmerman replied that there were a few and that no exclusion policy existed because that would have been contrary to the University's "inclusionary strategy" for Hispanics and Native Americans.[52]

Ethnic conflicts were not the only problem with the fraternities and sororities. When Zimmerman took office in 1927, more than half the student body belonged to these organizations. He observed that "a certain unfortunate spirit of petty rivalry" characterized some phases of Greek life at UNM. He was also concerned with attitudes that placed the fraternity or sorority above the University. One of the confrontations that arose revolved around elections for student government. The independents, students who did not belong to Greek organizations, opposed the concentration of student power in the tightly organized fraternity and sorority systems. They also accused the *Lobo* of favoring the Greek organizations and believed that students who did not have to work their way through college had more time to participate in student government and organizations.[53] The independents were in the minority, however, and their exclusion from leadership positions placed them at a disadvantage. Hence, despite the rhetoric lauding their contributions, it was a long time before there was any significant change.

Dean John Clark was an open advocate of Greek organizations. He viewed them as important contributors to the University's esprit de corps. Clark stated, "Contented, happy fraternity life leads to larger senior classes." He pointed out that at that time UNM had the only such organizations in the state and that they served as an effective recruiting tool for high school seniors. Clark thus encouraged the president and Regents to make land available east of the campus for fraternity and sorority houses. As enrollments grew, living space on campus became scarce, and dormitories had waiting lists. Furthermore, high rates for off-campus rentals and the threat of exposure to tuberculosis in rooming houses made those options less appealing. One solution was to accept Clark's recommendation to construct more fraternity and sorority houses, but that did not happen.[54]

Dean Lena C. Clauve

One of President Zimmerman's most significant appointments was the selection of Lena C. Clauve as dean of women, a post she held for thirty-two years, from 1929 to 1961. Dean Clauve was a 1925 BA graduate of UNM with a major in music. She had grown up in Indiana, and after graduation she taught in the Wabash consolidated county school for two years and then in the Wabash city schools, where she was supervisor of music for two years. One day, while teaching a class in Wabash, she was called to the telephone. The call was from President Zimmerman, who was attending a meeting in Chicago. He invited her to come to Chicago to be interviewed for the position of dean of women at UNM. Regretfully, she declined, pointing out that the invitation conflicted with the spring music festival for all junior and senior high school choruses at Wabash. Zimmerman replied he was sorry because it might mean she would not get the position. Two weeks later, she received a letter from Zimmerman offering her the job as dean of women. He said that her integrity in placing her students above the job made him realize she was just the person he wanted and needed. She was overjoyed. The president set no guidelines for her new position, just told her to use her common sense.

Clauve became a legend in her own time at UNM, with contributions that included writing the music for the school's fight song, "Hail to Thee, New Mexico." During World War II, as dean of both men and women, she was responsible for student employment, loans, housing, and supervision of fraternities and sororities, and she hired housemothers for both as well as for the dormitories. In 1930 she organized the Associated Women Students, which held tea parties and published a student handbook. For fifteen years, Dean Lena also continued to teach in the Music Department.

She was also a great founder, establishing chapters of Pi Lambda Theta, the education honorary, and Sigma Alpha Iota, the music honorary. Believing that each class should have an honorary to recognize outstanding young women, she founded Spurs for sophomore women and Las Campanas for juniors. She also was active with Mortar Board, the national honorary for senior women. In addition, Dean Clauve befriended foreign students, loaned students money, and got them jobs.

Betty Huning Hinton, a member of a pioneer New Mexico family and a recipient of both bachelor's and master's degrees from UNM, wrote a delightful tribute to Dean Clauve in 1989, which included this story.

Lena C. Clauve

> In the early years Lena sent out cards in early September to all new women students, assigning them an appointment time to come to her office. One night the campus police were patrolling and discovered a young woman sitting on the steps to the Administration Building. It was midnight. The policeman asked her what she was doing there. She said she had an appointment with Dean Clauve but Dean Clauve wasn't in. He looked at the card, and, of course, the card said 12 P.M.
>
> "Young lady, your appointment time is 12 P.M., and it is now 12 A.M. You'd better come back in the morning."
>
> The young student returned to the dormitory, rather shamefaced, to be greeted by the Dorm Mother who was almost frantic with worry.

Curfew in the 1930s was 10:00 P.M.

Another anecdote related to the opening of school one September in the 1930s. A dorm mother called Dean Clauve with the startling information that a young woman in the dormitory had a gun, and she refused to give it up. Dean Clauve went to the girl's room, where she saw the gun hanging on nails that had been driven into the inside of the door.

In her conversation with the girl Lena asked if her family did a great deal of hunting.

The girl said, "Oh, no."

Then Lena said, "Well, do you plan to hunt?"

Again the girl said, "Oh, no."

Lena's next question was, "Why do you have a gun?"

The girl's reply was, "My family was afraid we might have an Indian uprising."

"Why did you come to New Mexico then? We haven't had an Indian uprising in a hundred years."

"I came to study Anthropology because UNM has the best Anthropology Department in the Country. My family was opposed to my coming to New Mexico and the Wild West, so they bought me a gun."

Lena remarked, "You know we have Indian girls in the dormitory?"

The girl's rejoinder was, "No. How do they dress?"

"Well, they dress just like you and I do."

After the conversation, the girl finally unloaded the gun and gave it to Lena.

One of Dean Clauve's favorite stories on herself concerned a student-faculty dance held in the dining hall in the 1930s. As her partner danced her past President Zimmerman and his partner, Clauve caught her heel in the cuff of Zimmerman's tuxedo. They fell to the floor in a heap with her in Zimmerman's lap. Other dancers were helpless with laughter as they scrambled around to help the dean and the president to their feet. Zimmerman was a very dignified gentleman, but he, too, "was laughing when everybody was righted."[55]

Campus Development and Construction

While Tight is often praised as the president who first conceived the architectural style that led to UNM's image as the "pueblo on the mesa," President Zimmerman and the Regents of the late 1920s were responsible for bringing the style back into use. Through combinations of bond issues, federal programs, gifts, and legislative appropriations, many buildings that forever defined the University of New Mexico campus were erected during his tenure.

When Zimmerman was appointed president on a temporary basis on February 15, 1927, he hit the ground running. By March 14 the Board of Regents was approving the issuance of building and improvement bonds for four buildings. Final plans for the gymnasium, lecture hall, men's dorm, and biology building, all done in Pueblo Style, were presented to the board on August 2.

The board in its first meeting of 1928 approved the plan to move the sundial, the howitzer (a World War I memorial), and the drinking fountain to make way for a walk leading to the Administration Building from Sara Raynolds Hall. The board also approved a proposal to make land available to lease to fraternities and sororities.[56] President Zimmerman encouraged the building program of the fraternities and sororities, which added beauty and solidarity to the Pueblo Style campus. In rapid order, fraternities and sororities soon were building or acquiring their own houses.[57]

At Zimmerman's inauguration as president on June 4, 1928, he not only smoked the peace pipe with Indian chiefs for New Mexico tribes, but also took the lead in giving thanks for the bond funds to build four new buildings. He praised the architecture "so appropriate" to New Mexico's environment and emphasized the need for even more buildings and general campus development.

Mrs. Reed Holloman, as she was called in official documents although she signed her letters to Zimmerman as Alice, was elected president of the Board of Regents for the third time in 1928. The board gave approval to the president to borrow $8,000 to purchase trees and shrubs and install a sprinkler system and grass. The president later reported that a total of 481 trees had been planted. By 1929, the board had also approved a subdivision named Sorority Row on Roma, and the Chi Omega sorority was assigned a lot. Meeting on November 21, 1929, the executive committee of the board voted for completion of the final plans for a president's home and authorized preliminary plans for a women's dorm and a classroom building.

The Board of Regents, meeting on December 14, 1929, named the new gymnasium for Hugh Carlisle. He was one of five UNM students who had died during World War I.

Bids were received February 2, 1930, for some campus projects that had already been approved, including the president's home, which Miles Brittelle, Sr., designed. In December of that year, plans were approved for an addition to the Science and Engineering Building, sometimes called Hadley Hall II. A month later, on January 26, 1931, a contract was awarded and construction began.

In July 1931, the first of several contracts for a football stadium was awarded, and in early 1932, authorization was approved for a five-thousand-seat addition. Other recreational and athletic facilities constructed were an open-air swimming pool to the west of Carlisle Gym and tennis courts. Finally, after years of service and frequent relocations, the old wooden gymnasium was demolished during the winter of 1933–34.

By 1933, federal make-work programs financed many construction and landscape projects at UNM, including several large buildings. At that time John Gaw Meem, a Santa Fe architect famous for preservation of historic structures and adaption of the Spanish colonial, Pueblo, and Territorial styles for new buildings, was retained and began work on some of his finest buildings. Scholes Hall and Zimmerman Library, in particular, established a standard of design for all future buildings at the University of New Mexico.

In the spring of 1934 President Zimmerman told the governor and legislature that the University needed both state and federal funds for a long-term program to build substantial facilities.

Carlisle Gym was built around the facilities for the campus radio station and opened in 1929.

Scholes Hall

For four years, the plan of erecting small and absolutely necessary structures to take care of immediately pressing needs has been followed. Such a policy is short-sighted, costly in the long run, and can be justified only on the grounds that funds for an adequate, economical and long term building program have not been available.

We are in the process of filling up the campus with small, ordinary, and unimposing buildings, inadequate for the future, and making exceedingly difficult adequate building plans for the future.[58]

In August 1934, an application from UNM to the federal government for a grant and a low-interest PWA loan to construct an office-classroom-laboratory building was approved. The 1934 legislature passed a bill authorizing use of student fees and income from land and the permanent fund to obtain the matching funds for the PWA grant. Meem was selected to design the building, which eventually came to be called Scholes Hall.

At the time Terrace Street, the main street of the campus, was closed, and the new administration building was centered on the street, creating an axis all the way to Central Avenue. Meem based his exterior design on San Esteban del Rey Church at Acoma with its two towers. Bids were received on November 22, 1934, and construction was soon under way. When the building was completed, the president, bursar, registrar, and the deans moved into the west wing of the first floor. The Anthropology Department took the east wing, and the Anthropology Museum was located in the center portion of the same floor. Geology and physics moved into the second floor, and psychology was on the third floor. A campus-wide telephone switchboard was installed in the bursar's office.

Across the campus the old Administration Building in 1936 was renamed in honor of the late Charles Hodgin. In addition to the name change there were several relocations in this, the oldest building on the campus. Education stayed put, with Dean Simon Nanninga moving into the old president's office. The departments of English and Modern Languages were given space in the old facility. Classics, sociology, philosophy, and government were moved to the old Science Building.

J. Raymond Stuart, chief accountant of the University, recalled President Zimmerman telling him in 1935 or 1936 that the state had offered to sell about two thousand acres east of Albuquerque to UNM for $3 an acre. Stuart recommended the purchase after inspecting the tract. Later there were several land swaps with the City of Albuquerque. Stuart recalled in 1975, "A good part of the land thus acquired now embraces the University's South Campus, including the football stadium, the basketball gymnasium, and the golf course."[59]

At their first meeting in January, 1936, the Regents officially accepted the Administration Building, which opened on February 3, the beginning of the spring semester. The board also approved the sites for the new library and heating plant. At the prodding of the Dean of Engineering Marshall Farris, the board authorized houses for faculty members to be built on Roma and Las Lomas west of the president's home with Federal Housing Administration loans. A new building for the State Health Laboratory was bid in March 1936, and the Student Union Building (SUB) contract was approved in July of that year.

On September 25, 1937, more than a thousand people attended the dedication of the Student Union Building following a football victory. In December of that year the board approved lighting for the football field, which was ready for the 1938 season.

The University was notified in March 1937 that President Roosevelt had approved an allocation of $34,345 toward construction of a men's dormitory. This was built and called the Co-Op Dormitory (today it is the Naval Science Building). In addition, the WPA approved a project to remodel the old library for the Art Department.

In order to house the growing student body, the University administration planned to build a men's dorm, Bandelier Hall, on the west side of the dining hall and a women's unit on the east side of old Hokona Hall, to be named for alumna and former Regent Frances Halloran Marron. The construction of these new residence halls necessitated a new name for what had been called the New Men's Dormitory. The name was changed to Yatoka, which some thought to be an Indian word meaning "sun." Others said it was a Kiowa word meaning "thunderbird."[60] In any case, the dorm had a new name.

Meanwhile, construction on the library, the biggest, most important building on the campus, was under way. Bids were received on October 31, 1936; ground was broken on December 2, 1936; and on March 5, 1938, Mrs. James F. Zimmerman and students and faculty moved some of the books to the completed library with the University band leading the way.[61]

That same day, Kenneth Adams, artist in residence at the University, was commissioned to paint four murals on panels behind the library's circulation desk. A Carnegie Foundation grant funded the project. Van Deren Coke, director of the University Art Museum, wrote in his 1963 book *Taos and Santa Fe: The Artist's Environment, 1882–1942,* that Adams's style was "simple and unadorned" and that for the murals he "used a flat, linear technique to create a formal design suitable to the

Zimmerman Library in the winter of 1948.
Photo by Sherman Wengerd

architectural enframement and the Indian theme of the work."[62] Hughes noted that the murals added to the other Southwestern elements of the library building.

> The towering new building was designed and guarded in its architectural authenticity by John Gaw Meem . . . Colonnaded portals, wrought iron grilles, high wood ceilings with carved vigas and savions, authentic beams and corbels, diagonal latillas, carved doors and cases, Mexican tin lighting fixtures hand-made by native craftsmen under the direction of Walter B. Gilbert—all is beautifully created in the Spanish and Indian tradition of the Southwest.[63]

It may have been the age of the Great Depression for the rest of the country, and salary-wise it was a tough time for University employees, but seldom in the history of UNM has there been such a boom in campus development and construction. Big buildings, little buildings, grass and trees, athletic facilities—a marvelous physical plant had been created. The unique Southwestern architectural style gave the University campus a look of dignity and harmony as well as beauty.

Athletics

The late 1920s and the decade of the 1930s marked an important era in the history of sports in the United States. Athletics, both for participants and spectators, provided an outlet for interest and effort during the idleness of the Depression. In tune with the growing national interest in sports, UNM increased its emphasis on intercollegiate athletics. At this time there was no official intercollegiate athletics program for women at UNM or anywhere else. Women, however, participated rigorously and enthusiastically in intramural athletic competition.[64]

In order to have a football field, the UNM athletic director, Roy Johnson, in 1927 borrowed a plow and a team of horses and made the barren earth ready for seeding. Since the grass needed water, Johnson enlisted the aid of a friend and UNM sports fan, Clyde Tingley, then an Albuquerque city commissioner. In the spring of 1927, city construction crews were laying a water line from downtown to the heights directly east of the University. The water line ran beside Central Avenue, about two hundred yards from the football field. Tingley and Johnson conspired to connect another line from the field to the city's line, and soon the football field was green and grassy. It was years before their secret was discovered, and by that time the University had its own water supply.[65]

To be competitive in intercollegiate sports, it was necessary to improve the athletic facilities at UNM. In 1932 the football field was moved northward to a site just west of where the modern Student Union Building now stands. The field was seeded and maintained for varsity play. In 1934, an adjacent stadium was built at a total cost of $34,000, of which $9,000 came from federal PWA funds. The facility included space to house the departments of physical education and athletics, and together with Carlisle Gymnasium, UNM's athletic complex was proudly hailed as one of finest in the Southwest. Besides the varsity field, another grass practice field for football and other sports was constructed east of the main field. Bleachers to seat five thousand spectators were added at a later date.

On October 12, 1929, the Lobo football squad made what has been labeled as the first known flight of a football team to play an away game. The team flew to Pasadena, California, in two commercial Ford Tri-Motor airplanes to play Occidental College. Traveling for half-fare, receiving free hotel accommodations from a Pasadena establishment, and given a game guarantee of $5,000, the Lobos lost the game but made history. Johnson, never known to gamble, sent the first team by train while the rest of the squad traveled by air. Coming back to Albuquerque after the game, the first team was on the airplanes, and the reserves traveled by rail.[66]

An important reason for the growth of sports in this era was the use of a greater number of coaches. No longer was one individual expected to fill the fatherly role of coaching all sports, as head coaches were hired, fired, and subjected to the expectation of producing victorious teams. Winning in football was particularly important, as it provided much of the funding for the total program. Booster clubs were organized to promote the advancement of UNM athletics through fund raising and recruiting. Cheerleaders were appointed. A season ticket for home Lobo football games cost $5, a substantial savings over paying $2 per ticket for individual games. Crowds increased, including a record sixty-five hundred spectators at the 1938 UNM–Colorado A&M game in Albuquerque.

Zimmerman Stadium was built in phases as money became available. It was completed in 1934. Beneath the seat banks on the west side were offices and classrooms.

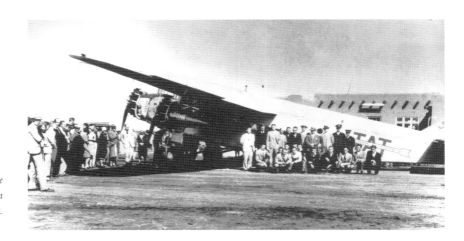

Players, coaches, and crew posed in front of one of the Ford Tri-Motor planes that that took them to Pasadena for a football game in 1927.

By far the most important development was the organization of the Border Conference in 1931. Its members were Texas Technological University at Lubbock, Arizona State University at Tempe, the University of Arizona at Tucson, Arizona State Normal School at Flagstaff, New Mexico A&M at Las Cruces, and the University of New Mexico. Leaders in the creation of this new conference were UNM's Roy Johnson and J. F. "Pop" McKale, the long time director of athletics at the University of Arizona.

Membership in the conference had many tangible benefits. Freshmen were ruled ineligible for varsity competition, thus giving first-year men an opportunity to familiarize themselves with University life. Standards for academic and residence eligibility were raised, as were those for transferring athletes. Scheduling became an orderly process with home-and-home arrangements. In addition, the so-called minor sports received more attention with healthy dual-meet schedules and annual conference championship meets. Football and basketball championships were determined by the number of wins and losses against conference opponents.[67]

With a stronger emphasis on winning, Roy Johnson, who had headed the UNM football program throughout the 1920s, came under heavy fire from off-campus boosters and sometimes the newspapers. Much of the criticism was aimed at his philosophy of not using freshmen players and what were regarded as his archaic recruiting practices. He actually scorned the whole idea of recruiting, especially those he regarded as tramp athletes. What the zealous alumni and Lobo football followers really wanted was a winning team. Although Johnson's overall record had been respectable—forty wins, thirty-two losses, and six ties—there were howls for his scalp. While there were those who supported him and his philosophy, he was relieved of his responsibilities for football in 1929. Because of his stature and integrity, he was retained as athletic director. After a two-year absence from coaching, Johnson once again assumed the duties as head coach of basketball and track and field.

The hunt for a football coach was on, and former Notre Dame star Charles Riley was appointed. Riley proved to be a big disappointment as his teams won but three games in three years. In the face of mounting criticism, Riley was fired in the spring of 1934.

The hunt resumed, and the search culminated in the hiring of Gwinn Henry, a "quiet, taciturn individual with a facility for producing solid results." A football, basketball, and Olympic-caliber track star at Southwestern University in Texas, he had been highly successful at the University of Missouri before becoming the head coach of the St. Louis Gunners, a professional team, a post he held when UNM hired him. Henry, a likable individual described as "shy, retiring, humble," in his first year as coach led the 1934 team to one of the University's finest football seasons ever. The team won eight games and lost one while also garnering the Border Conference championship.

Henry coached two more years at UNM, one successful with a six and four record, the other not so successful with two wins and seven losses. The 1936 season sparked heavy criticism from elements outside the University. Early in 1937 he resigned as coach to accept the position as athletic director at the University of Kansas.

Ted Shipkey, a former Stanford University football All-American and former football coach at Arizona State University, became UNM's fourth football coach in seven years. To even the most casual of observers, it became evident that football coaches at UNM in the 1930s were turning over almost as fast as members of the Board of Regents. Shipkey, however, turned out to be a willing and successful recruiter and soon built teams that were highly competitive. His records for the rest of 1930s were good and culminated in two outstanding campaigns, 1938 (eight wins and three losses) and 1939 (eight and two). The 1939 team also played in the Sun Bowl in El Paso, the first UNM team to participate in a bowl game.[68]

Basketball continued to compete with football for spectator interest during the thirties. It experienced its greatest success during the early and middle portion of the decade, but finished in a state of depression and despair for the future. The games were played in Carlisle Gym, which was considered to be a spacious facility. With membership in the Border Conference, scheduling became easier, and the number of games increased. Some of the trips to away games meant week-long absences by the student-athletes, though, a fact viewed with disfavor by the faculty and administration. Johnson coached UNM basketball in 1930–31. He relinquished the position for two years to focus on his duties as athletic director. Replacing him during that time, Tom Churchill, a former University of Oklahoma athlete, led the Lobos to two good seasons in which the team won twenty-three games while losing twelve and in 1933 won the Border Conference championship.

Johnson resumed the job of head coach in 1934–35, but the program went steadily downhill for the next six years. He ended his career as head coach in 1940.[69]

The Border Conference held its first annual championship track and field meet in 1932. The University of Arizona dominated the meet for the rest of the decade. The Lobos placed second four times and third four times. Roy Johnson continued as head coach of track and field during this era, except for the 1937 season when Gwinn

Henry was at the helm. Johnson never changed his philosophy about recruiting athletes, and as a result, little or no scholarship aid for track and field was provided. Johnson continued to rely on the talents of athletes who participated in other sports on the campus, primarily football and basketball.[70]

Through most of the 1930s, baseball was completely ignored, mostly because of the emphasis on track and field and the cost of travel. Signs of revival occurred in 1939, with the University's affiliation with the Border Conference and the leadership of former UNM athlete Johnny Dolzadelli.[71]

Interest in tennis soared in this decade as the sport began to be financed on a level necessary to compete with other institutions. The coaching of Benjamin Sacks resulted in outstanding success in dual meets against intrastate rivals. UNM finished second three out of the four times it competed in the Border Conference championship tournament between 1935 and 1939. Sacks resigned as coach in 1939 to devote full time to his duties in the History Department and was succeeded by the football coach, Shipkey.[72]

There was only a single dual meet in cross-country in this era, with the UNM runners losing to New Mexico A&M 10–11 in 1934.

The sport of swimming, which Jack McFarland introduced at the University in 1929–30, also experienced limited activity during the decade and disappeared from the UNM intercollegiate athletic scene in 1934.

Boxing in the 1930s at UNM experienced first a rapid rise in popularity and then a decline at the hands of fearful administrators. The Border Conference recognized boxing as a conference sport in 1934 and held conference tournaments every winter until 1938, when the sport disappeared from the conference. Under the leadership of Coach Willis Barnes, boxing enjoyed several successful seasons at UNM. In 1935 UNM captured the conference championship, with four members of the team winning their weight divisions.[73]

The Fiftieth Anniversary—1939

The year 1889, when the bill authorizing the creation of the University of New Mexico was passed, is celebrated as the official founding date of the institution, although it did not open its doors to students until the fall of 1892. Therefore, the time for celebrating the fiftieth anniversary of the founding was 1939.

The University's biannual report for 1939–41 provided glimpses of the progress of the first fifty years. There were four administrative officers and 139 faculty members. Fall-semester enrollment was 1,713 in 1941. Operating funds were slightly more than $63,000. Private donations in 1938–39 totaled almost $39,000 and included two gifts for the UNM community school in Nambé and one for the Taos County Adult Education Project. An anonymous donor gave $150 "to buy books in the field of wit and humor." Federal funding included more than $16,000 in student aid through the National Youth Administration and almost $158,000 from the Works Progress Administration for materials and labor at Chaco Canyon, the Harwood Foundation in Taos, and on the campus.[74]

The University was also celebrating enhancements to its library in 1939. The legislature appropriated $20,000 for the purchase of the Van de Velde collection of materials on the Southwest and Mexico. The Catron family, pioneers in New Mexico ranching, finance, and politics, donated its library. In addition, a Rockefeller Foundation grant allowed the purchase of the complete Library of Congress card catalog.[75]

One of the highlights of the semicentennial celebration was a charming history of the University written by Dorothy Hughes. She was a graduate student and teaching assistant in the English Department who went on to be an Edgar Award-winning mystery writer. In her preface to *Pueblo on the Mesa*, she related how she was called into the office of President James Zimmerman in February 1939. The president requested that she write the book.[76] The due date was June 1939, and she met it.

Hughes ends her book by quoting from one of Zimmerman's earlier speeches, one that captures the aspirations and tone of his long, distinguished tenure as the University's president.

The University of New Mexico has suffered too much by unfavorable comparisons with long-established institutions. Each new step taken has been toward a goal which many other universities reached long ago. Rightfully we may be proud of each advance. The University has been young, small, and poor; it is still so, in comparison with most universities in the country. Its youth, however, gives it a vigor that the old ones may lack . . . That the University is financially poor is not unusual in university histories; so was each university at one time, and each had to struggle through many years for sufficient maintenance. The University of New Mexico . . . has, in truth, scarcely begun.[77] ■

The north edge of the Central Campus (right) was anchored by the Anthropology Building, Scholes Hall, and Zimmerman Library in 1941—as it still was sixty years later. Hodgin and Rodey halls are at the upper left.

CHAPTER TEN

Administration of James F. Zimmerman, Part 2

1940–45

Albuquerque and the University of New Mexico in the 1940s both underwent their most significant social changes to date. The implications went much deeper than the ramifications of the First World War. World War II literally transformed Albuquerque from a peaceful, sun-drenched, slowly growing community into a major city humming with the nation's wartime effort.[1]

As early as 1938, the storm clouds of war in Europe had begun to throw a shadow over college campuses in the United States. The world had witnessed the capitulation of many European countries to Adolf Hitler, as well as President Lázaro Cárdenas's nationalization of Mexican oil production. At the same time, the U.S. House Un-American Activities Committee began to ferret out suspected Communist forces within American government, business, and educational institutions. The tension escalated in 1939 with Germany's invasion of Poland. Congress approved the Selective Service Act a year later, and the draft began to remove bright young students for military service that ultimately would take them to all parts of the world.[2]

As Marc Simmons says, when America entered World War II, "the strong trend toward economic recovery . . . blossomed into full-blown prosperity" for Albuquerque.[3] The city was in a good position to become a major center for military training, wartime industries, and weapons research. Further, Albuquerque's potential as a center for aviation attracted the attention of the federal government as well. A million-dollar municipal airport was opened on the East Mesa in August 1939. A year later the United States Army Air Corps designated the city as a service station for military planes. Land adjacent to the municipal air field was leased to the government in 1941 to train Flying Fortress crews. This became Kirtland Field in 1942.

The president of the National Academy of Sciences informed UNM President James F. Zimmerman of various federal research programs targeted for national security funding and requested names of UNM faculty who could work for them. Zimmerman suggested E. J. Workman of the Physics Department, an expert in weather and related meteorological phenomena. He became the director of a special research project that developed an explosive projectile the Navy would later use as a strategic weapon.[4] After the war it was revealed that the top-secret VT proximity fuse, which caused a shell or projectile to explode automatically when it neared an

Campus publicity photos during World War II often featured smiling coeds and sailors.

enemy target, had played a key role in the defense of Britain against Nazi bombs, in the defeat of the Germans at the Battle of the Bulge, and in the Pacific Ocean battles with the Japanese. The project earned Workman top honors from the Navy, Army, and New Mexico Academy of Science.[5]

Workman, who held a doctorate in physics from the University of Virginia, had been at the University since 1933. After the war he became president of the New Mexico Institute of Mining and Technology, serving there for eighteen years before moving on to the University of Hawaii.

In the meantime, not only in New Mexico but throughout the country, the daily lives of people changed. They saved cooking fat, old rubber tires, newspapers, and scrap metal, which various patriotic organizations collected for use in the nation's war factories. They bought war bonds and got used to ration books for gasoline. They gave up or cut back on such scarce luxuries as nylon stockings, metal toys, choice cuts of meat, and real butter. Even metal coat hangers were in short supply.

Family dining at restaurants increased, along with visits to nightclubs and supper clubs. Dancing was still a popular form of entertainment, especially the new craze, the jitterbug. The pin-up girls attired in scanty two-piece bathing suits could be viewed all the way from a soldier's locker on a military base to war theaters in the Pacific and Europe, or the front pages of Albuquerque's daily newspapers.

The effect on Albuquerque was profound and lasting. The establishment of Kirtland Air Force Base and, after the war, Los Alamos and Sandia National

President Zimmerman

Laboratories deeply influenced the economy of both state and city. The federally sponsored scientific research and development programs attracted highly educated men and women who brought with them a new, often more affluent lifestyle, including a hunger for better educational services at all levels.

At the University of New Mexico there also was a rapidly growing cosmopolitan atmosphere. During the war a large percentage of the University's enrollment was women. Of the men on the campus, almost three-quarters were in the Navy. They came from all parts of the country for specialized training leading to officer status.[6]

Zimmerman and Popejoy

As the threat of the war increased, Zimmerman suffered a setback of his own. In March 1939, while driving back from Hot Springs, New Mexico, he suffered a massive heart attack. At that time, the highway was unpaved, and there were no medical services along the way. Zimmerman and his wife managed to return to Albuquerque, but the time spent without medical care had its effect. The president lay seriously ill for several weeks, barely recuperating to participate in the celebration of the semicentennial of the University.[7]

During the time of his illness and recovery, indeed, for much of his remaining four years as president, Zimmerman relied heavily on Tom Popejoy, who had become the president's executive assistant in 1935. No stranger to the UNM campus,

Popejoy had received his degree in 1923. The former football hero had held a series of administrative posts, including comptroller, and was recognized for his ability to resolve fiscal and budgetary problems. Zimmerman released Popejoy from some of his responsibilities in 1935 to serve as assistant state director of the National Youth Administration, a critical feature of student recruitment and retention, under the supervision of Clinton P. Anderson, future New Mexico congressman and senator. Popejoy was named to replace Anderson as state NYA director in 1936. In January 1939, he moved to Washington, D.C., to become deputy director of the national office of NYA.

Popejoy enjoyed the support of Governor Clyde Tingley, who sought to strengthen the state by applying for every conceivable federal program. Popejoy returned to Albuquerque and UNM in February 1940, but while in Washington he had seen to it that New Mexico in general, and UNM in particular, remained favorites of New Deal officials.[8]

Clyde Tingley

Closely intertwined with the University of New Mexico and President James Zimmerman throughout the late 1920s, the 1930s, and the first half of the 1940s was Albuquerque city commissioner and self-proclaimed mayor Clyde Tingley. He also served as governor of New Mexico from 1934 to 1938. Described as a "gruff, thick-skinned, combative politician" who spoke "the rough and ungrammatical language of the laboring man," Tingley may have lacked polish, but he had the ability to lead.

Tingley was born in a log cabin in rural Ohio on January 5, 1881. While still in his twenties, he was superintendent of a motorcar company in Bowling Green, Ohio, when he met and wooed Carrie Wooster, a member of a wealthy and prominent family. Before they could get married, however, she became ill with tuberculosis. Upon the advice of her physician, she went west, getting off the train in Albuquerque. Tingley soon joined her, and they were married on April 21, 1911. They set up housekeeping with Carrie's mother in one of the health-seeker cottages on Iron Avenue.

Tingley, a natural politician, gloried in the limelight and public exposure that went with political offices and was elected to the City Commission in 1916. He served until 1934, and for twelve of those years he was chairman of the commission and anointed himself with the title of mayor, believing that the prestige of the city warranted a mayor. He left the post when he was elected governor of New Mexico.

While sometimes regarded as autocratic, he was scrupulously honest, which fit with his main aim in life: not to become rich but to get reelected. Under his direction, Albuquerque was beautified. Trees were planted, weeds were cleared from vacant lots, and windblown trash was swept from gutters. He led in the construction of public facilities, including railroad overpasses, the Little Theater, the zoo, an airport terminal, and buildings on the State Fairgrounds. His name was attached to many projects, including Tingley Drive, Tingley Field, Tingley Beach, and Tingley Coliseum. It was said that modesty was not part of his nature.

It was Tingley's ability to get things done that paid dividends during the darkest days of the Great Depression. In the federal relief agencies President Roosevelt created soon after his inauguration in March 1933, Tingley saw the opportunity to promote the economy and reputation of Albuquerque. As described by historian Marc Simmons: "His mind became a fertile field, sprouting a bumper crop of ideas about how to get and use public project funds."

When elected governor in 1934, Tingley parlayed his new rank and support of Roosevelt's New Deal into a personal friendship with the president. Tingley was said to have the president's ear. This gave him direct access to the White House and to heads of federal administrative agencies. He frequently traveled to Washington to seek aid for New Mexico, Albuquerque, and the University of New Mexico. With Tingley's advocacy and backing, UNM became the largest single beneficiary of WPA projects in New Mexico, which resulted in the construction of Zimmerman Library, Scholes Hall, the stadium, and many other facilities.[9]

George I. Sanchez

It should be noted that presidents of state universities often have their greatest success when there is a sympathetic governor in office. Zimmerman was certainly fortunate to have the friendship, support, and even the ear of Governor Tingley. Although lacking a formal education himself, Tingley appreciated the contributions of a great university to a city and a state.

George I. Sanchez—Again

George I. Sanchez, the researcher who had distributed the much-criticized ethnic questionnaire, returned to the UNM campus in 1934 from his PhD program at the University of California–Berkeley. He was eager to continue his social-science–based research and public policy advocacy on behalf of his fellow Hispanics. He also taught part-time at UNM in educational psychology.

That same year Sanchez became president of the New Mexico National Education Association and traveled the state to call for fairness in tax spending on public education. In the spring of 1935, the legislature and Governor Tingley approved the state's first redistribution of tax revenues based solely on per-pupil attendance. Sanchez accepted a fellowship from the Julius Rosenwald Fund of Chicago to duplicate his pioneering research in Mexico, which at that time was undergoing dramatic reform efforts. Based on that work, Sanchez wrote *Education: A Revolution in Mexico* in 1936.

Sanchez became highly critical of his native state in 1940 for what he viewed as exploitation of the Coronado Quarto Centennial celebrating the four-hundredth anniversary of the arrival of the Spaniards. Sanchez believed that the reality of illiteracy, disease, poverty, and loss of land among the state's Hispanic population did not square with plans for a celebration and took exception to those activities designed for tourist appeal and commercial gain.

In 1940 Sanchez moved from New Mexico to Texas. By this time his book, *The Prophet Without Honor*, had received national acclaim. The publication of *Forgotten*

People, his study of the plight of Hispanics in northern New Mexico, followed.[10] His fame and productivity blossomed in Texas, and Sanchez achieved national prominence for his research on education and ethnicity. He was considered the leading authority on bilingual education.

Zimmerman Administration Continues

The enrollment in the 1940 fall semester was 1,565. As the University entered the 1940s, Zimmerman's poor health and Popejoy's absence in Washington left the campus somewhat in limbo. The ailing president nonetheless continued to press for a link to the state's multicultural population. He built on the Latin American Studies program established in 1938 and sought to broaden it by emphasizing UNM's offerings in Spanish language and literature as well as Southwestern and Hispanic history. The head of the Modern Languages Department, Francis Kercheville, was organizing summer excursions to Mexico for students, faculty, and community participants.[11] UNM also added to the regional influence in anthropology, art, biology, economics, education, government, and sociology. The president further sought to prepare New Mexico students for participation in Latin American diplomatic, consular, and commercial relations and embraced FDR's Good Neighbor Policy of hemispheric defense and solidarity.[12]

For the quarto centennial President Zimmerman chaired a committee that put on a commemoration of the Spanish *entrada* to New Mexico in 1540, and the University library played a role in the celebration's research, exhibits, and presentations. In October 1940 the Southwestern Library Association held its convention in Albuquerque, with President Zimmerman and Librarian Wilma Loy Shelton playing prominent parts.

In 1941 the School of Inter-American Affairs was established, with Joaquín Ortega as its director. A native of Spain, Ortega had earned graduate degrees at the University of Wisconsin, then joined the faculty there and helped establish what he called "the leading Spanish department in this country," as well as the first interdepartmental curriculum in inter-American affairs.[13]

The bombing of Pearl Harbor and the actual outbreak of war in December 1941 profoundly affected UNM. The Biennial Report to the Regents from President Zimmerman on January 1, 1943, stated: "The first obligation of the University is its share in winning the war. The second obligation is the preservation of our educational effort on all fronts, and the third and final obligation is that of preparation for the tasks which will be required of all of us when peace comes." The president promised that the University would continue its programs in all its colleges.

Conversion to a wartime campus resulted in great changes at UNM. The April 1943 issue of the *UNM Alumnus* reported that the meteorology students in the Army Air Corps program had been assigned quarters in three dormitories and told to get ready for an accelerated program of studies in the Physics Department. Quarters for officers were established in the student union, and the patio of the SUB, "once a place for student loafing, was filled with soldiers waiting for instructions or standing at attention listening to orders." When they were not in class, the soldiers were drilling on the sandy lot by the side of Hokona Hall or studying at the library. Civilian pilot trainees who had formerly occupied one of the dorms were now moved into the Kappa Alpha fraternity house.[14]

Notwithstanding the large, vigorous Navy reserve unit on the campus, enrollments declined in every department. At the time of Zimmerman's report, twenty-seven members of the faculty were on leave for military duties, and the University's problems included replacing them, coping with fluctuating enrollments, dealing with students who left for service in the middle of a course, and maintaining academic standards. Almost every academic department made shifts in its programs to accommodate the war and foreign policy of the United States. Faculty morale and student spirit, however, were reported to be "excellent."[15]

Campus Development and Construction

World War II strongly influenced campus development and construction. Although the nation was not at war in 1940, many UNM students enrolled in a pilot-training program, which prompted Dean of Engineering Marshall Farris to send a memo to President Zimmerman recommending a school of aviation. The Regents approved an addition to a wing of the Engineering Building for an aeronautical engineering program. The University also bought material for the Co-Op Dormitory through the Government Procurement Office at a large discount, and ground was broken for the dormitory in September 1940.

The University was notified in late 1940 that it would receive a prefabricated steel building to house the National Youth Administration program. This caused great concern because its exterior did not conform to the Pueblo Style of architecture. The NYA added roughly $6,000 to modify the exterior, however, and John Gaw Meem added a portal with stuccoed corner walls, wood columns, corbels, and beams to give it the UNM look. The building was located just south of the Civil Engineering Building, but was demolished when the Mechanical Engineering Building was erected in 1979–80.[16]

After the bombing of Pearl Harbor in December 1941, a grant for a new wing on Hokona Hall was approved, but construction was deferred until the war ended. Sixteen other projects were also put on hold. The Co-Op Dormitory was completed and named Mesa Vista Hall (I), and Kwataka Hall was closed for remodeling into offices for Inter-American Affairs.

By 1943, construction was suspended on all projects except those with an immediate effect on the war effort. The Board of Regents appointed a building committee charged with surveying and listing the needs of the University for the next fifteen years.[17]

Athletics

Intercollegiate athletics at UNM were sharply curtailed once the country entered the war. Football and basketball teams played only limited schedules and all other sports were canceled. By 1942–43, the Border Conference had abandoned all athletic activities. There were not enough athletes on the respective campuses to participate in most sports. In addition, gasoline shortages and restricted train accommodations made team travel virtually impossible.[18]

On the UNM campus, the two decades popularly called the Johnson Era came to an end in the summer of 1940, when the venerated Roy Johnson reported for duty as a major in the U.S. Army.[19]

Officers in the Army and Navy urged President Roosevelt and the colleges and universities across the country to continue football. On the one hand, the Navy had its V-5 and V-12 programs at hundreds of collegiate institutions and allowed trainees to participate in varsity sports. Without this support, very few colleges would have found it possible to field teams. The Army, on the other, prohibited individuals in its programs from engaging in intercollegiate athletic programs. Most of the institutions affiliated with Army programs dropped varsity athletics. UNM had the Navy V-12 program, and therefore had the manpower to compete in both football and basketball.

Ted Shipkey, the successful UNM coach of the late 1930s, continued as head football coach until he entered the armed forces after the season of 1941. Willis Barnes, the assistant football coach who had been on the athletic staff at UNM since the 1920s, succeeded him. Shipkey returned to the University in 1945 shortly after the start of the football season and served as an assistant coach. A year later he entered the professional ranks as a coach of the Los Angeles Dons. UNM teams under Barnes achieved a five-year record of nineteen wins, twenty losses, and six ties.

Basketball continued at UNM throughout the war with only a slight decrease in the number of games played. Annual basketball schedules included Border Conference competition as well as regional and intersectional games. Conference play, however, was discontinued after the 1943 conference tournament.

The UNM basketball teams in the war years had a series of four coaches, of whom two were volunteers. The first volunteer was History Professor Benjamin Sacks, who had been an outstanding UNM player in the 1920s. Succeeding Sacks in 1941 was the football coach, Willis Barnes. Barnes guided the team for the 1942 and 1943 seasons, when UNM compiled records of six victories and six losses. The wartime athletic director, George "Blanco" White, replaced Barnes for the 1943–44 season and had an excellent record of eleven wins and two losses. In 1944–45, a second volunteer, Woodrow Clements, a graduate of Highlands University and a native New Mexican, coached the UNM team to another outstanding season in which the Lobos won thirteen games while losing only two.[20]

The Death of President Zimmerman

President Zimmerman suffered a fatal heart attack on October 20, 1944, and so did not see the end of World War II. Tom Popejoy, at that time comptroller of UNM as well as executive assistant to the president, chaired a committee made up of deans and the business manager that served in place of the president until a new appointment could be made.²¹ The committee had met weekly during the Zimmerman administration to advise the president.

James F. Zimmerman left a rich, enduring legacy. It is fitting that the most majestic building on the campus, Zimmerman Library, was named in honor of this dynamic and revered president. He inherited many problems from his predecessor David Hill, who had somehow managed to alienate virtually every constituency. Zimmerman rose from the ranks of the faculty. He knew them, he had their respect, and he listened to them. A teacher and scholar as well as an able executive, he made wise and strategic appointments in both the administrative and faculty ranks. He was looking for and could implement new ideas. He had a feeling for the Southwest—its languages, its Hispanic and Indian cultures, its religions, traditions, music, art, and architecture, and its rich literary productivity. He survived multiple turnovers in Regents and governors, and in the latter half of his time in office he won the support of the governor, the legislature, and federal authorities. He was proud but not pompous, modest but not a whiner, demanding but fair. He literally put his heart and soul into the University. Those who knew him testified they were aware that when around him, they were in the presence of greatness.

The *New Mexico Historical Review* published a tribute to Zimmerman in January 1945. It listed among his accomplishments the Harwood Foundation in Taos, the Chaco Canyon archaeology station, the San José experimental bilingual school, summer field schools, and extension courses. Paul Walter, Sr., who had worked with Zimmerman to establish the UNM Press, said: "In his inaugural address, Zimmerman outlined comprehensive plans for the growth of the University, so idealistic that many of his hearers doubted their practicality. It was given to him to achieve these but at the sacrifice of his health, his very life."²²

Tony Hillerman picked up on the fact that Zimmerman resented the constant comparisons to eastern institutions, knowing full well that it took Harvard and others hundreds of years to get where UNM was in half a century. "Like Dr. Tight before him, Zimmerman wanted to fit the school to its environment. Tight had objected to copying Eastern architecture; Zimmerman saw no profit in copying Eastern academic format."

In a state rich with the relics of bygone cultures, the UNM departments of anthropology and archaeology flowered to fame. The University became a center for study of Spanish and Latin American history, language and culture. A College of Education, deeply interested in bi-lingual teaching problems, was founded to provide the State with badly-needed teachers. The College of Fine Arts was added—again with orientation toward the Southwest. The long-neglected Extension Division was suddenly active in offering adult education to New Mexicans. The Graduate School was started to give New Mexico the full cycle of education. And important for our view, Zimmerman Library was built—big enough (it was thought) to meet scholastic needs into the dim, distant future.²³

Los Alamos, Trinity, and the Atomic Bomb

In 1945, several months after the death of Zimmerman, the world changed, and his adopted state and beloved University played a significant role in that change. Most narratives of this moment start with April 1943, when, as Marc Simmons wrote, the U.S. government "established the secret Los Alamos Laboratory on a beautiful, but almost inaccessible, shelf of the pine-clad Pajarito Plateau thirty-five miles northwest of Santa Fe."[24]

Albuquerque, with its excellent air and rail facilities, influenced the selection of a site for the Manhattan Project, the name given to the design and construction of the world's first atomic bomb. The Army's Albuquerque Engineering District, a branch of the Corps of Engineers, was assigned the task of constructing the laboratory and living quarters for the scientists and engineers who would be working on the highly secret mission.

Mystery surrounded this project from its very inception. "Throughout the country prominent physicists, chemists, and mathematicians suddenly dropped from sight. Unbeknown to the public, the government had spirited them away to remote Los Alamos."[25] Even New Mexicans were curious about the puzzling doings in Los Alamos but had no idea of the nature or magnitude of the endeavor.

> The uncertainty prompted much humorous speculation: the Army was said to be operating a nudist colony, or a home for pregnant WAC's [Women's Army Corps], or an internment camp for Republicans, or a factory producing windshield wipers for submarines.

Since there was no rail service to Los Alamos, the vast quantities of materials needed for the project were shipped through Albuquerque, addressed to E. J. Workman, professor of physics at the University of New Mexico. These materials never reached the campus but were diverted to a railroad siding on the outskirts of Albuquerque. Army engineers collected them there for transport by truck to the Trinity Site. As work on the bomb progressed, part of a gunnery and bombing range southeast of Socorro and near Alamogordo was selected as the testing ground for the first atomic explosion, the Trinity Site. By the evening of July 15, 1945, all air traffic was barred between Albuquerque and El Paso, Texas.

July 15, 1945, was a fateful day in the history of New Mexico and the world.

> At 5:30 [A.M.] . . . a shock-wave boom shook New Mexico and parts of Texas and Arizona. In Gallup, 235 miles from the Trinity Site, houses rattled and windows blew out. Guests in Albuquerque's Hilton Hotel tumbled from their beds in alarm and peering outside saw an awesome red glow filling the southern sky. The pyrotechnic display, visible for hundreds of miles, resembled nothing less than the fires of Hell.
>
> The world's first atomic explosion . . . marked, with a mushroom-shaped exclamation point, the commencement of a new age. For New

Mexico, as a center of nuclear research, the die was cast. The ancient land, which still showed on every side the influence of Indians and Spaniards, was now to become the permanent home of a growing battalion of scientists. For Albuquerque, that meant a new direction in its economy and a further swing toward the center of America's mainstream.[26]

The University of New Mexico, the city of Albuquerque, the state, the nation, and the world had entered the Atomic Age.

Sculptor John Tatschl seems more excited than the chilled Physical Plant workers about installing his bronze Lobo in front of Zimmerman Stadium. Photo by Alfred Gescheid, class of 1950

CHAPTER ELEVEN
Administration of John Philip Wernette
1945–48

John Philip Wernette

Atomic bombs dropped on Hiroshima and Nagasaki in August 1945 forced the Japanese surrender and marked the end of World War II. These events served to launch New Mexico, Albuquerque, and UNM into a whole new world. Tony Hillerman commented: "The Atomic Age had been born at Los Alamos and the wand of progress was touching New Mexico. Hobbs, Artesia, Grants, Alamogordo and other communities were booming. Albuquerque had become the fastest-growing city in the United States. Demand for higher education was skyrocketing."[1]

New Mexico, particularly Albuquerque, became one of the most important scientific centers of the world. The war had brought the city such enterprises as Kirtland Air Force Base and later the adjacent Sandia Base and Sandia National Laboratories. By 1949, the Atomic Energy Commission negotiated a contract with Western Electric Company, a subsidiary of Bell Telephone, to operate Sandia as a private corporation to manufacture and test nuclear weapons.

Within a decade the pace of research accelerated, bringing Manzano Base, a satellite of Sandia, designated as a storage space for atomic bombs. Around the same time, a vast uranium deposit was discovered an hour's drive west from Albuquerque, near the town of Grants. Later strikes in the area along with the continued development of advanced weaponry in Los Alamos made New Mexico a world leader in uranium mining and atomic science. Contractors, miners, and other skilled laborers, as well as engineers, technicians, and executives, were lured to New Mexico, and particularly to Albuquerque.

This huge influx of people, many of them highly educated and cosmopolitan in their attitudes and tastes, not only changed the economic and social life of Albuquerque, but also extended the city's boundaries. Where before World War II the campus marked the eastern boundary of the city, the postwar boom stretched the eastern and northern residential and business areas to the base of the Sandias and then some. What little more than a half-century earlier had been a slow-paced railroad town had blossomed by the mid-1940s into a booming, blooming metropolis.[2] These newcomers hungered for, demanded, and expected a program of higher education that would meet their aspirations and needs.

Edward F. Castetter

This postwar era was a time of great change in the political composition of the community. Where in prewar years the political power lay in the labor unions and working class, newcomers to Albuquerque tended to be more conservative, more sophisticated, and more inclined to embrace the philosophy of the Republican Party. They resisted political cliques and political machines. One of the casualties of this change was Clyde Tingley, who after completing two terms as governor in 1938 returned to Albuquerque and was elected to the city commission. As chairman of that body and again the city's ex-officio mayor, he was said to have run city hall in the same heavy-handed manner as he had in previous years. In 1947, however, his power was broken as the educated voters in the new precincts on the east mesa voted him and his supporters out of office. Clyde Tingley died at Bataan Memorial Methodist Hospital on December 24, 1960.[3]

The Appointment of President J. Philip Wernette

On the UNM campus, almost overwhelmed by the postwar surge in enrollments and the return of the veterans from the war, leadership was in limbo. President Zimmerman had died, and in his place Comptroller Tom Popejoy and a committee of deans and top administrators attempted to fill the gap. An anxious faculty, thinking to seize the moment and assume control of the University, hoped for a weak choice for president, someone who would delegate the real power to the faculty. Considerable power was lodged in the Faculty Budget and Education Policy Committee, chaired by Edward F. Castetter, a professor of biology. This committee sought to secure the authority to select the members of all standing University committees and thereby increase their influence over University affairs.

There was much speculation that Tom Popejoy would be the next president and that Zimmerman had actually groomed him for the job. Zimmerman was regarded as an intellectual and an accomplished scholar, but also as a man with idealistic tendencies when it came to solving problems. Zimmerman had frequently turned to Popejoy for advice and assistance, depending on the latter's common sense. It was said that Zimmerman directed while Popejoy got things done. Zimmerman's confidence in Popejoy gave the young administrator the opportunity to hone his own skills so that when the opportunity came, he was ready to assume more responsibilities.

There was some faculty criticism of Popejoy because his forte had been administration and finance rather than academics. He had no doctorate, and his highest faculty post was associate professor of economics. Thomas C. Donnelly, head of the Government Department, was the internal favorite of many faculty members. The Regents, moving slowly and cautiously, chose neither, deciding instead to go outside the University.

James Defibaugh, a research associate in the History Department during Popejoy's administration, had some thoughtful insights on presidential transitions.

Dr. Zimmerman's death, while he was still in office as president, presented serious problems for the University which it had never faced before. Ordinarily, the process of presidential succession is one which is planned well in advance of the fact, rather in the manner that kings and queens passed their power, in the Middle Ages, to chosen successors. In the normal order of things, the important elements of the University community are consulted, and a selection is made. . . . When presidents die in office, however, things are different; the competitive elements within the University all seek to achieve their own ends at the expense of others, and to advance their own candidates, who, it is hoped, will take special care to see that their particular interests are protected and advanced. Such was the case after the death of Dr. Zimmerman.[4]

On June 5, 1945, the Regents named J. Philip Wernette as UNM's eighth president. Holder of a PhD from Harvard University's School of Business. Wernette assumed office in August.

Wernette was born in Imlay City, Michigan, October 29, 1903. He received his bachelor's degree from the University of California–Berkeley in 1924 and a master's from the University of Southern California in 1926. He served as an instructor at Southern Cal, completed a master's degree at Harvard, and went on to earn his PhD there in 1932. He served on the faculty of the Harvard School of Business from 1927 to 1945. Wernette was on the committee of financial advisors to Columbia University in 1929 and a fellow of the Social Sciences Research Council from 1932–33. He wrote five books on economics and business and edited a book on executive philosophy and practice.

Wernette appeared before the Faculty Senate for the first time on August 13, 1945. He "delivered a general, non-controversial speech which gave little hint of the discord to come," Dabney reported.

> But it soon turned out that Wernette had no idea of going along with the view that he was [an] administrator and nothing more. He was determined to be a strong president, and before long a wide split had developed between the president and the power group in the faculty.[5]

The Administration of President Wernette

If the atomic bomb changed the world, certainly the G.I. Bill that emanated from World War II changed higher education in America forever. In a fireside chat to the nation on July 28, 1943, President Roosevelt advocated government-financed education as part of veterans' benefits. Congress responded quickly and enthusiastically, passing Public Law 346, the Servicemen's Readjustment Act of 1944, which soon became known as the G.I. Bill.

For the first time in history, the doors to higher education were opened to those who had the intellectual acumen and motivation for a college education but lacked the finances or opportunity or both to pursue a degree. Far exceeding expectations, the G.I. Bill lured millions of servicemen to college campuses. In addition, women

Some twenty-five barracks were brought to the campus after World War II, including this one that served as home for Mr. and Mrs. Ernest Sloan and their daughter Patricia Anne.

and the economically disenfranchised of the nation, especially Native Americans, Hispanics, and African Americans, also took advantage of federally sponsored programs and enrolled in unprecedented numbers.

Like universities throughout the country, UNM was unprepared for the flood of veterans in the postwar era. Early speculation was that few would take advantage of the G.I. Bill, as educators believed the veterans either were too old to return to the classrooms or would not make good students. By 1946 more than two million students were enrolled in the nation's universities, and half were veterans. In addition, there were sixty thousand women and seventy thousand African Americans who for the first time availed themselves of the opportunity to attend college. Enrollment for the fall semester of 1946 at UNM was just 924. By 1949, it was 4,921.

There was a shortage of everything: classrooms, laboratories, housing, even faculty to teach classes. This problem was made worse at UNM by numerous changes in staff and faculty, as well as resignations and retirements of key scholars and administrators. The latter list included heads of the History, Psychology, and Mathematics departments, the dean of the Graduate School, and the former dean of the College of Arts and Sciences, Lynn Mitchell.

Perhaps the greatest loss came when John Clark retired in 1945. A living link with the University's founding, he had been a professor of chemistry for thirty-eight years and had served as the first dean of the Graduate School, as dean of men, and as dean of students. A prominent figure on campus and a popular speaker, Clark delighted in addressing freshmen on the history of UNM, telling with special gusto of the burning of the science building and the loss of all the specimens.

Adding to the woes was the general shortage of faculty on campuses all around the country and UNM's inability to compete in salaries and benefits. In spite of these difficulties, the University was able to persuade France V. Scholes to return to New Mexico from the Carnegie Institution as well as hire additional gifted professors who would set a standard of excellence for many years.

One of the University's strengths was in the spotlight in 1945 when Professor Leslie Spier founded the *Southwestern Journal of Anthropology.* It had a multidisciplinary, international approach and rapidly achieved prominence. Its name was changed to the *Journal of Anthropological Research,* reflecting its international focus, under editor Henry Basehart in 1973.

The Wernette era marked the beginning of a number of professional programs at the University of New Mexico. Pharmacy became the fifth college at UNM in 1945 with Roy A. Bowers named as its first dean. He was also its only faculty member that first year. The college occupied rooms in the Science Lecture Hall, the Chemistry Building, and in temporary barracks until a building for pharmacy laboratories, classrooms, and faculty offices was constructed in 1948. The first class was graduated in 1949. In 1960, the four-year program was lengthened to five years.[6]

The Regents established a College of Business Administration in 1947. Before this time, the work in business was offered as a department in the College of Arts and Sciences. Vernon G. Sorrell, who had joined the UNM faculty in 1931, became dean of the new college in 1947 and remained in that post until 1959. The college offered programs in accounting, finance, general business, industrial administration, and marketing and an executive secretarial program. Three specialized programs were later added: the Bureau of Business Research, the Southwest Management Development Program, and the Data Processing Program.[7]

Also making a debut in 1947 was a four-year program in architectural engineering, with John Heimerich as chairman.[8]

There had been intermittent calls for a law school at UNM for decades, and in 1933 President Zimmerman recommended one, estimating that the first year would require only one instructor and a budget of $7,000.[9] It was not until 1947, however, that the Regents officially founded the School of Law "to meet the need of the state for men and women trained for the legal profession."[10] Professor Emeritus Henry Weihofen, writing of the school's first forty years, said, "Members of the bar were not unanimous in favoring the undertaking. Some feared the school would not be of high quality, and that it might be subject to political influence."

The first dean was Alfred Leroy Gausewitz, who had been a law professor at the University of Wisconsin. A Navy veteran of World War I, he had spent time in Albuquerque recuperating from tuberculosis. The other charter faculty members were Verle Rue Seed, Arie Poldervaart, and John A. Bauman. Four rooms were made available in the old Zimmerman Stadium, and some eleven thousand books were acquired. The first class numbered fifty-three, of whom twenty, along with seven transfers, graduated in 1950. Of those, 84 percent passed the state bar exam.[11]

Yet another professional program established at this time was the Journalism Department. Before 1947, journalism was a major in the English Department. Keen Rafferty, a former *Baltimore Sun* copy editor who had come to the University in 1942 as news service director and alumni secretary, was the new department's chairman. Under his leadership the program got off to a fast start, receiving its national accreditation in 1955, only six years after the graduation of its first class. In 1947 the first classes were held in World War II barracks near University Avenue, before construction of a new facility in 1949.[12]

Rafferty's successor in the renamed Office of Public Information was G. Ward Fenley, PhD, who would direct the growing media relations and publications program before moving on to write the popular "Old Man Action Line" column for the *Albuquerque Journal.* Jess Price succeeded him in 1967.

On June 7, 1947, the first doctoral degrees were presented. Hector H. Lee's dissertation was on American civilization, and Marie Pope Wallace's was on Spanish and Ibero-American literature.[13]

The president's relations with the faculty continued to deteriorate, as exemplified by the early retirement of Jay Carroll Knode, dean of the College of Arts and Sciences, effective in June 1947. A contest arose as to who would be his successor. The power group of the faculty wanted Edward Castetter, who subscribed to Knode's theory of a strong faculty and weak president. Wernette, however, chose Thomas Donnelly for the deanship.[14]

John Clark

A group of non-credit students posed with Lex Lewis Haas, center, head of the Art Department, for a feature on UNM's Community Evening College in January 1948. He was showing them how, in a darkroom, a photographic print is processed in a chemical bath.

In 1947, President Wernette, in his first and only appearance before the New Mexico Legislature, made a spirited appeal for substantial increases of the appropriation to UNM. He cited many statistics concerning UNM, New Mexico, and the nation pertaining to salaries, appropriations per student, and average expenditures for similar institutions. His pleas, protests, and lamentations were to no avail. His ineffectiveness with the legislature led faculty to believe he not only did not have their confidence but was also unable to hold a base of support among most of the Regents or political leaders of the state. Also, as reported by Dabney, "His dedication to his task was recognized, but his methods of operating were distasteful."[15] Defibaugh provides this description:

> Wernette was a man of strong convictions. He had attained high academic recognition. He lacked, however, any trace of tact, and seemed not to have any concept of political savvy. He made few friends, and his blunt character resulted in the loss of many . . . He seemed to lack that most essential attribute of the able administrator: common sense. He was a failure as a president.[16]

It should be noted, however, that throughout Wernette's short and stormy tenure as president, Comptroller Tom Popejoy was reputed to be a loyal supporter of the administration, one who calmed troubled waters and contributed significantly to the continuation of normal operations of the University. Popejoy revealed no ill will for his new boss, and indications were that Wernette soon came to rely on Popejoy as much as Zimmerman had.[17] It was no surprise to those in the many UNM constituencies when Wernette's contract was not renewed for 1948–49. Once again, a search for a new president was under way.

Campus Development and Construction

The postwar era on the UNM campus was not a time for construction. Lack of time and money to plan and build forced University administrators to look to other solutions for the problems of providing classes, labs, and housing for a student population that had almost tripled. Like colleges and universities all across the country, UNM began to scramble to acquire surplus military buildings.

Housing was in high demand and short supply. UNM negotiated with Kirtland Air Force Base for use of its bachelor officers' quarters to house some six hundred male students in seven base dormitories. At the same time, all the permanent dormitories on the campus, with the exception of Yatoka Hall, which was converted to offices and classrooms, were turned over to women students. Double-deck beds were employed to increase their capacity to 391. The University also had to deal with a whole new clientele of students, the married couples, some with children. To this end, in the summer of 1947 UNM contracted for concrete foundations, plumbing, heating, and power for seven barracks, which were moved from Bruns Hospital in Santa Fe to the campus. These buildings were then remodeled into eighty-three one- and two-bedroom apartments on Stanford Boulevard Northeast, about where the Basic Medical Sciences Building was eventually located.

Of the permanent buildings constructed in the mid-1940s, the first, begun in October 1946, was a small structure on University Boulevard for the Chemical Engineering Department. It was a one-story facility with a central, high-ceilinged area and offices, classrooms, and laboratories.

John Tatschl, a noted Viennese sculptor and professor in the Art Department, created the University's famed Lobo sculpture in 1947. The bronze statue was placed on a pedestal west of the Stadium Building. The Interfraternity Council commissioned the Lobo statue, and student contributions paid for it. A plaque on the side reads: "Dedicated to those students of the University of New Mexico who gave their lives in World War I and World War II."[18]

Rudy Krall

Athletics

Intercollegiate athletics at UNM after World War II underwent a significant change in both expansion of programs and emphasis. The growth in popularity of both football and basketball was associated with the quality of coaching and the excellence of play. Many sports that had been discontinued during the war enjoyed strong comebacks as spectators supported the total program in ever-increasing numbers.

Willis Barnes continued as UNM's head football coach during the seasons of 1945 and 1946. His 1945 team won six contests and tied for the Border Conference championship. UNM played the University of Denver in the Sun Bowl in El Paso, Texas, on New Year's Day, 1946, winning 32–24. One of the greats in UNM football history, Rudy Krall, a powerful running back, played on that 1945 championship team and was later invited to play in the East-West Shrine game in San Francisco.

In 1947, Berl Huffman, a graduate of Trinity University in Texas, replaced Barnes as head coach. Huffman was regarded as a gifted after-dinner speaker, but his short career at UNM was both "lackluster and unsuccessful." Over three seasons, his teams were 4–5–1, 2–8, and 2–8. His contract was not renewed for the 1950 season.

Track and field, cross-country, and swimming had irregular and limited activity in this era. Golf, however, achieved the ultimate in both physical facilities and coaching leadership. With the opening of the new golf course in the spring of 1942, and under the direction of George "Stormy" Petrol, the sport drew national attention, leading to the selection of UNM as the host for the 1949 NCAA championship tournament. Among the prominent collegiate golfers in the tourney was a young Wake Forest University player by the name of Arnold Palmer. UNM, taking advantage of playing on its own course, finished seventeenth in the tournament.[19]

After almost ten years of no activity, baseball was reorganized on a limited basis at UNM in 1938. John Dolzadelli, who had been instrumental in returning the sport to the varsity intercollegiate level, held the head coaching position for the early part of the 1940s. In 1946, Gus Zielasko took over the position. Beginning in 1947, Petrol gave up his duties as golf coach and became the head baseball coach. Under his leadership the quality of play improved, and varsity baseball became a serious rival to track and field as the leading spring sport.

The Beginning of the End

Referring to the Regents' search for a successor to Zimmerman, Dabney observed that the University's most successful presidents had been those like Zimmerman who knew the campus and the state. "Those brought in from the outside, like Hill, had problems."[20] Dabney's list of examples was limited, however, because Zimmerman was the only president appointed from within between 1889 and 1945. Certainly Herrick, Tight, and Boyd could also be on the list of successful presidents.

Wernette had a short honeymoon at UNM. By the summer of 1947, when there was talk that the board was considering terminating his appointment, a controversy arose over Wernette's dismissal of three University students who had been suspended for a series of campus pranks, which included repeatedly setting fire to a campus building. The Regents reinstated them.

On January 29, 1948, the Regents met in the chambers of U.S. Circuit Judge Sam Bratton, president of the board. At the conclusion of their meeting, it was announced that Wernette's contract would not be renewed in June of that year and that Tom L. Popejoy, University comptroller, had been selected to succeed Wernette. When asked whether President Wernette had resigned or been dismissed, Judge Bratton said, "Just say we didn't renew his contract." He did not elaborate except to say that the Board of Regents had been considering this action for a long time. President Wernette did not attend the session.[21]

The action of the Regents was lauded by the *Albuquerque News,* which carried an editorial lamenting "the long and unfortunate misrule of the University of New Mexico" under Wernette.

Dr. Wernette, a research worker in the field of economics, never at any time during his two and a half year tenure here, manifested the talents of a good administrator and as a result of this fact, conditions at the University have steadily deteriorated.

From the very start it was our earnest and sincere desire to call attention to conditions that needed to be corrected. At first we believed that Dr. Wernette might change his methods and might eventually grow to fit the very large position that he was brought here to fill. But as the months passed and conditions continued to grow worse, we openly and decisively advocated his removal.

Dr. Wernette is a very capable man in his own domain. We have come to know him very well during his residence here and have had numerous interviews and visits—all pleasant. And we have the greatest respect for his work and for his mind. Unfortunately for all concerned, he just didn't fit his job here.[22]

President Wernette and his wife, Eleanor, posed after the 1946 commencement ceremony.

Saturday morning, February 1, a group of UNM students scattered hundreds of pamphlets on campus protesting the action of the Regents in terminating Wernette. Unidentified student leaders said the purpose was not to "slam" Tom Popejoy, who was described as a "most honored man." The purpose instead was to charge the Regents with playing politics and to express students' concern that the board's action would result in a drop in UNM's scholastic standing.[23]

Wernette's dismissal did attract national attention as the February 16, 1948, issue of *Time* magazine contained an article critical of the University of New Mexico. The magazine blasted the Regents for ousting President Wernette "like a janitor" and reported he was fired without notice. *Time* lauded Wernette for bringing new faculty members of high caliber and gave him credit for increases in UNM's enrollment. It also raked the Board of Regents as "politics-ridden" by citing the reinstatement of the three students Wernette had suspended.[24]

The *Albuquerque Journal* rebutted the magazine's article, pointing out that Wernette was allowed to stay on in his post until June. The newspaper noted that he had appointed a dean of the College of Fine Arts who did not even have a degree in any of the fine arts fields and asserted that the president "had nothing to do with the suspensions of the students and didn't even publicly back up the dean who ordered the suspensions." Most of all, the newspaper took umbrage at *Time*'s poking fun at newly appointed President Tom Popejoy because he was a Rotarian.[25]

In addition, the dean of the College of Education, Simon Nanninga, circulated a petition supporting the Regents in their dismissal of Wernette and appointment of Popejoy. The petition was signed by 181 of the 241 faculty members, and a copy was sent to the editors of *Time*.[26]

Between January and June, the smoke cleared, and the fact remained. Wernette was out, and Popejoy was in. ∎

Gerald Nash of the History Department was a popular teacher, author, and scholar of the American West. Photo by Dick Meleski

Thomas Lafayette Popejoy

CHAPTER TWELVE

Academic Advances During the Administration of Tom Popejoy

1948–68

The Regents' dismissal of J. Philip Wernette in January 1948 was apparently preceded by considerable politicking on the UNM campus. It was no secret that Tom Popejoy, executive assistant to the president, and Thomas Donnelly, dean of the College of Arts and Sciences, both had their eyes on the job. Popejoy had loyal allies from many sectors, while Donnelly enjoyed strong support from the academic factions. According to James Defibaugh:

> The battle that ensued for the Presidency was fought in the grand tradition of political battles everywhere. There was no quarter given, and little asked. When the dust settled, and the blood ceased to flow, Tom Popejoy emerged victorious. The alliances he had built in years past within the University stood him in good stead. His allies without the University— and most especially in state government—made valuable contributions to his success. He was President of the University of New Mexico.[1]

President Thomas L. Popejoy

Appointed in January on the same day Wernette was notified his contract would not be renewed, Tom Popejoy officially took office July 1, 1948—the first native New Mexican to hold the position of president of the University of New Mexico. He was born December 2, 1902, on a ranch twenty-one miles east of Raton, a rural town in northern New Mexico just below Raton Pass that leads north to Colorado. His parents let him move to town, where he and his sisters kept house while attending high school. Tom met Bess Kimball at Raton High, and the two were married when he graduated from high school in 1921. An outstanding scholar and athlete, Popejoy enrolled at UNM that fall and brought his bride along. At that time he and Bess were one of only six married couples on the campus. While Tom was an undergraduate and graduate student and during his early years as a member of the faculty and staff at UNM, she worked as a clerk in a department store in downtown Albuquerque. She earned a bachelor of science in education in 1930.

The west façade of Zimmerman Library was a good location for publicity photos.
Photo by Dick Meleski

Popejoy graduated from UNM with a bachelor's degree in economics in 1925. After taking some courses at the University of Illinois and the University of California–Berkeley, he then finished his graduate work at UNM, earning a master's degree in economics in 1929.

In 1925 Popejoy was hired as an instructor in the UNM Economics Department, and he worked his way up in the academic ranks for eight years until he was an associate professor. For some of this time he was also the athletic business manager. He succeeded Frank D. Reeve as secretary of the Alumni Association in 1930. In 1937, he was appointed comptroller of the University, then later served as assistant to the president to both Zimmerman and Wernette. During the World War II years, Popejoy was also acting registrar. His career at the University was interrupted when he took brief leaves to work with the National Youth Administration and the Office of Price Control during World War II. From 1940 to 1944, Popejoy also served on several occasions as acting president when Zimmerman was ill.[2]

Administration of President Popejoy

The presidency of Tom Popejoy spanned two decades, longer than the tenure of any of his predecessors or indeed any of his successors through the year 2003. He presided over a period of the University's most dynamic growth. Enrollment jumped from 4,495 students in fall 1948 to more than 14,000 at the time of his retirement in 1968. Graduate and professional studies and research assumed new importance as the University became less of a provincial college and more of a center for serious scholarship. During these two decades the University grew in many ways to serve the people of New Mexico while meeting the demanding missions of a comprehensive research university.[3]

After World War II the Southwest emerged from obscurity to become a place of choice, not only for those seeking higher education but also for leaders of military and research institutions, corporations, health-care providers, and industrial and manufacturing concerns. Outdoor recreation, retirement living, in short, every human endeavor where climate, scenery, and sheer livability played a part, made the Southwest appealing, especially when ways were found to supply water and keep buildings cool. During the war, military programs had brought students to Southwest campuses from all over the nation, and after the war many of them came back. Like many universities, though, UNM had meager budgets, too few faculty, and inadequate facilities.

Time and events proved that Popejoy was up to the challenge. Like his predecessors the president was involved in a never-ending struggle for money. His prior work and connections within state government, especially the legislature, served him and the University well, however. Without retarding the physical growth of the institution, he was able to maintain the architectural integrity of the campus. A staunch defender of academic freedom, he defused the panic over alleged Communist infiltration of the campus while at the same time taking advantage of the national concern for eliminating the supposed technology gap separating the United States and the Soviet Union. With diplomatic firmness, he managed to placate the more radical elements of the faculty and student body during the rise of national social unrest and maintain a reasonable calm on the campus.

Popejoy did not do all these things alone, of course. He had a knack for selecting and organizing administrators, able men and women who worked with him and for him, people like Harold L. Enarson, Sherman E. Smith, John Perovich, Van Dorn Hooker, Myron F. Fifield, Harold Lavender, John Durrie, France V. Scholes, Chester C. Travelstead, and many other faculty and staff members. He was a master of delegating responsibilities to those more knowledgeable or experienced in specialized fields and eliciting from them the expert advice he needed. He was also one who generated strong loyalties from his associates. "He wasn't a saint, but he was very much a human being, and it was in his humanity that he and others found their strength."[4]

When he moved into the president's office, Popejoy did not have to get acquainted with the job. He knew the importance of getting people, especially faculty and students, involved in the planning and decision making. One of his first acts as president was to appoint a Committee on University Aims and Objectives. This committee advised that UNM could best serve the citizens of the state by carrying out four objectives: (1) providing general education so students could develop their personal aspirations and attain a liberal-arts education; (2) providing special and professional education in scholarly or technical fields; (3) emphasizing faculty scholarship and research to make contributions to learning; and (4) offering adult education and general cultural programs to enrich the lives of New Mexicans. These principles were the road map for his administration.[5]

The University's spectacular growth in research began early in Popejoy's presidency. Federal agencies such as the Atomic Energy Commission and the National Science Foundation initiated outside-sponsored research in 1951, with

Dudley Wynn

Virginia Crenshaw

grants totaling slightly more than $100,000, small change in today's sponsored research, but an important beginning. At the same time, faculty contributions in other fields of research multiplied in significance and volume, greatly enhancing the University's national prestige.[6]

The first major change in the administrative hierarchy of UNM came in 1951, when Roy Bowers, dean of pharmacy, accepted a similar post at Rutgers University. Elmon L. Cataline replaced him. That same year Popejoy promoted John Durrie, who had been the assistant to Academic Vice President France Scholes, to the new position of secretary of the University. For the next twenty-six years Durrie was in charge of Regents' minutes, faculty rosters, and a host of other official documents. He also organized commencement ceremonies for more than forty thousand graduates and served as a respected voice on matters of protocol.

A year later, Thomas Donnelly, dean of the College of Arts and Sciences, resigned and accepted the presidency of New Mexico Highlands University in Las Vegas. For that one year, 1952, Harold Reid served as acting dean. Then, in 1953, Dudley Wynn, who had been a professor of English at UNM and during the Wernette years served as director of the Humanities Program at the University of Colorado, was persuaded to return and accept the post.[7]

In 1955, the School of Nursing was the first of many professional schools added to the UNM academic program. Formal efforts to start a nursing program began in 1950 with a meeting between nursing leaders and UNM faculty members, who recognized the need for a second program in the state. In 1952, Edyth Barnes, nurse consultant to the U.S. Public Health Service, conducted a survey that recommended a four-year bachelor's degree program at UNM. This led to formation of a committee, which Marion Fleck, executive secretary of the New Mexico Nurses Association, headed, to approach lawmakers in Santa Fe. The legislature approved a $60,000 line item in the spring of 1955 to initiate the nursing program. A nationwide search led to the appointment of Eleanor King as the first dean. Virginia Crenshaw succeeded her in 1961.[8]

A small program combining architecture and engineering continued in the postwar years. The faculty included Don Schlegel and the architectural historian Bainbridge Bunting. Administration of the two-college program was awkward, and there was concern that no faculty members were registered engineers or architects.[9]

The University College was organized in 1956 to replace the General College. Under the new plan, all entering freshmen at UNM would begin in the University College and one or two years later transfer to a degree-granting college. A terminal two-year associate degree program was also available. It was hoped that University College would facilitate the recognition of particularly gifted students who might be drawn into an honors program.

The year 1956 marked the arrival of Chester Travelstead as dean of the College of Education. A Kentucky native whose mother was an educator, he saw action as a Navy officer in World War II before earning degrees in music and educational administration. He was dean of education at the University of South Carolina when the U.S. Supreme Court ruled in 1955 that segregated educational facilities were unconstitutional. Travelstead gave a speech calling on his university to comply with the order to admit Negroes, and soon after he was notified that his contract would not be renewed. President Popejoy learned of Travelstead's principled courage and invited him to come to UNM.

The biggest concerns of faculty in the mid-1950s revolved around low salaries, twelve-hour teaching loads, and ethics questions pertaining to faculty members earning extra remuneration for contracted research. Faculty who were not in academic fields that attracted outside funding were left to rationalize that the University as a whole probably profited from outside subsidies for research. The lure of better salaries in engineering, the applied sciences, and business proved to be attractive to students, resulting in larger enrollments in these disciplines. During these years, the University continued to grow in prestige and stature, as evidenced by its approval for a Phi Beta Kappa chapter in 1965.

To people on the UNM campus, these were the halcyon days. Enrollments were climbing, appropriations were higher, and salaries and fringe benefits were improving. Morale among faculty and students was high.[10] (Nina Ancona's may have suffered a bit between 1954 and 1960, when she held the title of acting chairman of the Music Department. Six years must be a record tenure in a supposedly temporary position.)

In 1956, a Graduate Center was established in Los Alamos by cooperative arrangement with the Los Alamos Scientific Laboratory, where UNM had been offering some graduate work since 1947. Biology, physics, and chemistry courses were in high demand as many employees of the laboratory aspired to earn doctorates while continuing their work. Using outstanding scientists at the laboratory as faculty was also attractive, while the availability of the scientific laboratories and state-of-the-art equipment expanded opportunities for significant research. Added prestige came from the fact that Los Alamos had the reputation of having the highest ratio of PhDs per capita in the world, while Albuquerque could claim to have the highest PhD ratio per capita for a major city.

Another outreach program initiated in that era was the founding of KNME-TV in 1958. It was organized in cooperation with the Albuquerque Public Schools and the state Department of Education as the first public educational television station in the state. The parallel to this in the private sector was the strong support the Bureau of Engineering Research and the Bureau of Business Research rendered to activities in their fields.

Popejoy also had his critics. One flap in 1959 revolved around Professor Josiah C. Russell. A specialist in medieval history, he had come to UNM in 1946 as professor and chairman of the History Department. Possessed of a contentious personality, he was often at odds with fellow faculty and the dean of Arts and Sciences, which led to his replacement as department chair in 1952. As tensions with other faculty increased, Russell also became highly critical of President Popejoy, denouncing him frequently, publicly, and immoderately. Finally, in 1959, Popejoy decided that Russell's

Chester Travelstead

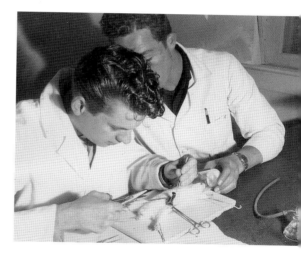

Another rat gave up life for the advancement of knowledge.

John Donald Robb

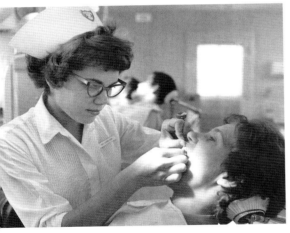

Working in one of the last World War II barracks on campus, dental hygiene students practiced on UNM employees and others who wanted low-cost teeth cleaning. Photo by Dick Meleski

attitude and deportment had reached a point that his usefulness to the University was outweighed by the damage he was doing. The president took advantage of a New Mexico law passed in 1957 that allowed the involuntary retirement of a faculty member at the age of sixty. Popejoy wrote a letter to Russell notifying him that he would be involuntarily retired when he reached that age, which was about a year and a half away. Russell appealed to the Academic Freedom and Tenure Committee, which supported the president but took issue with the law itself. Russell then appealed to the American Association of University Professors, which, after sending an investigating team to the campus, expressed support for the professor. Russell also appealed to the state district court, which in January 1961 ruled in his favor. He returned to the faculty, where he stayed until his voluntary retirement in 1965.[11]

In the College of Business Administration, William J. Parrish was named dean in 1959. He remained in that post until 1962, when he was named dean of the UNM Graduate School. Howard V. Finston, who joined the faculty in 1953, was appointed the new dean of business in 1962.[12]

A College of Fine Arts, consisting of the new Department of Architecture and the existing Art, Drama, and Music departments and the Art Museum, had a new dean when Clinton Adams was appointed in 1961. He arrived in time to supervise the completion of phase one of the Fine Arts Center and put into motion a broad program to stimulate further interest in the arts. The first dean, George St. Clair, held the post until 1939, when William McLeish Dunbar succeeded him. Dunbar served until 1945, including military leave in World War II. John D. Robb assumed the post in 1946 and was dean until 1957. Edwin E. Stein, who served from 1958 to 1960, followed.[13]

Robb, an eminent musicologist, published *Hispanic Folk Songs of New Mexico* in 1954. In the preface he told of his travels, tape recorder in hand, through northern New Mexico to persuade people to sing for him. The book, which UNM Press published, included lyrics, piano accompaniments, and commentaries on twenty-three Spanish-language songs that might otherwise have been lost.

A two-part dental program, one for dental assistants and one for dental hygienists, was initiated in 1961. Housed in renovated barracks, the programs were equipped to give practical training to students in addition to classroom work. A grant from the U.S. Department of Public Health supported the program, a part of the UNM College of Pharmacy. The first class of eighteen dental hygienists graduated in June 1963.[14] One of the prime movers in the development of the program was Professor and later Director Monica Novitski, who had earned dental hygienist and dentistry degrees at Marquette University.

The deanship of Arts and Sciences, UNM's largest college, turned over in 1961 when Dudley Wynn resigned to devote full time to directing the new General Honors program. Hoyt Trowbridge, a specialist in English literature, succeeded him. Trowbridge served in that post until 1970, with the exception of 1963–64, when he was acting academic vice president. During that year, Morris Hendrickson, chairman of the Mathematics Department, was acting dean.[15]

When President Kennedy signed an executive order creating the Peace Corps in 1960, a new opportunity opened for the University. The program would train young Americans to work side-by-side with people in underdeveloped nations. UNM students, like college students across the country, were eager to be a part of this service mission. President Popejoy saw the Peace Corps as a way to increase the University's presence in Latin America.

UNM students began lobbying Congress to establish a Peace Corps training center on campus. It took four tries, but in 1962 the University was designated the nation's first training center for Latin America. Its director was Marshall R. Nason, previously a professor of modern and classical languages, who had left the University for a year to direct the initial Peace Corps efforts in Chile.

Training was conducted for thirteen weeks on campus and at UNM's Lawrence Ranch. Students could receive up to fifteen hours of academic credit. Between 1962 and 1967, eighteen hundred volunteers were trained in Spanish, community development, and world affairs, with field exercises in construction and recreation. By 1965, however, the number of Peace Corps volunteers was declining nationally, and problems developed with the UNM training contract. The program was canceled in 1966, but the University continued as a Peace Corps recruiting center.

Nason remained at UNM and in 1982 was presented the Regents' Meritorious Service Medal. The first director of the Latin American Center (which later became the Latin American and Iberian Institute), he also established UNM's study and research center in Quito, Ecuador.

The Architecture Department had not succeeded in gaining accreditation by 1965, when Tim Vreeland, a Yale graduate who had worked for the well-known architect Louis Kahn, was appointed chairman. Accreditation came in 1966, and by 1968 the program had been reorganized to offer an undergraduate major and a master's degree. Don Schlegel succeeded as chairman in 1969, and the Design and Planning Assistance Center was founded to place graduate students and volunteers in low-income neighborhoods and outlying areas.[16]

Robert G. Lalicker, who had graduated from UNM in 1950, became the executive director of the Alumni Association in 1962, and Frank McGuire, a 1961 graduate and former student body president, was his assistant. Lalicker followed in the footsteps of the University's first alumni secretary, Frank D. Reeve. He was appointed in 1927 to work with former students and edit the alumni magazine. Reeve at that time was a graduate student and later became a professor of history. He also wrote a history of the University as his master's thesis. Winifred Reiter, who graduated in 1930, succeeded Reeve as editor of the *Alumnus*.[17] The editor during the 1970s was Nooley Reinheardt.

The *New Mexico Historical Review* became a wholly UNM publication in 1963. State funds previously allocated to its publisher, the Historical Society of New Mexico, were ruled illegal. The journal's editor, the same Frank Reeve, successfully appealed to President Popejoy for funds. The journal was produced at the UNM Printing Plant, which had been separated from the University Press in 1957. Reeve,

Hoyt Trowbridge

Marshall R. Nason

Robert G. Lalicker

President Popejoy met with the Regents in 1959 (from left): Howard C. Bratton, Ralph Lopez, Dorothy Woodward, Finlay MacGillivray, and Lawrence H. Wilkinson.

who had been editor since 1946, was also a consultant to the Navajo and Mescalero Apache tribes. In 1964 Eleanor B. Adams succeeded him as *NMHR* editor.

During Popejoy's long service as president of UNM, he was blessed by having several outstanding Regents, including Bryan G. Johnson, Dr. Lawrence H. Wilkinson, Cyrene Luthy Mapel, and Howard C. Bratton.

Perhaps Popejoy's greatest moment as president came in 1962 at the time of Red-baiting, blacklists, and confrontations with zealots of the purge movements that targeted university campuses as supposed hotbeds of Communism. Nationally, the movement was known as McCarthyism, named for U.S. Senator Joseph McCarthy, who had chaired sensationalized Senate investigative hearings in the early 1950s. In New Mexico, some of the accusations revolved around seven UNM professors who had signed a resolution calling for the abolition of the House Committee on Un-American Activities. A related issue centered on student and faculty dissension over a National Defense Education Act requirement that students sign a loyalty oath before being considered for a loan.

Members of the American Legion particularly were openly critical of the University. In July 1962, President Popejoy was invited to address the state convention of the American Legion in Carlsbad. In one-hundred-degree heat, he delivered a fiery speech entitled "Second-Class Citizenship," which not only silenced critics, but was later hailed as a classic defense of the rights of faculty and students to seek the truth and speak freely. Some excerpts demonstrate why.

During these turbulent times it has been my purpose to defend members of the faculty and student body, even though I may not necessarily have agreed with their statements. . . . It would seem that a state university without controversy or ferment might be investigated to see if there is any life or vitality in the brains of the faculty and students.

It goes without saying almost that the university is a place of learning, where students and faculty members in an uninhibited way are searching for the truth. . . . First-class faculty members will simply not take assignments at institutions of higher learning if they are aware that conditions of second-class citizenship prevail.

The free play of ideas in the classroom, free and easy access to books, journals, and pamphlets in the library, freedom to search out the truth in the laboratory, are the best guarantees of a free society. Students, when given these freedoms, will surely be on the side of our way of life. The battle will be lost, though, if we use subterfuge, half-truths, and practiced and planned hysteria.

As long as I am president of the University of New Mexico, I shall fight with all the acumen and energy that I have for the freedom of our faculty and our students. I shall do this because I think it is right and necessary. It is the one way that our democratic way of life will survive in the world, a large portion of which is trying to tear down and erode the dignity of man as an individual.[18]

President Popejoy (left) and Lincoln LaPaz, professor of mathematics and astronomy, celebrate the arrival of a meteorite that could still be viewed in the University's Meteoritics Museum in 2003.

Popejoy's leadership in higher education extended beyond the borders of New Mexico. He was one of the founders of the Western Interstate Commission on Higher Education (WICHE), which made it possible for students from western states to receive, at resident tuition cost, training in professional schools of other western states if the home state had no such program. Most of the demand was in the fields of medicine and veterinary medicine. Popejoy was also the first president of the Association of Rocky Mountain Universities, an organization formed to conduct cooperative scientific research projects. He served as president of the National Association of State Universities and Land-grant Colleges as well.[19]

Popejoy and two contemporaries, Robert Gordon Sproul of the University of California and James Lewis Morrill of the University of Minnesota, were referred to as "the three wonders of American Higher Education." It was a special tribute to their leadership abilities that each was elected to head a major university without having earned a PhD.[20] Sproul received an honorary degree from UNM in 1940.

The Founding of the Medical School

Popejoy often said that he regarded the establishment of the UNM School of Medicine in 1964 as one of the highlights of his career as president. Under his administration the groundwork was laid for the school's development in later years as a state, regional, and national center for medical research, education, and patient care. Jake W. Spidle, a UNM professor of history wrote in *Doctors of Medicine in New Mexico* in 1986 that "no single event in New Mexico's modern medical history has

Reginald Fitz

been more important than the decision in the late 1950s to build a medical school in the state."[21]

It had become apparent in the postwar era that the state was facing a physician shortage. Contractual arrangements with WICHE had provided a handful of New Mexico students an opportunity to get their medical educations in Colorado, California, Utah, and Washington. Leaders in the educational and medical communities believed a medical school within the state was essential if New Mexico was to meet the growing demands for health education, care, and research. Popejoy decided to ask first for a two-year medical school, where students would complete their classroom work before going to a hospital or other facility for clinical training.

Supporting the idea were the young specialists who had flocked to the state in the late 1940s and 1950s. They had trained in other states and realized the value of a nearby medical school. There were, though, "some fierce individualists who sneered at the idea that a medical school was needed," according to Professor Robert Loftfield, later a member of the first UNM Medical School faculty. "In their minds, any good doctor could drive into the Gila Wilderness and amputate a leg by flashlight with a pocket-knife without needing to call for the help of some medical school professor."[22]

One of the prime movers in the founding of the school was Reginald Fitz, who had gone to Colorado in 1948 for his medical residency and stayed on the faculty at the Department of Medicine at the University of Colorado. He later became chief of medical services at Denver General Hospital in the early 1950s and then associate dean of the CU Medical School in 1957.[23]

In an interview with Spidle, Fitz provided considerable insight into the people and events leading to the founding of the medical school. He credited the relationship between Popejoy and Dr. Ward Darley, executive director of the Association of Medical Colleges, as a strong link in the relationship between educators and physicians in Colorado with their counterparts in New Mexico.

Fitz proclaimed that the appointment of Harold L. Enarson, who had been executive director of WICHE, as academic vice president of UNM in 1960 was critical. A native New Mexican, Enarson had degrees from UNM, Stanford, and American University. He had taught political science at two universities and served in several important government posts before joining WICHE in 1954. An eloquent speaker and writer as well as a distinguished scholar and administrator, he made a major impact on the University during his brief tenure.

One of Enarson's responsibilities in his new post was to explore the possibilities of establishing a medical school. Through Darley, Popejoy had learned that the W. K. Kellogg Foundation of Battle Creek, Michigan, was developing a grant-in-aid program to assist in the establishment of new medical schools in this country.[24] Enarson had strong connections with the Kellogg Foundation and was later credited with drafting the Kellogg proposal, which received a grant of $1,082,000.[25]

Popejoy, with his legendary energy, enlisted the aid of influential figures in the New Mexico Medical Society, including its then-president, Dr. Lewis Overton, as well as Dr. Fred Harold of Albuquerque and Dr. Robert Derbyshire from Santa Fe. Especially effective, however, was Albuquerque surgeon Larry Wilkinson, who also was a member of the UNM Board of Regents.

Wilkinson was a Texas-born and -educated physician and a prominent member of that generation of ambitious young specialists who had come to New Mexico following the Second World War. After setting up his general surgery practice in 1948 at the old Santa Fe Railway Hospital, Wilkinson quickly became a powerful, respected force in Albuquerque medicine. Aggressively and successfully, he lobbied his fellow physicians for their support of the medical school. At its annual meeting in May 1960, the New Mexico Medical Society went on record endorsing the creation of a two-year medical school at UNM.[26]

With the UNM faculty, administration, and governing board in line and the backing of the state medical society, Popejoy turned his attention to the legislature. The Kellogg grant was Popejoy's trump card in convincing legislators to support the proposed school. Jack Campbell, the powerful speaker of the House of Representatives and a future governor, lent his aid, strongly supporting the president. After receiving approval in the House, the bill was deadlocked in the Senate until the majority leader, Fabián Chávez of Santa Fe, threw his support behind it, and an initial appropriation of $25,000 was approved. It was a narrow win, but a win nonetheless.[27] In 2001 an endowed chair in the School of Medicine was named for Chávez, and Dean Paul Roth said, "He was one, along with a few other key folks, who dreamed the dream and had the vision of a medical school in New Mexico."[28]

The appointment of Fitz in July 1961 as the UNM School of Medicine's first dean was hailed as brilliant. With both his father and grandfather having served as deans of medicine at Harvard University, he was well connected with the world of medicine. He was also familiar with both New Mexico and Colorado. Most of all, though, he was viewed as a person of vision and inspiration, one who had the courage to dream. In a region where many "quite reasonably saw empty, unattractive mesa-land dotted with scrubby desert plants and tumbleweeds," Fitz "envisioned buildings and a bustling medical center." One of his successors as dean, Leonard Napolitano, wryly commented: "He had a lot of the missionary in him. . . . He was a remarkable judge of horse flesh in terms of the people he recruited."[29]

The facilities at first were not much. The University bought an old Seven-Up bottling plant and the Exeter-Tonella Mortuary, and later added space in temporary buildings for the library.[30] In 1962 word came that Congress did not approve a bill to fund medical schools, but within months New Mexico's U.S. Senator Clinton P. Anderson announced a National Institutes of Health grant for construction. Dean Fitz and architect Robert Krueger presented their preliminary plans to the Regents on April 8, 1963. The estimated cost for construction was $3.74 million, which was to be covered by the federal grant, Kellogg Foundation funds, some University funds, and smaller grants. These, however, would provide for only two-thirds of the proposed building. Again, the state's supportive congressional delegation, Senator Anderson and Representatives Joseph Montoya and Thomas G. Morris, came to the

Harold L. Enarson

The former soft-drink plant that was the first home of the School of Medicine fit in with the campus's Spanish-Pueblo Revival architecture.

rescue, announcing in June 1964 the award of an additional grant so the building could be constructed as designed.

Fitz made arrangements with the trustees of the Bernalillo County-Indian (BC-I) Hospital, which bordered the campus, and the Veterans Administration Hospital for the School of Medicine to assume responsibility for their intern and residency training programs, which the University of Colorado had previously sponsored. (The county-Indian hospital was renamed Bernalillo County Medical Center in 1968, and a year later the University assumed operational control. The name was changed to University Hospital in 1979.)

The new dean's effort to assemble an excellent faculty was described as "remarkably successful." That new faculty included Solomon Papper, a nationally known nephrologist who came from the Bernalillo County-Indian Hospital to join UNM as chairman of the Department of Medicine; James S. Clarke, the first chairman of the Department of Surgery; Robert Loftfield as head of biochemistry; Leroy McLaren and Joseph Scaletti in microbiology; Sidney Solomon as chairman of physiology; Robert S. Stone, the first chairman of pathology and Fitz's successor as dean, who became director of the National Institutes of Health; Robert Anderson, later chairman of the Pathology Department; Aaron Ladman, first chairman of the Department of Anatomy; and Leonard Napolitano, a professor of anatomy.[31]

Fitz can be credited with developing "a unique pedagogical approach" that lured these talented doctors eager for an opportunity to reform their profession. They developed an interdisciplinary program that came to be called the "organ system or bloc system approach" in which "individual subjects were presented and analyzed with the several basic medical sciences contributing their particular perspectives."[32]

The first UNM Medical School class, consisting of twenty-four students chosen from more than two hundred applicants, began the program in the fall semester of 1964. The curriculum included anatomy, biochemistry, physiology, microbiology, pathology, pharmacology, clinical laboratory medicine, introduction to clinical medicine, history-taking, and physical diagnosis.[33]

To nobody's real surprise, within two years, the program at UNM became a full-fledged, four-year MD degree. Skeptical New Mexico legislators speculated that this was what Popejoy and Fitz had in mind all the time, and they probably were right.

An Anniversary and Some Administrators

The year 1964 marked the seventy-fifth anniversary of the legislation founding the University of New Mexico, and the institution sought to celebrate the occasion in style. It was a time for looking forward and a time for looking back. The *Albuquerque Journal* published a "Seventy-fifth Anniversary Edition" on the University of New Mexico, which included short histories of each of the institution's colleges.

A review of UNM's largest college, Arts and Sciences, covered its eighteen departments and traced its history back to its founding in 1899. In addition to awarding the largest number of bachelor's degrees of any college, Arts and Sciences at UNM has always been a feeder for the professional colleges and the Graduate School. At the time of the anniversary, more than seventeen hundred students were enrolled in programs leading to master's or doctorate degrees.[34]

The second oldest college at UNM was Engineering, founded in 1906. In 1964, the college had more than twelve hundred students in its four major departments: chemical engineering, civil engineering, electrical engineering, and mechanical engineering. The college proudly boasted that the biggest problem for its graduates was not finding a job, but deciding which job to take.[35]

The College of Education, founded in 1928, had had three deans since its inception. Simon Nanninga served first, succeeded by Charles R. Spain in 1954 and by Chester Travelstead in 1956. Travelstead initiated doctoral programs and established a multidisciplinary teacher education committee. He also strengthened ties with public schools throughout the state and expanded programs in Latin America. Principal departments in 1964 were elementary education, secondary education, music education, art education, home economics, physical education, industrial arts, science education, and counseling and guidance. Over and above its main job of educating teachers, the college served the state through its Bureau of Educational Service and Research.[36]

At the College of Law, Vernon Countryman succeeded A. L. Gausewitz as dean in 1959. A graduate of the University of Washington, he had clerked for U.S. Supreme Court Justice William O. Douglas, served in the U.S. Army Air Corps, taught at Yale, and practiced in Washington, D.C., before coming to UNM. Countryman had the name changed to School of Law in 1960. In his four years as dean he raised admission standards and was a spokesman for civil liberties and the United Nations. He resigned in late 1963 to join the faculty of Harvard Law School.

Countryman was succeeded by Robert Clark and then Henry Weihofen, who each served as acting dean for one year. The associate dean was Albert E. Utton,

Robert S. Stone. Photo by Dick Meleski

Thomas Christopher. Photo by Dick Meleski

who had been the first New Mexico native to join the faculty in 1962. Utton had been the undergraduate student body president at UNM and then a Rhodes Scholar in England, where he played basketball and earned two law degrees. An authority on water rights and natural resources law, he was faculty advisor for the Law School's highly regarded *Natural Resources Journal* and also chaired the regional Rhodes application board.

Thomas W. Christopher was appointed dean of the School of Law in 1965. He was a graduate of Washington and Lee University, the University of Alabama, and New York University and had served as a law professor at Emory University and the University of North Carolina. During Christopher's six-year term as dean a number of significant steps were taken, including the creation of the Institute for Public Law and Services and the Indian Law Center, which was partly responsible for doubling the number of Native American lawyers. In 1966 the Law School's degree was changed from LLB to Juris Doctor, reflecting a national trend. Christopher also led the planning for a new law building on the North Campus.[37]

Academic Vice President Harold Enarson was lured away in 1966, becoming president of Cleveland State University. He gained national attention with his handling of Vietnam War protests and went on to serve as president of the Ohio State University and president of the National Association of State Universities and Land-grant Colleges.

In 1965 Enarson wrote a profile of the University. "Our goal, shared by faculty, regents, and administrators, and by the business and political leadership of the city and the state, is the creation of a regional 'center of excellence'—a strong, vital, urban university attentive to state needs, demanding in its standards, and skillful in its exploitation of the distinctive regional opportunities in its environment." Enarson acknowledged that state funding limitations required the University to make "hard, sometimes cruel choices."

> But if institutional self-restraint is required, so also is institutional boldness. The State of New Mexico, alone and unaided, is not likely to build a strong and powerful university of true excellence; federal support, especially in key areas, will be essential. . . . A university indifferent to the federal dollar is blind to opportunity; but a university that is uncritical in its pursuit of the federal (or foundation) dollar risks the loss of its identity and the blurring of its purposes. A university, of all institutions, must seek to control and direct its own future.

UNM's specialization in Latin American art, culture, and languages was a key part of its profile, Enarson wrote. He cited the Peace Corps Training Center, a teacher-training program contracted by the Agency for International Development, and Ford Foundation grants for recruiting Spanish-speaking science faculty and providing interns in educational planning to Latin American governments and universities.[38]

As the University prepared for its centennial celebration in 1988, an article in the *New Mexico Business Journal* said Popejoy deserved credit for recognizing UNM's potential as a modern, comprehensive state university.

The list of changes during Popejoy's presidency is a chronicle of the University's coming of age: a fine law school, a medical school, about 40 new buildings (including a world-class concert hall and basketball arena) and the inauguration of teacher-training programs in Colombia and Ecuador, among many others.[39]

The campus at the University's seventy-fifth anniversary in 1964 included Bernalillo County Medical Center (upper left), the twin wings of Hokona dorm, the College of Education complex with its round kiva classroom, and the north wing of Mesa Vista Hall—and few empty parking spaces.

Chapter Thirteen
Other Aspects of the Popejoy Years
1948–68

Introducing President Popejoy at an academic honorary banquet, an English professor quipped, "If you would see his monument, try driving through the campus."[1] The professor could have been paraphrasing the tribute to the architect of several major London buildings, Sir Christopher Wren: "If you would seek his monument, look about you." The reference could also have been a subtle criticism of the closing of some streets through the campus during Popejoy's tenure.

To meet the demands of enrollment growth and expansion of teaching and research programs, the University needed a massive construction program. Popejoy, with his years of experience as comptroller and his genius for procuring land and using it wisely, planning buildings for the campus, and obtaining funds to finance these projects, was the right man for the job. Ferrel Heady, who succeeded Popejoy as president, later stated that Popejoy certainly could be considered the father of the state's modern institution of higher learning.[2]

An indication of the magnitude of the development of the campus during the Popejoy years is that Van Dorn Hooker's 299-page, first-century architectural history needed 100 pages to cover those two decades.

Hooker had great respect for Popejoy—for his energy, his vision, his love for the University. "Popejoy was keenly aware of the need for long-range campus planning, and he made shrewd decisions about expanding to the North and South Campuses and about buying and selling land."[3]

A quick, overall summary would begin with the completion of the chemical engineering building in 1947, followed by the journalism facility and a civil engineering building in 1949, the same year that preliminary planning began for a Law School building. Later highlights would include Mesa Vista dormitory for men in 1950; the physics-meteoritics building in 1952; buildings for chemistry, biology, and geology in 1953; Hokona Hall in 1956; Johnson Gymnasium in 1957; a thirty-thousand-seat football stadium in 1960; a new student union in 1958; the Alumni Memorial Chapel in 1962; and the concert hall in 1966.

Early in 1949 the Board of Regents authorized twenty small faculty apartments to be located on what is now Lomas Boulevard, east of Yale. They were occupied on October 24, 1949, and later became married student housing, then offices.

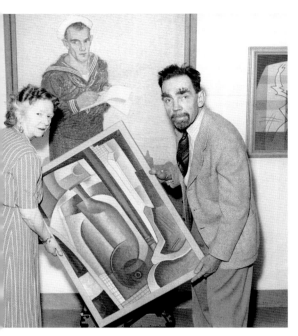

Mr. and Mrs. Raymond Jonson with some of his paintings

Jonson Gallery was the first art gallery on the campus, which John Gaw Meem's associates designed to provide living and studio space for noted Transcendentalist painter Raymond Jonson, as well as exhibition space for his paintings. Jonson and his wife financed it with friends from Santa Fe with the understanding that when he and his wife died, the structure would become University property. It was completed in 1949.

Also in 1949, Hugh B. and Helen Woodward established the Sandia Foundation to which they donated the bulk of their estates. Net income was distributed to UNM and Dickinson College as well as various charitable foundations. Woodward had been district attorney, lieutenant governor, and U.S. attorney and served as a UNM Regent from 1935 to 1937. He had purchased land in Albuquerque that later became very valuable. Years later, Woodward Hall was named for the couple.

With the beginning of a new decade, the 1950s, buildings were being planned and constructed as fast as the administration could conceive of them and architects could design them. With no money for construction forthcoming from the legislature, these buildings were financed by additional student fees and income from revenue-producing facilities, such as residence halls, dining, and athletics. A general classroom building was approved in May 1950, and the project was finished in June 1951. It was named for former Arts and Sciences Dean Lynn B. Mitchell.

North Korea invaded South Korea on June 15, 1950, and the United States was once again involved in a foreign war, although this four-year conflict officially was referred to as a police action. Congress established the National Production Authority (NPA), which had control of the use of construction material that might be necessary for the war effort. The University secured permission from the NPA to proceed with construction of the biology, chemistry, law, geology, and physics-meteoritics buildings, but with no guarantee of allotment of specific materials. The buildings were funded by a bond issue derived from a $10 building fee assessed on all students at registration.

At the August 1951 Regents meeting, the new chemistry building was named for legendary Professor John D. Clark, one of UNM's true founding fathers.[4]

Carlisle Gymnasium was still being used as a concert hall in the spring of 1951 when the *New Mexico Quarterly,* a UNM Press publication edited by English Professor George Arms, published an article entitled "An Exceptional New Mexican: Kurt Frederick." A Vienna native who had played with a prestigious contemporary-music quartet, Frederick was an associate professor of music at UNM and the conductor of the amateur Albuquerque Civic Symphony. Carlisle Gym's acoustics were fine, said the author, former UNM music faculty member Ernst Krenek, a well-known composer, but the atmosphere was not exactly classical.

The Law School building, the first Bratton Hall, was completed in October 1952. This was converted to house the Department of Economics when the Law School was moved to the North Campus in 1971.

In July 1954, ground was broken for a small astronomical observatory on what would be called the North Campus. Nearby, Bernalillo County-Indian Hospital,

Mitchell Hall, a key part of the University experience for all students since the mid-1950s, was a good example of modern adaptations of the classic Pueblo Style. This is the north side, now enhanced by landscaping; the seldom-photographed south side is a little-appreciated design asset in the heart of the Central Campus. Photo by Tyler Dingee

adjacent to University land on the north side of Lomas Boulevard, was completed in August and opened on October 15, 1954.

Meanwhile, with increasing enrollment, the University was reaching a crisis in housing. The University put an old Army barracks into use to house men, and two were renovated for women.

A state general obligation bond issue of $4.5 million was on the November 1954 ballot, but was meeting heavy opposition from the New Mexico Taxpayers Association. Top needs for UNM were listed as a women's dormitory and a new gymnasium. The voters approved the general bond issue, and UNM subsequently received $1.65 million to be used for the construction of a new gymnasium.

In anticipation of an enrollment of some ten thousand students, architect Edward Holien, Meem's partner, developed a campus plan to serve as a basis for planning and siting future buildings. The Campus Improvement Committee, headed by biology Professor Howard J. Dittmer, helped direct formation of the plan, but it lacked a central focus. It was superseded by the development plan done by John Carl Warnecke and Associates in 1959–60.

The Regents on December 18, 1954, approved plans for the first phase of a new women's dormitory. Popejoy arranged the financing, using revenue and land income bonds. At that time, a tunnel system connecting buildings to the main utility plant also was approved.

Two contracts for construction for the women's dorm were approved May 16, 1955, and the completion date set for the fall semester of 1956. The east wing was named Hokona-Zia, and the west wing was called Hokona-Zuni. The buildings inspired a lot of comment. The dean of women, Lena Clauve, wanted alarms on the gates to prevent entrances and exits after the 10 P.M. curfew. The coeds objected. After the dorm was occupied, students called it "the prison," or "the rock" (after Alcatraz). Some also called it "the brassiere" because of its two-wing shape.

Meanwhile, plans for the new gymnasium were nearing completion so bids could be taken in November 1955. The plan called for eighty-two hundred seats in

Kurt Frederick and the orchestra in Carlisle Gym. Photo by Goehring Photographic

Tom and Bess Popejoy greet Rowland Ajayi at a reception for foreign students in 1964. Like almost every other category, the number of foreign students increased greatly during Popejoy's tenure.

the basketball arena, a swimming pool, lockers for more than twenty-four hundred students, four handball courts, and a wrestling room. There were also to be offices, shower and locker rooms, and a training room.

A remodeling of the President's House in 1955 included adding about a thousand square feet to the living room, enlarging the kitchen and garage, installing new kitchen equipment, completely rewiring the house, and installing air conditioning. It was reported that Bess Popejoy was particularly pleased with the new kitchen, which she said would be a great help with entertaining large groups.

In October 1955, the State Highway Department, after eight years in the laboratory building on the northeast corner of the campus, decided to move the operation to Santa Fe. The Regents agreed to purchase the building to provide a home for government-sponsored research. It later became the Computer and Information Resources and Technology Building.

By 1956, planning for a new student union building was under way, and in April of that year students voted to increase their activity fee by $5, with $3.50 to be used to help finance a bond issue for construction of the facility.

An open house for the public was held at the new Hokona Hall on November 11, 1956, and more than seven thousand visitors toured the new facility. At the Board of Regents meeting a week later, Popejoy was given authorization to negotiate with the Public Service Company of New Mexico for a campus power distribution system that would allow UNM to put lines in the utility tunnel system.[5]

Frieda Lawrence, the writer's widow, bequeathed the D. H. Lawrence Ranch north of Taos to the University in 1956. Not a working ranch, the heavily forested 160 acres had spectacular mountain views. There was a house and the cabin where the author of *Sons and Lovers* had worked, as well as a small shrine and the graves of Lawrence and his widow. The University added thirty-one family-size cabins

and a multipurpose three-story building, named Lobo Lodge, and later twenty-one green plywood cabins. University conferences, retreats, workshops, and classes were held at Lawrence Ranch for many years, and employees, alumni, and graduate students rented the cabins for modest fees. In 1960 the D. H. Lawrence Fellowship was established to provide a writer or artist with a summer's residence at the ranch.

The new gymnasium that was still under construction in May 1957 was named for Roy W. Johnson. It is rare for a facility to be named for a person who is still on the job, but "Old Iron Head" had made enormous contributions to UNM's athletic and academic programs. The first basketball game in Johnson Gymnasium was played on December 6, 1957, before a crowd of 3,186. A dedication tournament was held on December 27–29, with the Universities of Wyoming, Michigan, Wisconsin, and New Mexico participating.

Meanwhile, the visionary president encouraged George M. Reynolds, president of Winrock Enterprises, to develop 160 acres of UNM land in the Northeast Heights as a shopping center. The result was a seven-million-dollar project, the largest shopping center ever built in New Mexico to that time. Construction began in 1959, and on March 1, 1961, the center opened. Through the years, millions of dollars flowed to the University from its share of gross receipts taxes and rentals.

The 1957 legislature was critical of Popejoy's proposed men's dormitory, charging that it was too plush and certainly did not need air conditioning. As a result, in August 1957, the Regents approved revised plans, which included eliminating the air conditioning, a costly mistake. In the early fall and late spring and summer, the building, Coronado, was so hot it was almost unbearable. Air conditioning was installed in 1981 at a cost of more than $300,000.

Comptroller and later UNM President John Perovich announced in the summer of 1957 that eight more World War II barracks would be turned over to the

Students of the 1960s describe registration as an hours-long ordeal. Step 1: Find a faculty member to approve your course choices. Step 2: Stand in line in Johnson Gym to get a card representing an opening in the course. If none is available, choose another course and repeat Steps 1 and 2 before progressing through Steps 3 through 12. The professor at right under the "Government" sign is Dorothy Cline.

Roy Johnson at the dedication of Johnson Gymnasium. In 1952 he had traveled to the Olympic Games in Helsinki, Finland, as a gift from the UNM alumni lettermen.

Alumni Chapel was designed by Edward O. Holein to resemble a Pueblo mission church. Its painted-wood altar screen is the work of santero John M. Gonzales. In 1974 a nine-stop baroque pipe organ was installed as a memorial to Walter Keller, former chairman of the Music Department. Photo by Michael Mouchette

Albuquerque Public Schools, which added to the total of seven APS had already received. He added that various departments would continue to use the remaining twelve barracks until permanent buildings could be erected.

On June 9, 1959, UNM Regents and the Albuquerque Board of Education agreed to an acre-for-acre land swap that would give the University enough space for a football stadium, married student housing, and research facilities on the east and west sides of University Boulevard that would be called the South Campus.

November 14, 1959, was a red-letter day as the New Mexico Union was dedicated in an elaborate ceremony. Representatives of the student body and alumni and the director of student affairs, Sherman E. Smith, were the speakers, and the University symphony and choir performed.

Earlier, in September 1959, the Regents had decided that since Zimmerman Field would no longer be used for football after the new stadium was completed, they would name the library for former President James Zimmerman. The old stadium building and field continued in use for intramural sports until 1969. At that same meeting, representatives of the Alumni Association asked the Regents to call for bids on the Alumni Memorial Chapel, pointing out that building costs had almost doubled since their fund-raising drive began. The Regents agreed, and the site was selected. The chapel, which members of the Meem firm designed, would be located between the old Student Union Building and the Administration Building.

The decade of the sixties at UNM began in January when four trees were moved to clear the site for the Alumni Memorial Chapel. The Alumni Association had raised $76,300, and President Popejoy said the University would loan the association the balance, $8,565. The building was dedicated on February 28, 1962.

The General Development Plan, also known as the Warnecke Plan, was presented to the Regents in January 1960. It projected an enrollment of twenty-five thousand and an increase of 1.6 million square feet for the Central Campus, which was to be used primarily for academic functions, with Zimmerman Library as the core. The plan also established what became the powerful Campus Planning Committee, whose first chairman was Sherman Smith.

At the June 8, 1960, commencement exercises, the University awarded John Gaw Meem an honorary doctor of fine arts degree. The citation read:

Nationally honored architect and recently retired founder and head of the firm which since 1933 has designed nearly forty buildings for the University, he has been the guiding influence in the creation of a homogeneous complex of campus structures which has been termed one of the outstanding examples of regional architectural style in the United States. By capturing the soft earth colors and characteristic shapes of the landscape, and through a sensitive use of symbolic design, he has been able to recall both form and spirit of the ancient and rich heritage of the Southwest while meeting the contemporary functional requirements of a growing University.

In 1960, the Lobo statue was moved from the front of old Zimmerman Stadium to the west side of Johnson Gymnasium. Professor John Tatschl, who had created the statue a decade earlier, commented, "You know quite often after looking at something for ten years, you want to disown authorship. But on the contrary, I look back on my work ten years later and I'm still proud I made him."[6]

President Popejoy now had visions of a new football stadium on the South Campus. He proposed using money from land sales to finance a thirty-thousand-seat stadium, and the Regents approved the project in February 1960. When the architect submitted his first plans, the president was not pleased with cost estimates and suggested doing away with the superstructure and putting the stadium in a bowl-shaped depression. This involved lowering the field ten feet and adding fifteen more rows of seats below the original grade level. The changes were approved, and construction began. By September 17, 1960, the stadium and football field were ready for the opening game with the National University of Mexico.[7]

A year later, in their meeting of November 11, 1961, the Regents approved remodeling the old Student Union Building for the Department of Anthropology and the Anthropology Museum. The board also authorized bidding for construction of the College of Education complex and phase one of the Fine Arts Center.

Also in 1961, Popejoy commissioned Bob Lalicker to create a full-scale fund-development program, originally in combination with the Alumni Office and later as a separate unit that grew into the UNM Foundation. Lalicker served as development director until 1965, when Lars Halama succeeded him. Halama hired Chuck Vickers as a student employee, and he stayed with the office until his retirement in 2000. Bill Weeks held the development director job briefly in 1971–72, and then Lalicker returned, serving until 1984.

During 1962, the University under Popejoy's direction bought, sold, and swapped many parcels of land. In addition to his other talents, Popejoy clearly was a wizard at real-estate transactions. He had realized after the war that the golf course on the east side of the Central Campus would have to make way for new buildings, so he commissioned a new eighteen-hole course north of Lomas Boulevard. The course was popular, and it also served as a land bank, a good way to hold on to the land until it was needed for buildings. Over the years it was whittled down to nine holes to accommodate the Law School and parts of the medical complex.

In January 1963, President Popejoy announced that the Research Park would be located on the South Campus on land bounded by University Boulevard, Saint Cyr, Coal, and Bridge. Mr. and Mrs. C. R. Davis sold the University the parcel of just over one hundred acres for $1.1 million, money derived from the sale of some University land near the airport. It was not until June 1965 that the first tenant was approved, the Dikewood Corporation, which dealt with operations research and systems analysis. Few at the time could envision the park's impact on scientific research and economic development in the community and state in the years to come.

The mounting pressure on the UNM campus for planning, designing, reviewing bids, awarding contracts, and supervising construction finally led to the establishment

Van Dorn Hooker

A new University logo was created for the seventy-fifth anniversary.

of the Office of the University Architect in 1963. After marathon interviews, Van Dorn Hooker, a partner in the Santa Fe firm of McHugh and Hooker, Bradley F. Kidder, and Associates, became UNM's first University architect.

By 1963, the first phase of the College of Fine Arts building was completed and occupied. Formal dedication did not occur until October 1964.

As the University celebrated its seventy-fifth anniversary, the new facilities for the College of Education were ready for dedication. The ceremony included presentation of a new University medal, designed by Art Professor Ralph Douglas, to U.S. Senator Clinton P. Anderson.

The eight-building Education complex included a round, kiva-like classroom building and a faceted, stained glass wall designed by Professor of Art John Tatschl on the administrative building. The architect was Max Flatow, a Texas native who had designed buildings for Los Alamos National Laboratory before founding his own firm in Albuquerque in 1947. The focus of early criticism for its unconventional design, the Education project was praised because "while it respects and draws inspiration from traditional architecture of this region, it also accepts modern technology without apologies . . . and rises . . . to a new and creative plane."[8]

The anniversary year also saw the first major exhibition in the University's new Art Museum. Fine Arts Dean Clinton Adams had hired Van Deren Coke to direct the museum, housed in the Fine Arts Center. The two decided the museum collection should emphasize prints and photographs, because outstanding examples of these relatively new media were available at reasonable prices. The museum also would track the offerings of the art and art history programs and would be affiliated with the Tamarind Institute of Lithography.

The Regents approved an eighteen-hole golf course on the South Campus in March 1964. The Campus Planning Committee on March 24 approved a site for a tower on the plaza north of the Student Union to mount the bell from the battleship *U.S.S. New Mexico.*

James Webb Young donated land near Cochiti Pueblo to the University in March of 1965. Nicknamed Old Jim Young, he had been a director of the influential J. Walter Thompson advertising agency and a part-time New Mexico resident. He developed an orchard on his 9,550 acres and sold apples by mail. The land was valued between $350,000 and $450,000 when it was donated, and the University planned to continue the orchard operation.

By the mid-1960s, so much building was going on that the campus looked like "one big construction yard."[9] Rerouting of old streets, opening new streets, new buildings, additions to old buildings, and utility extensions disrupted campus life, often to the consternation and downright exasperation of students, faculty, and staff. For the long run, though, beautiful things were happening.

In October 1965, the state Board of Finance approved a University revenue bond issue to finance a basketball arena, an Olympic swimming pool, new dormitories and dining hall, new KNME-TV studios, a utility package, and landscaping. That same month the Regents approved a contract for the Basic Medical Sciences Building.

This faceted-glass wall on the west side of the Education complex's administration building was designed by art Professor John Tatschl. Completion of the complex enabled Education Dean Chester Travelstead and his faculty and students to move out of their shabby quarters in Hodgin Hall. Photo by Dick Meleski

Van Deren Coke

Several months later, 1966, the Regents approved a lease-purchase arrangement for an existing store building on the southwest corner of Central and Stanford to house the Architecture Department.

At a Rotary Club meeting in April 1966, President Popejoy unveiled plans for a vastly expanded Medical School with $150 million of new buildings. That same year, an extension to the library was added.

The concert hall under construction in the Fine Arts complex was named for President Tom Popejoy. It is reported that Vice President Sherman Smith asked Popejoy if he would have preferred having the football stadium named for him. Popejoy replied that he would rather have the concert hall as his memorial. Another version of the story comes from Coleman Travelstead, who in the mid-1960s was a member of the Student Senate. He says the senate, after consulting with Popejoy, passed a resolution calling for the concert hall to be named for him.

Popejoy Hall, which in 2003 is still one of the state's premier venues, was dedicated in October 1966 with a performance by the Utah Symphony Orchestra. The design and acoustics received rave reviews, as did the art works in the foyer.

Also in 1966, plans were approved for an addition to the Biology Building, the construction of a building for the College of Business Administration, construction of an Engineering Center, and the building of a new dormitory complex. This was later named Laguna–DeVargas, with La Posada as the dining hall.

In addition, the athletic facility for basketball, later referred to as the Pit, was ready for the Lobos' opening game against Abilene Christian College, December 1, 1966. With a seating capacity of more than fourteen thousand (later enlarged to eighteen thousand), it was an engineering feat as well as an athletic structure that often is ranked among the best in the world.

The Regents began 1967 by approving designs for a new building for the Law School and plans for the Student Health Center–University College project; the Student Health Center building was completed in June 1968. The law building was to be funded from the 1967 legislative bond issue and the federal Higher Education Facilities Act, Title II, for graduate facilities, and it was completed in 1971.

The addition to the Biology Building was dedicated on November 10, 1967, with biology Professor Martin Fleck serving as chairman of the ceremonies. In June 1968, the Regents named the building for Edward F. Castetter, professor emeritus and former chairman of the department and academic vice president.

The Basic Medical Sciences Building was dedicated on November 18, 1967. The *Albuquerque Journal* ran a special section to help commemorate the event.

Planning, designing, and construction continued at a hectic pace as Popejoy entered the twilight time of his forty-seven years as a student, teacher, and administrator at his beloved UNM. Grinning shyly, and in his customary self-deprecating way, he acknowledged he did not want to wear out his welcome and announced plans for his retirement. On December 14, 1967, the Board of Regents announced that Ferrel Heady, then serving as academic vice president, had been selected to succeed Popejoy and would take office on July 1, 1968.[10]

The Gallup Campus

The University had offered extension courses in Gallup as early as 1957, and by the mid-1960s community leaders were lobbying for a two-year college. President Popejoy commissioned Bob Lalicker, the assistant to Academic Vice President Ferrel Heady, to prepare an implementation plan for a UNM campus. Voters approved a property tax levy in 1967, the legislature appropriated a modest $22,000 in 1968, Calvin Hall was named campus director, and the first classes were offered that September at Gallup High School.

In 1969 Bert Cresto donated six acres south of town. The Gallup Lions Club provided a building on the site, Lions Hall, the campus's first building. Clair Gurley, a Gallup car dealer, and his wife later gave fifty-two adjoining acres.

The University's famed Pit was consistently rated one of the best college sports facilities in the country. It was Tom Popejoy's idea to build it below grade level to save money, and he insisted that no columns block spectators' view.

Student Life

Reflections on student life are sometimes enhanced by the passage of years. Three UNM alumni presented their remembrances of the postwar era in articles published in the *Albuquerque Journal* on October 29 and November 5, 2000.

One of the authors, Ben Duncan, came to UNM from Alabama in 1947 and graduated in 1950. After taking his master's at Oxford, he chose to stay in England, where he eventually went into advertising, journalism, and broadcasting. He published two novels, and in 1976, he joined Cambridge University, where he taught until his retirement in 1989.

In his essay he related that his acquaintance with the University began in 1946 when a fellow soldier showed him a UNM catalog. Excited about this "exotic" place, he decided to use his G.I. Bill to study literature and psychology at UNM.

The new Student Union had a great wooden dance floor.

His journey by train across the South wound up in Albuquerque. His impressions of Albuquerque began with the piles of Native American crafts on the rail-station platform and the clothes of the people selling them.

Then the bustle of the downtown streets, hearing more Spanish than English spoken, the sound of cowboy boots on the pavements, the smell of spices, fruits and vegetables all new to me.

The university provided a bus . . . to take me and other students, predominantly veterans . . . out to Kirtland Field, the Air Force base where the university had rented housing for us all . . .

I'll never forget my first walk across campus, stepping into the real world promised by the catalog photographs, climbing the hill from Central up to Hodgin Hall, seeing the pueblo style for the first time. Who needed fake Gothic, Ivy League buildings when you could be going to classes in buildings that seemed to link you with a shadowy, unthinkably ancient past?

At registration in a huge room, I heard voices and accents all around me which themselves told me what a varied band I'd landed among. Later we heard that every one of the then 48 states was represented. But my ears told me almost as much.

Then of course, there were the Hispanic students . . . If anyone had a right to be at home in the place, they did. They were quiet, unassuming, warm, open. I wondered what thoughts were going through their heads as they watched the rest of us arrive in what was, after all, their land. . . .

UNM consisted of two worlds: one, the college life that could have taken place anywhere in the states, consisting of football, fraternities, college kids trying to be like college kids in films; the other, a world of rebellious, questioning, creative young men and women, unconventional in dress and lifestyle, quickly finding places to live in Old Town or other predominantly Hispanic parts of the city. I moved uneasily between the two worlds for a year, and then jumped into the second. . . .

Here's a memory: Six or eight young men and women, in jeans and T-shirts, lying in a sort of circle on the grass, using their textbooks as head rests. . . .

Newspapers of the time told of universities so crowded with GIs that football stadiums replaced lecture rooms. Some freshmen and sophomore classes were big at UNM, but thinned as we reached the last two years, and I have a sense of teachers aware of individual students, classes small enough for us to ask questions and share what we knew.

Duncan capped his essay by saying he could still close his eyes and remember hearing water "gushing into an irrigation ditch, a guitar, the sound of horses' hooves on a dusty road, growing more distant, and finally, out of hearing."[11]

Mel Firestone arrived on the UNM campus about the time Duncan was graduating, 1950. A native of Nebraska, he had a double major in anthropology and sociology and graduated in 1954. After later receiving his PhD in anthropology at the University of Washington, Firestone taught and conducted fieldwork at universities in the United States, Newfoundland, and Devon, England. Later he was a fellow of the American Anthropology Association and the Royal Anthropological Institute of Britain. He joined the faculty at Arizona State University in 1968 and retired in 1997.

Firestone had attended the University of Southern California in his freshman year, but on the drive home, "the University of New Mexico and its Anthropology department got in the way."

Firestone recalled that "in those mystic times of 1950–54, one could see with vivid, smogless clarity from the Sangre de Cristo Mountains all the way to Mount Taylor . . . New Mexico was exotic to an innocent young [Nebraska] Cornhusker."

With housing in great demand when he arrived on campus, Firestone finally found lodging in an apartment behind Okie Joe's, a popular bar on Central Avenue across from the campus.

Firestone's most vivid memories of UNM revolved around his relationships with members of the Anthropology Department. He cited several, beginning with Professor Frank Hibben, who was his boss and mentor on several digs. Firestone described Hibben as a "particularly colorful man" who was fond of using such expressions as "a trial for academic strength" for an examination, and "the late lamented misunderstanding" for World War II.

Firestone reported that he was greatly impressed by Professor Leslie Spier, one of the paramount anthropologists of his day. Retired from Yale, Spier taught at UNM for one semester each year. Firestone described Spier as a short, kindly, dignified, grandfatherly man, who wore a gray wool suit and a broad-brimmed cavalry campaign hat. Of the latter, Spier said, "Everyone is entitled to one eccentricity and this is mine."

Firestone's favorite professor was W. W. "Nibs" Hill, chairman of the department. A tall, gangly man with a sense of humor, he lectured sitting cross-legged on a table at the front of the classroom with a cigarette dangling from his mouth. Hill would light the cigarette with a kitchen match, then continue to lecture while the match burned closer and closer to his fingers. Forgetting the lecture, the students were focused on the match, but Hill would wait until the last second and then blow the match out.[12]

The third member of this trio of essayists was Phyllis (Flanders) Dorset, who arrived at UNM in the fall of 1949 after earning a master's degree from the University of Washington. Along with pursuing her doctoral program in English, she taught English composition. She was a technical editor, first with Sandia Corporation and then the Stanford Research Institute, retiring in 1991. She began her essay by saying that "sheer luck" freed her from the "sulky-skied Pacific Northwest to the clear blue skies and the warm, open people of New Mexico." She was advised that since

W. W. "Nibs" Hill

1957

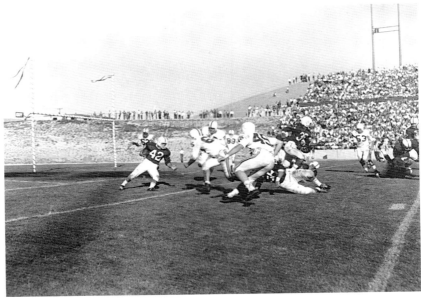

Quarterback Bobby Santiago (42) was a third-team All-American in 1962, leading UNM to the Western Athletic Conference title.

A three-year letterman, 1957–59, Don Perkins rushed for 2,001 yards in his career and received All-American honors following his senior season. He went on to play for the Dallas Cowboys.

she had earned a master's degree at the University of Washington, she should seek another institution for her doctorate, and she picked New Mexico. After a long train trip, she was deposited in Albuquerque in "the high, dry heat of a late summer afternoon, armed with considerable elan and a teaching assistantship."

New Mexico in the late 1940s and early 1950s was a feast, with its stunning, sun-baked vistas of tawny earth, blue mountains, endless skies and its energetic people, full of gratitude that the war was over and full of hope for their futures.

The spirit of the new was everywhere—new industries, new restaurants, new art galleries, new stores, new theater companies, new bookstores, new houses, new cars, new clothes, and, underlying all of it, new ideas. Discoveries were being made in all fields, from anthropology to art and literature, medicine and nuclear physics, geology and engineering.

True, that was happening all over America. What set New Mexico apart was its mythic past and its overlay of cultures—Native American, Spanish, Mexican and Anglo-Saxon. Looking back on it now, I see that the fusion of the ancient with the modern—energized by our youthful optimism—formed an explosively creative period in our lives.

The student body at UNM, as well as the campus, were relatively small compared with other schools, and it was easy to make friends. Most of us were from "away"—only being at UNM by happenstance. What we shared was the adventure of being there. . . .

Over half the students were ex-GIs. Older, smarter and sophisticated, the veterans were eager, probing, and flinty. They sparked the best in the rest of us. From this climate came searching questions that led to papers that were scholarly enough to reach print in professional journals. We had our own set of local icons—Witter Bynner, Oliver La Farge, Mabel Dodge Luhan, Frieda Lawrence, Dorothy Brett, Frank Waters, Paul Horgan. Our minds seethed with ideas, our discussions were lofty (some would say pompous).

New Mexico was a poor man's Paris. People lived art. The signs were everywhere, in its architecture, and its art, and in people's daily lives. Original paintings in a myriad of media and styles hung not only in galleries, but in restaurants, banks, shops, libraries, offices, hotels and public buildings. Prime movers in this artistic explosion at the University were Raymond Jonson . . . and Ada Yunkers, both of whom found New Mexico irresistible.

After graduation, most of us left New Mexico, fully believing that we would come back. In our brief stay, it had become "La Querencia," which the Spanish translate to "Land of the Heart's Desire."

But, we didn't come back; our paths took different directions. Yet, wherever we are, the merest nudge—a still, warm day in September, a stuccoed wall with an uneven surface, a random piece of red sandstone, and we are there.[13]

UNM cheerleaders

At the close of each academic term, at each commencement, alumni go forth from the University, each with a personal story of the long journey to earn a degree. Where they go, the University goes with them. They become the professionals, the leaders in their communities, large and small, in New Mexico, in their country, in the world. Whether they ever return to their alma mater, either physically or in their dreams, they always remember the warm days, the Pueblo Style campus, the gracious people, and the professors and friends they knew while they were there in that special, exotic place.

Athletics

President Popejoy had been a football player, not the kind of student most favored by some faculty, and he had not earned a doctoral degree. He had a certain degree of self-consciousness about these chinks in his armor. His sense of humor served him well, though. When asked if he liked his job as president, Popejoy once replied, "Well, the pay isn't so hot, but I sure do get to meet a lot of football coaches."[14]

Indeed he did. In his first twelve years as UNM president, Popejoy welcomed and said farewell to five football coaches: Berl Huffman (1947–49), Dudley DeGroot (1950–52), Bob Tichenal (1953–55), Dick Clausen (1956–57), Marv Levy (1958–59), and Bill Weeks (1960–68). Of these, only Levy, with a two-year mark of fourteen wins and six losses, had an overall winning record. He went on to coach in the National Football League and was elected to its hall of fame. However, DeGroot's 1952 team had the best defensive record in the nation, giving up only forty-six points in nine games. The Lobos were invited to the Sun Bowl, but Popejoy kept them at home, wanting to emphasize academics over athletics.

The Lobos' first true big man, Ira Harge was a first-team All-WAC performer in 1963 and '64. He was selected by the Philadelphia 76ers in the second round of the 1964 NBA draft. Photo by Dick Meleski

Pete McDavid served as UNM's director of athletics from 1956 to 1974. He also was a letterman for the Lobo football team, graduating in 1938.

Adolph Plummer works out in Zimmerman Stadium. He was a two-time All-American in the 440-yard run.

On the basketball court, Toby Roybal was a standout. In 1955 he scored a total of 110 points in three consecutive games, including 45 in one game—and this was before the 3-point shot.

Many fans believe the golden age of UNM athletics was the first five years of the 1960s. In the fall of 1963 Bill Weeks's football team beat the University of Arizona for the second of three straight conference championships; in the spring of 1964 Bob King's men's basketball team tied Arizona State for the first-ever conference crown and was runner-up in the National Invitational Tournament finals. That same spring Dick McGuire's men's golf team and Hugh Hackett's men's track team won conference titles. Hackett produced thirty-four All-Americans in track and field, including UNM's first, Buster Quist, named to the 1958 college track team. He had placed second in the NCAA javelin throw, becoming the first Lobo to place in a national meet. Quist was a two-time Skyline Conference javelin champion and also played baseball and skied.

Overall, between 1960 and 1965 UNM men's football, basketball, golf, and track and field combined for eleven conference championships. McGuire's golfers won nine titles in a row and ten in eleven years. Moreover, basketball "awoke from a long slumber, igniting a phenomenon called Lobomania."[15]

Pete McDavid had been appointed UNM athletic director in 1956. Described as "a friendly but hard-driving Illinois transplant," he had played football for UNM and coached at Santa Fe High School and Albuquerque High School, where his teams won a state championship in football and two state titles in track.[16]

At UNM McDavid proved to be a good judge of coaches, hiring Hackett, Weeks, and King as well as gymnastics coach Rusty Mitchell, whose teams gained national recognition. Among the outstanding athletes of the period were hurdler Dick Howard, a 1960 Olympic bronze medallist; half-miler Jim Dupree; Adolph Plummer, who set a world record in the 440-yard dash in 1963; and Bob Smith, who won the WAC championship in the trampoline in 1965.

The golden age of Lobo athletics did not last. When most Division I football teams went from one-platoon to two-platoon football in the mid-1960s, the UNM program was not given the resources to follow suit. This was an administrative decision tantamount to deemphasizing the sport. The team won only six games in the next three years. Weeks resigned as football coach but stayed at the University as a member of the legislative liaison team.

Lobo basketball, however, exceeded all expectations as a crowd-pleasing, money-making favorite. As *Albuquerque Journal* sportswriter Mark Smith pointed out, before Bob King came to UNM from the University of Iowa, the program was as dismal and barren as Albuquerque's Northeast Heights, and "everything east of Wyoming Boulevard was basically dirt. So were the Lobos."[17]

In King's second season, UNM, playing home games in Johnson Gym, tied for the championship and had a season record of twenty-three and six. By 1966, Lobo basketball was ready for the Pit, built at a cost of $1.5 million. President Popejoy was credited with the vision along with Athletic Director Pete McDavid and architect Joe

Boehning. Constructed across University Boulevard west of the football stadium, it employed the same concept that made the stadium so economical: the excavation of a bowl for the seating area. Coach King wanted the seats to be as close to the playing court as possible. President Popejoy said there should be no columns to interfere with any spectator's view.[18]

The UNM athletic program made giant strides under Popejoy in three different regional conferences. When he became president in 1948, UNM was a member of the Border Conference, which had been organized in 1933. Then, from 1952 to 1962, the University was a member of the Skyline Conference. In 1962, UNM became one of six charter members of the Western Athletic Conference (WAC), along with the University of Wyoming, Colorado State University, the University of Arizona, Arizona State University, and the University of Texas at El Paso.

Popejoy and Golf

While Popejoy was revered as a football hero and praised for his vision in the construction of the Pit and renaissance in basketball, it was his passion for golf that led to UNM's prowess in the sport.

Rather than letting large tracts of University land stand idle until needed for academic and research facilities, Popejoy built golf courses. Hooker wrote:

> Tom Popejoy loved the game of golf. While he was comptroller, working with President Zimmerman, he found funds to build the University Golf course, which extended from Central and Girard into what is now the North Campus. A good part of the funding came from PWA-WPA grants. When the course was reduced by the pressure for building sites, he headed the effort to build the South Course.[19]

By 1965 a $1.2 million course, designed by the famed golf course architect Robert Lawrence, was under construction southwest of the airport. President Popejoy officially opened the South Campus Golf Course in December 1966, with a long drive down the center of the fairway. Not long after that, *Golf Digest* rated the UNM course one of the five best in the country, and it was to serve as the site for later NCAA championship tournaments. The magazine also described the UNM course as "home to roadrunners, ducks, jackrabbits, and cottontails plus some trout in the ponds."[20]

Popejoy Remembered

For nearly half a century, Thomas Popejoy seemed almost larger than life. After his retirement, he was plagued by failing health, and he died in the Bernalillo County Medical Center on October 24, 1975, at the age of seventy-two. In many ways he was like a hero out of pulp fiction, bigger than Kit Carson, but smaller than a New Mexican grizzly. His visage was somewhere between Benjamin Franklin and Sam Houston, his personal demeanor someplace between Andrew Jackson and Abe

Toby Roybal was a slick-shooting guard from Santa Fe who scored forty-five points against Montana in 1956, a single-game Lobo record that stood for twenty-one years.

Head coach Hugh Hackett's track and field teams drew big crowds in the 1960s and early 1970s. Among the All-Americans he coached were Clarence Robinson, the NCAA outdoor champion in the triple jump and long jump in 1965, and Barbara Butler, the national discus champion in 1971.

President Popejoy recruited Marian "Sparky" Ipiotis, a secretary in the Physical Plant, to help Regents and other dignitaries put on their academic regalia before commencements and other ceremonies. She kept the job for many years.

Lincoln. Best of all, though, he was New Mexican to the bone. He was the stuff legends are made of, and there never was or will be a lack of tall tales about Tom Popejoy.

One of the most cited Popejoy stories relates to a time when Tony Hillerman was working as the president's assistant. Having completed his master's degree at UNM, the former newspaper reporter and editor was now also teaching journalism. Popejoy called him into the president's office and said, "You're going to get a call from the Sandoval County sheriff. He had a fire in his jail. See what you can do for him."

The sheriff did indeed call and report that some prisoners had acted up, started a fire in the cellblock, and burned eleven mattresses. He added that he had no budget to replace the mattresses and wondered whether he could get some from the University. Hillerman told him he would call him back.

Hillerman found out that while the dorms had no mattresses to spare, the University had recently completed a program for the Peace Corps. Abandoned Peace Corps mattresses were stored under the old football stadium. Hillerman told the sheriff where to pick them up.

Several months later in the Senate hallway at the Capitol in Santa Fe, Hillerman was accosted by the sheriff's brother, a state senator. "Hillerman," the senator said, "you're holding my IOU. I don't like unpaid debts. What do you need?"

Hillerman told him the University's top priority was to get the School of Medicine authorization out of the Senate Finance Committee, where a senator from an eastern county was holding it up. UNM was one vote short. The Sandoval senator examined the list of "ayes" and "nays" and tapped the name of one "nay" senator. "Change him from no to yes," he said. Hillerman explained that this particular senator was leading the opposition. "That's all right," the sheriff's senatorial sibling replied. "He owes me one." Thus, "evildoers in the Sandoval jail got mattresses and New Mexico got an incredibly expensive medical school."[21]

While Popejoy was hailed as a staunch advocate of academic freedom, irate New Mexicans often assailed him over some of the antics of UNM professors. He would smile wryly and reply, "I have told the faculty they have given me abundant opportunities to defend them."

President Popejoy was demanding of his subordinates, but he enjoyed their loyalty, friendship, and downright affection. At the time of Popejoy's death, senators; congressmen; businessmen; newspaper editors, columnists, and reporters; educational leaders; and the general public sang his praises. Some of the most moving words came from those who had worked closely with him on a daily basis. John Perovich, a fellow member of the "Raton ratpack," was Popejoy's vice president for business and finance. As an "apprentice genius," Perovich studied and learned from the master financier, enough to land in the president's seat himself in 1983. Perovich said at the time of Popejoy's death, "He took over a small institution and it grew into a large complex institution. The University and the State were very fortunate to have him at that time."

John Durrie, the University secretary, said of Popejoy, "He came to his conclusions wisely. He wasn't afraid to make any decision."

Sabine Ulibarrí, chairman of the Modern and Classical Languages Department, put it simply, saying, "Popejoy was the best president UNM ever had."

Edith Buchanan, an English professor who introduced thousands of undergraduates to the joys of Shakespeare, summed it up equally well when she said, "He took the time to be human."[22]

In 1964, at the time of UNM's seventy-fifth anniversary, Tony Hillerman had been given the task of writing a short overview of the history of the University of New Mexico. In carrying out the assignment, Hillerman took the elevator to the eighth floor of Zimmerman Library to get a look at the five-hundred-acre Central Campus. Peering out through the rows of small windows, this is what he saw and wrote.

If one could look back—as well as out—from these lofty windows he would see a far different scene. On another sunny February day just 75 years ago the seed from which this great University grew was planted. Then the East Mesa was empty. The village of Albuquerque lay quietly in the Rio Grande Valley a full two miles to the west with more than 50 years to wait before the Atomic Age would touch it with destiny. No roads marked the grassland. The only occupants were the inevitable colonies of prairie dogs and occasional transient coyotes and range cows. Anyone in 1889 who foresaw a "great all-embracing university" at this lonely site . . . could justly have been called a dreamer.

Today . . . the view from amid the topmost books of its [UNM's] library shows how well [the] dream has been realized. Beyond the windowpanes lie a College of Engineering of national prestige, and departments of languages and foreign studies whose brilliant reputations won the University the role as the nation's training center for the Peace Corps. Just to the east stands the most modern College of Education plant in existence. To the north, the first building of the University's new School of Medicine is taking shape. To the south, the first phase of a new Fine Arts Center awaits dedication. To the west lies the home of a UNM anthropology department rated second to none.[23]

For Hillerman, for the UNM faithful, the view from the top of Zimmerman Library was promising, even exhilarating. Much changed in the University's first seventy-five years. Much more would change in the next seventy-five. Meanwhile, if there are those who would seek Popejoy's monument, they would only have to go to the University of New Mexico campus and look about them. ■

UNM · 1970

Professor Van Deren Coke harnessed his art students' outrage over the war and the protests by assigning them to make posters.

Chapter Fourteen
Administration of Ferrel Heady
1968–75

Ferrel Heady

Tom Popejoy had a well-founded reputation for planning ahead. It thus came as no surprise that when he announced his retirement in 1967, his replacement was already on board at the University of New Mexico: Ferrel Heady, who had been named academic vice president in January 1967. Heady was known and respected as a distinguished researcher and teacher, having risen through the ranks in the political science program at the University of Michigan. A brilliant scholar in his field, he not only commanded the admiration and respect of colleagues and students, but also became known as a leader and spokesman for the faculty. Nationally, Heady was renowned as one of the foremost educators in his specialty, public administration in Latin American countries. Among his students at the University of Michigan was David Cargo, who, like Heady, was to migrate to New Mexico. Later, Cargo became its governor.

Writing his autobiography, entitled *One Time Around,* was a pretty smart thing to do because it enabled Heady to tell his own version of some of the events that haunted his presidency at the University of New Mexico.[1] He was born on Valentine's Day 1916 on a farm in Platte County in rural northwestern Missouri near a town called Ferrelview, named in honor of his grandmother, whose maiden name was Ferrel. To be more precise, this county and town are where the Kansas City Municipal Airport is today. His first name actually was Chester and until the death of his father, the appendage Junior followed. The Chester was then reduced to C when he entered the U.S. Navy in World War II.[2] The Navy only required a first name and middle initial. Most of Ferrel's friends called him Chet at that time.

The family moved to Kansas City, Missouri, when Ferrel was thirteen, and he attended East High School. His grades and talent as a speaker and debater led to a scholarship at Washington University in St. Louis. An excellent student, he was a member of Phi Beta Kappa and graduated in 1937 with an AB degree in political science and English literature. Forgoing plans to attain a law degree, he began graduate work at Washington University, specializing in political science and economics. In three years Heady earned both an MA and a PhD in political science.[3]

After teaching for a brief time at the University of Kansas City, Heady accepted an appointment as a fellow with the Brookings Institution in Washington, D.C. His

The 1969 catalog featured a simplified University seal that was still in use on diplomas and other official documents at the turn of the twenty-first century.

residency in Washington indirectly led to meeting Charlotte McDougall in the fall of 1940 and marrying her eighteen months later.[4]

In September 1942, Heady went on active duty as an officer in the U.S. Navy. After being at sea in the Pacific during most of World War II, he also saw postwar service in Japan until his release from the Navy in January 1946.[5]

He obtained a job teaching the spring semester at the University of Kansas City, and his career in higher education was under way. He and Charlotte moved to Ann Arbor and the University of Michigan in the fall of 1946. He rose rapidly through the faculty ranks, becoming a full professor in the Department of Political Science. He also moved onward and upward in administrative posts, and by 1950 was assistant director of the Institute of Public Administration. He became its director in 1960 and held the post until he moved to New Mexico, where he became the academic vice president of the University of New Mexico on January 1, 1967.[6]

In his memoirs, Heady reflected on the change in his life from professor to administrator, writing: "As it turned out, I really had only a vague preconception of what life as a university administrator in that period would be like."[7]

Ferrel Heady succeeded Popejoy as the University's tenth president on July 1, 1968. Little did he know at the time that he was trading the serenity and stability of the life of a humble faculty member for what at a later date must have seemed like a trip through hell in a paper shirt. Looking back on that time, Heady observed that after moving into the presidency at UNM, "the duties of the position proved to be far more demanding than I had anticipated . . . those years seem to make up a segment of my life distinctly separate from and different from what happened before and what has followed, despite the obvious connections with earlier and later events."[8]

Heady later called his presidency the "S&S" Years, a term he borrowed from political scientist Samuel P. Huntington. The term meant both the decades of the sixties and seventies and a period when society was at sixes and sevens, a time of "disorder," "disagreement," or "confusion," when factions of people were "at odds" or "estranged."[9]

UNM's new president was not alone in having to cope with the explosion of campus unrest in the late sixties and early seventies. More than four hundred colleges and universities in the nation shut down in the wake of the antiwar protests in 1970. For UNM, as well as its sister institutions nationwide, it was to be a period of "turmoil and transition," the title of a book written about that era by a UNM Regent, Calvin Horn.[10]

The first indications of campus unrest were reported to UNM's Arts and Sciences Dean Hoyt Trowbridge, who in 1964 received ominous news from colleagues at the University of California–Berkeley.[11] Students on the UNM campus, however, remained relatively peaceful until 1968. Horn pointed out that in the beginning, "nonviolence was the intent of the students and their supporters, who felt that numerous changes were needed both on and off campus." Then he added that "as the war in Southeast Asia wore on and nothing in the University or society appeared to really change, more and more students and professors, originally pacifists, found themselves progressively more disillusioned." As Heady assumed the presidency, antiwar protests and other incidents on the campus angered many New Mexicans, including members of the state legislature. This led to Horn's describing Heady's first year in office as "a trial by fire."[12]

Protests Overpower Academics

Protests at the University of New Mexico began in an orderly fashion in October 1968, with only a handful of the institution's thousands of students actively involved. As the war in Vietnam increased in intensity and the draft became a threat to male students, however, the hostility began to focus on the Navy and Air Force ROTC units. On a pleasant autumn afternoon in 1968, about a hundred demonstrators surged upon the field where the Navy ROTC was practicing close-order drill. Vice Presidents Harold Lavender, John Perovich, and Chester Travelstead were called to the scene and implored the demonstrators to leave. When they refused, the vice presidents ordered the demonstrators to leave or steps would be taken to remove them. Most complied, feeling they had made their point. Three, however, were defiant and were arrested by campus police. Subsequently, after hearings, they were suspended from the University. They appealed on the basis that the penalties were too severe and they had been denied due process. The students received strong support from the faculty. The suspensions were withdrawn, and the case went before the Student Standards Committee, a disciplinary body composed of students and faculty members. Again, the demonstrators were found guilty and suspended. Again they appealed, this time to the president. After reviewing the matter, Heady lifted the suspensions conditional upon the three apologizing for their actions. They apologized, and emotions cooled down, for a while.[13] As Regent Calvin Horn noted, though, the incident affected how the University was viewed.

> The University was coming under increasing scrutiny by New Mexicans, but unlike on previous occasions of public concern, the presidency was not in firm control of campus events and its stature and influence with many New Mexicans was vulnerable in a way it had not been for several decades.[14]

In March 1969, just as the state legislature was nearing completion of its regular session, one of the legislators announced that Lionel Williams, a teaching assistant in the English Department, had made available in a freshman English class copies of the poem "Love-Lust" by Lenore Kandel. While not required reading, the poem was introduced to the class as an example of poor modern poetry written in the language of the street, including vulgar words in the author's description of unconventional sexual behavior. Some legislators were outraged and directed the UNM Board of Regents to remove Williams. Thus, what began as a matter within the College of Arts and Sciences, specifically, the English Department, soon spread to the entire University and the state of New Mexico.

Student Chuck Reynolds (left) looks skeptical about a leaflet being handed out by David Johnson (right). Professor Paul Schmidt holds the sign.

President Heady suspended Williams from his teaching duties, which prompted Joseph Frank, chair of the department, to support Williams by refusing to assign someone else to take over his classes. Another teaching assistant in English, Kenneth Pollack, who was a guest lecturer in Williams's class, used the occasion to deliver a lecture on an allegedly obscene sexual theme. Heady suspended him as well and dismissed Frank as department chair.

Members of the Arts and Sciences faculty were outraged at what they considered the president's egregious assault on academic freedom. Most of the A&S faculty also denounced the state legislature, charging it with dictating to the University.

A special advisory committee appointed by the president recommended that Williams and Pollack be reprimanded with some statement of disapproval, but also be reinstated. Heady accepted the recommendation and allowed the assistants to return to their classes. These actions, however, infuriated most state legislators, Governor David Cargo, and many citizens. Cargo received a reported fifteen thousand letters and telegrams related to the poem. Editorials in newspapers around the state were hostile, and references were made to UNM as hippie-haven and school of pornography. Bumper stickers appeared urging the closing of the University.[15] The University's appropriation request was cut by $128,000. Of that amount, $40,000 was used to fund a Legislative University Study Committee to investigate problems at all the state-supported universities. According to the media, however, many New Mexicans were of the opinion that the committee's chief target was UNM.

In February 1970, a basketball game with Brigham Young University was marked by protests over BYU's policies pertaining to black students. The night before the game large bricks painted with the letters BYU were thrown through the windows of the homes of the UNM president, athletic director, and several of the coaches. BYU was operated by the Mormon Church, which held that blacks should be denied opportunities for full participation in church affairs. The basketball game attracted a capacity crowd to the Pit. The demonstrators threw a barrage of debris onto the court, delaying the start of the game for thirty-five minutes and interrupting it again after about two minutes. State Police officers then stationed themselves among the spectators, and the game proceeded without further interruptions.

During the game, President Heady was confronted with a difficult decision when police notified him that they had received a bomb threat. He reasoned that with the delay of the game, any bomb set prior to the tip-off would already have exploded and directed that the game should continue.[16]

In March 1970, the ultraconservative Senator Strom Thurmond of South Carolina was speaking in Popejoy Hall, but there was such an uproar that the speech had to be discontinued. Many members of the academic community were dismayed that those who had been so vociferous in their insistence upon freedom of expression saw fit to deny it.[17]

A few days after the Thurmond incident, workers discovered an explosive device under the Air Force ROTC building, a highly flammable wooden barracks, shortly before it was timed to go off. Fortunately, the explosion was averted.[18]

What was labeled the most savage event in the University of New Mexico's history began on May 4, 1970, following the deaths of four students at Kent State University. After a protest against the escalating war in Vietnam and Cambodia, the Ohio governor had ordered the Ohio National Guard to the Kent State campus. Provoked by rock throwing and taunting from students, the troops fired into the crowd. That same evening, on the UNM campus, actress Jane Fonda delivered an antiwar speech calling for nonviolent protest.[19]

Following the Fonda speech, an ad hoc group hatched a plan to shut down the University. Their demands included withdrawal of American forces from Cambodia, elimination of ROTC programs on the UNM campus, and more scholarships for Indian students. An estimated three hundred students then marched the two blocks to the President's House on the campus. They massed in the courtyard near the front door, some climbing up on the balcony and roof. President Heady did not believe he could do much about withdrawing the troops from Cambodia and declined to go outside. He did agree, however, to keeping the New Mexico Union open for a continuation of discussions.[20]

The following day, Tuesday, May 5, 1970, Eric Nelson, the newly elected president of the Associated Students of UNM (ASUNM, the undergraduate student body), and Bill Pickens, the president of the Graduate Student Association (GSA), endorsed a plan for a student strike on Wednesday, and plans were announced for a rally on the mall Tuesday night. Nelson also issued his own set of demands on behalf of strike advocates. These included that the state legislature pass a law giving citizens the right to refuse to be drafted in an undeclared war; that the UNM president and Regents notify President Nixon that they condemned the actions in Cambodia and at Kent State; that the University refuse to pay the federal telephone tax that had been imposed to help finance the war; and that requests of UNM physical plant workers who announced that they were on strike be met.

At the rally, much criticism was leveled at the Air Force ROTC program. The rally ended at about 10:30 P.M., and a crowd of about a hundred marched to the AFROTC building, where many entered and refused to leave. Another group reentered the New Mexico Union and also refused to leave. In a telephone conversation with Governor David Cargo that Tuesday evening, President Heady learned that the governor had mobilized the New Mexico National Guard. He was later informed that about a hundred guardsmen had been alerted around 7 P.M. and had gathered at the Albuquerque Armory, about two miles from the campus.

Meanwhile, negotiations continued into the wee hours of the morning at the ROTC building. The demonstrators were finally told they would have to leave by 6 A.M. Wednesday or be arrested. They agreed to hold a press conference early in the morning and then leave before the deadline. This is what happened, and no further action was deemed necessary.

On Wednesday morning, soon after the AFROTC building had been evacuated, strike advocates set up barricades, and student marshals were stationed to persuade students not to attend classes. President Heady refused to declare an official all-

A disciplined line of National Guard troopers passes the Fine Arts Center on the way to the Union, which was occupied by protesters after the May 5, 1970, shooting of four students during an antiwar action at Kent State University in Ohio. Photo by Chester Painter

University strike, but did announce a moratorium from 11 A.M. to 12:30 P.M. for ceremonies on the mall in memory of the Kent State students.

At about 7 A.M. a strike flag featuring three clenched fists was discovered flying from the flagpole on the mall. Two hours later, this flag was hauled down and burned. About 2 P.M. one group of protesters was trying to haul down the American flag and another group was trying to keep it at full staff. Three students were reported to have suffered minor stab wounds, and several other students had undetermined injuries.

Meanwhile, students who wanted to attend classes were able to do so, and most classes were held. There were rare incidents of deliberate interference, though, such as filling a lecture hall with strikers to prevent a scheduled test in a large biology class. Many professors also canceled classes out of sympathy with the strike or because of apprehension about their own safety or that of students.

By late Wednesday afternoon, President Heady determined that it was no longer possible to try to go on with business as usual. He telephoned Governor Cargo, and they agreed that the campus would be closed until the following Monday. In an announcement on KUNM, the campus radio station, Heady also asked that the campus be cleared of all persons except those who needed to be there. Most people did leave, but a core group of strikers entered the New Mexico Union where they reiterated their position that the building belonged to the students. While not concurring with their views, University officials and State Police did not attempt to remove the demonstrators, who for the most part were peaceful.[21]

Thursday turned out to be a relatively quiet day. The standoff at the Union continued, and a group of students met with Governor Cargo in Santa Fe. Concerned Regents took part in a conference phone conversation with President Heady in which it was agreed that the occupation of the Union building was illegal and that

University attorneys should be instructed to initiate proceedings to obtain a court injunction against the occupants to be enforced by campus and city police.

Early on the morning of Friday, May 8, 1970, Vice Presidents Chester Travelstead and Harold Lavender went to the Union, where Lavender read a statement directing that the building be closed at 8:30 A.M. When it was evident that there was to be no response, President Heady went to the Union to make a direct appeal to the occupants to leave. He was booed and called uncomplimentary names.

A court order requiring the protestors to vacate the Union was signed about 3:30 P.M. The Regents were on their way to meet with the president and the Faculty Policy Committee. When this group got together, actions to enforce the court order were under way. President Heady later learned that Governor Cargo at 9 A.M. had delegated authority to State Police Chief Martín Vigil to use the National Guard to implement the evacuation. The governor then departed on a fishing trip, so he was not in contact with persons or events later that fateful afternoon and evening.

The National Guard unit was activated about 3 P.M., and it was decided that the troops would go into action with bayonets unsheathed. This was said to be "standard operating procedure in unstable situations."[22]

At this point, communications disintegrated. Vigil had the impression that the University administration was aware of developments, and he expected to meet the president and other officials at the Student Union. President Heady was under the impression that he would be informed if and when police or the National Guard would be on campus. The president and Regents were still in a meeting when Heady learned the National Guard was on its way. Heady and his party were inside the Union before the guardsmen had been deployed around the building.

Heady and the other officials discovered that Major Hoover Wimberly of the State Police had already read the court order to the people inside, and those persons who had not left voluntarily were being arrested. One hundred and thirty-one people were quickly arrested and escorted through the west exit of the Union to buses waiting outside. Chief Vigil later described the arrests as "peaceful and passive."

About that time, the National Guard arrived and moved quickly to establish a perimeter around the Union to prevent anyone from entering and help secure the Union and other facilities. In addition, about 130 city police and 56 State Police officers with riot equipment took up positions inside and at the entrances to the Union. Shortly thereafter, and unbeknownst to the police, at about 6:20, the National Guard began its sweep around the Union.

What ensued has been the subject of much controversy. One critical oversight was not alerting people in the area that the Guard was surrounding the Union. Also at issue was the order to disperse, which was given only inside the Union; nobody outside heard it. The use of unsheathed bayonets was later viewed as unnecessary force and resulted in at least ten stabbings, including both Guard members and demonstrators or spectators. Some of the latter included reporters and photographers who assumed they would be bypassed as the Guard advanced, whereas the latter had been instructed not to let anyone through their lines. It was generally agreed later that had the evacuation been accomplished under the control of the police, there would have been no crisis.

Once the arrests had been made and the mall area outside the Union cleared, the emergency situation quickly calmed. The campus was quiet. The guardsmen left before midnight and were deactivated by midafternoon the next day.[23]

Classes having been canceled just before the semester's end, the UNM Law School, with Thomas Christopher as dean, had decided to allow students the option of taking final exams and receiving letter grades or earning credits without grades if they also involved themselves in the campus protests in a positive way. "Throughout the turmoil, they served as crowd marshals, striving to keep matters in hand," reports Professor Henry Weihofen in his history of the Law School. The students' most constructive contribution was the creation of the Practical Law Program, which allowed them to practice a more socially conscious kind of law. The program included a speakers' bureau and a clearinghouse for evidence gathering and legal research related to the war protests.[24]

Almost two years went by with no major disturbances. A lot of time and effort were directed toward analyzing what had happened during 1970. The Alumni Association backed the Regents and the administration while the American Legion demanded that members of the board either change their policies or resign. The Regents overruled President Heady's granting permission to the faculty to adopt a motion expressing opposition to the Vietnam War, while the Legislative University Study Committee released a report critical of Heady's assessment of the handling of the spring crisis of 1970. The relative calm that continued throughout 1971 ended when President Richard Nixon announced the mining of the harbor at Haiphong and other North Vietnamese ports on May 8, 1972.

The antiwar protestors around the country reacted immediately. The UNM action began on the University mall at noon, May 8, with about 150 protestors embarking on a march to downtown Albuquerque. On the way they erected a barricade across Interstate 25 near the Grand Avenue overpass. Traffic on the interstate was effectively halted. Police eventually fired tear gas at the demonstrators, clearing them from the highway and arresting two. During the encounter, two people were shot, and one, Carolyn Babb Coburn, a reporter for the *Lobo*, suffered buckshot wounds in the abdomen and chest.[25]

By coincidence, a regular meeting of the UNM faculty had been scheduled that same afternoon, and on the agenda was a motion of no confidence in the University administration. As news filtered in about the turmoil at the freeway, the no-confidence motion was adopted in a secret ballot by a vote of 141 to 103, the total vote representing about one-third of the faculty. Then a formal resolution was introduced on behalf of the faculty urging the impeachment of President Nixon. Heady, as presiding officer, ruled the motion out of order, but his ruling was overturned by the faculty present, and the motion was carried.

The following day, Wednesday, May 10, 1972, a peaceful march of about 250 persons moved from the UNM campus to an entrance to Kirtland Air Force Base. A sit-in led to the arrest of thirty-five persons. The disturbances spread during the day and evening, eventually stretching from the base back to the UNM campus. This led to other arrests, bringing the total to forty-three.

The demonstrators congregated at Yale Park on the southern edge of the campus. The rock-versus-tear gas battle ebbed and flowed, and the police finally occupied the park about 5:30 P.M., announcing that it was closed for the evening. Meanwhile, as some forty to fifty people were treated for minor injuries, the number of demonstrators increased to more than a thousand. President Heady was critical of the use of tear gas in an attempt to confine the demonstrators to the campus and stated that police were driving students out of the dormitories and into the demonstration.

Thursday, May 11, 1972, was the culmination of the crisis as Albuquerque police continued to round up protestors on or near the campus. On the campus, a 10 A.M. rally drew about four hundred people as speakers advocated various strategies ranging from peaceful demonstrations to all-out revolution. By early afternoon, another gathering on the UNM mall attracted about two hundred persons. Most of the group moved toward Yale Park, where they were dispersed by police firing tear gas canisters. Demonstrators ran into several campus buildings to escape and also to rally support, some disrupting large classes. The crowd of milling students grew to more than five hundred. Several attempts by demonstrators to move off campus were thwarted by police directed by a helicopter flying low over the campus.

The Associated Students of UNM issued a series of resolutions supporting a student strike, decrying violence, calling for the impeachment of President Nixon, and deploring the use by police of tear gas and shotgun fire.

The situation continued to deteriorate, leading President Heady to use the powers the Regents had granted him to declare a state of emergency and impose a campus curfew from 11 P.M. to 7 A.M. the next day, May 12. Heady reports: "As the evening hours passed, it looked more and more likely that the curfew order might spark a confrontation at 11 P.M."[26] So the gutsy president walked from his residence to the mall and spoke to the crowd there. He explained the necessity for the curfew to clear the mall and end the pattern of nightly forays off campus and returns to the campus as a sanctuary. He told the students that he would lift the curfew if the people on the mall would stay there, or, if they left, would promise not to return later during the night. Sensing that the students were in agreement, Heady then announced that he was lifting the curfew and would stay on the mall and talk with them as long as they wished. The students responded with enthusiasm, and Heady spent the next two hours with them. Within two hours after the eleven o'clock deadline had passed, almost nobody remained on the mall.

The next day, Friday, May 12, plans were worked out for the antiwar march that started on the edge of the UNM campus and ended at Ridgecrest Park with a twenty-minute candlelight vigil. An estimated fifteen hundred marchers participated with police clearing traffic and staying fifty yards to the front and rear of the marchers. Heady and other administrators and faculty members were in the march.

Calvin Horn

Generally in the hallowed groves of academe, members of a university governing board, sometimes called regents, serve as a lay body to oversee the affairs of the institution. Often such a board sees as one of its primary duties the appointment of a president of the institution, usually a person with a strong academic background, an appropriate academic degree, and experience as an administrator. While the board is recognized as the final authority on all aspects of university life, in truth most of the responsibility for running the institution is delegated to the president, who theoretically is an experienced professional. The president, in turn, often delegates actual operational decisions to subordinate administrators and to faculty, student, or alumni groups. Included in these responsibilities are recommendations for hirings, usually finalized at the level of the president and passed on to the governing board for official confirmation. Most of the time a board concurs with the president's choice. If so, is the board then a mere rubber stamp ratifying the president's decision?

When Calvin Horn was appointed to the Board of Regents on February 5, 1971, he made it clear to President Heady he did not intend for the board to be a rubber stamp. He wanted to be fully informed on all major decisions and personnel appointments before any presidential determination or announcement.

Horn, a 1939 UNM graduate, was a veteran politician with ten years of service in the New Mexico House and Senate, including one year as speaker of the House. He was also a successful businessman. Newly elected Governor Bruce King appointed Horn and Austin Roberts, an attorney from Farmington, to replace Norris Bradberry, head of the Los Alamos Scientific Laboratory, and Larry Wilkinson.[27] There was some speculation that Horn and Roberts were named as Regents to clean up the mess at UNM, but if so, the governor was not acting alone. The following winter the state legislature passed a joint memorial directing the governing board to "play a more vigorous and dynamic role in the control and direction of the educational institution."[28] In his first official meeting of the Board of Regents, March 8, 1971, Horn, by unanimous vote, was elected president of the board, a post he held for the next six years.

A repeated theme throughout Horn's ten years as a UNM Regent was "Who runs the University?" In his book *The University in Turmoil and Transition*, Horn introduced this theme when he recalled the "Love-Lust" poem debacle in March 1969 and the turmoil in May 1970. "Why, the townspeople asked, was the University doing nothing? Who, they asked, was running that damned place?"[29]

Armed with the belief that the Regents had ultimate responsibility, he began scheduling Monday afternoon conferences with President Heady to become familiar with the various problems arising on the campus.

> I soon realized in these weekly conferences that President Heady and I might differ on the role the regents should exercise in the management of the University. It appeared to me that the president felt it was his right and responsibility to run the University for the regents, that the regents

were only the directors of the institution and that their authority should be used primarily to dismiss a president who did not run the university according to their policies.[30]

Regent Horn also expressed repeated concern about the importance of upholding the image of the president. Specifically, he took exception to reports of a faculty meeting November 30, 1972, where a faculty member, following a sequence of obscene remarks, told the president to shut up. The faculty member received a letter of reprimand from Vice President Travelstead, but Regent Horn did not feel that was enough. He appeared to be mystified as to why Heady had not taken a more active role in disciplining the faculty member.[31]

Heady later wrote that he recognized that his lack of outrage at the faculty meeting incident was not pleasing to some Regents. He said he did not share the view that the flare-up during the heated session was an intolerable transgression and that mitigating circumstances helped explain the professor's outburst. He also expressed his disappointment in the failure of the faculty to take any decisive disciplinary action since he believed that the faculty itself had been more wronged than he by what had taken place.[32] This matter dragged out until December 1975, six months after the professor, mostly for other reasons, was denied tenure and terminated from the University.[33]

Another incident related to a faculty member's distribution of a folder containing a front view of a nude couple with President Heady's face pasted atop the male figure. At a meeting of the Legislative University Study Committee, a senator asked Heady if he thought a professor should be allowed to slander a president of a university. Heady replied that he had considered taking legal action but decided not to, whereupon another legislator chastised the president for choosing not to make an example of a person who had failed to show respect for the office and profession. The professor who distributed the folder also treated the committee disdainfully, saying it was none of their business.

Yet another professor was asked if on April 10, 1969, on the University mall, he had said that Heady was "a liar, a hypocrite, and intellectually bankrupt." The professor replied, "I believe I said that Dr. Heady is morally bankrupt."[34]

Horn, like many other observers, believed Heady weathered the storm over the charges against him and his administration from all segments of New Mexico, especially the Legislative University Study Committee. He credited Heady's ability to do so by "being gracious and humble and by completely under-reacting. He was fair and considerate to even those who abused him, possibly to a fault. It appeared that the president had a crisis swirling about his office at least once a year . . ."[35]

Back in the Classroom

Despite the uproar, the traditional life of the University rolled on. Students went to class, faculty lectured, papers were written, books were read, tests were taken, grades were given, credits were earned, and degrees were conferred.

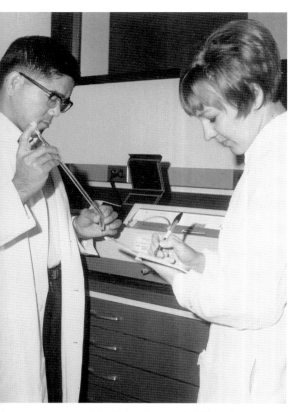

Microbiology Professor Sei Tokuda demonstrates a pipette technique while a student takes notes.

The summer of 1967 saw the initiation of a preparatory program at the School of Law for Native American students under the direction of Professor Fred Hart. By 1970 forty participants in the program were enrolled at various law schools. The following year, Yvonne Knight of Ponca City, Oklahoma, became the first Native American woman to graduate from the UNM School of Law. Dean Thomas Christopher resigned in 1971 to assume the deanship at his alma mater, the University of Alabama.[36]

In 1970 UNM began offering significant numbers of undergraduate courses at its center in Los Alamos, supplementing the graduate courses keyed to the needs of the national laboratory. In 1971 the architecture program, previously part of the College of Fine Arts, became a school in its own right, with Don Schlegel as the first dean. In 1973 UNM's Northern Branch in Española was absorbed into Northern New Mexico Community College.

In 1972 the UNM catalog announced that fellowships and assistantships in lithography were available at the Tamarind Institute, newly affiliated with the College of Fine Arts. Supported in part by the Ford Foundation, the institute offered training, study, and research as well as the production of high-quality lithographs. The UNM Art Museum's extensive collection of lithographs was an asset for the new program.[37]

A new division of the Maxwell Museum of Anthropology was organized in 1973. The Office of Contract Archaeology would undertake large-scale, interdisciplinary cultural resource studies, including projects that required both fieldwork and analysis. In the coming years its projects would include nominations for state and national historic registers, ethnology studies, and archival research.[38]

In 1975 Governor Jerry Apodaca appointed President Heady and the presidents of New Mexico State and New Mexico Tech to the new Committee on Technical Excellence. With private-sector representation from Sandia and Los Alamos National Laboratories, Kirtland Air Force Base, and White Sands Missile Range, the committee made up the Rio Grande Research Corridor. It made recommendations to the legislature for funds to upgrade scientific research, resulting in an additional $3 million a year for five years for buildings, equipment, and library holdings. The investment paid off, as the three universities were prepared to compete successfully for research grants.

In the early years of Heady's presidency the Greater UNM Fund, which the Development Office administered, was the major fund-raising initiative, supporting campus beautification, an addition to the library, and scholarships, among other things. In 1979 Professor Robert Desiderio of the School of Law laid the groundwork for the creation of the University of New Mexico Foundation. Jack Rust became the board's first president the following year.

One of the great losses in this era was the death of the long-time vice president for administration and development, Sherman Smith, on October 5, 1973, following complications from hip surgery. A man of many talents, Smith came to UNM in 1945 as chairman of the Chemistry Department, succeeding

John Clark. Like Clark, he also served as an effective administrator. Born April 10, 1909, in Custer, South Dakota, Smith earned a BS in chemical engineering from the South Dakota School of Mines in 1931 and a PhD in chemistry from the Ohio State University in 1935. After a year as a Dupont research assistant, he became a faculty member at the University of North Carolina, where he served until coming to UNM in 1945.[39]

In 1949, while still a faculty member, he was appointed director of student affairs, and that same year began representing UNM at the legislature. He became administrative vice president in 1965, under the leadership of Tom Popejoy. In 1970, his duties were expanded to include administration and development. In addition to handling UNM's affairs with the legislature and Board of Educational Finance, Smith guided the University through a period of great expansion in the physical plant and enrollment. In 1979, the central plaza on the UNM campus was named Smith Plaza in his honor.[40]

A letter from Smith to the Student Publications Board in 1961 showed his assertive side. That year's yearbook, the *Mirage*, had been mildly criticized in a newspaper column. Smith told the board, whose members selected the yearbook editor, that it was a "disgraceful production" that "celebrate[s] the follies of the 'collegiate sub-culture' at its worst." He urged the board to ensure that "the University will not again be embarrassed by a *Mirage* like this one."[41]

Mark Acuff, *Lobo* editor in 1962 and editor of the weekly *New Mexico Independent* at the time of Smith's death in 1973, reported that Smith was "for all his deep sensitivity and capacity for emotion, just about the toughest character I ever met."[42] V. B. Price, also writing for the *Independent*, reported that Smith was

> a complex individual in an intricate and demanding job—administrator, advocate, legislative diplomat and planner. . . . But more important than even that, Smith was the personification of that rarest and most valuable hero—the practical idealist, the man of vision who has the know how and tenacity to make his vision work.[43]

Price went on to quote the University architect, Van Dorn Hooker, as saying, "You create a campus. You create the most beautiful one you can; not a good campus, but a great one." Price observed that that was what Smith and Hooker had done. They had created a campus that awed people with its beauty, "a monument to modern New Mexican civilization, unpretentiously at peace with our Pueblo and Spanish traditions, but relevant to the present and capable of embracing the future."[44]

Personnel changes under Heady included the retirement of Hoyt Trowbridge, dean of the College of Arts and Sciences, in the spring of 1969. He was succeeded by Nathaniel Wollman, chairman of the Economics Department, in September 1969. A specialist in the economics of natural resources, Wollman had been on the UNM faculty since 1948. In addition to his support of excellence in teaching, Wollman also encouraged the faculty in research and publication by seeking funds

Sherman E. Smith

Smith Plaza. Photo by Michael Mouchette

Cyrene Mapel represented the Regents on the Campus Planning Committee and, reports Van Dorn Hooker, contributed much to the design process. Her fellow Regents are Albert Simms II (back row, center), Henry Jaramillo (back row, right), Calvin Horn (front row, center), and Austin Roberts (front row, right). President Heady stands at left in the back row.

for travel and participation in professional organizations. Among the major changes in his deanship was the implementation of the bachelor of university studies degree program in 1969, a development Wollman first supported, then later regretted.[45] The BUS degree was interdepartmental, and no major or minor was required.

One of the highly successful programs in this era was the Latin American Programs in Education (LAPE), offering training to foreign educators. The inspirational leader of this program was Dr. Frank Angel, professor and assistant dean in UNM's College of Education. Numerous students from this program eventually became university presidents, ministers of education, vice ministers, and directors general in various Central and South American countries.

Angel was a Las Vegas, New Mexico, native who began his educational career at age eighteen, teaching elementary classes in one- and two-room schoolhouses in rural San Miguel County. During World War II he served as a bomber pilot, amassing more than twenty-four hundred hours in flight time and receiving numerous decorations. He left UNM in 1971 to accept the post as president of New Mexico Highlands University, becoming the first Hispanic president of any public university in the country. He also served on President Nixon's Bicentennial Commission. He retired from Highlands in 1975.

In the fast-growing Health Sciences Center on the North Campus, several administrative changes were taking place. The founding dean of the School of Medicine, Dr. Reginald Fitz, retired in 1968. Robert S. Stone, who served until 1973, succeeded him, acquiring the title vice president for health sciences in 1970 and, working with his successor, Leonard Napolitano, consolidated the School of Medicine with the College of Nursing and the College of Pharmacy. Napolitano proved particularly adept at dealing with the legislature, and the school grew and prospered. Under Stone and Napolitano and the faculty they assembled, the center became a pioneer in expanding opportunities for women and minorities.

One of Dean Stone's earliest hires was Dianne Klepper, who had been chief resident in the Department of Internal Medicine 1967, as assistant dean for admissions and student affairs and an instructor in internal medicine. Dr. Klepper served a total of thirty-one years and continued to teach part-time after retirement.

In 1969 the nonprofit New Mexico Medical Foundation was incorporated. Its purpose was to process and collect professional fees earned by faculty members.

Dr. Morton Kligerman was named director of the Cancer Research and Treatment Center in March 1972, a post he held until 1980. In 1972 construction began on the center's facility with a grant from the National Cancer Institute and funds from the New Mexico Legislature. Among the center's research projects was a partnership with Los Alamos National Laboratory in the use of subatomic particles, called pions, to treat tumors.

Other developments included the creation in 1973 of the Office of the Medical Investigator within the School of Medicine and the opening of the state's Emergency Medical Services Academy on the medical school campus.[46]

At the Law School, a six-week institute to prepare minority and disadvantaged students was held in the summer of 1974. It was partly funded by the Council on Legal Education Opportunity (CLEO), a consortium of five western law schools. In 1975 the UNM School of Law received more than $1 million in scholarship funds, one of the largest such gifts ever made in the nation, from the estate of Roswell attorney W. E. Bondurant, Jr.

Fred Hart, the founding director of the American Indian Law Center, was named dean of the School of Law in 1971. He had studied law at Georgetown University and New York University, joining the UNM faculty in 1966. Centro Legal, a program providing legal counsel to poor persons charged with misdemeanors, evolved into the Clinical Law Program by 1973. Law students worked under the supervision of attorneys and judges to see firsthand how law is practiced.

Robert Bennett succeeded Hart as director of the American Indian Law Center and became a national spokesman for this specialized field based on the relationship between tribes and the federal government. He and Dean Hart agreed that the basic legal problem for Indians was the "ambivalent policy of the U.S. government toward the status of hundreds of defeated nations in this country." Cultural differences are compounded by the legal process, they said. "Indians," Bennett said, "see themselves as living in balance and harmony with nature, while whites try to master it and turn it to their own ends and so are in conflict with nature." Bennett retired in 1972, and Philip "Sam" Deloria took up the post.[47]

In 1975 Eleanor Burnham Adams retired after a thirty-four-year career as research professor and editor of the *New Mexico Historical Review*. An authority on the history of colonial Mexico and the Southwest, she was author or coauthor with UNM's France V. Scholes of seventeen works.

The end of 1974 marked Cyrene Luthy Mapel's final term as a UNM Regent. Appointed in 1962, she had served during the expansion years of Popejoy's presidency and the tumultuous years of Heady's term. Calvin Horn remembered her "as the member who insisted that we reconcile our differences if she were the swing vote."[48]

Martin "Jack" Campbell, a Yale PhD whose wide-ranging interests included the archaeology of the Arctic, succeeded W. W. "Nibs" Hill as chairman of the Anthropology Department in 1964. His colleague, J. J. Brody, an expert on Pueblo basketry, introduced him to Gilbert and Dorothy Maxwell. They had been traders of Native Southwest jewelry out of the trunk of their car until Gilbert discovered oil and became president of Occidental Oil Company. At Brody's suggestion, Campbell called on the Maxwells and hinted that if they provided support for construction of a new and much-needed facility for the Anthropology Museum, it would be named for them. They agreed and provided not only funds but also gifts of their outstanding collections of kachinas and Navajo blankets. Campbell succeeded Hibben as director of the museum and served until 1973.

In 1971, UNM and the National Park Service entered into an agreement to create a joint Chaco Project, to promote research on sites UNM formerly owned in Chaco Canyon in western New Mexico. The agreement called for a research

Fred Hart

center within the Anthropology Department and joint management of the resulting archaeological materials in Maxwell Museum.

While a new museum was being built south of the Anthropology Building, Jerry Brody became the first director of the Maxwell Museum with a UNM degree.

While New Mexico had been a home and an inspiration for writers for nearly a century, the 1970s have been cited as a milestone, because the University of New Mexico became the gathering place for Hispanic and Native American authors.[49] Rudolfo A. Anaya, the author of *Bless Me, Ultima,* headed a graduate program in creative writing for Indians and Hispanics. The first fellowship was awarded to Denise Chávez, who went on to a successful career. Among her early novels was the acclaimed *The Last of the Menu Girls.* Other UNM-connected writers included Leslie Marmon Silko, Simon Ortiz, N. Scott Momaday, Joy Harjo, Luci Tapahonso, Laura Tohe, and Sabine Ulibarrí, as well as Tony Hillerman, Stan Steiner, Paula Gunn Allen, John Nichols, and Geary Hobson.

Campus Development and Construction

The planning and building programs were little affected by the turmoil on the campus in this era. The Campus Planning Committee continued to meet, new contracts and projects were approved, and construction projects continued without interruption. By the early 1970s, the campus could still have been described as one huge construction site. Hooker wrote in his 2000 book:

> The area in front of Scholes Hall and the Alumni Chapel over to the future duck pond was torn up for a large landscaping project. The swimming pool addition to Johnson Gymnasium, the Psychology Building, the North Campus Chilled Water Plant, and the addition to the Anthropology Building were all under construction on the Central Campus, while on the North Campus a big parking lot, the Surge Building, and the chilled water plant were being built. To make matters worse, before all these projects could be completed, work was to begin on the Humanities-Lecture Hall project followed by the bookstore and the Cancer Research and Treatment Center (CRTC). At no time in the history of the University, before or since, has the campus been in such disarray.[50]

Among the contributions to campus development was the beautification project at University Stadium sponsored by the Lobo (booster) Club under the direction of Lee Galles. The project included irrigation, grass, and trees on the slopes of the stadium, along with large concrete disks, one with raised block letters "NM" and one depicting a football player, on the corners of the facility. Curbs were also added along with pine and cottonwood trees and chamisa.[51]

The Farris Engineering Center was completed in November 1968 and named for Marshall E. Farris, who served for twenty-nine years as dean of engineering. He had come to UNM from the University of Arkansas in 1931. Budgets were tight,

A thoroughly modern building, Farris Engineering Center was designed by architects Flatow, Moore, Bryan, and Fairburn. It has rows of long, narrow windows somewhat similar to those on Hodgin Hall, its neighbor to the south. Photo by Michael Mouchette

and he served as both dean and chairman of mechanical engineering. He and his colleagues did most of the design and construction supervision for the growing college's facilities. National accreditation came in 1937, and Farris retired in 1963.

Meanwhile, plans were going ahead on the construction and financing of a new building for the Law School. The Regents confirmed a contract for the project on November 8, 1969. At that same meeting they also ratified the agreement for UNM to operate the Bernalillo County Medical Center.[52]

A University landmark was removed from the campus in 1969 when the Zimmerman Field and Stadium complex was demolished to make way for new buildings. During the war years, the Navy's V-5 program had used the Stadium Building as a dormitory, and it later became the offices for the Navy ROTC program. The first classes for the School of Law had also begun in this building in 1947.[53]

The Law School's library in Bratton Hall overlooked the North Golf Course. Photo by Michael Mouchette

In their meeting of September 27, 1969, the Regents approved several building names. Ford Utility Center was named for Professor A. D. Ford, chairman of the Mechanical Engineering Department for many years and of the Campus Improvement Committee in the 1940s. The Administration Building was named for France V. Scholes, who had come to UNM in 1925 as a professor of history and served as academic vice president and dean of the Graduate School. Stuart A. Northrop, chairman of the Geology Department for thirty-three years, was the honoree for the Geology Building. The Civil Engineering Building was named for William C. Wagner, who was with the department for thirty-three years, seventeen years as chairman.

The addition to Clark Hall, the Chemistry Building, was designed by George Pearl and completed in December 1969 and named for Jesse Riebsomer, former professor and chairman. A few months later, March 1970, the Regents approved the purchase of the IBM building on the southeast corner of Central and Stanford to house the Technology Application Center.[54]

The new Bratton Hall, the Law School building on the North Campus, was dedicated on April 17, 1971. Byron "Whizzer" White, associate justice of the U.S. Supreme Court, was the honored guest and speaker.[55]

In 1972, the Electrical Engineering Building was named for Ralph W. Tapy, a long-time professor and chairman of the department. In June the physics laboratories and lecture hall project was completed and named Regener Hall in honor of Victor R. Regener, physics professor and researcher.

The Albuquerque fire marshall declared Rodey Hall too dangerous for use in 1971, and it was demolished. This made it possible to extend Redondo Drive, the loop road, between Tight Grove and the engineering complex. Built in 1908 in the style of a Pueblo church, Rodey Hall had served as chapel, auditorium, and archaeology museum before becoming the home of the Drama Department in 1933. The department's chair, Edwin Snapp, helped make the theater a key part of Albuquerque's cultural life.

In June 1973, Professor Emeritus of English T. M. Pearce wrote a memorandum to Myron Fifield, director of the Physical Plant. Pearce had heard that Hodgin

The Central Campus looked like a construction yard in late 1973, with projects including the Humanities Building, which faces Zimmerman Library across Smith Plaza.

Hall, Rodey's neighbor to the south, was on the demolition list and indicated that he would like to see the building kept as an alumni hall and visitor center. After a tour of the building with Fifield, he wrote another letter on July 1, 1973, advocating keeping and restoring Hodgin Hall. This led to the New Mexico Cultural Properties Review Committee placing Hodgin Hall on the National Register of Historic Places. Under the leadership of alums Tony Jackson and Bill Brannin, plans were soon under way to save and restore the building.[56]

Included in this spurt of activity was the South Campus athletic complex. Plans were implemented in 1973 to expand and improve the facilities for football and basketball, including a new press box for the football stadium and 2,370 balcony seats for the Pit. Space for the Lobo Club, a meeting room, expanded ticket sales areas, visiting-team dressing rooms, and storage for concession supplies, as well as widening the concourse were included in the changes for the basketball arena. The board approved the projects on April 23, 1974. Construction for the basketball alterations was to begin with the end of the 1974–75 season. For football, the target date was the start of the 1975 football season.[57]

At the end of 1973, Ortega Hall, which housed classrooms, language labs, and offices, was dedicated December 8. It was named in honor of Joaquín Ortega who had come to UNM in 1941 and for seven years was director of the School of Inter-American Affairs. He retired in 1954.

Also in 1973, the College of Business and Administrative Sciences was named the Robert O. Anderson Schools of Management. This was the first UNM academic division named for an individual. Anderson, board chairman of Atlantic Richfield, owned a ranch near Roswell and headed the Lincoln County Livestock Company.

By the end of 1973, six major buildings were under construction or just being completed. They included Woodward lecture hall, a humanities building, a new bookstore, the Nursing-Pharmacy Building, an addition to Zimmerman Library, and the Cancer Research and Treatment Center. Together they totaled about four hundred thousand gross square feet, equal to the total square footage of all the buildings on the University of New Mexico campus in 1941.[58]

Woodward Hall, which included facilities for Instructional Media Services, was occupied by the end of January 1974. The completion of the Humanities Building in August of that year precipitated a large relocation of departments and other functions. On the first floor were the Honors Program and the Graduate School; on the second floor was the English Department; the third floor housed American Studies, the Council for the Humanities, and Vo-Tech Education; on the fourth floor was the Department of Mathematics and Statistics; and on the top floor were the departments of Philosophy and Linguistics and the Navajo Reading Study.[59]

On December 31, 1974, Myron Fifield retired as director of the Physical Plant Department, after having served for more than twenty-three years. Floyd B. Williams, who had been the associate director since 1973, succeeded him.

At the UNM Gallup Branch, the campus had grown by sixteen acres, thanks to another gift from the Clair Gurleys. An administration and classroom building had been added in 1974. A Southwest-style building named Gurley Hall was new the next year, when an associate degree in nursing was offered.

The last year of Ferrel Heady's presidency, 1975, continued to be a time of extensive construction. The second-floor remodeling of Scholes Hall was completed in the spring. The deadlines for the alterations and expansions of the basketball arena and football stadium were met. The Cancer Research and Treatment Center was dedicated on August 8, 1975. Other UNM buildings completed in the summer of 1975 were the married-student housing complex on the South Campus and the Dale Bellamah Law Center adjacent to Bratton Hall on the North Campus. The last building to be completed under the administration of President Heady was the Nursing-Pharmacy Building, which was dedicated on October 18, 1975.[60]

Truly one of the high marks of Heady's presidency was a continuation of the phenomenal growth and development of the campus from the days of Tom Popejoy. Fittingly, the announcement of the establishment of the John Gaw Meem Archive of Southwestern Architecture in the UNM library came in May 1975. The gift included a substantial endowment for the maintenance of the collection of Meem's architectural drawings and papers.[61] Van Dorn Hooker, the university architect, was credited with soliciting the generous gift from Meem and arranging for its relocation. Meem and his firm designed twenty-six buildings for the University, and he became known worldwide for his creative architecture inspired by the Pueblo and Spanish colonial buildings of ages past. The beauty, majesty, and harmony of the UNM campus, which date back to the days of President Tight at the turn of the century, were preserved and expanded through the genius of Meem and his partners.

Athletics

In most accounts of athletic programs in a university, the coverage revolves around coaches, athletes, and won-lost records. For the University of New Mexico in the 1970s, however, the attention was focused on leadership in the athletic program and violations of rules.

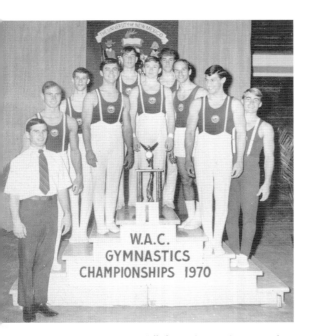

Rusty Mitchell (left), who won three national championships as a Southern Illinois University gymnast and was a member of the 1964 U.S. Olympic team, would stay at UNM as head gymnastics coach for thirty years. His 1995 team was the first to be ranked number one in any sport.

One of UNM's most famous athletes, Robin Cole was an All-American in 1976 before playing in two Super Bowls during his professional career with the Pittsburgh Steelers.

In 1973, when a new assistant athletic director was to be hired, Calvin Horn informed President Heady of his interest in previewing candidate applications. He said the Regents were concerned with the appointment because they thought both the former assistant athletic director and current athletic director, Pete McDavid, had not been very active.

Before there was any discussion with the Regents, however, the president called him to say the Athletic Council had recommended the current basketball coach, Bob King, for the position of assistant athletic director. President Heady said the Athletic Council wished to make an announcement of the appointment and that he concurred with the decision.

During the discussion Heady suggested that he should resign if Horn did not like the way he was running the University. Horn told Heady that while he would respect his decision to resign, he was not interested in being a Regent if it only meant rubber-stamping decisions. "Dr. Heady stated that regents confirmed, not rubber stamped, decisions. He admitted, however, when pressed that the terms were synonymous." The head Regent also told the president that he planned to discuss the selection procedure with other Regents and that this was the last time such a decision would be made without their input.[62]

Shortly thereafter, McDavid announced plans to retire in April 1973. Speculation immediately arose as to his replacement. King had strong support from Lobo boosters, the press, and the alumni. There was another candidate, Lavon McDonald, the associate director of student financial aid. McDonald was a former high school coach in Santa Fe, and coaches throughout the state began writing letters on his behalf. McDonald was also known to legislators and state officials, including Governor Bruce King.

Responsibility for screening the applicants was vested in the Athletic Council, which was to submit a panel of names to the president. The actual selection fell to the president, after consultation with the Regents. The Athletic Council on August 28, 1973, recommended King. The president pointed out, however, that the council was to submit a panel of names and was not authorized to recommend a specific person. Therefore, on September 4, 1973, the council submitted three names: Bob King, Dale Foster, and Bill Weeks. McDonald was not on the list. A member of the Athletic Council, Professor Robert S. Nanninga, wrote to President Heady objecting to the procedures. "I do feel that by failing to include the name of Lavon McDonald that the council is definitely limiting your latitude of responsibility as you make your recommendation to the regents."

On September 14, President Heady informed the Regents privately that in his opinion Bob King and Lavon McDonald should be the preferred candidates.

At the public meeting of the Regents on September 17, 1973, President Heady placed the name of Lavon McDonald before the governing board. Britton Ruebush, the student body president and a member of the Athletic Council, expressed anger and frustration. After allowing the dissenters their say, the Regents unanimously approved the appointment of McDonald.

The media lashed out at the president and the Regents. The Athletic Council passed a resolution that the appointment of McDonald was a blatant political intrusion into the affairs of the University. The council also condemned the president for his failure to resist the pressures of political interference.[63]

Heady responded that his preference for McDonald was based on the fact that five of the eight head coaches he had consulted, as well as several assistants he respected, supported McDonald. He also acknowledged that the Regents' interest in the appointment was obviously an influence and that he had no doubt that they preferred McDonald. Heady added, however, that he was convinced the Regents would have approved King had Heady recommended him.[64]

A disenchanted, disappointed, and no doubt disgusted Bob King left UNM to accept the head coaching job at Indiana State University, a relatively unknown school in NCAA history. He recruited what turned out to be one of the all-time greats in collegiate and professional basketball, Larry Bird. King coached the Indiana State University team, which lost to a powerful Michigan State University team in the national championship game of 1979. After retiring from Indiana State University, King settled in Bosque Farms in Valencia County, New Mexico, where he was residing in 2003.

A less contentious development in 1973 was the adoption of turquoise for the home jerseys of the football and basketball teams. Cherry and silver returned in 1980, however.

Women's athletics took a giant step forward in 1973–74, when the budget totaled $35,000, up from $4,300 the year before. Title IX, the federal law mandating equal opportunity for women in sports, got some of the credit, but Linda Estes, the associate athletic director, credited President Heady. He "was probably the first president in the nation to come out and do anything like that," she said. "We thought we were rich."[65]

Heady's Resignation

Heady had persevered "through all the attacks and allegations directed at him, and remained unflappable during even the most scurrilous statements about himself." Indeed, in the aftermath of a faculty no-confidence vote in May 1972, the Regents had given the president a unanimous vote of confidence to express their support.[66]

This was all on the surface, though. Behind the scenes, as early as March 1973 Horn discussed with Heady how long the latter might desire to continue as president of the University. Their talk stemmed from an editorial in the Farmington newspaper stating that Governor King had by that time appointed most of the Regents and that they were planning to dismiss Heady. Horn assured President Heady that neither the governor nor any one of the Regents had discussed any dissatisfaction, but he wanted to know Heady's plans. Heady, according to Horn, replied that he intended to step down as president in two or three years, but if the Regents were unhappy with his service, he would resign before that time and return to teaching. He also said he believed an evaluation of his presidency was in order.

Head basketball coach Bob King (left) hired Norm Ellenberger as an assistant coach. Photo by Dick Meleski

Cathy Carr was an All-American in the 100-meter breaststroke and won a gold medal at the 1972 Olympics.

Arturo Ortega

With two new Regents on the board, it was difficult to reach any consensus on an evaluation, and nothing further took place in 1973.[67]

The presence of two new Regents was pertinent. Heady's interpretation was that more changes were in the wind than just the turnover in board members. To Heady, the changes meant he was no longer working with the same Regents who had appointed him. The major difference, however, was that Arturo Ortega, who had always been completely supportive, was no longer on the board. Ortega, a UNM graduate and Albuquerque lawyer, had been a Regent since 1967 and continued to serve until 1973. He was later a regent at Georgetown University, where he had earned three degrees, and Colorado College. He served on the U.S. President's Committee on the Arts and Humanities in the early 1990s and worked to found the National Hispanic Cultural Center in Albuquerque.

What was a minor incident in August 1971 gave an early hint to Heady as to what he might expect later on. Returning from a vacation, Heady sported a small beard at the meeting of the Regents. The beard elicited a comment early in the session from Regent Horn, perhaps partly in jest, but also possibly a mild indication of disapproval. Horn inquired whether Heady expected the beard to expand, and the president responded that it had "reached its epitome." The story made the Associated Press wire and was printed in newspapers across the county, as at that time any facial adornment on university presidents was rare. Heady still had the beard in 2003.[68]

This time, however, it was Horn who persevered. He personally evaluated President Heady and when the report was completed on June 10, 1974, sent copies to members of the Board of Regents and the president. Horn pointed out that the rating was only his personal observation of the president and that his fellow Regents had not asked him to produce it. In the evaluation, he cited the president's strengths and weaknesses but refrained from drawing any conclusion. Upon receiving the evaluation, Heady asked to meet with the entire board. The meeting was held in late July at the home of Regent Horn, at which time Heady indicated he would like to continue as president for a while longer. The Regents and Heady finally agreed that he would retire as president no later than December 31, 1975. At that time he would be given a sabbatical leave to prepare for a return to teaching at UNM. Heady announced his retirement decision at the September 18, 1974, meeting of the board.[69]

After the Presidency

In his inaugural speech in 1968, Heady noted that President Herman Wells of Indiana University, when asked what was required of a university president to be successful, replied, "Be lucky!"[70] Heady was not lucky. He was a very decent man doing his best to try to lead a university in a very indecent time. He was not only a gentle man, but also a gentleman, a person sensitive to the feelings of others, a Navy veteran who had been in harm's way in World War II, but who had empathy for those who opposed all war. He listened to students, sought their counsel and ideas, appreciated their passion and commitment, and understood their impatience with an imperfect world. By the same token, he opposed lawlessness, destruction of property, and impositions on the freedom of others to express ideas or dissent. He did not believe in nonnegotiable demands, mob violence, or heavy-handed justice. He was honorable and fair, striving for justice and reason. Seeing others uncomfortable or troubled pained him. He put a priority on what he believed to be the best interests of the University as well as the rights of individuals. When he determined it was time to step down from the presidency, he conducted himself with the same stoic dignity that had characterized his tenure as head of the University. He returned to work as a teacher and researcher. He became a respected, treasured member of the faculty and served UNM until his retirement in August 1981. William Dabney described him as a "highly qualified administrator" who was also "a dedicated and gifted teacher."[71]

Ferrel and Charlotte Heady

On a part-time basis, Heady continued his involvement with the University and participated in federal programs such as those sponsored by the U.S. Agency for International Development. Even in his late eighties, he continued to travel frequently on assignments to Latin American countries, and, like the fabled Pied Piper, continued to gather the love and devotion of students both at home and abroad.

Ferrel Heady never lost his passion for teaching or his lust for tennis. At the National 1999 Senior Olympics in Orlando, Florida, Heady and his partner won the silver medal in tennis doubles for the 80 to 85 age bracket. Only the glitter of Ferrel's broad smile outshone the glitter of that silver medal. ■

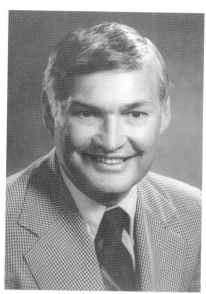

William E. Davis

CHAPTER FIFTEEN
Administration of William E. Davis
1975–82

BY V. B. PRICE

Expectations for the presidency of William E. "Bud" Davis were both full of high hopes and fairly gloomy when he took office in July of 1975. He was seen by some as a transitional figure who would take UNM to a new era of calm seas and respectability, and by others as a hopelessly bad choice, someone inclined by experience to be an advocate for athletics rather than academics. If the naysayers had bothered to check Davis's full résumé at the time, their apprehensions would have seemed as silly as they were. But they fretted publicly that Davis would squander UNM's precarious resources on an approach to progress that involved big-time sports draining funds and focus from the University's academic mission.

Optimists hoped the Davis presidency would help UNM move far away from the years of trauma and malaise in the late 1960s and early 1970s. They looked to him, and his down-home demeanor, to guide the University away from its violent and embarrassing past and lead it through the treacherous shoals of meddlesome micromanagement practiced by some state legislators.

But despite an overwhelming growth in student population and a transition in faculty leadership from an altruistic college old guard devoted to the University to an ambitious generation of scholars, young and old, without much connection to New Mexico, for most of Bud Davis's tenure the school's reputation as a worthy university with a growing potential for contributing to New Mexico's economic future was restored with the legislature and the community at large.

Then the fates threw UNM another knuckle ball, one quite as sensational as the "Love-Lust" poem controversy of 1969, but far stupider than the life-threatening trauma of bayonet-ready National Guard troops on campus stabbing students in 1970 and police firing shotguns into student crowds protesting the Vietnam War near the Big I in 1972. The idiotic catastrophe that weakened UNM's public image was called Lobogate. It attacked the University's biggest and most secure anchor in the community at large, the beloved Lobo basketball team on whose fortunes, it seemed, the mental health of the state collapsed in depression or rose in manic jubilation. Lobogate—with its accounting frauds, its faked grades and transcripts,

Facing page: Not an ivory tower but replicas of the bell towers in Pueblo churches top Scholes Hall, the administration building. Photo by Michael Mouchette

Klaus Keil (right) of UNM's Geology Department had research grants from the National Aeronautics and Space Administration, including a role in the 1975 Viking mission to Mars. He also analyzed samples of rocks brought back from the moon.

and alleged incentives like cars and apartments doled out to prime players—also exposed a vast network of sports gambling that involved so many people and deals that gamblers illicitly used the high-powered office computers at Sandia Labs to keep track of it. The scandal defined, albeit unfairly and inaccurately, the Davis presidency in the public eye. Rendered invisible for a while were Davis's successes building library and research funds, adding new faculty positions, internationalizing many of the University outreach programs, his work for minority empowerment, his spotlighting departments of academic excellence, his economic development collaborations with other New Mexico universities, his strong relationships with many legislators, and the voluminous interactions he initiated while reestablishing a healthy network of UNM supporters around the state.

Davis's focus on what he called centers of excellence tried to counterbalance, in some small way, the avalanche of bad press UNM had received since the late 1960s. He compiled a list of twenty-five of UNM's national-caliber departments and talked about them at virtually every venue in which he spoke. He focused on the early man and Mayan specialties of the Anthropology Department, on the world-class photography history program in the Art Department, on the nationally ranked radiopharmacy program. He always tried to highlight the diversity of UNM's academic achievement, pointing to the school's flagship status in the state. He paid as much attention to UNM's world-famous lithography program at the Tamarind Institute as he did to the School of Law's highly rated Clinical Law Program. He liked to draw attention to the Museum of Southwestern Biology, which had at the time, he said, the twelfth largest collection of recent mammals in the New World. Davis focused on Rudolfo A. Anaya's presence in the English Department, Tony Hillerman's roles in the Journalism Department and the national literary scene, and on UNM's laser optics program and its outstanding School of Medicine, with outreach programs for adults and children that covered the state.

Davis also continued the presidential sponsorship of the Annual Research Lecture, spotlighting, perhaps, a curious debate among the faculty concerning whether research contributed to strong teaching or undermined it.

Lobogate, however, came to overshadow the University's solid accomplishments, made all the more extraordinary owing to New Mexico's chronic status as one of the poorest states in the union. But UNM's problems didn't end with Lobogate, though Davis's career here did. The politicization of the Board of Regents since the 1960s had fostered confusion among the leadership about the basic roles, autonomy, and hierarchy of University life. Upon Davis's resignation to become chancellor of the University of Oregon system, the Board of Regents launched a series of disastrous presidential searches that spanned the better part of twenty-five years, with absolutely no institutional learning taking place that anyone could see. Doing as much damage as all the scandals put together, these presidential searches gave the greater community the image of a university with a slapstick Board of Regents, out of control, administratively inept, culturally insensitive, and ignorant of national and local issues of university governance. Local media coverage didn't help matters.

UNM allowed itself to be defined by outside opinion, most of it hostile, instead of investing resources in a sustained program of media management and public relations, explaining to the public the school's intellectual and social missions and its admirable fiscal and academic successes. After the Lobogate hurricane had blown itself out and Davis had moved on, the University fell prey to another scandal, a full-scale uprising involving the showing on campus of a film called *Hail Mary* that the state's Catholic hierarchy found objectionable. The Regents bungled the matter by banning the film, only to have a federal judge tell them in no uncertain terms their action was unconstitutional. Bud Davis, by now ensconced in the Oregon system, must have found the hubbub in New Mexico farcical and too familiar for comfort.

Davis's career as a university president or chancellor spanned thirty-one years—ten as president at Idaho State University, seven at UNM, seven as the chancellor of the Oregon system, and seven as the chancellor of Louisiana State University, where he retired from his leadership position in 1997 and as a professor of higher education in 2000. He returned to New Mexico and settled in Corrales where he continues to write and prepare speeches on issues of university governance.

These students in a Computer Science lab in 1977 were learning on that era's state-of-the-art equipment, even if it was the size of a refrigerator.

The controversy over Davis's hiring as president in 1975 agitated the mainstream and alternative media. Despite his ten years as president of Idaho State in Pocatello, Davis was seen by the UNM faculty as someone wholly unprepared to lead a major university. His record as an interim football coach at the University of Colorado following a scandal there, which he helped to clean up, and his years as a championship high school coach, with an EdD instead of a PhD, were derided by the more ambitious faculty. The Regents hired him because he was seen as an ideal "outside" president for a major university in a rural, conservative state. A charming, courtly man with a kind smile and unstoppable enthusiasm, a Marine who had served in Korea, he was old-fashioned enough to disapprove of coed dormitories. Davis's personality seemed tailor-made to communicate successfully with the legislature and its constituents around the state.

I was never one of those people who found Bud Davis's background troublesome. In fact, right from the start I liked the man. And my consideration of his years at UNM is colored by the warm regard in which I hold him. Lobogate, I must admit, dimmed my enthusiasm for UNM's leadership, both faculty and administration. But I always thought it was preposterous to accuse Davis of covering up the scandal, or of conspiring to thwart the FBI's and NCCA's investigations. Quite the opposite is the case. Davis is a civil libertarian, and his views about due process tended to slow down a rampaging political issue that called for heads to roll as fast as possible to appease the public, the media, and more cannibalistic faculty members. And until Lobogate, Davis's progressive administration left many alumni, older faculty, and students with a feeling of optimism they hadn't had in years.

As I wrote of UNM in a column in the *New Mexico Independent* in August 1976, "There are lots of things going on these days that give me a refreshing sense of confidence about the future of the school. Davis seems to be doing all the right things: He has surrounded himself with respected and influential people from

A new University logo echoed the clean lines of modified Spanish-Pueblo architecture in the 1970s. It was designed by Joyce "Steve" Rhodes of the Public Information Office.

the University community—most notably Tony Hillerman from the journalism department and former Fine Arts Dean Clinton Adams. He's been tirelessly aggressive about building a large and diversified constituency for UNM around the state. He's instigated an internal reorganization that might, if it's staffed [properly], . . . have positive effects on the quality of the relationship between those with something to teach and those with the desire to learn. And, as crucial as anything else, he's gotten UNM substantially more money from the state legislature."

In 1976, a year after his arrival, Davis gave a commencement speech that impressed me with his sincerity and savvy. I commented in the column, "Though some cynics have criticized his commencement speech this year as being little better than a locker room pep talk, I've got to admit that I think it's one of the best speeches of its kind I've ever encountered. Somebody has to say these things," I emphasized, "and I'm grateful that Davis has the guts and enthusiasm to do it."[1]

In retrospect, what I found so stirring in Davis's remarks was his idealism and sincere call for excellence. It reminded me of the passing generations of UNM faculty—the likes of Katherine Simons, Dean Dudley Wynn, France Scholes, "Nibs" Hill, and dozens of others who devoted themselves selflessly to the University and their students. Being a professor was for them a privileged life that came with a personal commitment to the ongoing betterment of their school, salary hikes or no salary hikes. Students in the fifties could tell UNM was a special place because of that commitment on the part of its faculty. When Dudley Wynn and Katherine Simons, with a core of other faculty, created the soon-to-be nationally acclaimed UNM Honors Program in 1962, they sought, in part, to counteract the more transitory attachments and mercenary inclinations of newer faculty seeking academic reputations and looking at UNM as a stepping-stone to greater glory.

Bud Davis's commencement address echoed the ambition for excellence of that older generation of faculty. After pledging to work to make UNM financially competitive with "the best in the West and in the nation among land-grant and state universities," Davis went on to encourage in the faculty and alumni a personal attachment to the institution.

> Money alone, however, is not the answer. I realize that within the institution we must use our resources in the most productive manner. This entails a deep commitment from each member of the University community—students, faculty, administrators, staff, and alumni. This means a total commitment to excellence in each of our endeavors, unremitting hard work, and pride in and loyalty to the institution and the state.

Davis thought that a university had a wider obligation to the state's residents than research and instruction. He told the 1976 commencement audience,

> In our academic programs, in our cultural centers of museums and art galleries and theaters, in our laboratories and institutes, we do have great

treasures. And we must share these treasures with more and more people all the time. To truly open the doors of knowledge, the University must continue to see itself as an educational resource for the whole community. Excellence and access must go hand in hand.[2]

Perhaps if Lobogate hadn't appeared like a nightmare in the later years of Davis's tenure he might have remained at UNM as long as Tom Popejoy had. It's fair to say, I think, that before that disaster Davis had done all the important things right. Even the faculty had sheathed their long knives for a while. And they had good reason to. Davis was something of a phenomenon when it came to working with the legislature for faculty salaries and new positions. Since 1975, Davis had increased the faculty by 217 positions, according to his final report to the University, and had overseen a 65 percent raise in faculty salaries in seven years. "This is one of the nation's better records," Davis observed in his report. In addition to reemphasizing the Annual Research Lecture, he created an outstanding teacher award and moved the Regents to create a Regents' Meritorious Service Medal.

By the time he moved on from UNM in 1982, major research grants had nearly doubled in seven years and, even more significantly, the legislature reduced the state's take of overhead money from contracts and grants from 50 to 20 percent, leaving 80 percent to the University itself to pay for utilities and other indirect costs of research. When it came to prodding the legislature to find more money, Davis's record was little short of astonishing, although the nation's rampaging inflation and the state's booming oil and gas industry helped. As he wrote in his summation report, "Legislative support for the instruction and general portion of the University's main campus budget rose from $28.7 million in 1975–76 to $73 million in 1982–83." Medical School funding, owing to Davis's backing of Medical School Dean Leonard Napolitano's aggressive and persistent lobbying at the legislature, jumped from $4.9 million to nearly $21 million.

The North Campus with its concentration of both the law and the medical schools experienced a building boom under the direction of University Architect Van Dorn Hooker, including the School of Law's Bratton Hall expansion, the Children's Psychiatric Hospital, the Family Practice Center and North Campus Bookstore, the Dental Building, and the Health Sciences Learning Center. The Davis years also saw the construction of the Art Building, the UNM Stadium Press Box, and the Biomedical Research Facility, as well as renovation of the Student Union Building.

During the Davis years, programs that now seem always to have been part of University life actually began, such as the Presidential Scholarship Program, the Office of Student Financial Aid and Career Services, the Latin American Institute, the Southwest Hispanic Research Institute, and the UNM Foundation, the school's major private fund-raising effort. Davis was also instrumental in creating the Los Alamos and Valencia County branch campuses.

After voters defeated a hotly contested proposal for the creation of an Albuquerque community college in 1979, Davis's administration created the General

In 1975 the fast-growing North Campus included a new addition to University Hospital (foreground) and the Law School's Bratton Hall addition, the Cancer Center, and the Nursing-Pharmacy Building.

A student spirit group, Trailblazers, was organized by President Davis and Vice President "Swede" Johnson. Members posed outside the newly remodeled New Mexico Student Union with their advisor, Gary Thomasson of the Alumni Office (left).

College to offer associate degrees and basic skills education. The General College was coordinated with the Albuquerque Technical Vocational Institute (TVI) and created an entry process for unprepared high school graduates. This was key to Davis's goal of raising admission requirements for credit programs. UNM Regent Calvin Horn has written that the General College was "perhaps President Davis's greatest achievement . . . [as] a partial answer to a state university's dilemma for how to admit ill-prepared high school graduates and still maintain high academic standards."[3] (Since its founding and well into the mid-1960s, however, UNM had an informal remedial program in place, which the author of this chapter sampled to his advantage in 1958.)

Davis evidenced great pride in his presidential report in UNM's status as the "27th university in the nation to have its Affirmative Action Plan approved," allowing for "steady improvement in numbers of minorities and women employed. Furthermore, the University is among the top two or three major state universities in both absolute numbers and percentages of Hispanic and American Indian students." It was also under Davis's tenure that UNM took over the management of the Bernalillo County Medical Center, the former Bernalillo County-Indian Hospital. Davis proudly listed UNM's General Library reaching the million-volume mark, with over a quarter of a million new books added during his years, as one of his most satisfying accomplishments.[4]

Davis's understanding of the wider New Mexico community, with its multitudinous and often contrary interests and associations, was keenly honed. As he struggled to improve faculty conditions and salaries, he worked to raise entrance standards without rejecting students who might be late bloomers in need of early remedial help. As he helped open UNM to the diversity of the state's population by seriously recruiting the best students from rural and urban communities alike, he appealed to New Mexicans' conservative, commonsense nature, sometimes with what now seem like hilariously contentious results. As serious as Davis was, and is, about higher education, he's never lost his sense of humor, as interviews with him for this chapter have reminded me.

After traveling the state and realizing that many parents detested the notion of coeducational dormitories and were refusing to send their kids to UNM because of them, Davis embarked on what he once described as "My Lonely, Losing Battle Against Co-Education in the Dorms."[5] He tried to segregate the dorms by gender when he was president at Idaho State, with mixed results. When he did the same thing at UNM, in 1976, in the heyday of the counterculture, he met with intense student resistance and the kind of scoffing that echoed throughout his remaining years at UNM. But he prevailed. And the use of UNM's dorms rose dramatically.

He delighted conservatives and appalled First Amendment advocates when he agreed to have something called a "Religion and Life Week" at UNM designed to, in Calvin Horn's words, "bring awareness on campus of the religious aspects of modern living."[6] Davis created an annual President's Prayer Breakfast, reminiscent of some post-Watergate prayer breakfasts carried out by defrocked Nixon appointees prominently in the news at the time. Even basketball coach "Stormin'" Norman Ellenberger, a future defrockee himself, agreed to have a team chaplain whom he referred to as "the free throw coach."[7]

UNM was still under intense legislative scrutiny in Davis's early years on campus. The stink raised by "Love-Lust," the counterculture, and Vietnam War protests lingered in the Roundhouse. And as life would have it, a week before the opening of Davis's first legislative session, the world-famous Pilobolus Dance Company had scheduled a show at Popejoy Hall with the last dance to be performed in the nude. The specter of legislators' reactions was too much for the politically savvy Davis to bear, and he, according to Horn, "ordered the nude scenes eliminated from the program . . . without consulting with the cultural committee or any student group. . . . There were harsh cries of censorship," the Regent observed with the understatement of a P. G. Wodehouse novel.[8] Professors and their spouses, students, and dancers were furious and ever more confirmed in their view that UNM's new president really was just a football coach in disguise. But 1976 was a breakthrough year for UNM at the legislature. Davis got along well with Governor Jerry Apodaca and Senator Aubrey Dunn, the most powerful voice in the legislature. Largely because of Bud Davis, UNM's instructional funding was increased by some 20 percent that year, which calmed much of the antagonism directed at the new president.

Davis got into other scrapes that flared up and then died down. He intervened in an internecine power struggle between Medical School Dean Leonard Napolitano and Vice President for Health Sciences Robert B. Kugel, MD, over who should run the UNM Medical Center. Davis had a nose for spotting gifted administrators and sided with Napolitano, who is generally regarded as the founding father of UNM's nationally acclaimed medical program.

Banning nude dancers on campus and canceling a seminar on the decriminalization of marijuana were bad enough, but when Davis addressed the faculty and acknowledged their justifiable complaints about the University's support for its academic calling, he made a modest, tongue-in-cheek proposal that set the faculty against him. Wondering how many of their number would forgo a raise

"Cindy" was a traveling evangelist who appeared frequently on campus in the 1970s, debating vigorously with students about religion, morality, and ethics.

in salary for one year to fund library and other research and equipment needs, Davis was figuratively pelted by rotten tomatoes. Underlying much of the faculty's response was their growing belief that increases in athletic funding were coming at the expense of academics. Some even called Davis an academic traitor, and many faculty members saw him as the enemy, which set the stage for faculty reaction to the disaster that no one could have guessed was lying in wait down the road.

As naturally as the Greek goddess of strife, Eris, would have it, the tragic battleground that Davis found himself on was all about athletics and its ever-increasing dominance in University affairs. Lobogate demonstrated once and for all how entangled a university's allegiances can be. Some legislators and community members find Lobo sports to be the most compelling reason to have a university at all. In contrast, many in the public schools and universities maintain that athletics drain attention and money from learning.

When Lobogate broke on the awareness of New Mexico, it acted like a massive particle accelerator smashing together atoms of competing athletic and academic interests with old University scandals and their wounds that Davis had tried so ably to heal. Davis later described his position in the Lobogate scandal as resembling that of the U.S. Navy admirals caught in the Tailgate sex scandals of 1991. Davis knew a number of the retired admirals. He told me they found themselves in a whirlwind they thought they didn't cause, brought about by actions none of them knew about or condoned. When you get in a situation like that, with so much hostility, Davis said in an interview, the only honorable thing to do is withdraw. And it took Davis two years to do so, during which time he re-created the Athletic Department and was exonerated of any wrongdoing not only by the University Athletic Council but also by the widely respected and unimpeachable Franklin Jones, who conducted a painstaking investigation of Lobogate for the Regents.

Regent Horn assessed the impact of Lobogate this way: "Not since 'Love Lust' in 1969 had the University experienced an internal crisis that startled the institution, shocked the alumni, and rocked the state as did the series of athletic scandals in the fall of 1979."[9] "The type of University desired by the public, legislators, alumni, and taxpayers was the objective of President Davis," Horn wrote.

> This was reflected in the legislative appropriation increases to the University in the instruction and general category of over $18 million or a 70.1 percent increase in the four year period from 1975 to 1979 . . . Yet the new image of the University, so clearly visualized by President Davis, fell and shattered in the fall of 1979 as did his dream of "creating a positive climate for the University to project to the state" as he became embroiled in the 1979–1980 athletic scandal.[10]

Reams of newsprint have been spent documenting every last hangnail of the Lobogate mess. And the Franklin Jones investigation has a step-by-step chronology of key happenings. What follows is a condensed version of the sequence of events, charges made against the Davis administration, the results of independent investigations, the reaction of the media, and the remarkable trials of former Lobo Coach Norm Ellenberger.

Nobody in New Mexico could really believe it when in the fall of 1979 they heard that the NCAA was charging UNM with fifty-seven violations of its code of conduct. It seemed utterly preposterous and came right out of the blue for most sports fans in the state. The Lobos and their southern rivals, the Aggies, were basketball icons of underdogs making good through true grit and the infectious optimism of their fans. Major college basketball teams, the Lobos and Aggies had more than modest success and even brought occasional national recognition to the state. They inspired fierce pride and fiercer loyalty. But attachment to the Lobos got a little out of hand in Albuquerque. Many people in the metro area, whether cheering at the Pit or glued to the radio or TV, lived and died on the fortunes of the darlings of the town, Ellenberger's Lobos. The year before, they had been ranked at one time fourth in the nation, to the utter joy of everyone. And Ellenberger himself had almost been elected coach of the year by the U.S. Basketball Writers Association. Ellenberger was a beloved figure. He got the most out of his kids. They all seemed to worship him. He had a 134–62 record at UNM since 1967, with two Western Athletic Conference titles and four postseason tournaments, including the NCAA. This was a far cry from the 1950s, before Bob King and Ellenberger, when BYU's basketball team would come into Johnson Gym and literally laugh at the fans and the hapless Lobos.

It was unthinkable that UNM's Athletic Department had been so miserably administered that fifty-seven NCAA violations, including all kinds of improprieties and payoffs to basketball players, were actually true. There must have been a colossal mistake. But the charges proved to be accurate. No, basketball was not just about the idealism of the Pit, the work ethic of student athletes, and their commitment to team spirit that sportswriters like to make it out to be. To many students and professors, as well as townspeople, Lobogate proved the long-held suspicion that intercollegiate athletics was undermining not only the reputation of the University and its ability to fulfill its primary missions of teaching and research, it was also corrupting the moral underpinning of the entire institution. Lobogate brought national disgrace and glaring notoriety to the whole state. And then denial set in.

In light of the NCAA's allegations, Davis promptly reassigned Athletic Director Lavon McDonald, a virtual appointee of then-Governor Bruce King before Davis's arrival. The NCAA violations that stunned the state had been objects of gossip for months among people in the know. Davis avowed he asked McDonald repeatedly if any of the rumors were true and was assured they were absolutely false.

More than a month passed from the NCAA revelations to the unthinkable moment on November 28 when nearly two dozen FBI agents "swarmed," to use Calvin Horn's description, onto the South Campus, home of the athletic complex, with questions and search warrants for Ellenberger, his coaching staff, and members of the University administration, including President Davis. At issue were false academic transcripts, doctoring grades so student athletes could play ball. The real blow, though, came when the FBI released a transcript of a wiretap, collected by the Albuquerque Police Department, from the home phone of a city gambler under investigation. The caller was an assistant UNM basketball coach, Manny Goldstein. At the gambler's house the phone was answered by head coach Ellenberger. And just like that the whole state heard two basketball coaches, of the beloved Lobos, discuss, in language one might use to order a pizza to go, the forgery of an academic transcript. It was a stunner. Jokes had abounded over the years about well-placed phone calls to professors from coaches begging them to give a mercy C-minus to the star player so he could play in the big game. But to actually forge a grade and then just play it coolly like it was the real McCoy—not even the most jaded of sports fans in New Mexico would have imagined that.

Such trickery, however, wasn't the fate of UNM to suffer alone. Bud Davis, who sat on numerous NCAA committees, recalled to me that some fifty-five schools were involved in Lobogate-like forgeries, many of them involving crooked administrators at small junior colleges around the country. In UNM's initial case, the transcript scam was complicated and brazen. An administrator at Oxnard Junior College in California was paid $300 to accept a forged transcript from Mercer County Community College in West Windsor, New Jersey. Manny Goldstein had in his apartment, an FBI search revealed, an embosser for Mercer College and other official materials. Eventually five other Lobo basketball players and three football players were found to have bogus credits from Ottawa University in Kansas, a source of many other sports scandals across the country. All of the UNM student athletes admitted they had never taken an Ottawa class. And all UNM games that they'd played in were forfeited.

Davis fired both Ellenberger and Goldstein in mid-December 1979, and the contracts for UNM's football coaching staff were not renewed. Ellenberger also had to face both federal felony charges and an investigation by the state attorney general's office into travel voucher double dipping that was said to have been going on since 1976. Ellenberger consistently deflected the accusations, and nothing was made of them by the University administration or the public media. The NCAA added to UNM's woes another set of charges involving boosters, gifts to parents, paying student transportation costs, cash rewards for making rebounds, discounts on stereo equipment—ninety-two violations in all.

Now all hell broke loose. The Alumni Association argued about supporting or calling for the firing of President Davis, the Lobo (booster) Club was up in arms, and the national media got the story and made mincemeat of Davis, the Regents, and the University. Every suspicion about the corruption of amateur athletics in the United States suddenly found a target in UNM. CBS's *60 Minutes* did a piece, the *Chronicle of Higher Education* reported on the scandal, and *Newsweek* and *U.S. News and World Report* had their say, venting outrage and sarcasm at will. And the *Albuquerque Journal,* though not the *Tribune,* called for the resignations of President Davis and the entire Board of Regents.

Mark Acuff, former *Lobo* editor and long-time editor and co-owner of the weekly *New Mexico Independent,* in his closely read media column, described the *Journal's* response as a "jihad" to "get Davis." Acuff defended Davis, quoting the UNM faculty Athletic Council's finding in January 1980 that Davis and his administration "had acted 'responsibly, decisively, and expeditiously' in investigating and moving to clear up the matter."

Acuff continued, "Responsibility is the key word, because it has not been stressed enough that President Davis is a civil libertarian and has taken great precautions to protect the individual rights of anyone accused in the 'scandal.'"[11]

In the *Lobo,* sports editor Paula Easley summarized the denial and rationalization behind the scandal at UNM and other schools, such as UCLA, Arizona State, and Oregon. She quoted a piece in *Newsweek* by sports columnist Pete Axthelm who wrote, "The shame of the system can be defined in all too many unpleasant contexts. It is fiscal: football and basketball are big business for most schools. It is educational: when a kid is cheated out of all chance of learning, the institution is also cheated out of all reason for being. It is social and racial: many victims of the 'dumb jock' syndrome, [*sic*] 1980 version are black. But most of all, it is moral. In the pursuit of victory, the vast majority of fans, alumni, and even coaches and administrators have accepted the notion that a winner may have to cheat."

The *Lobo* then quoted Ellenberger's contribution to the *Newsweek* article.

Nobody grows up wanting to come to UNM. How can we be as selective as Notre Dame or North Carolina? I had to compete under a bunch of rules that don't work. Every university president wants to fill the seats and get the publicity. Everybody wants a team where everybody loves their mother and has a B average. But it doesn't work that way. I recruited kids who never had a book in their homes. Maybe I didn't get them that magical college degree. But maybe I helped them be better people.[12]

Ellenberger's two trials—in federal court and in New Mexico District Court in Bernalillo County—were amazing media events. As in the *Newsweek* article, Ellenberger defended himself with what most people saw as down-to-earth common sense. The gist of his defense was that he'd done nothing wrong, everyone did it, and he was really just helping kids out of academic and money jams.

The federal trial of Ellenberger was held in Roswell in February 1980. He was charged with mail fraud, wire fraud, and an interstate travel violation. Ellenberger's lawyer, Leon Taylor, was a well-known, hard-charging defense attorney who said that Ellenberger was "a sacrificial lamb" for a rotten system. Ellenberger defended himself by saying he couldn't find a victim in the proceedings and that everything he did was for the good of the University. The federal jury found Ellenberger innocent of all charges brought against him. The NCAA also took a light-handed approach, putting UNM on a three-year probation beginning in 1980, with no TV games and no postseason play.

In June of 1981, Ellenberger went on trial in state district court charged with twenty-two counts of filing false travel vouchers and fraud. Ellenberger argued that he never used the money for himself, but put it all into a fund for the players. He was found guilty on twenty-one counts. In sentencing, district Judge Phillip Baiamonte said that Ellenberger "was only one cog in the machine of college basketball. Everyone looked the other way as the rules and laws were bent and broken. The real hypocrisy is with the colleges and universities across the country that maintain and establish professional ball clubs while purporting to operate under amateur rules." The judge gave Ellenberger a one-year deferred sentence on unsupervised probation.[13]

President Davis found the whole exercise exasperating, to say the least. He was not given the chance to argue in open court against implications that he had contributed to a permissive atmosphere in the Athletic Department. In a statement after the last Ellenberger trial, he said forthrightly that any implications of his "complicity" in Lobogate and its violations of NCAA rules and state laws were "false."

> It is important also to put another fact clearly on the record. Contrary to certain testimony in the trial, it is possible to operate a successful athletic program without violating the rules the University has pledged itself to honor. . . . At the University of New Mexico we are operating now a program in which all NCAA rules are being scrupulously enforced. . . . We can win without cheating.

Ever the admirable idealist, Davis generously took an opportunity in which he could have focused solely on his own rectitude to affirm the fundamental honor and worthiness of sport. In his statement, Davis said he questioned the athletic director on all the many rumors of shenanigans in the Athletic Department, and "in every instance" he was "assured" the rumors were not true. He continued,

> Where appropriate, other University officials were involved in investigations of such reports or rumors. However, it was not until receipt of the NCAA allegations followed by federal and state investigators using their authority for wiretaps, search warrants, subpoenas, and to take testimony under oath that the University received reliable information on which to act. It was only then that I learned about the forgery of transcripts, the secret travel account, and other serious NCAA violations.[14]

Despite Davis's frankness and logical refutation of implications that his administration was at fault for Lobogate, UNM and the community at large wanted a definitive answer as to who should take the blame for the whole sordid mess. Franklin Jones, of the law firm Sutin, Thayer & Browne, long considered by state government insiders to be a man of impeccable integrity, conducted an exhaustive investigation in his own orderly, detailed manner. It took him nearly five months, from January to May 1980. Blame, it turned out, could be spread pretty much across the board. In his letter of transmittal that accompanied the 102-page report entitled "Intercollegiate Athletic Problems at the University of New Mexico," he wrote with pointed clarity. "I have found no substantial evidence of active participation by the Regents or the President of the University or his immediate staff in the improprieties nor have I found any evidence of a cover-up or attempted cover-up by these officials." That being said, the Jones report outlined in withering detail the violations, procedural and chain-of-command errors, and general community attitudes that allowed glaring violations of NCAA rules to take place for all to see who wanted to see. Most folks, it seems to me, couldn't believe their eyes, some were in a state of denial, and many really diehard fans just plain didn't give a hoot.

The gist of Jones's analysis put Lobogate in a national context and placed blame with several boards of Regents, several University administrations and their athletic directors, as well as naïveté about what Jones called "the winning syndrome." Jones wrote:

> Major intercollegiate athletic programs at UNM went out of control mainly because of the combination of problems of the type which have plagued intercollegiate football nationally for at least seventy-five years with problems of institutional immaturity at UNM. This conclusion is not meant to overlook the failure of individuals and groups responsible for the improprieties which have surfaced since early 1979. This conclusion emphasizes the risks which accompany the failure to develop appropriate institutional patterns of control.

He continued, saying that the "history of intercollegiate athletics nationally clearly indicates that the pressures leading to improper practices are neither new nor isolated." As early as 1905, President Teddy Roosevelt told a group of coaches that would create the NCAA a year later that colleges had "to clean up the win-at-any-cost philosophy and brutality or he would stop all college football."

The "winning syndrome," Jones concluded, "is characterized by behavior in sports that tends to justify any means if the end result is victory, and by the beliefs that failure consists of 'getting caught,' and that rules apply to those 'too stupid' to figure out how to evade them."[15]

The Jones report exonerated Davis and the Regents, and so did an earlier report by another respected and trusted figure, Law School Professor Albert E. Utton. Utton wrote, for the UNM Athletic Council, "It is the considered conclusion of the Athletic Council that . . . the University administration acted ethically, and responsibly. The Council further concludes that the Administration acted in a timely manner, given the complexities involved in checking transcripts transferred from other institutions."[16]

In partial defense of the Lobos' devoted and perhaps overzealous fans, it should be noted that after Ellenberger was fired and the team was reduced to four scholarship players and walk-ons, and a young assistant coach, Charlie Harrison, was thrown into the breach, the Pit was packed for every game of what turned out to be the dismal but honest remainder of the season. Davis's reorganization of the Athletic Department brought in no-nonsense John Bridgers as athletic director; the decent and ultimately successful Gary Colson as head basketball coach, who proved he could win without cheating; and Joe Morrison as football coach, who eventually took the Lobos to one of their best seasons, 10–1, in the early 1980s. Davis had shored up and revamped the athletic structure at UNM, but that accomplishment was largely overshadowed by the scandal.

One might think the president of an NCAA-penalized university might be persona non grata in the inner workings of the NCAA. This was not so in Davis's case. He served on the NCAA Committee on Governance, Organization, and Services from 1979 to 1982. In an address to NCAA institutional executive officers on "institutional control of intercollegiate athletics" in September 1981, Davis used the occasion to reflect on his own experiences and observations during Lobogate.

Athletics "are becoming more commercialized and not less" in the "past few years," he said. "Commercial considerations influence objectives, levels of intensity, policies and decisions, even to the point at which television contracts now are influencing decisions affecting this organization [the NCAA] and our respective institutions."

Institutional control, he said, "is undermined seriously when there is direct involvement of regents or trustees in the immediate management of the intercollegiate athletic program."

Davis hit hard on his wisely contrarian view in opposition to the freshmen eligibility rule. "I'd still like to go back to the time when most of us were undergraduates, when students had to come and prove themselves as bona fide students for at least the freshman year. Now they may start in the football program three weeks before they ever attend classes at an institution."

As for Lobogate, Davis's advice was direct. "Thus, as a battle-scarred veteran and a university president, and with great humility, I would state that the first principle for a president in ensuring institutional control is to be sure that those he trusts can be trusted. There is no substitute for integrity at all levels—administrators, directors of athletics, coaches, players, alumni and boosters. Murphy's law states that 'nature always sides with a flaw.' If there is a flaw in any link of the command chain of responsibility, the flaw will surface."

Alumni and booster clubs get unfair finger pointing when it comes to the pressure to win, he said. "If it could be documented, it is my premise that most often those responsible for under-the-table inducements, payoffs for rebounds, illegal travel and other taboos are miscellaneous individuals closely associated with the head coach." Davis likened the glamour of a successful coach to that of a movie star. "People vie for his favor. . . . And often, they are willing to do ridiculous things for that opportunity."

The best advice he could give to a university president about being in control of doings in the Athletic Department "is to hire athletic directors and coaches he thinks he can trust and then scare the daylights out of them. . . . [Above] all, let them know that if in any way they embarrass the university, compromise its integrity or violate or transgress any of the rules, that their exit will be certain, sudden, and final."[17]

Davis had other fine moments with the NCAA, the most far-reaching of which was his role with a half-dozen others in drafting guidelines for Title IX of the Educational Opportunity Act Amendments of 1972, guaranteeing equal opportunity and support for women in athletics. Davis presented the guidelines to the NCAA at its annual meeting in 1979 and made the motion two years later to authorize NCAA championship competitions for women.

Davis hired as UNM women's athletic director Linda Estes, a nationally recognized long-time Title IX advocate and a faculty member in UNM's Physical Education Department. Estes sided with Davis in squabbles with the NCAA over what the exact nature of equal opportunity meant, but it was under Estes's leadership that virtual parity between men's and women's athletic programs was achieved.

A university president, however, has a lot more to think about than the Athletic Department and its various media-driven frenzies. And a university itself is vastly more than its president. A compelling history of a university could be written from the perspective of its students, or the accomplishments of its faculty, or the pressures and vision of its regents. While Bud Davis's presidential tenure here was dominated in the media by athletics, Davis himself saw one of his major roles as an advocate of the complex resources, services, and associations that make up a university's interaction with the greater community. Davis was, in fact, a tireless spokesman and defender of UNM around the state. At a time when universities were under attack from the business community and conservative legislators who looked upon UNM's faculty and students as having what Davis jokingly referred to as "funny ideas," Davis presented himself in seemingly hostile environments time and time again, building his argument for the irreplaceable role a university plays in the economic, intellectual, and cultural life of its state.

At the Albuquerque Rotary Club in 1977, Davis built his case for UNM's pervasive positive influence in the life of New Mexico, saying that the school "is one of the few institutions that touches, in some direct way, the lives of the majority of the people" in the state. From its branch colleges, continuing education services, medical school, health center, and emergency hospital to its museums and other cultural institutions, its libraries, its university press, its huge payroll, its television and radio stations, not to mention its core research and instructional roles, UNM is "a major repository of information, intellectual talent, and physical resources. It aspires to place all its human and material resources in service to New Mexico in every way possible and practical."[18]

That commitment to expanding UNM's energies and talents beyond the so-called ivory tower to benefit the New Mexico community as a whole is President Davis's true legacy. ■

The parlor in Hodgin Hall acquired period wallpaper, lighting, and furnishings but kept its original wood floor. Each of the building's three lower floors was designed in the style of one of the University's first three decades by John Meigs, executive director of the Lincoln County Trust. The top floor is a large meeting room with three of the WPA hand-tinned chandeliers from the 1937 Student Union ballroom. Photo by Adam Eidelberg

Chapter Sixteen
Administration of John Perovich
1982–84

John Perovich

I t was rather unusual that a presidential search for the University of New Mexico should be concluded with an announcement of the appointment at the halftime of a football game. From its very beginnings, though, it had been an unusual search for the institution's twelfth president. John Perovich, vice president for finance, was named the interim president in April 1982, when it was announced that William E. Davis would be leaving for Oregon at the end of June. Perovich took office July 1, 1982, and it was anticipated that he would serve until sometime in the fall. The Regents appointed a thirteen-person search committee, chaired by Provost Emeritus Chester Travelstead. This committee was to seek out and screen applicants and nominees and recommend a slate of final candidates to the Regents. Perovich made it clear he had no aspirations for the job on a permanent basis.[1]

In the course of the search, six finalists emerged. Two were from within UNM: McAllister Hull, a Yale graduate in physics who had served on the World War II Manhattan Project in Los Alamos and had succeeded Travelstead as UNM provost, and Albert E. Utton, a professor of law. Alex Mercure, a Hispanic, also had UNM connections, having served as UNM vice president for external affairs. He also had been an assistant secretary of agriculture in the Carter administration. The three external candidates were a vice chancellor from Syracuse University, the liberal arts dean at the University of Arizona, and the deputy director of the National Science Foundation of Washington, D.C. John Aragón (a UNM alumnus), the popular president of New Mexico Highlands University, and Warren Armstrong, president of Eastern New Mexico, also were rumored to be dark horses.[2]

Amidst rumors that the Regents would select a president who was not on the list, Faculty Senate President Steven Kramer warned that going "off the list" would be "dangerous" to the University and cripple a process the Regents themselves had engineered. He also stated that it would be an insult to the six candidates who were interviewed and would discourage any viable candidates in the future.[3]

June Perovich

Regents Select John Perovich

On late Saturday afternoon, November 20, 1982, four of the Regents met, with the fifth, Colleen Maloof, whose mother had died that morning, in contact by telephone. Board President Henry Jaramillo reported that the members of the board could not reach a consensus on any of the six final candidates and turned to John Perovich with the request that he continue indefinitely as interim president. Perovich agreed. Following the meeting, one of the Regents attended the UNM-Hawaii football game. Asked what had transpired at the meeting, he replied that Perovich had been appointed. Word spread like wildfire, and at halftime the appointment was announced over the stadium loudspeaker. Horrified at the turn of events, Travelstead rushed to his office to notify the six former candidates.

The self-effacing Perovich stated, "I really wasn't a candidate until today."[4]

The repercussions were vicious, as the *Albuquerque Journal* reported. "The tortuous search for a new University of New Mexico president has ended in discord that could plague the institution for months." The newspaper was quick to point out, however, that the controversy was not about Perovich's qualifications but the way he was picked. The lead editorial in the *Journal* of November 23, 1982, said:

> Few will argue with the naming of John Perovich to be president of the University of New Mexico. The UNM Board of Regents, however, discredited itself by failing to follow the selection process it established and then later failing to clearly support Perovich as the permanent president of the institution.[5]

Kramer praised Perovich but called the selection process "disgusting." All the finalists, however, graciously extended their best wishes to Perovich.

Perovich was born near Raton in 1924. Like his mentor, Tom Popejoy, he grew up in that small, coal-mining community and set his sights on attending the University of New Mexico. He entered UNM in 1942. During World War II, he served with the Army Air Force as a navigator. Following the war, Perovich married his hometown sweetheart, June Brewer. He also returned to his studies at UNM on the G.I. Bill, graduating in 1948 with a bachelor's degree in business. A year later he earned a master's in business administration while also working in the University's business office. Perovich rapidly rose through the ranks as administrative assistant to the comptroller, comptroller, chief financial officer, and, finally, vice president for business and finance. Fifty-eight years old at the time of his appointment, Perovich had served under three UNM presidents, Popejoy, Heady, and Davis. He was often credited with much of the University's success with the legislature. His outstanding management of the institution's fiscal affairs included real-estate transactions, bond issues for capital improvements, contracts and grants, and creation and management of foundations and complex service centers like the UNM medical facilities. Regarded as a person of "unquestionable integrity and commitment to the well being of UNM," Perovich was warmly hailed from all quarters.[6]

Described as modest and low-keyed, Perovich was a task-oriented administrator and like Tom Popejoy was respected as a man who could get things done. He stated that the dissent with the search process had not and would not interfere with his work at the University.[7]

Well into the month of December, there was still no final word from the Regents pertaining to his title or the length of time he might serve as president. Finally, on December 11, 1982, Perovich announced that if necessary he would serve longer than two years but that his preference was to serve only until a permanent president was named.

While the Regents were deliberating, Travelstead published his personal observations on the search. Some of his comments were critical of the board. It was his opinion that from the beginning most of the search committee leaned toward bringing in one of the highly qualified candidates from outside New Mexico.[8]

Henry Jaramillo, president of the board, and two other Regents, Calvin Horn and Dr. Phillip Martinez, defended the search and selection. Jaramillo stated:

> Collectively, the Regents felt that Mr. Perovich came closer to fulfilling all the varied qualities needed to move our university forward than any of the recommended final candidates. The Regents decided upon a known person, instead of turning to an unknown candidate. Thus, Mr. Perovich became the choice of the Board of Regents.[9]

Jaramillo also reported that University legal counsel was researching whether Perovich could legally become permanent president under the search guidelines since he was not an official candidate for the position.

Resignation of Regent Calvin Horn

In a letter dated December 23, 1982, Regent Calvin Horn asked the governor-elect, Toney Anaya, not to consider him for an appointment to a third six-year term, thus ending campus speculation. The sixty-three-year-old Horn had served twelve years on the board, six as president. He received generous praise from the newspapers, Governor Anaya, and other sources for his dedicated service to higher education and the University of New Mexico.[10]

The Administration of President John Perovich

In 1982 and 1983, as Davis moved out and Perovich moved in, the University could identify a number of centers of excellence. Some were in the tradition of Southwestern and Latin American studies that had been a priority since the earliest days, and others reflected the postwar emphasis on science and engineering.

The School of Law's Clinical Law Program, which placed law students in real-world work, its Indian Law Program, and its Institute for Public Law and Services had earned a national reputation. Professor Robert J. Desiderio had succeeded Fred Hart as dean in 1979. The thirty-eight-year-old Desi had received his law degree from Boston College, studying under Hart, and had joined the UNM faculty in 1967. After the turbulence of the 1960s and 1970s, the School of Law was fairly quiet. In 1983 a milestone was reached when women made up more than half the student body.[11]

The College of Engineering sponsored annual student design-build competitions, including this one for the fastest wheeled contraption.

At the School of Architecture and Planning, Dean George Anselevicius had initiated a lecture series, a visiting foreign instructor program, and two professional publications. A native of Lithuania who studied in England, he had worked for Skidmore, Owings and Merrill and been a professor and administrator at the Illinois Institute of Technology, Washington University, Harvard, and the State University of New York at Buffalo before coming to UNM in 1981.[12]

One of many faculty members contributing to the University's excellence was Raymond R. "Tim" MacCurdy, who was selected to deliver the Annual Research Lecture in 1980. Holder of a doctorate from the University of North Carolina, he had been at UNM since 1949, serving as chairman of the comparative literature program and of the Department of Modern and Classical Languages and becoming an authority on Spanish poetry.

A significant development in research came in 1984 with the establishment of the Institute for Space and Nuclear Power Studies within the College of Engineering. In addition to professional training and research in space nuclear power and space systems technology, the institute hosts a major international forum in space technology that includes a design competition for secondary students.[13]

In December 1984, Perovich issued a report on the key developments at UNM during his years as president. He noted that UNM had become one of the Southwest's major institutions of higher learning with more than twenty-four thousand students on the main and branch campuses and in community service programs throughout the state. Whereas in the pre–World War II period the average student at UNM was a recent high school graduate, by the 1980s the student body also included growing numbers of nontraditional students, and the average age was twenty-seven. Many had families or full-time jobs, necessitating more than 850 late-afternoon and evening classes. More than half the UNM students were women, and more than 38 percent were minorities.

More rigorous admission requirements adopted in 1983 had resulted in closer cooperation between the University and the public schools of the state. Some 84 percent of the freshmen came from New Mexico high schools. The thrust of the new requirements was to produce a generation of students coming to UNM prepared to succeed. For those who were not quite ready, the General College continued to administer UNM's basic skills or preparatory courses. It had an open admission policy with no specific subject matter or grade-point requirements. The goal was to provide access as well as excellence to a broad range of New Mexico citizens.

Perovich took a strong personal interest in the institution's financial aid programs, specifically the Presidential Scholarship Program where the amount of the stipend per student was increased from $800 to $1,500 per year. Alumni and friends of the University donated funds to support this program, and by 1984, UNM was offering 290 Presidential Scholarships to the incoming class.

Other programs included the Excel Scholarship, which provided $1,000 per year for four consecutive years to the upper 10 percent of each high school graduating class, plus the UNM ACT Scholarship to cover full tuition for students who scored at least a composite score of twenty-six on the American College Test (ACT). Further, the University had twenty-four National Merit Scholars in 1984. New Mexico was also one of only five states with an operational state work-study program, which included more than three hundred students per year in on-campus jobs.

In the spring of 1984 the University published the first volume of *Quantum,* a journal of research and scholarship. There was an article about history Professor John Kessell's work on don Diego de Vargas, who led Spain's reconquest of New Mexico in 1692. Another article was about fieldwork in Mayan Mexico by archaeologist Jeremy Sabloff, who later became a distinguished professor at the University of Pittsburgh.

Meanwhile, voters approved bond issues for new branch-campus facilities in Los Alamos ($1.2 million), Valencia County ($2.5 million), and Gallup ($4 million).

Among the most dramatic developments at the University during Perovich's presidency was the expansion of the Medical Center. The center now included the Carrie Tingley Hospital for treatment of children's orthopedic problems, which had relocated from Truth or Consequences in 1981. The UNM Hospital dedicated a new seventy-four-thousand-square-foot, three-story critical care addition that housed an emergency department, a level I trauma center, a burn center, pediatric services, and new medical and surgical care units. Construction was financed through a bond issued passed in 1981. Before the dedication of the building, Bernalillo County voters, by an overwhelming margin, approved an eight-year mill levy to support both the UNM Hospital and the UNM Mental Health Center.

Another major development was designation of the Center for Non-Invasive Diagnosis as one of the centers of excellence in the Rio Grande Research Corridor. The center, directed by neurosciences Professor Nicholas Matwiyoff, was established in collaboration with Los Alamos National Laboratory. In this program, scientists and physicians from both the University and the national lab focused on developing

The Center for Non-Invasive Diagnosis on the North Campus was honored by the New Mexico Society of Architects for its design. Because steel interferes with magnetic imaging, the building's wood frame has aluminum nails.

magnetic resonance imaging as a safe, noninvasive diagnostic tool. The Rio Grande Research Corridor involved UNM, New Mexico State, and New Mexico Tech in a collaborative effort funded by the legislature. UNM's other program in the research corridor was the Center for High Technology Materials.

Private support through the UNM Foundation and its Heritage Club, President's Club, Century Club, and Tom L. Popejoy Society funded endowed chairs for outstanding faculty with a goal of improving their productivity and supporting their research and scholarship. Sponsored research increased from $7 million in 1974 to more than $41 million in 1983. UNM was becoming one of the leading universities in the country in federal grants for research, the report noted.

Continued growth in the collections of the UNM General Library was augmented by an additional $330,000 in the 1983–84 budget, plus another additional $350,000 in the 1984–85 budget.[14]

By the 1980s, there were eighteen departments in the College of Arts and Sciences: American studies, anthropology, biology, chemistry, communicative disorders, economics, English, geography, geology, history, journalism, modern and classical languages, philosophy, physics and astronomy, political science, psychology, sociology, and speech communication. In addition there were interdisciplinary programs such as comparative literature and religious studies, as well as area study programs for Latin America, Russia and East Europe, Asia, and others, in which baccalaureate degrees could be earned but which drew their faculty from the various departments.[15]

The middle 1980s found UNM's School of Law faculty involved in key issues that remain vexing in the twenty-first century. James Ellis presented papers at international conferences and testified before Congress on the legal rights of the mentally ill. Charles DuMars was the governor's appointee to a commission studying water allocation and at a conference in 1984 he predicted "growing competition for increasingly scarce water." Al Utton was an expert presenter at a conference on U.S.-Mexico border issues.[16]

The spring of 1983 saw the graduation of the first students in the School of Medicine's Primary Care Curriculum (PCC). An outgrowth of the innovative, interdisciplinary program the school's founders had developed twenty years earlier, the PCC gave students the option of studying basic medical sciences alone or in small tutorial groups and working with physician preceptors instead of attending standard lectures.

In 1984 the UNM School of Medicine could cite a long list of accomplishments during its first two decades. A total of 837 doctors had graduated, and 152 of them had completed postgraduate training and gone on to practice in New Mexico. The school was not only increasing the number of doctors and improving the quality of medical practice; it and its companion institutions were also providing services not readily available elsewhere through the Burn and Trauma Unit, Cancer Center, Children's Psychiatric Hospital, and other programs. The school remained true to the philosophy that good teaching could not exist apart from good research. There were successful programs in immunobiology, cell biology, arthritis and rheumatology, aging, cancer, and diabetes treatment. One of the most promising efforts, which Dr. Philip Eaton led, was an insulin delivery pump that could be implanted in a diabetic to deliver insulin.

Given the outstanding success of the research program at the School of Medicine, it seemed only logical that the University's first director of research should come from the school: Joseph Scaletti of the Department of Microbiology. At the time, Scaletti was simultaneously serving as associate provost for research and coordinating director of the Allied Health Sciences Programs, which had been established with a federal grant in 1972. By example, he demonstrated to colleagues on both the Central and North campuses that writing grant proposals and carrying out sponsored research are both art and science.

Developing a research park became a priority for Scaletti, who along with Regent John Paez visited successful facilities in Utah, Arizona, and North Carolina. A planning and development firm was hired for the site on the South Campus. A new Research Park tenant was the New Mexico Engineering Research Institute, headed by Del Calhoun.

During his tenure as vice president, Scaletti pursued collaborations with Sandia National Laboratory and Hughes Aircraft, among others. Outside funding from government and foundation grants quadrupled.[17]

Campus Development and Construction

Perovich was renowned as a builder, and his brief stint as UNM's president only enhanced his reputation. Like Popejoy, Heady, and Davis before him, he enjoyed the wise counsel of Van Dorn Hooker, the University architect. Between Hooker's appointment in 1963 and Davis's departure in 1982, eighty-seven new buildings were constructed, and under Perovich, more were in the pipeline. Although Hooker and

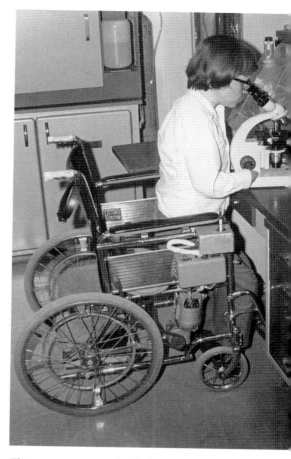

This microscope station in the School of Medicine was typical of adaptations made for handicapped people. A study by the state Board of Educational Finance in 1972 estimated that making all higher education facilities barrier-free would cost at least $3 million.

Registration was in Bandelier Hall in the early 1980s. The "ladder man" placed colored gel blocks over squares representing class sections that were open, closed, or restricted. However, he was usually running behind the central registration computer. An all-electronic system was in place in the new Student Services Center in 1983, and by 2003 students registered on-line without standing in line.

his staff did not design buildings, they had a strong role in selecting the architects who received commissions and collaborating with them to see that their buildings suited the University style. In 1982, Hooker was made a fellow of the American Institute of Architects at an investiture ceremony in Hawaii. Anna Dooling wrote in the *Albuquerque Journal* that when he arrived in 1963, the UNM campus was at a turning point. Its Pueblo Style was being threatened by the kind of architectural thinking that was putting glass boxes in urban downtowns all over the country.

Dooling wrote that under Hooker's guidance, the campus returned to preserving its regional character. Although nothing since the 1950s rigidly adhered to the Pueblo Style, the feeling that John Gaw Meem sought was maintained "by a conformity in color and texture, in a casual, almost informal massing of forms within buildings, and in an avoidance of symmetry." For example, the buildings clustered around Smith Plaza in front of the library appear like a network of buildings in a pueblo, she said.

The University of New Mexico and its architect had their critics. Hooker had to walk a tightrope between the University's mandate "to maintain a style and the danger of mummifying it with slavish adherence." He also had to contend with binding fiscal limitations, not to mention politics and occasional intrusions by governors. Hooker kept the faith, though, and the mood. The *Journal* reporter praised him as a low-keyed but forceful man who worked almost invisibly and possessed an incorruptible integrity.[18]

During the Perovich years, construction was started on a new track-and-field facility and an addition to Johnson Gymnasium. Planning began on an eight-hundred-car parking facility on Lomas Boulevard, a new Schools of Management/Social Sciences building, a new Science and Engineering Center, and expansion and improvement of the football stadium. The new Student Services Center was completed, bringing closely related offices together under the same roof for the first time. Among those who had fought hard for the student center were Regent Ann Jourdan and Vice President Marvin "Swede" Johnson, who pointed out that students walked miles to complete admission, registration, advisement, and counseling tasks each semester.

Environmental improvements on campus included new landscaping on the south side of La Posada, around the Cancer Center, and in front of Hodgin Hall. A joint venture with the city resulted in a landscaped bus stop with a sculpture on the corner of Girard and Central, and a contract was negotiated to landscape medians on Central.

Negotiations for the return of Yale Park to the University were proceeding, and a design plan was developed. In 1983, at the urging of Hooker and Dean Rupert Trujillo of the Division of Continuing Education and Community Services, UNM purchased the Masonic building on University Boulevard for a conference center and continuing education facility, part of the University's commitment to the concept of lifelong learning. Also, long-range planning began on land UNM owned at Eubank and I-40 and on the Research Park on the South Campus.

A project near and dear to all alumni was the remodeling of Hodgin Hall at a final cost of $1,355,000, which included $154,595 for furnishings. Along with presidents of the Alumni Association, Alumni Director Gwinn "Bub" Henry was a spark plug for the fund raising. The project turned Hodgin into a showplace of period furnishings and a museum for University memorabilia. It also provided a home for the Alumni Association and the UNM Foundation and was used for entertaining alumni and friends, as well as becoming a popular stop for visitors touring the campus. Hodgin was unveiled to the public at the UNM Homecoming, November 5, 1983.

The Bernalillo County Mental Health–Mental Retardation Center opened a $1.6 million wing for adolescent and geriatric patients on January 10, 1984. Not long after, ground breaking for the critical care wing in the UNM Hospital was held in April 1983. The two-story wing was financed by a county bond issue that had been approved in 1980, and the facility was dedicated in November 1984.

On November 6, 1984, New Mexico voters approved a $64 million education bond issue, which enabled UNM to finance the Lomas Boulevard parking structure and a building for the Anderson Schools of Management, economics, and social sciences.[19]

Ibrahim Hussein was an All-American in the 1,000-yard run in 1983. He went on to become one of the world's premier long-distance performers, winning the New York City Marathon in 1987 and the Boston Marathon in 1988, '91, and '92.

Athletics

The University of New Mexico enjoyed a moment in the national spotlight as the Pit was the site for the NCAA Final Four Basketball tournament on April 2–4, 1983. The facility was given a fresh coat of paint, and signs welcomed the NCAA participants and guests. Additional fixtures were installed to increase the light level on the court; NCAA logos were painted on the floor; fourteen rows of seats were taken on the west side for the press; and four TV camera mounts were built. A new building on the south side, designed to be used later for gymnastics, was completed in time to provide interview and work space for the sportswriters and broadcasters who covered the event. North Carolina State University defeated the University of Houston in the final seconds in one of the most memorable NCAA basketball championship games of all time.[20]

Another highlight in John Perovich's presidential tenure was the outstanding football season of 1982. At the game in which it was announced that Perovich had been appointed president, the Lobo football team defeated the University of Hawaii, 41–17, to finish the season with an all-time UNM best of ten wins and one loss. In spite of a season that was among the best in the nation, the bowl committees ignored the University. Sadly, the University lost head coach Joe Morrison, who in three years had built an outstanding program. He departed to take the head coaching job at the University of South Carolina, which he turned into a national power.

Gary Colson took over a basketball program that was in shambles and coached teams that improved year by year. Athletic Director John Bridgers provided strong and stable leadership to the overall program and aggressively developed the physical plant as well as the overall quality of the program.

Gary Colson's eight UNM teams compiled a 146–106 record with five straight trips to post-season play.

Perovich's Replacement Sought

When Perovich first accepted the job of president on an interim basis he said he would serve two years. Thus, he announced his retirement in December 1984, effective January 1, 1985, after forty years of employment at UNM.

In his final report as president, Perovich remained true to form, generously praising those who had worked with him to move UNM ahead. His integrity, fairness, concern for people, and love for UNM marked his departure as he cleared the way for yet another presidential search.

On March 20, 1984, the Regents named a New York consulting firm to assist the board in its search. The PA Executive Search Group was retained for $26,000 plus expenses. Earlier in the month, the board had outlined procedures for the search process and indicated it would serve as its own search committee. The board also stated that it intended to name a new president by June 30, 1984.

The 1982 search process had received strong criticism from candidates for being too open. In contrast, the 1984 search was criticized by University faculty for being too secretive. Richard King, an associate professor in educational administration, was quoted as saying: "There is a noticeable lack of direct involvement by faculty, staff, students, and alumni in establishing criteria, screening applicants, and interviewing candidates."[21]

The Regents missed their target date of June 30, but on August 7, 1984, board President Jaramillo announced that John Elac would be appointed president at the next public meeting of the board, which was scheduled for September 4.

Elac was chief of the General Studies Division of the Inter-American Development Bank of Washington, D.C. Born in Chile of Lebanese parents, his first language was Spanish. He had lived in the Southwest and been a banking executive and a university faculty member and was regarded as an expert in Latin American affairs. He held MA and PhD degrees from the University of California at Los Angeles (UCLA) and had taught at the University of California–Berkeley, Georgetown University, and UCLA. He had also worked with the Agency for International Development, the Inter-American Development Bank, and the Panama Canal Company. In the latter post, he had been the personal choice of President Lyndon Johnson.[22]

Following the announcement of Elac's pending appointment, howls of protest erupted on the UNM campus. Among the loudest was that Elac had personal ties with Robert Cox, the head of the consulting firm. In a news conference, Elac acknowledged that he had submitted his application at the suggestion of Cox, a friend of twenty years. Faculty also focused on the alleged "secretive manner in which the Regents conducted the search and Elac's lack of academic and administrative experience." The faculty met on Monday, August 20, 1984, and voted no confidence in the Regents. The Regents responded with a statement on August 23, calling the no-confidence vote "a reckless act that can have no positive results."[23]

Meanwhile, Elac, responding to an invitation from the deans to visit the UNM campus, arrived in Albuquerque at noon, Wednesday, August 22, and met for two hours with the Council of Deans. Donald McRae, dean of the College of Fine Arts, reported: "It was generally agreed that none of the deans would make any comment out of courtesy to Mr. Elac." Elac had no comment.[24]

That same day, August 22, the Associated Students of the University of New Mexico unanimously passed an emergency resolution condemning the Regents. ASUNM President John Schoeppner said, "John Elac is not qualified to be the president of the University of New Mexico. Henry Jaramillo and the Board of Regents have violated their trust to the faculty, students and residents of this state."[25]

An open meeting of the faculty for the morning of Thursday, August 23, was announced by Faculty Senate President Pauline Turner. Faculty members were to be permitted to "observe" only.[26] Approximately three hundred faculty members filed silently into UNM's Popejoy Hall and listened as Turner and four members of the Faculty Senate Operations Committee interviewed Elac.

Following this interview, the operations committee asked Elac not to accept the presidency. Late Thursday night, Elac refused to say whether he would comply with the faculty's request. He canceled all meetings with students and administrators Friday morning. He did meet with Governor Toney Anaya, who had said that if he were unsatisfied with Elac's credentials, he would ask him not to accept the presidency. Following the two-hour closed meeting, Governor Anaya commended Elac's "professional manner" and thanked him for visiting the state. Anaya declined to express his opinion on Elac's qualifications. Elac stated: "Until I sign a contract, the decision is not irrevocable. I have not resigned my position at the Inter-American Development Bank. I'm here on my own vacation time."[27]

Elac returned to his Washington, D.C., home. He later contacted the Regents and notified them that he would not accept the presidency of UNM. The Regents then turned to another finalist in the search—Tom Farer, who became the thirteenth president of the University of New Mexico effective January 1, 1985. ■

University Architect Van Dorn Hooker mandated that the Health Sciences and Services Building not obstruct the view of the Sandias from the medical library. When the design was submitted, Hooker laid the building footprint out and set helium balloons the height of the building to check the view. Photo by Michael Mouchette

Chapter Seventeen
Administration of Tom Farer
1985–86

Tom Farer

When John Elac turned down the presidency of the University of New Mexico, Governor Toney Anaya was irate and blamed the Regents for the failed process. Speaking to a crowd of UNM students as part of a Labor Day celebration, he said that if the Regents had another "disastrous" presidential search, "they should all resign or be removed through the legal system." He further stated: "This is not the first time this has happened. The University's, the public's, and the governor's patience are all at an end. Maybe this Board of Regents has had one chance too many. Maybe they should not make the decision."[1]

Campus morale was low; emotions were high. The governor heaped more fuel on the fire by saying he would encourage anyone the current Regents selected to turn down the appointment. He would tell whoever was chosen that the governor's support would not be forthcoming, and that if an offer were accepted, he would seek to have the Regents void the contract. Governor Anaya was also reported to have said he might demand that all new UNM Regents submit a letter of resignation in advance that he could use to oust any board members who ignored his wishes.[2]

The Regents, however, pressed on, but not before some internal reorganization. Board President Henry Jaramillo announced that Regent Dr. Phillip U. Martinez would serve as spokesman for the board for the duration of the search because he "represented the majority opinion." At that time Regents Martinez, Ann Jourdan, and John Paez constituted the majority, which favored the continuation of the search. By a three-to-two vote, the board thus invited Tom Farer, one of the finalists when Elac was chosen, to interview for the job.[3]

Farer, a professor of law at Rutgers University, held a bachelor of arts degree from Princeton University and a law degree from Harvard Law School. He was a 1983 fellow of the Woodrow Wilson International Center for Scholars and had been a senior research fellow of the Carnegie Foundation and the Council on Foreign Relations. He also had served on the Inter-American Commission on Human Rights from 1976 to 1983, and in 1975 had been a special assistant to the assistant secretary of state for inter-American affairs. He was also special assistant to the general counsel of the Department of Defense. Farer served as well as a member of the Congressional Presentation Staff, the Agency for International Development, and Delta Capital Corporation and as an adviser to the commanding general of the police force of the Somali Republic.[4]

Early in September, Farer visited the campus. While the faculty reacted favorably to his candidacy, its members also expressed a desire to review additional candidates. Student body president John Schoeppner reported that the students would also like to meet more finalists before a decision was made, but it was not to happen.[5]

On a three-to-two vote, September 18, 1984, the Regents approved hiring Tom Farer, with Regents Henry Jaramillo and Coleen Maloof dissenting. Farer's appointment would not become official until contract details were worked out, and he would not assume the office until early January 1985.[6] By the end of September, the Faculty Senate decided to urge support for the incoming president and called upon the governor and Regents to back the new head of UNM.[7]

But Henry Jaramillo, president of the Board of Regents, refused to sign Farer's contract. Part of his reluctance was the fact that Farer had played a part in writing it. The matter was referred to the New Mexico attorney general, Paul Bardacke, who declared the contract was legal when the vice president of the board, Phillip Martinez, signed it. Jaramillo finally agreed to sign it "with reservations," so by late November, it appeared that the matter was settled.[8]

Just as it seemed that the furor over Farer's appointment had quieted, it was discovered that Farer had billed UNM $2,750 as a consulting fee for his interview visit to the campus. Farer claimed that this was standard procedure, but after talking to President John Perovich, Farer withdrew his request for the fee and was reimbursed for only his travel, lodging, and meals.[9]

Tom Farer took office effective January 1, 1985. When he arrived in New Mexico, he described his immediate impression of UNM as that of "a great ship in dry-dock—beautiful, full of a sense of excitement and adventure. But like any great ship in dry-dock, she was neither rotting nor going forward."[10]

Farer viewed his job as helping to push UNM forward and identified his first task as setting goals and orienting faculty and staff to the future. He said, "We as a university had been hampered by the absence of a structure that permits the creation of programs designed to assist in reaching institutional goals."[11] Thus, he endeavored to institutionalize a budgeting process in which academic criteria could dominate.

Early in the spring of 1985, Farer created the Strategic Planning Committee to carry out what he described as the most comprehensive planning effort at UNM since World War II. The committee included eighty-six faculty, staff, and community leaders and was charged with the examination of almost every major department of the University. Farer was determined to do away with the "we-they" thinking he had found on the campus and, in nautical terms, launch the ship finally out of the dry-dock.[12] At that point, perhaps he was unaware that the Rio Grande was not only shallow but also full of quicksand.

A Transition Time

Farer reported he was "moving carefully" during the transition period. He said he did not believe in change for the sake of change. He estimated the transition period would last about six months.

Among the major changes that spring of 1985 was the resignation of Marvin "Swede" Johnson as vice president for student affairs, alumni relations, and development. Johnson had accepted a top administrative position with the Adolph Coors Company in Golden, Colorado. Farer said that Johnson's position covered a "much wider" range than was usual at other universities and should be divided between two administrators, one for University relations and one for student affairs.[13]

Moving rapidly in his reorganization of the administration, Farer appointed Mari-Luci Jaramillo as interim vice president for student affairs March 6, 1985. At the time, Jaramillo was associate dean of the UNM College of Education. Over some twenty years, she had served in a number of capacities, including professor in the former Department of Elementary Education and later that department's chair. She had also worked with UNM's Latin American Programs in Education and had been the United States ambassador to Honduras.

At the time of Jaramillo's appointment, Farer announced that Alumni Relations, Development, and KNME-TV would be transferred to the Office of Public Affairs and the evolving Office of Intergovernmental Relations.[14] This reorganization was in turn revised in later years.

Farer also appointed Robert Desiderio, who had been dean of the School of Law, as vice president for academic affairs, succeeding McAllister Hull. Former Law Dean Fred Hart resumed the post on an acting basis. Desiderio resigned as vice president after one year and returned to the School of Law as a faculty member.

Mari-Luci Jaramillo had been a popular teacher, mentor, and consultant on education and minority affairs. Her autobiography described her childhood in northern New Mexico as one of monetary poverty but spiritual wealth.

Finance

Following the pattern of virtually all those who had preceded him, Farer announced early in his tenure that the highest priority on his requests to the legislature was raising faculty and staff salaries.[15] The House Appropriations and Finance Committee on February 20, 1985, approved a proposed budget with a staggering 16 percent increase in tuition. This raised howls of protest and was eventually adjusted to a 9 percent increase, which seemed to satisfy most students.[16]

As if the tense atmosphere around the University during the first few months of Farer's tenure were not enough, a full-fledged tornado hit the campus on September 22, 1985. It set down near the Student Services Building and continued northeast. While it broke windows, upended trees, and downed power lines, prompting reports of power outages in some areas of the city, there were no major injuries.[17]

Robert Desiderio

Academics

A slew of resignations and retirements marked the spring of 1985. Heading the list of departing faculty was award-winning author and journalism professor Tony Hillerman. Among others leaving UNM were Clinton Adams, director of the Tamarind Institute; Richard H. Clough, Cornie Hulsbos, José Martinez, and George Triandafilidis, professors of civil engineering; Ahmed Erteza, professor of electrical and computer engineering; Robert Evans, director of the Honors Program; William Huber, dean of University College; Harold Meier and Charles Woodhouse, both from the Sociology Department; Beaumont Newhall, visiting professor of art; Loren Potter, professor of biology; and Glenn Whan, professor and chairman of the Chemical and Nuclear Engineering Department.[18]

The New Mexico Advisory Committee to the U.S. Commission on Civil Rights attacked the University for its poor minority hiring practices. George Anderson, of the New Mexico Rainbow Coalition, said that the University had a system of "apartheid," and accused the institution of being "racist, sexist, ethnocentristic, and bigoted." President Farer, in turn, called Anderson's statements "slanderous."[19]

The nearly continuous furor during the spring semester of 1985 began to take its toll. F. Chris Garcia, dean of the College of Arts and Sciences, commented, "There is no doubt in my mind that faculty morale is in its lowest ebb in several years." James Thorson, a UNM English professor, agreed, saying, "There's no question in my mind that people are really down."[20]

There was some sunshine in that gloomy spring of 1985 as in April the Board of Regents approved the removal of seventeen buildings between Las Lomas Road and Roma Avenue to create parking areas. An alternative plan was produced to turn the area into an "ethnic mall," where departments such as Native American Studies, Afro-American Student Services, and Chicano Student Services would be located. The ethnic groups concerned strongly endorsed the proposal inasmuch as it would preserve the buildings that housed their activities. President Farer was reported as being impressed with it, but it was never adopted.[21] Later, most of the buildings were torn down to make room for a new classroom building.

Additional positive news in 1985 was the opening of the Zuni Campus (or "twig") of the UNM Gallup Branch. Cooperative efforts of UNM, the Zunis, and the Zuni School District led to renovation of an old high school. The following year saw Governor Toney Anaya and President Farer dedicate an addition to Gurley Hall and Zollinger Library on the Gallup campus.

Construction was under way in Tomé in the summer of 1986 for a new campus for the fast-growing UNM Valencia Branch. The first classes had been offered in the fall of 1978 at the Eastern Valencia County Satellite Center, after a successful fund-raising campaign in the Belen–Los Lunas area. The following year the New Mexico Legislature mandated that the satellite centers become branch campuses, funded by local mill levies, general fund appropriations, and tuition. The Valencia Branch began offering technical certificates and associate degrees in 1981.

More Dissention

Storm clouds continued to gather around the operation of the University radio station, KUNM. The news director, Marcos Martinez, was fired in mid-April 1985. This led to an accusation of racism from the Southwest Organizing Project (SWOP), which, in turn, led to various student groups demanding a public hearing of Martinez's case. Within a month, President Farer reinstated Martinez. Shortly thereafter the general manager of the station, Wendell Jones, who had fired Martinez, resigned. Several months later, in January 1986, Tim Singleton, a long-time public broadcasting official in Indiana, became the new general manager of the station. [22]

Seeking to stem the tide of overexpenditures in the Athletic Department, President Farer in August 1985 placed Athletic Director John Bridgers on probation. Farer reported that he held Bridgers responsible for the deficit of $780,000. He further stipulated that if Bridgers failed to regain the University's confidence and meet certain conditions, he would have no other choice but to dismiss him. [23]

A Change in Board Leadership

Adding to the stormy atmosphere of Farer's first few months as president was a decisive turnover on the Board of Regents with the departure of Henry Jaramillo and Phil Martinez. Former New Mexico Governor Jerry Apodaca was appointed to the board by Governor Toney Anaya in January 1985 and was elected president at his first meeting. Apodaca later commented about the board's dealings with Farer: "I can't point to one incident or event that caused the breakdown. It's as complicated as what ends a marriage. This relationship just didn't work out." [24]

Jerry Apodaca had been a strong supporter of education as a state senator and governor, but the native New Mexican and the Easterner Tom Farer saw things differently.

Farer viewed Apodaca as a "thorn in my side." He reported that the former governor had once told him that he would drive him off the campus. Apodaca denied ever making that threat. Almost from the day Apodaca joined the board, Farer and Apodaca were engaged in a running battle, sometimes within the allegedly quiet halls of academe, more often in the newspaper or on the radio or television. The UNM campus squabbles attracted national media attention.

The issues varied. In April 1986, Farer took exception to the Regents' order that UNM not show the controversial movie, *Hail Mary,* which had sparked protests from Catholic organizations for its modern portrayal of the Virgin Mary. [25] According to Apodaca, however, Farer was out of town during part of the crisis. In an emergency meeting April 7, 1986, upon advice of legal counsel, the Regents rescinded their earlier action and permitted the film to be shown. [26]

On another occasion, Farer protested about the pressure three Hispanic Regents brought to bear by demanding that UNM hire more minorities. He also charged that Regents exerted political pressure to influence a pending promotion. In yet another instance, the president protested when the board overturned the suspension of a law student who had falsified some information on his admission application. [27]

Farer, described as "a polished, articulate man" who was often seen on the campus wearing his "trademark fedora," proclaimed that he wanted to be "an agent of change." In assembling his own administrative team, which some faculty leaders criticized as "destabilizing," Farer demoted Joel M. Jones, vice president for administration and planning. When Farer first arrived on campus, Jones was one of his primary advisors. Jones apparently fell out of favor after he said at a faculty meeting that the current Regents were no more intrusive than past boards. The president promptly ordered four divisions that had been under Jones to report directly to the president, and Jones was suddenly on the outside looking in. Farer said his differences with Jones prevented them from working together. Academic Vice President Robert Desiderio tried to put things in perspective by saying, "No president can turn this place around in one year."[28]

Chris Garcia, dean of the College of Arts and Sciences, was alarmed that the internal bickering and highly publicized conflicts between the president and the Regents were detracting from the real problems of the University.

> We're already a skeleton of what we should be. People say we have to cut the fat out of the budget. Well, the fat went a long time ago, along with the muscle and tissues. We're talking bone marrow here . . . I hope this is simply a bad dream we wake up from. Then we can get on with the real problems of this university.[29]

Frustrated by the competing demands of multiple constituencies during his first year in office, Farer expressed his opinion that the demands of the office of president were unending. One particular surprise was the media. He described their fascination with the University as "unusual," unlike any community he had ever seen. He commented: "The number of front page stories and the sheer proportion of UNM news to other educational institutions in the state certainly make an impact on the public's perception of UNM." He registered his particular dismay at the level of controversy surrounding issues in the UNM sports program, inasmuch as the athletic budget represented only 1 percent of the total University budget.

Continuing his nautical metaphor, Farer said after the year of planning and preparation, the ship (the University) was "on the open seas with a clear destination on . . . an exciting, perhaps difficult, but certainly worthwhile voyage ahead."[30]

Apodaca was quoted in the *Lobo* on April 22, 1986, as saying Farer "has been here 16 months too long. I'm convinced he doesn't care about the University of New Mexico." Apodaca asked, "Is it in the best interest of the University to renew the contract of someone who is only interested in his own career?"[31]

Farer appeared on the KNME-TV public affairs program *Illustrated Daily* on April 23, 1986, and acknowledged he had clashed repeatedly with Regents. He alleged there had been a number of cases of cronyism but did not identify any specific instances. The television interview was being taped at the same time the Regents were meeting in a closed session to discuss his contract. Farer publicly accused three Regents of various derelictions, including gross policy meddling, hiring pressure, and commercial self-favoritism.[32]

Columnist V. B. Price stated that the governor and/or the attorney general should investigate Farer's harsh accusations. If they were found to be true, Price believed the Regents could be removed for malfeasance. If false, in the eyes of Price, the president deserved a swift kick. Price also asserted: "The ideal solution . . . would be a complete internal house cleaning—president and regents, then—a fresh start with new blood." Price colorfully described the atmosphere in that spring of 1986.

Albuquerque used to be a college town. Now it smells like an academic battlefield littered with politicians bloating in the sun.

It is enough to break your heart, this spectre of carnage and morbid egos. . . . The school is being massacred by a political Lobogate of accusations, strong-arm "public relations," anti-intellectualism, posturing and puffery.

The reputation of the university resembles that of a corrupt mini-state in the middle of a massive civil war. The reality, of course, is not so far from that—except when the stuffed shirts and the power mongers are put aside and the university is seen for what it is behind the public dumb show, a community of largely hard-working and gifted faculty and their students who want to get on with the business of learning.

The behavior at UNM signals a leadership vacuum caused by the cyclonic tensions between political polarities, political celebrities and a climate of economic, demographic and ideological change. The state can't expect much from itself until political warlords and hacks backbite themselves out of existence and a new generation of leaders has the guts to move in among the carnage and take charge.[33]

Meanwhile, board President Apodaca was more than a little disturbed when he learned that Farer had been interviewed in mid-April as one of the finalists for the job of chancellor of the university system of New Hampshire. Unconfirmed reports in the media also alleged that Farer was being considered for posts at Rutgers University, Cornell University, the University of Minnesota, and the University of North Carolina. Furthermore, Apodaca and Regent Robert Sanchez charged that Farer was seldom on campus, cared little about the University, and was trying to boost his career at the expense of UNM.

On Thursday, May 1, 1986, Farer announced that he would not accept a new contract from the Regents in December, regardless of terms. On Friday, he added that he had no intention of stepping down before his contract expired. Before he became president in January 1985, the UNM School of Law faculty had voted him a tenured professorship, which meant that the school had to find a position for him if he did not choose to go elsewhere before the end of his contract.

Four of the Regents stated they were not interested in conducting a presidential search until Farer's contract expired on December 31, 1986, when the board might have three new members. Regent Ann Jourdan's appointment expired on that date, and she had stated she was not seeking reappointment. If voters approved a constitutional amendment (which they did) in November, the five-member Board of Regents would increase to seven.[34]

Reactions on the campus were varied. The student newspaper, the *Lobo*, reported that it had received Farer's statement announcing he would not seek a new contract. Sympathetic to Farer, the editor of the *Lobo* apologized to the president for the rudeness of the Board of Regents. A letter from a biology graduate student, Kerry

S. Kilburn, suggested that one solution to the problem would be to blow up the University, which he would consider a mercy killing.[35]

Strong segments of the faculty supported the beleaguered president. A petition was signed by the appropriate number of faculty members to call a special meeting on Thursday, May 8, 1986. President Farer designated Professor David Sanchez to preside. Sanchez, chair of the Mathematics and Statistics Department and former Faculty Senate president, was leaving to become vice president at Lehigh University.[36]

Thursday afternoon, May 9, 1986, more than seven hundred faculty members out of a total of approximately twelve hundred voted no confidence in the UNM Board of Regents and called on all five Regents to resign by the end of the year. In what was called the largest faculty meeting in the history of the University, the faculty approved the strongest censure it could give. About two dozen members voted in support of the Regents. The resolution the faculty approved gave three reasons for the vote of no confidence.

> The board has brought discredit to the university through its divisive actions; the board has brought instability by inappropriate and arbitrary interference in the administration and academic operations of the university; and the board has failed to provide leadership in support of the university before the Legislature and the public.[37]

Vice President Joel Jones was booed lustily, as were others who sought to speak on behalf of the Regents.

On May 23, 1986, Farer left Albuquerque for a three-week trip to Europe and was expected to return June 16, a day before the Regents' next scheduled meeting. On June 4, Apodaca announced that Farer and the Regents had reached an agreement on buying out Farer's contract.[38] On that same day, Farer issued a statement outlining his reasons for stepping down before the expiration of his contract.

> My discussions with members of the Board of Regents over the past several weeks have made it clear to me that the majority of the Board are intent that for the remainder of my term as president of the University I will not be permitted to exercise fully the powers of the office.
>
> I have been told that not only does this majority of the Board of Regents not support my policies and decisions, but in addition they are prepared to move affirmatively to restrict the established powers of the office, including the power to make decisions, such as those involving senior personnel, necessary to the effective functioning of the University.[39]

Farer also said he was "tired of the controversy, and of attempting to manage institutional change in an unpropitious environment."[40]

The turmoil at UNM caught the attention of the national media, and the events on the campus received front-page coverage in the *New York Times* (May 12,

1986) and the *Chronicle of Higher Education* (June 4, 1986). The opening paragraph of the *Times* story featured Farer's complaint that the Regents treated him like a butler who might steal the family silver. The *Times* further reported:

> The decision of the president . . . to quit grows partly out of his view that the board majority had engaged in "petty malice and day-to-day pecking at the heels of the administration." The leader of the majority, former Gov. Jerry Apodaca, the board's president, says the Regents are only trying to represent the taxpayers' point of view on operation of the university.[41]

The *Times* called the ethnic issue an "underlying theme; one that turns on the century-old tensions between the state's old Hispanic society pushing against the dominance of the Anglo-Saxon culture."[42]

> Viewed in that context . . . the departure of Mr. Farer, a non-Hispanic white . . . is a victory for the Chicano side and for its champion, Mr. Apodaca, who is a Hispanic American. Mr. Farer's appointment in 1984 came after several years in which state leaders sought [as president of UNM] a Hispanic American from within the state.
> "What we're dealing with here is a post-World War II phenomenon," said E. A. Mares, a Chicano writer who is curator of education at the Albuquerque Museum. "That is, of a Chicano middle class that has come of age and that is critically aware of the deficiencies and shortcomings in terms of ethnic representation at the university, and this is a deeper issue than the personalities involved."[43]

As the *Times* pointed out, Farer barely concealed his distaste for the Regents who opposed him. The way Apodaca got rid of Farer made the latter look like a quitter, but the campus itself was squarely behind its departing president, the article said.[44]

With Farer leaving, Apodaca was hailed as the victor, but the *Times* reported that the *Lobo* ran a cartoon depicting Apodaca bare-chested, a weapon in one hand and Mr. Farer's severed head in the other. "Mission Accomplished," the caption said.[45]

Farer returned from Europe to attend the meeting of the Regents on June 17, 1986. Apodaca began by praising Farer. The agreement with Farer stipulated that he would be offered a position as professor at the UNM School of Law. The agreement stated that he would not begin there until the spring 1987 semester and that he would be granted a leave of absence to write books, shepherd the Strategic Planning Committee, and "recover from the presidency."[46]

Meanwhile, in what was rightly perceived as a done deal, Gerald W. May, dean of UNM's College of Engineering, was announced as the University's interim president without a search. Some of the University's constituents may have wondered if, deep down in their souls, sitting Regents wanted to be sure they were out of office before a real search for a permanent president was under way. ■

The building housing some management and social sciences programs was designed as a transition between its neighbors, the Spanish-Pueblo Revival Old Bratton Hall and the modern School of Medicine complex. Photo by Van Dorn Hooker

Chapter Eighteen
Administration of Gerald W. May
1986–90

Gerald W. May

With all the flap about the open conflict between Jerry Apodaca, president of the Board of Regents, and Tom Farer, president of UNM, it came as no surprise when on June 4, 1986, Apodaca announced that there had been an agreed-upon buyout of Farer's $90,000-a-year contract scheduled to expire December 31, 1986. Apodaca also announced that at the next board meeting, scheduled for June 17, Gerald W. May would be appointed president for a term of two years.[1]

May, who had been a faculty member in civil engineering since 1967, had been named acting dean of engineering when Bill Gross left in the spring of 1980. A national search was then conducted, and May was selected as dean in 1981. When Farer resigned five years later there really was no national search for his replacement; May was promoted to the presidency from within.

At UNM, he was a known quantity, a quiet, serious, highly moral man viewed as one who knew the University and whose interim appointment would allow time for controversy to subside before a presidential search began. May himself speculated that the Regents had appointed him to bring stability to the institution and was optimistic that his appointment would be well received by the faculty, which in the late spring had voted no confidence in the Regents.[2]

The son of missionaries, May was born in Kenya and grew up on a farm in Illinois. Before coming to the University of New Mexico, he received his undergraduate degree in civil engineering from Bradley University in Peoria, Illinois, and earned his master's and doctorate degrees in that field from the University of Colorado. May had been an engineer for Sandia Laboratories and the Illinois Highway Department. He and his wife, Mary Joyce, were the parents of three children, Erica, Heidi, and Chris.

Forty-five at the time of his appointment, May was reported to be "cautiously excited" about taking the reins of the University after President Farer left office July 1. When members of the Board of Regents first approached him in the spring of 1986, he told them to look somewhere else. He did not know the members of the board or whether he would have their full support. What the soft-spoken May hoped was "to be the peacemaker in trying to bring together the people who

Like many first couples at the University, Mary Joyce and Gerald May posed at the gate in front of the President's Residence. Photo by Michael Mouchette

sided with Tom [Farer] and those who backed the Regents. I was too far from the situation to place blame on anyone. From my standpoint, things were just not working out." May thought of himself as "someone who would be brutally honest if he needed to be and would listen carefully to different views from people in the University and community."[3]

Board of Regents Expanded

The voters in November 1986 passed a proposition that added two new members to the Board of Regents, making a total of seven. Along with the seat vacated by Ann Jourdan, Governor Garry Carruthers named three new members to the board when he took office in January 1987: Ken Johns, an Albuquerque car dealer; Sigfried Hecker, director of Los Alamos National Laboratory; and former astronaut Frank Borman, a car dealer in Las Cruces.[4]

Funding Down, Tuition Up

The mild-mannered May inherited a fiscal nightmare. In February, the New Mexico House of Representatives had unanimously passed a funding bill that cut appropriations to all state agencies, including higher education.[5] The Senate topped this by passing an even harsher budget.[6] The University responded by increasing tuition and cutting its budget by 2 percent. This was followed within the year by a 3 percent decline in enrollment and an exodus of faculty, including several professors from the School of Medicine.[7] A survey of undergraduates revealed that their chief concerns were the underpaid and diminishing faculty, rising tuition, and parking.[8]

The following year, 1987, the financial situation worsened as the House voted to raise tuition at state institutions of higher learning by 24 percent.[9] The Senate modified this somewhat by reducing the increase to 16 percent. The two houses eventually compromised on 20 percent while limiting raises for faculty to just under 3 percent, which still left the pay for faculty at UNM some 10 percent below salaries at peer institutions. President May and the board came under criticism when it became known that the president had received a 10 percent salary increase, although he too earned less than his peers.[10]

As part of the response to the budget crisis, the University announced that the Child Care Center would be closed. This raised such a storm of protest that the directive was quickly rescinded, changes were made, and the center stayed open.[11]

Funding woes persisted, and in order to avoid budgets cuts in 1988, President May proposed a tuition rate of $120 more than the legislature had recommended. After much furor, the Board of Regents approved an increase of 16.5 percent.[12]

A year later, the board approved another tuition hike, this time $100 per student. The students, supported by some faculty members and the Reverend Jesse Jackson, turned the April 1989 meeting of the Board of Regents into a shouting match. They then organized a sit-in in the president's office, which they occupied for two weeks.

In keeping with a national trend, universities across the country began selling off their investments in companies that did business in South Africa as a part of their protest against the apartheid regime governing that nation. UNM followed suit when in 1986 it began divesting approximately $1.23 million, a process that was completed by October of that year. Supporters of divestment were critical of President May and other UNM officials, however, for not acting sooner and more aggressively.[13]

Financial news for a select group of UNM students was positive, however. In 1989 the Regents, endeavoring to attract the best and brightest of New Mexico's high school graduates, authorized twenty "full-ride" scholarships per year. The Regents' Scholarship provides for tuition and fees, room and board, and books, all renewable for four years for students who maintain a 3.5 grade average for fifteen or more credit hours per semester.

The standards for the scholarships are rigorous. The student must be valedictorian of his or her class at a state high school, have a GPA of 3.9 or better, and score 31 or higher on the ACT. All recipients are admitted to the General Honors Program (called the University Honors Program as of 1998) and are expected to represent the University at various functions.

By 2003 nearly three hundred students had been selected as Regents Scholars and 99 percent of them had gone on to graduate school. They had won Rhodes and Truman scholarships and many other prestigious academic awards.

Scott Altenbach was an outstanding teacher as well as a renowned researcher.

Academic Programs and Faculty

All the while academic life on the campus just kept chugging along. After a national search, former Arts and Sciences Dean F. Chris Garcia was appointed vice president for academic affairs. One of the big issues in 1987 was the January announcement of the closing of the General College, which had served as a means of entrance for students whose high school academic record would not allow them to enter a regular college degree program. Taking remedial courses permitted students to build up their academic records and enter the University on a regular basis. People particularly concerned with the education of minorities viewed the closing as a threat to their inclusion, since many of them did not meet the standards for full admission. The Albuquerque Technical Vocational Institute and community and branch colleges throughout the state, however, stepped forward to offer the pre-college-level courses.

Two examples of UNM research were publicized in 1986. The University's magazine *Quantum* had an article about the Harding Pegmatite Mine in southern Taos County, which the Geology Department operated as a research site. *New Mexico Magazine* published an article about biology Professor J. Scott Altenbach, an internationally known authority on bats. He was one of the first to explain how bats fly by devising a way to film them at high speed, and his footage was used in the BBC's *Life on Earth* series.

That year a new agreement with the National Park Service brought added responsibilities to the Maxwell Museum of Anthropology, now under the direction of Garth Bawden. The museum became co-owner of the archaeological collections

Computers were becoming more and more important for both administration and academics, but these students found the learning curve a bit steep.

from years of research at Chaco Canyon. The agreement denoted a landmark in collaboration between the federal government and a local institution on behalf of scholarly work and public education, and it represented an early example of a long-term cooperative plan for upkeep and use of a valuable collection.

The year 1987 also saw the debut of a UNM Biology Department course that became one of many shining examples of the University's efforts in research, teaching, and public service. Bosque Biology taught undergraduates about the riparian areas adjoining the middle Rio Grande and introduced them to scientific processes. Under the leadership of Clifford Crawford, the course evolved into an interdisciplinary program with substantial grant funding for faculty and graduate students. Expertise and information from these projects have been applied to important restoration efforts, especially after the drought and fires of the early twenty-first century.

Perhaps the greatest impact on the academic scene was the implementation of the evening and weekend degree programs in 1987. UNM had earlier made several unsuccessful attempts to establish a program that would allow students to earn degrees by attending class in the evenings and on weekends. With a few exceptions, such as the College of Education, there were only scattered and uncoordinated offerings. Administrators received many complaints from people in the community about their inability to earn a degree because they had work or child-care obligations on weekdays.

When Chris Garcia became academic vice president in 1987, he was determined to meet these community needs and establish an articulated evening and weekend degree program. He found the right man to lead the program in David Stuart, a professor of anthropology. With skill and perseverance, Stuart managed to develop the program, not only persuading departments to offer more evening and weekend courses but also arranging for extended hours in the libraries, student union, and student service offices. Vice President for Administration David Mc Kinney came up with start-up funds for the program. It flourished beyond all expectations, both financially and by fostering good will in the community.

A major development in research came in the fall of 1988 with the dedication of the Sevilleta Long-term Ecological Research Project. One of only seventeen sites in a study network funded by the National Science Foundation, it was led by biology Professor James R. Gosz. Sevilleta National Wildlife Refuge, about fifty miles south of Albuquerque, is at the juncture of at least four major biological regions, offering unique combinations of land forms and climate and great species diversity. Faculty and graduate students later researched the effects of El Niño winter storms on New Mexico, monitored pollution by observing bees, and measured water vapor with ultraviolet lasers, among other things.

The nation's first Center for Disaster Medicine was created at the School of Medicine in 1990. The center houses the Disaster Medical Assistance Team (DMAT), which not only responds to state and national disasters, but also provides consultation and training to individuals and teams.

One of the hottest faculty issues revolved around Margaret Randall, an adjunct professor in American studies and women studies. She had given up her U.S. citizenship in 1967, when she became a Mexican citizen by marrying a man from that country. Back in the States, she became a harsh critic of U.S. foreign policy, especially when it involved Central American countries. Under the McCarran-Walter Act of 1952, people could be denied residency in the United States if they had been affiliated with a Communist organization. After Randall gave up her citizenship, an Immigration and Naturalization Service judge ordered her deported under the McCarran-Walter Act. This evolved into a heated civil liberties and free-speech controversy taken up by supporters all across the United States and Mexico, including well-known authors such as Norman Mailer, Kurt Vonnegut, Alice Walker, Arthur Miller, and Adrienne Rich. The judge turned down Randall's appeal because he claimed her writings supported world Communism. Although she was ordered to leave the country on December 1, 1986, her appeal kept her teaching at UNM in the spring semester of 1987. She accepted another teaching position at Trinity College in Hartford, Connecticut, for the fall semester of 1987.

A purely local freedom of speech issue erupted in 1987 when the University's radio station, KUNM, decided to change its format after almost twenty years. The station had traditionally used a free-form programming format during the day, which allowed the disk jockeys to play whatever they wanted. Looking to improve listener ratings, KUNM officials decided to abandon free-form.[15]

The controversy heated up with board members resigning and threats of violence against staff and fear of destruction of the radio station's property. This led to the station closing entirely at the end of June 1987. Opponents of the program changes filed a lawsuit against the University. In addition, Pat Conley, program director at KUNM, was found guilty of assault and battery after attacking station volunteer Andres Mares-Muro while on the air. The long battle over control of KUNM finally ended when the station's general manager, Tim Singleton, resigned in January 1989.[16]

One of the changes in the central administration was the appointment of Joel Jones as vice president for administration and planning in 1987 after an unsuccessful search. Jones had been associate provost under McAllister Hull and was then named vice president for administration by President Farer. Jones left UNM in 1988 to become president of Fort Lewis College in Durango, Colorado. After an extensive search, Orcilia Zuniga Forbes, who was named vice president for student affairs in 1989, replaced him.

Carroll Lee, comptroller and associate vice president for business, retired from UNM December 31, 1986, after thirty years of service. Lee, a UNM graduate and certified public accountant, had served in state government before joining the University.[17] Following an intensive search, David McKinney was named vice president for finance.

In 1986 the UNM School of Law for the first time named one of its own graduates as dean: Theodore Parnall. He returned to New Mexico after practicing with a New York firm that did extensive work in the Third World. Under his administration Henry Weihofen wrote his history of the School of Law.[18]

Bryan Hobson Wildenthal was named as the new dean of the College of Arts and Sciences effective July 1, 1987. He came to UNM from Drexel University in Philadelphia, Pennsylvania, where he had been a faculty member in the Physics Department. Fred Sturm, who had served as the acting dean of arts and sciences, returned to his position as chair of the Philosophy Department.

Three other deanships were confirmed in 1987. Raymond Radosevich became the new dean of the Anderson Schools of Management; Estelle Rosenblum was named dean of the School of Nursing; and Robert Migneault was appointed the dean of library services. All three were formerly acting deans.

Also in 1987, Van Deren Coke retired. The founding director of the UNM Art Museum was "credited with putting New Mexico on the photographic map" by focusing the museum's collection on photography and prints. He also served as chair of the Art and Art History Department. An author, sculptor, and collector, he donated many pieces to the museum.[19]

Another 1987 retiree was Van Dorn Hooker. Appointed the first University architect in 1963, he had overseen major changes to the campus while upholding the special Pueblo Revival atmosphere.

A further change among top administrative positions was the departure of Alex Sanchez, UNM vice president for community and international programs. It was announced July 1, 1989, that Sanchez was resigning to accept the presidency of Rio Hondo Community College in Whittier, California. Sanchez, who earned his doctorate at New Mexico State University, had come to UNM as a professor of educational administration in 1979. Before that, he had been academic dean at the New Mexico Military Institute in Roswell.[20] He returned to New Mexico in 1993 to be president of Albuquerque Technical Vocational Institute.

Conflict and Lawsuits

Incoming President May did not have to look for controversy and conflict when he took office in the summer of 1986—they were waiting for him.

Before he took office the Regents, against the advice of their attorney, had ruled that the controversial film *Hail Mary*, a modern retelling of the story of the Virgin Mary, would not be shown on the campus. Two UNM students filed a lawsuit protesting the action. Five days later, the Regents reversed themselves, and the film was shown without incident. Subsequently, however, it was learned that the Regents' attempt to ban the film had cost the taxpayers of New Mexico more than $18,000 in attorneys' fees. Of the total, the University paid only $4,244.78. The New Mexico Risk Management Department, the state's liability insurer, was to pick up the balance. A U.S. District Court judge ordered the University to pay $6,885.94 in attorneys' fees to the two UNM students who had sued the board.[21]

Several lawsuits against the president and/or other administrative officials were filed during the May years alleging racial or gender discrimination. In 1987, the former director of African-American Studies, Harold Bailey, sued UNM for alleged violations of his civil rights, charging that he was denied interviews for University positions for which he had applied. A judge, finding there was not sufficient evidence to substantiate his charges, threw the case out.[22]

Also that year, a male teaching assistant in the English Department was charged with racial discrimination. A student claimed she was given a low grade because she was Hispanic. The department and numerous students, including several Hispanics, stood by the teaching assistant, and the charges were refuted.[23]

A history professor charged that the Latin American Institute was racist because he was not included on a television program for the Public Broadcasting System on the history of Mexico.[24] The allegation was never substantiated.

A female department chair accused President May of gender discrimination for saying there were no women on the campus qualified for high-level administrative positions. She was joined by other female professors and staff on the campus who questioned the president's stand on affirmative action.[25]

Orcilia Zuniga Forbes

Although charged with saying that there were no qualified women on campus, May thought the truth was more complex. In a meeting with women leaders, there was agreement that there were not enough women in administrative posts. May stated that the problem was a shortage of qualified women in the candidacy pools when the University conducted searches. He asked the women on the faculty and staff to help by serving on search committees, applying for positions, and working their networks to encourage women from other campuses to apply. The women were unmollified and wrote May a letter, which was also released to the news media, expressing their opinion that his administration was misogynistic.

It should be noted that May appointed Judy Jones as assistant to the president, Karen Abraham as alumni director, and Orcilia Zuniga Forbes as vice president for student affairs. Meanwhile, in 1989, the Women Studies Program on the campus celebrated its twentieth anniversary.[26]

In February 1988, the University found itself in violation of the 1973 Rehabilitation Act. Specific charges were a failure to provide proper accessibility to the new Electrical and Computer Engineering Building for people who use wheelchairs. The University took steps to ensure compliance.[27]

No one sued when in 1988 a campaign was undertaken to ban smoking, including in the Pit. In a poll, almost 90 percent of more than eleven hundred respondents agreed that smoking should be banned. The University also identified limited smoking areas for the New Mexico Union building in December of that year.[28]

Facilities

Construction on campus in the late 1980s included completion of a building housing social sciences, Parish Library, and the Graduate School of Management on the north end of the main campus. On February 1, 1988, the Electrical and Computer Engineering/Centennial Library building was opened.[29] The Health Sciences and Services Building on the North Campus opened in 1989.

A fifth classroom building was added at the Los Alamos Branch in 1987. The branch had begun operations at an elementary school in 1980 and the following year had contracted with Los Alamos National Laboratory to take over operation of the Center for Graduate Studies. The branch facility had been remodeled and expanded in 1982–83.

1960 Protests Revisited

A forerunner of things to come characterized the nearly four-hour meeting of the Board of Regents on Tuesday, April 13, 1988, when more than a hundred students packed the boardroom. The students complained that their voices had not been heard. Campus police tried to limit the number of people coming into the meeting at Scholes Hall, but after Regents President Ken Johns responded to students' demands, they packed the boardroom and overflowed into the hallway. During the tense, somewhat informal meeting, the Regents voted against a resolution relating to the problems at radio station KUNM and refused to vote on a resolution on eight campus issues. Following the rowdy, sometimes stormy meeting, Johns commented that the students had "certainly gotten the Regents' attention."[30] As the *Lobo* reported,

> A year later, April 11, 1989, members of the Board of Regents faced a jeering, shouting crowd of about four hundred students in Popejoy Hall when they voted unanimously to approve a $100 per year tuition hike.
>
> The Regents, bathed in spotlights and seated at long tables on Popejoy's stage, listened quietly. The students in the audience spoke for almost two hours. The Board reached its decision in less than 30 seconds. The Regents took no bows.[31]

From the beginning of the April 11 meeting, the board's attempt to conduct business seemed futile as shouted comments from the crowd interrupted speakers with boos, cheering, whistles, and applause.[32]

After the meeting was adjourned, more than one hundred students stormed May's office and about forty stayed for the night. The students labeled Scholes Hall "Solidarity Hall," and the President's Office became the "People's Office." T-shirts were made to commemorate the occasion and, as the days passed, professors and administrative staff joined in the protest. The Faculty Senate objected to the administration's tactic of tying the 5 percent faculty salary raise to the 7.5 percent tuition increase.

A negotiation meeting on April 12 included student representatives, faculty and staff, and Board of Regents President Robert Sanchez. In the students' view, Sanchez took a hard line and refused to negotiate on tuition. The meeting was deemed a failure.

On April 13, the Faculty Senate presented a resolution to President May asking him to request that the Regents meet with the students and reconsider the tuition increase. The protest grew and drew support from not only the faculty, but also some legislators. Rallies, bands, speakers, and the occupying of the President's Office drew reporters and TV cameras to cover what many described as a return to the protests of the 1960s.[33]

On April 24, the fourteenth day of the protests, the students announced they would pull out of Scholes Hall at 11:30 A.M. and hold a victory rally on the mall, but they made it clear they planned to continue their activities. Students reported that Sanchez had announced that the Regents would reconvene on April 27 to discuss the tuition-increase issue. ASUNM Senator Antonio Anaya threatened that if the Board of Regents disregarded the protesters' requests, they would take over the Student Services Center and the New Mexico Union. Other student leaders said the protest activities would escalate if the Regents ignored students again.[34]

Amidst a fanfare of horns and drums playing "Yankee Doodle" and led by a student carrying an American flag, more than one hundred protesters with shouts and signs marched out of Scholes Hall on April 24, 1989. They took with them their sleeping bags, mattresses, books, and computers as they vacated what had been their home for two weeks. The crowd grew to more than two hundred when they had a victory celebration on the mall. The *Lobo* reported:

> Single mothers, widows, returning students, graduate and undergraduate students were among those protesting. Philosophy and business majors slept side by side on the hard concrete floor of Scholes Hall, working together day and night to keep alive the spirit of the protest.
>
> The movement crossed all ethnic, economic and social paths, uniting the entire University community, said student leader Glenn Smith.[35]

For more than three hours in a five-hour board meeting April 29, 1989, in the Lecture Hall of the Anthropology Building, the Regents listened to student speakers. They then unanimously voted to sustain the 7.9 percent tuition increase. They did, however, add a $200,000 safety net for grants to students who might be hurt by the hike. The room was filled to capacity by 205 students, while more than 60 students listened outside to the live broadcast by KUNM.[36]

Some protesters claimed a victory after the Regents maintained the tuition hike. About seventy-five marched from the meeting to the flagpole in front of Scholes Hall, chanting, "We have just begun to fight." Several speakers at the brief rally shouted of victory and accomplishment. One student, Steve Laboueff, said the protesters should be happy with what they accomplished and added, "We asked for the impact study. We asked for involvement in the budgetary process. In the process we made a stance and people all over this country have looked at us. We did it in a non-violent way, and I don't think the struggle is over, but I think we have won many things."[37]

President May drew praise from some quarters for his handling of the sit-in. Law Professor Garrett Flickinger, former president of the Faculty Senate, stated,

Australian Luc Longley was the seventh player taken in the 1991 NBA draft, by Minnesota, and went on to play for three world championship teams with the Chicago Bulls. At UNM he scored in double figures for sixty-one consecutive games in 1989.

"Jerry kept his cool and preserved the status quo. That's the kind of leadership we appreciate."[38]

Athletics

Several changes in athletic leadership positions characterized the May years. Athletic Director John Bridgers submitted his resignation November 24, 1986, to be effective July 1, 1987. He had been named to the post in 1979 following the Lobogate scandal that had resulted in indictments of three basketball coaches. Bridgers denied he had been fired from the job, but said he did not think he could run a successful program under the existing financial restraints. Earlier in the year he had made plans and begun fund raising for a major expansion of University Stadium. He believed that the future success of football and the entire athletic program was dependent on building a bigger, better stadium and expanding the funding for athletics by producing more revenue. Bridgers, who had developed one of the dominant football programs in the nation as coach and later athletic director at Florida State University, was hopeful that UNM or the state legislature would help fund the stadium expansion. The plan failed to gain the support of the Regents, however, and was abandoned.[39]

By April 1987, the Regents had finished their nationwide search, and John Koenig was named UNM athletic director. The forty-three-year-old Koenig, who at that time was associate athletic director at the University of Illinois, assumed the post May 1. Before his stint at Illinois, Koenig had been assistant vice president for academic services and an active member of the Faculty Senate at Southeast Missouri State College.[40]

In the football program, Joe Lee Dunn, who had been a defensive coordinator under Joe Morrison before the latter departed for the University of South Carolina, had been the head coach of the Lobos for four seasons, 1983–86. His teams had posted seventeen wins against thirty defeats. He announced his resignation and departed to join Morrison at South Carolina. Mike Sheppard replaced him.

Assessing his first few months as president in February 1987, Gerald May included changes in the Athletic Department as among the most significant developments on the campus. He said "the whole scene of things has turned over" with the imminent retirement of Bridgers, the hiring of Sheppard, and budget-saving program cuts.[41] Little did he know that the worst was yet to come. Citing lack of legislative support, President May had announced the elimination of four varsity athletic programs: wrestling, baseball, women's basketball, and women's swimming. He estimated that this action would save the University $480,000.[42] Through the support of donors from the private sector, all but wrestling were later revived in the UNM athletic program.

The next year there was a major change in the basketball program, when, after several days of negotiation in April 1988, Coach Gary Colson resigned. The announcement was made in an emotional meeting. Colson had accepted the position in 1980 at a time when the basketball program was in shambles as a result of the

Lobogate debacle. He inherited a weakened squad with few experienced players and literally had to rebuild the entire program. Over the next eight seasons, his teams had won 146 games while losing 106. During Colson's tenure, the Lobos played in five National Invitational Tournaments and posted two twenty-win seasons. In his last years, though, he was under heavy fire from sports writers, fans, and boosters who were critical of his failure to lead the team to the NCAA playoffs.[43] Dave Bliss, who came to UNM from Southern Methodist University, replaced Colson.

Just as it looked as if the UNM athletic program might enjoy a brief period of stability, in late 1988 and early 1989 another scandal broke. The new athletic director, John Koenig, and his two associate directors faced charges that included fraud and embezzlement of UNM money following reports that they had received double reimbursements for entertainment and travel expenses. In February 1989 a grand jury indicted them on fifty-eight criminal counts. Koenig resigned his post in July after only fifteen months on the job. Although found guilty, he received a suspended prison sentence.[44] Gary Ness, a professor of health, physical education, and recreation, succeeded him.

UNM athletics did not bring much joy to the life of President May. He had to endure the embarrassment of fraud by high-ranking officials in the program, their later resignations, and the clamor over the shutdown of four athletic programs, and he had to oversee searches for two athletic directors, a head football coach, and a head basketball coach. Football particularly suffered through four miserable years with a record of eight wins and thirty-nine losses.

Centennial

Staff and alumni spent more than two years preparing for a wide-ranging celebration of the hundredth anniversary of the founding of the University. Led by Centennial Director Rose Mary "Redd" Torres Eakin and University Secretary Anne Brown, the celebration was intended to involve all members of the University community and build a base of support for its second century. Much historical research was conducted, many works of art and publications were commissioned, and the official calendar of events filled four pages.

A special supplement to *New Mexico Magazine* appeared under the title "A Century of Scholarship." The University of New Mexico shared the coverage with New Mexico State University and New Mexico Institute of Mining and Technology, as all three were created in the same bill the Territorial Legislature passed on February 28, 1889. In the section of the publication devoted to UNM, the University in its hundredth year was described.

> Today's UNM campus is a 600-acre monument to planning, design, tradition and innovation. It has a genuine sense of place. This campus could be nowhere else but New Mexico . . .
>
> The 28,000 students on UNM's five campuses have access to the broadest curriculum in the state. There are 4,000 courses, 125 degrees and

The Centennial logo, designed by the Public Affairs Department staff, features a tower commonly thought to be that of Zimmerman Library, but it is in fact Mesa Vista Hall.

Redd Eakin and Dorothea Powell dressed in period costumes to take their Centennial exhibit, "Then and Now," on the road.

nationally recognized programs in Latin American studies, anthropology, laser optics, environmental studies and photography. In addition to law and medicine, UNM has the state's only schools of pharmacy and architecture and planning. It enrolls 80 percent of the state's PhD candidates and is a national leader in minority enrollment.[45]

Activities on the UNM campus opened with an academic convocation on October 30, 1989, featuring an address by former Congress member Shirley Chisholm in University Arena. Professors and students marched in academic regalia, and staff, alumni, and friends of UNM were in attendance. A series of centennial speakers came to the University, including Arthur Schlesinger, Beaumont Newhall, Richard Leakey, Robert Redford, Tom Wolfe, Susan Sontag, and Tom Peters. Centennial offerings included a symposium on Hispanic life and an international symposium, a campus architecture exhibit, a performance by the Royal Philharmonic Orchestra, lecture series in academic departments, and a celebration of UNM's ties to the nation's space program. The actual hundredth birthday party featured the Centennial Ball on February 25 and a commemoration of the founding of the University in Santa Fe on February 28, 1989.[46]

The celebration also saw the naming of the building housing the Counseling and Family Studies Department for Elizabeth Simpson, who had served as dean of the predecessor department, home economics, for thirty-four years. During her early years at UNM she had also supervised the students' dining hall, which had tables reserved for faculty. Librarian Wilma Loy Shelton recalled, "As we gathered around these tables where we felt the best and cheapest food in town was served, our hearty appetites were satisfied, and lots of social chitchat and banter indulged in."[47]

During the centennial year Marcus Price, a professor of physics and astronomy, compiled what he called "the incomplete history" of science and research at UNM.

He noted the founding in 1898 of a series of publications on biology, geology, physics, and chemistry and wrote tersely, "One of last of series is 1938 commentary on 'Menace of Fluorine to Health' as UNM Chemistry Department develops techniques for removing fluorine from drinking water to fight what was thought to be a health hazard."

Price also recorded these landmarks: 1932: "physics master's program added" and 1946: "Lincoln La Paz brings noted meteor studies to UNM. Established meteoritic museum still recognized today as outstanding collection. His studies form basis for present Institute of Meteoritics." In 1980, Price continued, the Institute for Modern Optics was established.

> Within a few years, this program has 20 grad students, 10 research staff members, more than $1 million in sponsored research, and gains state and national visibility for UNM. Today, UNM science programs move forward. From Institute for Modern Optics has grown a Center for High Technology Materials, an enterprise between departments of Physics and Astronomy and Electrical and Computer Engineering. Collaborations between UNM and Sandia National Laboratories offered by this center enhance opportunities for UNM students and faculty. A Center for Ceramic Sciences, also established with government support, brings together faculty and students from science and engineering.[48]

Resignation of May

For a conscientious, dedicated man like May, who had malice toward none and charity for all, his three years as president of UNM must have been like a bath in a cement mixer. May did not even have the opportunity to initiate a dignified resignation. With information from an anonymous source, the morning *Albuquerque Journal* carried a front-page story June 30, 1989, proclaiming in bold headlines "UNM Board to Discuss May's Fate." The Regents scheduled an emergency meeting for 2 P.M. that day, to be followed by an open session. Then there was to be a news conference. The unnamed source, an administrator who reported to May, stated that the purpose of the news conference was to discuss the president's status.[49]

As the *Journal* reported the following day, the somber UNM president stated that his job had exacted a heavy personal toll and he would step down June 30, 1990. May added: "This decision has been mine, arrived at after weeks of discussion with my family, the Regents, and others." He had no comments on his plans for the future.[50]

Later in the June 30 meeting, the Regents approved a $5,000 raise for the president's final year in office and set in motion the search for his replacement by voting to use a national consulting firm as well an internal search committee. For the third time in six years UNM had a vacancy in its top administrative position.[51]

The announcement of May's pending departure was met with mixed reviews. The *Journal* editorialized:

University Secretary Anne Brown carried a specially commissioned Nambé staff during the procession into the Pit to begin the Centennial convocation.

May has certainly done his level best as president, but to say that UNM is enjoying a period of strength or stability is an exaggeration. Due to circumstances that may well have been beyond the president's control, the university finds itself in a painful period of financial hardship, battling against a rising sense of mediocrity . . .

May has faced his share of crises, in which he has found himself confronted with allegations of discrimination against women and minorities, the resignation and criminal indictment of his athletic director, and a 1960s-style student protest over tuition increases.

To his credit, May has kept his ego out of these confrontations. He is a good listener, obviously dedicated to the university. On Friday he asked for continued support in his final year as president, and he deserves it.[52]

The University of New Mexico in Its 100th Year

During 1989–90, his last year in office, President May oversaw the publication of a report on the University of New Mexico, covering the years of his administration. It described the University as a comprehensive community of more than forty thousand students, faculty, and staff on campuses in Albuquerque, Los Alamos, Santa Fe, Gallup, and Valencia County. In addition, another forty thousand people were enrolled in continuing education classes.

UNM's enrollment reflected the multicultural nature of the state, and a total of 28,615 students on five campuses marked an all-time high. Some 24,525 were enrolled on the main campus, of whom 4,497 were graduate or professional students. The two-year branch campuses served another 3,727 students, while the graduate and other programs at Los Alamos, Santa Fe, and Gallup served 362.

In 1989–90, more than 4,200 degrees were awarded in 125 programs, including 2,449 bachelor's degrees, 1,110 master's degrees, 204 doctoral degrees, 117 law degrees, and 72 medical doctorates. In addition, 324 associate degrees were conferred, primarily at the branch campuses.

The students reflected the cultural diversity of the Southwest with almost a third coming from historically underrepresented groups. Hispanics comprised roughly 25 percent of the total student body, and the more than 1,000 Native American students were the largest number attending an American university.[53] The average age of the students was twenty-seven, and about 2,450 lived on campus.

President May's report also noted that members of the University's excellent faculty were awarded more than $85 million for research, public service, and sponsored programs in 1989–90, placing UNM among the top fifty research universities in the nation. The title of distinguished professor represented the most prestigious academic rank granted at UNM, and in 1989 Professors Lewis Binford in anthropology, Henry Ellis in psychology, and Marlan Scully in physics all held the title.

UNM had the state's only schools of medicine, law, pharmacy, and architecture and the only divisions of public administration and dental programs, the report said. The University also oversaw two of the state's five Centers of Technical Excellence and a joint research program in semiconductor circuitry with Sandia National Laboratories.

Other outstanding programs cited in the report were the Center for Non-Invasive Diagnosis, the Center for Southwest Research, the Center for Micro-Engineered Ceramics, the Center for Advanced Studies, and the New Mexico Engineering Research Institute.

At the UNM Medical Center there were more than 370,000 outpatient visits to its clinics in University Hospital, the Cancer Center, Children's Psychiatric Hospital, Mental Health Center, Family Practice Center, and Carrie Tingley Hospital for disabled children. Each year the hospital system with a total of 477 beds treated more than seventeen thousand patients.

The University had celebrated the acquisition of its millionth library book in 1980. By 1990, the size of the collection had doubled, making UNM's General Library system one of the largest in the state and one of the most important research facilities in the Southwest. UNM also gained national and international acclaim for its University press, which in 1989 had a record sales year of $3 million and published more than fifty titles.

The UNM Development Office was reorganized during the May administration. Development officers were hired for several schools and colleges, and agreements were formalized to link the UNM Foundation to these efforts. By 1988 there was a 30 percent increase over the preceding year in gifts from individuals and the private sector, from $13 million to $16.9 million. In addition, the University's first capital campaign began during the centennial celebration in 1989. Its goal of raising more than $65 million in five years was met and doubled.

President May's report demonstrated that all too often the truly magnificent accomplishments of the University and its faculty and students are lost in the furor over incidents that soon become yesterday's news. May, a devout, dedicated leader, provided stability and momentum as UNM continued its upward struggle to enlighten and serve the people of New Mexico. In June 1990, he stepped down from his duties as president and returned to the security, serenity, and sanity of the classroom and laboratory. ■

Students work on a copper laser in Dr. Kim's laboratory in the Physics and Astronomy Department. Photo by Michael Mouchette

Richard E. Peck

CHAPTER NINETEEN
Administration of Richard E. Peck
1990–98

Richard E. Peck's credentials were impeccable: an impressive academic record with degrees in English, supplemented by a succession of posts as he moved through the academic ranks at major state universities. After a conscientious committee composed of UNM students, faculty, administrators, and Regents completed an intensive national search, Peck turned out to be everybody's All-American, the first choice of almost anybody who had anything to say about the selection of the University of New Mexico's fifteenth president. When Peck assumed the job on July 1, 1990, he became the fifth president in eight years.

The search narrowed down to two finalists in mid-January 1990. Peck, who at that time was serving as the interim president of Arizona State University, was the favorite. Born in 1936 in Milwaukee, Wisconsin, he had earned a bachelor's degree at Carroll College in Wisconsin and master's and PhD degrees in English from the University of Wisconsin. He served in the Marine Corps as a helicopter pilot from 1954 to 1959. Early in his academic career he taught English at the University of Wisconsin, the University of Virginia, and Temple University.

In 1984, Peck was dean of the College of Arts and Sciences at the University of Alabama, moving on to Arizona State University as provost and vice president for academic affairs in 1988. In June 1989 he became the interim president at that institution, but he was not a candidate for the permanent post.

Peck was a sports fan and a dedicated golfer and skier. He had written plays, teleplays, travel articles, humorous columns, and seven books in addition to many academic works. Among his publications were a novel titled *Something for Joey* and a play, *The Cubs Are in Fourth Place and Fading*. Peck was described as an energetic, warm individual who had won a wide circle of admirers in the eighteen months he had been at Arizona State. Faculty, students, and administrators praised his sense of humor and his personality, while ASU alumni proclaimed that he had been important in maintaining good relations between the school and outside groups.

He certainly met with high approval when interviewed by various groups on the UNM campus. Professor Gil Merkx, director of the UNM Latin American Institute, who was sometimes known as a caustic critic of administrators, reported, "No one has a negative thing to say about him."[1]

Facing page: Sacks, candles, and sand make the University House, previously known as the President's House, glow.

Donna and Dick Peck

On the morning of January 18, 1990, Regents' meeting the *Lobo* reported that Peck had the endorsements of the Associated Students of the University of New Mexico, the Graduate Students Association, the Chicano Student Union, and the United Mexican American Students. Some fifty faculty members in an informal meeting the previous afternoon endorsed Peck with one faculty member dissenting. The president of the Faculty Senate, Professor Marion Cottrell, commented that Peck had unique qualities that would enable him to serve the University well. Pauline Turner, professor of counseling and family studies, said that Peck was the man because he would make faculty feel good about themselves.[2]

The only blip on the search radar was a lawsuit against the Board of Regents filed by a former UNM vice president, Alex Mercure, Las Mujeres de LULAC, the American GI Forum, IMAGE of Albuquerque, and MECHA de UNM . Mercure, one of the five finalists for the presidency, and the organizations were requesting an injunction, charging that the Regents had violated Mercure's constitutional rights to due process and equal protection. The board met, then recessed. After a lengthy hearing, District Court Judge John Brennan refused to halt the search on the basis that there was not enough evidence to conclude that the search had discriminated against Hispanics as a group. The Regents reconvened and announced the appointment of Richard Peck about 8:45 P.M. January 18, 1990.[3]

The choice was met with strong approval. Bryan Hobson Wildenthal, dean of the College of Arts and Sciences, reported that he had conferred with the twenty department heads in the college and they were the most hopeful they had been in several years.[4]

While appointed in January, Peck did not actually sign a contract until April 16, 1990. Robert Sanchez, president of the board, signed it April 25. The board's final approval came on May 8. The contract stipulated that President Peck was also to be a full professor with tenure in the English Department.[5]

Meanwhile, outgoing President May announced that he intended to stay at UNM as a tenured member of the College of Engineering faculty. He stated: "I've been here twenty-three years. This is my institution. I anticipate staying here." James Thompson, dean of engineering, stated that there had been an active effort to encourage May to return to the faculty.[6]

University House

Inclusion of provisions to repair and renovate the President's House was a key item in Peck's contract. He and his wife, Donna, had decided that they would resume the tradition of living on the campus, but the house needed work inside and out.

The 1946 student yearbook, the *Mirage,* included a caption stating that "the President's House captures the entire spirit and warmth of the Southwest. Built in the traditional pueblo style, the house is a successful blending of the Indian and Spanish cultures. Its unique charm greatly enhances the beauty of the campus."[7]

Archivist Terry Gugliotta prepared a delightful history of the house at the time of its renovation. Architect Roger Lujan, director of the Department of Facility

Planning, supervised the work. Interior designer Amy Walton suggested that the house combine the ambiance of the 1930s with the convenience of the 1990s. Furniture and fixtures for the public areas were chosen to achieve the 1930s effect. Gil Berry, UNM's landscape architect, designed the landscaping to emphasize native plants.[8]

Renovations were completed in time for the Pecks to move in by Thanksgiving. Although the total area was more than fifty-seven hundred square feet, the family living area on the second floor was modest at about nine hundred square feet.[9]

The Pecks requested that the house be renamed University House with the intent that it be used to bring together University and community members from Albuquerque and throughout the state, as well as serve as a meeting place for national and international visitors. It was to become a major entertainment center for guests and a showcase for the University.[10]

An Inauguration, Not a Coronation

Peck swept into office with a flourish. The University held its first formal inauguration of a president since 1968, when Ferrel Heady took office. On November 8, 1990, nearly four thousand people attended the celebration in University Arena. It was an academic ceremony with distinctly New Mexico touches. Eagle dancers from Laguna Pueblo led representatives from more than a hundred colleges and universities dressed in full academic regalia, and a mariachi band provided the recessional music.

During Peck's twenty-minute address, he outlined goals he said would allow the University to "achieve a position of authority and respect and of great pride to the citizens of New Mexico." In addition to ensuring an outstanding undergraduate education, the goals were for UNM to become a university for the Americas and a model in cultural diversity. They also included the formation of an Honors College, enhanced by the announcement of the Carruthers Chair in Honors, with a $1 million endowment from Burlington Resources Foundation and named for Governor Garrey Carruthers.

After Peck received the official president's medallion from Regents President Robert Sanchez, a young man in the audience began shouting his objections to the inauguration. He was promptly escorted out.

Later several student leaders called for a protest over the cost of the inauguration, an event they called a "fifty-thousand-dollar coronation." The student body president, John Webber, reported that student members had quit the University's Budget Committee, which had been formed following the fourteen-day occupation of then-President May's office in April 1989, when the students were protesting tuition hikes.[11] The *Albuquerque Journal* carried a supportive editorial on November 10 that called the inauguration "a worthwhile ritual."[12]

Administrative Posts

The frequent comings and goings of presidents from 1982 to 1990 were accompanied by numerous turnovers in the top administrative positions at UNM. With the departure of President May, Vice Presidents Chris Garcia and Alex Sanchez resigned.

Karen Glaser

Paul Risser was appointed by Peck to be provost/vice president for academic affairs and research. David McKinney, vice president of business and finance, and Orcilia Zuniga Forbes, vice president for student affairs, were both carryovers from the May administration.

Risser accepted an offer to become president of Miami University in Oxford, Ohio, effective January 1, 1993. Chris Garcia, who had returned to the political science faculty after serving as vice president for academic affairs from 1987 to 1990, was named interim provost, but stated he was not a candidate for the permanent position.[13]

In August 1993, it was announced that Mary Sue Coleman had been appointed the new provost and vice president for academic affairs. She had received her bachelor's degree in chemistry from Grinnell College in 1965 and her PhD in biochemistry from the University of North Carolina four years later. From 1972 until 1990, Coleman had a variety of posts on the faculty at the University of Kentucky, rising to the rank of full professor. She was also director of graduate studies in biochemistry and associate director for research at Kentucky's cancer center. From 1990 to 1992, she served as associate dean of research at the University of North Carolina. Her tenure as provost at UNM, however, was of short duration. In the fall of 1995, she was appointed president of the University of Iowa.[14] She later became president of the University of Michigan. William C. Gordon, a UNM professor of psychology, succeeded Coleman as provost.

Meanwhile, Alonzo Rodriguez in 1995 was selected as vice president for student affairs to replace Zuniga Forbes. The offer was rescinded, however, when University officials became aware that Rodriguez was facing felony charges for hunting elk in Colorado in October 1994. He had not disclosed that information to UNM administrators.[15] The dean of students, Karen Glaser, assumed the duties as interim vice president for student affairs.

The position of director of the budget opened in December 1992, when long-time UNM employee James Wiegmann retired. Wiegmann's former assistant, Tom Stephenson, became acting budget director pending a search.

Soon after taking office President Peck asked his executive assistant, Judy Jones, to assume supervisory responsibility for the Development Office, Alumni Office, and Public Affairs Department. In 1992 the assignment was passed to Paul Nathanson, director of the Institute for Public Law, for two years. In 1995 Zuniga Forbes was named vice president for institutional advancement, and when she left in 1998 Jones became the interim vice president. Development Director Dennis Eloe brought Carolyn Tinker from the Health Sciences Center to be associate director of development, and she became interim director in 1993. Karen Stone then served as development director from 1994 to 1998.

The University Archive, which the Regents established in 1985 when they approved a proposal from Paul Vassallo, dean of the libraries, acquired a new archivist, Terry Gugliotta, in 1993. In addition to photographs, minutes, building plans, and countless reports and official publications, the archive houses every book ever published by the UNM Press, original drawings of the University seal, and oral histories of important figures in University history.

Dr. Jane Henney was named vice president for health sciences after the retirement of the dean of the School of Medicine, Leonard Napolitano. Henney was a former deputy commissioner of the Food and Drug Administration and a former administrator at the University of Kansas School of Medicine. The Health Sciences Center included the hospitals and the academic programs in medicine, nursing, pharmacy, and allied health, and interdisciplinary training was a goal.

Another first for women was chalked up in December 1995 when Kathleen Guimond, a lieutenant at Northern Illinois University's Public Safety Division, was appointed as UNM's police chief.[16]

Regents

Governor Bruce King appointed two new Regents in January 1991, Gene Gallegos of Santa Fe and Arthur D. Melendres of Albuquerque. Both were graduates of the UNM School of Law.[17] Two months later, at their March 17 meeting, the Regents elected Roberta Cooper Ramo, an Albuquerque attorney, as the board president, the second woman to hold the post. Two more new Regents were added in 1993, when Governor King named Barbara Brazil and Penny Taylor Rembe to replace Ken Johns and Frank Borman. Brazil was a public affairs officer for Intel Corporation in Rio Rancho. Rembe was owner of a North Valley business. Sigfried Hecker was appointed for a second six-year term.[18]

In November 1994, New Mexico voters approved a constitutional amendment mandating that a position on the board of regents of each state university be reserved for a student. Accordingly, in March 1995 Governor Gary Johnson named former UNM basketball player Eric Thomas to the board. Thomas, a UNM undergraduate, had entered the University in 1990 on a basketball grant-in-aid, but relinquished the scholarship in 1993 because of heart surgery. Originally from Oxnard, California, he was a biology major, chaired the Student Athletic Advisory Committee, and was a member of the Faculty Senate Subcommittee on Intercollegiate Athletics. He also was on the athletic academic honor roll.

In 1994 Governor Johnson appointed Mary Tang, a Jemez Pueblo woman, to the board. She had worked at Sandia National Laboratories for fifteen years. She had earned a PhD in education from UNM.[19]

Three new Regents were added to the board in January 1997, when David Archuleta, Richard Tolliver, and student Kimberly Richards were appointed.

Academic Developments

In a lead story published shortly after the announcement of Peck's appointment as president in January 1990, the *Lobo* reported that the new president would face stormy times. The newspaper article pointed out: "Richard Peck hasn't felt the sting of UNM's blizzards—cruel winds remindful of weak budgets, faculty disputes, and athletic scandals."[20]

Eric Thomas was both the youngest and the tallest Regent in 1995. He served with (front row, from left) Barbara Brazil, board President Art Melendres, Penny Taylor Rembe, and (back row) Gene Gallegos, Larry Willard, and Mary Tang.

Peck got a glimpse of what lay ahead from the "UNM 2000" report, begun under the administration of President May. Among the goals set for the University by the turn of the century were to level off tuition increases, place the University on better financial footing, increase cultural pluralism, improve the quality of both faculty and students, and expand UNM's research facilities.[21]

One of the University's premier researchers, Dr. R. Philip Eaton of the School of Medicine, was awarded a federal patent in August 1990 for a method of analyzing biological fluids. With a grant from Sandia National Laboratories, Eaton was developing a biomedical engineering research program. His previous work had included many studies of diabetes. Eaton delivered the 1979 Annual Research Lecture and received a Regents' Meritorious Service Medal in 1981. He won the School of Medicine's award for outstanding clinical teaching in 1995 and became UNM's vice president for health sciences in 2001.

In 1992, the departments of Journalism and Communications merged. It was hoped the effort would cut the costs of teaching, scholarship, and research.[22]

A long-term historical translation and editing undertaking, the Vargas Project, continued in 1993. The purpose of the multivolume project, headed by noted author and historian John L. Kessell and Rick Hendricks, was to make available in English the papers of don Diego de Vargas, whose governorship of colonial New Mexico had begun in 1692. According to Professor Jonathan Porter, History Department chair, UNM could boast that it had the leading program in the world on the American West.[23]

In 1993, George Anselevicius returned to teaching after thirteen years as dean of the School of Architecture and Planning. He was succeeded by Richard Eribes, who reorganized the school and appointed Edith Cherry as director of architecture and Ric Richardson as director of planning. In 1994 Don Schlegel retired after forty years of service.[24]

In November 1997, UNM learned that cultural landscape historian John Brinkerhoff Jackson, who had died in August 1996, left a $2.5 million bequest to the School of Architecture and Planning. One of New Mexico's most influential and eye-opening thinkers, Jackson had been an international traveler and man of inherited wealth. After World War II, he settled in New Mexico. In 1951, he founded *Landscape Magazine* in Santa Fe, which he edited and published until 1968. He taught graduate seminars at Harvard University in the fall and the University of California–Berkeley in the spring, then spent his summers in La Cienega, New Mexico, traveling by motorcycle. He urged UNM to look to its strengths and focus on Latin American issues and Southwest culture.[25]

The UNM Bureau of Business and Economic Research (BBER) was fifty years old in 1997. Under Brian McDonald's direction, the BBER provided research and analysis on economics and demographics, including the census, and published a monthly statistical report. The bureau's FOR-UNM Economic Forecasting Service developed short-term projections of employment and personal income in New Mexico.

Appropriations, Budgets, and Tuition

Continuing a trend of the previous decade, dwindling support from the legislature resulting in tuition increases led to organized student protests that became almost an annual rite of spring during the Peck administration. In 1981, the tuition for a full-time New Mexico resident undergraduate student was $666 per year. By 1991, it had more than doubled to $1,453.[26] The rationale was salary increases for faculty and staff, the need to hire more faculty, increased emphasis on research and graduate study, and higher costs for almost everything, especially library materials.

President Peck fought to keep expenditures at an appropriate level that reflected the national and state fiscal recession of the early 1990s. An increase in administrative salaries in 1992 created some concern among faculty and staff whose pay lagged far behind that of peer institutions. The following year, 1993, the legislature approved a 6 percent increase in the University's appropriation and the Regents enacted an 8 percent increase in tuition.[27]

In 1994, the Regents approved yet another hike in tuition, an increase of 5.4 percent. Governor Johnson vetoed $2.5 million of expenditures for UNM programs in his 1995 budget. Johnson stuck with his pledge to force all state agencies, including higher education, to cut funding by 3 percent. This led to the UNM Regents imposing another 6 percent tuition raise, which provoked noisy protests from student groups.[28] Some camped out in front of Scholes Hall to protest. The protestors won what they proclaimed to be a victory when the administration agreed to a town hall meeting to discuss the increase. Roughly two hundred students attended the meeting, which ended in the Regents' vow to ensure student representation in all future tuition decisions and to generate better publicity pertaining to Regent meetings.[29] However, the Regents did not rescind the tuition increase.

As 1996 began, more tuition increases were threatened, leading to a demonstration at the governor's office in Santa Fe.[30] There was also criticism of President Peck, who decided not to attend a town hall to discuss the projected tuition hikes.[31] Twenty students camped out in front of Scholes Hall to protest the proposed tuition hike, and two were charged with trespassing.[32]

When the Regents voted approval of a 3.7 percent tuition increase, additional protests led to the jailing of fourteen students. They claimed their actions were justified because the Regents had ignored their demands and were unwilling to negotiate or discuss the increase. The students also faced academic sanctions and possible suspension. Criminal charges filed by University officials were dismissed in the Metro Court of Albuquerque, and no students were suspended or expelled.[33]

In a new twist to the almost annual protests against tuition increases, Faculty Senate President Beulah Woodfin in February 1997 called UNM's tuition "too low." She added that UNM's relatively modest tuition was a bargain.[34] The Regents approved a 4.5 percent tuition increase for the 1997–98 academic year, followed by another 3.5 percent increase the next year.[35]

University employees were grateful for a legislature-authorized 4.5 percent raise during the 1998 session.[36] Also welcomed was the end of a four-year court battle between UNM and its employees when the New Mexico Supreme Court ruled that UNM faculty and staff had the right to collective bargaining.[37]

During the Peck administration, tuition had risen from $1,372 in 1990 to $2,242 in 1998, an average increase of 4.85 percent a year.[38] More bad news loomed as early reports were that Governor Johnson was going to propose upping it another 13 percent in the 1999 legislative session.

Good News at Last

In 1994 the New Mexico Legislature approved $700,000 for the Graduate Student Association, $200,000 for computer hardware and software, and $500,000 to fund research, travel, and seminars. Senator Manny Aragon from Albuquerque helped sponsor the bill and worked for its passage.[39]

Even better news for New Mexico scholars came with the legislature's establishment of the New Mexico lottery scholarships in February 1997. The first awards were to be distributed that fall, and it was estimated that twenty-eight hundred 1997 high school graduates would be eligible. The New Mexico Commission on Higher Education was to administer the program, and the money would come from a surcharge on sales of lottery tickets. To qualify for the scholarship students had to be New Mexico residents and graduates of a New Mexico high school or have a New Mexico GED. They then had to enroll for twelve credit hours at any of the state's twenty-three public colleges or universities in the first regular semester following high school graduation. Students also had to have a 2.5 grade point average to be eligible for the tuition scholarship and earn a 2.5 during the first college semester. The scholarship could be renewed for up to eight consecutive semesters if they continued to meet the academic requirements.[40] President Peck told the Board of Regents: "This is potentially the most dramatic thing for higher education that's been done in New Mexico in years."[41]

There was a slight decline in UNM enrollment between 1993 and 1996, when the fall total was 30,534, down 665. Many attributed the decline to more rigorous admission standards and the elimination of the General College. President Peck sought to reverse this trend by personally visiting the state's high schools to recruit students. The results were good, as in the fall of 1997 the UNM freshman class was 2,050 students, the first time since 1988 that UNM had an entering class topping 2,000. In all, the total enrollment on the UNM Albuquerque campus in August 1997 was 22,361 students. Many were attending because of the New Mexico lottery scholarship program.[42]

Student Protests and Rallies

Aside from the almost yearly rallies and protests against increases in tuition, most of the student demonstrations during the Peck era revolved around the 1991 Persian Gulf War in the Middle East. The threat of war brought an end to alleged UNM student apathy on January 15, 1991, when about five hundred people filled Smith Plaza south of Zimmerman Library. The Lobo Peace Groups, organizers of the event, provided an effigy of U.S. President George Bush, which they set afire. While supporters of the war chanted, "Kill Saddam," antiwar protesters answered, "Peace now!" Prowar students waved a U.S. flag; antiwar students suggested burning it.

As reported in the *Lobo,* "Meanwhile, skateboarding middle-schoolers raced around the crowd in shouting swarms. A man standing on a wall reciting radical poetry and preaching love, stripped nude and raised his arms, and repeatedly shouted, 'No!'" Campus police remained silent during the nudity scene but arrested the poet after the plaza had cleared. He was charged with indecent exposure.[43]

Two days later, another clash on the UNM campus broke out when ROTC students supporting the war exchanged jibes with about forty individuals who were planning a march on the federal building to protest the war. Early on the following Monday, January 28, 1991, about thirty people protesting what they termed UNM's involvement in military research were removed by a dozen helmeted campus police from the office of the UNM Center for High Technology Materials.[44]

Emotions smoldered but did not erupt until February 8, when about 150 people listened to students speak about antinationalism as they burned paper replicas of flags of several nations. The theatrics turned violent when onlookers stormed the stage in front of Zimmerman Library after an American flag was set afire. An angry mob split into two groups and assaulted both the student holding the flag and a student who was speaking. Although uniformed police were standing by, no arrests were made as the crowd melted away.[45]

Other demonstrations having nothing to do with war tended to be more peaceful. On February 6, 1991, for example, protestors surrounded a Jeep parked on an access ramp for the handicapped outside Mitchell Hall. They placed fluorescent stickers on the vehicle's windows and literature under the windshield wiper next to the $5 ticket for parking in a yellow zone.[46]

Students and their children hoped to attract the attention of UNM officials when they staged a sit-in at the Duck Pond. They said that student parents wanted the administration to work with the Albuquerque Public Schools to coordinate their vacation dates. The problem had arisen when UNM and APS recesses scheduled for spring did not coincide.[47] The dates were not changed.

In hotter weather, July 24, 1991, five students set up camp on the lawn of University House. They were protesting the University's out-of-state tuition policy. When given the choice of either being arrested or leaving peaceably, they chose the latter.[48]

Carrying over from the May administration, the troubles with KUNM continued as accusations of racism and lack of professionalism plagued the campus radio station. Alleging that the general manager, Malcolm Gault-Williams, had not increased the role of students, staff, volunteers, community members, and minorities in the station's activities, the KUNM Radio Board gave him a vote of no confidence.[49]

Later, in January 1991, Gault-Williams was accused of trying to censure free speech by cutting back on the station's air time for editorializing. In July 1991, new

charges alleged racial discrimination, followed by additional accusations that he was intoxicated at a party. He was replaced.

Minorities

When Peck assumed the UNM presidency veteran administrators, Regents, faculty members, students, and state and community leaders told him to find a consensus on University priorities, a feat many believed only Tom Popejoy had accomplished. Peck was eager to accept the challenge and said, "Watch me." He found that many constituencies were pulling apart rather than uniting. He went to work to find accord between faculty and management, students and campus police, Hispanics and Anglos, blacks and whites, community interests and Regents, and the legislature and the University's proposed budget. He established three major goals: to see UNM offer the best undergraduate education in the Southwest; to become a model in diversity of student, faculty, and staff populations; and to seek intellectual and educational partnerships in Latin America to make UNM the university for the Americas. As one reporter stated, the Regents were looking for "a salesman with a soul, one who could not only sell UNM to Albuquerque, but to New Mexico and the nation, as well."[50]

Peck was not on the job long before being sued by Harold Bailey, a former director of African-American Studies. The $1 million action filed December 3, 1990, alleged top University administrators conspired to deny him the right to compete for two administrative positions at UNM.[51] The suit was dismissed.

Aside from this, smooth relations with the minority students, faculty, and staff characterized Peck's first year as president. One incident drew attention, however, when after a football game some fraternity boys, allegedly from Sigma Alpha Epsilon, reportedly yelled racist epithets at some minority students. SAE officials could not be reached for comment. One member of SAE said, "I'm a Hispanic, and I know nothing about it."[52] African American and Hispanic students later said they were assaulted. These actions sparked a rally, as some 150 students gathered on the mall on October 19, 1991, but there were no further developments.

On the good news side, in 1992, a U.S. Department of Education survey showed that New Mexico ranked third nationally in percentage of minority students. Only Hawaii and Washington, D.C., had more.[53] Further, enrollment of African Americans had increased by 8.33 percent for the 1991–92 school year, and they accounted for 481 of the Albuquerque campus's total of 24,199 students.[54]

In May 1992, President Peck and other UNM officials decided it would be more cost effective to combine the University's three minority student services centers into one multicultural student center. The directors of the centers, African American, American Indian, and Hispanic, were told their contracts would not be renewed. This led to a week of turmoil. On June 3, President Peck announced that he had decided to delay the change for a year to allow a more thorough review of the impact of the reorganization plan and consideration of alternatives.[55] Meanwhile, the mural *The Three Peoples of New Mexico* in Zimmerman Library, which Kenneth

Adams had painted in 1938, was vandalized in March 1993 for the third time. The mural was said to be racist and offensive to Hispanics and Native Americans, but no one ever claimed responsibility for the vandalism. Debate was so heated over a resolution pertaining to this mural, as well as three others on display, that ASUNM Senator Lino Trevinio resigned from his elected post.[56] The mural was repaired, but no further action was taken.

The Mercer Report and More Protests

UNM's hiring and grievance procedures were fraught with problems, resulting in a "climate of fear and retaliation," according to a report mandated by the New Mexico Legislature and commissioned by the University. Dubbed the Mercer Report and released in October 1994, it followed an investigation costing $100,000 conducted by the Dallas-based William M. Mercer Company. It said there were severe pay inequities for women and minority faculty and staff as well as a poor grievance process. UNM officials asserted that the differences in pay had nothing to do with discrimination.[57]

The Mercer consultants judged the University's Human Resources Department to be slow, bureaucratic, and uncommunicative. The report also stated that there was a climate of fear and possible retaliation.[58] Employees filed thirty-seven discrimination suits against the University in 1992-93, and eighteen the following year.

The *Lobo* reported on October 26 that many members of the UNM community believed the Mercer Report validated claims of discrimination, a charge the administration denied. President Peck immediately prepared a response, saying the Mercer Report did not conclude that pay inequities were the result of discrimination. He also said the administration was trying to understand why these inequities were occurring. The Board of Regents was scheduled to review the study at its November meeting.[59]

A month later, headlines in the student newspaper proclaimed "Zimmerman Gutted by Hate Crime." It went on to report that more than $20,000 worth of journals dealing with homosexuality and feminism were missing and might have been stolen. A library employee stated that some time on Friday night, November 18, 1994, vandals removed five shelves of material and replaced them with books on the Nazis. A few journals were left behind with swastikas and phrases like "Bitch propaganda" scrawled on the pages.[60]

The defacement of materials and alleged theft provoked a rally of about two hundred persons who came together to denounce hate crimes. Sandrea Gonzales of the UNM Women's Center called upon the UNM administration to take the problem of hate crimes seriously and fight the problem with action, not words.

President Peck responded by reporting what was being done to apprehend the perpetrators. He stressed that hate crimes could only be eradicated when people could collectively reject hatred and put an end to intolerance. He cited racism, sexism, and homophobia as evils the entire UNM community must condemn. Following Peck, there was a long line of speakers ready to take the microphone.[61]

On November 30 it was reported that while shelving other journals, a staff member and two student employees used a ladder to reach some high shelves and discovered the missing volumes near the ceiling, hidden behind the stacks. The perpetrators remained unknown.[62]

A milestone in the history of UNM was reached in March 1994 when the University changed its employee benefits policy to add same-sex partners to health, dental, and vision coverage as well as basic life insurance policies. Long-term disability benefits, however, still applied only to UNM employees. The transition was smooth, and within a year 125 domestic partners were receiving benefits.[63]

Big news in 1995 was the decision of the University of California Board of Regents to terminate affirmative action programs, including college admission. When queried on how this might affect UNM, President Peck replied that UNM would not change its policy. He added, "Since we're not admitting students on the basis of ethnicity, all we can do is increase the applicant pool of those underrepresented groups." Chris Garcia, professor of political science, said, "Government can still promote equal opportunity without promoting discrimination against any group, including white males."[64]

A five-year study on the number of Hispanic and Native American faculty at UNM, which President Peck had ordered soon after he took office, was released in October 1995. The number of full-time Hispanic faculty at UNM was four times greater than the national average, and the number of Native American teachers five times greater. As of March 1995, Hispanics made up 8.9 percent of UNM's full-time faculty, while full-time Native American teachers represented 1.7 percent. The report also showed that 43.7 percent of UNM's full-time faculty were women, 2.9 percent better than the national average. While UNM officials were pleased with the progress and national standings, they believed the institution could and should do even better.[65]

The ugly issue of racism cropped up again in November 1995, when a racist flyer was distributed on the campus. On a Thursday afternoon, November 16, UNM faculty, administrators, and students gathered on the north SUB mall. President Peck met with the group and urged students to come up with "mutually supportive" solutions for dealing with racism.

The rally quickly turned into a shouting match, with students saying they were tired of hearing the same message every time a crisis occurred. Peck retorted that he would be glad to hear their suggestions and take them to the Regents, but he would not let students tell him that nothing had been done. "I will not stand for the same old rhetoric," Peck fired back. "For you to say nothing has been done is a lie."[66]

Near the end of Peck's administration, 1997, the enrollment on UNM's main and branch campuses was 35.5 percent Hispanic, 10.7 percent Native American, 2.5 percent Asian/Pacific Islander, and 2 percent African American. That spring, UNM graduated 185 Native Americans, a national high. That fall, 36.3 percent of incoming students were Hispanics from New Mexico high schools.[67]

Academic Kudos

More dollars do not always translate into more kudos, but they often make the difference between good and great. For UNM students and faculty, more money in specific areas during the Peck years meant great.

On the national scene, the UNM School of Medicine began receiving well-deserved recognition in 1994 when *U.S. News and World Report* rated it thirteenth in the nation. The school had also received high rankings the previous years and had been widely praised for its innovative primary-care curriculum. That was the good news. The bad news was that the future doctors would be faced with a 10 percent tuition increase the following year.[68]

Another turn of the wheel brought good news, though, when on March 22, 1995, the *Albuquerque Journal*, both a strong ally in getting the word out about the University's successes and an outspoken critic about the failures, carried an editorial after *U.S. News and World Report*'s high ranking of the School of Medicine.

> Like a finely crafted building, a good reputation is assembled bit by bit, day by day. Over the years, the University of New Mexico School of Medicine has accomplished that difficult task, earning a reputation as one of the top medical schools in the nation.[69]

In 1993 the legislature funded a locum tenens program, assigning UNM medical faculty, staff, and residents to fill in for sole practitioners, many in small communities, so they could attend conferences or take vacations. That same year Paul Roth, associate dean for clinical affairs, and Joseph Scaletti, director of Allied Health Sciences, developed a telemedicine capability that allows physicians around the state to send X-rays and other diagnostic images by phone line for UNM radiologists to review. In 1997 the first class of physician assistant students began studying to serve in rural areas of New Mexico.[70]

UNM's General Library was ranked among the nation's top fifty for the second straight year by the Association of Research Libraries. Lynn Trojahn, the library development officer, said, "It's really like being in the top one percent of academic and research libraries." She pointed out that the rankings involved more than thirty-two hundred libraries.[71] The library also received a generous gift from Regent Larry Willard and named the reading room for his parents.

One of the great treasures of UNM was the University of New Mexico Press. In 1991, the paperback edition of *The Education of Little Tree* was number one on the *New York Times* paperback bestseller list. In 1986, the director of the UNM Press, Elizabeth Hadas, had paid a few hundred dollars for the publication rights. The story was about a boy who lost both parents and was raised by his Cherokee grandparents in Tennessee during the Depression. It sold more than a million copies, the highest grossing book the press had ever produced.[72]

The Association of American University Presses recognized Hadas's sharp marketing instincts and elected her as their president, effective June 1992. Hadas

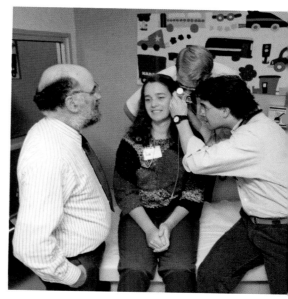

Scott Obenshain (left) wrote an article describing the primary care curriculum, entitled "How Students Learn," for the winter 1990 issue of Salud, the School of Medicine publication. His students posed for a mock ear examination. Photo by Dennis Clark

The new UNM Bookstore continued to threaten the bank balances of book lovers with an array of best sellers, classics, references, how-tos, travel guides, software, and too much more.

had worked at UNM Press for more than twenty years and been instrumental in publishing the first works of many authors.

Campus Development and Construction

The mid-1990s saw the completion of the UNM long-range master plan, which projected a maximum enrollment of thirty-five thousand and an additional 4.9 million square feet of facilities. It also provided a design framework and guidelines for long-term development of Central Campus and North Campus. The plan had its origins in the "UNM 2000" vision statement.

During the years of the Peck administration the University was involved in land sales, land swaps, gifts of property, and much remodeling and new construction. In 1993 land adjacent to Winrock shopping center was sold for $2.3 million, with the proceeds going to a scholarship endowment.

The New Bookstore

The easternmost part of what had been Yale Park was intended as the site for the new University Bookstore. In addition, a high-rise parking complex was to be erected just south of Johnson Gym. In October 1993, however, the Regents voted to cancel the parking garage and focus on the bookstore. Area bookdealers and merchants, fearing the competition, suggested that a better name for the facility would be "Lobomart." The Regents nevertheless forged ahead in developing final plans, although the size of the bookstore was reduced.[73]

Later in 1995, a writer for the *Lobo* reported that in tearing up Yale Park the Regents had dug themselves a nice hole. One of the major areas of contention was wiping out what had been considered a greenbelt on the south side of the main campus. The issue became so contentious that ASUNM leaders put a resolution to save Yale Park on a ballot and called upon the Regents to find a different site for the proposed bookstore. The resolution passed by a four to one margin.[74]

Even Albuquerque Mayor Martin Chavez got into the act. In July 1995 he offered the city reservoir at the northeast corner of Yale and Redondo as an alternative site for the bookstore. A city public works official said plans to give UNM the reservoir site had been in the works since 1987. President Peck said he appreciated the mayor's offer and added that the University was considering the reservoir site for a future facility for the School of Architecture and Planning. He declined the offer of the reservoir as a site for the bookstore, saying that paperwork and site preparation would take too much time. He added that the final decision lay with the Regents.[75]

In his report to the Regents August 9, 1994, Peck said, "The best site [for the bookstore] is the site in Yale Park, even if the reservoir site were available." He added that choosing the reservoir site would delay the project up to two years. The Regents then formally rejected the city's offer, and despite protests and students taking up residence at the site, preparation of the site and construction were soon under way.[76] Students moved in to save the trees in Yale Park, and a neighborhood resident made the television news by climbing one of the trees and chaining herself to it to stop the chain saws. The planners and builders nonetheless plunged on.[77]

In April of that year the *Lobo* reported that plans for the new bookstore were still rolling. It was predicted that actual construction of the $4.3 million facility would begin by May. The new deadline for the structure was estimated to be June 1996. After the facility was completed, it was estimated it would take another month to move the old bookstore out of the existing building, which was to be divided between the College of Arts and Sciences and the College of Fine Arts.[78]

Finally, after more than two years and $5 million, the 48,500-square-foot bookstore opened July 22, 1996. On the corner of Central Avenue and Cornell Drive, it was about one-third bigger than the old store. A Starbuck's coffee counter, a convenience store, and a ticket office for fine arts and sporting events supplemented the stacks of textbooks and racks of UNM sweatshirts.[79]

The Research Park

By 1992 the University had more than twenty-five thousand students, seventy-five hundred faculty and staff, a $187 million payroll, and a budget in excess of $502 million, not including University Hospital. The University was renowned for sending trained people out to the community—people who earned more, bought more, paid more taxes, and became leaders. The University was also working to bring added research dollars to the state, which in turn would create new private-sector jobs and attract venture capital. Much of that effort was concentrated in the hundred-acre Research Park on its hill overlooking downtown Albuquerque and close to the airport, Sandia National Labs, and Kirtland Air Force Base. By 1992 an additional one hundred thousand square feet of office and laboratory space had been built. Efforts were being made to find tenants for another 840 acres of UNM-owned property southwest of the airport, and it was announced February 15, 1993, that Southwest Airlines would set up shop on the property. UNM's real-estate advisers were hopeful this attention would spark interest in the park, which eventually was expected to earn a million dollars per year for the University.[80]

By the summer of 1993 the Research Park's tenants included the Social Security Administration and several University programs. When Martin Marietta assumed management of Sandia National Laboratories in July it formed a subsidiary to support commercial technology ventures and planned to house it at the Research Park. The facility was expected to increase total lease revenues at the research park to $160,000 a year.[81]

The Research Park's success showed business and industry that the University was ready and able to form strong partnerships, according to an article in the *New Mexico Business Journal*. Soon there were contracts for research and development in materials fabrication, an optoelectronics program, the Business Assistance and Research Center, and the UNM Technology Ventures Division.

In March 1993, the Board of Regents approved a lease with the Sandia Foundation for the building of a microelectronic research center and parking structure near the basketball arena on University Boulevard. Once completed, the center would join such high-tech facilities as the Advanced Materials Laboratory and New Mexico Engineering Research Institute buildings at the Research Park.[82]

The University formed a nonprofit corporation, the Science and Technology Corporation @ UNM (STC) in 1995. Its goals were to market faculty inventions, support increases in corporation-sponsored research, and participate in New Mexico's economic development. The STC licenses technology developed at UNM, including optics, high-performance materials, medical devices, and drug-discovery tools.

The Center for High Technology Materials was dedicated in 1997. It was one of five Centers of Technical Excellence the New Mexico Legislature created to strengthen collaboration among UNM, private industry, and national laboratories with the goal of providing more jobs. Research would be conducted into fiber optics, computer components, fabrication technologies, and manufacturing techniques for products to create, store, or transfer information.[83]

The University was strengthening the business community in other ways, as well. The Anderson Schools of Management's weekend MBA program had produced four hundred graduates since 1971, the Small Business Institute was training students to work in teams for start-ups, and UNM had one of the nation's few master's degree programs in manufacturing.[84]

Main Campus Changes

The most massive construction project during Peck's administration was the $11 million Dane Smith Hall, the first new classroom building on the UNM campus since Mitchell Hall in 1951. Named for a former UNM English professor, the eighty-thousand-square-foot building was located on a site between Roma and Las Lomas Road, northeast of Scholes Hall. Dane Smith Hall housed forty-two classrooms, including four instructional television classrooms, and computing facilities, a copy center, and a snack bar. Before construction could start, however, more than four hundred UNM employees had to be relocated so that the nine buildings where they worked could be demolished.[85] Among the casualties in these old buildings, many of which had originally housed faculty members and their families, were the Faculty Club, the buildings housing the Hispanic, Native American, and African-American programs, the Women's Center, and the Campus Police headquarters.

Other new construction included an electrical distribution substation for the North Campus and an athletic training facility on the South Campus.

The Board of Regents in June 1990 voted to approve $2 million for a facelift for Zimmerman Library. The project entailed remodeling the original west wing of the library into the Center for Southwest Research; renovating the lobby, circulation desks, and catalog area; adding an entry on the north; and improving services with an additional $5 million from federal funds.[86]

Other changes on the main campus included the addition to Hokona Hall in 1994 of a new access ramp for the handicapped, new ceilings in the corridors of the Zuni wing, and new windows and heating and air conditioning for all rooms. The

The new south façade of Zimmerman Library may seem to be a fitting companion to John Gaw Meem's classic original, but the first addition keeps the building off the National Register of Historic Places.

three-floor, 187,000-square-foot Hokona Hall was built in 1956 as a women's dorm but was used for offices at the time of the renovation.[87]

The hottest news relating to the residence halls, however, was the spectacular fire in Santa Clara Hall in March 1997. In one of the Albuquerque Fire Department's largest dispatches, sixteen units responded to the call when the dorm's main power distribution unit burst into flame. The fire and power failure forced about twenty students out of their rooms for three days.[88]

Other renovation projects included Popejoy Hall, where acoustics were improved, and the foyer of the Fine Arts Center, the chemistry addition known as Reibsomer Hall, Johnson Center, and the University Hospital's outpatient clinic. The Continuing Education complex received an addition, and the Cancer Center was expanded.

The *Lobo* announced in March 1991 that construction had begun on the first phase of the Yale Mall between Redondo Drive and the *Center of the Universe* sculpture west of Ortega Hall.[89] The Cornell Mall linking the Fine Arts Center, the Student Union, and the College of Education complex also was renovated.

New uses were found in the 1990s for one of UNM's oldest buildings. Constructed in 1916 as the Chemistry Building and now listed on the National Register of Historic Places, it had housed art studios and classrooms before being transformed into the Engineering and Science Computer Pod.

In the fall of 1996 the School of Architecture and Planning took over a remodeled office building south of the Central Campus. It would have classroom and studio space and house the Design and Planning Assistance Center. Dean Richard Eribes saw the building, one of at least five converted facilities the school used, as yet another temporary step before it could have its own home.

In September 1991 the Student Union Board voted to ban smoking throughout the facility. Smokers grumbled about the action and charged that this was just one more way UNM was making life difficult for students.[90]

In addition to its scientific and technical offerings supporting Los Alamos National Laboratory, the UNM Los Alamos Campus hosts a Small Business Development Center and offers a Southwest Studies program, which boasts a collection of about 1,800 books and other historic documents posted in an on-line catalog. Photo by Steve Borbas

The Valencia Campus, at the foothills of the Manzano Mountains, continued to grow thanks in part to local funding. Photo by Steve Borbas

Stunning views and large-scale outdoor sculpture mark the UNM Taos Campus, where the offerings include preparatory courses, freshman- and sophomore-level classes, and vocational programs. Photo by Steve Borbas

The University also became a local leader in the recycling movement when a pilot project to recycle as many paper products as possible began in March 1991. Between January and June of 1991, the University recycled 113 tons of paper, saving the institution $1,600 in fees it would have paid to have the waste hauled away.[91]

The American Association of Botanical Gardens and Arboreta recognized the University's six hundred acres as an arboretum in 1994. Three tours were developed to showcase more than two hundred plant varieties.

UNM around the State

During Peck's administration enrollment at UNM's Gallup Branch had passed twenty-six hundred. An adult basic education facility and a classroom/computer lab had been built and a bond issue approved to fund a building for the Zuni Campus and expand the Gallup Campus.

At the Los Alamos Branch, a learning resource center was added, and the student service building was renovated. Training partnerships were in place with Los Alamos National Laboratory and Northern New Mexico Community College.

The third phase of the UNM Valencia Branch learning resource center was completed. Voters approved funding for a new community/student center at the branch, which was one of many educational institutions developing new programs to help welfare recipients transition into careers.

Enrollment at the Taos Education Center reached 887 in the fall of 1997, and more than two hundred classes were offered on the eighty-acre site with its $2.1 million building.[92] The Klower family of Iowa had donated land for the campus to the town of Taos in 1993 shortly after UNM took over the Taos Education Center from Northern New Mexico Community College.

Also in Taos, the Harwood Museum of Art reopened after a $1.2 million renovation project. Called perhaps the best-kept secret in Taos, the museum displays works by members of the early 1900s Taos Society of Artists as well as American Modernist works, including those of the famed Agnes Martin.[93]

The Harwood's history began in 1916, when Burt and Lucy Harwood purchased a small adobe house south of the Taos plaza. After Burt's death in 1923 his widow established the Harwood Foundation in his honor. She expanded the house and opened a lending library, and the facility became a cultural center. Local artists and members of the foundation board, including Mabel Dodge Luhan, donated paintings, and the permanent collection was born. In 1936 Mrs. Harwood donated the property to the University. Federal funds helped pay for a new library and gallery designed by John Gaw Meem. Through the years the University maintained the growing facility, which in 1976 was added to the National Register of Historic Places. In 1984 the library came under the jurisdiction of the town of Taos and moved to another building. The director of the Harwood Museum of Art, Robert Ellis, who had taught art at UNM for twenty-three years before retiring and moving to Taos, worked with Curator Davis Witt to raise funds to upgrade the museum.

Athletics

The decade of the 1990s was a tumultuous period for UNM athletics, a time of firings and hirings, a new athletic director, a WAC championship, NCAA penalties, and faculty resolutions. The football stadium was enlarged, and a training facility was built.

The first big change occurred at the end of the football season of 1991 when University officials dismissed Head Football Coach Mike Sheppard. Sheppard, whose five-year record at UNM was eight wins and forty-nine losses, received $155,000 for the remaining two seasons on his three-year contract.[94] The athletic director, Gary Ness, stated that Sheppard's replacement should be a recognizable coach who had the personality to attract community interest as well as someone who could recruit highly talented student athletes. John Bridgers, who had been the UNM athletic director from 1979 to 1987, said, "I don't think any coach could've won with the support [Sheppard] had. One coach is not going to do it. It takes a whole community."

Less than thirty days after Sheppard's departure, Dennis Franchione was announced as the new UNM head football coach. The former head coach at Southwest Texas State, Franchione had a collegiate coaching record of 80–19–2 in nine years, including serving as head coach at Southwestern State (Kansas) and Pittsburg State (Kansas).[95]

Franchione's arrival was a rousing success with a season-opening 24–7 win over Texas Christian University, a team that had defeated UNM the previous season by a score of 60–7. Ironically, seven years later, in 1997, Franchione, who was highly successful at UNM, announced his resignation to take the head coaching job at Texas Christian University.[96] He went on to the University of Alabama and later to Texas A&M. Rocky Long, who had been UNM's quarterback from 1969 to 1971, succeeded Franchione in 1998.

There also was a turnover in the top job in UNM athletics when in November 1992 Rudy Davalos, the athletic director at the University of Houston, was appointed to the post at UNM. Davalos, a native of San Antonio, Texas, was an alumnus of Southwest Texas State, graduating in 1960 with a degree in education.[97] He received his master's degree in education from Georgetown, Kentucky, in 1962. As a point guard on the Southwest Texas State basketball team, he led them to an NAIA title. Over a long career, he coached or was an athletic administrator at Georgetown College in Kentucky, the University of Kentucky, Auburn University, the University of the South, the University of Texas at San Antonio, and finally, the University of Houston.

On November 28, 1992, UNM took time out from the basketball wars to honor a beloved former coach, Bob King. More than fifteen thousand friends, family, and past heroes of Lobo basketball converged to fill the Pit to honor one of their own during pregame and halftime ceremonies. King had the most wins in Lobo basketball history, 175, against 89 losses. He led his teams to Western Athletic Conference championships in 1964 and 1968, three National Invitational

Two-time All-American Brian Uhrlacher had a lot to celebrate as a Lobo. The Lovington, New Mexico, native was taken by the Chicago Bears as the ninth overall selection in the 2000 NFL draft.

Kenny Thomas's four years as a Lobo—when he scored in double figures in 105 games—was the most successful period for men's basketball: an overall mark of 102–30, including 71–3 in the Pit and four straight trips to the NCAA tournament.

Tournament appearances, and one NCAA championship tournament. Governor Bruce King and Albuquerque Mayor Louis Saavedra had proclaimed Bob King Day, and UNM officially unveiled the new Bob King Court in the heart of the arena.[98] Some people questioned why the entire arena was not named for King. Perhaps the reasoning was that no matter what its official name, it would always be known as the Pit.

The UNM athletic program swung from high to low in less than a month as December 8, 1992, was the day the NCAA imposed five-year sanctions on men's track and cross-country and women's gymnastics for recruiting and financial aid violations. The latter penalty was moot because the women's gymnastics program had been dropped. There were no cross-country infractions, but penalties were imposed because of its close association with the spring program.[99]

Two years later, UNM hit another high when the men's basketball team won the Western Athletic Conference championship in March 1994, with a final conference win over Brigham Young University on the latter's home court in Provo, Utah. The win ended a sixteen-year dearth since the last UNM basketball championship and was Coach Dave Bliss's first win in Marriot Gym.[100]

A championship basketball season, however, had little impact on a faculty determined to deemphasize athletics. After struggling to get a quorum, eventually 136 members of the faculty were mustered to a meeting March 29, 1994. English Professor Hugh Witemeyer led the attack, charging the UNM Athletic Department with unethical procedures over the last fifteen years. He stated, "We are not talking about a few bad apples. The barrel itself is rotten." Witemeyer then proclaimed that universities exist primarily to further teaching, learning, and research, not to participate in the semiprofessional sports entertainment industry. He added, "Therefore, like slavery, the athletic industry needs to be abolished because it's based on false principles." After fiery discussion, the faculty members voted in favor of a symbolic resolution abolishing sports at UNM.[101] The resolution had no legal standing, however, and was ignored by University officials.

The Peck Era Nears Its End

On August 8, 1997, President Peck announced that he was stepping down as president at the end of the spring semester, 1998. Then, after a year-long sabbatical, he planned to return to UNM as a professor of English. Peck, who had been president since 1990, said he looked forward to reading what he wanted to and writing some plays.[102]

In early July, Peck had announced an administrative reorganization in which the University's vice presidents would no longer report directly to him, but instead to Provost and Vice President for Academic Affairs William C. Gordon. When asked whether the reorganization would hurt academics by forcing Gordon to spend more time on administrative rather than on academic matters, Peck said, "No." He stated that "the reorganization reinforced the idea that academics are the center of the University." He added that he would continue to work with the vice presidents.[103]

Looking Back

In 1998, the final year of Peck's presidency, the University's annual report cited the year's highlights in various academic programs. These included a NASA grant to the Colleges of Engineering and Arts and Sciences to support undergraduate education related to space science and technology; a Sloan Foundation grant for minority doctoral candidates in engineering; a top-25 national ranking for the master's degree program in architecture; and an exchange program between the School of Law and a law school in Chihuahua, Mexico, as well as a top-10 ranking for the clinical law program and a top finish in the national Native American moot court competition. The Anderson Schools of Management reported graduation placement rates exceeding 80 percent, and a Native American Management Education Center was launched. The master of public administration program received accreditation. The Kellogg Foundation underwrote recruitment and training of minorities in early childhood education.[104]

The 1997–98 annual report also noted that a new cancer research facility had opened, and the Health Sciences Center library was developing an on-line database of American Indian and Alaska Native health studies. A study of hantavirus survivors was under way, and the Robert Wood Johnson Foundation was helping UNM train health-care providers in rural areas.

The School of Medicine's primary-care curriculum was praised again by *U.S. News and World Report*. The magazine also ranked the UNM College of Nursing ninety-fifth out of five hundred graduate programs and sixteenth out of one hundred nurse-practitioner programs.[105]

A survey of undergraduate programs conducted for the *Gourman Report* published by the *Princeton Review* ranked UNM among the top 11 percent and placed nine programs among the nation's best. The programs cited were American studies, anthropology, art, art history, environmental design, geology, Latin American studies, nuclear engineering, and Spanish and Portuguese.

A study published by the Johns Hopkins Press placed UNM twenty-ninth out of 109 public research universities. Other national surveys gave high marks to certain graduate and professional programs, including primary care, rural, and family medicine; clinical law; photography, print making, and fine arts; intercultural communication; anthropology; Latin American studies; and psychology.[106]

Praise for the Pecks

President Peck and his wife Donna provided warm, gracious hospitality to an estimated ten thousand visitors a year, and Donna became a renowned hostess. As a token of the Regents' esteem and appreciation for her tireless activities on behalf of UNM, Donna Peck was awarded the Regents' Meritorious Service Medal in the fall of 1997.

As Peck's time of departure drew near in the spring of 1998, Mary Conrad, the talented editor of the alumni magazine *Mirage*, published this exit interview with the retiring president.

Richard E. Peck was inaugurated as UNM's 15th president in November, 1990, approximately 63,000 hours before the time of our interview.

Over the course of those hours, Peck hoisted boxes into dorms; hobnobbed with the rich and famous; tolerated slights, rudeness, and an occasional tough insight from campus constituents; aggravated a few parties and entertained even more; wooed legislators; wowed regents; suffered the disappointment of faculty and staff over pay raises; presided over countless meetings and banquets; cheered for the cherry and silver; played more than a few rounds of golf; carved out an occasional moment for his own intellectual and creative pursuits; listened; proposed; bit his tongue; and devoted just a few moments to being grandfather, father and husband.

There is a pattern to the hours, however, a cycle of university life among students, faculty, staff, and regents which, while it may impede accomplishment, also reminds us of the nature of teaching, learning, and growing. Students graduate, faculty and staff leave, regents fulfill their terms.

"You offer the same explanations, urge the same arguments to new groups of people," Peck says of the short cycle's frustrations.

As a consequence, he says, the president who survives the complete turnover of a board of regents is a rarity. After the board turns over "the once new president appears to be part of the old guard."

Still, Peck doesn't dismiss the cycle's value, especially when it involves first-year teaching and learning. The president must well remember his first year of teaching, he says. "That goes on every year for some people, and it's very significant." And while it may be more fun to teach graduate students already intrigued by the professor's own academic interest, Peck says it is "important to lead freshmen to a respect for scholarship."

The repetitive nature of the job means the president needs a high threshold to resist frustration, says Peck. To that he adds patience—"not my lifelong suit"—and "the willingness to listen to arguments without having to win them."

To buoy the president in the mire of contention and consensus, a supportive family becomes critical. "I couldn't have done it without Donna," Peck says.

But when it comes right down to it, the president must want to be at UNM, a part of the ongoing community. "If someone thinks they can change the culture, they would fail quickly," he says. The new president "must recognize the virtues of the people he or she is joining and want to be part of what they're doing."

Peck has respected the culture of UNM and New Mexico, trying always to build on strengths inherent to the university and the state—such as diversity and ties with Latin America—since his arrival. Perhaps this sensitivity as much as anything earned him his acceptance for eight years, a record length of service in recent times. He calls his tenure and its "implicit stability" a "peculiar measurement of achievement" since the 1980s had seen five UNM presidents, including Peck.

A dramatist, Peck had watched university presidents before he acceded to the role. He had served in university administrations as department chair, dean of arts and sciences, and even interim president.

From the outside, Peck says, the presidency appears to be a powerful position. From the inside, he says, "it really isn't," and "maybe it shouldn't be." But the trade-off means "it doesn't allow for the individual intervention it once did" or the 20-year terms such as Tom Popejoy's. And it means that Peck will be leaving UNM before realizing some of his vision for it.

Peck speaks less, however, of a vision for the school as motivating his presidency than of a belief in scholars' paying their dues to the place that allows them to pursue their scholarship. Both he and Donna speak in terms of his returning to teaching as his true love, "what he really wants to do."

What next? Peck quotes former UNM President John Perovich as saying that retired presidents go from *"Who's Who* to who's he?" Peck says he will miss the invitations, but puts them into perspective as he has put the gibes and puff into perspective: "[The invitations] go to the president, not to Richard Peck. I hope after eight years some will come to Richard Peck."[107]

As the sun set on his presidency, Peck had turned philosopher. He wisely noted that he had survived multiple turnovers in governing boards, emphasizing that the board that hires a president often is not the same board three years later. He was bold and had a stiff backbone when it came to standing up for his beliefs, but in many ways he also was a shy, conscientious person, one who was sensitive to what others thought and went out of his way to make people feel good about themselves and UNM. He had the heart of a lion and the soul of a poet. ▪

William C. Gordon

CHAPTER TWENTY
Administration of William C. Gordon
1998–2002

In August 1997, President Peck announced his resignation, effective July 1, 1998. That gave the UNM Board of Regents almost a year to select his successor. It could be argued that after conducting five presidential searches in nineteen years, the board must have had more expertise in this process than virtually any in the country. Such was not the case. Its last search had been the selection of Peck, who took office in July 1990. With a complete turnover in the board, all institutional memory was gone. Once again, a UNM governing board had an abortive search, adding another chapter to what was becoming a familiar story.

The process began quietly enough. On March 9, 1998, the Regents named three presidential finalists, one of whom was the UNM provost, William C. (Bill) Gordon. The search came to a halt, however, when Bernalillo County District Court Judge Theresa Baca issued a preliminary injunction that prevented UNM from hiring a president until it complied with a 1991 consent decree. The latter required the University to disclose a candidate's name when he or she was interviewed by two or more Regents or members of the search committee. The New Mexico Foundation for Open Government and the *Albuquerque Journal* had requested the injunction. Two of the three final candidates subsequently withdrew, including Gordon.

This led to an emergency meeting of the Regents on April 13, 1998, at which time the members of the board unanimously agreed to abandon the search. Finally, in June 1998, the Regents named Gordon as interim president, which gave them another year to look for a permanent president.[1]

Gordon came to the post with an impressive academic and administrative record and a reputation for a low-key approach and coolness under fire. He was a known quantity to UNM, having joined the Psychology Department faculty in 1978. In 1990, he was appointed chair of the department, which he then guided successfully through its national accreditation process. In the fall of 1992, he became interim dean of the College of Arts and Sciences and in 1993 dean, following a national search. As dean, Gordon fully eliminated a sizable budget deficit. He worked with the faculty to produce the college's first comprehensive strategic plan and implemented a highly successful program to recruit exceptional new senior faculty. He also established the college's first full-scale development and alumni outreach programs.

Facing page: The mezzanine is the heart of the remodeled Student Union, which features conference facilities upstairs, offices for student organizations, a food court, and plenty of room to lounge. Decorative accents are in the "Cherokee Red" color favored by Frank Lloyd Wright. Photo by Tom Brahl

In 1996, Gordon assumed the posts of provost and vice president for academic affairs at UNM. As provost, he was directly responsible for overseeing and developing all Central Campus academic, research, and public service programs. He also directed all branch campus operations and managed the academic affairs budget. He created thirty new graduate assistantships and steered a significant amount of new funding to library acquisitions. He also put into place the University's first comprehensive research overhead budget and implemented student outcomes assessment programs across the campus. In addition, Gordon created a special office at UNM to coordinate and foster Native American program development.

Before coming to UNM, Gordon earned his bachelor's and master's degrees from Wake Forest University and his PhD in experimental psychology from Rutgers University. He began his academic career in 1973 as an assistant professor of psychology at the State University of New York at Binghamton. While there he received the SUNY System Chancellor's Award for excellence in teaching.

The Interim Months

One of Gordon's first actions as interim president was to appoint F. Chris Garcia, professor of political science, as interim provost in July 1998. The selection of Garcia came as no surprise, for he had served in that post from January 1987 to June 1990 and again for seven months in 1993. He joined Judy Jones, interim vice president for institutional advancement, David McKinney, vice president for business and finance, and Eliseo "Cheo" Torres, vice president for student affairs.[2]

The Regents wasted no time in implementing a new presidential search, approving a preliminary time line at their September 8, 1998, meeting. By February 1999, they announced the names of five finalists, and a month later, by a unanimous vote, selected Bill Gordon for the permanent post.[3]

When Gordon had been named interim president in 1998, one of his first challenges was the tremendous increase in freshman students for the fall semester. Departing President Peck's recruiting efforts were paying off. The entering class increased by 26 percent over the previous year, and since 1996 had grown 56 percent. More than 63 percent of the students who applied for admission actually enrolled in the fall. Both classroom space and housing posed special problems, but these the University was happy to handle.[4]

What was not new was yet another rally protesting Governor Johnson's proposed 13 percent increase in tuition, but only fifteen students participated.[5]

In academic developments that fall of 1998 was the Regents' approval of two new academic majors, African-American Studies and Women Studies.[6] The University also was honored that Manuel Montoya of Mora, New Mexico, was named a Rhodes Scholar, UNM's first since the 1970s. Montoya, a student in the University Honors Program, was majoring in English and economics and was also a Truman Scholar in 1998.[7]

January 1999 saw the appointment of three new Regents: Jack Fortner, Judith Herrera, and student Jason Bousilman. They replaced Penny Taylor Rembe, Barbara

Brazil, and Kimberly Richards, whose terms expired in December. Larry Willard, the board's president, was reappointed.[8]

In January 1999, the North Central Association accreditation team evaluated UNM. They reported they were "impressed" by the overall review, but had some concerns about the lack of Hispanic faculty members.[9]

In the spring of 1999 the University's research magazine, *Quantum,* reported that the U.S. Patent Office had recently approved two patent claims filed by the University. One was a device developed by Samuel Slishman of the School of Medicine allowing physicians to enter the chest cavity rapidly, especially in emergencies. The other was a test for hantavirus, a deadly disease rodents transmitted to humans. It was developed by a team led by Brian Hjelle of the Pathology Department and Nora Torrez-Martinez of the UNM Center for Emerging Viruses.

Hantavirus, which had put New Mexico in the national spotlight during an outbreak in 1998, was the subject of much research at UNM. The Centers for Disease Control and Prevention were funding a study of the causes and timing of outbreaks of the disease under the direction of Terry Yates, professor of biology and later vice provost for research. The National Science Foundation was supporting Yates's studies of rodent tissues in UNM's Museum of Southwestern Biology proving that hantavirus had been present in New Mexico for thousands of years. In addition, research at the UNM Long-term Ecological Research Center at the Sevilleta National Wildlife Refuge showed that rodent populations had increased dramatically in 1993 after several warm, rainy El Niño winters and that a rising number of human plague cases were associated with that weather. Two years later the Sevilleta project was named one of the nation's "Nifty Fifty" funded by the National Science Foundation.

Wide vistas and ample research opportunities characterize the Sevilleta National Wildlife Refuge, which sits on both sides of Interstate 25 between Belen and Socorro. Photo by Michael Mouchette

Gordon's Long-term Goals

It was jokingly reported in the *Lobo* that after Gordon crossed the word "interim" off his business cards, he proclaimed that his first order of business would be to establish a long-term plan for UNM that would serve as a road map to the future. The Regents praised him for having demonstrated successful leadership at all levels of an extremely complex and highly diverse research university.[10]

His speech at his inauguration on October 10, 1999, focused on recognizing the University's responsibility to reach out to the statewide community, capitalizing on the state's natural resources, and improving recruitment and retention of strong faculty, students, and staff. He emphasized that he would strive to offer students the atmosphere his mentors provided for him when he was a student. He would seek to have faculty members bring to the classroom the excitement they experienced as researchers.[11]

Finance

As expected, the legislative session of 1999 was stormy. Governor Gary Johnson vetoed the appropriations bill, which meant that University officials had to prepare their 1999–2000 budget without knowing how much state money would be available.[12] UNM's Board of Regents raised student fees from $487 per semester to $523. The funds would offset renovation costs of the Student Union Building and the Child Care Center. A campus poll showed that students generally approved the increase, which was less than the $50 increase that had been anticipated.[13]

The good news from Santa Fe, however, was Governor Johnson's signing of a bill to repeal the sunset clause and save the lottery scholarship program. His signature meant that 1,468 students on UNM's main campus would continue to receive full-tuition scholarships, which amounted to more than $1 million.[14]

In October 1999 the Regents authorized $61.5 million in revenue bonds, some backed by student fees, to finance nearly a dozen capital improvement projects, including $25 million to renovate the Student Union Building, $12.6 million for a new residence hall complex, and $3.5 million for unspecified parking improvements.[15]

Former President Peck Stays Busy

In the fall of 1999, it was reported that former President Peck had been nominated as interim president at the University of South Florida. Peck said he would take unpaid leave from his position as an English Department faculty member.[16] Peck continued to indulge in his other passion, writing. By 2002, he had four books on the market: *The New Mexico Experience*, a look at the people and events that shaped modern New Mexico; *Something for Joey*, the true story of courage and love between Heisman Trophy winner John Cappeletti and his brother Joey; *All the Courses in the Kingdom*, a tour of Fife, Scotland, combining history and golf; and *Dead Pawn*, a mystery novel interweaving three cultures in the Southwest.

Academics

Spotlighted in Gordon's tenure as president were the new freshman learning communities, which put first-year students in seminar-style classes with experienced professors. About 350 freshmen in a class of 2,400 participated in the two-year-old program in the fall of 2001. The program also enrolled about 25 students in two or more classes together in an effort to foster a supportive academic community to help freshmen succeed. By the fall of 2002, it was estimated that more than half of UNM freshmen would be enrolled in some kind of seminar program. The seminars had a profound effect on UNM's historically poor retention rate, as more than 88 percent of the first-year students in the fall of 2001 returned for the spring semester.

The University of New Mexico introduced its first online classes in January 2000. The Internet classes allowed students living in rural communities to take classes without having to commute to the Albuquerque campus. These students paid regular tuition rates, but also had to pay a $100 delivery fee.[17]

The School of Architecture and Planning was ranked among the top twenty-eight programs in the country in 2003, and its faculty were ninth in the number of teaching awards.[18] Previously, the school's Design and Planning Assistance Center had been recognized for contributions to public understanding of the profession.[19]

In 1999 Roger Schluntz was appointed as dean, and a master's program in landscape architecture was approved and accredited. Ted Jojola, the first Native American on the school's faculty, was appointed to head the community and regional planning program. An endowment from the late architect George C. Pearl helped fund a certificate program and research fellowship in historical preservation studies. In 2001 Chris Wilson was named chair of the school's cultural landscape studies program.[20]

The spring of 1999 saw the renewal of the Institute of Medieval Studies' popular spring lecture series. The topic was "Medieval Scandinavia: The Vikings and Their Culture." The institute also offered seminars and peer mentoring for secondary teachers.

Biology Professor Randy Thornhill became an overnight media sensation in January 2000 with his controversial theory on rape. A book he coauthored with Craig T. Palmer of the University of Colorado, *A Natural History of Rape: Biological Bases of Sexual Coercion,* led to his appearance on several national and local TV news programs, including NBC's *Today* show. The thesis of the book was that the practice of rape had evolved over time as an instinctive strategy for a male to produce children and keep his genes alive in a new generation.[21]

Fred Harris

UNM made other national news in June 2000, when the *Wall Street Journal* reported that the University was far above the norm for the number of women receiving the MBA, with women comprising 43 percent of the enrollment in the Anderson Schools of Management. The national average for women in business schools at that time was 30 percent.[22]

Anthropology Professor Lawrence Straus was also in the news in the fall of 2000, announcing that he and his student researchers had obtained four more radiocarbon dates from El Mirón, a cave in northern Spain, showing that ancestral humans had used it tens of thousands of years ago. Straus was an internationally recognized expert on the Upper Paleolithic period in Europe who had been bringing undergraduate and graduate students to excavate El Mirón annually since 1966. He was also editor of the *Journal of Anthropological Research,* published at UNM.

The University received $1.5 million in 2001 for an endowed chair in information science. Named for Spain's Prince of Asturias, it was funded by a Spanish electric utility. Credit for the gift went to President Gordon and Albuquerque's Ed Romero, the U.S. ambassador to Spain.

UNM's Fred Harris received awards as the nation's outstanding teacher in political science from the American Political Science Association and Pi Sigma Alpha, the national honorary, in August 2001. A former U.S. senator from Oklahoma and a member of the national board of Common Cause, Harris had published eighteen books, including *Locked in the Poorhouse: Cities, Race, and Poverty in the United States.* He also practiced what he taught in political science, serving on many committees, providing issue analysis, and supporting candidates.

The 2001 fall semester saw the debut of a new biomedical sciences graduate program. After seven or eight years of study, candidates would receive both PhD and MD degrees.

In November 2001, it was announced that Dr. Karl M. Johnson, an internationally famous virologist and adjunct professor of medicine and biology at UNM, had been awarded Panama's highest scientific honor. Johnson had helped isolate many viruses, such as Ebola and hantavirus.[23]

In March 2001, the United Staff of UNM won the right to represent educational support employees at the bargaining table. The union had met the minimum number of votes required to make the election valid—60 percent—and the Board of Regents soon ratified the results.[24] Gordon's emphasis on faculty and staff interests also were high points of his administration, as salaries and legislative support increased significantly during his time in office.[25]

The University's impact on the community was highlighted in a 2001 report from the Office of Institutional Advancement and the Office of Research Services. The ten hospitals and clinics of the Health Sciences Center scheduled nearly 669,000 patient visits; more than 19,000 faculty, staff, and student employees earned paychecks totaling $480 million and paid $18.2 million in state and local taxes; and the University purchased $368 million in goods and services in New Mexico. The report also noted that UNM was one of only nine universities in the United States classified as both a "minority institution" and a "Carnegie doctoral/research university-extensive."

The main campus received $140 million in research grants, awards, and contracts in 2000, and the Health Sciences received $77 million, the report said. Fifty-seven percent of the total was federal funds. Among the largest research projects were the Center on Alcoholism, Substance Abuse, and Addictions; the Center for High Technology Materials; the Center for Micro-engineered Materials; and the High Performing Computing, Education, and Research Center. The latter operated in Albuquerque and Maui, Hawaii. The report also said the National Science Foundation had ranked UNM fifty-sixth out of the top one hundred universities for research and development expenditures in 1999.[26]

Berthold and 9/11

September 11, 2001, was a day of infamy for citizens of the United States. Not unlike the Japanese attack on Pearl Harbor on December 7, 1941, the terrorist attacks on the World Trade Center of New York and the Pentagon will forever be etched in the memories of those who watched the hideous drama unfold. Raw sensitivities were further inflamed by the remarks a UNM history professor, Richard Berthold, made to his classes. Hours after the terrorist attacks, Berthold told students in his Western civilization and Greek history classes, "Anyone who can blow up the Pentagon has my vote." As the *Lobo* reported on September 24, 2001,

> UNM history professor Richard Berthold is no stranger to controversy. He has never wavered in standing by his opinion, whether it is reprimanding the University in a column, supporting Palestine or criticizing affirmative action. He has never wavered, that is, until Sept. 11.[27]

Berthold later apologized, saying he regretted those words. Some legislators, however, were not satisfied, especially Representative William Fuller from Albuquerque. Fuller acknowledged that it would be hard to fire Berthold because he had worked at the University for thirty years and had tenure. He also stated, though, that any instructor who said what Berthold had should face serious consequences. Fuller added that he was sure President Gordon would take appropriate action.

Gordon issued a statement on September 21, calling Berthold's comments "irresponsible and deeply offensive." The statement also reported that Berthold expressed deep regret at what he had said.

Gordon added, "I know that many others—both on this campus and in the community—have had the same reaction. While we all know that the First Amendment protects a broad range of speech, the fact that Professor Berthold's speech is protected does not make the comments any less repugnant."[28]

The backlash was incredible. The *Albuquerque Journal* editorialized, saying "the University found itself under fire in a manner it had not suffered since the notorious 'Love Lust Poem' controversy of the '60s." It called upon Berthold to resign to spare his institution further grief over his intemperate tongue. Then the editorial called upon all New Mexico to be unanimous "in the resolve that we will not let one irresponsible, faculty-tenured bigmouth make the University of New Mexico another casualty of the tragedies of Sept. 11."[29]

Angry letters from an outraged citizenry filled the op-ed pages of the *Albuquerque Journal*, the *Tribune*, and the *Lobo*. Berthold had a few defenders, but very few. President Gordon personally received more than a thousand calls, letters, and e-mails concerning Berthold's remarks. To his credit, Gordon kept his cool. In a beautifully crafted letter published in the *Albuquerque Journal* on October 4, Gordon discussed the issue in a calm, rational tone and came down on the side of free speech.[30]

Rudolfo A. Anaya

If some professors incite angry letters to the editors or university presidents, others bring joy and pride. So it was with Rudolfo A. Anaya, whom many considered to be the dean of Chicano literature. Anaya received a National Medal of Arts Award in 2001 from President George W. Bush. The sixty-four-year-old Anaya, a UNM professor emeritus of English, called the award "an honor. It's humbling."

Anaya had earlier received a national Hispanic literature award for his first novel, *Bless Me, Ultima*, published in 1972. It had become a standard text in high school and college literature courses worldwide. He also wrote four cultural mysteries—"The Albuquerque Quartet"—as well as children's books, including *The Farolitos of Christmas*, and essays and plays. His play, *The Season of La Llorona*, began as a novella and was adapted for the stage. Anaya also had mentored many would-be authors as the director of the UNM Creative Writing Program before his retirement.

Charlotte Black, writing about Anaya's background, said:

Growing up on the llano, in the small rural village of Pastura, Rudolfo Anaya had a dream. He wanted to be a writer, and a writer he is. His books tell of life as it has been lived in New Mexico for centuries, and of the legends that give structure to that life. He talks of families on the llano and in the barrios, of the richness of their culture and the beauty of their beliefs.[31]

The *Albuquerque Journal* paid him homage in a glowing editorial March 16, 2002, saying "he captured the heart and soul of Hispanic New Mexico."[32] Indeed, Anaya made all New Mexico proud.

Clinton Adams and Peter Walch

UNM lost one of its great leaders and characters when Clinton Adams, eighty-three, died of liver cancer May 18, 2002. He was a respected printmaker and painter, cofounder of the Tamarind Lithography Workshop, and long-time dean of UNM's College of Fine Arts. He also served the University as interim provost and as associate provost. According to Peter Walch, the former director of the UNM Art Museum and a long-time friend of Adams, the private Adams was "an old curmudgeon, and the term may well have been invented to describe him. He was a first-class poker player, who was rarely caught bluffing, a skill, of course, highly relevant to being a successful, high-level university administrator."

Marjorie Devon, director of UNM's Tamarind Institute of Lithography, paid high tribute to Adams, saying, "A deep, independent thinker, his research and publications on American lithography have contributed significantly to art history." Adams was also a historian and the author of more than one hundred articles, most of them related to the history of lithography. *The New York Times* praised as "definitive" his 1983 book *American Lithographers, 1900–1960: The Artists and Their Printers*. He also wrote several other books on art and a memoir about his early life. In 1985, he received the Governor's Award for Outstanding Contributions to the Arts of New Mexico.[33]

Peter Walch retired in 2001 after serving as Art Museum director for sixteen years and, before that, a professor of art and art history for fourteen years. He viewed the museum as "the physical and spiritual home" for exhibits, lectures, and cultural studies as well as teaching and research. During his tenure the permanent collection grew to more than forty thousand objects, including many outstanding photographs. Walch also arranged to have artwork displayed around the campus, including works on paper by Garo Z. Antreasian in Dane Smith Hall and a sculpture by Bob Haozous west of the bookstore.

Minorities

UNM's emphasis on Hispanic programs began paying off as the University twice was ranked among the leaders in the nation in attracting Hispanic students during Gordon's administration. In September 2001, the UNM School of Law and the

Anderson Schools of Management were ranked fourth and eighth, respectively, for Hispanic students by *Hispanic Business* magazine. The recognition was based on enrollment, faculty, student services, retention rate, and reputation. Hispanic students comprised nearly one-fourth of the student population in the UNM School of Law, and 35 of the 110 law degrees awarded that year went to Hispanic students.[34]

Several months later, March 2002, *Hispanic Magazine* listed UNM as one of the top twenty-five colleges and universities committed to being a Hispanic-serving institution. The list mentioned the architecture of UNM's campus, which reflects both Pueblo and Spanish colonial influences, as well as two of the University's strongest academic programs, Latin American Studies and Southwest Hispanic Studies. The magazine also named institutions that were successful in recruiting and retaining Hispanic students. In order to be included, universities had to show that their student bodies were reflective of the overall U.S. population of Hispanics and that a significant number of Hispanics were graduating from the institution. Other criteria included the number of Hispanic-related degree programs, Hispanic student organizations, minority support programs, and Hispanic faculty.[35]

Students

In January 2000, Randy'L He-dow Teton, a senior majoring in art history, was the model for Sacagawea, the Indian who served as a guide for Lewis and Clark in their expedition to the West Coast in 1803. Glenna Goodacre was the artist who designed the one-dollar coin commemorating the epic journey. Teton was a member of the Shoshone Bannock tribe, while Sacagawea was a Shoshone Lemhi. Teton, who was proud but modest over being selected, smiled when she said, "Similar tribes, different bands."[36]

More kudos accrued to UNM students when Jennifer Halbleib, a biochemistry student, was selected as one of forty national Marshall Scholarship recipients in January 2001. She planned to use the scholarship, valued at roughly $50,000, to study cellular and molecular biology at Oxford University in Great Britain.[37] Then, in early 2002, Lobo placekicker Katie Hnida became the first woman to play in an NCAA Division 1 game at the Las Vegas Bowl.

Fraternity Woes

Fraternities made for unhappy times during the Gordon administration. The UNM chapter of Sigma Alpha Epsilon was found responsible for allowing consumption of alcohol at the fraternity's house in August 1999. The University also determined that the fraternity's record during the previous four years warranted a three-year suspension of its charter. The chapter filed an appeal but as of 2003 the suspension was still in effect.[38]

The next problem was Sigma Chi. The *Lobo* reported on December 7, 2000, that an African American engineering student, Candace Majedi, had parked her car illegally in the fraternity's dirt parking lot on Las Lomas across from Dane Smith

Dane Smith Hall features classrooms of various sizes, computer labs, a copy center, a snack bar and commons area, and the offices of the Evening and Weekend Degree Program. Photo by Van Dorn Hooker

Hall. When she returned to her car after class, she saw about ten men standing around the vehicle. She noted a taped swastika on the roof of the car and later discovered that the door lock was filled with gum and the windshield was covered with duct tape. Further inspection revealed the car had been vandalized and a crude note had been taped to the window."[39]

Members of the University community were outraged, and despite an apology from the fraternity, a large group of students gathered outside the Sigma Chi house to protest the incident. Majedi's attorney filed a federal lawsuit on her behalf against the fraternity and also accused the University of condoning behavior that promoted racism, sexism, gay bashing, discrimination, and acts of violence against minorities, women, gays, and disabled persons.[40] After further demonstrations, UNM officials met with Majedi and her attorney, who agreed to drop the lawsuit if the University promised to take swift, appropriate action.

Time passed, and in February 2001, it was announced that the University had suspended the Sigma Chi fraternity through the fall semester. This failed to appease Majedi, however, and her attorney said the University's action was but "a slap on the wrist."[41]

A year later, April 20, 2002, the national office of Sigma Chi revoked the UNM chapter's charter, meaning that the group could not use the fraternity name and that it had effectively been dissolved. A month later, the *Lobo* reported that members of the fraternity were forced to move out of the house because the City of Albuquerque had condemned the property for safety-code violations.[42]

Campus Development and Construction

The UNM campus during the Gordon administration was once again a massive construction site. Prominent were major new buildings, infrastructure upgrades, and both gains and losses of coveted parking spots.

One significant development was the Regents' approval on December 8, 1998, of a policy requiring all new buildings to adhere to the Pueblo Style and creating a committee to inventory and maintain the campus's architectural treasures. Fittingly, the state chapter of the American Institute of Architects in 1999 named Zimmerman Library the best building in New Mexico in the twentieth century. A jury said John Gaw Meem's now-classic example of Pueblo Revival architecture "contribute[s] to the architectural heritage of the state."[43]

In the spring of 1998 a rusty bolt securing a thirty-year-old underground water line failed and more than a hundred thousand gallons of water poured into a utility tunnel, shorting out electrical cables and steam lines. It was only one of many infrastructure problems on the campus, and in April 2001 revenue bonds totaling $52.7 million were issued to renovate Ford Utility Center and replace a fifty-year-old chilling plant. The bonds were to be repaid with energy savings resulting from greater efficiency, partly through a new cogeneration unit to allow UNM to produce up to 80 percent of its own energy. The new chiller was dedicated in June 2003. The building, on Redondo across from the Anderson Schools of Management, was praised for displaying the Pueblo Style in an industrial facility and called a beautiful and functional anchor to the campus.[44]

Dane Smith Hall, planned and built under the Peck administration, was dedicated on August 30, 1998. The main feature of the hall was a three-story courtyard with balconies on each level. Fifty-four classes were scheduled in the hall for the fall semester.[45]

In December 1998 plans for a new apartment-style dormitory complex were approved. The $12.6 million complex was to be at the southeast edge of the Central Campus, replacing some tennis courts. Twenty-eight two- and three-story structures would include studio, two-, and four-bedroom apartments with bathrooms and kitchens as well as a large commons area. The complex, named Redondo Village Apartments, was completed in August 2001 and accommodates four hundred students.[46]

Meanwhile, the new bookstore on the Cornell Mall opened. The old bookstore was renovated to accommodate the Biology Department and the College of Fine Arts Media Arts programs.[47]

Ribbon cutting for the renovated Johnson Center was held in August 1999. Funds authorized by a student referendum and additional monies from a state general obligation bond financed the $5.8 million renovation project. Locker rooms were updated to meet the Americans with Disabilities Act, and the bilevel weight room, joined by a spiral staircase, had many new machines. The bike shop was moved and expanded to include the outdoor shop, where students could rent camping gear and other recreational items. The final areas upgraded were the dance room, racquetball courts, the Johnson Field pool, and the wrestling/yoga room.[48]

Another major renovation undertaking was the New Mexico Union, or the Student Union Building, often referred to as the SUB. In July 1998 the Regents' Facility and Finance Committee approved a $25 million plan to add 8,000 square feet to the northwest corner of the building and renovate 147,000 square feet. UNM system revenue bond proceeds and a 2 percent increase in student fees funded the project.

After many revisions to the plans, what was described as "a form of open-heart surgery" on the campus began in January 2001. The SUB was closed and food was trucked in from a former car dealership, while outside vendors set up tents on the mall. The project was slated for completion in seventeen months, but in February 2003 it was far from finished, and the University replaced the general contractor with a new firm, which got the job done by year's end.[49]

The renovation included an expanded theater and computer lab and new space for food franchises. New entrances were added facing Smith Plaza and the Cornell Mall. The second floor housed an enlarged ballroom and a banquet facility as well as offices, and there were more offices and conference rooms on the third floor. The forty-year-old facility received a new coat of stucco, energy-efficient windows and doors, and all-new infrastructure, including wiring for the University computer network. A new atrium brought in natural light and connected the three levels.[50]

The new building for the School of Architecture and Planning would be "an important showpiece," said a gratified Dean Roger Schluntz in mid-1999 when the project was announced.[51] After more than three decades in makeshift quarters on the south side of Central Avenue at Stanford, the school would move across the street. A year later came the announcement that Antoine Predock, a UNM alumnus with an international reputation, would design the building and that it would include a new home for the Fine Arts Library. Predock was chosen after a national competition funded by the New Mexico Legislature. The next news was that the facility would be named for George C. Pearl, a prominent Albuquerque architect and historic preservationist whose campus projects included Ortega Hall, the first addition to Zimmerman Library, and additions to the Chemistry Building and to Bratton Hall. By late 2003 fund raising for the $12 million project was still under way.

In 1999 the Regents also approved the plan for a $4 million facility just south of the Maxwell Museum of Anthropology. The thirty-five-thousand-square-foot Frank C. Hibben Center for Archaeological Research would include classrooms, a lecture hall, and storage space.

By mid-2001, the University was preparing a new parking lot at University and Lomas on land formerly leased to a car dealer. Plans also were being made for a three-level parking structure east of Popejoy Hall. Other projects under way or recently completed were an expansion of University Stadium, an addition to Bratton Hall for the School of Law, and a new child-care facility on University Boulevard.

A prosperous era came to an end in November 2001, when the Regents approved a plan to sell the eighty acres on which Winrock shopping center sits near Louisiana Boulevard and Interstate 40. The center had been built in 1959 when Winthrop Rockefeller leased the land and began making sizeable payments. He sold it to a real estate firm in the mid-1980s, and by 2001 it was described as an "under-performing asset."[52]

In Tomé, a new student/community center was dedicated at the Valencia Branch in the fall of 2000. A new sixty-five-hundred-square-foot library was built at the Gallup Branch, and the Zuni Campus, which included a health careers building, was dedicated in 2002.

Athletics

One of Bill Gordon's first actions as UNM's interim president in August 1998 was signing the official letters withdrawing the University from the Western Athletic Conference (WAC). UNM joined seven other universities that announced they were leaving the WAC in June to form a new conference. Albert Yates, president of Colorado State University, was the president of the new conference, which in time would be named the Mountain West Conference.[53]

Gordon took over the same fall that Rocky Long began his first season as head coach of the Lobo football team. Long had been an outstanding quarterback at UNM from 1969 to 1971 and had graduated from the University in 1974. After coaching football at Albuquerque's Eldorado High School, he worked as an assistant coach at UNM, the University of Wyoming, Texas Christian University, Oregon State University, and UCLA, as well as one year with the professional British Columbia Lions. He returned to UNM in 1998 and coached the team to a three-win, nine-loss record that year. The following year, his team won four games. The next year it won four, and in 2001 it won five. Long developed a reputation for creative, tenacious defenses, but the team improved in all phases of the game. Gordon had the luxury of attending games with a Lobo team that was always competitive.

On the sad side of his duties as president, Gordon also had to approve the athletic director's "painful, but very necessary decision" to cut three sports for the 1999–2000 fiscal year: men's swimming, men's gymnastics, and men's wrestling. Athletic Director Rudy Davalos said the cuts were necessary because the Athletic Department did not have enough resources to support twenty-four men's and women's programs. Elimination of the three sports was expected to reduce expenditures by approximately $175,000 in 1999–2000, and the savings would eventually grow to more than $300,000 annually.[54]

Dave Bliss, who had succeeded Gary Colson as basketball coach in 1988, left UNM in 1999 to accept the head coaching job at Baylor University. His replacement was Fran Fraschilla. In March 2001, after his Lobo team lost a lopsided game to the University of Minnesota in the opening round of the National Invitational Tournament, Fraschilla resigned, citing what he regarded as insurmountable negative public opinion and intense media scrutiny. The team had posted a sixteen-and-fourteen record, their worst since 1993. Fraschilla's three-year record at UNM ended with his teams winning fifty-five games while losing forty-one. He did, however, guide the team to three National Invitational Tournament appearances.[55]

In less than a month, Davalos was naming a new UNM head coach for basketball: Ritchie McKay, the thirty-six-year-old coach of Oregon State University. McKay had coached six years, including a stint at Colorado State University, but had never stayed more than two years at one place. He was given a five-year contract at UNM with a base salary of $175,000 per year. Radio and television contracts, plus other incentives, made the contract worth about $500,000 per year. First, though, the University had to buy out McKay's two remaining years at Oregon State for $225,000. UNM also had to pay departing coach Fran Fraschilla about $500,000 for the remaining years on his contract.[56]

Emphasis Makes the News

A sports information director at another college once commented that the athletic program received less than 1 percent of the total university budget, but 99 percent of the publicity. This is surely true in most communities. An excellent example involves the news stories, pictures, and editorials in one metropolitan newspaper, the *Albuquerque Journal,* covering the period from March 17 to April 24, 2002, and relating to three events: the resignation and hiring of a basketball coach; the naming of a noted Hispanic author, Rudolfo Anaya, as a recipient of the National Medal

Ritchie McKay became the eighteenth head men's basketball coach at UNM in 2002. His father, Joe, played at UNM from 1960 to 1963.

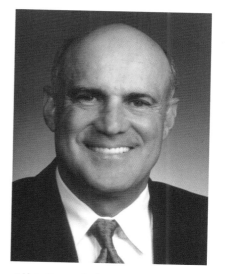

Athletic Director Rudy Davalos was still on the job in 2003.

of Arts by the president of the United States; and the resignation of Gordon as the president of the University of New Mexico.

In the forty-one-day period, the figures compiled were as follows:

Event	Column Inches	Front Page	Pictures	Editorials
Basketball Coaches	2,007	9	9	11
Rudolfo Anaya	31	1	1	1
Bill Gordon	155	2	3	1

Gordon's Resignation

Friends and colleagues of Gordon who had worked with the affable former psychology professor for twenty-four years were stunned and saddened to hear on March 14, 2002, that he was leaving to accept the post of provost at Wake Forest University. The move would return him to the North Carolina school where he had received a bachelor's degree in 1968 and a master's degree in 1970.[57]

Wake Forest had a combined graduate and undergraduate enrollment of about six thousand and long-standing ties with the Southern Baptist Church. There was some speculation that Gordon might be in line to become the university's next president when Thomas K. Hearn, Jr., sixty-four, retired. Hearn had been the Wake Forest president for almost twenty years. Gordon, however, said he was not looking to be anything other than provost.[58]

There was no doubt that Gordon was a hot prospect for presidencies. Although he had not applied for the job, he was one of three finalists for the position of chancellor of the University System of Georgia in the fall of 2001. Earlier, in 1998, the *New York Times* had listed him as a candidate for chancellor of the City University of New York.

The departing UNM president received high grades from many sources. Described as "low-key and approachable," he nonetheless had a reputation for being "dogged" when it came to faculty salaries and academic issues. He was very popular with UNM faculty and staff.

Some Hispanic leaders criticized him, however, for not hiring more Hispanics for leadership positions. Leaders of the New Mexico Hispanic Round Table reported they met monthly with Gordon and other top UNM officials and often recommended Hispanic candidates for administrative vacancies. They complained that of four cabinet-level administrators hired during Gordon's term, only one was Hispanic.

Gordon rebutted the criticisms, pointing out that three of UNM's cabinet-level administrators were Hispanic. He added that of eighty-one administrators and managers hired between November 1999 and November 2001, 32 percent were ethnic minorities.[59]

Overwhelmingly, however, UNM's many constituencies regretted Gordon's departure. An *Albuquerque Journal* editorial paid him high tribute, saying that Gordon had served well as the president of UNM:

Bill and Kathy Gordon. Photo by Tom Brahl

Gordon's calm, analytical style of governance endeared him to UNM insiders and earned him the respect of the larger community.

Gordon made staff salaries a priority, and the Legislature approved significant raises for three straight years, including a 7 percent increase last year.

"I'm proudest of what we've done to improve the quality of undergraduate education," Gordon said. His emphasis on that area was refreshing—after all, that's the primary mission of a state university.

Gordon came to UNM in a time of turmoil over the institution's goals and governance, and over the presidential selection process. He has restored UNM's relations with the community and Legislature, and brought the university closer to the calm, reflective atmosphere appropriate for a center of learning.

New Mexico owes William Gordon a debt of gratitude for his service. We would have been quite happy for him to have stayed a while longer, but we wish him well in his new post at Wake Forest.[60]

In his announcement that he was moving, Gordon said university presidents needed to make their mark quickly and bow out before their enthusiasm waned. "It really takes an investment of your whole self. That is hard to maintain over a long period."

An articulate and activist faculty member, Beulah Woodfin, professor of biochemistry, put it well when she said, "Four years is about as much as you can expect. But, for heaven sakes, the basketball coach gets a longer contract."[61] ■

Freshmen get campus tours and tips from fellow students during "LOBOrientation." Photo by Brian Lucero

Chapter Twenty-One
Administration of F. Chris Garcia
2002–3

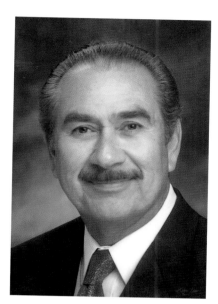

F. Chris Garcia

For its first 113 years, the University of New Mexico had not had a Hispanic president. When in 2002 it finally did, he had to be drafted. In a move that some Hispanic leaders considered long overdue, and despite F. Chris Garcia's reluctance to take the job, on June 20, 2002, the Regents announced they had unanimously approved his appointment as the UNM president for a period of one year. Garcia, a professor of political science, said he accepted the presidency reluctantly, emphasizing that he had no permanent interest in the job.[1]

Preoccupied with illnesses in his family, Garcia had at first rejected efforts to appoint him to the presidency. Then, ninety-three faculty members circulated a petition urging Regents to hire him. Regent Jack Fortner and former Regent David Archuleta later visited Garcia's office, urging him to take the job.

Garcia said that encouragement from all walks of UNM life, including faculty, staff, and students, was what convinced him to accept the job. "When so many people seem to think you ought to do the job, you should at least give it serious consideration," he said. "Still, it was tough because I very much enjoy being a faculty member."

The appointment came as no surprise to many, as Garcia had overwhelming support from many sectors on and off campus, including the Hispanic community and legislators. He also was a well-known television personality, serving as a pollster and later an analyst on election nights. All who knew him and respected his many accomplishments expressed their belief that Garcia would be an ideal person to lead the University. His fixed-term appointment for one year would also give the Regents the time and opportunity to conduct a national search for a permanent president.[2]

Garcia brought a long history of administrative experience. Beginning in 1976 he served five years as associate dean of the College of Arts and Sciences, the University's largest college. Then, after a national search, he was named dean, becoming the first Hispanic to hold the title and serving six and a half years, until 1986. The next year, following another search, he was named vice president for academic affairs and served for three and a half years during Gerald May's tenure as president. In 1993 Garcia was asked to serve as interim provost and vice president for academic affairs under President Peck. After seven months Garcia returned to the faculty. Then in 1998–99 he served as the top academic administrator with President Gordon.

Garcia's sojourns in these posts proved invaluable as prelude to his presidency. He knew first-hand the importance of the schools and colleges and the critical roles their deans played. Further, he had worked closely with three presidents and observed their widely varied styles. He also had been an active member of the three presidents' executive councils. In all, fully half his thirty-four years at UNM had involved administration. He would later say with tongue in cheek, "Surely, going back and forth from the faculty to administration to faculty (four times) is unusual (unprecedented? crazy?) to say the least."[3]

Garcia had been nominated in 1984 when the Regents ultimately chose Tom Farer for the job. Garcia, then in his fourth year as dean of the College of Arts and Sciences, said at that time he did not expect to be considered as a finalist and that he saw himself as primarily a teacher and researcher.[4]

Garcia, an Albuquerque native, graduated from Valley High School in 1957. He earned a UNM bachelor's degree in government in 1961 and a master's in government and education in 1964. He went on to earn a PhD in political science at the University of California, Davis, in 1972. He taught political science at UNM starting in 1970. He was assistant and associate dean of the College of Arts and Sciences from 1975 to 1980 and then served as dean from 1980 to 1986.

Garcia took on the presidency at a critical time—but then, it is always a critical time for UNM. The state budget had been delayed because of Governor Johnson's fight with the legislature and their failure to agree on a compromise for issues such as Medicaid spending. Finally, in late May, the legislature reconvened for an extraordinary session to override Johnson's veto and pass the state budget, allowing UNM to work out its own financial plan. In the end, UNM wound up losing roughly $167,000 from the original legislative appropriation.[5]

More important to the University and its many constituents, however, was a philosophic problem that had plagued the institution since its founding in 1889: the question of access versus quality.

Hugh Witemeyer, a professor of English and president of UNM's chapter of the American Association of University Professors, compared the University of New Mexico to a circus performer "riding two different horses and hoping they don't get too far apart." He pointed out that New Mexicans looked to UNM to serve a broad cross section of the state's undergraduates while at the same time the school was expected to excel as a premier national research university. He noted that in states with a well-developed system of community colleges, the flagship universities are not called upon to perform this dual role.

Departing President Gordon had stated that the mission of UNM and the state's other universities should be better defined and that the state needed a higher education agenda. Incoming President Garcia, who had a national reputation for his studies on the role of Hispanics in U.S. society and politics, went on to state that New Mexico held a singular position among states in that no single ethnic group constituted a majority. Garcia believed that UNM had to serve a unique mix of ethnic and socioeconomic groups as well as pursue an ambitious research agenda, accommodating top scientific minds as well as students who were minimally prepared for college.

UNM Regent Jack Fortner agreed that UNM had little choice but to take on widely different roles because it was in a state with large populations of Hispanics and Native Americans who sometimes spoke a language other than English at home. He believed that as the state's largest university, UNM could not require high scores on admissions tests.

Another Regent, Richard Tolliver, had a different opinion. Higher admission standards would in the long run attract New Mexico students who shunned UNM to attend out-of-state colleges and universities, he said.

It would be up to the new president to provide the initial leadership in UNM's newly developed strategic plan intended to guide the school over the first decade of the twenty-first century. This called on the University to develop a handful of programs to a high degree of excellence, while at the same time provide New Mexico citizens with access, a term often synonymous with lenient or open admission standards. According to Provost Brian Foster, programs at UNM deemed likely to be identified for emphasis and excellence included some liberal arts programs, such as Latin American studies, art, and anthropology, as well as several programs in the health sciences. Other strong programs would include engineering fields such as nanotechnology, the science of building materials at the atomic level.[6]

Also in the spotlight was the College of Engineering's Materials Science Research Center, directed by Steve Brueck. One of the Rio Grande Research Corridor's centers of excellence, it had a state-of-the-art facility in the Research Park funded by its research grants.

There was widespread agreement that President Garcia was well suited for his leadership role at UNM. He possessed not only the academic credentials, but also other qualities essential for the head of a public university: the credibility with the governor and legislature and the political savvy he would need as the one responsible for the University's lobbying effort. This obviously entailed knowledge of the University and its relationship to the diverse populations of the state. Garcia summed it up well when he said, "We are not an ivory tower. We reflect the socio-economic environment of our state. You have to be willing to deal with a great deal of diversity, a great deal of ambiguity."[7]

Academics

One of the first bits of news accompanying Garcia's assumption of the presidency was that the 2002 freshman class would set new records with more than twenty-eight hundred students, an increase of 18.5 percent over the previous year. Credit for the increase was assigned to recruitment visits UNM staff made at least once a month to high schools around New Mexico, an enhanced web site, and the widespread dissemination of scholarships and tuition options available to incoming students,

Dean Scarnecchia

specifically, the lottery scholarships. In addition, it was anticipated that the number of entering freshmen from fall of 2001 who returned as sophomores would increase.[8] The student body became increasingly diverse, especially because of the greater number of Native American students.

As the fall semester began, it was announced that Suellyn Scarnecchia, associate dean for clinical affairs and a clinical law professor at the University of Michigan, had been appointed as the new dean of the UNM School of Law. She would teach clinical and negotiations courses and begin her services January 1, 2003. The former dean, Robert Desiderio, tendered his resignation effective June 30 but planned to remain at UNM until Scarnecchia arrived.[9]

On the good news agenda, in October 2002 *U.S. News and World Report* reported that UNM's College of Engineering ranked forty-sixth nationally, tied with Dartmouth College, the University of Massachusetts, and Vanderbilt University. Joseph J. Cecchi, dean of the college, said the graduate research programs and the diverse student population were two characteristics that set the UNM program apart from other schools. He also cited the student job and internship opportunities at Sandia and Los Alamos National Laboratories, the Air Force research labs, Intel Corporation, Philips Semiconductor, and partnerships with the College of Arts and Sciences and the Medical Center.[10]

A month later, the magazine *Hispanic Engineer & Information Technology* ranked the School of Engineering seventh best as a school for Hispanics. Robert LeFarge, director of diversity programs for the School of Engineering, said that Hispanics were the predominant minority in the engineering programs, making up 33 percent of the student body.[11]

In the fall of 2002 it was announced in UNM's *Mirage* that *Community College Week* had credited the UNM Gallup Branch with having awarded more college diplomas to Native Americans than any other public school in the country. Most degrees were in education. In its decade of existence, the bachelor of science in elementary education program had graduated 540 teachers in Gallup and 382 in Farmington, nearly half of them Native American and Hispanic.[12]

Also in 2002 word came that S. Scott Obenshain, MD, who had retired from the School of Medicine faculty in 1993 after twenty-three years, had received a prestigious award sponsored by the Harvard Medical School and the Beth Israel Hospital for his innovations in clinical education and his long-standing contributions as a clinician-teacher and scholar.

UNM's Health Sciences Center received six research grants of more than $1 million each in fiscal year 2001 and thirteen in 2002. Subjects included diabetes prevention, biomedical genomics, asthma, respiratory diseases in Native Americans, and many clinical studies. A major focus was "translational research" intended to carry scientific understanding promptly to patient care. A total of nineteen patents were issued to Health Sciences Center researchers in 2001 and 2002.[13]

The freshmen learning communities, which President Bill Gordon had inaugurated with great success, were continued under the Garcia administration. The

program also was expanded in the form of a service-learning component that was added to the second semester of the freshman year and later to the sophomore year.

The Extended University, which delivered courses and degree programs by telecommunication, media, and computers, continued to expand. Enrollments increased to 5,618 students in the fall of 2002. Course offerings grew by 9 percent, and online courses increased 79 percent. To handle the administrative load, the combined position of vice provost for extended education and dean of continuing education was separated. Jerónimo Domínguez, the outdoing dean, who was key in the establishment of the Extended University, was named vice provost, while Rita Martinez-Purson came from Northern New Mexico Community College to become dean of Continuing Education.

In October 2002 the *Lobo* reported that the UNM Communication and Journalism Department had withdrawn its application for reaccreditation from the national accrediting body. Brad Hall, department chair, said members of the department decided that withdrawal of the application was their best option considering the feedback they had received from the visiting accreditation team. Hall said loss of accreditation would not affect students graduating in the 2002–3 academic year and that accreditation might not be necessary in the future. The report of the accreditation team, received in early December, stated that the department did not comply with six of the twelve criteria used to evaluate programs.[14]

In Gallup, Elizabeth Miller was appointed director of what she described as "a branch community college" in 2003. The UNM Gallup Branch offered sixty certificate and degree programs, including five bachelor's and one master's, and enrolled more Native Americans than any postsecondary institution in the nation.[15]

In the spring of 2003 the UNM Opera Theatre celebrated its twentieth anniversary with a performance of Mozart's *The Marriage of Figaro.* The program,

The Gallup Campus, set in the mesa lands of western New Mexico, is a neighbor to the Navajo, Zuni, and Hopi tribes and boasts the nation's largest enrollment of Native Americans.

Marilyn Tyler

Bill Miller

directed since its inception by Marilyn Tyler, had won three National Opera Association awards. Earlier that year Andrea Clayton, a senior majoring in vocal performance who was scheduled to sing the role of Cherubino in *Marriage*, placed first in the association's annual performance competition.

The latest in a long series of academic publications from William R. Miller, distinguished professor of psychology and psychiatry, appeared in 2003. "Matching Alcoholism Treatments to Client Heterogeneity (Project MATCH)" was the largest clinical study ever conducted to compare alcoholism treatment methods. Some tests were conducted at UNM's Center on Alcoholism, Substance Abuse, and Addictions, providing insight into the relationship of Hispanic ethnicity to drinking problems. In addition to attaining a national reputation in research on alcoholism, Miller had studied motivational interviewing as a stimulus for behavior change and the relationships between spirituality and health outcomes.[16]

Sabine Ulibarrí

Sabine "Uli" Ulibarrí, a pioneer in the field of bilingual books, well-known author, poet, and UNM professor, died in January 2003 at the age of eighty-three. He was regarded as one of the few "true" Chicano writers, who wrote in Spanish but also in English on a facing page. He had joined the UNM faculty in 1947, taught courses in creative writing, and was chair of the Department of Modern and Classical Languages from 1971 to 1980.

He was author of about fifteen books, including *Tierra Amarilla: Cuentos de Nuevo Mexico*. During World War II, he distinguished himself by flying thirty-five missions over Europe as a B-17 ball-turret gunner and received the Distinguished Flying Cross. He returned to UNM and earned bachelor's and master's degrees, and later a doctorate in Romance languages from the University of California at Los Angeles. Ulibarrí said, "To know language is to enter into intimacy of a people. To know it is to become committed to a people, a culture, a way of life. The teacher has the magic key that will open this treasure house of love."

Ulibarrí received a number of accolades, including the 1987 Governor's Award, the UNM Regents' Meritorious Service Medal in 1989, and the Alumni Association's Zimmerman Award in 1992. Perhaps the highest honor was the one that came from his students, who called him "a great professor."[17]

Campus Development and Construction

During the summer of 2002, final work was being done on the Frank C. Hibben Center for Archaeological Research. The late UNM professor had funded the project's $4 million cost for a building to house a collection of artifacts. The center was located south of the Maxwell Museum of Anthropology. After retirement, Professor Emeritus Hibben's continued interactions with students gave him the desire to give financial help to struggling students and led to his establishing the Center for Archaeological Research, the home of the Hibben Trust, which provided scholarships. He also made annual grants to graduate students conducting research

Sabine Ulibarrí was photographed with a student at UNM's Quito Center in Ecuador in the early 1960s.

in archaeology. Hibben was a world-renowned author, explorer, and researcher deeply dedicated to his work and to the University of New Mexico.[18]

On the North Campus, the Outpatient Surgery and Imaging Building was constructed and opened on University Boulevard. The Magnetic Resonance Imaging Facility was being expanded to accommodate an enlarged mission in brain research and a new name: the Pete and Nancy Domenici MIND Institute. The Health Sciences Center opened its $6.6 million Research Incubator Building in 2003, providing easily modified lab and office space for short-term research projects.

The new Lomas Chilled Water Plant, which supplied cooling for the entire campus, was dedicated. Its opening marked the completion of the first of three projects to upgrade and renew the University's utility infrastructure.

In addition, a 397-space parking structure across the mall from Popejoy Hall was approved. Construction began, and it was slated for completion in October 2003, but it too was delayed.

On November 5, 2002, New Mexico voters passed Bond Issue B, which enabled UNM to raise $6 million to upgrade and remodel some of the campus's oldest and most heavily used buildings. The sale of the bonds would provide funds to upgrade utilities in Castetter Hall, Northrop Hall, the Physics and Astronomy Building, and Mesa Vista Hall. In addition, some of the money would be used to upgrade mechanical systems, which required a lot of traffic-snarling work in the utility tunnels.[19]

The College of Education's administration building was named for Chester Travelstead in 2003, and an endowed professorship was established in his name. Having served from 1956 to 1977 as dean of education, academic vice president, and

Jordan Adams led the Lobo women's team to the NCAA "sweet sixteen" in 2003. She is the only player in school history to record 1,000 points, 700 rebounds, and 300 blocked shots.

the University's first provost, Travelstead had continued in voluntary capacities for many years.

The fall of 2003 saw an important new chapter in the long, unfinished tale of Mesa del Sol. The State Land Office held this thirteen-thousand-acre tract between Kirtland Air Force Base and Interstate 25 in trust for the University. In 1997 plans had been announced for a pioneering development combining work sites, retail facilities, and residences for up to eighty thousand people. Later an environmental demonstration project was added and a master developer was selected for the project. By the turn of the century an outdoor amphitheater had been built and named Journal Pavilion for its sponsor. Then, on October 14, 2003, the Regents approved a land swap intended to jump start the development of Mesa del Sol. The University would give the state the Young Ranch, ninety-three hundred acres near Cochiti Dam, in return for twenty-four hundred acres at Mesa del Sol. UNM would lease about two thousand acres to the Cleveland-based developer, most likely for use as an industrial park. Details proved difficult, however, and the deal remained in limbo into 2003. [20]

Athletics

During Garcia's one-year term as president, the UNM athletic program had amazing success. The football team had its best record in five years, including a bowl appearance. The women's basketball team reached the "sweet sixteen" in the NCAA championship competition. Teams in other sports made championship or postseason appearances, including men's and women's golf; men's tennis, soccer, and outdoor track; and women's indoor track and skiing. What pleased Garcia most of all was that UNM athletes earned a record-breaking cumulative grade point average for both the fall and spring terms. This led to the University's first Academic Athletics Recognition Dinner at which some two hundred student athletes were present. Other good news included the athletic budget ending the year in the black. President Garcia was also an active participant on the board of directors of the newly formed Mountain West Conference. [21]

Meanwhile, Linda Estes, who had retired in 2000 after serving as assistant athletic director and a tireless advocate for women's sports, was rejoicing over the fact that President George W. Bush had decided to make no changes in Title IX, the federal legislation enacted in 1972 that prohibited gender discrimination in college athletics. The president's action came after he had established a committee in 2002 to review Title IX. *Albuquerque Journal* sports columnist Rick Wright wrote, "Often a controversial figure during her 31 years in UNM athletics, Estes will let others fight the battles from here. But she's pleased that battles already won won't have to be fought again." [22]

Regents

Larry Willard, after six years as president and more than eight years as a member of the UNM Board of Regents, resigned in July 2003 to become chairman of the New

Computers were sleek and ubiquitous at the turn of the twenty-first century.

Mexico Governor's Economic Development Corporation. Willard, regional president and CEO of Wells Fargo Bank New Mexico, had also served on the boards of the Anderson Schools of Management and UNM Hospital. He was highly respected as a visionary leader who had brought a strong business background to UNM.[23] In addition he was a generous contributor to the University.

Governor Bill Richardson in 2002 had appointed five new Regents: Jamie Koch, Mel Eaves, Maria Griego Raby, Donald Salazar, and Angela Cook. Doug Brown was later appointed when Salazar died. After conducting some personal research, Eaves proposed a rule that would bar UNM from doing business with Regents or their companies. Both Eaves and Koch said they were not alleging any wrongdoing, but they believed UNM should change its policies to avoid any appearance of a conflict. Willard also said in an interview that he never used his position to bring business to Wells Fargo and that he actually discouraged the bank from pursuing UNM business during his eight years as a Regent. "The company would have been a hell of a lot better off if I'd been off the board," he said.[24]

On July 15, 2003, the Regents approved a policy that stated UNM "may not engage in business with any firm or corporation in which a regent has a financial interest." It also barred UNM from doing business with an immediate family member of a Regent. The policy further required Regents to submit annual statements listing any potential conflicts of interest.[25]

Garcia's Agenda

When Garcia assumed the presidency of UNM in August 2002, he had in mind an agenda for his one and only year in office. A year later, in reporting on his activities and accomplishments, he reviewed the record, comparing goals with outcomes.

His top priority was strengthening the sense of community on the UNM campus and uniting the many constituencies that sometimes manifested conflicting objectives. He believed that the University itself was often fragmented along several lines: cultural, socioeconomic, geographical, and organizational. He resolved to work to promote good relations with faculty, students, and staff in an atmosphere of mutual trust and support. To this end, he met regularly with representatives of the Faculty Senate and the undergraduate and graduate student governments. Moreover, he worked with a group of retired faculty and staff members to charter the long-overdue UNM Retirees Association. These varied groups worked collaboratively under Garcia's leadership to advance the major objectives of the University, his report noted.

Being Hispanic, he knew much was expected of him in reaching out to the Hispanic communities around the state. He attended numerous functions of the Hispano Chamber of Commerce. He addressed eight hundred Hispanic high school juniors and seniors from throughout New Mexico as the keynote speaker at Hispano Student Day at UNM. He talked to Hispanic students all over the state about college life and the processes of getting admitted to UNM. Governor Richardson also appointed him to the board of directors of the National Hispanic Cultural Center in Albuquerque.

President Garcia expressed his pride in the University of New Mexico and its commitment to diversity. In January 2003, after a two-year vacancy, he appointed a director of the Office of Equal Opportunity. In addition, he worked closely with a newly appointed special assistant for diversity. He sought to make UNM a model for other major universities and institutions throughout the nation. Some campus traditions, such as the Yuletide hanging of the greens at the president's house, were modified to bring some additional native New Mexican traditions into holiday celebrations.

A second group Garcia endeavored to reach was the Native Americans. His report cited the allocation of $19,000 from the president's office, which the All Indian Pueblo Council and other entities would match, as seed money for a major summer scholarship fund drive for Indian students.

Garcia also sought to strengthen UNM's evening and weekend degree programs, begun with the support of then-Vice President Garcia in 1987. By 2003, forty-three degrees and thirty-seven minors or concentrations were available during the off-peak hours. More than eleven thousand students were taking some one thousand evening or weekend courses each semester. About half of all graduate courses were being offered at night.[26]

Garcia was also pleased by the Graduation Project, which he had helped inaugurate in 1997 to lure dropouts back to complete their degrees. Like the evening and weekend program, it was headed by the man who dreamed it up, David Stuart, vice provost for academic affairs and the long-time champion of nontraditional students. Stuart tracked down students who had left after earning more than ninety-eight credit hours, sometimes using a collection agency to find them. He talked them into returning to finish their degrees and helped ease their way by, for example, getting them into filled classes. By 2003 the program had brought 1,684 dropouts back, of whom 1,124 graduated.[27]

The fourth group Garcia targeted was the business community, especially those concerned with economic development. He created a position of special assistant to the president for economic development and appointed a faculty member on a part-time basis to the post, believing that the University needed one central, visible spokesperson in this area. Garcia also supported the appointment of a director of the Economic Development Center in the Schools of Management. He endeavored to add endowed chairs in areas such as microtechnology and commercialization and was involved in the creation of the Prince of Asturias Endowed Chair in Information Science and Technology. Garcia was also active in many organizations promoting education and economic development. In addition, he worked with Sandia National Labs and New Mexico State University to form the New Mexico Consortium for Bioresearch, plus a new joint Center for Policy, Security and Technology bringing together Sandia, UNM, and Lockheed-Martin.

Chris and Sandy Garcia

In government relations, President Garcia sought a stronger liaison with the state's congressional delegation as well as with others in the national legislature and executive branch. UNM retained a lobbying firm in Washington, which was credited with being a major influence in increasing UNM's federal appropriation in 2002–3 by a factor of five.

Garcia was proud that the Health Sciences Center under the leadership of Vice President R. Philip Eaton, Medical School Dean Paul Roth, and UNM Hospital Director Steve McKernan continued to thrive as one of the preeminent facilities in the Southwest for health care, research, and education. The center's programs included clubs promoting health-care careers for middle and high school students, an enrichment program for undergraduates, a clinical program for preprofessionals, and a postbaccalaureate support program. Asked if financial support was the most important ingredient for success in these programs, Dr. Eaton said, "No—caring."[28]

In funding, Garcia worked closely with the UNM Office of Development and the UNM Foundation. Judy Jones, the vice president for institutional advancement, reported that more than $42 million had been raised in 2002–3, exceeding the previous year's total by about 4.5 percent. The number of members of the President's Club nearly doubled in a year's time. The faculty received a record $260 million in research contracts and grants, exceeding the $247 million of 2001–2.[29]

"Overall," Garcia said modestly, "we had a successful year."

Praise for Garcia's leadership came from many quarters as he received high marks for communicating well with faculty and students. English Professor Hugh Witemeyer reported that Garcia had been especially good about consulting with the faculty. He stated that Garcia held regular meetings with faculty and "kept his ear to the ground."

Garcia's year as president would likely be remembered by many as a prosperous time for UNM. The University's overall budget grew a robust 10.3 percent to about $1.4 billion, equal to about a third of the state's $4.1 billion budget. The legislative appropriation to UNM also increased 5.8 percent. Government grants and contracts, a measure of UNM's research activity, grew 11.5 percent.

Life on the UNM campus, however, was not all sunshine and roses. Turmoil in the outside world created some reverberations at UNM, including antiwar protesters who regularly used UNM as a staging ground. In addition, the federal government demanded that UNM tighten controls on anthrax and other infectious agents used in medical research.

Albuquerque Journal reporter Olivier Uyttebrouck pointed out, however, that compared with the final year of Gordon's presidency in 2001–2, which Gordon dubbed "the year from hell," Garcia's term was remarkable for its lack of controversy. By contrast, the biggest news at UNM during Garcia's tenure centered on the search for his successor.[30]

As the time drew near for Garcia to step down from the presidency, he said he looked forward to getting reacquainted with his family and shedding some of the fifteen pounds he had packed on during his year in office. He joked that people were constantly shoving food under his nose at the endless round of dinners, meetings, and social events he attended. From references to his work schedule, it was clear that Garcia, like many university presidents, put in roughly seventy to eighty scheduled hours a week. Many of these hours involved being with pleasant people, doing interesting things, and eating delicious food, but the constant pressure to sit at head tables and make gracious and appropriate remarks at public functions leads to strain and stress. Among other things, the demands on a university president call for endurance and stamina. Garcia was thus grateful to hand his office over to Louis Caldera, whom the Regents selected in May 2003 after a nine-month search.

Chris Garcia, the sixty-three-year-old political science professor, said he enjoyed his year as president but looked forward to returning to his academic career. At the top of his agenda was completing a book on Hispanics in U.S. politics. Given the nature of his topic and his year as university president, a Garcia book on Hispanics in politics might start with his own autobiography.

An editorial in the *Albuquerque Journal* was appropriately entitled "Garcia made UNM Leadership Look Easy."

> Outgoing University of New Mexico President F. Chris Garcia will turn over the keys to his successor at the beginning of August. He leaves the one-year appointment with praise from nearly everyone who ventures an opinion.
>
> That's not a surprise. But it's a fitting tribute to one of UNM's most accomplished administrators in recent memory.
>
> Beyond administrative skills, Garcia, a fixture in the political science department since 1970, is an astute communicator and a nationally known authority on Hispanics in American politics.
>
> Though Garcia's tenure as president might initially have been seen as a caretaker's job, much has been accomplished.
>
> The university budget grew by more than 10 percent; legislative

appropriations grew by 6 percent. Without a doubt, it helped to have a president universally respected by the state's elected officials, many of whom were once his students.

New training for faculty members who manage large grants and contracts also came on line during his watch. A rebuilt Student Union Building opened as well.

An academic who took this job reluctantly will soon return to the classroom and his own writing.

It will be a time to finally take a breath, as he notes, and take stock of a job well done.[31]

¡Viva Garcia! UNM's first Hispano president opened the door for the second one.

¡Viva Caldera! ■

Louis Caldera

CHAPTER TWENTY-TWO
Appointment of Louis Caldera

2003—

With Chris Garcia serving as UNM's president for a fixed term, the Board of Regents had a year for the search and selection of a new president. One might think that with so much time and practice, this time the Regents, the UNM officials, and perhaps even the media would get it right. Once more, though, there was turmoil and tension surrounding the search.

After a six-month national search, on March 18, 2003, an eleven-member search committee chaired by UNM Regent Maria Griego-Raby was slated to announce recommendations based on interviews of twelve to fifteen candidates. Surprisingly, though, members of the many constituencies of UNM opened their morning edition of the *Albuquerque Journal* to a blistering editorial lambasting the presidential search committee for "inexcusable bias against a couple of home-state applicants with outstanding credentials." The editorial staff of the *Journal* took issue with the committee's failure to interview two native New Mexicans: Dan Lopez, president of New Mexico Institute of Mining and Technology in Socorro since 1993, and Manuel Pacheco, who had been president of both the multicampus University of Missouri and the University of Arizona. Some people found it difficult to believe that neither warranted an interview. Some Hispanic groups especially thought that the search committee was disinclined to consider a Latino.[1] Even Governor Bill Richardson got into the act, saying the search committee should have interviewed two high-profile Hispanics, both of whom were UNM alumni.[2]

The UNM Regents on Friday, March 21, 2003, announced five presidential finalists. The list included a former secretary of the Army, a former chancellor of the University of Colorado at Colorado Springs, a vice president of the Ohio State University, a vice president in the State University of New York system, and the dean of the School of Business at Arizona State University. The Regents said they were pleased with the selections and voted unanimously to approve them, but Juan José Peña, former president of the New Mexico Hispanic Round Table, noted the list did not include any New Mexican Hispanics or university presidents. Regent Donald Salazar stressed that most of the finalists held high administrative posts just under the presidency at large universities and said: "They may be No. 2, but they are a tier below the president at significant institutions."[3]

Facing page: Photo by Tom Brahl

The editorial writers at the *Albuquerque Journal* felt so strongly about the issue that on Wednesday, March 26, they blasted the search committee for a second time.

> If the goal of search committee members in snubbing Lopez and Pacheco was to prove they are an independent body responsible only to themselves, they did so splendidly. And they did so in a shroud of secrecy.
>
> Regrettably, they needlessly culled two good candidates from the search and greatly disappointed many New Mexicans and Hispanics in the process.
>
> The search committee's message—intentional or not—is that New Mexico is incapable of producing the quality of leaders needed to even be considered, let alone to run, its own universities.[4]

On April 4, 2003, it was announced that the five finalists had been scheduled for campus visits, starting April 8. Each was to spend two days on campus and participate in public forums with students, faculty, staff, and townspeople and alumni.

Following the visits, the Regents scheduled a meeting on April 28 to discuss the five candidates. Regents reported no intensive lobbying from off-campus groups or individuals. It was known, however, that the New Mexico Hispanic Round Table was supporting Louis Caldera.

Faculty members called on Regents to select a president with strong academic credentials. In an e-mail survey of thirty faculty members, a slight majority, sixteen, favored Carlos Santiago, chief academic administrator at the University of Albany, State University of New York, who was also an economist and Latin American scholar.

Regent Sandra Begay-Campbell said she expected the president to spend a lot of time working off campus building strong relations with legislators, donors, and others. She said, "I'm looking for a leader that will take the university to the next level. The president needs to build UNM's national reputation and find additional state and private funding. I don't need them to write papers."[5]

UNM Regents on Monday, May 6, 2003, named former secretary of the Army Louis Caldera as their choice for the University's top job. Caldera, age forty-seven, would be UNM's first noninterim Hispanic president. The Regents praised his demonstrated leadership as the Army's top civilian. He also had been a California legislator and was currently vice chancellor for advancement of the California State University system. The Regents planned to take formal action on the appointment at their regular meeting scheduled for May 13. Although some faculty had objected to Caldera, mostly because of his lack of credentials in teaching and research, several made conciliatory comments about him after his selection.[6]

The choice of Caldera was considered a turning point for the status of Hispanics in New Mexico, according to outgoing UNM President Chris Garcia.

"This is a good signal to everyone," he said. "As the pool of qualified Hispanic candidates grows, ethnicity will cease to be a significant consideration in presidential searches."

Charles Montaño, president of the New Mexico Hispanic Round Table, said he believed Caldera was chosen because Hispanic groups had demanded for years that UNM hire a Hispanic president. He went on to say he hoped Caldera would be a role model for young people in New Mexico, increase the number of Hispanics in UNM graduate programs, and improve UNM's record for hiring Hispanics.[7]

Even the *Albuquerque Journal,* which had been critical of the search process, had nice things to say about Caldera's emergence as the top pick.

It has the potential to be a historic selection. If nothing else, it clearly upends past conventions about prospective university presidents.

The selection of Louis Caldera, the 47-year-old former Army secretary, to lead the state's flagship institution of higher learning is probably not expected, but it is instructive.

The University of New Mexico Regents' selection shows their inclination toward management and fund-raising skills over traditional scholarship. As the corporate world increasingly finds leadership and strategic vision more valuable than coming up through the company, universities may begin to emphasize the need to recruit can-do managers.
. . .

His Mexican-American heritage would make him UNM's first permanent Hispanic president since the university was founded. With his reputation for hard work and eloquence in two languages, he has the makings of a fine role model.[8]

In the ensuing days there seemed to be support for considering administrative skills versus academic experience. Columnist Harry Moskos of the *Albuquerque Journal* pointed out that the selection of Caldera was not the first time that administrative ability had swayed a selection of a UNM president. He was alluding of course to the successful tenure of Tom Popejoy, who served as UNM president from 1948 to 1968. As Moskos pointed out, Popejoy did not have an earned PhD.[9]

In the days following his selection, UNM Regents often referred to Caldera as an "untraditional" choice for president. They considered his professional experience in the Army and politics a plus. It also did not bother Regents that Caldera sat on the board of directors of four large corporations, including Southwest Airlines.

Some faculty, however, renowned for thinking otherwise, believed Caldera was "too untraditional, lacking a background in scholarly research." They were critical that his job experience at a university was limited to two years as a nonacademic administrator in the California State University system. English Professor Hugh Witemeyer told the *Journal* that Caldera's appointment represented "a step in the militarization and corporatization of the university. I think the notion that the

President Caldera (left) and his wife, Professor Eva Caldera (right), attended a reception in Zimmerman Library's west wing with Rudolfo Anaya and his wife, Patricia.

president of the university doesn't have to be an educator is a dangerous notion."

Caldera's response was that the president's role has changed in an era when universities are more dependent on federal and corporate research funding. He said, "The president is the resource gatherer of the university. The president must be 'out there' seeking money from corporations, foundations, state and federal agencies. Policy makers want universities to be relevant to the lives of ordinary people in the state. If the university is going to succeed, it has to be successful in attracting resources."[10]

Olivier Uyttebrouck, whose coverage of the UNM Regents would make a book in itself, wrote the detailed story in the *Albuquerque Journal* of Caldera's path to the presidency and called it "Up the Ranks."

> Louis Caldera's life is a classic story of a first-generation American. He rose from hamburger flipper at Bob's Big Boy to Secretary of the Army. Other stops along the way: West Point, Harvard, a prestigious West Coast law firm, three terms as a California assemblyman . . . Vice Chancellor of the Cal State System . . . President of the University of New Mexico.

Caldera's parents, Benjamin and Soledad Caldera, emigrated from Chihuahua, Mexico, to El Paso in 1956 with their one-year-old daughter, Lori. Louis and a younger brother and sister were born in El Paso. The family moved to Los Angeles in 1960, where the fifth child in the family was born. The family later settled in Whittier.

Benjamin Caldera demanded that his children speak English and that they make good grades. But, strapped with health and financial problems, the father was in and out of the family and finally returned to Mexico. Louis, a high school student, became head of the family.

His hard work and good grades earned him an appointment to West Point after his graduation from high school in 1974. He was grateful for the opportunity to get an education in addition to a salary that he used to help his family in Whittier. After graduating from West Point in 1978, he led a military police platoon at Fort Dix, New Jersey, and was promoted to captain while serving on active duty with the Army from 1979 to 1983. While at Fort Dix, he was joined by his mother, his sister, and a brother.

Leaving the army after five years, he attended Harvard University, where he earned both a law degree and a master of business administration in 1987. While at Harvard, he met Eva, and they were married in 1981.

A good student at Harvard, he was hired out of law school by the Los Angeles law firm O'Melveny & Myers, one of the nation's largest and most prestigious law firms, where he worked in a department that handled public financing for government agencies and schools.

In 1992, Caldera was elected a California Assembly member, representing a downtown district of Los Angeles. He was reelected in 1994 and 1996. He became involved in national Democratic politics, and President Clinton appointed him to one of the nation's highest profile jobs as secretary of the Army. Serving from 1998 to 2001, he oversaw an annual budget of more than $70 billion. High points of his tenure included beefing up recruitment efforts and improving educational opportunities for soldiers. The Army changed its slogan to "An Army of One" to emphasize career opportunities for soldiers. He announced a plan in 1999 to improve recruitment by offering soldiers a wide number of college-level courses through the Internet. By 2003, the program was enrolling more than one hundred thousand soldiers worldwide. Under Caldera the Army also tailored its recruitment message for Hispanics, emphasizing educational and training opportunities.[11]

In 2002, he became the vice chancellor for university advancement at the California State University System office in Long Beach and president of the California State University Foundation.

Louis Caldera, a son of Mexican immigrants, moved up the ranks from El Paso to East Los Angeles to the Pentagon to the "pueblo on the mesa." And the Caldera chapter has just begun. ▪

University of N. Mex.
Albuquerque

Epilogue

Leaps Forward, Presidents, and Observations

Louis Caldera, president of the University of New Mexico when this history was being finished, is the twenty-second individual to hold the job. For the most part, his predecessors had been men of high hopes and short tenures, with only two, Zimmerman and Popejoy, serving more than ten years. Looking back on the first 114 years of the University, it seems appropriate to touch on some of the great leaps forward during the administrations of some of its most productive presidents.

When the University first opened its doors in the summer of 1892, its primary task was to prepare students to take college courses in a territory that had no public school system. In those early years, what was called a university actually was a prep school. The first administrators were really not much more than glorified principals presiding over a faculty of half a dozen teachers and fewer than a hundred students. Not all the academic work was even on the high school level, as subpreparatory courses had to be added in reading, writing, and arithmetic. This galled some presidents and grieved others.

In the fall of 1892, the University moved from rented quarters in downtown Albuquerque into the new building on the mesa roughly two miles east of the railroad tracks. Access to the campus was a steep, rutted dirt road. There were no residence halls, and a student had to walk, ride a horse, or be hauled in a wagon. The only place to live was Albuquerque, a bawdy, brawling, end-of-the-track railroad town that had little of the trimmings or trappings of civilization. In short, for most parents, it probably did not seem like a good place to send young-uns.

Albuquerque itself was isolated. In fact, the whole New Mexico Territory was isolated. Not until after statehood in 1912 and the end of World War I in 1918 did Albuquerque and New Mexico begin to connect with the rest of the world through the radio and automobiles and highways.

The University of New Mexico's first president was Elias S. Stover, a prominent Albuquerque merchant who was also a member of the Board of Regents. He held the title while first a principal and then a vice president, Hiram Hadley, administered the University's academic affairs.

The first academic president was Clarence L. Herrick, a talented man whose academic career and life were cut short by tuberculosis. He was appointed in 1897.

In the fall of 1898, the first student enrolled for college-level courses, while the prep school had an enrollment of 103. By 1901, the college enrollment had increased to 14, and the prep enrollment had dropped to 88. The first graduate courses were offered under Herrick, and the subpreparatory courses were discontinued.

Herrick's successor was one of his former students, a man referred to as "the human dynamo," the six-foot-two, effervescent William G. Tight. Tight could repair a roof, pitch a baseball, or inspire students to plant trees. He envisioned a UNM campus that would reflect the architecture of the native Southwest. He was a doer and a charmer. But he also was married and the father of a child and had left them both when he came to his post in New Mexico. Two members of the Board of Regents, a Catholic priest and a Baptist minister, probably did not view with favor a later divorce. Also, the fact that he had taken a female member of the faculty buggy riding was hot gossip in Albuquerque, where the number of churches had surpassed the number of saloons and brothels. And Tight felt obligated to dismiss two faculty members and expel one student, to the consternation of some of the Regents. So, in spite of his popularity and dynamic leadership, Tight was abruptly fired as president in 1909. He died shortly after; some said from a broken heart.

These early UNM presidents confronted a vexing problem, namely, determining what kind of curriculum would best suit the fledgling institution. In a true university, a student read and spoke Latin and Greek and mastered subjects common to those citadels of classical education in New England or the upper Midwest. In this raw territory scrambling to become a state, there were not many students well versed in Latin and Greek—or in grammar or algebra, for that matter. Admission standards were low but aspirations were high, so, in trying to make a university out of a prep school, both Herrick and Tight pledged allegiance to the classical curriculum.

Edward Dundas McQueen Gray, a real English dandy, succeeded Tight. He was a recognized scholar, spoke several languages, and aspired to make the University of New Mexico an Oxford on the Rio Grande. He also wanted male students to wear bow ties. He fell short of achieving either goal.

Finally, in 1912, New Mexico was granted statehood. This was also the year the Regents hired a real pro to head the University, Davis Ross Boyd, who had been the founding president of the University of Oklahoma. He got the University organized, stabilized, and through World War I. He brought some realism and sanity to the curriculum and laid the foundations for the University's later emphasis on regional strengths.

Boyd's successor, the persnickety David Spence Hill, came across as a fastidious bachelor who was deeply concerned about the manners and morals of the students, especially their fondness for check-to-cheek dancing. He managed to unite the campus and the community, against him, but succeeded in restoring the policy that curriculum should be structured to meet the standards of prestigious universities.

The presidencies of James F. Zimmerman and Tom Popejoy were turning points in the development of UNM. Between the two of them they served in positions of leadership for forty-one years, through Depression, war, and postwar boom.

While each appreciated the necessity of meeting national and regional standards of accreditation for undergraduate and graduate programs, each also saw the wisdom of exploiting UNM's strategic locale in the Southwest and its proximity to Latin America.

Zimmerman had the vision and energy to ground the University in its special setting, and its nickname the "pueblo on the mesa" was coined on his watch. A former professor of history, he was the first of an eventual seven UNM presidents to rise from within the faculty of the University. Among his major contributions was relating the University to its special opportunities in the Southwest, namely, the architecture, geology, geography, anthropology, folklore, and language that evolved from the Hispanic and Native American heritages and cultures.

Further, with the help of a young comptroller by the name of Tom Popejoy, he took advantage of New Deal agencies to support academic programs and pay for many buildings, including the landmarks Zimmerman Library and Scholes Hall. He saw the University through hard times and died of a heart attack at the very beginning of what would be termed the Atomic Age.

After Zimmerman's death there were two in-house candidates for UNM president: the comptroller, Tom Popejoy, and Government Department head Thomas C. Donnelly. The Regents chose neither, selecting instead J. Phillip Wernette, a Harvard PhD. Between Zimmerman's death and Wernette's arrival, however, the faculty assumed a great deal of authority in administrative affairs, a power they desired to retain. It was their hope that Wernette would be a weak president. His time in office was filled with discord, and he received word of his dismissal in February 1948 after thirty months in office.

Passed over for the presidency in 1945 because he did not have a PhD, Thomas Lafayette Popejoy was named as UNM's president in 1948. A homegrown New Mexican, he embarked upon what would be the longest tenure of any UNM president, twenty years. His experience in Washington and his positive relations with the New Mexico Legislature were augmented by widespread approval of his defense of academic freedom. He was a revered, effective president. During his many years in office he oversaw a massive expansion of the campus, including the early years of the School of Law and the beginnings of the Health Sciences Center. But when it came time to choose something on the campus to bear his name, he opted for Popejoy Hall. John Perovich, his right-hand man and eventual successor, later observed that it was interesting that the Regents should name a home for the performing arts after a Raton cowboy whose idea of classical music was a fiddler from Springer and a banjo player from Wagon Mound.

Under Popejoy, with expansion of graduate programs, increasing emphasis on research, and alliances with such scientific enterprises as Sandia and Los Alamos National Laboratories, UNM became a university in fact as well as in name. The phenomenal growth in enrollment after World War II led to visionary land acquisition as well as extensive construction on the Central Campus and the new North and South campuses. The academic program also underwent significant

Photo by Dick Meleski

change with the development of professional schools—medicine, pharmacy, nursing, law, architecture, and business—as well as emphasis on the graduate programs in the sciences, engineering, social sciences, and humanities. The University further capitalized on its cultural and geographic setting with programs indigenous to the Southwest and countries in Latin America, including the Peace Corps and Latin American Institute.

Popejoy also attained Lincolnesque stature as a defender of free speech with a rousing address to the New Mexico American Legion. The talk became a legend in University lore and endeared him in perpetuity to faculty everywhere.

Presidents Face New Challenges

When Popejoy retired in 1968, his departure marked the end of an era. The university presidency was never the same—at UNM or anywhere else.

As the war in Vietnam escalated and social issues from women's rights to the plight of the poor and the length of young men's hair polarized the nation in the 1960s, campuses across the nation changed forever. Student activism took many forms. Protestors occupied and trashed more than a few buildings, but in many cases the activists brought about positive change. For better or for worse, students stopped paying automatic respect to their titled elders. Presidents, once revered as philosopher-kings of the academic world, became targets for both demonstrators and people off-campus who longed for law and order.

At UNM, President Ferrel Heady was the first of the institution's presidents to be caught in this vise. Torn between legislators and Regents who demanded he assert himself and faculty whose ever-changing demands could rarely be met, Heady sometimes disappointed both sides. He nonetheless emerged with his honor intact, although the campus was sometimes bathed in tears emanating from both tear gas and frustration.

It is worth remembering that most UNM students, faculty, and staff carried on in the midst of this chaos. Academic programs were strengthened, the Health Sciences Center flourished, and the School of Law became a model nationwide for its special programs for minorities and women.

Exercising the author's prerogative, I am skipping over the Davis years from 1975 to 1982 and moving on to my trusted vice president and successor, John Perovich. After working at UNM for his entire career, he had the opportunity to lead his alma mater during a calmer, more positive time. A financial wizard, he invigorated the fledgling Research Park and oversaw the expansion of the North Campus. A champion of the poor, struggling student, he garnered the resources for extensive student aid programs.

Tom Farer came in as a stranger in a strange land, took on the Regents by publicly criticizing them on the University television station, and lost. He departed after eighteen fiery months with a final blast against his governing board in the national media.

Gerald May had the countenance of an eagle and the faith of a devout Christian. Conscientious, attentive to detail, he undertook the demanding tasks of the job with courage, patience, and diligence. Notable advances during his tenure included strengthening the University's capabilities in scientific research by creating research centers and nourishing the evening and weekend degree program. It also was his lot to preside over the celebration of the University's centennial and reorganization of the Development Office.

Richard Peck was a powerhouse, a no-nonsense administrator who came into office with a heavy agenda. The campus grew and changed. The Research Park lured new tenants, and residence halls sprang up on the playing fields east of Johnson Gym. Research grants and contracts doubled, then doubled again. Peck polished community relations as he and his wife Donna entertained thousands of guests. In his spare time, he turned golf games into fund-raising bonanzas. He got the University ready to enter a new century, then rode off to Florida to serve as an interim president before coming back to writing and retirement in Placitas.

William Gordon, a quiet, respected professor of psychology turned dean and provost, stepped up to take on the job as UNM president just in time to cope with the 9/11 terrorist attack and Professor Richard Berthold's callous quip. Gordon did the impossible, upholding academic tradition and Berthold's right to freedom of speech without alienating his critics. It helped that Berthold apologized and soon after left the campus. Gordon ended his four years as president by accepting a post as provost at his alma mater, Wake Forest University. Whether by accident or design, he departed while he was well ahead of the game and enjoyed the high regard of all.

Out of the classroom and away from his election prognostications, Chris Garcia emerged as a twenty-first-century Don Quixote, ready to joust with all the demons arrayed against UNM, but only for a year. A native New Mexican and UNM alumnus, and the first Hispanic to sit in the president's chair, Garcia was a charmer. With made-for-television good looks and eloquence, he had many admirers and allies, and his presidency appeared to be a year of smiling celebration.

Then came Louis Caldera, riding in like Zorro to write a blazing new chapter of UNM history. As he moved into the president's house, he had the assurance that all of the many constituencies of the University would be watching. New Mexico has never lacked for experts ready and willing to give their advice—whether graciously, gratuitously, or gleefully.

A Time of Many Presidents

In 1968, when Tom Popejoy retired from UNM, there were at least four state university presidents in the Rocky Mountain region alone who had served twenty years or more: Bill Morgan of Colorado State University, Ray Olpin at the University of Utah, Duke Humphrey at the University of Wyoming, and Richard Harvill at the University of Arizona. In the last third of the twentieth century, however, serving as a college president was not so much a matter of leadership as a battle for survival. Short tenures and high turnover were common nationwide—presidents seemed to turn over faster than losing football coaches or one-term governors.

From 1968 to 2003, UNM had nine presidents. There are several reasons for this high turnover. One has to be the politicization of the governance of public higher education. UNM Professors Stanley Pogrow and F. Chris Garcia wrote in 1976: "Nowhere is the influence of politics in education decision making more apparent than in the confused and uncoordinated manner in which higher education has developed in New Mexico."[1] In New Mexico, after several abortive attempts to centralize the governance of higher education, relations between the six state universities and the legislature came down to a competitive lobbying effort.

At UNM, there seems to have been at least a century of confusion over the respective roles of the president and the Regents concerning governance of the University. On more than one occasion, the Regents proclaimed they were not a mere rubber stamp, but the ultimate authority. At other times, presidents believed the board should determine overall policy goals, primarily by hiring the president, but delegate the actual running of the University to the president. Historically there have been gentler and kinder times when the board and the president have worked together. When serving as UNM's president, I was queried as to who was running the University and asked the students to conduct a poll. The results revealed that the person really running the University was John Perovich, the vice president for finance. As a student so accurately stated, "Every time President Davis makes a decision, he says that he first has to ask John Perovich."

An additional influence in the short terms of presidents is the media. In another time the media often supported university leaders and led the cheers for their local university. Toward the end of the twentieth century, however, the media began to substitute suspicion for confidence, hostility for advocacy, and cynicism for trust. Perhaps this was more of a problem for UNM than for other universities in smaller cities with fewer media outlets.

Television brought the public into boardrooms, and meetings of the Regents became media events. Names of nominees or candidates for presidencies became headline news, which had a chilling effect on potential candidates, particularly those who held good jobs and wanted to keep them. Public meeting laws also changed the relationship between presidents and governing boards, limiting opportunities for the president to discuss sensitive issues in the presence of the whole board. For the news media, there also seemed to be the hovering specter of the Watergate syndrome in the desire to break a big story fast and the questioning of leadership in high places. Investigative reporters loved to ask, "What did the president know and when did he know it?" Going along with that line of thinking was, "If he did not know what was going on, he should have known." The media are well aware that the fall of university presidents, once viewed as philosopher-kings, makes for juicy news.

Universities are built on trust. For example, one trusts that grades determined by faculty are based on merit. The president must have confidence in the judgment of faculty and administrators because he often has to rely upon their decisions. Thus, the president hopes that those he trusts can be trusted.

At times in the history of UNM and other institutions, the downfall of a president stemmed from just plain bad luck in having bad things happen on his watch, like an antiwar riot, a scandal in the athletic program, or even an expelled student and his powerful father who take their case to the public. While perhaps not guilty of committing questionable acts or even knowing of them, the president's credibility and ability to lead are fractured. In such cases, thoughtful, caring presidents take the bullet or fall on their swords.

Some of the high turnover in presidencies can be traced to the politicization of the governing boards, once deliberately held at arm's length from any suggestion of political interference. Appointments to governing boards of public institutions of higher learning occasionally became political plums, and governors dole out the appointments, sometimes to reward support and sometimes to get control of the institution—and sometimes both.

Perhaps the cause of the heavy turnover in university presidents is not one of these, but all. Unrelated discontent can coalesce, especially on a college campus, where it used to be said that the politics were so vicious because the stakes were

Photo by Mel Buffington

so small. That too has changed. The stakes are no longer small. Universities are now major players in state economies and interact with business and industry, sometimes as partners and sometimes as recipients of grants and contracts for research, endowments for faculty professorships and chairs, or financial aid or jobs for students. The payroll of a major university is certainly a significant element in its local community, the state, and even the nation.

Finally, there is that old adage that every man can do three things: build a fire, coach a football team, and run a university. There are always plenty of people ready to tell a president how to run the university. As my grandmother used to say, "You knew that when you hired on for the job."

Multicultural Education

From the day UNM opened its doors in 1892, it faced many challenges from a territory and later a state in which the predominant ethnic group was what we now call Hispanic. Should the curriculum meet the needs of the young people on a raw frontier or conform to standards designed for colleges in the East? Specifically, how could UNM make education relevant to the lives of the young students indigenous to the territory? How could UNM alleviate the conflict between the family's need for the labor of a child versus sending the child to school? How could the University resolve language barriers of the Hispanic and Indian populations? How could it make the use of a second language a bonus, not a handicap? How could the University capitalize on the Spanish, Mexican, and Indian cultures to initiate and expand relations with Latin American countries? And how could UNM allay the suspicions of Hispanics and Indians who were leery of sending their precious children off to be educated as Gringos (a pejorative term for Anglos), perhaps never to return to their people and culture? These were questions still begging for answers at the beginning of the twenty-first century.

In 2003 low enrollment of minority students and the shortage of minority professional employees on the campuses of the state's universities still continue to draw sharp criticism from those who believe these percentages should reflect the demographic makeup of the state.

In New Mexico in 2003, the combined minorities were 54.6 percent of the total population, which means they outnumbered the Anglos. Hispanics comprised the largest group with 42.1 percent, Native Americans were 9.5 percent, African Americans 1.9 percent, and Asians 1.1 percent. However, the Anglo culture was dominant as reflected in the language. Spanish was spoken widely, and in recent years official state documents have been printed in both English and Spanish. But in spite of New Mexico's desire to be viewed as a mosaic of peoples and cultures, there were and are great disparities in college enrollments and in the attainment of degrees. Nationally in the year 2000 Hispanics and Native Americans combined received only 5.4 percent of the total doctoral and professional degrees.[2]

Although the percentages of Hispanics and Native Americans attending college and earning degrees are better in New Mexico than in other states, the numbers still fall far short of both expectations and aspirations. This difference in levels of education is reflected in minority representation in positions of professional leadership. This is particularly true in administrative and faculty posts in colleges and universities, most of which require a doctoral or professional degree and most of which are filled by Anglos. Critics of the shortage of Hispanic and Native American faculty at UNM insist that the institution employ them in the same proportion as their percentage of the state population: more than half. Attempts to refute this argument often are based on statistics, but answers based on statistics are seldom palatable to those who are the statistics. The problem is exacerbated by that fact that across the country virtually all collegiate institutions, including many richer than UNM, are striving to promote diversity within their faculties and student bodies and aggressively recruit members of minority groups.

Basically, the problem is that not enough Hispanics and Indians get the professional degrees required for faculty or administrative positions. What can we do about it? Prime the pump from the top. In a similar situation, in another state, the legislature appropriates $600,000 a year for PhD fellowships for African American students at its major research university. The attorney for the federal government in resolving a desegregation case in Louisiana approved this action. In the chemistry program alone, there are thirty-two African American PhD candidates. Fellowships in New Mexico for Native Americans and Hispanics on the doctoral level would dramatically increase the number of terminal degrees earned by students from these ethnic groups.

How do we get more bilingual teachers into the K–12 program, especially those who speak Spanish or one of the native languages? The legislature could appropriate money to pay an annual bonus to every teacher who is fluent in two or more languages. Many Hispanics and American Indians are fluent in English. They have to be to compete. Too few Anglos are fluent in Spanish or Indian languages. It could and should be a two-way street. What a difference it would make in our schools and state!

Another problem is the economic barrier. Minority families often do not have the financial resources to send their children to college. State universities were founded on the principle of no or low tuition. Let's get back to that philosophy. In-state tuition should be low, or better yet, nonexistent. Free tuition should be provided for students who have taken the courses and prepared themselves for the college experience. This would have a dynamic impact on their selection of courses in middle school and high school. Several states in the Deep South already have such programs.

What about those minority students who are on the bubble and need preparatory courses? This has always been a challenge for frontier universities like UNM, which had to begin with a prep school to get students ready for college work. Preparatory courses can be provided at little expense, especially during the summer months. Use the dorms and engage summer faculty to teach the basic core courses in English, math, science, and social studies that will count toward graduation. Admit

Photo by Michael Mouchette

these students to full standing if they have a C average or better after the summer. Give each student the same mentoring and support you would a 225-pound halfback who can run the 40 in 4.2 seconds. This program proved to be 100 percent effective in another state.

How do we increase the number of minority administrators in our public school systems and improve their competence and use their insight into applied research? Organize courses leading to doctor of education degrees for school administrators at their regional colleges. A brief commute to attend core courses in block sessions on Tuesday and Thursday evenings would allow administrators to keep their jobs, learn new skills, and earn advanced degrees. They could also conduct research pertaining to the needs of minority students in their respective school systems. Such programs elsewhere have been highly successful and cost effective.

Educators, as well as politicians, often pay a lot of lip service to increasing the number of minorities in our student bodies and faculties. But too often they do nothing tangible to make a difference. The first step is to define the problem. The second is to find a solution. In New Mexico, our racial and cultural heritage is too great to fritter away. The question should never be "How little can we spend and keep the Natives sullen but not rebellious?" It should be "What does it take to have the best state university in the country, one that meets the needs of all its students regardless of race or color or ethnic background?" Let us find the way.

Some Personal Observations

Since 1960, I have held some kind of post at institutions of higher learning, including state universities in Colorado, Wyoming, Idaho, New Mexico, and Louisiana, as well as Oregon, where I served for seven years as chancellor of the state system. I also have been an alumni director, head football coach, dean of men, tenured professor of higher education (since 1963), executive assistant to the president for student affairs, president or chancellor (for thirty-one years), and finally a member of the board of regents for a state university. Along the way, I have had the opportunity to analyze trends and issues in higher education from different points of view. Here are some of my personal observations.

College Costs Are Going Up. The annual report, "Trends in College Pricing," which the College Board released in October 2003, states that the cost of higher education has increased more than 40 percent over the last ten years and that tuition over that period of time has jumped 47 percent. In the past year alone, tuition has increased 14.1 percent.

State Support Is Going Down. This increase in the cost to students and their families is attributed to declines in state funding, leading the president of the College Board to comment, "In a troubled economy, colleges are faced with holding down prices without sacrificing education quality."[3]

Will Potter, writing in the *Chronicle of Higher Education* in mid-2003, summed it up by saying, "The burning question for public-college officials these days is, 'Can it get any worse?'"

Last year increases in state appropriations for higher education were the smallest in a decade. Now they have dropped yet again. As colleges eliminate faculty and staff positions, restructure programs and increase tuition, some say the 2003–4 fiscal year . . . may be the worst in memory for higher education. . . . Last year, 37 states made midyear cuts to their budgets. . . . The cuts amounted to the deepest reduction in the 27-year history of the survey. The rainy-day funds that states put aside have dried up. . . .

About half of the states reduced spending on higher education in 2003–4, with an average cut of about 5 percent. . . . Eighteen states raised their higher education budgets, although most of the increases were measly.[4]

Some educators attribute the disenchantment of state legislators to a dwindling lack of confidence in the direction our public universities are going. In many states, public universities sometimes are viewed as islands of liberalism in a sea of conservatism. Conversely, faculty sometimes view their campuses as oases of enlightenment in deserts of ignorance.

Chasing the Dollar. As higher education in the United States entered the twenty-first century, more and more emphasis seemed to be placed on chasing the dollar: evaluating institutions on their ability to attract federal, state, and private dollars to subsidize contracted research. Fund raising reached a new level of importance as individual schools and colleges on university campuses began to have their own development directors. Aspirations for artistry in writing grant proposals inspired training sessions for faculty as well as conferences for professional fund raisers. Furthermore, allegiance to the goal of generating large outside gifts became a basic theme in presidential inaugural speeches, matched in eloquence only by the past fund-raising success recorded in the president's personal vita when he or she was a candidate for the job. Within the institution, within the school or college, a major reason for continued employment of neophyte professors on the tenure track often became how much money they could bring to the table through outside support for research. Many a college administrator privately hoped that the ability to attract money was one of the characteristics to be considered in evaluating a scholar or department or university, but not the only one.

Should Every Faculty Member Be a Researcher? Reduced teaching loads for faculty deeply involved in research are both desirable and justifiable. Studies have shown, however, that a high percentage of PhDs never publish anything after their dissertation. Legislators are suspicious. Some are of the opinion that a lot of faculty getting released time for research are not researching. Further, one of the truly sad fallouts of the mania for research emphasis is the number of tenure-track teachers who never publish anything and never get tenure. Because of the publish or perish push, some truly great student-centered faculty bite the dust, often to the chagrin of students, colleagues, department chairs, and even deans.

Photo by Michael Mouchette

Lower-division Undergraduates Are Balancing the Budget. Some of the disenchantment of legislators might be attributed to the fact that in some state graduate research universities, graduate assistants are teaching the bulk of the lower-division undergraduate classes. Usually the rationale is that this practice frees up the more experienced full-time faculty for research and publishing. What seldom is mentioned is that graduate assistants are cheaper than full-time faculty, but they may not be as knowledgeable about the subject or as skilled in presenting it.

Identity Crisis and Classifications. The emphasis on research has become a driving force in higher education, resulting in an identity crisis for many institutions. The Carnegie Foundation in 1996 came up with the classification of Doctoral/Research I universities, which was very satisfying to those universities receiving the ranking. For some other institutions, however, chiefly those that were something other than Doctoral/Research I universities, it was a put-down. They looked upon themselves as second-class citizens in the academic pyramid, a real kick in the old self-esteem. The foundation in 2000 changed its classifications to Doctoral/Research—Extensive and Doctoral/Research—Intensive, which meant that all those who wanted to be research universities could and nobody's feelings were hurt.

Colleges and Normal Schools: Gone with the Wind. Further, as we enter the twenty-first century, very few institutions are satisfied with being colleges. Many want to call themselves universities, which some consider a more prestigious term. A university used to be generally defined as "a collection of colleges at an institution which also offered doctoral degrees," but no more. A postsecondary institution has almost unlimited autonomy, especially in what it chooses to call itself. Thus, many highly respected colleges and normal schools are gone with the wind in a higher education landscape of universities only.

State-assisted Universities. A new term in "pedaguese" that raises the blood pressure of legislators is "state-assisted," which is used in place of the old term "state-supported." Sometimes it is just a new way of bookkeeping. In days gone by, many activities that were allegedly self-supporting and generated both revenue and expenditures, such as residence halls, food services, athletics, bookstores, interest on endowed funds, grants and gifts, state and government contracts, university presses, and others, were classified as auxiliary services. The general operating budget terminology was usually used in reference to funds that were generated from tuition and fees in addition to legislative appropriations. Someone, somewhere, came up with a new way to crunch the numbers in which all an institution's revenues and expenditures were lumped together. In this way, an institution could show that it generated more funds than the legislature appropriated and could thus claim to be merely "state-assisted," rather than "state-supported." This ploy can make legislators feel unappreciated.

National Rankings. National magazines have sold lots of copies by featuring their choices of the nation's best colleges and universities. Readers are not really surprised, though, that the rating game seems to be heavily stacked in favor of the elite institutions in the East, the upper Midwest, and California, meaning the criteria give brownie points for the number of applicants turned away or the emphasis on graduation and retention rates. Most penalized are those colleges and universities in urban areas with large numbers of minority students or working students, namely the lower-income, often underprepared, second-chance students who may be discovering their own abilities and ambitions for the first time. Sometime, some magazine is going to get around to ranking the "people's colleges" on how well they serve their communities or all the people of a state.

Governance of Higher Education. In some states, where each institution or system has its own governing board, it continues to be open season on the members of the legislature. Hordes of lobbyists hound these holders of public office as universities and colleges compete for public dollars. While from time to time, one or more institutions in a state seem to forge ahead, quite often this competition results in an overall watering down wherein all institutions are treated the same— badly. Some legislators are delighted to have good reasons to say no. Competing institutions quarreling over insufficient funds often provide them with good reasons to say no. Thus, changes in the governing structure have been of great interest in the last half century. In some states, officials have put their intramural squabbles behind them and organized strong centralized governing boards with jurisdiction over all postsecondary education. Like Solomon, other states have split the baby, creating a central board for the state-supported colleges and universities, but leaving the community, technical, and junior colleges with boards of their own. Some states have taken a third route by creating coordinating councils with limited power, leaving the institutions and systems with their own governing boards and direct access to the legislature. Other states, including New Mexico, have stayed with the status quo, which usually suits the big universities, which are the power brokers.

Intercollegiate Athletics. Even the purists in academe have to admit that sometimes a great athletic program can attract favorable national attention for a university. Notre Dame's prowess on the football field preceded its academic reputation. It is no accident that Stanford University, one of the truly elite national universities, also ranks near the top in its athletic program. Arizona State University's rapid growth was not damaged by its outstanding football and baseball programs. When graduation rates of athletes are published and university presidents are quoted, however, there is much hand wringing about the overemphasis on college athletics, particularly football and basketball. Most of the problems could be resolved by going back to the rules of half a century ago when athletes had to complete one year of solid academic work before they were eligible for varsity competition. Today, a freshman can participate in as many as three football games before ever darkening the door of a classroom.

Faculty Salaries. Studies have repeatedly shown that where there is great education, there are great teachers. Lock-step salary schedules, paying bad teachers as much as good ones, have been the bane of public schools and too often of universities. One way to recognize and reward great teaching is through endowed chairs and professorships with the interest on endowments used as salary supplements. Matching funds from the state legislature often provide attractive lures for support from the private sector for endowed chairs and professorships. Some states, for example, provide a 40–60 match: $40,000 is appropriated for an endowed professorship against a $60,000 donation, or $400,000 for an endowed chair to match a $600,000 gift. In a very short time, this can have a tremendous impact on retaining valued professors as well as recruiting nationally for new professors.

The Curriculum. Several of UNM's most successful presidents emphasized the anthropology, geology, history, literature, political science, language, and cultural diversity of the Southwest and Latin America. Tom Popejoy oversaw the founding and flourishing of a vast medical complex that emphasized family practice and service to rural areas, a law school that excelled in practical law clinics and special programs for Native Americans and Hispanics, and professional programs in science and engineering that led to strong alliances with national laboratories such as Sandia and Los Alamos. Along with all this, the University was striving to adhere to the standards by which great universities are judged, wherever they are.

Balancing Access and Quality. While striving to fulfill the dual role of serving a cross section of New Mexico undergraduates and also meeting national standards for research institutions, UNM takes a drubbing in *U.S. News and World Report's* annual publication, "America's Best Colleges." UNM's rankings are consistently in the lower two tiers of collegiate institutions. Factors considered in these rankings often include high school class rank and standardized test scores of entering freshmen, student retention and graduation rates, academic reputation, faculty pay, and spending per student. Rankings often reward highly selective schools that admit only top high school students. As UNM Provost Brian Foster has pointed out, if a university accepted only a tiny portion of the applicants, it received a higher ranking. He said, "My position is that quality and access are not opposed ideas."[5]

In the standards used for national rankings, public colleges or universities located in urban areas (commuter institutions as opposed to residential colleges) with large numbers of students who work full-time or part-time while attending school, and/or with large minority enrollments, often fare poorly. Some higher education officials, usually in the low-ranking institutions, are of the opinion that the ranking standards often reflect values typical of the preWorld War II era when less than 25 percent of college-age students attended college and higher education was for a select socioeconomic and intellectual elite.

The Beat Goes On

If these observations about the present state of higher education seem to emphasize the problems, it is heartening for me to remember the people I knew at UNM who had the solutions for the problems of their day. It makes me hopeful that new people will find solutions for the current problems.

It is easy to look at the sprawling campuses and facilities that keep multiplying or expanding and think those things just happen. People with long memories, however, recall that what is now the Health Sciences Center had humble beginnings in a former mortuary and soda bottling plant, or that the School of Law began in the old football stadium with only a few courses. Sometimes the beginnings were more than humble—they were downright impoverished. Those involved in the struggle know that every building, every appropriation, every program represents a battle fought and won.

The battles are not fought by presidents alone, of course. Most of a university's accomplishments derive from the work of its faculty, administrators, and staff. Each person ever associated with UNM will have his or her own list of great teachers or colleagues. While this version of UNM's first 114 years is finished, the history of the University of New Mexico will go on and on. Remember that Oxford University started in the twelfth century and is still going on. Perhaps in eight hundred years some student will pick up this volume and get some insight into what the University of New Mexico was like as it entered the twenty-first century.

Sunset on the Sandias

Meanwhile, to get the feeling of the University of New Mexico, walk the campus in the early evening, that time of day when the Pueblo Style buildings turn a warm gold and the shadows spread across the duck pond and Smith Plaza. Near the pond, you can hear the tinkling of the fountains, the chirping of the birds, the hum of the campus with students hurrying to wherever they are going. Watch the last rays of the sunset turn the Sandias that watermelon color for which they have been named. Join in spirit those who for more than a century have been a part of this miracle on the mesa—this University of New Mexico—*el milagro en la mesa.* ■

Appendices

Editor's Note: Many of these appendices were compiled from the UNM catalogs, which are the only authoritative source for much of the University's history. Because catalogs are prepared months before their publication and many catalogs cover two academic years, they are often late in announcing the creation of a new department, the appointment of a new dean, and other changes. Corrections to the historical record will be welcomed by the University Archives.

Facing page: Tight Grove, west of Hodgin Hall, is still the "front entrance" to the Central Campus. Many of the pines planted by Tight and his students are still alive. The bronze Lobo, sculpted by Michelle Middleton and cast by Richard Wortman, was a gift to the University from the Alumni Association during its hundredth-birthday celebration in 1997. Photo by Tom Brahl

Appendix 1: Snapshots of the University at 25, 50, 75, and 100 Years

1914

Fall Enrollment	137
Degrees Awarded	12
Faculty	19
Buildings	8
Library Volumes	12,000
Estimated Resident Student Cost per year	$238

Academic Units

College of Letters and Science (departments of biology, chemistry, English, French, geology, German, Greek, history and international law, Latin, library science, mathematics, physics, physical training, psychology and philosophy, social science, Spanish)

School of Education

School of Fine Arts

School of Applied Science (departments of civil engineering, electrical engineering, home economics)

Extension Division

Preparatory Department

1939

Fall Enrollment	1,565
Degrees Awarded	242
Faculty	139
Total Assets	$3.2 million
Buildings	23
Library Volumes	75,724
Tuition for Resident Undergraduate	$10 per credit hour
Estimated Resident Student Cost per year	$425
Private Donations	$38,957.73

Academic Units

College of Arts and Sciences (departments of anthropology, architecture, biology, chemistry, economics & business administration, English, geology, government & citizenship, Greek & Latin, history, mathematics, modern languages & literatures, philosophy, physics, psychology, sociology)

College of Education (departments of elementary education, secondary education, educational administration, educational psychology, health, home economics, library science, physical education)

College of Engineering (departments of civil engineering, electrical engineering, mechanical engineering, petroleum engineering)

College of Fine Arts (departments of art, architecture, dramatic art, music)

General College

Graduate School

Summer Session

Field Sessions

1964

Fall Enrollment	10,723
Degrees Awarded	1,363
Total Degrees Awarded 1901–64	17,353
Faculty	452
Revenues	approximately $20 million
Campus	$60 million plant, 500 acres
Buildings	64 plus Los Alamos Graduate Center

Libraries (Volumes)

Zimmerman (362,315),

Fine Arts (15,000),

Law (59,000),

Tuition for Resident Undergraduate	$17 per credit hour
Estimated Resident Student Cost per year	$761
Research	$4.59 million in contracts
Private Donations	$1.13 million

Academic Units

University College

College of Arts and Sciences (Division of Foreign Studies; departments of anthropology, biology, chemistry, economics, English, geography, geology, government, history, journalism, mathematics & statistics, modern & classical languages, philosophy, physics & astronomy, psychology, sociology, speech)

College of Business Administration (concentrations in accounting, finance, general business, industrial administration, marketing, executive secretary, data processing)

College of Education (departments of art education, educational & administrative services, elementary education, health, physical education & recreation, home economics; secondary education; curricula in business education, industrial arts, library science, music education)

College of Engineering (departments of chemical engineering, civil engineering, electrical engineering, mechanical engineering)

College of Fine Arts (departments of architecture, art, dramatic art, music, music education)

Graduate School

School of Law

School of Medicine

College of Pharmacy (Dental Hygiene Program)

1989

Fall Enrollment	28,615
Degrees/Majors Offered	74
Degrees Awarded	4,266
Total Degrees Awarded 1901–89	approximately 87,000
Faculty	2,300
Budget	$350.5 million
Buildings	137

plus Los Alamos Branch, Gallup Branch,
Northern Branch, Valencia Branch,
Santa Fe Graduate Center

Libraries (Volumes)
General (Zimmerman, Centennial Science &
Engineering, Fine Arts, Tireman Learning
Materials, and William J. Parish: 1.3 million volumes)
Medical Center (110,000)
Law (150,000)

Private Voluntary Support	$13.4 million
Alumni	101,000
Tuition for Resident Undergraduate	$57.50 per credit hour

Academic Units

Robert O. Anderson Schools of Management

School of Architecture and Planning

College of Arts and Sciences (departments of American studies, anthropology, biology, chemistry, communication, communicative disorders, economics, English, geography, geology, history, Ibero-American studies, international studies, journalism, Latin American studies, linguistics, mathematics & statistics, modern & classical languages, philosophy, physics & astronomy, political science, psychology, religious studies, sociology)

Division of Dental Programs

College of Education (departments of art education, counseling & family studies, curriculum & instruction in multicultural teacher education, educational administration, education foundations, health promotion, physical education & leisure programs, nutrition, special education, technological & occupational education, business education, industrial/ technical education)

College of Engineering (departments of chemical-nuclear engineering, civil engineering, computer science, electrical engineering & computer engineering, mechanical engineering)

College of Fine Arts (departments of art, music, music education, theatre arts, dance, film/television)

Interdisciplinary Studies and Special Programs (ethnic programs, general honors, Reserve Office Training Corps, women studies)

School of Law

School of Medicine

School of Nursing

College of Pharmacy

Division of Public Administration

University College

Division of Community Service

Graduate Programs

Evening and Weekend Programs

Appendix 2: Enrollment*

Year	Enrollment		Year	Enrollment
1931	1,000		1972	19,637
1932	1,037		1973	20,547
1933	1,063		1974	21,462
1934	1,062		1975	23,014
1935	1,209		1976	23,685
1936	1,352		1977	23,043
1937	1,413		1978	22,687
1938	1,442		1979	23,561
1939	1,482		1980	24,482
1940	1,565		1981	25,200
1941	1,713		1982	26,692
1942	1,500		1983	27,095
1943	1,205		1984	27,767
1944	1,078		1985	27,988
1945	941		1986	27,484
1946	924		1987	28,157
1947	3,649		1988	28,015
1948	4,495		1989	28,615
1949	4,921		1990	29,165
1950	4,795		1991	30,129
1951	4,643		1992	30,443
1952	3,796		1993	31,199
1953	4,086		1994	30,668
1954	4,163		1995	30,964
1955	5,028		1996	30,534
1956	5,854		1997	30,107
1957	6,648		1998	30,241
1958	6,914		1999	30,871
1959	7,824		2000	29,888
1960	7,595		2001	30,048
1961	8,086		2002	31,975
1962	8,642		2003	32,696
1963	9,494			
1964	10,723			
1965	12,186			
1966	12,979			
1967	13,830			
1968	14,440			
1969	15,692			
1970	18,061			
1971	19,541			

*Official fall-semester head count from Office of the Registrar. Figures before 1931 are unreliable; branch campus and off-campus enrollment included beginning 1958.

Appendix 3: Regents

Governor	Term	Regents Appointed	Term
L. Bradford Prince	1889–93	Mariano S. Otero	1889–94
		G. W. Meylert	1889–94
		Henry L. Waldo	1889–1908
		Elias S. Stover	1889–1910
		Frank W. Clancy	1889–1912
William T. Thornton	1893–97	William B. Childers	1894–99
		James H. Wroth	1895–97
Miguel A. Otero	1897–1906	Juan C. Armijo	1897–1903
		James H. Wroth	1899–1909
		E. V. Chavez	1903–8
Herbert J. Hagerman	1906–7		
George Curry	1907–10	Fletcher Cook	1908–9
		A. M. Mandalari (Mandalaria)	1909–12
		W. D. McBee	1909–11
		R. W. Hopkins	1911
William J. Mills	1910–12	W. J. Johnson	1910
		James H. Wroth	1910–12
William C. McDonald	1912–17	R. W. D. Bryan	1912–13
		John A. Reidy	1912–27
		Howard L. Bickley	1912–17
		Nathan Jaffa	1912–27
		A. W. Cooley	1912–13
		George L. Brooks	1913–19
		W. G. Hayden (Haydon)	1913–17
Ezequiel C. de Baca,	1917–19	Antonio Lucero	1917–19
Washington E. Lindsey		John R. McFie, Jr.	1917–20
		Nestor C. Montoya	1919–21
		Antonio A. Sedillo	1919–27
Octaviano A. Larrazolo	1919–21	William E. Gortner	1920–21
		Mrs. Rupert F. Asplund	1921–23
		Thomas F. Keleher, Jr.	1921–23
Merritt C. Mechem	1921–23	Mrs. Frances Nixon	1922–27
		Charles H. Lembke	1922–27
James F. Hinkle	1923–25		
Arthur T. Hannett	1925–27		

Richard C. Dillon	1927–31	Mrs. Reed Holloman	1927–31
		John F. Simms	1927–31
		Mrs. Laurence F. Lee	1927–29
		Frank Light	1927–31
		A. C. Torres	1927–31
		Orie L. Phillips	1928–31
		W. R. Lovelace	1931–37
Arthur Seligman	1931–33	M. Ralph Brown	1931–33
		Glenn L. Emmons	1931–33
		Henry G. Coors, Jr.	1931–34
		Mrs. O. N. Marron	1931–33
Andrew W. Hockenhull	1933–35	Margaret Page Hood	1933–35
		John J. Dempsey	1933–35
		John W. Hernandez	1933–35
Clyde Tingley	1935–39	P. G. Cornish, Jr.	1936–37
		Adolfo C. Gonzales	1936–47
		Hugh B. Woodward	1936–37
		Mrs. Floyd W. Lee	1936–47
		Joseph L. Dailey	1938–39
		R. Fred Pettit	1938–39
John E. Miles	1939–43	Sam G. Bratton	1939–51
		Jack Korber	1939–59
		Mrs. John Milne	1939–51
John J. Dempsey	1943–47		
Thomas Jr. Mabry	1947–51	David Chavez	1947
		Tibo J. Chavez	1947–51
		Mrs. George W. Savage	1947–51
Edwin L. Mechem	1951–55	Mrs. Franklin Bond	
		(Later Mrs. Oscar B. [Ethel] Huffman)	1951–57
		Jack Walton	1951–54
		Wesley Quinn	1951–59
		Paul F. Larrazolo	1951–55
John F. Simms	1955–57	Ralph R. Lopez	1955–61
		Finlay MacGillivray	1955–61
Edwin L. Mechem	1957–59	Dorothy Woodward	1957–60
John Burroughs	1959–61	Howard C. Bratton	1959–68
		Lawrence H. Wilkinson	1959–70
		Mrs. J. P. (Dorothy) Brandenburg	1960–63
Edwin L. Mechem	1961–62	Thomas R. Roberts	1961–68
		Bryan G. Johnson	1961–67
Tom Bolack	1962	Edwin L. Mechem	1962–63

Jack M. Campbell	1963–67	Mrs. Fred C. Luthy	
		(later Mrs. Frank A. [Cyrene] Mapel)	1963–74
David F. Cargo	1967–71	Arturo G. Ortega	1967–72
		Walter F. Wolf, Jr.	1968–72
		Norris Bradbury	1969–70
Bruce King	1971–75	Calvin Horn	1971–82
		Austin G. Roberts	1971–76
		Albert G. Simms II	1973–77
		Emmett E. Garcia	1973
		Henry Jaramillo	1973–84
Jerry Apodaca	1975–79	Mrs. William A. (Ann) Jourdan	1975–86
		Phillip U. Martinez	1977–84
		Colleen Maloof	1977–88
Bruce King	1979–83		
Toney Anaya	1983–87	John D. Paez	1983–88
		Jerry Apodaca	1985–90
		Robert L. Sanchez	1985–90
Garrey Carruthers	1987–91	Frank Borman	1987–92
		Sigfried Hecker	1987–95
		Ken Johns	1987–92
		Roberta Cooper Ramo	1989–94
		C. Gene Samberson	1989–94
Bruce King	1991–95	J. E. (Gene) Gallegos	1991–96
		Arthur D. Melendres	1991–96
		Barbara G. Brazil	1993–98
		Penny Taylor Rembe	1993–98
Gary Johnson	1995–2003	Mary A. Tang	1995–2001
		Eric A. Thomas*	1995–97
		Larry D. Willard	1995–2003
		David A. Archuleta	1997–2003
		Kimberly A. Richards*	1997–99
		Richard Tolivar	1997–2003
		Jack L. Fortner	1999–
		Judith C. Herrera	1999–2003
		Jason Bousliman*	1999–2000
		Sandra K. Begay-Campbell	2001–
		Eric Anaya*	2001–2
Bill Richardson	2003–	Donald M. Salazar	2003
		John M. (Mel) Eaves	2003–
		Maria Griego-Raby	2003–
		James H. (Jamie) Koch	2003–
		Andrea L. Cook*	2003–

*student Regent

Appendix 4: Chief Administrators of the University of New Mexico*

A. Presidents and Chief Academic and Administrative Officers

President	Chief Academic Officer	Chief Administrative Officer
Elias S. Stover 1892–97	Vice President in Charge Hiram Hadley, 1894–97	
Clarence L. Herrick 1897–1901		
William George Tight 1901–9		
Edward D. M. Gray 1909–12		
David Ross Boyd 1912–19	Dean of the University Charles E. Hodgin, 1911–12, 1914–16 Vice President Charles E. Hodgin, 1917–25	
David Spence Hill 1919–27		
James F. Zimmerman 1927–44		
John P. Wernette 1945–48		
Thomas L. Popejoy 1948–68	Academic Vice President France V. Scholes, 1949–57 Edward F. Castetter, 1957–61 Harold L. Enarson, 1960–66 Ferrel Heady, 1967–68	Administrative Vice President Harold L. Enarson, 1960–61 Sherman E. Smith, 1967–70 Vice President for Business and Finance John Perovich, 1968–82
Ferrel Heady 1968–75	Academic Vice President Chester C. Travelstead, 1969–70 Vice President for Academic Affairs Chester C. Travelstead, 1970–77	Vice President for Administration and Development Sherman E. Smith, 1970–73

*Acting or interim appointments omitted.

President	Chief Academic Officer	Chief Administrative Officer
William E. Davis 1975–82	Provost Chester C. Travelstead, 1977–79 McAllister H. Hull, 1979–87	Administrative Vice President for Student Affairs, Alumni Relations, and Development Marvin D. Johnson, 1977–85 Vice President for Administration and Planning Joel M. Jones, 1987–88
John Perovich 1982–84		
Tom Farer 1985–86	Vice President for Academic Affairs Robert J. Desiderio, 1985–86	
Gerald W. May 1986–90	Vice President for Academic Affairs F. Chris Garcia, 1987–90	Vice President for Administration and Planning Joel M. Jones, 1987–88 Vice President for Business and Finance David L. McKinney, 1987–99
Richard Peck 1990–98	Provost/Vice President for Academic Affairs Paul G. Risser, 1991–93 Provost Mary Sue Coleman, 1993–97 Provost/Vice President for Academic Affairs William C. Gordon, 1997–99	
William Gordon 1998–2002	Provost/Vice President for Academic Affairs F. Chris Garcia, 1998–99 Brian L. Foster, 2001–	Vice President for Business and Finance Julie C. Weaks, 1999–2002
F. Chris Garcia 2002–3		Vice President for Business and Finance Julie Weaks Gutierrez, 2002–

B. Chief Research Officers

Vice President for Research
George Springer, 1969–73

Associate Provost for Research and Academic Services
Paul H. Silverman, 1977–79

Associate Provost for Research
Joseph V. Scaletti, 1979–87

Vice President for Research
Paul Risser, 1987–93

Associate Provost for Research
Ellen Goldberg, 1993–97

Associate Vice President/Research
Lee. B. Zink, 1997–2001
Lee Renis, 2001–3

Vice Provost for Research
Terry Yates, 2003–

C. Chief Health/Medical Officers

Vice President for Health Sciences
Robert S. Stone, 1973–74
Robert Kugel, 1975–77
Leonard Napolitano, 1977–79

Director of the Medical Center and
Dean of the School of Medicine
Leonard Napolitano, 1979–95

Vice President for Health Sciences
Jane Henney, 1995–99
R. Philip Eaton, 2001–

D. Vice President for Student Affairs

Harold W. Lavender, 1968–77
Mari-Luci Jaramillo, 1985–89
Fred M. Chreist, Jr., 1989–91
Orcilia Zuniga Forbes, 1991–97
Eliseo Torres, 1997–

E. Chief External Affairs Officers

Vice President for Regional and Community Affairs
Alex Mercure, 1975–77

Associate Provost for Community Education
Alex Sanchez, 1979–87
Vice President for Community and International Programs
Alex Sanchez, 1987–89

Vice President for Institutional Advancement
Orcilia Zuniga Forbes, 1995–98
Judy K. Jones, 1999–2002
Vice President for Advancement
Judy K. Jones, 2002–

Appendix 5: Degree Programs*

1896–97	Bachelor of Pedagogy†
1897–98	Bachelor of Arts
	Bachelor of Science
	Bachelor of Literature†
	Master of Arts
	Master of Science
1916–17	Bachelor of Arts in Commerce†
	Bachelor of Fine Arts
	Bachelor of Music
	Bachelor of Science in Chemical Engineering (Engineering Chemistry)
	Bachelor of Science in Civil Engineering
	Bachelor of Science in Electrical Engineering
	Bachelor of Science in Geological Engineering†
	Bachelor of Science in Home Economics†
1929–30	Bachelor of Arts in Education
	Bachelor of Science in Education
1933–34	Bachelor of Science in Physical Education (Health and Physical Education; Bachelor of Science in Health; Bachelor of Science in Physical Education)†
1935–36	Bachelor of Science in Mechanical Engineering
1936–37	Bachelor of Fine Arts in Art (Bachelor of Arts in Fine Art)
	Bachelor of Fine Arts in Dramatic Art†
	Bachelor of Fine Arts in Music†
1937–38	Doctor of Philosophy
1938–39	Bachelor of Business Administration
	Bachelor of Science in Petroleum Engineering†
1941–42	Bachelor of Arts/Bachelor of Science with ensign's commission, United States Navy†
1944–45	Bachelor of Science in Pharmacy (Bachelor of Pharmacy)†

---

* By date of first listing in catalog; later names in parentheses.

† No longer listed as a degree in 2003–5 catalog.

Bachelor of Science in Naval Science (Naval Science Engineering)†
Bachelor of Science in Industrial Arts†
Bachelor of Science in Industrial Arts Education†

1948–49   Bachelor of Laws (Juris Doctor)
Bachelor of Science in Architectural Engineering†

1950–51   Master of Business Administration

1956–57   Bachelor of Science in Nursing

1957–58   Bachelor of Architecture

1958–59   Bachelor of Science in Medical Technology (Bachelor of Science in Medical Laboratory Sciences)
Doctor of Education

1961–62   Doctor of Science in Engineering†

1962–63   Bachelor of Arts in Recreation†

1965–66   Master of Fine Arts

1966–67   Bachelor of Music Education
Bachelor of Science in Home Economics Education†

1967–68   Doctor of Medicine

1969–70   Bachelor of Science in Health Education†

1970–71   Master of Architecture
Bachelor of University Studies
Associate of Arts in Human Services†
Associate of Science in Dental Hygiene†
Bachelor of Science in Dental Hygiene

1971–72   Bachelor of Science in Home Economics†
Associate of Arts in Education†
Associate of Arts in Human Services†
Associate of Science in Laboratory Technology†

1972–73   Associate of Arts in Community Services†

1973–74   Bachelor of Engineering
Associate of Science in Medical Engineering Technology[†]
Associate of Science in Instrumentation Engineering Technology[†]
Associate of Science in Radiologic Technology[†]
Associate of Science in Nuclear Medicine Technology[†]

1974–75   Associate of Science in Pre-Engineering[†]
Associate of Science in Medicine for Physician's Assistant[†]

1975–77   Master of Industrial Administration[†]
Master of Science in Computing and Information Science
Associate of Arts in Community Services[†]
Associate of Science in Radiologic Technology[†]
Associate of Science in Nuclear Medicine Technology[†]
Bachelor of Science in Physical Therapy[†]

1977–79   Master of Management
Bachelor of Science in Computing and Information Science
Associate of Science in Instrumentation Engineering Technology[†]
Associate of Science in Laser Engineering Technology[†]

1979–81   Bachelor of Science in Electrical and Computer Engineering
Bachelor of Arts in Environmental Design

1981–83   Bachelor of Science in Computer Science
Master of Science in Nursing

1983–85   Master of Community and Regional Planning
Bachelor of Science in Nuclear Engineering
Bachelor of Science in Computer Engineering
Associate of Professional Studies in Commercial Skills[†]
Associate of Applied Science in Computer Programming[†]

1985–87   Master of Accounting (Master of Accountancy)
Master of Science in Pharmaceutical Sciences[†]
Doctor of Science in Pharmaceutical Sciences (Doctor of Pharmacy)
Master of Science in Industrial Technical Education[†]

1987–89   Bachelor of Science in Construction Engineering
Bachelor of Science in Construction Management[†]
Associate of Applied Science in Business Technology[†]
Associate of Applied Science in Secretarial Studies[†]
Associate of Applied Science in Quality Control[†]

1989–91   Master of Engineering[†]
            Associate of Applied Science in Respiratory Therapy[†]

1993–95   Master of Public Health
            Master of Music
            Master of Water Resources Administration

1991–2001   Master of Landscape Architecture
            Master of Occupational Therapy

2002–5   Master of Engineering in Hazardous Waste Engineering
            Master of Engineering in Manufacturing Engineering
            Master of Physical Therapy

Appendix 6: Academic Deans and Department Chairs[a]

A. Preparatory Programs

Preparatory Department	George S. Ramsay	1892–94
	Marshall R. Gaines	1894–95
Commercial Department	Josephine Parsons	1894–1911
Preparatory School	D. M. Richards	1909–10
General College	Jay Carroll Knode	1935–48
	Thomas C. Donnelly	1948–53
	Dudley Wynn	1954–55
	John R. Rinaldi	1983–87

B. College of Education[b]

Normal Department	George S. Ramsay	1892–94
	Alcinda L. Morrow	1894–96
	Charles E. Hodgin	1896–99
School of Education	Charles E. Hodgin	1906–15
College of Education	Simon P. Nanninga	1928–54
	Charles R. Spain	1954–56
	Chester C. Travelstead	1956–69
	Richard E. Lawrence	1969–74
	David W. Darling	1974–83
	David Colton	1983–91
	Peggy Blackwell	1993–97
	Viola Florez	1998–
Physical Education for Men	Roy W. Johnson	1926–35
	Gwinn Henry	1935–38
	Roy W. Johnson	1947–58
	Armand Seidler	1958–60
Physical Education for Women	Mary Cheshire	1933–37
	Catherine Ruth Campbell	1937–39
	Leo Lindsey Gleaves	1939–46
	Mercedes Gugisberg	1946–60

[a] By date of first listing in catalog. Central Campus degree-granting units only (for some other academic units see appendix 7). Units appearing in catalogs before about 1920 did not necessarily confer degrees; conversely, degrees in education were conferred between 1915 and 1928 although there was no school or college of education. Acting or interim appointments omitted.

[b] Name in effect in 2003.

Health, Phy Ed & Recreation for Women	Mercedes Gugisberg	1960–61
Health, Phy Ed & Recreation for Men	Armand Seidler	1960–63
Elementary Education[c, d]	Loyd S. Tireman	1933–60
	Harold D. Drummond	1962–68
	David Darling	1968–73
	Mari-Luci Jaramillo	1973–75
	Herman E. Warsh	1975–77
	Donald E. Kelly	1979–81
	Marlis Mann	1981–83
	Donald Kelly	1983–85
School Administration	Simon P. Nanninga	1933–57
	Paul V. Petty	1957–59
Educational & Administrative Services	Paul V. Petty	1959–68
Educational Administration[c]	Richard Holemon	1968–71
	Ronald E. Blood	1971–74
	Paul A. Pohland	1974–87
	Mike Milstein	1987–91
	Paul A. Pohland	1991–93
Home Economics[e]	Elizabeth Simpson	1933–53
	Grace Long Elser	1953–66
	Ednell Snell	1966–75
	Mary M. Smith	1979–81
	Richard M. Smith	1981–83
	Mary M. Smith	1983–85
Family Studies	Richard M. Smith	1985–87
	Virginia C. Shipman	1987–93
Secondary Education[c]	John W. Diefendorf	1933–58
	Bonner M. Crawford	1953–58
	Wilson Ivins	1958–67
	Robert J. Doxtator	1968–74
	Roderic L. Wagoner	1974–81
Secondary & Adult Teacher Education[c, d]	Paul W. Tweeten	1981–83
	Roderic L. Wagoner	1983–85

[c] Chairs not named after 1992–93.

[d] Included in Curriculum & Instruction in Multicultural Teacher Education 1985–93.

[e] Offered as separate curriculum through other colleges until 1936.

Art Education^c	Alexander S. Masley	1948–69
	Donald J. McIntosh	1970–74
	Howard McConeghey	1974–77
	James J. Srubek	1977–93
Guidance & Special Education	George L. Keppers	1966–69
	Louis C. Bernardoni	1969–73
	Wayne R. Maes	1973–74
Special Education^c	Gary W. Adamson	1974–77
	Billy L. Watson	1977–79
	Gary W. Adamson	1981–85
	Deborah D. Smith	1985–93
Guidance & Counseling	Wayne R. Maes	1974–77
	Darrell E. Anderson	1979–83
Counselor Education	Darrell E. Anderson	1983–87
	Marion J. Heisey	1987–89
Counseling & Family Studies^c	Virginia Shipman	1989–91
	Wayne R. Maes	1991–93
Educational Foundations^c	Albert W. Vogel	1968–72
	Louis A. Rosasco	1972–83
	Albert W. Vogel	1983–85
	John T. Zepper	1985–87
	Gladys Levis-Pilz	1987–91
	Joseph G. R. Martinez	1991–93
Curriculum & Instruction in	David W. Darling	1985–87
Multicultural Teacher Education	William A. Kline	1988–91
	Sigmund A. Mierzwa, Jr.	1991–93
Technological & Occupational Ed	Frank R. Field	1985–91
Training & Learning Technologies^c	Frank R. Field	1991–93

C. College of Arts and Sciences^f

College of Arts and Sciences	Lynn Boal Mitchell	1919–29
	George Pope Shannon	1929–35
A&S Upper Division	George P. Hammond	1935–38

---

^f College of Science, Literature and Arts, 1898–1901; College of Letters and Science(s) 1903–9 and 1912–16; College of Letters and Arts 1909–12; College of Arts, Philosophy and Science(s) 1916–19.

A&S Lower Division	Jay Carroll Knode	1935–38
College of Arts and Sciences	Jay C. Knode	1938–47
	Thomas Donnelly	1947–52
	Dudley Wynn	1953–61
	Hoyt Trowbridge	1961–69
	Nathaniel Wollman	1969–81
	F. Chris Garcia	1981–86
	B. Hobson Wildenthal	1987–93
	William C. Gordon	1993–96
	Michael R. Fischer	1997–99
	Reed Way Dasenbrock	2001–
Anthropology & Archaeology	Edgar Lee Hewett	1933–35
Anthropology	Donald D. Brand	1935–45
	Willard W. Hill	1948–64
	John M. Campbell	1964–73
	Henry W. Basehart	1973–75
	Philip K. Bock	1977–81
	Jeremy A. Sabloff	1981–85
	Linda S. Cordell	1985–87
	Karl H. Schwerin	1987–93
	Erik Trinkaus	1993–97
	Marta Weigle	1997–2003
	Carole Nagingast	2003–
Art[g]	Dorothea Fricke	1933–36
Architecture[h]	William E. Burk, Jr.	1936–44
Biology	Edward F. Castetter	1933–57
	Loren Potter	1959–72
	Paul Silverman	1972–75
	Clifford Crawford	1975–79
	James S. Findley	1979–83
	David W. Duszynski	1983–92
	J. David Ligon	1992–95
	Terry L. Yates	1995–99
	Kathryn G. Vogel	1999–2003
	Eric S. Loker	2003–

[g] Included in College of Fine Arts after 1937.

[h] College of Architecture 1949–58; College of Fine Arts 1960–70; School of Architecture and Planning 1971– .

Chemistry	John Dustin Clark	1933–46
	Sherman E. Smith	1946–50
	Jesse L. Riebsomer	1950–64
	Raymond N. Castle	1964–71
	Guido H. Daub	1971–81
	Riley Schaeffer	1981–89
	Richard W. Holder	1989–91
	Cary J. Morrow	1991–97
	Fritz S. Allen	1997–2001
	Thomas Niemczyk	2001–
Classics	Lynn B. Mitchell	1933–44
Economics & Business Administration	Vernon G. Sorrell	1933–48
Economics	Julian S. Duncan	1949–61
	Nathaniel Wollman	1961–70
	Sanford Cohen	1970–73
	Gerald Boyle	1973–79
	Alfred L. Parker	1979–88
	Ronald Cummings	1988–93
	David Brookshire	1993–2003
	Richard Santos	2003–
English	George St. Clair	1933–39
	Thomas M. Pearce	1939–52
	George Warren Arms	1952–58
	Hoyt Trowbridge	1958–62
	Franklin M. Dickey	1962–67
	Joseph W. Frank	1967–70
	Joseph Zavadil	1970–79
	Hamlin Hill	1979–87
	David McPherson	1987–89
	Lee A. Bartlett	1989–93
	Michael R. Fischer	1993–97
	Robert E. Fleming	1997–98
	Scott P. Sanders	1998–
Geology	Stuart A. Northrop	1933–64
	Vincent C. Kelley	1964–70
	Lee A. Woodward	1972–77
	Douglas L. Brookins	1977–79
	Rodney C. Ewing	1979–85
	Cornelis Klein	1985–87
	Klaus Keil	1987–91
	Stephen G. Wells	1991–93

Earth & Planetary Sciences	Barry S. Kues	1993–99
	Leslie D. McFadden	1999–
History & Political Science	Marion Dargan	1933–35
History		
	George P. Hammond	1935–45
	Josiah Cox Russell	1948–53
	Benjamin Sacks	1953–58
	Edwin Lieuwen	1958–67
	Frank Iklé	1967–74
	Gerald D. Nash	1974–81
	Janet Roebuck	1981–87
	Jonathan Porter	1987–97
	Richard Robbins	1997–2001
	M. Jane Slaughter	2001–
Political Science	Edwin C. Hoyt	1967–71
	Michael Gehlen	1971–74
	Edwin C. Hoyt	1974–77
	Robert J. Sickels	1977–83
	James L. Ray	1983–85
	Paul L. Hain	1985–91
	Karen L. Remmer	1991–95
	Neil J. Mitchell	1995–2003
	Kenneth M. Roberts	2003–
Mathematics	Carroll V. Newsom	1933–46
Mathematics & Astronomy	Lincoln LaPaz	1946–53
Mathematics	Morris Hendrickson	1957–65
Mathematics & Statistics	Julius R. Blum	1966–69
	Lambert Koopmans	1969–74
	Arthur Steger	1975–77
	Richard J. Griego	1977–81
	Walter T. Kyner	1981–83
	David Sanchez	1985–87
	Richard J. Griego	1987–89
	Frank L. Gilfeather	1989–91
	Alexander P. Stone	1993–97
	Ronald Schrader	1997–2003
Modern Languages	Francis M. Kercheville	1933–42
	Robert M. Duncan	1942–51
	Raymond R. MacCurdy	1951–52

Modern & Classical Languages	Robert M. Duncan	1952–64
	Raymond R. MacCurdy	1964–69
	William H. Roberts	1969–74
	Sabine R. Ulibarrí	1974–83
	Tamara Holzapfel	1983–87
	Dick Gerdes	1987–93
Foreign Languages & Literatures	Diana Robin	1993–97
	Walter Putnam	1997–2001
	Monica S. Cyrino	2001–3
	Warren S. Smith	2003–
Psychology	Benjamin F. Haught	1933–44
	George M. Peterson	1949–64
	Frank A. Logan	1964–75
	Henry C. Ellis	1975–85
	Douglas P. Ferraro	1985–91
	William C. Gordon	1991–95
	Michael J. Dougher	1995–2003
	Mark A. McDaniel	2003–
Philosophy	Jay Carroll Knode	1933–48
	Hubert G. Alexander	1948–65
	Paul F. Schmidt	1965–77
	Howard N. Tuttle	1977–83
	Fred Gillette Sturm	1983–91
	Russell Goodman	1991–97
	George Frederick Schueler	1997–2001
	Russell Goodman	2001–
Physics	Robert S. Rockwood	1933–34
	Everly John Workman	1934–44
	Victor H. Regener	1947–61
	Walter M. Elsasser	1961–63
Physics & Astronomy	Victor H. Regener	1963–79
	R. Marcus Price	1979–87
	Daniel Finley	1987–93
	David Wolfe	1993–99
	John K. McIver	1999–2003
	Bernd Bassalleck	2003–
Government & Citizenship	Arthur S. White	1934–40
	Thomas C. Donnelly	1940–42
	Victor Ernest Kleven	1942–43
	Thomas C. Donnelly	1943–50

Government	Howard J. McMurray	1950–58
Government & Citizenship	Howard J. McMurray	1958–61
	Edwin C. Hoyt	1961–67
Sociology	Paul F. Walter, Jr.	1935–61
	David L. Varley	1961–68
	Richard F. Tomasson	1968–73
	Pedro R. David	1973–83
	H. Laurence Ross	1983–87
	Richard M. Coughlin	1987–91
	Gary D. LaFree	1991–97
	Richard M. Coughlin	1997–2001
	Susan B. Tiano	2001–
Journalism	Keen Rafferty	1948–67
	Anthony G. Hillerman	1967–75
	James P. Crow	1975–81
	Robert H. Lawrence	1981–87
	Fred W. Bales	1987–93
Communication & Journalism	Everett M. Rogers	1993–99
	Karen A. Foss	1999–2001
	Bradford Hall	2001–
Division of Speech	Robert E. B. Allen	1949–51
Speech	Wayne C. Eubank	1951–71
Speech Communication	Wayne C. Eubank	1971–72
	R. Wayne Pace	1973–79
Speech Communication	Kenneth Frandsen	1979–89
Communication	Kenneth Frandsen	1989–91
	Robert K. Tiemens	1991–93
Speech & Hearing Sciences	Amy B. Wohlert	2001–
Geography	Burton L. Gordon	1961–66
	Richard E. Murphy	1966–83
	Rodman E. Snead	1983–85
	Stanley A. Morain	1985–93
	Bradley T. Cullen	1993–95
	Olen Paul Matthews	1995–2003
	Stanley A. Morain	2003–

Latin American Studies	Martin C. Needler	1969–81
	Nelson P. Valdes	1981–83
	Jon B. Tolman	1983–87
	Susan B. Tiano	1987–89
	Garland D. Bills	1989–93
	Robert Himmerich y Valencia	1993–95
	Linda Hall	1997–2001
	William Stanley	2001–3
	Claudia Isaac	2003–
Communicative Disorders	Lloyd E. Lamb	1972–85
	Richard B. Hood	1985–91
	Linda L. Reinsche	1991–97
Linguistics	John W. Oller	1973–77
	Garland Bills	1977–83
	Alan Hudson-Edwards	1983–91
	Jean Newman	1991–97
	Garland Bills	1997–99
	Joan L. Bybee	1999–2003
	Sherman E. Wilcox	2003–
American Studies	Sam B. Girgus	1977–85
	Marta Weigle	1985–95
	Vera Norwood	1995–2001
	A. Gabriel Melendez	2001–
Religious Studies	Andrew Burgess	1981–
Spanish & Portuguese	Erlinda Gonzales-Berry	1993–97
	John M. Lipski	1997–2001
	Anthony Cardenas-Rotunno	2001–3
	Tey Diana Rebolledo	2003–
International Studies		
Asian Studies	Noel Pugach	1995–97
	Jonathan Porter	1997–2001
	Fred Gillette Sturm	2001–3
	Jonathan Porter	2003–
European Studies	Charles McClelland	1995–2001
	Carolyn Woodward	2001–3
	Steve Bishop	2003–
Russian Studies	Natasha Kolchevska	1995–97
	Byron Lindsey	1997–2001
	Natasha Kolchevska	1998–99
	Byron Lindsey	2001–

Women Studies	Shane Phelan	1999–2001
	Cheryl D. Learn	2001–3
	Gail Houston	2003–
Biochemistry	Jeffrey K. Griffith	1999–

D. Dean of the University

	Charles E. Hodgin	1902–4
		1908–12
		1914–16
	Lynn Boal Mitchell	1917–18

E. School of Engineering[b]

College of Science and Engineering	Martin F. Angell	1909–12
School of Applied Science	Martin F. Angell	1912–13
College of Engineering	Thomas T. Eyre	1921–26
	Philip S. Donnell	1927–28
	Robert S. Rockwood	1929–31
	Marshall E. Farris	1932–61
	Richard H. Clough	1961–69
	Richard C. Dove	1969–75
	William A. Gross	1975–81
	Gerald W. May	1981–87
	Richard Williams	1987–88
	James C. Thompson	1988–95
	Paul A. Fleury	1997–2001
	Joseph L. Cecchi	2003–
Electrical Engineering	Francis M. Denton	1933–35
	Chester Russell, Jr.	1935–39
	Ralph W. Tapy	1939–57
	Richard K. Moore	1957–63
	Arnold H. Koschmann	1963–70
Electrical Engineering & Computer Science	A. H. Koschmann	1970–71
	Victor W. Bolie	1972–77
	Peter Dorato	1977–81
Computing & Information Science	Donald R. Morrison	1979–81
Electrical & Computer Engineering	Peter Dorato	1981–85
	Russell H. Seacat	1985–89
	Nasir Ahmed	1989–97
	Kenneth Jungling	1997–99
	Christos Christodoulou	2001–

Computer Science	Cleve B. Moler	1981–87
	Edward S. Angel	1987–89
	Brian T. Smith	1989–93
	James D. Hollan	1995–99
	Deepak Kapur	1999–
Mechanical Engineering	Marshall E. Farris	1934–42
	Albert D. Ford	1942–53
	Charles T. Grace	1953–64
	Richard C. Dove	1964–69
	Maurice W. Wildin	1970–72
	Frederick D. Ju	1972–77
	William E. Baker	1977–81
	Alan D. Lebeck	1981–85
	Mo Shahinpoor	1985–89
	Frederick D. Ju	1991–93
	Joe F. Mullins	1993–95
	David E. Thompson	1995–2001
	Marc S. Ingber	2001–3
Civil Engineering	John H. Dorroh	1934–43
	William C. Wagner	1943–60
	Richard H. Clough	1960–61
	J. R. Barton	1961–65
	Cornie L. Hulsbos	1965–85
	Stephen P. Shelton	1987–91
	Jerome W. Hall	1991–99
	Timothy J. Ward	1999–
Chemical Engineering	Sherman E. Smith	1946–48
	Thomas T. Castonguay	1948–72
	Robert L. Long	1975–79
Architectural Engineering	John J. Heimerich	1949–58
Nuclear Engineering	Glenn A. Whan	1967–75
	Robert L. Long	1975–79
Chemical & Nuclear Engineering	E. James Davis	1979–81
	David M. Woodall	1981–83
	Frank L. Williams	1987–93
	Norman F. Roderick	1993–95
	Joseph L. Cecchi	1995–2001
	Julia E. Fulghum	2003–

F. Graduate Studies[b]

Graduate School	John Dustin Clark	1919–26
Graduate Division	Benjamin Franklin Haught	1926–19
Graduate School	Benjamin Franklin Haught	1919–36
	George P. Hammond	1936–47
	France Vinton Scholes	1947–50
	Edward F. Castetter	1950–63
	William J. Parish	1963–66
	George P. Springer	1966–73
	Bernard Spolsky	1977–81
	Charlene McDermott	1981–87
	R. Marcus Price	1987–89
	Richard J. Griego	1989–93
	Ellen Goldberg	1993–97
	Nasir Ahmed	1997–2001
	Kenneth Frandsen	2001–2
Graduate Studies	Teresita Aguilar	2003–

G. College of Fine Arts

	George St. Clair	1936–39
	William McLeish Dunbar	1939–45
	John Donald Robb	1946–57
	Edmund Eugene Stein	1958–60
	Clinton Adams	1961–77
	Donald C. McRae	1979–87
	Ernest D. Rose	1987–91
	Thomas Dodson	1993–2003
	James S. Moy	2003–
Music	Grace Thompson	1933–41
	John Donald Robb	1941–48
	Hugh H. Miller	1948–58
	Edwin Gerschefski	1960–61
	Joseph Blankenship	1961–68
	Walter B. Keller	1969–70
	William M. Seymour	1972–74
	William E. Rhoads	1974–79
	Peter L. Ciurczak	1981–89
	Harold Van Winkle	1989–93
	Nancy Uscher	1993–95
	John M. Clark	1995–98
	Chrisopher Shultis	1998–99
	Stephen Block	1999–

Art	Ralph W. Douglass	1936–47
	Lez Louis Haas	1948–64
	Van Deren Coke	1964–70
	Leonard Lehrer	1971–74
	Nicholai Cikovsky, Jr.	1974–79
	Wayne Lazorik	1979–81
	Garo Z. Antreasian	1981–85
	Christiane Joost-Gaugier	1987–89
	Harry Nadler	1989–91
Art & Art History	Nick Abdalla	1991–93
	Christopher Mead	1993–97
	Elen Feinberg	1997–98
	Flora Clancy	1998–2001
	Joyce Szabo	2001–3
	Martin Facey	2003–
Dramatic Art	George St. Clair	1936–40
	Edwin Snapp	1940–70
	Joseph E. Yell	1971–72
Theatre Arts	Joseph E. Yell	1972–73
	Robert F. Hartung	1973–77
	Peter Prouse	1977–79
	Brian Hansen	1981–85
	James Linnell	1987–91
Theatre & Dance	James Linnell	1991–99
	Denise Schulz	1999–2003
	Judith Chazin-Bennahum	2003–
Architecture	James J. Heimerich	1960–66
	Thomas R. Vreeland, Jr.	1966–70
Media Arts	Ira Jaffe	1997–2003
	Susan Dever	2003–
H. College of Pharmacy	Roy A. Bowers	1945–51
	Elmon L. Cataline	1952–71
	Carman A. Bliss	1971–87
	William. Hadley	1987–2003
	John A. Pieper	2003–
I. Schools of Management[b]		
College of Business Administration	Vernon Guy Sorrell	1947–59
	William J. Parish	1959–62
	Howard V. Finston	1962–70

School of Business & Administrative Sciences	Robert R. Rehder	1970–75
Robert O. Anderson SBAS	Robert R. Rehder	1975–79
R. O. Anderson Schools of Management	Morgan Sparks	1981–85
	H. Raymond Radosevich	1987–89
	Kenneth D. Walters	1991–95
	Howard L. Smith	1997–

J. School of Law[b]

College of Law	Alfred L. Gausewitz	1947–59
School of Law	Vern Countryman	1960–63
	Thomas W. Christopher	1965–71
	Frederick Michael Hart	1971–79
	Robert J. Desiderio	1979–86
	Theodore Parnall	1986–91
	Leo Romero	1993–99
	Robert J. Desiderio	1999–2002
	Suellyn Scarnecchia	2003–

K. College of Nursing

	Eleanor M. King	1956–61
	Virginia C. Crenshaw	1961–68
	Reina F. Hall	1968–69
	B. Louise Murray	1969–77
	Carmen R. Westwick	1979–83
	Barbara Lippincott-Rees	1983–87
	Estelle Rosenblum	1987–95
	Kathleen G. Bond	1995–97
	Sandra L. Ferketich	1997–

L. University College

	William Huber	1958–87
	John Rinaldi	1987–95
	Janet Roebuck	1995–99
	Richard Holder	1999–2001
	Peter White	2001–

M. School of Medicine

	Reginald H. Fitz	1961–68
	Robert S. Stone	1969–73
	Leonard Napolitano	1973–95
	Paul B. Roth	1995–

N. School of Architecture & Planning

Morton Hoppenfeld	1977–81
Donald P. Schlegel	1971–75
George Anselevicius	1981–93
Richard Eribes	1993–96
Roger L. Schluntz	1999–

O. Dental Hygiene[i]

Monica Novitski	1962–71
William E. Creighton	1972–74
Anthony C. Michelich	1975–77
Julie Sharp	1979–81

Dental Programs

E. B. Yudkovsky	1983–91
Ann Dinius	1995–97

Dental Hygiene

Demetra Logothetis	1999–

P. Division of Public Administration

Albert H. Rosenthal	1970–75
Leonard Stitelman	1975–81
T. Zane Reeves	1981–89
F. Lee Brown	1989–93

School of Public Administration

F. Lee Brown	1993–95
Bruce Perlman	1995–97
T. Zane Reeves	1997–2003
Kenneth G. Baker	2003–

---

[i] In College of Pharmacy or Extension Division 1963–81; in School of Medicine 1997– .

Appendix 7: Academic Units*

1892	Normal and Preparatory Departments (Schools)
1893	College Courses (Department)
1894	Commercial Department (School)
	School of Pharmacy (temporary)
1897–98	College of Letters and Science(s) (College of Literature and Arts; College of Arts, Philosophy, and the Sciences; College of Arts and Sciences)
	Bacteriological Laboratory
1902	School of Music
1903–4	Hadley Climatological Laboratory
1905–6	Engineering School (College of Science and Engineering; School of Applied Science; College of Engineering; School of Engineering)
1906–7	School of Education (College of Education)
1914	Extension Division (Extension and Adult Education; Extension, Summer Session, and Community Services; Continuing Education)
1915–16	Graduate School (Graduate Studies; Graduate Programs)
1916–17	College of Fine Arts (School of Fine Arts)
1919	Department of Hygiene
1927–28	Physical Education and Athletics
1933–34	Field Sessions
	San José Training School
1935–36	General College
1938–39	Nambé Demonstration School
1940–41	Taos County Project
1941–42	School of Inter-American Affairs (Division of Inter-American Affairs; Division of Foreign Studies)
	Department of Naval Science and Tactics
1946–47	College of Pharmacy
	Division of Government Research
	Bureau of Business Research (Bureau of Business and Economic Research)
	Navy Reserve Officer Training Corps Unit
1947–48	Institute of Meteoritics

*By date of first listing in catalog; not a complete list; later names in parentheses. For academic departments see appendix 6; for degree programs see appendix 5.

1948–49   College of Business Administration (School of Business and Administrative Sciences; Robert O. Anderson Schools of Business and Administrative Sciences; Robert O. Anderson Schools of Management)

College of Law (School of Law)

Engineering Experiment Station (Bureau of Engineering Research)

Division of Research and Development (Office of Research and Fellowship Services)

1951–52   Air Force Reserve Officer Training Corps Unit

1952–53   *New Mexico Historical Review*

Southwestern Journal of Anthropology (Journal of Anthropological Research)

1956–57   College of Nursing

1957–58   Los Alamos Graduate Center (Los Alamos Residence Center; Los Alamos Branch Campus)

Division of Architecture (School of Architecture and Planning)

1958–59   University College (University College and Counseling Center; Office of Undergraduate Studies)

Research Center (Research Computing Center)

1959–60   Holloman Graduate Center

1961–62   Sandia Corporation Graduate Program

Engineering Research Program

1962–63   School of Medicine

General Honors Program (General Honors and Undergraduate Seminar Program; University Honors Program)

1963–64   Dental Hygiene Program

Peace Corps Training Center (Peace Corps Training Center for Latin America)

Natural Resources Journal

1964–65   Natural Resources Research Center

Research Computer Center

1966–67   Eric C. Wang Engineering Research Facility

1967–68   Sandia and Kirtland Educational Programs

Language and Area Center for Latin America

1968–69   Gallup Branch

1969–70   Bureau of Educational Planning and Development

Institute for Social Research and Development

Andean Study and Research Center, Quito, Ecuador

Tamarind Institute

1970–71	Instructional Media Services (Instructional Media Center; IDEA Center)
	Division of Public Administration (School of Public Administration)
	Albuquerque Veterans Administration Hospital
	Bernalillo County Medical Center (University of New Mexico Hospital)
1971–72	Latin American Center (Latin AmericanInstitute; Iberian Institute)
	Ethnic Studies Programs
1973–74	Northern Branch
1974–75	Women's Studies (Women Studies)
	Black Studies (African-American Studies)
	Chicano Studies
	Native American Studies
	Division of Computing and Information Science
1977–79	Provost's Office
	Allied Health Sciences Center
	Health Sciences Library
	Santa Fe Graduate Center
1979–81	Eastern Valencia County Satellite Center (Valencia County Branch)
1989–91	Evening and Weekend Degree Programs
	Military Studies
1991–93	Aging Studies
1997–99	Taos Education Center

Appendix 8: Librarians[*]

1895–1902	M. Custers
1902–3	Kate Cunningham
1903–5	Julia D. Brown
1905–17	Della J. Sisler
1918–19	Pearl Anjanet Stone
1920–44	Wilma Loy Shelton
1945–49	Arthur McAnally
1949–73	David Otis Kelley
1973–75	John F. Harvey
1975–87	Paul Vassallo
1987–2003	Robert Migneault
2003–	Camila Alire

[*] By date of first listing in catalog.

Appendix 9: Administrative Units*

1896	Custodian and Librarian (General Library; University Library; Library Services)
1897–98	Director of the Gymnasium (Director of Physical Education; Director of Physical Education and Athletics)
1903–4	Matron of the Ladies' Cottage (Chaperon; Women's Dormitory; Residential Hall)
	Stenographer
1909–10	Registrar (Registrar and Bursar; Student Enrollment Services)
	Dean of Women (General Supervisor of Women)
	Proctor of the Men's Dormitory (Residential Hall)
1910–11	Secretary of the Faculty (Secretary of the University)
	Preceptress and Mistress of the Dining Hall
1912–13	Superintendent of Buildings and Grounds (Campus Superintendent; Physical Plant)
	Director of Music
1914–15	Director of Publicity (Editor of Publications and Director of Publicity; News Bureau; Public Information Office; Information and Publications; Public Affairs Department)
1916–17	Student Employment Secretary
	Student Adviser
1917–18	Financial Secretary (Business Manager; Comptroller)
1926	Dean of Men (Director of Student Personnel; Student Personnel Office)
1927–28	Office of the Bursar
	University Health Service (Student Health Center; University Physician)
1928–29	Dean of Students (Student Personnel Office)
	Dining and Residential Halls (Food Service; Housing)
1932–33	Faculty Manager of Athletics and Student Activities Adviser (Business Manager of Athletics)
1934–35	Secretary, Alumni Association (Alumni Office)
	Manager of University Press (Scholarly Publications; Publications Series; Director of University Press)
1940–41	Bureau of Tests and Records
1942–43	Placement Bureau (Placement Center; Vocational Information; Career Services Center; Student Financial Aid and Career Services; Career Counseling and Placement)
	Personnel Office (Non-Academic Personnel; Human Resources)
	Golf Course Business Manager (Golf Course)
	Landscape Architect
1944–45	Navy V-12 Unit
	Clerk of Admissions (Director of Admissions; Admissions Office; Admissions and Records Office; Admissions and Outreach Services)
1947–48	Counseling and Testing Services (Counseling Center)
1948–49	Veterans Affairs Office
1950–51	Student Affairs Office
1954–55	Fund Development (Development Office; UNM Foundation)

*By date of first listing in catalog; not a complete list; later names in parentheses.

1957–58	Student Affairs Division
	Printing Plant
1958–59	Division of Intercollegiate Athletics (Athletics)
	Director of Research (Office of Research Services; Office of Research Administration; Research and Graduate Affairs)
1959–60	New Mexico Union
1960–61	Educational Television (Station KNME-TV)
1964–65	Foreign Student Office (Office of International Services [Programs]; International Programs and Services)
	Data Processing Center (Computing Center; Computer and Information Resources and Technology; Information Systems)
	University Architect's Office (Facilities Planning)
1965–66	Campus Security (Campus Police; Police and Parking Services; Police Services; Parking Services)
1966–67	Student Aids Office (Student Financial Aid and Career Services)
	Campus Safety Office
	Purchasing
1967–68	University Concert Hall (Popejoy Hall)
	Institutional Research (Planning and Policy Studies)
1968–69	Radiological Safety
	Institute for Applied Research Services
1969–70	Auxiliaries and Services (Business Services)
1971–72	Student Activities
1972–73	Budget Office
1973–74	Women's Coordinating Center (Women's Center)
1974–75	University Counsel
	University Relations
	Administration and Development[a]
	Academic Affairs (Provost's Office)[a]
	Research[a]
	Health Sciences[b]
	Student Affairs (Student and Campus Affairs)[a]
	Business and Finance[a]
	Energy Research Center
1975–77	Regional and Community Affairs[a]
	Chicano Student Services

---

[a] Headed by a vice president.

[b] Including Veterans Administration Hospital, Bernalillo County Medical Center, Bernalillo County Mental Health/Mental Retardation Center, Cancer Research and Treatment Center, School of Medicine, College of Nursing, College of Pharmacy.

1977–79   Student Affairs, Alumni Relations, and Development[a]

School Relations (Student Outreach Services)

New Mexico Energy Institute

Equal Employment Opportunity Office (Affirmative Action Program)

1983–85   Director of Women's Athletics (Associate Athletic Director for Olympic Sports/University Relations)

African-American Cultural Center

Chicano Cultural Center

Native American Cultural Center

1985–87   Administrator, UNM Hospital

Director, Cancer Research and Treatment Center

Director, Bernalillo County Mental Health/Mental Retardation Center (UNM Psychiatric Hospitals)

Director, Dental Programs

1997–99   Director of Public Events

Appendix 10: Student Personnel Deans[*]

1909–10	Dean of Women	Della J. Sisler
1911–13	Dean of Women	Nellie Dean
1913–14	Dean of Women	Margaret Gleason
1920–22	General Supervisor of Women	Edna Mosher
1922–27	Supervisor of Women	Wilma Loy Shelton
1926–27	Dean of Men	John D. Clark
1927–29	Dean of Students	John D. Clark
1928–29	Adviser of Women	Elizabeth Simpson
1929–36	Dean of Men	Jay C. Knode
1929–62	Dean of Women	Lena C. Clauve
1936–46	Dean of Men	Jabez Leland Bostwick
1946–47	Dean of Men/Director of Student Personnel	Jabez Leland Bostwick
1948–69	Dean of Men	Howard Mathany
1962–71	Dean of Women	Helen Whiteside
1969–70	Dean of Students	Howard Mathany
1970–71	Dean of Men	Charles P. Roberts
1972–99	Dean of Students	Karen M. Glaser
1999–2003	Associate Vice President for Student Affairs	Randy Boeglin
2003–	Dean of Students/Director of Residence Life	Randy Boeglin

[*] From first listing in catalog; acting and interim appointments omitted. See appendices 4 and 9 for other positions.

Appendix 11: Alumni Association Presidents

1897	Charles Hodgin, Class of 1894	1966–67	Alfred A. Valdez, '61
1898	Josephine Hamm, '95	1967–69	Jack Mulcahy, '55
1899	Charles W. Ward, '97	1969–70	Joe Boehning, '53
1900	Mabel Wakefield Moffit, '98	1970–71	Rodney Shoemaker, '50
1901	Maynard C. Harding, '97	1972–73	F. Collister Redmond, '59
1902	Mata E. Tway, '01	1973–74	Judge Ben Hernandez, '41
1903	Lucy Hazeldine, '00	1974–75	Bobby John, '64
1907	Roy A. Stamm, '98	1975–76	S. Y. "Tony" Jackson, Jr., '51
1908	J. Ralph Tascher, '03	1977–78	Peggy Ritchie, '50
1909	Charles E. Hodgin, '94	1978–79	Stanley L. Hultberg, Jr., '64
1910	Rose M. Harsch Lynwalter, '07	1980–81	Judge Joseph F. Baca, '60
1911	Thomas Keleher, Jr., '02	1981–82	Jim Beckley, '62
1913	Erna Fergusson, '06	1982–83	Rose Mary "Redd" Eakin, '67
1914	Allan F. Keller, '08	1983–84	John P. Salazar, '65
1915	Lawrence F. Lee, '10	1984–85	Ray Berube, '60
1916	Pearce C. Rodey	1985–86	Jerry Atkinson, '67
1917	Pearce C. Rodey	1986–87	Karla (Bramer) Wilkinson, '73
1918	Erna Fergusson, '06	1987–88	Brian G. Burnett, '78
1927–28	Kenneth C. Balcomb, '16	1988–89	Judy Zanotti, '61, '73
1928–29	George Bryan, '23	1989–90	Robert Matteucci, '57
1929–30	Harold Mulcahy, '27	1990–91	Gloria Mallory, '60, '69, '72
1930–31	Ray McCanna, '17	1991–92	Steve Malnar, '65
1931–32	John Scruggs, '21	1992–93	Alex Beach, '69
1932–33	Allen E. Bruce, '17	1993–94	Chris Schueler, '85
1933–34	George Savage	1994–95	Marty Wilson, '71, '78
1934–35	Owen B. Marron	1995–96	Michelle Coons (Polk), '83
1935–36	Frank Schufflebarger	1996–97	Sandy Seligman, '69, '83
1936–37	Willis Morgan, '25	1997–98	George Friberg, '62
1937–39	Pearce C. Rodey	1998–99	Laura Hueter-Bass, '73, '80
1939–40	Dan A. MacPherson	1999–2000	Maria Griego-Raby, '80, '86
1940–41	Richard W. Thorne	2000–1	Gary Golden, '81
1941–42	Frederick H. Ward	2001–2	Connie Beimer, '71, '78
1942–43	Thomas J. Mabry	2002–3	Stephen Ciepiela, '77, '79
1943–44	Robert Elder, '26	2003–	Stephen Bacchus, '66, '68
1944–45	Albert R. Kool, '28		
1945–46	Gino Matteucci, '31		
1946–49	Glenn L. Emmons, '18		
1953–54	Floyd Darrow, '41		
1964–65	James Paulantis, '40		
1965–66	George Ambabo, '54		

Appendix 12: Foundation Leaders

A. Board of Directors Chairperson

1980–84	Jack Rust
1984–88	Jerry Geist
1988–92	Maxine Friedman
1992–94	Maralyn Budke
1994–96	Wayne Davenport
1996–98	Dick Morris
1998–2000	Ann Rhoades
2000–2	Mary D. Poole
2002–	Robert M. Goodman

B. Director of Development

1961–65	Bob Lalicker
1965–71	Lars Halama
1971–72	Bill Weeks
1972–84	Bob Lalicker
1984–86	S. Y. "Tony" Jackson and Peter Hunter
1986–89	Joe Skehen
1989–93	Dennis Eloe
1994	Carolyn Tinker
1995–98	Karen Stone
1998–2000	Duffy Swan
2000–1	Ray Ziler
2001–3	Leslie Elgood
2003–	Duffy Swan

Appendix 13: Student Government Presidents

A. Undergraduate Presidents

1907–8	J. Ralph Tascher
1908–9	E. M. Albright
1909–10	L. R. Lee
1910–11	A. R. Seder/Charles H. Lembke
1911–12	W. Coburn Cook
1912–13	W. Coburn Cook/John G. Pease
1913–14	J. G. Pease/J. J. Emmons
1914–15	J. J. Emmons
1915–16	J. J. Emmons/Ernest Hall
1916–17	Joseph McCanna/Floyd Lee
1917–18	James E. Hoover
1918–19	Donovan Richardson
1919–20	Donovan Richardson
1920–21	J. M. Scruggs
1921–22	Frank Neher
1922–23	Edward Horgan
1924–25	Roy Hickman
1925–26	Paul Fickinger
1927–28	Barney T. Burns, Jr.
1928–29	Thomas E. Moore
1929–30	Frank Stortz
1930–31	George Morrison
1931–32	Clifford Dinkle
1932–33	Jason Kellahin
1933–34	Fred Huning, Jr.
1934–35	George Seery
1935–36	John Kennedy
1936–37	Lyle Saunders
1937–38	Stanley Koch
1938–39	Stephen Reynolds
1939–40	Albert Simms
1940–41	Cy Perkins
1941–42	Trudelle Downer (Harden)
1942–43	Gerald Fischer
1943–44	Charles Gunderson
1944–45	Robert Blaise
1945	Bob Ferris
1946	Bob Oakley
1946–47	James Garliepp
1947–48	Brice Evans
1948–49	Bob Taichert
1949–50	Bill Fields
1950–51	Joe Passaretti
1951–52	Edward Driscoll
1952–53	Al Utton
1953–54	Jerry Matkins
1954–55	Jim Bruening
1955–56	Vince Gormley
1956–57	Bob Matteucci
1957–58	Jack Little
1958–59	Don Fedric
1959–60	Turner Branch
1960–61	Frank McGuire
1961–62	Linden Knighten
1962–63	Dennis Ready
1963–64	Tim Bennett
1964–65	John Salazar
1965–66	Jim Branch, Jr.
1966–67	Dan Dennison
1967–68	John Thorson
1968–69	Jim Dines
1969–70	Ron Curry
1970–71	Eric Nelson
1971–72	Ken White, Jr.
1972–73	Jack O'Guinn
1973–74	Ross Perkal
1974–75	Gilberto Gonzales
1975–76	Alan Wilson
1976–77	Damon Tobias
1977–78	Thomas Williams
1978–79	Mimi Swanson
1979–80	Mario Ortiz
1980–81	Mario Ortiz
1981–82	Michael Austin
1982–83	Michael Gallegos
1983–84	Dan Serrano
1984–85	John Schoeppner
1985–86	Marty Esquivel
1986–87	Mark Hartman
1987–88	Lillian Montoya (-Rael)
1988–89	Jim Spehar

1989–90	Charles Penny
1990–91	John Webber
1991–92	Karen Brownfield
1992–93	David Standridge
1993–94	Marcus Goodloe
1994–95	Alberto Solis
1995–96	Alberto Solis
1996–97	Shane Evangelist
1997–98	Jason Bousliman
1998–99	Fred Melendres
1999–2000	Eric Anaya
2000–1	Jennifer Liu
2001–2	Andrea Cook
2002–3	Jennifer Onuska
2003–4	Jennifer Onuska

B. Graduate Student Association Presidents[*]

1969–70	Richard Elliot
1970–71	William Pickens
1971–72	Bert Hansen
1972–73	Ray Schowers
1974–75	Stan Read
1975–76	William Tryon
1976–77	Carl Bradford
1977–78	Margaret Moses (-Branch)
1978–79	Steve Mapel
1979–80	Mike Daley
1980–81	Paul Kruse
1981–82	Ellen Foppes
1982–83	Dolph Barnhouse
1983–84	Jeffrey Evans/Marie Mound
1984–85	John Hooker
1985–86	John Hooker
1986–87	Charles Lee/Dave Longley
1987–88	Mimi Swanson
1988–89	John Schoeppner
1989–90	Lila Bird
1990–91	Mike Ordaz
1991–92	Johnnie Scott
1992–93	Mike Horcacitas
1993–94	Ahmad Assad
1994–95	CiCi Aragon
1995–96	Ray Sharbutt
1996–97	David Gillett
1997–98	David Miertschin
1998–99	Annie Shank
1999–2000	Brian Colon
2000–1	Monica Eshner
2001–2	Rachel Jenks
2002–3	Lorena Olmos
2003–	Aaron Kugler

---

[*] Later Graduate and Professional Students Association.

Appendix 14: Student Publications and Editors

A. Newspapers

The Cactus

1895	Floyd J. Gibbons

The Mirage

1888–89	G. E. Coghill/Douglas W. Johnson
1889–1900	Elizabeth Hughes
1900–1	Mata E. Tway
1901–2	Minnie Craig
1902–3	J. Ralph Tascher
1903–4	Wilfred H. Wroth/Lilian G. Huggett
1904–5	Lilian G. Huggett
1905–6	Edmund Ross
1906–7	Edwood M. Albright/J. Ralph Tascher
1907–8	Frank C. Light
1908–9	Elwood M. Albright/David R. Lane/ Roy A. Baldwin/Grover E. Emmons

The UNM Weekly

1909–10	Hugh M. Bryan
1910–11	A. R. Seder
1911–12	Erna Fergusson
1912–13	Clifford Nichols
1913–14	W. J. Higgins
1914–15	L. C. Murphy/W. J. Higgins
1915–16	Lee W. Walker
1916–17	Roy McCanna
1917–18	Ernest Hammond
1918–19	Ernest Hammond/Clyde Morris
1919–20	Clyde Morris
1920–21	George S. Bryan
1921–22	George W. White
1922–23	Fred T. Wagner

New Mexico Lobo

March 1923	Fred T. Wagner
May 1923*	Dan C. Burrows
September 1923	Willis Morgon
September 1923	Woodford Heflin
October 1923	Harris Grose
October 1923	Charles Barber
October 1923	Paul L. Fickinger
September 1924	Harris W. Grose
September 1925	Charles A. Williamson
January 1926	Alton E. Bailey
September 1926	Ted Gallier
November 1927	Jack Watson
July 1928	Winifred Stamm
September 1929	Raymond Stuart
October 1930	Stanley Miller
October 1931	E. L. Mayfield
October 1932	Howard Kirk
September 1933	Dan Minnick
September 1934	Gordon Greaves
September 1935	Marie Jenson
September 1936	Sam Marble
September 1937	Lyle Saunders
June 1938	Paul Weeks
September 1938	Afton Williams
September 1939	Reynolds Johnson
June 1940	O. A. Emerson
September 1940	Lewis Butler, Jr.
August 1941	Eddie Apodaca
September 1942	Edwin Leopold
September 1942	Judy Chapman
July 1943	John Baisley
November 1943	Betty Ellen Hearn
June 1944	Mary Catherine Darden
March 1945	Muriel Collins
June 1945	Connie Schutte
November 1945	Jane Yust
March 1946	R. Roger Reeve
September 1946	Melvin Morris
September 1947	Doug Benton
September 1948	Hank Trewitt
March 1949	Ed Glaser
July 1950	Troy Kemper
September 1950	Wright Van Deusen
June 1951	Bub Babb

*Date of appointment.

September 1951	Jack Gill	*Daily Lobo*	
February 1952	Joe Aaron	Spring 1974	Roger Makin
June 1952	Elaine Janks	Summer 1974	Michael Minturn
September 1952	Lionel Linder	1974–75	Michael Minturn
October 1953	David F. Miller	Summer 1975	Orlando R. Medina
June 1954	Mac Sebree	1975–76	Orlando R. Medina
September 1954	Bob Lawrence	Summer and Fall 1976	Susan Walton
May 1955	Bob Chatten	1977–78	Tim Gallagher
June 1955	Ken Siner	Summer and Fall 1979	Debbie Levy
September 1955	Bob Chatten	Spring 1980	Charles Poling
1956–57	Eric McCrossen	Summer 1980	Jeff Gardner
Fall 1957	Danny Zeff	1980–81	Ken Clark
Spring 1958	Paul Sweitzer	Summer 1981	Helen Gaussoin
Summer 1958	Sofia Chmura	1981–82	Helen Gaussoin
1958–59	Jim Irwin	Summer and Fall 1982	Marcy McKinley
Summer 1959	Joan E. Miller	Spring 1983	Kelly Gibbs
1959–60	Ernest Sanchez	Summer 1983	Stacy Green
1960–61	Linden Knighten	1983–84	Stacy Green
April 1961	Jamie Rubenstein	Summer and Fall 1984	Camille Cordova
1961–62	Mark Acuff	Spring 1985	Camille Cordova
1962–63	John C. McGregor IV	Summer 1985	Jo Schilling
Summer 1963	Lyn O'Connor	1985–86	Jo Schilling
1963–64	Fred Julander	Summer 1986	Kelly Clark
1964–65	Carroll Wayne Cagle	1986–87	Kelly Clark
Summer 1965	Jack Weber	Summer 1987	Charlie C. Clark IV
Fall 1965	Dennis Roberts	1987–88	Charlie C. Clark IV
Spring 1966	Jim Jansson	Summer 1988	Mike Kaemper
Summer 1966	Jo Ann Bailey	1988–89	Mike Kaemper
Fall 1966	Jim Jansson	Summer 1989	Marcos F. Montoya
Spring 1967	Lynne Frindell	1989–90	Marcos F. Montoya
Summer 1967	Melissa Howard	Summer 1990	Geoffrey D. White
1967–68	Chuck Noland	1990–91	Geoffrey D. White
Summer 1968	G. Roy Cornelius	Summer 1991	Eric Updegraff
1968–69	Rob Burton	1991–92	Eric Updegraff
1970–71	Wayne Ciddio	Summer and Fall 1992	Kandice McDonald
1971–72	Sarah Laidlaw	Spring 1993	Arturo Montoya
Summer 1972	Casey Church	Summer and Fall 1993	Laura Bendix
1971–72	Casey Church	1994–95	Kristin Davenport
1972–73	Aaron Howard	1995–96	Glen May
Summer 1973	John Ahearne	1996–97	Bruce Ross
Fall 1973	Janice Harding	Summer 1997	Susan Montoya
		1997–98	Dan McKay
		1998–99	Zac Shank

1999–2000	Aimee McNamara
2000–1	James Barron
2001–2	Iliana Limón
2002–3	Angela Williams
2003–	Arthur Simoni

B. Yearbook: *The Mirage*

1906	J. Ralph Tascher
1907	J. Ralph Tascher
1908	Elwood M. Albright
1909	William B. Wroth
1910	Harold E. Marsh
1911	A. R. Seder
1912	Erna M. Fergusson
1913	Evelyn Everitt
1914	L. M. Harkness
1915	B. O. Brown
1916	Milan L. Doering
1917	Myrl Hope
1918	Lina Fergusson
1920	Anne G. Cristy
1921	Dorothy Stephenson
1922	Irene B. Wicklund
1923	Walter E. Bowman
1925	Paul L. Fickinger
1928	Jack McFarland
1929	Robert S. Palmer
1930	J. Wilson Shaver
1931	J. O. Koch
1932	Otto W. Reutinger
1933	George P. Seery
1934	T. H. Tripp
1935	Lawrence Lackey
1936	George Schubert
1937	Stanley Koch
1938	William Beeken
1939	C. E. Standlee
1940	Richard Arnold
1941	Steve Koch
1942	Jean Mullins
1943	Edward L. Harley
1944	Dorothy Mace
1945	E. E. Zwicky, Jr.

1946	Diana Wolf
1947	Edwin Leupold, Jr.
1948	Betty Angelos
1949	Jene Lyon
1950	Fran Jones
1951	Bob Colgan
1952	Nancy Gass
1953	Ruth Carmel
1954	Carolyn Ramsey
1955	Joyce Simmons
1956	Shirley Irving
1957	Jo Ann Clauve
1958	Velma Martinez
1959	Carol Kutnewsky
1960	Lorena Bramlett
1961	Libbi Poch
1962	Kate Corbin and Diana Beal
1963	Diana Beal
1964	Bev Sorensen
1965	Barbara Knott
1966	Thomas Ormsby
1967	Pete Kendall
1968	Leslie Argo
1969	Mike Trujillo
1970	Lynn Hudson
1974	Cathy Mendius
1975	Jan Holland

C. Magazines
The Thunderbird

1945	Marjorie Tireman
1946	Barbara Jane Bailey
1947	Edith Davenport
1948	Jene Lyon
1949	Richard Lloyd-Jones
1950	Tom Sleeth
1951	Ed Abbey
1952	Warren Kiefer
1953	George Taylor
1957	A. Roberto Martinez
1958	Tom Weeks
1959	Joel L. Markman
1960	Janus Kozikowski

1961	Janus Kozikowski
1962	Richard Kovash
1963	Ron Swigger
1964	Richard Simms/Leon Coburn
1965	Gwyneth Jones Cravens
1966	Diane Casey
1967	Luis Calvillo-Capri/
	Mary Alinder
1969	Lynn Hudson
1970	Will Pike and Jim Willig
1974	Jeff Nighbert/Annetta Barnes
1975	Jeff Nibert

The Juggler

1967	Rob Burton
1968	Rob Burton

Conceptions Southwest

1978	Rick Celum
1979	Gail Krueger
1980	Robert Masterson
1981	Leslie Donovan
1982	Elizabeth Cohen
1983	Patrick Anastacio Chavez
1984	Christopher A. Gonzales
Spring 1985–Fall 1985	Martha P. Hogan
Spring 1986–Fall 1986	C. S. Webb
Spring 1987–Fall 1987	Steve Aunan
Spring 1988–Fall 1988	Thane Kenny
Spring 1989–Fall 1989	Lee G. Hornbrook
1990	Annemarie Neff
Spring 1991–Fall 1991	Tracy Aldel McInvale
Spring 1992–Fall 1992	Victoria Lynne Lucero
Spring 1993–Fall 1993	T. D. Cameron
Spring 1994	Kim Susanne Barber
Fall 1994–Spring 1995	Elissa M. Hannam
Fall 1995–Spring 1996	Maya E. Allen (-Gallegos)
Fall 1996–Spring 1997	Christina Faulkner
Fall 1998–Spring 1999	Antoinette C. Vinel
Fall 1999–Spring 2000	Eric Whitmore
Fall 2000	Elizabeth Butler
Spring 2001	Angela Williams

2002	Angela Williams
2003	Sahar Anwar

Best Student Essays

Spring 1989–Fall 1989	Editorial Board: Georgia Babb, Paul Bleicher, Lori K. Green, Larry R. Smith
Spring 1990–Fall 1990	Tami Toops
Spring 1991	Betty Karp, Jane Bowerman
Fall 1991	Jane Bowerman
Spring 1992	Lawrence Hoess
Fall 1992	Jane Bowerman
Spring 1993–Spring 1994	Naomi Reinhardt
Fall 1994–Spring 1995	Joseph Carpenter
Fall 1995–Spring 1997	Viqui Sanchez
Fall 1997–Spring 1999	Sonnin Dahl
Fall 1999–Spring 2000	Sarah Woods
Fall 2000–Spring 2001	Ashley Farmer
Fall 2001–Spring 2003	Maryalice Erickson

Appendix 15: Regents' Medals

A. Regents' Recognition Medal

1979	Dorothy B. Hughes
	Cyrene F. Mapel
1980	Martin W. Fleck
	Roy D. Hickman
1981	Vincent C. Kelley
	Lawrence H. Wilkinson
1982	John N. Durrie
	Alice King
	Peggy Ritchie
1983	John L. Rust
1984	Robert Dobell, Sr.
	Ralph R. Lopez
1985	Van Dorn Hooker
	Concha Ortiz y Pino de Kleven
1986	Marian Ipiotis
	Robert J. Stamm
1989	Manuel Lujan, Jr.
1990	Arturo G. Ortega
1994	Theda Douglas Rushing
1995	Ernest S. Romero
1996	Maralyn Budke
1997	Donna Peck
1998	George J. Friberg
	Richard S. Morris
1999	James B. Mulcock, Jr.
2000	Governor Bruce King
2001	Ambassador Edward L. Romero

B. Regents' Meritorious Service Medal

1979	Porfirio Apodaca
	John Perovich
	Victor Regener
1980	Donald H. Power
	Janet Roebuck
	Edwin J. Schodorf
1981	William H. Bowen
	Lorain F. "Tow" Diehm
	R. Philip Eaton
	William J. Spencer
1982	Karen Abraham
	Leo Lucero, Jr.
	Marshall R. Nason
1983	Beatrice Cappelli
	Gerald W. Earickson
	Klaus Keil

1984	Rupert A. Trujillo
	Jean Stebner
1985	Clinton Adams
	Isabel Darr
	Regina Prouse
1986	Richard L. Griego
	Laura V. Grissom
	Beverly White
1987	Carman A. Bliss
	John S. Daly
	Arleta L. Pickett
	Neddy A. Vigil
1988	Ruth Bowen
	Carroll J. Lee
	May Polivka
	Sidney Rosenblum
1989	Anne J. Brown
	Sabine R. Ulibarrí
1990	Rudolfo A. Anaya
	Rose Mary Torres Eakin
	Rita M. Padilla
1991	James S. Findley
	Raquel I. Martinez
	Floyd S. Williams, Jr.
1992	Henry C. Ellis
	Marge Merrills
	Harold N. Shaw
1993	Leonard M. Napolitano
	Estelle H. Rosenblum
1994	Donna Dionne
	Dr. Albert H. Rosenthal
1995	Alice H. Cushing
	Theo Crevenna
1996	F. Chris Garcia
	Karen Glaser
1997	Robert M. Ellis
1998	Charles R. Key
1999	Donald L. Mackel
	Olga M. Eaton
2000	Marilyn A. Burrows
	Lee B. Zink
2001	Henry L. Trewhitt
2002	Joel M. Jones
	Ralph Williams

Appendix 16: Annual Research Lecturers

1954   Leslie Spier, Anthropology, "Some Aspects of the Nature of Culture"

1955   Henry Weihofen, Law, "Crime, Law, and Psychiatry"

1956   Edward F. Castetter, Biology, "The Vegetation of New Mexico"

1957   France V. Scholes, History, "The Spanish Conqueror as a Businessman: A Chapter in the Life of
         Hernando Cortez"

1958   Lincoln LaPaz, Astronomy, "Some Aspects of Meteoritics"

1959   William J. Parish, Business Administration, "The German Jew and the Commercial Revolution in Territorial
         New Mexico"

1960   Victor H. Regener, Physics, "Science in Space"

1961   Stuart A. Northrop, Geology, "New Mexico's Fossil Record"

1962   Thomas M. Pearce, English, "The Lure of Names"

1963   Ralph D. Norman, Psychology, "Intelligence Tests and the Personal World"

1964   Milton Kahn, Chemistry, "Radioisotopes in the Study of Unweighable Amounts of Matter"

1965   Edwin Lieuwen, History, "Men on Horseback: The Latin-American Military Elites"

1966   Richard C. Dove, Mechanical Engineering, "Advances in Man's Ability to Measure His Environment"

1967   Stanley S. Newman, Anthropology, "Relativism in Language and Culture"

1968   Archie J. Bahm, Philosophy, "Philosophy—1968"

1970   Gerald D. Nash, History, "The American West in the 20th Century"

1971   James Yao, Civil Engineering, "Earthquake Engineering and Structural Safety"

1973   Hugh M. Miller, Music, "Humor in Music"

1974   Frank A. Logan, Psychology, "Learning Theory and Higher Education"

1975   Ralph C. Williams, Jr., Medicine, "Suppressor T-cells: Their Possible Relationship to Autoimmunity and Cancer"

1976   Clinton Adams, Art, "Mind, Eye, Hand and Stone"

1977   Garo Z. Antreasian, Art, "Some Aspects of Process and History in My Work"

1977   Martin C. Needler, Political Science and Sociology, "The Logic of Conspiracy: The Latin American Military
         Coup as a Problem in the Social Sciences"

1978   Henry C. Ellis, Psychology, "Strategies and Flexibility in Human Memory"

1979   R. Philip Eaton, Medicine, "Problems in Human Biology: The Necessity for Collaborative Research"

1980   Raymond R. MacCurdy, Modern & Classical Languages, "Don Francisco de Rojas Zorrilla: Seventeenth-Century
         Spanish Dramatist and Feminist"

1981   Klaus Keil, Geology and the Institute of Meteoritics, "Meteorites: The Asteroid Connection"

1982 Hamlin Hill, English and American Studies, "Huckleberry Finn's Humor Today"

1983 Beaumont Newhall, Art History and Photography, "The Unreality of Photography"

1984 Lewis R. Binford, Anthropology, "Changing Views of the Human Past"

1985 Howard C. Bryant, Physics & Astronomy, "A Physicist's Journal: From the Glory to the Two-electron Ion"

1986 Randy Thornhill, Biology, "Sexual Selection: The Nature of the Traits It Favors and What Controls Its Operation"

1987 Marlan O. Scully, Physics & Astronomy and the Center for Advanced Studies, "From Laser Physics to the Life Sciences: The Ramblings of a Quantum Cowboy"

1988 Ellen H. Goldberg, Microbiology, "Genetic Basis of Sexual Expression"

1989 Rudolfo A. Anaya, English, "Aztlan: A Homeland Without Boundaries"

1990 Jonathan M. Samet, Medicine, "The Hazards of Breathing: Cigarette Smoking, Radon, and Public Policy"

1991 Richard W. Etulain, History, "Reimagining the American West: Toward a Postregional Culture"

1992 William R. Miller, Psychology and Psychiatry, "The Value of Being Wrong: Two Decades of Unexpected Findings in Treating Alcohol Problems"

1993 Roger Y. Anderson, Earth & Planetary Sciences, "Climates of the Future: A Retrospective"

1994 Albert E. Utton, Director, U.S.-Mexico Transboundary Resource Center, "Water in the Arid Southwest: An International Region Under Stress"

1995 Robert T. Paine, Chemistry, "Exercises in Molecular Assembly: Some Designs and Accidents"

1996 Kathryn G. Vogel, Biology, "The Extracellular Matrix of Connective Tissue: Studying the Sticky Stuff"

1997 Louise Lamphere, Anthropology, "From Mill Town to Multinational: Gender, Family and Policy in Working Class Communities"

1998 Vera John-Steiner, Language, Literacy & Socio-cultural Studies, "Creativity and Collaboration: A Socio-cultural Approach"

1999 James Brown, Biology, "The Scale of Life: Of All Creatures Great and Small"

2000 Linda Biesele Hall, History, "The Virgin Mary, Coatlicue, and Pachamama: Thoughts on the Sacred Feminine in Latin America"

2001 Mohamed S. El-Genk, Chemical & Nuclear Engineering and the Institute for Space Nuclear Power Studies, "Space Exploration: A Journey into the Future"

2002 Everett M. Rogers, Communication & Journalism, "Applications of the Diffusion Model: Spread and Consequences of the Internet"

2003 Jane Buikstra, Anthropology, "Dialogues with the Dead: Mummies, Monuments, and Mallquis"

Appendix 17: Outstanding Teachers

A. Outstanding Teacher Award Recipients

1974–75	William Coleman, Chemistry
1975–76	Howard D. Rodee, Art & Art History
1976–77	George Arms, English
	Edith Buchanan, English
1978–79	Richard Ellis, History
	Frances Steinberg, Psychology
1979–80	Vivian H. Heyward, Health, Physical Education & Recreation
	Donald A. Neamen, Electrical & Computer Engineering
1980–81	Pham Chung, Economics
	William M. Dabney, History
1981–82	Jerry L. Born, Pharmacy
	Ferrel Heady, Public Administration and Political Science
1982–83	Roy D. Caton, Chemistry
	Jean M. Civikly, Speech Communication
	Vera John-Steiner, Educational Foundations and Linguistics
1983–84	J. Scott Altenbach, Biology
	Erlinda Gonzales-Berry, Spanish & Portuguese
	Wayne Moellenberg, Educational Foundations
1984–85	Ferenc M. Szasz, History
	Vonda O. Long, Counselor Education
	Rafael M. Diaz, Psychology
1985–86	Paul R. Kerkof, Biology
	John C. Condon, Speech Communication
	Patrick McNamara, Sociology
	George Peters, Modern & Classical Languages
1986–87	Breda Bova, Educational Administration
	Elsie Morosin, Nursing
	Samuel Roll, Psychology and Psychiatry
	Leo Romero, Law

1988–89	Richard Grassl, Mathematics & Statistics
	Jan Schuetz, Speech Communication
	Fritz S. Allen, Chemistry
	Nasir Ahmed, Electrical & Computer Engineering
	Elizabeth Poley, Gallup Branch
1989–90	Michael D. Cook, Art & Art History
	Jeffrey Davis, Mathematics & Statistics
	Harold D. Delaney, Psychology
	Bernard M. Moret, Computer Science
	Mary Ann Smith, Pharmacy
1990–91	Frank Kelly, Mathematics & Statistics
	Jerome Shea, University College
	Jane Caputi, American Studies
	Kenneth Jungling, Electrical & Computer Engineering
	Michele Blazek, Management
1993–94	Jennifer Dear, English
	Laura Little, Psychology
	Nancy Nelson, Psychology
	Kathleen Rick, Art & Art History
	Dan Wolne, Philosophy
1994–95	Richard Hermann, Music
	Richard Melzer, History, Valencia Branch
	Mary Anne Nelson, Biology
	Jon Tolman, Spanish & Portuguese
1995–96	Patricia Boverie, Training & Learning Technologies
	Manuel Molles, Biology
	Nagesh Rao, Communication & Journalism
	Ron Yeo, Psychology
1996–97	Quincy Spurlin, Elementary Education
	Mark J. Peceny, Political Science
1997–98	Candace Schau, Psychological Foundations of Education
	Phyllis Wilcox, Linguistics
1998–99	Keith Lemmons, Music
	Elizabeth Nagel, Individual, Family, Community Education
1999–2000	Deborah Evans, Chemistry
	Gail Houston, English

2000–1   Susan Dever, Media Arts
          Pedro Embid, Mathematics & Statistics
          Anne Skinner-Jones, Communication &
              Journalism and Women Studies
2001–2   Ralph Dawson, Electrical & Computer
              Engineering
2002–3   Gordon Hodge, Psychology
          Michael Nakamaye, Mathematics & Statistics
          John Caffo, Physics & Astronomy
          Marisa Clark, English
          Dan Wolne, Religious Studies
              and Development

B. Presidential Teaching Fellows

1993–95   Edward Angel, Computer Science
           Gordon Hodge, Psychology
1995–97   Cornelis Klein, Earth & Planetary Sciences
           Jean Civikly-Powell, Communication &
               Journalism
1998–2000 Jane Slaughter, History
           Helen Damico, English
2000–2   Monica Cyrino, Foreign Languages &
               Literatures
           Keith Lemmons, Music
2002–   Karen Foss, Communication & Journalism
           Elen Feinberg, Art & Art History

Appendix 18: Gerald W. May Outstanding Staff Awards

1991   Letha Allen
        Rudy Dominguez
        Kate Downer
        Joe Gonzales
1992   Charlie Gallegos
        Maria Martinez
        Magdalena Ortiz
        Theresa Rivera-Carabajal
        Ida Whitworth
1994   Pamela Burkhardt
        Fernando Chavez
        Lawrence Roybal
        Patricia King
        Roberto Espinosa
1995   Carolyn Casias
        James Davis
        Joyce Lisbin
        Eleanor Sanchez
        Lessley Foust
1996   Eppie Jaramillo
        Sandra Mitchell
        Sandra Carter-Mayes
        Doreen Miller
1997   Laura Valdez
        Michael Vigil
        Lynn Trojahn
1998   Judith Larson
        Terry Gugliotta
        Robert Harper
1999   Jan Dodson Barnhart
        Roxanne Littlefield
        Diana Torres
2000   Frances Duran
        Andrew Gonzalez
        Lisa McHale
        Genevieve Padilla
        Jerry Pilkinton

2001	Norma Boyd
	Ly Flock
	Joe McKinney
	Lydia Salas
	Lori Sloane
2002	Ray Mora
	Lucille Cordova
	Carolyn Gonzales
	Susan Quintana
	Carole Vollbrecht
2003	Randy Erwin
	Karin Retskin
	Robert Trujillo

Appendix 19:
Honorary Doctoral Degree Recipients

1924	John J. Tigert
1925	William A. Pusey
1926	John C. Futrall
1927	Charles E. Hodgin
1927	David Ross Boyd
1928	Ray Lyman Wilbur
1929	Clarence Cook Little
1930	Thomas Reed Powell
1931	Herman G. James
1933	Mary Austin
1933	Florence M. Bailey
1934	Aurelio Macedonia Espinoza y Martinez
1934	Edgar Lee Hewett
1934	Frederick Webb Hodge
1934	Alfred Vincent Kidder
1935	Rexford G. Tugwell
1936	Robert MacDonald Lester
1937	Herbert E. Bolten
1938	Rufus B. von Kleinsmid
1938	Clyde Kay Maben Kluckhohn
1939	Harold L. Ickes
1939	Harry Llewellyn Kent
1940	Robert Gordon Sproul
1941	Robert Lincoln Kelly
1941	James Ross McCollum
1941	Joaquín Ortega
1942	Douglas Wilson Johnson
1943	Erna Fergusson
1943	Fabian Garcia
1943	Homer Price Rainey
1944	Jaime Torres Bodet
1944	Alfonzo Caso y Andrade
1944	Rudolpho Brito Foucher
1944	Pablo Martinez del Rio
1944	Francisco Villagran Prado
1944	Ernest T. Pyle
1944	Alexander Grant Ruthven
1946	Howard Landis Bevis
1946	Robert L. Stearns
1947	Kirk Bryan

1947	Clarence Addison Dykstra		1964	William Orville Douglas
1947	J. Robert Oppenheimer		1964	Richard Buckminster Fuller
1948	J. Anton de Haas		1964	Rene d'Harnoncourt
1950	Harold Walter Stoke		1964	Lulu Wolf Hassenplug
1951	George Boas		1964	Robert Moody McKinney
1952	Father Berard Haile, DFM		1964	Georgia O'Keeffe
1952	James Stokeley Ligon		1964	John Dale Russell
1953	Norris Edwin Bradbury		1964	William Howard Schuman
1953	Ross Calvin		1964	Everly John Workman
1953	Myrtle Greenfield		1964	Henry Merritt Wriston
1954	Sam Gilbert Bratton		1965	Palmer Hoyt
1954	Harper Collins Donaldson		1965	Ernest Krenek
1954	George Peter Hammond		1966	Robert O. Anderson
1954	George Gaylord Simpson		1966	Ward Darley
1955	Francis Fergusson		1966	Roman Jakobson
1955	Judson Eugene Owens		1967	John O'Hea Crosby
1955	Thomas Lafayette Popejoy		1967	John Wainwright Evans
1955	Paul Alfred Francis Walter		1968	Brand Blanshard
1956	Thomas Sydney Bell		1968	William A. Keleher
1956	John Milne		1968	Galo Plaza Lasso
1956	Howard Riley Raper		1968	H. Vearle Payne
1957	Frank Harold Hanna Roberts		1968	Frederick Chapman Robbins
1957	James Webb Young		1968	Ramón José Sender
1958	Harriet Silliman Cosgrove		1969	Stanislaw M. Ulam
1958	Andrew Dasburg		1969	Robert Wendall Young
1958	Carl Michael Richter		1970	Laura Gilpin
1958	Estella Ford Warner		1970	Reuben Gilbert Gustavson
1959	Emil Walter Haury		1970	William Morgan, Sr.
1960	Rosser Lynn Malone		1971	Howard C. Bratton
1960	John Gaw Meem		1971	Raymond Jonson
1960	Arthur Newton Pack		1972	Shirley Mount Hufstedler
1961	Victor Babin		1972	France Vinton Scholes
1961	Clara Brignac Gonzales		1972	Ignacio Tinoco, Jr.
1961	Joseph Wood Krutch		1974	Fray Angélico Chávez
1962	Horace Marden Albright		1974	Clayton S. White
1962	Witter Bynner		1975	Peter Hurd
1962	Winfield Townley Scott		1975	Natachee Scott Momaday
1963	John Walter Gruner		1976	Roland C. Rautenstraus
1963	Kenner Fisher Hertford		1976	Robert M. Utley
1963	Paul Horgan		1977	Theodore Cooper
1963	Agapito Rey		1977	Glenn Leonidas Emmons
1963	Hugh Beistle Woodward		1977	John B. Jackson
1964	Felix Candela		1978	Cecil Andrus

1978	Cesar Sepulveda	2000	John Nichols
1978	Pablita Velarde	2001	Antoine Predock
1978	Frank Waters	2001	N. Scott Momaday
1979	Kurt Frederick	2002	Angela Vachio
1979	Arturo Ortega	2002	Simon J. Ortiz
1979	Louis Rosen	2003	Klaus Keil
1980	John Lewis	2003	Jimmy Santiago Baca
1980	Chester C. Travelstead		
1980	Morgan Sparks		
1981	Harold L. Enarson		
1981	Caswell Silver		
1981	Douglas Schwartz		
1982	Frank Angel, Jr.		
1983	Pete Domenici		
1983	Nathaniel Owings		
1984	David Tenney Kimball		
1984	Gordon Randolph Willey		
1985	Annie Dodge Wauneka		
1985	Richard Diebenkorn		
1986	Frank Ortiz		
1986	Charles Tomlinson		
1986	John D. Robb		
1987	Eliot Porter		
1988	Florence Hawley Ellis		
1988	Stephen Reynolds		
1989	Robert Holzer		
1989	George Kubler		
1990	Alberto Szekely		
1990	Carl Gorman		
1990	Tony Hillerman		
1991	Anne Noggle		
1992	Garrett Eckbo		
1992	Andrew Ciechanowiecki		
1993	Ferrel Heady		
1993	Robert Creeley		
1994	Henry Roth		
1996	George Clayton Pearl		
1996	Leonora Curtin Paloheimeo		
1996	Rudolfo A. Anaya		
1997	Harrison Schmitt		
1997	Angel Gonzalez		
1998	Bill Richardson		
1999	Sabine R. Ulibarrí		

Appendix 20: Alumni Association Awards

A. Award of Distinction/Erna S. Fergusson Award

"Given in recognition of exceptional accomplishments, or for commitment or distinguished service to the University of New Mexico. The recipient need not be an alumnus."

1969	Don Perkins
1970	Guy Rogers
	Reese Cagle
	H. L. "Hickum" Galles
	Tom Donnelly
1971	Hugh Graham, Sr.
1972	Charles H. Lembke
1973	Arturo Ortega
1974	Eugene R. Cinelli
	Gordon K. Greaves
1975	Ferrel Heady
	H. I. "Iggy" Mulcahy
1976	Rosalie Doolittle
	Gwinn "Bub" Henry
1977	Pete Domenici
	George Fischbeck
1978	Frances Marron Lee
	Marie G. Milne
1979	Bruce King
	Roy Johnson
	Calvin Horn
1980	Nelson Tydings
1981	Ned Elder
	Lena Clauve
1982	Robert M. "Bobby" Lee
	Carlton Daniel Spriggs
1983	John Whitmore
1984	Henry Jaramillo, Jr.
1987	Phillip U. Martinez
	Ann Jourdan
1988	Maralyn Budke
1989	William D. "Bill" Brannin
	Edward Tixier
1990	Pablita Velarde
	Joseph Baca
1991	Allan Fuhs

1992	Robert F. Gish
1993	Jean Mullins Macey
1994	Rudolfo A. Anaya
1995	Marvin D. "Swede" Johnson
1996	Maxine Friedman
1997	Bob Lalicker
1998	Clinton Adams
1999	John Perovich
2000	Van Dorn Hooker
2001	Archie Westfall
2002	V. B. Price
2003	John H. Morrison

B. Bernard S. Rodey Award

"Made to those persons who have devoted an unusual amount of time in a leadership capacity and whose efforts have contributed significantly to the field of education. The recipient need not be an alumnus."

1964	Albert G. Simms II
	D. A. MacPherson, Jr.
	Ben C. Hernandez
	Alfred A. Valdez
1969	Lynn B. Mitchell
1974	Lena Clauve
1976	Cyrene Mapel
1977	Chester C. Travelstead
1978	S. Y. Jackson
1980	Lawrence H. Wilkinson
1982	Marion and Martin Fleck
1983	John Donald Robb
1987	Leonard J. DeLayo, Sr.
1989	Jerry Geist
	Arturo Ortega
1990	Tibo Chavez
	Katherine Simons
1991	Leonard Napolitano
1992	Alice Cushing
1993	Stephanie M. Bennett-Smith
1994	Vernon E. Lattin
1995	David A. Sanchez
1996	Les Adler
1997	George E. Omer, Jr.

1998	Joel M. Jones
1999	J. Charles Jennett
2000	Ted F. Martinez
2001	Karen Glaser
2002	Daniel H Lopez
2003	James Hulsman

C. James F. Zimmerman Award

"Given to an alumnus of the University of New Mexico who has made a significant contribution which has brought fame and honor to the University of New Mexico or to the state of New Mexico."

1968	Tom L. Popejoy
1969	N. Scott Momaday
	Tom Wiley
1970	Donovan Richardson
1971	Eldred Harrington
	Roy Hickman
1972	J. Caldwell Wilson
	Shirley M. Hufstedler
1973	May S. Denham
1976	Harold L. Enarson
1977	Glenn L. Emmons
1978	John A. Lewis
1980	Stephen Reynolds
1982	Pete Domenici
1984	Ben C. Hernandez
1985	John Davis
	Ed Lewis
1986	H. L. "Hickum" Galles
1988	Klaus Keil
1989	Robert J. Stamm
1990	Lovola W. Burgess
1991	Antoine Predock
1992	Sabine Ulibarrí
1993	Larry Gordon
1994	Frank C. Hibben
1995	Anthony G. Hillerman
1996	Henry Trewhitt
1998	Betty Sabo
1999	Jack Samson
2000	Ann Rhoades

2001	Dennis C. Jett
2002	Milton H. Ward
2003	John M. Palms

D. Zia Award

"Made to New Mexico residents with a UNM degree who have distinguished themselves in any one or more of the following categories: philanthropic endeavor, public office, service to the University community and other volunteer activities, business or professional fields, or who have made a contribution to education."

1994	Adrian Bustamante
	Tom Cooper
	Cleta Downey
	Pete Gibson
	John Heaton
	Rick Johnson
1995	John T. Ackerman
	Charlie Carrillo
	James P. Miller, Sr.
	Teresa C. Moulds
	Robin Dozier Otten
	Glojean Todacheene
1996	Gwen Speer Clouthier
	Don Perkins
	Richard E. Ransom
	Maria Estela de Rios
	Butch Worthington
	Judy Zanotti
1997	Bruce A. Black
	Arthur Blumenfeld
	Ruth Frazier
	F. Chris Garcia
	Martha Lebert
	Seledon C. Martinez
1998	George J. Friberg
	John A. Garcia
	Robert Ghattas
	Van Gilbert
	John and Frances Hernandez
	Doris Rhodes

1999	Margaret Hopcraft Dike
	Nasario Garcia
	Debbie Ulrich-Johnson
	Michael S. Sanchez
	Myrna Smyer
	Thomas J. Steele, SJ
2000	Jose Abeyta
	Jackie Baca
	Maria Griego-Raby
	Arthur Melendres
	Thomas B. Ryan
	Louis L. Weller
2001	Randolph Barnhouse
	Laura Hueter Bass
	Sam J. Butler
	Michael J. Glennon
	Angela J. Jewell
	J. Howard Mock
2002	Alex Beach
	Fred Begay
	Breda Bova
	Thomas E. Chavez
	Ramon Huerta
	William R. Federici
2003	Gary Golden
	Yolanda Jones King
	James Lewis
	Petra F. Maes
	Mary Torres
	Robert Wertheim

E. Lobo Award

"Presented to an (adopted) alumnus of UNM who has given outstanding personal service to UNM or for special achievement in his/her career which reflects credit on the University."

1950	Mrs. James F. Zimmerman
1951	Mrs. Lynn B. Mitchell
	Lillian Huggett
1952	Mrs. Tom L. Popejoy
1953	Clarissa Fuller
1954	Lena Clauve
1955	Elizabeth Simpson
1956	Elizabeth Elder
1957	Mary Hickox
1958	Winifred Reiter
1960	Esther Thompson
1961	Nina Ancona
1962	Marion Fleck
1963	Petty Perkins
1964	Shirley M. Hufstedler
1965	Jane Mabry
1966	Katherine Simons
1967	Virginia LaPine
	Josephine Hammons
1968	Mrs. Sheldon Dike
1969	Mrs. Lloyd Sallee
1970	Mrs. John Milne
1971	Mary Nicolai
	Charlotte Heady
1972	May Denham
1973	Petty Perkins
1974	Francine Neff
1975	Peggy Ritchie
1976	Teresa Moulds
1977	Maralyn Budke
	Thelma Mock
1978	Polly Davis
	Maxine Friedman
1979	Iona Gamertsfelder
1980	Gale Doyel
1981	Redd Eakin
1982	Ann Jourdan
1983	Marie Hays
1984	Gwinn "Bub" Henry
1985	Judy Burton Chreist
1986	Paula Holland Grieves
1987	Ruth Goldsworthy
1988	Tony Hillerman
	Karen Abraham
1989	Henrietta Loy
1990	Judy Zanotti
1991	Karen Glaser
1992	Betty Hinton
1993	Alex Beach

1994	Gloria Mallory
	Mary McGregor
1995	Donna Peck
1996	Jo Ann Parish
1997	Dell Miera
1998	Yolanda King
1999	Jean Mullins Macey
2000	Dorothy S. Harroun
2001	Marjorie Bell Chambers
2002	John Perovich
2003	F. Chris Garcia

F. Distinguished Woman Award

1979	Lillian Dolde
1980	Louise Coe
1981	Alice King
1982	Dora Rosenbaum
1983	Concha Ortiz y Pino de Kleven
1984	Estelle Rosenblum
1985	Mari-Luci Jaramillo
1986	Betty Sabo
1987	Marilynne McKay
1988	Lena Clauve
1989	Lovola W. Burgres
1990	Marjorie Bell Chambers
1991	Nancy Domenici
1992	Sheila Garcia
1993	Judge Mary Walters
1994	Judge Diane del Santo
1995	Roberta Ramo

G. Ann Jourdan Award

1980	Iona Gamertsfelder
1981	Jack Little
1982	Paula Grieves
1983	Stephanie Stinnett
1984	Marie Hays
1988	Ken and Marsha Merritt
1988	Gwen Clouthier
1997	Ed Zamora
	Gary Bednorz

Appendix 21: Rhodes Scholars

1906	Thomas S. Bell
1908	Frank C. Light
1910	Hugh M. Bryan
1911	Karl G. Karsten
1914	William Coburn Cook
1916	George Adlai Feather
1920	Donovan M. Richardson
1920	Wayne Garrett
1923	Fred T. Wagner
1926	Woodford A. Heflin
1932	Critchell Parsons
1951	Robert Dean Pue
1953	Albert E. Utton
1955	John H. Morrison
1956	Michael T. McNevin
1978	Frank H. Allen III
1998	Manuel Montoya
2001	John Probasco

Notes

Chapter 1

1. Tony Hillerman, *The Great Taos Bank Robbery and Other Indian Country Affairs* (Albuquerque: University of New Mexico Press, 1973), 115.

2. Tony Hillerman, with David Muench, *New Mexico* (Portland: Graphic Arts Center Publishing Co., 1974), 31.

3. Michael Welsh, "History of the University of New Mexico" (University of New Mexico Archives [UNMA]), chap. 2, 8; Jane C. Atkins, "Who Shall Educate: The Schooling Question in Territorial New Mexico, 1846–1911" (PhD diss., University of New Mexico, 1982, and UNMA), 324.

4. Welsh, "History of the University," chap. 2, 11.

5. Welsh, "History of the University," chap. 2, 12; Atkins, "Who Shall Educate," 290.

6. Welsh, "History of the University," chap. 2, 21–22; Marc Simmons, *Albuquerque: A Narrative History* (Albuquerque: University of New Mexico Press, 1982), 308.

7. Welsh, "History of the University," chap. 2, 22–23; Simmons, *Albuquerque*, 308–11.

8. Van Dorn Hooker, *Only in New Mexico: An Architectural History of the University of New Mexico* (Albuquerque: University of New Mexico Press, 2000), 3–4.

9. Henry Ward Beecher quoted in Robert E. Spiller et al., eds., *Literary History of the United States*, 3rd ed. (London and Toronto: The Macmillan Company, 1963), 655.

10. Simmons, *Albuquerque*, 209–10.

11. Simmons, *Albuquerque*, 212–13.

12. Simmons, *Albuquerque*, 215–16.

13. Simmons, *Albuquerque*, 338.

14. Simmons, *Albuquerque*, 337.

15. Simmons, *Albuquerque*, 230.

16. Simmons, *Albuquerque*, 227.

17. Simmons, *Albuquerque*, 211.

18. Simmons, *Albuquerque*, 205.

19. Simmons, *Albuquerque*, 218.

20. Simmons, *Albuquerque*, 285.

21. Simmons, *Albuquerque*, 303.

22. Welsh, "History of the University," chap. 2, 21–24.

23. Welsh, "History of the University," chap. 2, 24–25.

Chapter 2

1. Spiller et al., eds., *Literary History*, 662.

2. Dorothy Hughes, *Pueblo on the Mesa* (Albuquerque: University of New Mexico Press, 1939), 13.

3. Hughes, *Pueblo on the Mesa*, 13.

4. Hughes, *Pueblo on the Mesa*, 15.

5. Welsh, "History of the University," chap. 2, 27–28.

6. Welsh, "History of the University," chap. 2, 27–28; Lee Ann Pricer, "Bernard Shandon Rodey" (undergraduate research paper, UNMA, April 16, 1982), 1–2.

7. Tom Popejoy, "Address to the Newcomen Society" (manuscript, UNMA, June 6, 1942).

8. Gary Karsh, "Birth of a Frontier University," *UNM Alumnus*, March 1979, 4–5.

9. Tony Hillerman, "Birthday for a College," *New Mexico Magazine*, February 1964, 3–5.

10. Hughes, *Pueblo on the Mesa*, 15–17.

11. Simmons, *Albuquerque*, 312.

12. Welsh, "History of the University," chap. 2, 32, 33; Frank D. Reeve, "History of the University of New Mexico" (master's thesis, University of New Mexico, 1928, and UNMA), 2–7.

13. Welsh, "History of the University," chap. 2, 33–34.

14. Simmons, *Albuquerque*, 312.

15. Simmons, *Albuquerque*, 312.

16. Simmons, *Albuquerque*, 312.

17. Hooker, *Only in New Mexico*, 6.

18. Welsh, "History of the University," chap. 3, 1.

19. Welsh, "History of the University," chap. 3, 7–8.

20. Welsh, "History of the University," chap. 3, 8–9; Minutes of the University of New Mexico Board of Regents (hereinafter Regents' Minutes), November 3, 1889, Office of the Secretary, University of New Mexico, 1.

21. Welsh, "History of the University," chap. 3, 8–9; Regents' Minutes, November 3, 1889.

22. Welsh, "History of the University," chap. 3, 9–10; Regents' Minutes, May 28, June 18, September 15, 1890, 5–8.

23. Welsh, "History of the University," chap. 3, 12.

24. Welsh, "History of the University," chap. 3, 12–13; Regents' Minutes, May 31 and June 11, 1892.

25. Welsh, "History of the University," chap. 3, 13.

26. Hooker, *Only in New Mexico*, 8.

27. Hooker, *Only in New Mexico*, 12–13; *Catalogue of the University of New Mexico*, 1892 (hereinafter UNM Catalog), 4, 7–8.

28. John D. Clark, "History of the University of New Mexico," originally published in "Freshman Week, 1934," UNMA.

29. John D. Clark quoting Charles B. Hodgin, "Campus Memories," *The Alumni News*, 1928, 3.

30. Clark quoting Hodgin, "Campus Memories," 3.

31. Hughes, *Pueblo on the Mesa*, 21.

32. Hillerman, "Birthday for a College," 3.

33. Karsh, "Birth of a Frontier University," 5

34. Melissa Howard, "The University of New Mexico, a Hundred Years of Partnership with Albuquerque," *New Mexico Business Journal*, September 1988, 52.

35. Hooker, *Only in New Mexico*, 8.

36. Charles B. Hodgin, *"Campus Memories," The Alumni News*, University of New Mexico, 1928, 40.

37. Hodgin, *"Campus Memories,"* 41.

38. Popejoy, "Address to the Newcomen Society."

Chapter 3

1. Simmons, *Albuquerque*, 314–15.

2. Hooker, *Only in New Mexico*, 11.

3. Hughes, *Pueblo on the Mesa*, 19–20; UNM Catalog, 1892.

4. Hughes, *Pueblo on the Mesa*, 20.

5. Hughes, *Pueblo on the Mesa*, 48.

6. Hughes, *Pueblo on the Mesa*, 48.

7. William B. Dabney, "A History of the College of Arts and Sciences," The College of Arts and Sciences: A Centennial History: 1889–1990 (manuscript, UNMA), 3.

8. Welsh, "History of the University," chap. 3, 4; Regents' Minutes, October 28, 1892, 2.

9. Welsh, "History of the University," chap. 3, 14–15.

10. Dabney, "A History of the College of Arts and Sciences," 1–2.

11. Welsh, "History of the University," chap. 3, 15; Regents' Minutes, February 1, 1894, 22–23.

12. Welsh, "History of the University," chap. 3, 15–16.

13. Welsh, "History of the University," chap. 3, 16–17.

14. Hughes, *Pueblo on the Mesa*, 103.

15. Hughes, *Pueblo on the Mesa*, 102.

16. Welsh, "History of the University," chap. 3, 17; Regents' Minutes, July 17, 19, 1894, 34–35.

17. Welsh, "History of the University," chap. 3, 17–18.

18. Welsh, "History of the University," chap. 3, 18–19; Simon Kropp, "Hiram Hadley and the Founding of New Mexico State University," *Arizona and the West*, Spring 1967.

19. Simon Kropp, *That All May Learn: New Mexico State University, 1888–1964* (Las Cruces: New Mexico State University, 1972), 15–19; Kropp, "Hiram Hadley," 30.

20. Welsh, "History of the University," chap. 3, 19–20; Kropp, "Hiram Hadley," 31–37.

21. Welsh, "History of the University," chap. 3, 19–20; Kropp, "Hiram Hadley," 31–37.

22. Welsh, "History of the University," chap. 3, 22.

23. Welsh, "History of the University," chap. 3, 22–23; Regents' Minutes, March 6, 1895, 48.

24. Welsh, "History of the University," chap. 3, 24.

25. Welsh, "History of the University," chap. 3, 24–27.

26. Welsh, "History of the University," chap. 3, 27.

27. Welch, "History of the University," chap. 3, 28; Regents' Minutes, April 12, 1895, 53; June 1, 1895, 53–55.

28. UNM Catalog, 1895, 17.

29. Welsh, "History of the University," chap. 3, 29–30; Regents' Minutes, February 11, April 18, May 12, and August 25, 1896, 72–76.

30. Welsh, "History of the University," chap. 3, 30; Regents' Minutes, May 15, 1896, 78.

31. Welsh, "History of the University," chap. 3, 32.

32. Welsh, "History of the University," chap. 3, 30.

33. Welsh, "History of the University," chap. 3, 33–34; Regents' Minutes, February 19, 1897, 94.

34. Welsh, "History of the University," chap. 3, 65.

35. Robert Knight Barney, *Turmoil and Triumph* (Albuquerque: San Ignacio Press, 1969), 72.

36. Hughes, *Pueblo on the Mesa*, 115.

37. Hughes, *Pueblo on the Mesa*, 37–38.

38. Hughes, *Pueblo on the Mesa*, 116–17.

39. Hughes, *Pueblo on the Mesa*, 117.

40. Hughes, *Pueblo on the Mesa*, 59.

41. Hooker, *Only in New Mexico*, 11.

42. Barney, *Turmoil and Triumph*, 9–13.

43. Barney, *Turmoil and Triumph*, 13–14.

44. Barney, *Turmoil and Triumph*, 23–31.

45. Barney, *Turmoil and Triumph*, 38.

46. Barney, *Turmoil and Triumph*, 33–34.

47. Hooker, *Only in New Mexico*, 11.

48. Hughes, *Pueblo on the Mesa*, 88.

49. Hooker, *Only in New Mexico*, 11–12.

50. Dabney, "A History of the College of Arts and Sciences," 3.

51. Hooker, *Only in New Mexico*, 11.

Chapter 4

1. Hillerman, "Birthday for a College," 6.

2. Lynn B. Mitchell, ed., *Remembrance Wakes—Memorial Day Exercises of the University of New Mexico, 1928–1941* (Albuquerque: University of New Mexico Press, 1941), 87–88.

3. Hughes, *Pueblo on the Mesa*, 101.

4. Welsh, "History of the University," chap. 3, 38.

5. Welsh, "History of the University," chap. 3, 39; Mitchell, *Remembrance Wakes*, 89–93.

6. Mitchell, *Remembrance Wakes*, 88–92.

7. Welsh, "History of the University," chap. 3, 37.

8. Simmons, *Albuquerque*, 343.

9. Simmons, *Albuquerque*, 343–44.

10. Simmons, *Albuquerque*, 344.

11. Simmons, *Albuquerque*, 345.

12. Van Dorn Hooker, "The Right-Hand Man," *UNM Alumnus*, March 1979, 7–10.

13. Mitchell, *Remembrance Wakes*, 144–53.

14. Welsh, "History of the University," chap. 3, 34.

15. Dabney, "A History of the College of Arts and Sciences," 3.

16. UNM Catalog, 1904–5, 90–91.

17. Welsh, "History of the University," chap. 3, 38.

18. Welsh, "History of the University," chap. 3, 41.

19. Welsh, "History of the University," chap. 3, 42–44; Dabney, "A History of the College of Arts and Sciences," 2; Judith R.

Johnson, "John Weinzirl: A Personal Search for the Conquest of Tuberculosis," *New Mexico Historical Review* 63, no. 2 (1988): 141–55.

20. Welsh, "History of the University," chap. 3, 34; Hughes, *Pueblo on the Mesa*, 19, 88; Hooker, *Only in New Mexico*, 11.

21. UNM Catalog, 1897–98, 21.

22. Welsh, "History of the University," chap. 3, 45; Johnson, "John Weinzirl," 1–2; Hughes, *Pueblo on the Mesa*, 69.

23. Welsh, "History of the University," chap. 3, 45.

24. Welsh, "History of the University," chap. 3, 46–47.

25. Welsh, "History of the University," chap. 3, 48.

26. Welsh, "History of the University," chap. 3, 48–50.

27. Welsh, "History of the University," chap. 3, 50.

28. Hughes, *Pueblo on the Mesa*, 100.

29. Hughes, *Pueblo on the Mesa*, 115.

30. Hughes, *Pueblo on the Mesa*, 60.

31. Hughes, *Pueblo on the Mesa*, 73.

32. Hughes, *Pueblo on the Mesa*, 23.

33. Welsh, "History of the University," chap. 3, 55; Regents' Minutes, May 22, 1899, 152–56.

34. Hooker, *Only in New Mexico*, 12.

35. Welsh, "History of the University," chap. 3, 55–56.

36. Barney, *Turmoil and Triumph*, 11.

37. Terry Gugliotta, "A Lot of Hooplore" (manuscript, UNMA, July 11, 2003), 1.

38. Barney, *Turmoil and Triumph*, 60.

39. Barney, *Turmoil and Triumph*, 49–50.

40. Hughes, *Pueblo on the Mesa*, 71.

41. Welsh, "History of the University," chap. 3, 58.

42. Welsh, "History of the University," chap. 3, 57.

Chapter 5

1. Karsh, "Birth of a Frontier University," 5.

2. Hughes, *Pueblo on the Mesa*, 25, 35.

3. Hughes, *Pueblo on the Mesa*, 35; Hillerman, "Birthday of a College," 7; Karsh, "Birth of a Frontier University," 7; Melissa Howard, "UNM: For 100 Years a '*Pueblo on the Mesa*,'" *New Mexico Magazine*, October 1988, 3.

4. Welsh, "History of the University," chap. 4, 3; Regents' Minutes, June 25, 1901, 215.

5. Welsh, "History of the University," chap. 4, 4; Ronald L. Stuckey, "William George Tight and the Naming of the Teays River and Lake Tight," *Bulletin of the Geological Society of America*, supplement A, 22 (1910): 7.

6. *Granville Times* (Granville, OH), December 14, 1905.

7. Hillerman, "Birthday for a College," 6.

8. Clark, "History of the University of New Mexico," 3.

9. Mitchell, *Remembrance Wakes*, 83–84.

10. Mitchell, *Remembrance Wakes*, 77.

11. Mitchell, *Remembrance Wakes*, 77.

12. Mitchell, *Remembrance Wakes*, 78–79.

13. Hughes, *Pueblo on the Mesa*, 23, 105–6.

14. Hillerman, "Birthday for a College," 7.

15. Hillerman, "Birthday for a College," 7.

16. Hooker, *Only in New Mexico*, 26.

17. Welsh, "History of the University," chap. 4, 4.

18. Welsh, "History of the University," chap. 4, 5–6.

19. Welsh, "History of the University," chap. 4, 8; Regents' Minutes, April 11, 1902, 233.

20. Welsh, "History of the University," chap. 4, 10.

21. Welsh, "History of the University," chap. 4, 11.

22. Welsh, "History of the University," chap. 4, 11–13.

23. Welsh, "History of the University," chap. 4, 13.

24. UNM Catalog, 1908–9, 115.

25. Welsh, "History of the University," chap. 4, 17–20

26. Welsh, "History of the University," chap. 4, 21.

27. "T. S. Bell, '05, Visits Alumni Offices," *UNM Alumnus*, June 1946.

28. Dabney, "A History of the College of Arts and Sciences," 4.

29. Dabney, "A History of the College of Arts and Sciences," 4–5.

30. Welsh, "History of the University," chap. 4, 9.

31. Hughes, *Pueblo on the Mesa*, 51.

32. Clark, "History of the University of New Mexico," 3.

33. "Architecture, Antics, Legacy of Early President," *Mirage*, Spring 1988, 6.

34. Melissa (Noland) Howard, "The Human Dynamo," *UNM Alumnus*, March, 1979, 13.

35. Charles Hodgin, "*Campus Memories*," 41–42.

36. "Architecture, Antics," 6.

37. Bart Ripp, "William George Tight, Early UNM President Added Color, Life to a Young Campus," *Albuquerque Journal*, metro sec., May 17, 1983.

38. Hodgin, "*Campus Memories*," 24–25.

39. Hodgin, "*Campus Memories*," 24–25; Mitchell, *Remembrance Wakes*, 71.

40. Hughes, *Pueblo on the Mesa*, 39.

41. Hughes, *Pueblo on the Mesa*, 61–65.

42. Hughes, *Pueblo on the Mesa*, 119–20.

43. Hughes, *Pueblo on the Mesa*, 122–25.

44. Welsh, "History of the University," chap. 4, 16–17.

45. Welsh, "History of the University," chap. 4, 14.

46. Hodgin, "*Campus Memories*," 26; David B. Mitchell, letter to the editor, *UNM Alumnus*, June 1, 1979; Hooker, *Only in New Mexico*, 16.

47. Hooker, *Only in New Mexico*, 17.

48. Hooker, *Only in New Mexico*, 18–20.

49. Hooker, *Only in New Mexico*, 27.

50. Hooker, *Only in New Mexico*, 21–22.

51. Karsh, "Birth of a Frontier University," 6.

52. Bainbridge Bunting, "It Could Only Happen Here," *UNM Alumnus*, March 1978, 12.

53. Hooker, *Only in New Mexico*, 24.

54. Mitchell, *Remembrance Wakes*, 75.

55. Barney, *Turmoil and Triumph*, 14–15.

56. Barney, *Turmoil and Triumph*, 15–16.

57. Barney, *Turmoil and Triumph*, 16.

58. Barney, *Turmoil and Triumph*, 13.

59. Barney, *Turmoil and Triumph*, 13.

60. Barney, *Turmoil and Triumph*, 32–33, 63–70, 307–9.

61. *Granville Times* (Granville, OH), July 2, 1908.

62. (Noland) Howard, "The Human Dynamo," 15.

63. Hillerman, "Birthday for a College," 7.

64. Karsh, "Birth of a Frontier University," 6.

65. Simmons, *Albuquerque*, 315–16.

66. Ripp, "William George Tight."

67. Dabney, "A History of the College of Arts and Sciences," 5.

68. (Noland) Howard, "The Human Dynamo," 15.

69. Welsh, "History of the University," chap. 4, 24–27.

70. "Architecture, Antics," 7.

71. Welsh, "History of the University," chap. 4, 24–27.

72. Mitchell, *Remembrance Wakes*, 79.

73. Welsh, "History of the University," chap. 4, 27–32.

74. "Architecture, Antics," 6.

75. "Architecture, Antics," 6–7.

76. "Architecture, Antics," 7.

77. Welsh, "History of the University," chap. 4, 33; Regents' Minutes, May 1, 1909, 458; Dabney, "A History of the College of Arts and Sciences," 5.

78. "Architecture, Antics," 7; Mitchell, *Remembrance Wakes*, 79.

79. Mitchell, *Remembrance Wakes*, 66.

Chapter 6

1. Dabney, "A History of the College of Arts and Sciences," 5.

2. Welsh, "History of the University," chap. 4, 39.

3. Mitchell, *Remembrance Wakes*, 115.

4. Welsh, "History of the University," chap. 4, 40.

5. Mitchell, *Remembrance Wakes*, 117.

6. Welsh, "History of the University," chap. 4, 40–42; Dabney, "A History of the College of Arts and Sciences," 5.

7. Welsh, "History of the University," chap. 4, 44–45; Regents' Minutes, February 7, 1910, 483.

8. Welsh, "History of the University," chap. 4, 46–47.

9. Welsh, "History of the University," chap. 4, 48; Regents' Minutes, April 7, May 2, 29, 1910, 494, 498–99.

10. Hughes, *Pueblo on the Mesa*, 125–26.

11. Hughes, *Pueblo on the Mesa*, 126.

12. Hughes, *Pueblo on the Mesa*, 126.

13. Welsh, "History of the University," chap. 4, 50–52.

14. Hooker, *Only in New Mexico*, 25–26.

15. Welsh, "History of the University," chap. 4, 52–54.

16. Hughes, *Pueblo on the Mesa*, 127.

17. Hughes, *Pueblo on the Mesa*, 129.

18. Hughes, *Pueblo on the Mesa*, 129–30.

19. Hughes, *Pueblo on the Mesa*, 132.

20. Mitchell, *Remembrance Wakes*, 124–25.

21. Welsh, "History of the University," chap. 4, 53, 56–57.

22. Hughes, *Pueblo on the Mesa*, 76–77; Barney, *Turmoil and Triumph*, 37.

23. Welsh, "History of the University," chap. 4, 44–46; Regents'

Minutes, February 7, 1910, 493.

24. Barney, *Turmoil and Triumph*, 91.

25. Barney, *Turmoil and Triumph*, 40–42.

26. Barney, *Turmoil and Triumph*, 32–33, 51–52, 63–65, 72.

27. Welsh, "History of the University," chap. 4, 54; Regents' Minutes, August 1, October 24, 1910, 510, 513, 518.

28. Welsh, "History of the University," chap. 4, 54–58.

29. Mitchell, *Remembrance Wakes*, 124.

30. Welsh, "History of the University," chap. 4, 63–65; Regents' Minutes, September 18, October 2, 1911, 545, 551; January 13, 1912, 563.

31. Welsh, "History of the University," chap. 4, 64–65; Regents' Minutes, September 18, October 2, 1911, 545, 551.

32. Simmons, *Albuquerque*, 352.

33. Simmons, *Albuquerque*, 352.

34. Welsh, "History of the University," chap. 4, 71–73; Regents' Minutes, March 25, 1912, 2–3.

35. Dabney, "A History of the College of Arts and Sciences," 7.

36. Welsh, "History of the University," chap. 4, 75–76; Mitchell, *Remembrance Wakes*, 120–21.

37. "Observations of John D. Clark," 1956, UNMA.

38. Welsh, "History of the University," chap. 4, 75.

39. Welsh, "History of the University," chap. 4, 76–80; Edward D. Mc. Gray, "The Spanish Language in New Mexico," *Sociological Series* 1, no. 2 (1912): 37–38.

Chapter 7

1. Barney, *Turmoil and Triumph*, 74–75.

2. Barney, *Turmoil and Triumph*, 76.

3. Barney, *Turmoil and Triumph*, 78.

4. Barney, *Turmoil and Triumph*, 77–80.

5. Welsh, "History of the University," chap. 5, 1–2.

6. Mitchell, *Remembrance Wakes*, 187.

7. Welsh, "History of the University," chap. 5, 2–3.

8. Welsh, "History of the University," chap. 5, 5–8.

9. Welsh, "History of the University," chap. 5, 5–8.

10. Welsh, "History of the University," chap. 5, 8.

11. Welsh, "History of the University," chap. 5, 10–12.

12. Welsh, "History of the University," chap. 5, 16.

13. Welsh, "History of the University," chap. 5, 19.

14. Dabney, "A History of the College of Arts and Sciences," 7.

15. Dabney, "A History of the College of Arts and Sciences," 9; Hughes, *Pueblo on the Mesa*, 108–11.

16. Welsh, "History of the University," chap. 5, 40.

17. Welsh, "History of the University," chap. 5, 45.

18. Welsh, "History of the University," chap. 5, 45–46.

19. Welsh, "History of the University," chap. 5, 46–47; Regents' Minutes, January 11, 1915, 6; Dabney, "A History of the College of Arts and Sciences," 10.

20. Dabney, "A History of the College of Arts and Sciences," 10.

21. Welsh, "History of the University," chap. 5, 47.

22. Welsh, "History of the University," chap. 5, 49.

23. Hughes, *Pueblo on the Mesa*, 53.

24. Welsh, "History of the University," chap. 5, 50; Dabney, "A

History of the College of Arts and Sciences," 8.

25. Dabney, "A History of the College of Arts and Sciences," 8.

26. UNM Catalog, 1915–16, 247.

27. Welsh, "History of the University," chap. 5, 50–52.

28. Welsh, "History of the University," chap. 5, 56–57.

29. Welsh, "History of the University," chap. 5, 57–58; Regents' Minutes, December 16, 1916, March 21, 1917, 90, 95, 120.

30. Welsh, "History of the University," chap. 5, 61–62.

31. Hooker, *Only in New Mexico*, 32.

32. Hooker, *Only in New Mexico*, 32.

33. Hooker, *Only in New Mexico*, 32.

34. Hooker, *Only in New Mexico*, 32–33.

35. Hughes, *Pueblo on the Mesa*, 30–31.

36. Hooker, *Only in New Mexico*, 31–34.

37. Hooker, *Only in New Mexico*, 37.

38. Hooker, *Only in New Mexico*, 40

39. Hooker, *Only in New Mexico*, 34–40, 44.

40. Hooker, *Only in New Mexico*, 44, 51.

41. Hughes, *Pueblo on the Mesa*, 63–67.

42. Hughes, *Pueblo on the Mesa*, 132–33.

43. Clark, "History of the University of New Mexico," 6.

44. Hooker, *Only in New Mexico*, 38.

45. Hooker, *Only in New Mexico*, 37.

46. UNM Catalog, 1981–82, 1982–83, 7.

47. Barney, *Turmoil and Triumph*, 91–96.

48. Barney, *Turmoil and Triumph*, 97–99.

49. Barney, *Turmoil and Triumph*, 100–106.

50. Barney, *Turmoil and Triumph*, 110–12.

51. Welsh, "History of the University," chap. 5, 62–63.

52. Welsh, "History of the University," chap. 5, 63–65.

53. Hughes, *Pueblo on the Mesa*, 137–38.

54. Dabney, "A History of the College of Arts and Sciences," 10–11.

55. Dabney, "A History of the College of Arts and Sciences," 11.

56. Welsh, "History of the University," chap. 5, 72–75.

57. Hughes, *Pueblo on the Mesa*, 138–39.

58. Welsh, "History of the University," chap. 5, 80–81.

59. Hughes, *Pueblo on the Mesa*, 139–40.

60. Welsh, "History of the University," chap. 5, 84–87.

61. Welsh, "History of the University," chap. 5, 87–88.

62. Hooker, *Only in New Mexico*, 43.

63. Welsh, "History of the University," chap. 5, 90.

Chapter 8

1. Barney, *Turmoil and Triumph*, 115–24.

2. Welsh, "History of the University," chap. 6, 4.

3. Welsh, "History of the University," chap. 6, 5–9.

4. Welsh, "History of the University," chap. 6, 9–16.

5. Dabney, "A History of the College of Arts and Sciences," 13.

6. Michael Welsh, "Often Out of Sight, Rarely Out of Mind: Race and Ethnicity at the University of New Mexico, 1889–1927," *New Mexico Historical Review* 71, no. 2 (1996): 126.

7. Welsh, "History of the University," chap. 6, 20–21.

8. Dabney, "A History of the College of Arts and Sciences," 13–14.

9. Welsh, "History of the University," chap. 6, 25–26.

10. Welsh, "History of the University," chap. 6, 32–32.

11. Dabney, "A History of the College of Arts and Sciences," 13.

12. Dabney, "A History of the College of Arts and Sciences," 14.

13. Welsh, "History of the University," chap. 6, 34–35.

14. Welsh, "History of the University," chap. 6, 44–45.

15. Welsh, "History of the University," chap. 6, 36–48.

16. Welsh, "History of the University," chap. 6, 50–53.

17. Dabney, "A History of the College of Arts and Sciences," 14.

18. Welsh, "History of the University," chap. 6, 55–57.

19. Welsh, "History of the University," chap. 6, 58.

20. Welsh, "History of the University," chap. 6, 63–64.

21. Welsh, "History of the University," chap. 6, 67–68.

22. Welsh, "Often Out of Sight," 127–30.

23. Welsh, "History of the University," chap. 6, 70–71.

24. Welsh, "History of the University," chap. 6, 75–77.

25. Welsh, "History of the University," chap. 6, 79–81.

26. Welsh, "History of the University," chap. 6, 86.

27. UNM Catalog, 1926–27, 48.

28. Welsh, "History of the University," chap. 6, 87.

29. Welsh, "History of the University," chap. 6, 89.

30. UNM Catalog, 1924–25, 130–31.

31. Welsh, "History of the University," chap. 6, 91–95.

32. Welsh, "History of the University," chap. 6, 95.

33. Welsh, "History of the University," chap. 6, 97.

34. Welsh, "History of the University," chap. 6, 107.

35. Welsh, "History of the University," chap. 6, 107–9.

36. Welsh, "History of the University," chap. 6, 109–10.

37. Welsh, "History of the University," chap. 6, 134–37.

38. Welsh, "History of the University," chap. 6, 141–42.

39. Welsh, "History of the University," chap. 6, 109–10.

40. Welsh, "History of the University," chap. 6, 112–17.

41. Welsh, "History of the University," chap. 6, 118–22.

42. Dabney, "A History of the College of Arts and Sciences," 14–15.

43. Welsh, "History of the University," chap. 6, 25–27.

44. Welsh, "History of the University," chap. 6, 42–44.

45. Welsh, "History of the University," chap. 6, 83–85.

46. Welsh, "History of the University," chap. 6, 124.

47. Welsh, "History of the University," chap. 6, 147.

48. Hooker, *Only in New Mexico*, 45–51.

49. Mary Ellen Hanson and Carl A. Hanson, "Wilma Loy Shelton: Library Leader in New Mexico, 1920–1950," *New Mexico Historical Review* 20, no. 1 (1989): 54.

50. Hughes, *Pueblo on the Mesa*, 89–92.

51. Hooker, *Only in New Mexico*, 58.

52. Hooker, *Only in New Mexico*, 52–53.

53. Welsh, "History of the University," chap. 6, 81.

54. Barney, *Turmoil and Triumph*, 130–31.

55. Robert K. Barney, *Roy W. Johnson—A Short Biography* (Albuquerque: self-published, UNMA, 1963), 43.

56. Hooker, *Only in New Mexico*, 56.

57. Hooker, *Only in New Mexico*, 133–35.

58. Welsh, "History of the University," chap. 6, 62; Hooker, *Only in New Mexico*, 56.

59. Barney, *Turmoil and Triumph*, 136; Welsh, "History of the University," chap. 6, 81–82.

60. Barney, *Turmoil and Triumph*, 137–45.

61. Barney, *Turmoil and Triumph*, 159–64.

62. "The Lobo Mascot," *2002 New Mexico Football*, University of New Mexico Media Guide, 2002, University of New Mexico Media Relations Department, 20.

63. "The Lobo Mascot," 20.

64. Welsh, "History of the University," chap. 6, 128.

65. Welsh, "History of the University," chap. 6, 155–56.

66. Welsh, "History of the University," chap. 6, 139–40.

67. Welsh, "History of the University," chap. 6, 156–58.

68. Welsh, "History of the University," chap. 6, 158.

69. Welsh, "History of the University," chap. 6, 133.

Chapter 9

1. Barney, *Turmoil and Triumph*, 178–80.

2. Barney, *Turmoil and Triumph*, 176–77.

3. Barney, *Turmoil and Triumph*, 180–87.

4. Welsh, "History of the University," chap. 7, 6.

5. Welsh, "History of the University," chap. 7, 3–7.

6. Welsh, "History of the University," chap. 7, 10–11.

7. Welsh, "History of the University," chap. 7, 11–18.

8. Welsh, "History of the University," chap. 7, 19–21.

9. Welsh, "History of the University," chap. 7, 30.

10. James T. Stensvaag, "Fifty Years of the *New Mexico Historical Review*: An Archival Record," *New Mexico Historical Review* 51, no. 4 (1976): 275.

11. Hooker, *Only in New Mexico*, 59.

12. Hughes, *Pueblo on the Mesa*, 33–34.

13. Welsh, "History of the University," chap. 7, 50–61.

14. Welsh, "History of the University," chap. 7, 64–65.

15. Dabney, "A History of the College of Arts and Sciences," 16.

16. Welsh, "History of the University," chap. 7, 68.

17. "Grace Edmister Dies; Founder of NMSO," *Albuquerque Journal*, July 10, 1984.

18. Welsh, "History of the University," chap. 7, 89–91.

19. Welsh, "History of the University," chap. 7, 116–18.

20. Welsh, "History of the University," chap. 7, 123.

21. Welsh, "History of the University," chap. 7, 121–23.

22. Dabney, "A History of the College of Arts and Sciences," 16–17.

23. Welsh, "History of the University," chap. 7, 42–43.

24. Welsh, "History of the University," chap. 7, 134–35, 148–50.

25. Welsh, "History of the University," chap. 7, 130, 133–35.

26. Howard, "A Hundred Years of Partnership with Albuquerque," 53.

27. Welsh, "History of the University," chap. 8, 1–3.

28. Dabney, "A History of the College of Arts and Sciences," 18.

29. Welsh, "History of the University," chap. 8, 5–7.

30. Welsh, "History of the University," chap. 8, 8.

31. Welsh, "History of the University," chap. 8, 10–11.

32. Phillip B. Gonzales, "Spanish Heritage and Ethnic Protest in New Mexico: The Anti-Fraternity Bill of 1933," *New Mexico Historical Review* 61, no. 4 (1986): 283–93.

33. Welsh, "History of the University," chap. 8, 15–19.

34. Welsh, "History of the University," chap. 8, 22–23.

35. Welsh, "History of the University," chap. 8, 23–33.

36. Welsh, "History of the University," chap. 8, 33–38.

37. Michael Welsh, "A Prophet Without Honor: George I. Sanchez and Bilingualism in New Mexico," *New Mexico Historical Review* 69, no. 1 (1994): 19–34.

38. Welsh, "History of the University," chap. 7, 2.

39. J. D. Arnold, "Senator Bronson Cutting," *New Mexico Magazine*, May 2003, 28–33.

40. Mitchell, *Remembrance Wakes*, 143–53.

41. Dabney, "A History of the College of Arts and Sciences," 20.

42. Hughes, *Pueblo on the Mesa*, 55.

43. UNM Catalog, 1934–35, 148.

44. Don Schlegel, "History Notes: School of Architecture and Planning" (unpublished manuscript, UNMA, October 20, 2004), 1.

45. Dabney, "A History of the College of Arts and Sciences," 21.

46. Dabney, "A History of the College of Arts and Sciences," 22.

47. Barney, *Turmoil and Triumph*, 191–93.

48. Nick D. Mills, Jr., "The Origins of Latin American Programs at the University of New Mexico, 1927–1948" (manuscript, UNMA, 1981), 13–14.

49. Hughes, *Pueblo on the Mesa*, 96–98.

50. Welsh, "History of the University," chap. 7, 58, 111, 153.

51. Marie Hays, UNM Traditions: The First Hundred Years (manuscript, UNMA, n.d.).

52. Welsh, "History of the University," chap. 7, 113.

53. Welsh, "History of the University," chap. 7, 57–58.

54. Welsh, "History of the University," chap. 7, 16, 56–57.

55. Betty Huning Hinton, *UNM's First Dean of Women, Lena C. Clauve* (Albuquerque: Guynes Printing Company of New Mexico, 1989), 1–34.

56. Hooker, *Only in New Mexico*, 58–60.

57. Hughes, *Pueblo on the Mesa*, 65.

58. Hooker, *Only in New Mexico*, 70.

59. Raymond J. Stuart to James Defibaugh, research associate, History Department, University of New Mexico, Jan. 8, 1975, cited by Welsh, "A History of the University," chap. 7, 63.

60. Hooker, *Only in New Mexico*, 61–79.

61. Hooker, *Only in New Mexico*, 80–83.

62. Van Deren Coke, *Taos and Santa Fe: The Artist's Environment, 1882–1942* (Albuquerque: University of New Mexico Press, 1963), 68.

63. Hughes, *Pueblo on the Mesa*, 92–94.

64. Barney, *Turmoil and Triumph*, 137.

65. Barney, *Roy W. Johnson*, 44.

66. Barney, *Turmoil and Triumph*, 145–47.

67. Barney, *Turmoil and Triumph*, 191–97.

68. Barney, *Turmoil and Triumph*, 197–211.

69. Barney, *Turmoil and Triumph*, 216–20.

70. Barney, *Turmoil and Triumph*, 220–25.

71. Barney, *Turmoil and Triumph*, 211–12.

72. Barney, *Turmoil and Triumph*, 214–15.

73. Barney, *Turmoil and Triumph*, 225–30.

74. University of New Mexico 1939–1941 Biennial Report, Office of the President, UNMA, 9–15.

75. Biennial Report, 9–15.

76. Hughes, *Pueblo on the Mesa*, vii.

77. Hughes, *Pueblo on the Mesa*, 147.

Chapter 10

1. Barney, *Turmoil and Triumph*, 242.

2. Welsh, "History of the University," chap. 7*, 18 (7* is Welsh's second chap. 7).

3. Simmons, *Albuquerque*, 366

4. Simmons, *Albuquerque*, 367.

5. "Secret Fuse Tiny But Deadly," *All Hands*, U.S. Navy magazine, September 1945, 23–24; "Workman to Head Hawaii Lab," *Albuquerque Tribune*, November 13, 1964.

6. Barney, *Turmoil and Triumph*, 242–61.

7. Welsh, "History of the University," chap. 7*, 34.

8. Welsh, "History of the University," chap. 7*, 8–9, 26, 28, 36–37.

9. Simmons, *Albuquerque*, 361–67.

10. Simmons, *Albuquerque*, 15–17, 21, 32, 35, 39–40.

11. Mills, "The Origins of Latin American Programs," 16.

12. Simmons, *Albuquerque*, 25.

13. Mills, "The Origins of Latin American Programs," 26.

14. *UNM Alumnus*, April 1943.

15. Dabney, "A History of the College of Arts and Sciences," 23–24.

16. Hooker, *Only in New Mexico*, 86.

17. Hooker, *Only in New Mexico*, 85–87.

18. Barney, *Turmoil and Triumph*, 263.

19. Barney, *Roy Johnson*, 55.

20. Barney, *Turmoil and Triumph*, 265–66, 269–70, 284–89.

21. Hooker, *Only in New Mexico*, 87.

22. Paul A. F. Walter, Sr., "Necrology: James Fulton Zimmerman." *New Mexico Historical Review* 20, no. 1 (1945): 83–89.

23. Hillerman, "Birthday for a College," 31.

24. Simmons, *Albuquerque*, 367

25. Simmons, *Albuquerque*, 367

26. Simmons, *Albuquerque*, 367–68; Lansing Lamont, *Day of Trinity* (New York: Atheneum, 1965), 10, 53, 154, 240–41; James W. Kunetka, *City of Fire, Los Alamos and the Birth of the Atomic Age, 1943–1945* (Englewood Cliffs, NJ: Prentice Hall, 1978), 43.

Chapter 11

1. Hillerman, "Birthday for a College," 31.

2. Simmons, *Albuquerque*, 370–71.

3. Simmons, *Albuquerque*, 371.

4. James Defibaugh, "A New Mexico Legend," *UNM Alumnus*, December 1975, 1.

5. Dabney, "A History of the College of Arts and Sciences," 24–25.

6. "College of Pharmacy," *Albuquerque Journal*, February 23, 1964.

7. "College of Business Administration," *Albuquerque Journal*, February 23, 1964.

8. Schlegel, "History Notes," 1.

9. Henry P. Weihofen, "History of the Law School, 1947–1987" (manuscript, UNMA, 1988), 1.

10. "The School of Law," *Albuquerque Journal*, February 23, 1964.

11. Weihofen, "History of the Law School," 1–7.

12. "Journalism Department at U. Having Own Little Celebration," *Albuquerque Journal*, February 23, 1964.

13. UNM Catalog, 1948–49, 284.

14. Dabney, "A History of the College of Arts and Sciences," 25–26.

15. Dabney, "A History of the College of Arts and Sciences," 27.

16. Defibaugh, "A New Mexico Legend," 1.

17. Defibaugh, "A New Mexico Legend," 1–2.

18. Hooker, *Only in New Mexico*, 87–90; Barney, *Turmoil and Triumph*, 262.

19. Barney, *Turmoil and Triumph*, 289–96.

20. Dabney, "A History of the College of Arts and Sciences," 24.

21. "Regents Select Popejoy to Take Over Next June," *Albuquerque Tribune*, January 29, 1948.

22. Larry La Rouche, Albuquerque News, January 30, 1948.

23. "Pamphlets Over Campus Protest Regents' Action," *Albuquerque Journal*, February 1, 1948.

24. "Out Like a Janitor," *Time*, February 16, 1948.

25. "Time and Wernette," *Albuquerque Journal*, February 14, 1948.

26. "Petition Lauds Popejoy Choice," *Albuquerque Tribune*, February 14, 1948.

Chapter 12

1. Defibaugh, "A New Mexico Legend," 2.

2. Art Bouffard, "Tom Popejoy, Ex-U Head, Dead at 72," *Albuquerque Journal*, October 25, 1975; Urith Lucas, "UNM Leader Popejoy Dies," *Albuquerque Tribune*, October 25, 1975; Orlando Medina, "Popejoy Remembered," *New Mexico Daily Lobo*, October 28, 1975; Myron F. Fifield, "My Personal Association with President Thomas Lafayette Popejoy," *New Mexico Professional Engineer*, September 1968, 4–6, 9–10, 14; Carlos Salazar, "UNM's 'First Lady' Was Partner, Hostess and Mother," *Albuquerque Tribune*, August 23, 1996.

3. Defibaugh, "A New Mexico Legend," 2.

4. Defibaugh, "A New Mexico Legend," 2.

5. Gerald D. Nash and Gunther E. Gothenburg, "Expanding Horizons, A Pictorial History of the University of New Mexico," *UNM Alumnus*, July 1964, 29.

6. Nash and Gothenburg, "Expanding Horizons," 30.

7. Dabney, "A History of the College of Arts and Sciences," 28.

8. "College of Nursing," *Albuquerque Journal*, February 23, 1964.

9. Schlegel, "History Notes," 2.

10. Dabney, "A History of the College of Arts and Sciences," 28–31.

11. Dabney, "A History of the College of Arts and Sciences," 32–33.

12. "College of Business Administration," *Albuquerque Journal*, February 23, 1964.

13. "College of Fine Arts," *Albuquerque Journal*, February 23, 1964.

14. "Two-Part Dental Program Offered at University," *Albuquerque Journal*, February 23, 1964.

15. Dabney, "A History of the College of Arts and Sciences," 33.

16. Schlegel, "History Notes," 3.

17. "Alumni Association Always Ready to Be of Service to University," *Albuquerque Journal*, February 23, 1964.

18. "'Free Play of Ideas' Guided Popejoy," *Campus News*, November 6, 1975.

19. "Free Play of Ideas."

20. "Free Play of Ideas."

21. Jake W. Spidle, *Doctors of Medicine in New Mexico: History of Health and Medical Practice, 1886–1986* (Albuquerque: University of New Mexico Press, 1986), 309.

22. Spidle, *Doctors of Medicine*, 310, citing a July 20, 1984, interview with Dr. Robert Loftfield.

23. Reginald H. Fitz, MD, interview by Jake W. Spidle, May 14, 1988, UNM Medical Center Library Oral History of Medicine Project, Albuquerque, New Mexico.

24. Spidle, *Doctors of Medicine*, 313.

25. Fitz interview.

26. Spidle, *Doctors of Medicine*, 314.

27. Spidle, *Doctors of Medicine*, 316.

28. Veronica Hefner, "Reluctant Visionary," *Albuquerque Tribune*, July 5, 2001.

29. Spidle, *Doctors of Medicine*, 317.

30. Van Dorn Hooker, A Conversation with Reginald Fitz, First Dean of the Medical School (unpublished manuscript, UNMA). University of New Mexico, May 13, 1993. 1.

31. Spidle, *Doctors of Medicine*, 318–19.

32. Spidle, *Doctors of Medicine*, 319–21.

33. "Medical School Opening to Be Climax of Long Campaign," *Albuquerque Journal*, February 23, 1964.

34. "College of Arts and Sciences," *Albuquerque Journal*, February 23, 1964.

35. "UNM Graduates Find That Jobs Are Plentiful," *Albuquerque Journal*, February 23, 1964.

36. "To Emphasize Academic Subjects," *Albuquerque Journal*, February 23, 1964.

37. Weihofen, "History of the Law School," 27–41.

38. Harold L. Enarson, "Profile of the University of New Mexico," *New Mexico Business Report*, University of New Mexico, March 1965, 1, 2, 4, 5.

39. Howard, "A Hundred Years of Partnership with Albuquerque," 53.

Chapter 13

1. Dabney, "A History of the College of Arts and Sciences," 32.

2. Bouffard, "Tom Popejoy."

3. Hooker, *Only in New Mexico*, 229.

4. Hooker, *Only in New Mexico*, 108.

5. Hooker, *Only in New Mexico*, 103–24.

6. Hooker, *Only in New Mexico*, 146.

7. Hooker, *Only in New Mexico*, 127–46.

8. Bainbridge Bunting in *New Mexico Architecture*, cited by Hooker, *Only in New Mexico*, 163–64.

9. Hooker, *Only in New Mexico*, 158.

10. Hooker, *Only in New Mexico*, 147–89.

11. Ben Duncan, "Ben Duncan's Story," *Albuquerque Journal*, October 29, 2000.

12. Mel Firestone, "Mel Firestone's Story," *Albuquerque Journal*, November 5, 2000.

13. Phyllis Dorset, "Phyllis Dorset's Story," *Albuquerque Journal*, November 5, 2000.

14. Milton W. Holt, athletic director at Idaho State University, quoting Tom Popejoy, September 15, 1967, personal communication to William E. Davis.

15. Rick Wright, "Lasting Legacy for Lobos," *Albuquerque Journal*, October 17, 2004.

16. Wright, "Lasting Legacy."

17. Mark Smith, "Coach Made Lobo Basketball," *Albuquerque Journal*, September 19, 1999.

18. Hooker, *Only in New Mexico*, 170–73.

19. Hooker, *Only in New Mexico*, 229.

20. Hooker, *Only in New Mexico*, 183.

21. Tony Hillerman, *Seldom Disappointed* (New York: Harper Collins, 2001), 238–39.

22. Medina, "Popejoy Remembered."

23. Hillerman, "Birthday for a College," 3.

Chapter 14

1. Ferrel Heady, *One Time Around* (Albuquerque: School of Public Administration, University of New Mexico, 1999).

2. Heady, *One Time Around*, 6–7.

3. Heady, *One Time Around*, 33–42, 43–67.

4. Heady, *One Time Around*, 67–73.

5. Heady, *One Time Around*, 76–107.

6. Heady, *One Time Around*, 107–39.

7. Heady, *One Time Around*, 142.

8. Heady, *One Time Around*, 142–43.

9. Heady, *One Time Around*, 143, citing Samuel P. Huntington, *American Politics: The Promise of Disharmony* (Cambridge, Mass.: Harvard University Press, 1981), chap. 7.

10. Calvin Horn, *The University in Turmoil and Transition: Crisis Decades at the University of New Mexico* (Albuquerque: Rocky Mountain Publishing, 1981).

11. Dabney, "A History of the College of Arts and Sciences," 34.

12. Horn, *The University in Turmoil*, 15–16.

13. Horn, *The University in Turmoil*, 16–19.

14. Horn, *The University in Turmoil*, 19.

15. Dabney, "A History of the College of Arts and Sciences," 137–38.

16. Heady, *One Time Around*, 169–72.

17. Dabney, "A History of the College of Arts and Sciences," 38.

18. Heady, *One Time Around*, 173.

19. Dabney, "A History of the College of Arts and Sciences," 38–39.

20. Heady, *One Time Around*, 173–76.

21. Heady, *One Time Around*, 177–83.

22. Heady, *One Time Around*, 186.

23. Heady, *One Time Around*, 183–89.

24. Weihofen, "History of the Law School," 42–45.

25. Heady, *One Time Around*, 202.

26. Heady, *One Time Around*, 208.

27. Horn, *The University in Turmoil*, 75.

28. Heady, *One Time Around*, 241.

29. Horn, *The University in Turmoil*, 47.

30. Horn, *The University in Turmoil*, 202.

31. Horn, *The University in Turmoil*, 153–58.

32. Heady, *One Time Around*, 248.

33. Heady, *One Time Around*, 249.

34. Horn, *The University in Turmoil*, 211–12.

35. Horn, *The University in Turmoil*, 214.

36. Weihofen, "History of the Law School," 72–76.

37. UNM Catalog, 1972–73, 256.

38. University of New Mexico, http://www.unm.edu/~oca (accessed March 2005).

39. "UNM Official Dr. Smith Dies," *Albuquerque Journal*, October 5, 1973.

40. Hooker, *Only in New Mexico*, 217.

41. Sherman E. Smith to the Student Publications Board, July 11, 1961, UNMA.

42. Mark Acuff, "Off the Cuff," *New Mexico Independent*, October 12, 1973.

43. V. B. Price, "We'll Miss Sherman Smith," *New Mexico Independent*, October 12, 1973.

44. Price, "We'll Miss Sherman Smith."

45. Dabney, "A History of the College of Arts and Sciences," 38–39.

46. Shannon Carter, History of the University of New Mexico School of Medicine (Manuscript, University of New Mexico School of Medicine, 2005), n.p.

47. Weihofen, "History of the Law School," 91–94, 146–47, 151–57.

48. Tom Sanchez, "Former UNM Regent Cyrene Mapel, 81, Dies," *Albuquerque Journal*, September 7, 1992.

49. Tony Hillerman, *The Spell of New Mexico* (Albuquerque: University of New Mexico Press, 1976); David King Dunaway and Sara Spurgeon, *Writing the Southwest* (Albuquerque: University of New Mexico Press, 1995); Rozanna M. Martinez, "Book Samples Works of Southwest Writers," *Rio Rancho Journal*, March 9, 2004.

50. Hooker, *Only in New Mexico*, 199, 208.

51. Hooker, *Only in New Mexico*, 192–94.

52. Hooker, *Only in New Mexico*, 195–96.

53. Hooker, *Only in New Mexico*, 197.

54. Hooker, *Only in New Mexico*, 199.

55. Hooker, *Only in New Mexico*, 201.

56. Hooker, *Only in New Mexico*, 212–14.

57. Hooker, *Only in New Mexico*, 216–18.

58. Hooker, *Only in New Mexico*, 218.

59. Hooker, *Only in New Mexico*, 220–21.

60. Hooker, *Only in New Mexico*, 224–27.

61. Hooker, *Only in New Mexico*, 222.

62. Horn, *The University in Turmoil*, 202–4.

63. Horn, *The University in Turmoil*, 215–18.

64. Heady, *One Time Around*, 254.

65. Horn, *The University in Turmoil*, 218.

66. Horn, *The University in Turmoil*, 216–17.

67. Horn, *The University in Turmoil*, 218–19.

68. Heady, *One Time Around*, 242–43.

69. Horn, *The University in Turmoil*, 219–21.

70. Heady, *One Time Around*, 145.

71. Dabney, "A History of the College of Arts and Sciences," 36.

Chapter 15

1. V. B. Price, "Bud Davis Really Seems to be Doing What He Set Out to Do at the U," The *New Mexico Independent*, August 13, 1976.

2. Price, "Bud Davis."

3. Horn, *The University in Turmoil*, 319–20.

4. William E. Davis, "The University of New Mexico Presidential Report: William E. Davis, 1975–1982," UNMA.

5. William E. Davis, "My Lonely, Losing Battle Against Co-education in the Dorms," *Empire Magazine, Denver Post*, October 17, 1971.

6. Horn, *The University in Turmoil*, 286.

7. Horn, *The University in Turmoil*, 287.

8. Horn, *The University in Turmoil*, 293.

9. Horn, *The University in Turmoil*, 295.

10. Horn, *The University in Turmoil*, 293.

11. Mark Acuff, "Bad Days at UNM: Journal Goes from Irresponsibility to Pathology," *New Mexico Independent*, January 4, 1980.

12. Paula Easley, "Newsweek Reminds UNM of Past," *New Mexico Daily Lobo*, September 24, 1980.

13. Horn, *The University in Turmoil*, 316.

14. William E. Davis, statement published in the *Albuquerque Journal*, July 8, 1981.

15. Franklin Jones, "Intercollegiate Athletic Problems at the University of New Mexico," report for the Regents of the University of New Mexico, May 5, 1980, UNMA.

16. Albert E. Utton, "Athletic Council Opinion Regarding Matters Contained in a Statement of Professor Charles Coates," December 17, 1979, UNMA.

17. William E. Davis, "Address to NCAA Institutional Executive Officers on Institutional Control of Intercollegiate Athletics," September 29, 1981, UNMA.

18. William E. Davis, "Beyond the Adobe Walls," speech presented to the Albuquerque Rotary Club, August 18, 1977, UNMA.

Chapter 16

1. Arturo Sandoval, "John Perovich Named Acting UNM President," *Albuquerque Journal*, April 2, 1982; Nancy Harbert and Dennis Latta, "UNM's Interim President to Remain on Job, *Albuquerque Journal*, November 21, 1982.

2. Mary Engel, "UNM: 'Open' Presidential Search Breeds Rumors," *Albuquerque Journal*, November 14, 1982.

3. Engel, "UNM: 'Open' Presidential Search."

4. Harbert and Latta, "UNM's Interim President."

5. "New UNM President," editorial, *Albuquerque Journal*, November 23, 1982.

6. Christopher Miller, "New UNM Leader Praised, Selection Process Panned," *Albuquerque Journal*, November 22, 1982.

7. Mary Engel, "Modesty Key to Perovich's Administration," *Albuquerque Journal*, January 1, 1983.

8. Chester C. Travelstead, "Here's Travelstead's Opinion of the Search Process," *Albuquerque Journal*, December 3, 1982.

9. Calvin Horn, Henry Jaramillo, and Dr. Phillip Martinez, "UNM Regents Reply to Criticisms of Presidential Search," *Albuquerque Tribune*, December 7, 1982.

10. Mary Engel, "UNM Regent Calvin Horn Resigns," *Albuquerque Journal*, December 30, 1982.

11. Weihofen, "History of the Law School," 159–61.

12. Schlegel, "History Notes," 12.

13. University of New Mexico, http://www.unm.edu/~isnps (accessed March 2005).

14. John Perovich, "The University of New Mexico Presidential Report," University of New Mexico, December 1994, 13.

15. Dabney, "A History of the College of Arts and Sciences," 42–44.

16. Weihofen, "History of the Law School," 174–79.

17. Joe Scaletti, unpublished oral history, UNMA, 2004.

18. Anna Dooling, "One Man Credited with UNM's Style—or Lack of It," *Albuquerque Journal*, June 6, 1982.

19. Hooker, *Only in New Mexico*, 265–78.

20. Hooker, *Only in New Mexico*, 270.

21. Mary Engel, "N.Y. Firm to Aid UNM Presidential Search," *Albuquerque Journal*, March 21, 1984.

22. "Forum," *New Mexico Daily Lobo*, August 23, 1984.

23. Kristie Jones, "Elac Speaks to Council; UNM Deans Mum," *New Mexico Daily Lobo*, August 23, 1984.

24. Jones, "Elac Speaks to Council."

25. "Resolution Condemns Regents," *New Mexico Daily Lobo*, August 23, 1984.

26. Harrison Fletcher, "'Open' Meeting for Elac and Faculty," *New Mexico Daily Lobo*, August 23, 1984.

27. Mary Engel, "Elac Returns Home to Ponder UNM Post," *Albuquerque Journal*, August 24, 1984.

Chapter 17

1. Harrison Fletcher, "Presidential Search Should Wait," *New Mexico Daily Lobo*, September 4, 1984.

2. Harrison Fletcher, "Regents Will Invite Farer to Visit," *New Mexico Daily Lobo*, September 5, 1984.

3. Fletcher, "Regents Will Invite Farer."

4. Harrison Fletcher, "Second on Candidate List to Meet UNM Personnel," *New Mexico Daily Lobo*, September 10, 1984.

5. Harrison Fletcher, "Faculty Gives Farer High Marks," *New Mexico Daily Lobo*, September 12, 1994; Maria DeVarenne, "Regents Could Name Farer U.N.M. President Today," *New Mexico Daily Lobo*, September 18, 1984.

6. Harrison Fletcher, "Regents in Favor of Hiring Farer as UNM President," *New Mexico Daily Lobo*, September 19, 1984.

7. Kristie Jones, "Faculty Urges Support for Farer," *New Mexico Daily Lobo*, October 1, 1984.

8. Harrison Fletcher, "Jaramillo Declines to Sign Farer Contract, *New Mexico Daily Lobo*, October 10, 1984; Marie DeVarenne, "Bardacke Counsels Farer Contract Legal," *New Mexico Daily Lobo*, October 17, 1984; Harrison Fletcher, "Jaramillo Signs Farer's Contract with 'Reservations,'" *New Mexico Daily Lobo*, November 19, 1984.

9. Maria DeVarenne, "Jaramillo 'Appalled' over Fee Charged by Farer During Visit," *New Mexico Daily Lobo*, November 26, 1984; Maria DeVarenne, "Farer Says Dispute Has No Justification," *New Mexico Daily Lobo*, November 27, 1984; Maria DeVarenne, "Farer Withdraws Fee Request," *New Mexico Daily Lobo*, November 28, 1984.

10. "The First Year of a New President," *Mirage*, Spring 1986, 14.

11. "The First Year," 14.

12. "The First Year," 17.

13. Juliette Torrez, "Farer Seeks Short Transition Period," *New Mexico Daily Lobo*, February 19, 1985.

14. David Morton, "Farer Names Jaramillo as Student Affairs Veep," *New Mexico Daily Lobo*, March 6, 1985.

15. David Morton, "'Highest Priority' for Staff Salary Increases," *New Mexico Daily Lobo*, April 10, 1985.

16. Harrison Fletcher, "Compromise Fails; Tuition Increase Included in Bill," *New Mexico Daily Lobo*, February 21, 1985; Harrison Fletcher and David Morton, "Regents Discuss Tuition Raises," *New Mexico Daily Lobo*, April 3, 1985.

17. Ben Neary, "Eyewitnesses Describe Tornado's Impact," *New Mexico Daily Lobo*, September 23, 1985.

18. Stacy Green, "Hillerman Latest to Resign," *New Mexico Daily Lobo*, May 6, 1985.

19. Camille Cordova, "Hearing Focuses on UNM Employment," *New Mexico Daily Lobo*, May 6, 1963.

20. David Morton, "Administrators Concerned about Low Faculty Morale," *New Mexico Daily Lobo*, May 30, 1985.

21. Harrison Fletcher, "Regents Approve Removal of 17 UNM Buildings for Parking Spots," *New Mexico Daily Lobo*, April 4, 1985; Juliette Torrez, "Proposal Submitted to Stop Destruction of Buildings," *New Mexico Daily Lobo*, July 11, 1985.

22. David Morton, "KUNM-FM Fires News Director," *New Mexico Daily Lobo*, April 16, 1985; Camille Cordova, "Group Denounces KUNM-FM Racism," *New Mexico Daily Lobo*, April 22, 1985; Kelly Clark, "Student Groups Demand Public Martinez Hearing," *New Mexico Daily Lobo*, April 26, 1985; Juliette Torrez, "KUNM Manager Selected," *New Mexico Daily Lobo*, January 13, 1986.

23. Jay Reborn, "Athletic Director on Immediate Probation," *New Mexico Daily Lobo*, August 26, 1985.

24. Liz McMillen, "Feud Between President and Regents Debilitates University of New Mexico," *Chronicle of Higher Education*, June 4, 1986, 1.

25. McMillen, "Feud Between President and Regents," 21.

26. Jegot Ortega y McKenzie, "Regents Rescind Film Ban," *New Mexico Daily Lobo*, April 8, 1985.

27. McMillen, "Feud Between President and Regents," 21.

28. McMillen, "Feud Between President and Regents," 23.

29. McMillen, "Feud Between President and Regents," 23.

30. "The First Year," 17.

31. Associated Press, "Apodaca Says Farer 'Doesn't Care' About UNM," *New Mexico Daily Lobo*, April 22, 1986; Kelly Richmond, "Farer Won't Seek New UNM Contract," *New Mexico Daily Lobo*, May 2, 1998.

32. Richmond, "Farer Won't Seek New UNM Contract."

33. V. B. Price, "Viewpoint: How Did UNM Ever Get to Be Such a Mess?" *Albuquerque Tribune*, May 2, 1986.

34. Jeff Awalt, "Farer Says He Will Not Quit Early," *Albuquerque Journal*, May 3, 1986.

35. "An Open Apology to Farer," editorial, and Kerry S. Kilburn, "Blow Up the University," *New Mexico Daily Lobo*, May 2, 1986.

36. Kelly Richmond, "Board of Regents to Face Vote by Faculty Members," *New Mexico Daily Lobo*, May 2, 1986.

37. Jeff Awalt, "Faculty Votes No Confidence in Regents," *Albuquerque Journal*, May 9, 1986.

38. Jeff Awalt, "Farer to Leave Office July 1," *Albuquerque Journal*, June 4, 1986.

39. Kelly Richmond, "Regents, Farer Agree on Early End to Contract," *New Mexico Daily Lobo*, June 5, 1986.

40. Richmond, "Regents, Farer Agree."

41. Iver Peterson, "U. of New Mexico Leader Says He's Had Enough," *New York Times*, May 12, 1986.

42. Peterson, "U. of New Mexico."

43. Peterson, "U. of New Mexico."

44. Peterson, "U. of New Mexico."

45. *New Mexico Daily Lobo*, May 2, 1983.

46. Kelly Richmond, "Regents Approve Deals with May, Farer," *New Mexico Daily Lobo*, June 19, 1986.

Chapter 18

1. Andy Aldrette, "Engineering Dean Named Acting UNM President," *Albuquerque Tribune*, June 4, 1986.

2. Mary Driscoll and Jim Martin, "Farer to Leave Office July 1," *Albuquerque Journal*, June 4, 1986; David Morris, "Regents, Farer Agree on Early End to Contract," *New Mexico Daily Lobo*, June 5, 1986.

3. Aldrette, "Engineering Dean."

4. Kelly Richmond, "1986 UNM Stories Abounded in Conflicts," *New Mexico Daily Lobo*, December 15, 1986; Maria DeVerenne, "May Reflects on State of the University," *New Mexico Daily Lobo*, February 25, 1987.

5. David Gomez, "House Votes to Raise Tuition, Slash Funding," *New Mexico Daily Lobo*, February 6, 1986.

6. "State Budget Faces Tightening by Senate," *New Mexico Daily Lobo*, February 10, 1986.

7. Kira Jones, "Low Pay Blamed for Faculty Departures," *New Mexico Daily Lobo*, August 27, 1986; Jo Schilling, "Student Enrollment Down from Year Ago," *New Mexico Daily Lobo*, August 27, 1986.

8. Walt Smith, "Poll of UNM Students Reveals Top Concerns," *New Mexico Daily Lobo*, December 4, 1986.

9. "House Votes to Raise Tuition 24 Percent," *New Mexico Daily Lobo*, February 18, 1987; Kelly Richmond, "Committee OKs 16 Percent Jump in School Tuition," *New Mexico Daily Lobo*, March 10, 1987; Kelly Richmond, "Legislature OKs 20 Percent Tuition Hike," *New Mexico Daily Lobo*, March 24, 1987.

10. Mike Kaemper, "May's Pay Raise Sees Opposition," *New Mexico Daily Lobo*, December 14, 1987.

11. Kira Jones, "Money Woes Close Child Care Center," *New Mexico Daily Lobo*, June 4, 1987; Kira Jones, "Conditions for Child Care Center Are Named," *New Mexico Daily Lobo*, June 8, 1987; Ken Cunningham, "Child Care, New Budget Discussed," *New Mexico Daily Lobo*, June 11, 1987.

12. Heather Bennett, "May Will Propose Extra Tuition Hike," *New Mexico Daily Lobo*, March 9, 1988; Anne Clancy, "Regents Vote Unanimously to Raise Tuition," *New Mexico Daily Lobo*, March 21, 1988.

13. Evan Leland, "Divestment Policy Unclear," *New Mexico Daily Lobo*, July 10, 1986; Charlie C. Clark IV, "UNM's S. Africa Divestment Done," *New Mexico Daily Lobo*, October 14, 1986.

14. Carter, History of the University of New Mexico School of Medicine

15. Fiona Urquhart, "KUNM Changes Format," *New Mexico Daily Lobo*, June 4, 1987.

16. Charlie C. Clark IV, "KUNM Closes Amid Threats and Controversy," *New Mexico Daily Lobo*, July 2, 1987; John Montoya, "KUNM Program Director Found Guilty of Assault," *New Mexico*

Daily Lobo, December 1, 1987; Anne Clancy, "Supreme Court Rules Against UNM Petition in KUNM Legal Battle," *New Mexico Daily Lobo,* February 2, 1988; Juliette Torrez, "General Manager for KUNM Resigns," *New Mexico Daily Lobo,* February 1, 1989.

17. Fiona Urquhart, "Goodbye, Carroll Lee," *New Mexico Daily Lobo,* June 11, 1987.

18. Weihofen, "History of the Law School," 191.

19. "Photog Led UNM Art Department," *Albuquerque Journal,* July 25, 2004.

20. "UNM Official Takes California College Job," *Albuquerque Journal,* July 1, 1989.

21. Kelly Richmond, "1986 UNM Stories Abounded in Conflicts," *New Mexico Daily Lobo,* December 15, 1986; Kelly Richmond, "State Picks Up Tab for *Hail Mary* Suit," *New Mexico Daily Lobo,* July 3, 1986.

22. Charlie C. Clark IV, "UNM Accused of Racial Discrimination," *New Mexico Daily Lobo,* July 16, 1987; John Montoya, "Officials Named in Lawsuit," *New Mexico Daily Lobo,* July 23, 1987.

23. Leslie Slaymaker, "English TA Faces Racism Charges," *New Mexico Daily Lobo,* July 23, 1987.

24. Mike Kaemper, "History Professor Claims Racism, Lack of Respect," *New Mexico Daily Lobo,* February 15, 1988.

25. Matthew Hoffman, "Women Faculty Allege Discrimination," *New Mexico Daily Lobo,* April 25, 1988.

26. Rhonda A. Gregg, "Women Studies Program Celebrates 20 Years at UNM," *New Mexico Daily Lobo,* October 6, 1988.

27. Charlie C. Clark IV, "UNM in Violation of Federal Regulations," *New Mexico Daily Lobo,* February 10, 1988.

28. Mike Kaemper, "Groups Urge UNM to Ban Smoking in Pit by Next Season," *New Mexico Daily Lobo,* March 1, 1988; Enrique Caraveo, "Union Reduces Smoking Areas for SUB Patrons," *New Mexico Daily Lobo,* December 2, 1988.

29. Eric de la Harpe, "Campus Construction Ahead of Schedule," *New Mexico Daily Lobo,* October 17, 1986; Heather Bennett, "New Library Almost Open for Business," *New Mexico Daily Lobo,* January 1, 1988.

30. Anne Clancy, "Students Crowd into Regents' Meeting," *New Mexico Daily Lobo,* April 13, 1988.

31. Veronique de Turenne, "Regents Disregard Protest, OK Hike," *New Mexico Daily Lobo,* April 12, 1989.

32. Turenne, "Regents Disregard Protest."

33. Grace Belinda del Valle, "Faculty Calls for Regents to Reconsider," *New Mexico Daily Lobo,* April 14, 1989; Enrique Caraveo, "Student Protest Gains Support," *New Mexico Daily Lobo,* April 17, 1989.

34. Enrique Caraveo, "Student Protesters Will Continue Efforts," *New Mexico Daily Lobo,* April 24, 1989.

35. Enrique Caraveo, "Protesters Vacate Scholes Hall," *New Mexico Daily Lobo,* April 25, 1989.

36. B. Barton Lee, "Regents Sustain $100 Hike Decision," *New Mexico Daily Lobo,* April 28, 1989.

37. Ronald David Hidalgo, "Some Protesters Claim Victory After Regents Maintain Tuition Hike," *New Mexico Daily Lobo,* April 28, 1989.

38. Johanna King, "Term Marked by Controversy," *Albuquerque Journal,* July 1, 1989.

39. Eric Snouffer, "Bridgers to Call It Quits Next June," *New Mexico Daily Lobo,* November 25, 1986.

40. Eric Snouffer, "New AD Stresses Rapport," *New Mexico Daily Lobo,* March 24, 1987.

41. Maria DeVarenne, "May Reflects on State of the University," *New Mexico Daily Lobo,* February 25, 1987.

42. Maria DeVarenne, "UNM Ax Slashes Four Athletic Programs," *New Mexico Daily Lobo,* February 18, 1987.

43. Chris Harris, "Basketball Coach Colson Resigns," *New Mexico Daily Lobo,* April 27, 1988.

44. Anne Clancy, "Grand Jury to Decide Merits of University Case," *New Mexico Daily Lobo,* February 13, 1989; Anne Clancy, "Koenig Indictment Ends Era of Tumult, UNM President Says," *New Mexico Daily Lobo,* March 20, 1989.

45. Melissa Howard, "A Century of Scholarship," special supplement to *New Mexico Magazine,* October 1988, 5.

46. Howard, "A Century of Scholarship," 8.

47. Hooker, *Only in New Mexico,* 49.

48. Marcus Price, "The Incomplete History of Science and Research at UNM," *Quantum,* Fall 1988, 10.

49. "UNM Board to Discuss May's Fate," *Albuquerque Journal,* June 30, 1989.

50. Nancy Tipton, "UNM President Gerald May Resigns," *Albuquerque Journal,* July 1, 1989.

51. Tipton, "UNM President."

52. "UNM Leadership," editorial, *Albuquerque Journal,* July 1, 1989.

53. *The University of New Mexico, 1986–1990* (Albuquerque: University of New Mexico Office of Public Affairs, 1990), 3–4.

Chapter 19

1. "Finalists a Study in Contrasts," *Albuquerque Journal,* January 19, 1990.

2. Jay Levine and Beth Velasquez, "ASUNM, GSA, Some Faculty Endorse Peck," *New Mexico Daily Lobo,* January 18, 1990.

3. Regents' Minutes, January 18, 1990, 195.

4. Nancy Tipton and Ellen Marks, "Peck Named UNM President," *Albuquerque Journal,* January 19, 1990.

5. Linda J. Mott, "Regents Talk $, Peck Listens," *New Mexico Daily Lobo,* June 7, 1990.

6. Linda J. Mott, "President to Stay at UNM in Engineering Post," *New Mexico Daily Lobo,* February 6, 1990.

7. *Mirage* yearbook (1946), the University of New Mexico, UNMA, 4.

8. Terry Gugliotta, "University House" UNMA, 1990.

9. Edgar Thompson, "University House Ready for Unveiling," *New Mexico Daily Lobo,* November 1, 1990.

10. Gugliotta, "University House."

11. John Fleck, "UNM Students Protest $50,000 Coronation," *Albuquerque Journal*, November 10, 1990.

12. "A Worthwhile Ritual," editorial, *Albuquerque Journal*, November 10, 1990.

13. Steve O'Neil, "Too Late to Apply for Provost Position," *New Mexico Daily Lobo*, January 29, 1993.

14. Glenn May, "Provost Seeks Tenured Diversity," *New Mexico Daily Lobo*, March 3, 1994; "Coleman Named U. of Iowa President," *New Mexico Daily Lobo*, October 3, 1995.

15. Doug Johnson, "UNM Rescinds Position Offer to Rodriguez," *New Mexico Daily Lobo*, June 15, 1995.

16. Miguel Navrot, "First Female UNM Police Chief Will Begin Next Spring," *New Mexico Daily Lobo*, December 5, 1995.

17. Marcos Montoya, "New Regents Have Strong UNM Background," *New Mexico Daily Lobo*, January 16, 1991.

18. "King Nominates Newest Regents," *New Mexico Daily Lobo*, January 11, 1993.

19. Doug Johnson, "Board of Regents Gets Two New Members, Land and a President," *New Mexico Daily Lobo*, March 20, 1995.

20. Jeff Perrine, "Peck Faces Rocky Problems During His Term," *New Mexico Daily Lobo*, January 23, 1990.

21. Perrine, "Peck Faces Rocky Problems."

22. Dianne DeLeon, "Departments of Communication, Journalism to Merge," *New Mexico Daily Lobo*, March 12, 1992.

23. Jason Harper, "History Department Studies Spanish Colonial Era in N.M.," *New Mexico Daily Lobo*, September 3, 1993.

24. Schlegel, "History Notes," 14.

25. Jessica Salazar, "Gift to School of Architecture Largest in University History," *New Mexico Daily Lobo*, November 24, 1997; V. B. Price, "How UNM Should Spend a Scholar's Rich Legacy," *Albuquerque Tribune*, April 3, 1998.

26. Mike Earnest, "Tuition, Pay Increases Approved," *New Mexico Daily Lobo*, April 16, 1991.

27. Steve O'Neil, "UNM Board of Regents Approves Tuition Increase," *New Mexico Daily Lobo*, April 14, 1993.

28. Doug Johnson, "Regents Raise Tuition 6 Percent," *New Mexico Daily Lobo*, March 24, 1995; Doug Johnson, "Johnson's Cuts Upset Program Directors," *New Mexico Daily Lobo*, March 22, 1995; Rory McClannahan, "Governor Johnson Delivers Promised Funding Rollbacks," *New Mexico Daily Lobo*, September 13, 1995.

29. Doug Johnson, "Rally Ends in Camp-Out at Scholes," *New Mexico Daily Lobo*, March 30, 1995; Chris Cervini, "Administration Grants Professor Demands," *New Mexico Daily Lobo*, April 3, 1995; Doug Johnson, "Meeting Ends in Vow of Representation," *New Mexico Daily Lobo*, April 6, 1995.

30. Glenn May, "PSA Protestors Rattle Roundhouse," *New Mexico Daily Lobo*, January 17, 1996.

31. Dan McKay, "Peck, Splinter Groups Discuss Meeting," *New Mexico Daily Lobo*, March 6, 1996.

32. Dan McKay, Juliet Casey, and Chris Cervini, "Campus Police Arrest Tuition Protestors," *New Mexico Daily Lobo*, March 21, 1996.

33. Miguel Navrot, "Protestors Blame Regents' Inflexibility," *New Mexico Daily Lobo*, March 25, 1996; Dan McKay, "Student Pleas, Noisemakers Fail to Halt Tuition Increase," *New Mexico Daily Lobo*, March 22, 1996; Doug Johnson and Chris Cervini, "Demonstrators Shake Up Regents Meeting with Chants and Rattles," *New Mexico Daily Lobo*, March 22, 1996; Miguel Navrot, "Protestors Face Academic Sanctions," *New Mexico Daily Lobo*, April 19, 1996.

34. Dan McKay, "Faculty Senate Calls UNM Tuition Too Low," *New Mexico Daily Lobo*, February 5, 1997.

35. Dan McKay, "Regents OK 4.5 Percent Tuition Increase," *New Mexico Daily Lobo*, March 25, 1997; Dan McKay, "It's Final: Tuition Hiked 4.5%," *New Mexico Daily Lobo*, March 28, 1997.

36. Kate Nash, "Legislature Gives UNM Top Priorities," *New Mexico Daily Lobo*, February 20, 1998.

37. Kate Nash, "UNM Loses in Supreme Court," *New Mexico Daily Lobo*, June 25, 1998.

38. Kate Nash, "Regents Approve 3.5 Percent Increase," *New Mexico Daily Lobo*, March 27, 1998.

39. Lori J. Montoya, "GSA Hits the Jackpot," *New Mexico Daily Lobo*, March 1, 1994.

40. Angela Coffey-Henderson, "Lottery Scholarships Soon to Be Available," *New Mexico Daily Lobo*, February 17, 1997.

41. Juliet Casey, "Lottery Dough to Be Dished Out to Freshmen," *New Mexico Daily Lobo*, April 11, 1997.

42. Mott Giles, "UNM Sees Its Biggest Entering Class in a Decade," *New Mexico Daily Lobo*, August 27, 1997.

43. Tema Milstein, "Bush Burns," *New Mexico Daily Lobo*, January 15, 1992.

44. Tema Milstein, "Peace Protest Not Quite Peaceful," *New Mexico Daily Lobo*, January 18, 1991; Sean McAfee and Michelle Melendez, "Student Sit-in at Materials Center," *New Mexico Daily Lobo*, January 29, 1991.

45. Betty Karp, "Violence Erupts as 'Old Glory' Burns," *New Mexico Daily Lobo*, February 11, 1991.

46. William B. Untiedt, "'Sit In' Protests Insensitive Parker," *New Mexico Daily Lobo*, February 7, 1991.

47. Tema Milstein, "Students to Sit In with Children at Duck Pond," *New Mexico Daily Lobo*, March 28, 1991.

48. Kandice McDonald, "University Rains on Protest," *New Mexico Daily Lobo*, July 25, 1991.

49. Michelle Melendez, "KUNM Vote Shows 'No Confidence' in Gault-Williams' Performance," *New Mexico Daily Lobo*, November 14, 1990.

50. Michelle Melendez, "Peck Accepts Challenge for Consensus Among UNM's Multiple Interest Groups," *New Mexico Daily Lobo*, September 24, 1990.

51. Edgar Thomason and Michelle Melendez, "Lawsuit Alleges UNM Discriminated," *New Mexico Daily Lobo*, November 7, 1990.

52. Jahanshah Javid, "Racial Slurs Spark Rally," *New Mexico Daily Lobo*, October 9, 1991.

53. Tema Milstein, "New Mexico Third in Nation in Minority Student Count," *New Mexico Daily Lobo*, February 20, 1992.

54. Tema Milstein, "Enrollment of Black Students Up 8 Percent," *New Mexico Daily Lobo*, February 20, 1992.

55. Laura Bendix, "Peck Reverses Ethnic Centers Decision," *New Mexico Daily Lobo*, June 4, 1992; Molly Trafican, "Ethnic Centers Still in Limbo," *New Mexico Daily Lobo*, August 17, 1992.

56. Rene Henderson, "ASUNM Senator Resigns in Protest Over Mural Debate," *New Mexico Daily Lobo*, March 11, 1993.

57. Glenn May, "Regents Recommend 5.4 Percent Tuition Hike," *New Mexico Daily Lobo*, March 21, 1994.

58. Jason H. Harper, "UNM Hiring and Pay Discriminatory," *New Mexico Daily Lobo*, October 24, 1994.

59. Jason H. Harper, "Peck, Staff Respond to Mercer Report," *New Mexico Daily Lobo*, October 26, 1994.

60. Mike Malello and William C. Reichard, "Zimmerman Gutted by Hate Crime," *New Mexico Daily Lobo*, November 21, 1994.

61. Glenn May, "Rally Conveys Community Outrage," *New Mexico Daily Lobo*, November 23, 1994.

62. William C. Reichard, "Journals Found Hidden in Library," *New Mexico Daily Lobo*, November 30, 1994.

63. Juliet Casey, "Same-Sex Partners Eligible to Receive UNM Benefits," *New Mexico Daily Lobo*, October 16, 1995.

64. Dan McKay, "Affirmative Action: Peck Says It Stays," *New Mexico Daily Lobo*, August 25, 1995.

65. Curtis W. Berry, "Peck Wants Supplement NRC Study," *New Mexico Daily Lobo*, October 14, 1995.

66. Miguel Navrot, "Rally Calls on Community to Fight Hatred and Racism," *New Mexico Daily Lobo*, November 19, 1995; Doug Johnson, "Peck Tells UNM, 'We Need to Find Ways to Feel Safe,'" *New Mexico Daily Lobo*, November 15, 1995.

67. "Students," 1997–1998 Annual Report, University of New Mexico, August 1998, 8.

68. Gerald A. Henderson, "UNM Ranked One of Best Med Schools," *New Mexico Daily Lobo*, March 23, 1994.

69. "UNM School of Medicine Ranks in Top Ten," editorial, *Albuquerque Journal*, March 22, 1995.

70. Carter, History of the University of New Mexico School of Medicine.

71. Kate Nash, "With Tight Budget, UNM's Library Among Nation's Top 50," *New Mexico Daily Lobo*, April 28, 1998.

72. Jahanshah Javid, "UNM Press Book No. 1 Bestseller," *New Mexico Daily Lobo*, September 18, 1991; Natalia Blacksmith, "UNM Press Focuses on Southwest," *New Mexico Daily Lobo*, November 16, 1993.

73. Glenn May, "Regents Forge Ahead with Plans for New Bookstore," *New Mexico Daily Lobo*, April 4, 1994.

74. Bruce Ross, "Recent ASUNM Resolution Could Play a Part in the Rescue of Condemned Yale Park," *New Mexico Daily Lobo*, April 22, 1994.

75. Glenn May, "Peck Declines Offer, Yale Park Site Confirmed," *New Mexico Daily Lobo*, July 21, 1994.

76. Chris Cervini, "Bookstore Construction Begins in Park This Week," *New Mexico Daily Lobo*, August 15, 1994.

77. Doug Johnson, "Regents Dig Themselves a Nice Hole," *New Mexico Daily Lobo*, January 8, 1995.

78. Doug Johnson, "Plans for New Bookstore Still Rolling," *New Mexico Daily Lobo*, April 29, 1995.

79. Bruce Ross, "UNM Bookstore: It Means Business," *New Mexico Daily Lobo*, July 25, 1996.

80. Steve O'Neil, "UNM to Benefit from Its New Business Park," *New Mexico Daily Lobo*, February 15, 1993.

81. Nancy Tipton, "UNM Expects Boost from Martin Marietta," *Albuquerque Journal*, July 29, 1993.

82. Steve O'Neil, "Regents Have High Hopes for UNM Research Park," *New Mexico Daily Lobo*, March 9, 1993.

83. Lawrence Spohn, "UNM Dedicates High-tech Learning Site," *Albuquerque Tribune*, October 17, 1997.

84. "University of New Mexico," *New Mexico Business Journal*, September 1992, 14–15.

85. Sarah Duffy, "Department Move Delays Construction of Dane Smith Hall," *New Mexico Daily Lobo*, August 27, 1996.

86. Linda J. Mott, "Regents Boost Zimmerman Facelift Funds," *New Mexico Daily Lobo*, June 14, 1990.

87. Eric J. Brown, "Renovated Hokona Hall Scheduled to Reopen in Summer," *New Mexico Daily Lobo*, May 9, 1994.

88. Kate Nash, "Fire Forces Residents Out of Dorms for 3 Days," *New Mexico Daily Lobo*, March 24, 1997.

89. Marcus Montoya, "Yale Mall Project Breaks Ground," *New Mexico Daily Lobo*, March 19, 1991.

90. Glenn May, "Smoking Room in SUB to Be Closed," *New Mexico Daily Lobo*, September 15, 1991.

91. Paul A. Fulginiti, "UNM to Get into the Recycling Act," *New Mexico Daily Lobo*, March 10, 1991.

92. "The Peck Years," 1997–1998 Annual Report, University of New Mexico, August 1998, 18.

93. Dennis Wall, "Little-known Museum Might be Taos' Best-Kept Secret," *New Mexico Magazine*, September 1993, 46.

94. Associated Press, "Coach Sheppard Fired," *New Mexico Daily Lobo*, November 5, 1991.

95. Greg Archuleta, "New UNM Football Coach: Franchione," *New Mexico Daily Lobo*, December 5, 1991.

96. Martin Salazar, "Franchione to Head TCU Football," *New Mexico Daily Lobo*, December 15, 1997.

97. Greg Archuleta, "Davalos to Be UNM Athletic Director," *New Mexico Daily Lobo*, November 17, 1992.

98. Wende Schwingendorf, "Bob King Given Court, Holiday," *New Mexico Daily Lobo*, November 30, 1992.

99. Wende Schwingendorf, "UNM Athletic Department on Probation," *New Mexico Daily Lobo*, December 9, 1992.

100. Phil Bundy, "Lobos Win WAC Championship," *New Mexico Daily Lobo*, March 4, 1994.

101. Guillermo Contreras, "Faculty Members Support Resolution to End Athletics," *New Mexico Daily Lobo*, March 30, 1994.

102. Kate Nash, "Pres. Peck Will Reappear as Professor," *New Mexico Daily Lobo*, August 18, 1997.

103. Martin Salazar, "Peck to Retire with Plenty of Perks," *New Mexico Daily Lobo*, August 25, 1997.

104. "A Tour Through Campus Colleges and Schools," *1997–1998 Annual Report, University of New Mexico,* August 1998, 12–13.

105. 1997–1998 Annual Report, University of New Mexico, August 1998, 17.

106. "Achievements, Memories and Milestones from 1997–98," 1997–1998 Annual Report, University of New Mexico, August 1998, 6.

107. Mary Conrad, "Exit Interviews," *Mirage,* Spring 1998, 8–10.

Chapter 20

1. Don McKay, "Regents Name Presidential Finalists," *New Mexico Daily Lobo,* March 10, 1998; Kate Nash, "Judge Halts President Search," *New Mexico Daily Lobo,* April 8, 1998; Martine Salazar, "Regents Abandon President Search," *New Mexico Daily Lobo,* April 19, 1998; Stephen Rabourn, "Gordon Is Interim President," *New Mexico Daily Lobo,* June 4, 1998.

2. Ryan Wallace, "Gordon Names Garcia Interim UNM Provost," *New Mexico Daily Lobo,* July 30, 1998.

3. Alexis Kerschner, "Regents Approve New Presidential Search," *New Mexico Daily Lobo,* September 9, 1998; Iliana Limón, "Regents Announce Search Finalists," *New Mexico Daily Lobo,* February 17, 1999; Iliana Limón, "Gordon Selected to Top UNM Post," *New Mexico Daily Lobo,* March 26, 1999; Juan A. Lozano, "Gordon Named President," *Albuquerque Journal,* March 26, 1999.

4. Kate Nash, "Freshman Class Is Top on Gordon's List," *New Mexico Daily Lobo,* August 26, 1998.

5. Alexander Krughoff, "Students Rally to Protest Tuition Increase," *New Mexico Daily Lobo,* October 8, 1998.

6. Stephen Rabourn, "Regents Approve Two New Majors," *New Mexico Daily Lobo,* December 9, 1998.

7. "UNM Gets First Rhodes Scholar Since the '70s," *New Mexico Daily Lobo,* December 7, 1998.

8. Iliana Limón, "UNM Regents Induct New Members," *New Mexico Daily Lobo,* January 20, 1999.

9. Iliana Limón, "Accreditation Team 'Impressed' by UNM," *New Mexico Daily Lobo,* January 27, 1999.

10. Iliana Limón, "Gordon to Establish Long-Term Guidelines," *New Mexico Daily Lobo,* March 26, 1999.

11. Iliana Limón, "Gordon to Focus on Community," *New Mexico Daily Lobo,* November 11, 1999.

12. Mike Dano, "Johnson's Veto Disrupts Budgets," *New Mexico Daily Lobo,* April 14, 1999.

13. Iliana Limón, "Regents Raise Fees to $523," *New Mexico Daily Lobo,* November 13, 1999.

14. Mike Dano, "Johnson Signs Bill to Save Scholarship," *New Mexico Daily Lobo,* April 16, 1999.

15. Frank Zoretich, "UNM Regents Move Ahead on New Buildings," *Albuquerque Tribune,* October 13, 1999.

16. Iliana Limón, "Peck Nominated for Florida Post," *New Mexico Daily Lobo,* September 29, 1999.

17. Mike Dano, "Students Attend UNM's First Online Classes," *New Mexico Daily Lobo,* January 24, 2000.

18. "Architecture Program Ranked 28th," *New Mexico Daily Lobo,* December 15, 2003.

19. Carolyn Gonzales, "DPAC Earns Architecture Award of Distinction," *Campus News,* November 13, 2000.

20. Schlegel, "History Notes," 14–16.

21. Mike Dano, "Professor Develops Rape Theory," *New Mexico Daily Lobo,* January 27, 2000; Mike Dano, "Media Blitz Works for Thornhill," *New Mexico Daily Lobo,* February 4, 2000.

22. Alma Olarchea, "Women Top U.S. Average at Anderson," *New Mexico Daily Lobo,* June 22, 2000.

23. Carla Medina, "Panama Honors UNM Professor," *New Mexico Daily Lobo,* November 26, 2001.

24. Iliana Limón, "Staff Votes for Unionization," *New Mexico Daily Lobo,* March 21, 2001.

25. Oliver Uyttebrouck, "Departing UNM Boss Earns High Grades," *Albuquerque Journal,* April 1, 2002.

26. "UNM: Information Overview," Office of Research Services, April 2001.

27. James Barron, "Professor Sorry for 'Pentagon' Remark," *New Mexico Daily Lobo,* September 24, 2001.

28. Barron, "Professor Sorry."

29. "Condemn Berthold, Not University," editorial, *Albuquerque Journal,* September 30, 2001.

30. William C. Gordon, "Professor's Words Test University," *Albuquerque Journal,* October 4, 2001.

31. Charlotte Black, "The Land, the Man, His Work," *Albuquerque Tribune,* October 14, 1977.

32. David Steinberg, "Author Anaya Humbled by National Arts Honor," *Albuquerque Journal,* March 15, 2002; "Roudolfo Anaya Gets Deserved Recognition," editorial, *Albuquerque Journal,* March 16, 2002.

33. David Steinberg, "Clinton Adams: Ex-Dean Was Noted Lithographer," *Albuquerque Journal,* May 18, 2001.

34. "UNM Schools Ranked Top-10 by National Hispanic Magazine," *New Mexico Daily Lobo,* September 25, 2001.

35. "UNM Named to *Hispanic Magazine* List," *New Mexico Daily Lobo,* March 25, 2002.

36. Mike Dano, "UNM Student Models for Coin," *New Mexico Daily Lobo,* January 28, 2000.

37. Alma Olarchea, "UNM Student Earns Marshall Scholarship," *New Mexico Daily Lobo,* January 8, 2001.

38. Iliana Limón, "SAE Appeals Loss of Charter," *New Mexico Daily Lobo,* November 11, 1999.

39. Iliana Limón, "Car Damaged in Fraternity Parking Lot," *New Mexico Daily Lobo,* December 7, 2000.

40. Iliana Limón, "Fraternity Violations Reach Boiling Point," *New Mexico Daily Lobo,* April 24, 2002; Iliana Limón, "Students Rally Against Racism," *New Mexico Daily Lobo,* December 11, 2000.

41. Iliana Limón, "Sigma Chi Suspended Through Fall," *New Mexico Daily Lobo,* February 22, 2001.

42. Jason Gil Bear, "UNM Sigma Chi House Condemned," *New Mexico Daily Lobo,* May 1, 2002.

43. Carolyn Gonzales, "Zimmerman Library Named Century's Best Building in New Mexico," *Campus News,* November 22, 1999.

44. Peggy Rhodes, "New Water Plant Keeps Campus Cool," *New Mexico Daily Lobo*, May 16, 2003.

45. Cohal Acevedo, "Dane Smith Dedication Set for Friday," *New Mexico Daily Lobo*, August 27, 1998; Matthew Travis, "Larger Freshmen Classes Force Dane Smith to Open Early," *New Mexico Daily Lobo*, August 1, 1998.

46. David Hyde, "New Apartment-Style Dorms Due by Fall 2000," *New Mexico Daily Lobo*, December 14, 1998; Olivier Uyttebrouck, "UNM's New Student Digs Rival Private Apartments," *Albuquerque Journal*, August 15, 2001.

47. Slobhan Hadley, "Biology, Media Arts to Unite in Old Bookstore," *New Mexico Daily Lobo*, March 9, 1999.

48. Starr Alexander, "Johnson Center Renovation Gets Nod of Approval," *New Mexico Daily Lobo*, August 26, 1999.

49. Frank Zoretich, "UNM Prepares for Renovation on Campus Core," *Albuquerque Tribune*, November 22, 2000.

50. Iliana Limón, "SUB Gets Closer to Renovation," *New Mexico Daily Lobo*, March 4, 2000.

51. Frank Zoretich, "New Architecture Building to Eat up UNM Parking Spots," *Albuquerque Tribune*, October 5, 1999.

52. Olivier Uyttebrouck, "UNM Selling the Land Under Winrock," *Albuquerque Journal*, November 14, 2001.

53. James Barron, "UNM Officially Leaves WAC," *New Mexico Daily Lobo*, August 27, 1998.

54. James Barron, "Three Men's Sports Cut for 1999," *New Mexico Daily Lobo*, April 1, 1999.

55. Ron Gonzales, "Fraschilla Era Ends with Resignation," *New Mexico Daily Lobo*, March 18, 2001.

56. James Barron, "McKay Inks Deal as Lobo Head Coach," *New Mexico Daily Lobo*, April 1, 2002.

57. Oliver Uyttebrouck, "UNM's Gordon to Join Wake Forest," *Albuquerque Journal*, March 15, 2002.

58. Scott Sandlin, "2nd Presidency Rumored for Gordon," *Albuquerque Journal*, April 1, 2002.

59. Uyttebrouck, "Departing UNM Boss."

60. "Gordon Served Well As President of UNM," editorial, *Albuquerque Journal*, March 18, 2002.

61. Uyttebrouck, "Departing UNM Boss."

Chapter 21

1. Olivier Uyttebrouck, "Who Is Fit to Lead?" *Albuquerque Journal*, August 12, 2002.

2. Angela Williams, "UNM Professor to Take on Presidency," *New Mexico Daily Lobo*, June 13, 2002; Olivier Uyttebrouck, "UNM's Garcia Ready to Get Back to Basics," *Albuquerque Journal*, July 11, 2003.

3. F. Chris Garcia to William E. Davis, November 11, 2004.

4. Uyttebrouck, "Who Is Fit to Lead?"

5. Williams, "UNM Professor."

6. Olivier Uyttebrouck, "A School for All Seasons," *Albuquerque Journal*, August 11, 2000.

7. Uyttebrouck, "A School for All Seasons."

8. Colleen Banet, "'02 Freshman Class Size Breaks Records," *New Mexico Daily Lobo*, August 28, 2002.

9. Julian R. Lucero-Emmons, "New School of Law Dean Introduced to University," *New Mexico Daily Lobo*, August 28, 2002.

10. Rivkela Brodsky, "School of Engineering in Top 50 List," *New Mexico Daily Lobo*, October 4, 2002.

11. Rivkela Brodsky, "Engineering School Ranked 7th in Hispanic Magazine," *New Mexico Daily Lobo*, November 26, 2002.

12. Laurie Mellas-Ramirez, "Training Teachers at a 'Gallup,'" *Mirage*, Fall 2002, 23.

13. "Research for the 21st Century," Health Sciences Center Annual Report on Research, Fiscal Years 2001–2002, n.p.

14. Arthur Simoni, "C&J Declines Reaccredidation," *New Mexico Daily Lobo*, October 31, 2002; Arthur Simoni, "Report Details Journalism Program Faults," *New Mexico Daily Lobo*, November 11, 2002.

15. Elizabeth Miller, "Thirty-five Years of Excellence," UNM-Gallup publication, September 15, 2003, 1.

16. University of New Mexico, http://casaa.unm.edu (accessed March 2005).

17. Paul Logan, "UNM Professor Shares Love of Literature," *Albuquerque Journal*, January 8, 2002.

18. Colleen Banet, "Hibben Center Nearly Finished," *New Mexico Daily Lobo*, July 2, 2002.

19. Clay Holtzman, "UNM to Use Bond Funds to Remodel Buildings," *New Mexico Daily Lobo*, November 26, 2002.

20. Tanya Soussan, "Interest in Mesa del Sol Booms," *Albuquerque Journal*, September 20, 1997; Olivier Uyttebrouck, "UNM to Consider Land Exchange," *Albuquerque Journal*, October 14, 2003; Olivier Uyttebrouck, "UNM Stalls Mesa del Sol Development," *Albuquerque Journal*, February 26, 2004.

21. F. Chris Garcia, "Administrative Activities and Accomplishments: A Year-end Report to the UNM Regents," President's Office, July 31, 2003, 3.

22. Rick Wright, "For Estes, Friday Was Banner Day," *Albuquerque Journal*, July 13, 2003.

23. Jeff Proctor, "Willard Resigns as Regents' President," *New Mexico Daily Lobo*, July 3, 2003.

24. Olivier Uyttebrouck, "Regents Examine Business Conflicts," *Albuquerque Journal*, July 15, 2003.

25. Olivier Uyttebrouck, "UNM Gets Tough with New Policy," *Albuquerque Journal*, July 16, 2003.

26. University of New Mexico, http://www.unm.edu/preview/evening.html (accessed November 11, 2004).

27. Danita Gomez and Vanessa Shields, "Report on the Graduation Project," Office of the Vice Provost for Academic Affairs, September 14, 2004.

28. R. Philip Eaton, "Made in New Mexico," UNM Health Sciences Center, n.d.

29. Garcia, "Administrative Activities and Accomplishments," 1–7.

30. Olivier Uyttebrouck, "UNM's Garcia Ready to Get Back to Basics," *Albuquerque Journal*, July 14, 2003.

31. "Garcia Made UNM Leadership Look Easy," editorial, *Albuquerque Journal*, July 17, 2003.

Chapter 22

1. "UNM President Search Misses 2 New Mexicans," editorial, *Albuquerque Journal*, March 18, 2003.

2. Olivier Uyttebrouck, "Gov.: UNM Applicants Deserve Look," *Albuquerque Journal*, March 20, 2003.

3. Olivier Uyttebrouck, "UNM President Search Narrows to 5," *Albuquerque Journal*, March 22, 2003.

4. "UNM List of Finalists Ignores State's Leaders," editorial, *Albuquerque Journal*, March 26, 3002.

5. Olivier Uyttebrouck, "UNM Regents Tackle Big Decision with Style," *Albuquerque Journal*, April 28, 2003.

6. Olivier Uyttebrouck, "Caldera Selected to Run UNM," *Albuquerque Journal*, May 6, 2003.

7. Olivier Uyttebrouck, "Hispanics Applaud Caldera's Selection," *Albuquerque Journal*, May 7, 2003.

8. "Caldera Emerges As Top Presidential Pick," Editorial, *Albuquerque Journal*, May 8, 2003.

9. Harry Moskos, "Popejoy Won Job on Skills," *Albuquerque Journal*, May 18, 2003.

10. Olivier Uyttebrouck, "Up the Ranks," *Albuquerque Journal*, May 13, 2003.

11. Uyttebrouck, "Up the Ranks."

Epilogue

1. Stanley Pogrow and F. Chris Garcia, "The Governance of Public Education," in *New Mexico Government*, ed. F. Chris Garcia and Paul L. Hain (Albuquerque: University of New Mexico Press, 1976), 187.

2. *Chronicle of Higher Education*, Almanac issue, Vol. 1, No. 1, August 29, 2003.

3. Elizabeth F. Farrell, "Public-College Tuition Rise Is Largest in 3 Decades," *Chronicle of Higher Education*, October 31, 2003.

4. Will Potter, "State Lawmakers Again Cut Higher-Education Spending," *Chronicle of Higher Education*, August 8, 2003.

5. Uyttebrouck, "A School for All Seasons.

Index